# THE ENCYCLOPEDIA OF ETIQUETTE

# THE ENCYCLOPEDIA OF ETIQUETTE

*A guide to good manners in today's world*

*by*

## LLEWELLYN MILLER

WITH AN INTRODUCTION BY
## CLEVELAND AMORY

GRAMERCY PUBLISHING COMPANY • NEW YORK

To
Marie Rodell
and
Caroline MacChesney
with
love and gratitude

© MCMLXVII, by Crown Publishers, Inc.
Library of Congress Catalog Card Number: 67-27041
Printed in the United States of America
This edition published by Gramercy Publishing Company,
a division of Crown Publishers, Inc.
a b c d e f g h

# CONTENTS

## ACKNOWLEDGMENTS

During the five years devoted to the research and writing of this book, hundreds of people came to my aid with time, talent, special knowledge and skills—not to mention sympathy, wise counsel, and no small measure of forbearance.

Foremost among the many whom I can never thank enough for help far beyond the demand of duty or affection is Marie Rodell, best of friends, best of agents. The format and character of this book originated with her, and she played an important part in its growth from the first card-index outline to galley proofs. Quite literally, this book would not have been possible without her advice, critical judgment, taste, and time.

Appreciation, beyond words, goes to Nat Wartels for his unfailing encouragement and generosity, which, along with his exacting publishing standards, are reflected throughout the staff of his Crown Publishers, Inc. My gratitude and admiration go also in fullest measure to editor-in-chief Herbert Michelman for his understanding of writers, and his kindness as well as swift good judgment in helping me past the scores of emergencies, big and little, that mark the development of any book as complicated as this one. My particular gratitude goes to him for his choice of Kay Pinney as my immediate editor during the last three years. Besides being armored with a merry wit and a vast professional competence, she has the most remarkably retentive mind for detail that I have known in my long experience as reporter, editor, and writer. Her ability to keep count of the twigs without losing sight of the forest has been of immeasurable value both to me and in the coordinating of the work of researchers. My gratitude also to Naomi Rosenbach, production editor, for reading all sections relating to Jewish customs and amalgamating the information gathered from authorities in that field; and to Warren Potter and Ruth Walsh, whose attention to content as well as commas in months of editing and proofreading were contributions of the greatest importance.

I owe a very special debt of gratitude to my sister, Caroline MacChesney, who took time away from her own interests for the mammoth job of preliminary organization of outlined material, and who joined me at various other times in a major part of the research, which we began in Spain and continued in France, New York, Washington, California, Mexico, and way points.

Very special gratitude also to Harold Baron, my editor throughout the period when the style and organization of this book were being explored. His technical knowledge, his interest and encouragement, both while he was at Crown and during the years since, have sustained me during many times when the task seemed endless.

Invaluable help was given through the years by scores of other distinguished men and women in many fields. For generous aid in matters relating to Washington protocol and precedence, and to forms of address, special thanks to members of the U.S. State Department, particularly George Abell, Assistant Chief of Protocol; Louise K. Nichols, Protocol Officer; and Frances Bourne of The Directives Staff; for answers concerning the White House, gratitude to Barbara Keehn, Carol Carlyle and Sanford L. Fox; for aid in compiling and for checking the Forms of Address charts and other matters relating to the Armed Services, greatest appreciation to Lieutenant Colonel Robert A. Webb, Lieutenant Commander Herbert Pendergast, and Major Barbara Smith of the Directorate for Information

Services for the Department of Defense; and also to Rear Admiral George van Deurs, USN (Ret.), Lieutenant Colonel C. V. Glines, USAF; Colonel Robert E. Collier, USMC; and Margaret Ratcliffe, of British Information Services, for help with the Forms of Address section.

For kindness and patience in answering many questions concerning religious matters, my thanks go to Wilmer C. Fields of the Southern Baptist Convention; The Reverend Thomas McGovern of the Archdiocese of New York; The Reverend Canon Charles Guilbert of the National Council of the Protestant Episcopal Church; Rabbi Philip R. Alstat; Rabbi Abraham Avrech, Associate Director of the Community Service Division of Yeshiva University; Rabbi Balfour Brickner, Director of the Commission on Interfaith Activities of Reform Judaism of the Union of American Hebrew Congregations; Rabbi Neil Gillman of the Jewish Theological Seminary of America; Rabbi Malcolm Stern of the Central Conference of American Rabbis; The Reverend Norman Temme of the Lutheran Church; The Reverend Dr. Everett C. Parker of the United Church of Christ; Arthur West, Director of the Commission for Methodist Information; Arthur Dore, Director of Information for the Greek Orthodox Church in the Americas; Dr. Emanuel Rackman, Yeshiva University; the officers of the Church Information Service of The Church of Jesus Christ of Latter-Day Saints; Major Arthur S. Miller of The Salvation Army, and Louise (Mrs. Malcolm) Stern for reviewing the section on Jewish wedding ceremonies.

At Tiffany & Co., special thanks to Mab Wilson, director of publicity; her assistant, Barbara Edgerton; George O'Brien, director of design development; and Alexander Bennett of the stationery department, for their very kind help on the big sections on social correspondence and visiting cards. For assistance in checking details of business correspondence and manners, particular thanks are due to The Katharine Gibbs School, and also William Rapley, Chief of the Management and Records Section of the U.S. Post Office Department. For information in other specialized fields, gratitude to Blanche Burnett, former society editor of the San Francisco News Call-Bulletin; Dr. Katharine Bain of the U.S. Children's Bureau; Dr. Sandra Forman and Ioan V. Beckham of Harrison Forman World Travel, Inc. Thanks also to Vice Admiral William J. Marshall, USN (Ret.), President of The Bourbon Institute, for reviewing and amending the sections on whiskies, wines, and their service; to Professor John Sokol, Teachers College, Columbia University, and Bonnie Edwards of the Office of University Relations; Herbert J. Herrlich, President, Frank E. Campbell The Funeral Church; Luther Meyer, Vital Statistics editor of the San Francisco News Call-Bulletin; Walter Stevens and Mildred Schlesinger of Brooks Brothers; Joseph Miller, Miller Harness Co., Inc.; James Blackwell, Executive Secretary of American Horse Shows Association, Inc.; Raymond Gurney, Real Estate Board of New York; The Light House, The New York Association for the Blind; for informed counsel on musical matters, Elizabeth North of Town Hall and Sam Morgenstern, composer and director; and for special information on the entertainment world, Leonard L. Levinson.

Among the many manufacturers, groups, and associations that provided informative material were the Billiard Congress of America, Greeting Card Association, National Live Stock and Meat Board, American Water Ski Association, National Rifle Association of America, American Bowling Congress, ITT World Communications, the New York City Department of Parks, United States Golf Association, Women's International Bowling Congress, U.S. Lawn Tennis Association, National Travelers Aid Association, United States Ski Association, The Jewelry Industry Council, American Glassware Association, American Bowling Congress, Red Arrow Bonded Messenger Service, American Bowling Congress, and the American Movers Conference.

My thanks go also to many others, unknown to me by name—to the librarians, taxi drivers, trained nurses, theater ushers, hairdressers, the employees of airlines, hotels, restaurants, caterers, florists, and garages, to the staffs of state departments of information, to guides and guards, policemen, teachers, teenagers, pet owners, and the countless others to whom my questions have been directed as our paths crossed.

In deepest gratitude,

Llewellyn Miller

New York, October, 1967

# INTRODUCTION

## by Cleveland Amory

This book is a dictionary of etiquette. The word "etiquette" itself goes back to Louis XIV and, of all things, to the familiar expression "Keep Off the Grass." Louis XIV's head gardener, it seems, in an effort to keep trespassers off his newly laid Versailles gardens, put up warning signs or tickets—*etiquettes*—to keep such trespassers on the straight and narrow. And, when no one paid any attention to them, the gardener went to the King, who promptly issued an edict commanding one and all "to keep within the *etiquettes*." Soon the word came to stand not only for all matters of court deportment, but deportment in other spheres as well.

My dictionary defines etiquette as "the forms, manners and ceremonies established by convention as acceptable." And the reason this encyclopedia is highly acceptable to me is that Llewellyn Miller has come up with an etiquette book that has a minimum of snobbery and a maximum of common sense as well as a format that is ideally suited to the practicality of her approach to good manners as they are today. Above all, working as a reporter and not as a Miss Naughty Naughty, she has come up with a book that is chock full of nondidactic and highly readable vignettes—not just the what's what of etiquette but the far more important reasons why (and explicitly how) certain of our long-established rules are being modified by our fast-changing times. Etiquette is, after all, when all is said and done, not something like Tennis or Bridge in which there are Official Rules. There is no one Recognized Expert capable of laying down the law, and the best one can hope for is to get, by example and case history, combined with common sense, workable ground rules and foul lines.

That is exactly what you will get here—the ground rules and guidelines for today's protocol and best practice, whether they relate to the traditional, intricate, and fixed procedures of the ceremonial wedding, the brand-new social headache of the party-crashing fever, or manners in the business world. Yesterday, for example, the business world was almost entirely a section for men only. Today, with close to half of our adult female population in that world, it's not just a question of man-manners but woman-manners, too.

But, make no mistake about it, although this is a present-day book, Llewellyn Miller has, like the good reporter she is, done her homework—in the fascinating field of the past history of etiquette. She has, for example, included the amusing *Rules of Civility and Decent Behavior in Company and Conversation* that young George Washington, at the age of fifteen, wrote down in his school copybook. And if the accent in his precepts seems to be on the what *not* to do's—"Bedew no man's face with your Spittle"—young George also learned some important what *to* do's, such as how to "walk in company with another":

> "If he be a Man of Great Quality, walk not with him Cheek by Jowl but somewhat behind him; but yet in Such a Manner that he may easily speak to you."

Young George also learns such important things as "how to doff his hat":

> "In Pulling off your Hat to Persons of Distinction, as Noblemen, Justices, Churchmen, &c make a Reverence, bowing more or less according to the Custom of the Better Bred, and Quality of the Person."

Pursuing this past history further, even as comparatively recently as 1870, the gentleman's hat was still giving trouble in etiquette books. *The Bazar Book of Decorum*, for example, published in that year and written by a Dr. Robert Tomes, had this tip for hat-tippers:

> "When you salute a lady or a gentleman to whom you wish to show

particular respect, in the street, you should take your hat entirely off and cause it to describe a circle of at least ninety degrees from its original resting place."

Finally, in that era, in typically forthright American fashion, came an automatic hat-tipper. Indeed, a patent was actually taken out at the United States Patent Office for a machine to be installed in one's hat—one that set off a spring which, released by a slight tip of the wearer's head, promptly tipped the whole hat.

The nose, too, gave trouble. One of the earliest etiquette books, Eleazar Moody's *The School of Good Manners*, in between such age-old advice as "If thy superior be relating a story, say not 'I have heard it before,' " also counsels persons at the table to "spit not, cough not, nor blow thy nose." But, by the time of *The Bazar Book of Decorum*, the news about the nose was that no news was good:

> "The nose should never be fondled before company, or, in fact, touched at any time, unless absolutely necessary. The nose, like other organs, augments in size by handling, so we recommend any person to keep his own fingers, as well as those of his friends or enemies, away from it."

No early-day problem of etiquette was more fraught with danger than the matter of calling cards. It underlay, one book declared, the "very structure of society." "You can hardly," this book warned, "invite people to your house until you have called and have left a card. And thus one has a safeguard against intrusive and undesirable acquaintances. To stop an acquaintance, one has but to stop leaving cards. It is thus done quietly but securely."

At the height of the mania, the rigamarole was rigid:

> "When the visitor herself rings the door-bell and the message is 'not at home,' the butler, or maid, proffers the card tray on which the visitor lays a card of her own and her daughter's for each lady in the house and a card of her husband's and son's for each lady and gentleman. But three is the greatest number ever left of any one card."

And, as if this were not complicated enough, one also had to observe the proprieties of turning down the upper right-hand corner for a personal visit, the upper left-hand corner for congratulations, the lower right-hand corner for adieu, the lower left-hand corner for condolences, and the entire left end for a call on the entire family.

One early-day book of etiquette tried to take in the whole sphere of the human condition under the title *The Gentleman's and Lady's Book of Politeness and Propriety of Deportment*. Written by Elizabeth F. Bayle-Mouillard, it was, like so many early American books, a translation of a French work. In any case, for all its general approach, it was also specific in its catalogue of bad manners:

> ". . . to balance yourself upon your chair . . . to extend your feet on the andirons; to admire yourself with complacency in a glass; . . . to laugh immoderately; to place your hand upon the person with whom you are conversing; to take him by the buttons, the collar of his cloak, the cuffs, the waist &c; to seize ladies by the waist, or to touch their person; . . . to beat time with the feet and hands; to whirl round a chair on one leg."

In the old books, the etiquette for "gentlewomen," as they were called, was perhaps the strictest of all. One of the most widely read of these was *The Young Lady's Friend*, a small volume published in 1838 by Mrs. John Farrar, the wife of, of all things, a Harvard professor. From behavior at the lecture in the morning to the formal dinner at night, Mrs. Farrar's book was a bible. She frankly defined her ideal "gentlewoman" as "the daughter of a rich man." At lectures, such a girl must never "run, jump, scream, scramble or push, in order to get a good seat." At the formal, or what Mrs. Farrar calls the "ceremonious," dinner, her girl's behavior was carefully outlined from the very moment of entry through her hostess's door.

"With erect carriage and firm step," Mrs. Farrar advised, "enter the drawing-room, either with your parents, three together, or following them alone, or on the arm of a friend or sister." She made clear that there were to be no distractions until her young lady had properly curtsied to her hostess.

The dining room also was full of perils. The young lady must not play with the cutlery, make pellets of the bread, blow her nose or touch her hair. Indeed, in her closing remarks on the ceremonious dinner, Mrs. Farrar made no bones about the pace of the whole bygone era:

> "Be sure to get through with your dessert and have your gloves on, all ready to move, by the time the lady of the house gives the signal . . . the sooner you can depart after taking coffee the better. . . . A dinner, well performed by all the actors in it, is very fatiguing and, as it generally occupies three hours or more, most persons are glad to go away when it is fairly done."

Even in those days, however, youth was beginning to give trouble to etiquette writers. And Mrs. Farrar was stern indeed to prehistoric "twisters":

> "Some girls have a trick of *jiggling* their bodies (I am obliged to coin a word to describe it); they shake all over, as if they were hung on spiral wires, like the geese in a Dutch toy; than which nothing can be more ungraceful or unmeaning. It robs a lady of all dignity, and makes her appear trifling and insignificant. Some do it only on entering a room, others do it every time they are introduced to anybody, and whenever they begin to talk to anybody. It must have originated in embarrassment, and a desire to do something, without knowing exactly what; and being adopted by some popular belle, it became, at one time, a fashion in New York and spread thence to other cities."

Mrs. Farrar's "fashion" becomes downright "folly" when another etiquetteer, Florence Howe Hall, daughter of Julia Ward Howe, author of "The Battle Hymn of the Republic," had her say in a book published in 1888, *The Correct Thing in Good Society*:

> "There is a form of folly quite prevalent in New York which seems to be peculiar to the place. It is for women who are entirely respectable and well-behaved members of Society to imitate the dress of a fast, loose class, because they think it is rather knowing to do so. Thus, one will often see a middle-aged, quiet-looking woman resplendent with gold-dyed hair and a very showy costume, the incongruity between the garments and the wearer often quite startling."

In many cases these rules of etiquette reach remarkable heights. Mrs. Hall decrees, for example, that the mark of a gentleman was his removal of his hat with his left hand; only by doing so could he leave his right hand free for a possible handshake. Mrs. Hall also points to the exemplary upbringing of a girl who, though only three years old, would never help herself at table from a dish unless it was one passed from the left side. Another writer cautions the male dinner-table partner of a lady who in the course of a meal "may perchance raise an unmanageable portion to her mouth." The dictum was stern: "Cease all conversation with her and look steadfastly into the opposite part of the room."

As might be expected, the Number One problem of all was the relationship between the male and the female. Mrs. Farrar was a strong believer in the good influence that sisters could be on brothers:

"I have been told by men, who had passed unharmed through the temptations of youth, that they owed their escape from many dangers to the intimate companionship of affectionate and pure-minded sisters. They have been saved from a hazardous meeting with idle company by some home engagement, of which their sisters were the charm; they have refrained from mixing with the impure, because they would not bring home thoughts and feelings which they could not share with those trusting and loving friends; they have put aside the wine-cup and abstained from stronger potations, because they would not profane with their fumes the holy kiss, with which they were accustomed to bid their sisters good night."

The advent of the waltz coincided with the heyday of the early etiquetteers, and virtually all of them warned of its pitfalls. "A gentleman," one counsels, "never encircles the lady's waist until the dance begins and drops his arm as soon as it ends." Another codifier washed her hands of any attempt to tell young things how to behave during such a dance. "The waltz," she declared, "is suitable only for married persons." If they had been left entirely to the manners mentors, one thing is certain—the Nineties would never have been known as Gay. The era of the Plush Age man was also the era of what has been called the "antimacassar approach to womanhood," and Mrs. Farrar, for one, took firm steps against the male animal:

"If the natural feelings of modesty are not sufficient to guard you from all personal familiarity with the young men of your acquaintance, let good breeding, and good taste, aid you in laying down rules for yourself on this head. Never join in any rude plays, that will subject you to being kissed or handled in any way by gentlemen. Do not suffer your hand to be held or squeezed without showing that it displeases you by instantly withdrawing it. If a finger is put out to touch a chain that is round your neck, or a breast-pin that you are wearing, draw back and take it off for inspection. Accept not unnecessary assistance in putting on cloaks, shawls, overshoes, or anything of the sort. Be not lifted in and out of carriages, on or off a horse; sit not with another in a place that is too narrow; read not out of the same book; let not your eagerness to see anything induce you to place your head close to another person's. These and many other little points of delicacy and refinement deserve to be made fixed habits, and then they will sit easily and gracefully upon you, heightening the respect of all who approach you, and operating as an almost invisible, though a very impenetrable, fence, keeping off vulgar familiarity, and that desecration of the person which has too often led to vice."

Above all, the early-day etiquette books were firm on the subject of the chaperon. In one of the most famous of nineteenth-century etiquette books, *Manners and Social Usages*, Mrs. John Sherwood left no doubt as to just what a chaperon was:

"She must accompany her young lady everywhere; she must sit in the parlor when she receives gentlemen; she must go with her to the skating rink, the ball, the party, the races, the dinners, and especially to theatre parties; she must preside at the table and act the part of a mother, so far as she can; she must watch the characters of the men who approach her charge,

and endeavor to save the inexperienced girl from the dangers of a bad marriage, if possible."
Remarkably enough, not even an engaged girl escaped. Said Mrs. Sherwood:

"A chaperon is indispensable to an engaged girl. . . . Nothing is more vulgar in the eyes of our modern society than for an engaged couple to travel together or to go to the theatre unaccompanied, as was the primitive custom. . . . Society allows an engaged girl to drive with her fiance in an open carriage, but it does not approve of his taking her in a closed carriage to an evening party."

Everywhere women's lives were circumscribed. In the matter of calling, for example, Mrs. Sherwood counseled that even an "elderly girl" of twenty-five—shades of the "over-thirty" syndrome of today!—was very "unwise," as she put it, to visit an artist's studio alone—even though, she added, "there is, in art, an ennobling and purifying influence which should be a protection." Another book, Hill's *Manual of Social and Business Forms*, published in 1887, also counseled even "business ladies" about calling on gentlemen. "Do not, if a lady," it said —and the "if a lady" was itself an era mark—"call upon a gentleman unless he may be a confirmed invalid."

Mrs. Farrar was particularly stern about the business lady. She should, it was said, avoid like the plague "the pretty little arts and graces, the charming ways which are so delightful in a parlor, but which are so utterly out of place, have even been dangerous, in the arena of daily struggle for bread and butter."

Hill's *Manual*, on the other hand, was equally stern about the matter of how a gentleman should make, we presume, a "businesslike" proposal:

"He may write to the lady, making her an offer, and request her to reply. He may, if he does not trust to words, even in her presence, write the question on a slip of paper, and request her laughingly to give a plain 'no' or 'yes.' He may ask her if in case a gentleman very much like himself was to make a proposal of marriage to her, what she would say. She will probably laughingly reply that it will be time enough to tell what she would say when the proposal is made. And so the ice would be broken."

The most amazing propriety of all was reserved for, of all places, the library. "The perfect hostess," declared an etiquette pamphlet of the year 1863, "will see to it that the works of male and female authors be properly separated on her bookshelves. Their proximity unless they happen to be married should not be tolerated." Surely no etiquette book could go further.

With all the nonsense in these early books, however, there is also some touching advice. Hill's *Manual* has, for example, along with an elaborate code of etiquette between husband and wife, a pretty set of rules:

"Never should both be angry at the same time. Let the angry word be answered only with a kiss. Always leave home with a tender good-bye and loving words. They may be the last."

Conversation itself was, in fact, a fertile field for all early-day etiquette books —and nowhere will you find a better example of just how different from the old-timers is the approach of Llewellyn Miller. Here in this book, for instance, you will find, on the subject of conversation, a whole conversational essay—what conversation is and what it is not—and, after reading it, you are still, conversationally speaking, a free soul.

Not so in the old books. Etiquetteers warned of the woman whose conversation was bounded, as they said, "on the north by her servants, on the east by her children, on the south by her ailments, and on the west by her clothes." And well they might have, for one etiquetteer, our old friend Mrs. Farrar, actually boiled down what she called "the proper topics of conversation before dinner" to five—"a child," she said, "a picture, an animal, a vase of flowers and a worked ottoman."

Logan's *Home Manual* went so far as to give whole sample conversations— one for an afternoon tea, another for a dinner party, another for a musicale, another for a reception and still another for a ball. The one for a dinner party was in itself almost a ball:

"The gentleman must say, 'We must be careful not to step on that elaborate train,' referring to the costume of a lady preceding the pair.

" 'Yes, indeed, that would be a mishap. But trains are graceful in spite of their inconvenience.'

"Her companion must answer: 'Oh! I admire them, of course. Only I have such a dread of stepping on them and bringing down the wrath of the fair wearer on my devoted head.' . . .

"Having seated themselves, and exchanged a few comments (of course flattering), on the table decorations, the lady, wishing to ascertain whether her companion was one of the silent diners-out, might say, 'Some people do not care to eat and talk at the same time, but prefer to let what few comments they make come in between the courses.'

" 'A man must be a dull fellow who cannot do both, with satisfaction to his neighbor if not to himself.'

" 'Then I may talk to you without fear of interrupting your enjoyment of your dinner? But you speak as though it were easier to please your neighbor than yourself.'

" 'Set down that speech to my gallantry.' "

One of the most remarkable facts in the history of the etiquette of conversation was that, in the old days, being invited to someone's house for dinner did not, unless the guests were specifically introduced to each other by the hostess, entitle them to speak to each other. But at least one etiquetteer, Mrs. John Sherwood, in *Manners and Social Usages*, bravely spoke out against this practice and compared it unfavorably with British Society:

"Dinner parties in stiff and formal London have this great attraction: a gentleman steps up and speaks to a lady, although they have never met before, and often takes her down to dinner without an introduction. The women chat after dinner like old friends; everyone knows that the roof is a sufficient guarantee. This is as it should be; but great awkwardness results in the United States if one lady speaks to another and receives no answer. 'Pray can you tell me who the pianist is?' said a leader of society to a young girl near her at a private concert. The young lady looked distressed and blushed, and did not answer. Having seen a deaf-mute in the room whom she knew, the speaker concluded that this young lady belonged to that class of persons, and was very much surprised when later the hostess brought up this silent personage and introduced her.

" 'I could not speak to you before because I had not been introduced —but the pianist is Mr. Mills,' remarked this punctilious person. 'I, however, could speak to you although we had not been formally presented. The roof was sufficient guarantee of your respectability, and I thought from your not answering that you were deaf and dumb,' said the lady.

"The rebuke was deserved. . . . We hold it proper, all things considered, that at dinner-parties and receptions a hostess may introduce her friends to each other. . . . All well-bred people recognize the propriety of speaking to even an enemy at a dinner-party, although they would suffer no recognition an hour later."

Modern etiquette may be said to have begun with the close of the First World War. In the years 1918–1929, no less than sixty-eight different works on the subject were published, and from 1930 to 1945 came seventy-eight more. Included among these were books and revisions of books by such well-known authorities as Lillian Eichler, whose first *Book of Etiquette* was published in 1921; Emily Post, who was first published in 1922; as well as a host of others, including such well-known names as Hallie Erminie Rives, Inez Haynes Irwin, and Margaret Culkin Banning. But there seemed to be no end to new readers for etiquette books. Vogue's *Book of Etiquette*, brought out in 1948, and Amy Vanderbilt's *Complete Book of Etiquette*, first published in 1952, won outstanding success among the scores of less ambitious works published in the last twenty years—without slowing the steady sale of Emily Post's regularly updated work.

Of all these, the origin of Mrs. Post's book was probably the most interesting. For many years the literary adviser of Funk and Wagnalls had tried unsuccessfully to persuade Mrs. Post, who was the daughter of the architect of Tuxedo Park and the author of several novels contrasting European with American standards, to undertake such a book; Mrs. Post had steadfastly refused. One day the Funk and Wagnalls man surreptitiously left another book on the subject, published by Doubleday, in Mrs. Post's Tuxedo cottage. Picking it up one night, Mrs. Post was horrified by gaucheries. "Doubleday," she said, recalling the event, "Doubleday! And I know they were ladies and gentlemen, too."

One thing is certain. Mrs. Post's early works, with their wonderfully imaginatively named characters, were landmarks in their field. Her hero and heroine of those early editions were, for example, Mr. and Mrs. Oldname, who are not to be confused, of course, with Mr. and Mrs. Upstart, Mr. and Mrs. Unsuitable, Mr. and Mrs. Spendeasy Western, Mr. and Mrs. Jameson Greatlake or, for that matter, Mr. and Mrs. Littlehouse—even though, we are told, Mrs. Littlehouse *was* Sally Titherington. And when you, as Mrs. Newwed, decided to give a dinner party and ask to *your* little house Mrs. Toplofty, Mr. Clubwin Doe, the Worldlys, the Gildings, and the Wellborns—well, you just know there's going to be trouble even though Mrs. Kindhart is there too. And, sure enough, trouble there is—from the first awful moment when the fire smokes just as Mr. Clubwin Doe enters, to the final dreadful *crise* when your Swedish maid says, instead of the preferred "Dinner is served"—ah, the horror of it—"Dinner's all ready!"

Edmund Wilson once wrote that Scott Fitzgerald had been inspired with the idea of writing a play about etiquette—one in which all the motivations would consist of everyone trying to do the right thing. "The element of dramatic conflict," Wilson noted, "would be produced by setting people at cross-purposes through stalemates of good form, from which the only salvation would be the intervention of some bounder as *deus ex machina* to put an end to the sufferings."

Llewellyn Miller is no bounder. But she may well be the *dea*, if not the *deus*, *ex machina*, we have been waiting for. She spells out the standard rules with crisp, exact precision, explains which customs or details of customs have become antiquated, and includes hundreds of new topics. In other words, her book sweeps through the old world of etiquette like a new broom, and, for the new world of etiquette, for our own present tense times, she has not only opened the windows but the doors too.

# HOW TO USE THIS BOOK

Main subject entries follow one another in strict alphabetical order: **ANTIPASTO**, **ANTIQUES**, **APARTMENTS**, and so on. When a subject requires lengthy analysis and discussion, it is broken down into sections that are also alphabetically arranged. For example, the long entry on **TRAVEL** is broken down into more than a dozen major divisions, and many of these are likewise alphabetically subdivided to assist the reader in finding the specific information he needs. The division **PLANES**, under **TRAVEL**, for instance, is further divided as follows:

**TRAVEL**

    **PLANES**

        **Bargains in Airports**
        **Checking**
        **Clothes**
        **Delays**
        **Drinks**
        **Foods**
        **Forms of Address**
        **Illness**
        **Luggage**
        **Packing**
        **Radios**
        **Reservations**
        **Special Services**
        **Tipping**
        **Toilets**

Rather than repeat text material with every subject entry to which it might possibly apply, often the reader is provided simply with a cross-reference to another subject entry where the information is thoroughly discussed. At the subhead **INTRODUCTIONS** under **BUSINESS MANNERS**, for example, the reader is referred directly to the main entry **INTRODUCTIONS**.

In addition to this alphabetical organization of subjects and breakdown into subdivisions, a complete index at the back of the book lists all references to *any* subject by page number so that the minor or specialized information can be found as readily as the major rules.

# A

## A LA CARTE

*A la carte* (according to the card) means that each item on a menu is priced separately. *Table d'hôte* (table of the host) means that a complete meal is served for a fixed price, always less than the same number of courses ordered *à la carte*. A host is clearly indicating that he would rather not order *à la carte* when he asks, "Do you see anything you like on the dinner?" Any guest with his social wits about him takes the hint, out of consideration for his host's pocketbook and for another reason—dining out is a more pleasant and formal occasion, with less confusion in the serving, if all at a table follow the host's lead and take either the complete dinner or the same number of courses *à la carte* that he does. A host cannot feel anything but somewhat hurried and awkward if someone at his table is waiting with an empty plate while he and his other guests finish the appetizer and soup courses.

## ABBREVIATIONS

Certain abbreviations have found their way into such common use that the complete words sound stilted and old-fashioned. "Aeroplane" is a good example. It was first shortened to "airplane"; and now "plane" is so generally accepted that the abbreviation is no longer printed with an apostrophe " 'plane." "Phone" is as often heard as "telephone," and TV is well on its way to replacing "television" in the speech of college professors as well as kindergartners. Other shortened words, like "perm" for "permanent" (the "wave" having already been dropped), no doubt will be as standard, before long, as is "bus" for the long-since-outmoded "omnibus."

The excessive use of abbreviations is a harmless affectation of youngsters, but clinging to a multisyllabic word no longer in wide use is no less an affectation on the stuffy side.

The use of abbreviations like "Ave.," "Blvd.," "Yrs. Tly.," and so on, in personal letters is a matter of individual choice, but there is no such latitude in correspondence that has any pretensions to formality—particularly in formal invitations and replies.

For examples of correct abbreviations, *see* CORRESPONDENCE; FORMS OF ADDRESS; INVITATIONS; VISITING CARDS.

**FRENCH ABBREVIATIONS.** R.S.V.P. stands for *Répondez s'il vous plaît.* These initials are in very wide use in this country, though their translation, "Please reply," is equally correct. "Please reply" is never abbreviated to initials because "p.r." stands for *pour remercier* (to thank). R.S.V.P. (or R.s.v.p.) may be engraved or printed on any formal invitation, or written on any informal one. Periods after each letter are standard, but are often dropped when R.S.V.P. is handwritten. What is important, though, is observing the rule that an answer must be given to any invitation on which this abbreviation appears.

The following abbreviations of French terms are used only on visiting cards under circumstances explained in detail under CALLS. Capital letters may be used, but are not usual:

p.c. stands for *pour condoléance* (to express sympathy).

p.f. stands for *pour féliciter* (to congratulate).

p.p.c. stands for *pour prendre congé* (to take leave), meaning that one is leaving town.

p.r. stands for *pour remercier* (to thank).

**ACCEPTANCES.**  *See* INVITATIONS and WEDDINGS.

## ACCESSORIES

This somewhat vague term generally means most of the smaller items of a wardrobe: belts, gloves, handkerchiefs, neckties, and scarves, for example. However, umbrellas, shirts, blouses, shoes, hats, and handbags are included when "matching" accessories are under discussion. All authorities agree on one thing, though, and ban "men's furnishings" as a substitute term. Styles in women's accessories change rapidly. Rules concerning men's accessories are more exact and less subject to change.

*See* CLOTHES for details.

## ACCIDENTS

Everyone involved in an accident is a loser to some degree. The single most important thing for the victim to remember is that, by dictionary definition, an accident is an unintended injury or damage. The person who causes an accident is obligated to repair the damage to whatever extent possible, but the victim is equally obligated to relieve the embarrassment of the person at fault. The first words spoken by anyone should be an expression of concern for the hurt or damage. Nothing is less soothing than to hear "It wasn't my fault," or "If you hadn't—" before "Are you all right?" or "Let me help you."

*See* APOLOGIES AND EXCUSES; AUTOMOBILES; DAMAGE (for rules about possessions); TABLE MANNERS (for accidents at meals).

**ACTORS, ACTRESSES.**  *See* CELEBRITIES; ENTERTAINERS; THEATERS.

## ADDRESSES

Any message worth mailing deserves the protection of a return address on the envelope. It is especially important to put a return address on formal announcements and Christmas cards. Hundreds of thousands of them go astray each year because the addresses are incorrectly written. Other hundreds of thousands are not acknowledged because the recipient does not have the sender's address. In either case, hurt feelings can result—the sender's because he does not receive an answer; the intended recipient's because he seemingly has been ignored.

A zip-code number is a standard part of an address, and should be used on all mail—no exceptions.

**CHANGING ADDRESSES.** Common consideration for the hard-pressed postman, as well as selfish interest, calls for announcing a change of address promptly to one's entire circle of acquaintances, and also to shops, magazine publishers, and all others who are in regular touch by mail. The local post office will supply change-of-address postcards at no charge. Card shops carry a wide assortment of "new address" cards. For business purposes or for a very large circle of social acquaintances, either a printed postcard or an engraved or printed announcement sent in an envelope is the standard choice. Sometimes the announcement of a new business connection or an invitation to an open house is combined with the change-of-address announcement. Otherwise, the standard form is:

NEW ADDRESS:  *After June 15. (year)*

*Miss Jane Jones*

*45 East Street*

*New York. N. Y. 00000*

*Plaza 0-1234*

*(Until June 15: 54 West Street. Stamford. Ohio 00000)*

*See also* CORRESPONDENCE; INVITATIONS; VISITING CARDS; and the Index.

**ADMIRALS.**   *See* FORMS OF ADDRESS (Armed Services).

## ADMITTANCE CARDS

A card of admission serves as an entrance ticket. Such a card is issued only for very large balls, banquets, receptions, weddings, or other gatherings where it is necessary to guard against party crashers. An admittance card may be enclosed with an invitation, or sent after an acceptance is received. Any specialist in formally engraved stationery has samples of the correct forms for different events.

## ADOPTIONS

An adoption is celebrated just as a birth would be—from the handing out of the traditional cigars to the issuing of formal announcements.

**ANNOUNCEMENTS.**   In almost all states, the law requires a year's delay between the time a child is given to the adopting family and the final court proceeding that makes the adoption legal. In the majority of cases, this waiting period is no more than a formality. However, many people feel that formal announcement is premature before an adoption is legal, and anticlimactic after the child has been with them for a year. When announcements are sent, the child's birth date or approximate age is used, not the adoption date.

*Before legal proceedings are complete,* a formal announcement gives the child's first name only:

*Mr. and Mrs. John Brown Smith*

*have the happiness to announce*

*the arrival and prospective adoption of*

*Joan*

*aged four months*

*(or born on the eighth of March. 19—)*

*After legal proceedings are complete,* a formal announcement gives the child's full name:

Mr. and Mrs. John Brown Smith
have the happiness to announce
the adoption of
Joan Marilyn Smith
aged sixteen months

OR

Mr. and Mrs. John Brown Smith
take pleasure in announcing that
Joan Marilyn Smith
born on the eighth of March, [year]
has been adopted as their daughter

*For a child whose last name is publicly known,* a formal announcement gives the old and the new name fully, and the relationship, if any:

Mr. and Mrs. John Brown Smith
take pleasure in announcing that Mrs. Smith's niece
Miss Joan Greene
has been adopted as their daughter
and will henceforth be known as
Miss Joan Greene Smith

**Replies.** A formal announcement of either a birth or an adoption does not require an answer. However, the arrival of a child is a family event of major importance. If the parents have shared their happiness by sending an announcement, it is only a routine courtesy to send a note of congratulations, no matter what the rules say.

**GIFTS.** An announcement of either a birth or an adoption does not require a present in response, but a very close friend usually sends or takes one.

## ADVERTISEMENTS

Nearly everyone knows that specific permission in writing must be obtained before a person's name and picture can be legally used in an advertisement of a commercial product or service; but many people do not know that the same rule applies to the use of a name or picture in an advertisement of a charity or other nonprofit enterprise. Officers of a club or members of a committee drafting an advertisement should not take for granted permission to use the names of members, patrons, or contributors. Few people object to such use of their names to advertise a cause they support, but some feel that it will expose them to appeals from too many other organizations. Their right to refuse should be respected.

For the rules governing paid "advertisements" of personal matters in the Vital Statistics columns of newspapers, *see* Announcements (Press) in the Index.

## ADVICE

> "Advice is seldom welcome; and those who want it most
> always like it least."—Lord Chesterfield

How did the saying "Advice is cheap" ever win wide acceptance? Advice may be valuable or useless, sound or silly, but anyone who gives it must be prepared to pay its price, which can be high. The person who gives advice shares responsibility for the result if his advice is followed—and must expect to take part of the blame if the outcome is unhappy.

If advice, solicited or unsolicited, is not followed, keep silent. "I told you so!" is among the least helpful—and least endearing—of comments.

By all the rules, asking a broker, lawyer, doctor, or any other professional for personal advice under social circumstances is taboo. Ask a professional about any general aspects of his field, but not what specific stocks to buy, what specific legal action to take, or what to do about Johnny's tonsils.

## AFFECTATIONS

Any extreme affectation in dress, manner, accent, and choice of words usually defeats the purpose that inspires it, which is not just to attract attention—but to attract favorable attention.

**IN ACTIONS.** The daintily crooked little finger and other carefully contrived "genteel" mannerisms have been pretty well laughed out of use, but no less affected is the studied mannerlessness of the beatnik.

**IN SPEECH.** The best practice is to choose the short familiar word or phrase rather than try too hard for the long, pretentious one. "Buy" is better choice than "acquire"; "met," than "made her acquaintance"; "read," than "perused." Anyone who comes back after a short stay elsewhere and struggles to substitute a pronunciation such as "vahze" when everyone locally says "vace" risks the charge of affectation to no gain, since both pronunciations are correct. It is inconsiderate as well as affected to use foreign words and phases unless one is certain that a listener understands their meaning, and patronizing to use a foreign word and follow it immediately with a translation.

James Thurber put it neatly in his *Fables for Our Time:* "You might as well fall flat on your face as lean over too far backward."

## AGE

> "Youth is grand for kids, but that's no excuse for making it
> a life sentence."—*Russell Baker*

Age is a touchy subject. Many people guard the number of their years as if it were the guiltiest of secrets. Others have accepted the fact that they, like everyone else, grow a year older with each passing twelve months, and speak of age freely, to the consternation of some of their contemporaries. To be on the safe side, it is a good rule never to mention the age of any adult in general conversation, even if the person under discussion is absent. A woman, particularly, may feel uncomfortable if the age of a mutual acquaintance is discussed. Though her own is not mentioned, she may feel that speculation about it is in the air.

There is no excuse for asking a child to tell the age of an adult relative. It is equally taboo to ask any adult how old he is, except under a few business circumstances. An employer may ask the age of a job applicant, since that information has a bearing on company insurance and retirement plans. The employer is not free to ask that personal question in the presence of others, however, and records containing personal information should not be kept in open office files.

The correct date of birth must be given on such documents as applications for insurance, a passport, a driver's license, a marriage license, and a Social Security number. Otherwise, an adult is entitled to answer, "Over twenty-one."

**AGE OF CONSENT.** The age at which a person may marry without parental consent varies from fourteen years in certain states to twenty-one in others. *See* "Licenses" under WEDDINGS.

**AIR FORCE.**  *See* FORMS OF ADDRESS (Armed Services).

**ALCOHOLIC DRINKS.**  *See* BEER; PUNCH; WHISKIES AND OTHER SPIRITS, WINES; and also separate entries, including BANQUETS; TOASTS, etc.

**ALCOHOLICS.**  *See* INTOXICATION.

## ALFRESCO

This term comes to us from Italy. Its literal translation is "in freshness." When applied to a painting, "alfresco" means that the work (a fresco) was done on fresh, damp plaster. When applied to any meal, it means "in the open air." Technically, picnics and cookouts are alfresco meals, but as commonly used, "alfresco" means a somewhat more formal meal served on a terrace or in a garden or patio. Unless otherwise specified in the invitation, rules for arrival and departure are the same as for a meal served indoors. Manners at table are also the same, and the lack of a roof is not an invitation to use a lawn, flower bed, or terrace floor as an ashtray.

**ALIBIS.**  *See* APOLOGIES AND EXCUSES.

## ALLERGIES

A food allergy is a personal problem that is best not mentioned at the table. A guest allergic to one particular food, like cucumbers, need say only, "No, thank you," when it is offered. Such explanations as "They give me hives" or the weary cliché "I like them but they don't like me" are thoughtless because it is too late for the hostess to change her menu without becoming a short-order cook.

It is dismaying to a hostess to see several of her carefully prepared main dishes go untouched. Therefore, the unfortunate person who is allergic to a number of commonly served foods does best to refuse her invitation with the frank explanation that his diet problem is extreme. She is then free to avoid the seafood, onions, chocolate, or whatever else may be troublemaking for him; or, if for some reason her menu is not open to change, to accept his refusal with sympathy, regret, and no misunderstanding.

The procedure above holds for anyone allergic to animals. It is much better to explain than to leave the owner of a cat, for example, in doubt about the reason her invitations are consistently refused.

## ALLOWANCES

Giving a child a regular income can be a good way to teach him how to manage money, but many authorities on child guidance advise against an allowance set up as payment for the performance of routine household tasks. They believe that the child who shares family chores without pay and as a matter of course, just as he shares family pleasures (such as a holiday trip), is being taught the individual's proper social relation to others in any group—in other words, the responsibility for doing one's fair part that is the basis of all good manners.

Under any circumstances, the amount of an allowance should not be based on the parents' ability to afford a large one, but rather on what is the going rate in the child's circle. It is poor taste, as well as poor judgment of what is best for a child, to give him an allowance conspicuously larger than that of others in his camp or school.

**AMBASSADORS.**   See FORMS OF ADDRESS (Diplomatic).

## AMERICAN

Travelers need to remember that "American" does not mean "citizen of the United States" in Central and South America. Anyone who says, "I am an American," invites the correction "We are Americans too." Ask for the "United States" embassy, not the "American" embassy; say "history of the United States," not "American history," when speaking with a citizen of any of the countries to our south. This rule does not hold, as it logically should, in Canada. Canadians are quite accustomed to calling us "Americans," and themselves "Canadians."

## AMERICAN PLAN

At a hotel or resort, "American Plan" means that meals are included in the quoted price. Customs vary about tipping. If waiters rotate, they are tipped after each meal. Otherwise, tips are given at the end of a short stay, weekly during a long stay. Anyone giving extra or one-time service is tipped at the time. If in doubt, ask the manager.

**ANECDOTES.**   For the extensive list of rules concerning the timing and subject matter of anecdotes, and manners of the listener, see CONVERSATION.

**ANNIVERSARIES.**   See BIRTHDAYS; HOLIDAYS; WEDDING ANNIVERSARIES.

## ANNOUNCEMENTS

The rules concerning the announcement of news, whether business or social, are standardized.

For details about who properly makes an announcement—and when and how—
see separate listings from ADOPTIONS to WEDDINGS, and also the Index for mention
within other subjects.

## ANNULMENTS

The news of a marriage annulment is usually told to friends in an informal
fashion. It is not customary to send out a formal engraved announcement, to
send a release to the press, or to insert a paid notice in the Vital Statistics
columns—though of course this is a matter for individual decision.

## ANSWERS

Certain formal announcements and invitations require an answer. Others require none. The list is long.

Details are given under INVITATIONS and also under separate headings from
BIRTH ANNOUNCEMENTS to WEDDINGS. For answers to spoken questions, see "Questions and Answers" under CONVERSATION.

## ANTIPASTO

The literal translation of the Italian word *antipasto* is "before the meal," Antipasto is an assortment of such appetizers as salami, anchovies, pâté, hard-boiled
eggs, olives, radishes, tomato slices, pimientos, celery, pickled mushrooms,
chick-peas, and so on, served as a first course and eaten with a fork. Individual
servings may be put at each place shortly before dinner is announced, or a
platter may be passed after guests are seated. Antipasto usually is served with
bread and butter. A cruet of oil and one of vinegar, and salt and freshly
ground black pepper are the classic accompaniments.

## ANTIQUES

Beautiful possessions of great age all too often become booby traps for servants
and guests. It is not fair to trust the handling of irreplaceable or extremely
valuable breakables to a servant, nor is it sensible to leave them within the
reach of a little child.

Lovely possessions are really valuable only to the degree that they give
pleasure. The hostess who is so busy putting coasters under glasses that she
does not have time to listen to her guests would do better to lend her great-
great-great-grandfather's piecrust table to a museum or put it in her bedroom;
if her antique chairs will not carry a man's weight, they should be put out of
the way of guests altogether.

## APARTMENTS

A community roof is not an introduction, and any move toward social involve-
ment with fellow apartment-dwellers is properly made slowly and informally.
Only in exceptional circumstances does a resident of an apartment house
make a formal call on a newcomer, as is usual in many suburban communities
of separate houses.

**COMPLAINTS.** The conveniences of life in an apartment house have their
price. A main cause of discomfort and friction is the sounds that inevitably
echo from adjacent apartments. Each tenant has to meet this problem with
resignation. It is only fair to count ten before registering a complaint about
an occasional festivity that goes on past the normal hour for quiet. Chronic
disregard of community peace is another matter, and calls for action.

In general, complaints about one's neighbors are best made through the
superintendent or elevator man if the annoyance is shared by other tenants—
a dog that barks constantly during his owner's absence, for example. In any
case, a diplomatic protest nearly always gets best results. "I'm sure you don't
realize that you wake us when you turn on the Late Late Show" usually is

much more effective than the outraged shout "Turn down that TV!"—which in itself may startle another neighbor out of a sound sleep.

**ENTERING AND LEAVING.** An apartment elevator is considered a part of each tenant's personal quarters. Therefore, a man takes off his hat when sharing an apartment elevator with a woman, even a stranger, unless he is so burdened with bundles that it would be absurd to do so.

Men and boys stand aside and let women and girls get on and off first unless the elevator is so full that this routine politeness would be senseless. However, a hostess with a mixed group ushers all her guests into her elevator, and only one man stands aside until she is aboard.

To a certain extent, corridors too are treated as part of the tenant's dwelling. When a guest leaves, a host usually goes to the elevator, rings, and waits until it comes. A hostess sometimes does the same for a woman guest. If the elevator door is in sight, a hostess stands in her own door until the elevator arrives to pick up either a man or woman guest. When a man is seeing a woman home, he leaves her at the street entrance if there is a doorman. Otherwise, he sees her to her elevator. In a walk-up apartment, he sees her safely inside the street door but does not climb the stairs to say good night at her own door. On the other hand, when a man is calling to take a woman out, he presents himself at her own door under all usual circumstances.

In all other ways, entering and leaving an apartment are the same as for any other dwelling. A host or hostess opens the door and invites the guests to enter first, but if the place is dark or there is a crowd of guests, he or she does the sensible thing and goes first to find lights or show the way.

**GREETINGS.** The doorman, elevator operator, or any other building employee must be given some greeting each time he is encountered. There is no excuse for failing to nod, smile, say "Good evening," or give some other acknowledgment of the presence of an employee, or to say or indicate "Thank you" to an elevator man when leaving his car. Under no circumstances should a member of the building staff be treated like a piece of furniture.

No greeting is required between fellow tenants who live on different floors. In many big apartment houses, people share the same address for years without speaking. However, it is a pointed snub to sail past someone who lives on the same floor without some kind of greeting, and it is customary to nod to a fellow tenant seen month after month in the elevator. The resident of longer tenure usually makes the first advance, though there is no hard-and-fast rule.

**TIPPING.** It is customary for a resident to tip a staff member for any service beyond his regular duties—when he is asked to walk a dog, move furniture, or run out to mail a letter for example. In addition, an elevator man is generally tipped for the extra work entailed by a very large party. The guest of a resident is expected to tip an attendant who handles any sizable luggage, parks a car, and so on. Staff members usually are tipped in cash at Christmastime, but a superintendent with managerial status is often given a bottle or other present rather than money.

## APOLOGIES AND EXCUSES

The whole matter of apologies is confused by two popular but essentially senseless maxims. The first, the sweeping "Never apologize and never explain," is an absurd policy for anyone to follow—unless it be the person with the unfortunate habit of apologizing constantly for everything: his appearance, clothes, house, car, and so on. In essence, he is an insatiable demander of attention and reassurance, practicing what Oliver Wendell Holmes termed "egotism wrong side out."

An apology is always called for when one person puts another to inconvenience, discomfort, disadvantage, embarrassment, or loss. The person who misapplies the "Never apologize . . ." maxim in such cases not only shows a thick-skinned indifference to the feelings of his victim but also builds up an extremely difficult situation for himself. All it takes is "I'm sorry." But to skip completely any expression of regret leaves the victim first baffled and then understandably both hurt and indignant.

The second doubtful maxim—"Least said, soonest mended"—does not mean "Say nothing," except in one case. If apologizing for a thoughtless comment made in the presence of others might do double damage by emphasizing the embarrassment of the victim, it is better to skip the matter at the moment and mend things later, in private. "Least said, soonest mended" is best interpreted as "Let the apology fit the crime." Nothing is helped, and conversation is interrupted, if a guest makes a long, abject apology for something like spilling a glass of water at the table, for example.

A more emphatic apology is of course due after any mischance that causes real pain, damage, or inconvenience—if a spilled drink burns someone or stains or soaks his clothing, for instance. But even then the most considerate procedure is to apologize with unmistakable concern, help mend the damage if possible, and let the unfortunate victim retreat from the embarrassing spotlight of attention.

The manner and the tone in which an apology is offered are more important than the words. "Please excuse me," "I'm so sorry," and "I beg your pardon" are among the standard expressions of apology, but "Oh-oh" or any other spontaneous exclamation of sincere concern can serve in many situations. A brusque "I'm sorry" fulfills the form but not the spirit of an apology, and usually only adds resentment to the distress of the victim. And the apology that shifts the blame or puts emphasis on the excuse rather than the regret ("I'm sorry, but if you hadn't—") is no apology at all.

In any circumstance where an apology is needed, expression of concern for the other person comes first, and this rule holds even if both parties to an accident or mischance are partly to blame or if no one is directly responsible. "I'm sorry" or some other indication of regret is the small coin of courtesy due from anyone who jostles another passenger on a bus, for example—even if the driver's heavy foot on the brake is clearly responsible.

No more than a forgiving gesture or understanding grimace is necessary in answer to a routine polite apology for a minor mishap, but some response other than a stony, enduring silence is just as essential as the apology itself.

Any sincere apology must be accepted with good grace; and what is of major importance in achieving good grace in both an apology and a response is exchanging them promptly and with sympathetic awareness of the other person's distress.

**ALIBIS.** By dictionary definition, an alibi is a provable claim that a person was not in a specific place at a specific time. The dictionary also gives an alternate meaning, "a plausible excuse, especially for failure or negligence," but this second meaning is best forgotten because "alibi" used in that sense has come to mean the weaseling out of blame or responsibility by a palpably flimsy, or even a false, excuse. "What's your alibi?" can have an insulting implication, and is not a good substitute for "What was your reason for . . ."

**EXCUSES AND EXPLANATIONS.** Everyone causes trouble for someone else at one time or another. When the mischance is due to thoughtlessness, carelessness, or just plain stupidity, little can be done except to admit the fact and express regret. But in the countless cases where the difficulty is caused by a circumstance that could not be anticipated or controlled, in simple justice to everyone concerned the reason should be fully explained—if it is possible to do so without making matters worse by being a tattletale. An example on the simplest level is the difference between "We had a flat tire" and "I *told* Joe that we had a soft tire, but he simply would not listen."

## APPETIZERS

Any food served just before a meal or as a first course to sharpen the appetite is an appetizer. This includes the snacks served with cocktails and such salty foods as pâtés, pickled fish, eggs à la Russe, seafood cocktails, and the items that Italians call *antipasto*. Fruit salads, fruit juices, and soups are not technically appetizers even if served as a first course.

In this country, the appetizers that are eaten from the fingers are usually called "canapés." The appetizers served at the table and eaten with a fork are generally called "hors d'oeuvres," but no one makes any great point of this distinction.

Plates are rarely provided for the finger foods served with drinks, though of course they may be; but cocktail napkins are an essential. When appetizers are offered speared with a toothpick, they are eaten in one bite and the toothpick is put on an ashtray—never back on the serving platter.

## APPLAUSE

Common courtesy calls for applause on certain specific occasions. Common sense and custom forbid such interruptions at other specific times. It is more unsophisticated than ill-mannered to break the rules, though applause at the wrong time can be a disaster to a performer, speaker, and a participant in some games and sports events.

Clapping can be vigorous, but clapping with the hands cupped to make a louder noise, yelling, booing, stamping, and whistling are generally saved for certain sports events, though by no means all. Booing is part of the show at professional wrestling matches, for example, but is never correct during collegiate or other amateur contests. Squealing is for kids, and even they are out of line in making a show of themselves in this fashion when applauding any serious artist. Shouts of "Bravo" and so on are not incorrect, but they make the admirer somewhat conspicuous in this country.

Those seated in the front rows are obligated to give at least a token demonstration of applause when a speaker or performer takes a bow. This is no more than compassionate recognition that he did his best, no matter how inept it may have been. It is unkind to sit immobile in the direct view of a performer at the end of a show, or to move out of the front rows during a final curtain call. Also, as a general rule, a guest applauds to the most cordial degree he can manage, as a courtesy to his dismayed host, rather than maintain a pointed silence after dull entertainment.

**BALLET.** The conductor is always applauded when he makes his first appearance. A set may be applauded if the mood of the music and action will not be spoiled. A burst of applause sometimes follows the execution of an especially difficult solo or sequence, but it should be cut short so that the mood of the work will not be damaged seriously. When in doubt, don't applaud.

**CHURCHES.** Applause is never appropriate during or following any service in a church or other place of worship.

**COMPETITIONS.** Applause is never correct during tournament play at a bridge, chess, tennis, or other similar competition.

**CONCERTS AND RECITALS.** The conductor and the soloists are applauded each time they make an entrance and an exit. Applause is appropriate only at the end of each selection. It is never given following each of a group of related though separate selections offered as a unit, even though there is a marked moment of silence between them; or between the movements of a concerto, a symphony, or any other large, integrated musical work.

**CONDUCTORS.** A conductor is applauded when he enters the pit at the opera or a musical comedy, or takes the podium at any concert. He acknowledges this greeting by facing the audience, and bowing. When he turns to face the orchestra, applause ceases.

**ENCORES.** Persistent applause for a number in a musical comedy and calls for "Encore" are permissible and very pleasing to the performers. At all other musical events, the audience waits until the intermission or, more usually, the end of the program before calling for encores. The performer usually offers an added number or numbers of his choice, though an audience may call for the repetition of any short item on his program or something else in his repertoire.

**LEAVING DURING APPLAUSE.** Whenever possible, members of an audience, and especially those in the front rows, remain seated until the performers have received the final round of applause.

**LECTURES.**  *See* "SPEAKERS," below.

**MOVIES.** Applause, if any, is best saved for the end unless the audience is, as a whole, having a sportive time at an old silent melodrama.

**NATIONAL ANTHEM.** The playing or singing of our national anthem is never applauded if the rules are followed.

**OPERA.**  *See* OPERA.

**SACRED MUSIC.** Even if performed in an auditorium or concert hall, sacred music such as the *Messiah* and the Bach B minor Mass and *St. Matthew Passion* must not be applauded during or after its performance. Only the first entrance of the conductor, the orchestra, and choir may be applauded, though frequently this too is omitted. However, it is correct to applaud the performance of a sacred work that is interspersed among secular pieces at a recital.

**SPEAKERS.** A lecturer or other speaker should be given a welcoming round of applause when introduced, and at least a token round of applause at the end of his talk—in relief that he has at last shut up, if for no other reason. A speaker may be interrupted by applause, and a great many deliberately invite this evidence of approval. When in doubt, however, don't start applause. Thin, scattered applause from a few overeager enthusiasts is worse than none, and too many interruptions can damage a speaker's timing of major points.

**SPORTS EVENTS.** Applause is a major breach of manners at certain times during some competitive events, but customary during others. The rules are explicit. For details, *see* separate sports listings. One rule applies to all spectators, however. It is poor sportsmanship to applaud a poor shot or a miss during the playing of tennis, billiards, golf, or any other competitive sport, no matter how delighted a spectator may be at the advantage this failure gives his favorite player or team.

**STANDING OVATIONS.** These are the supreme compliments that audiences can pay. The standing ovation honoring an exceptional performance comes at the end of a speech or when a star or company appears for a curtain call.

**SYMPHONIES.** It is customary to applaud the conductor each time he takes the podium or leaves it. A soloist in a concerto also is applauded when he makes his first appearance, but applause for his solo must be saved until the entire work is finished. The individual movements of a symphony should not be applauded.

**THEATERS.** Applause is the very breath of life to people of the theater. It is customary to applaud an effective set when the curtain rises. A star is applauded on his first entrance, and frequently a well-known member of the supporting cast is given this greeting. On occasion, the end of an extraordinarily effective scene or long, difficult speech is applauded, but, as a general rule, applause that interrupts the action and breaks into the mood of a drama is not welcome. An audience is privileged to call for an encore of a musical comedy number, but not to demand repetition of a scene in a drama.

**APPLES.** *See* FRUITS.

## APPOINTMENT TO OFFICE

During a meeting, the appointment of someone present to a committee or other office does not require a spoken acceptance. Silence can give consent. If it is necessary to refuse, an answer should be given immediately. When news of an appointment is telephoned or given in any other informal fashion to someone absent from a meeting, acceptance or refusal on the telephone is enough. However, a written notification of appointment to an office requires a written answer.

## APPOINTMENTS

An appointment is an agreement to be at a specified place at a specified time, and should be considered a word-of-honor promise, not to be broken except in an emergency.

**BREAKING.** An explanation of some kind is called for when it is necessary to break an appointment. The excuse must be accepted without any such reproach as "But I was depending on you!" The best answer is "I am so sorry," and, if applicable and practical, "Can I help in any way?" When the explanation is flimsy, offhand, or palpably false, it is hard to find a more impeccable and effective reproof than an indifferent "Oh. I'm sorry."

**FOR SERVICES.** An appointment with a doctor, dentist, hairdresser, or others providing similar services is an agreement for the purchase of a commodity—his time. Failing to keep such an appointment or breaking it at the last moment means loss of income to the person providing the service, and deprives some other client who could have been given that time.

**FORGETTING.** Completely forgetting an appointment is one of the most embarrassing of mishaps. The only sensible remedy is for each person involved to put himself in the other's place. After a reasonable wait, the victim should telephone to find out if perhaps he is mistaken about the time and place (which he just might have been). Or he can bring the matter up later in person, by telephone or letter, but the mischance should not be ignored. No matter how inconvenienced or annoyed the victim may be, he must accept an apology with as much calm as he can muster. The person at fault, on the other hand, must apologize in no uncertain terms, and suggest another appointment forthwith.

**HOST AND HOSTESS.** When an appointment is in a public place, the host or hostess is expected to arrive a few minutes before the appointed hour in order to be on hand to welcome the guest.

**TARDINESS.** There is no other description for people who are chronically late than "chronically rude" because they callously waste other people's time. Occasionally, tardiness is unavoidable, but even so it calls for special procedures. The first requirement always, whenever possible, is to telephone if the delay is to be fifteen minutes or more.

For lateness at meals and other details relating to making, breaking, and keeping appointments, *see* Tardiness in the Index.

**APRICOTS.** *See* FRUITS.

## ARMBANDS

An armband that is tied on as a temporary badge of authority is called a "brassard." A black band attached to the left sleeve of a man's suit or overcoat is called a "mourning band."

See MOURNING.

**ART GALLERIES.**    See MUSEUMS, ART GALLERIES, AND EXHIBITS.

## ARTICHOKES

This delightful vegetable usually is served as a first course—hot, chilled, or at room temperature. Before cooking, each thorny leaf point is snipped off with kitchen shears, and the stem is cut off so that the artichoke will stand upright on a flat base. A very small artichoke may be served on a salad plate, but any sizable one needs a plate of dinner size. The standard artichoke plate has a center section for the whole vegetable, a smaller section for the sauce, and a large one for the discarded leaves. These plates are a pretty and useful addition to a china service, but are by no means essential. An ordinary dinner plate is equally correct. Any firm sauce, such as mayonnaise, is spooned to one side. Melted butter and other liquid sauces are served on the dinner plate in a tiny separate container. Some excellent recipes call for cooking artichokes in water, oil, and spices, but this method of preparation is better avoided unless finger bowls can be provided.

One leaf at a time is pulled off, its base dipped in the sauce, and then pulled between the teeth to detach the soft edible portion. The remainder of the leaf is discarded on the side of the plate, and anyone experienced in the handling of artichokes does this neatly, since an untidy heap of leaves is an unattractive sight.

The bottom of an artichoke is called the *fond,* which is a French word for "bottom," and it is frequently also called the "heart," though technically the heart of an artichoke is the *fond* with a few of the tender inside leaves attached. The whole hearts of only the very youngest artichokes are served, since a prickly thistle-like fuzz known as the "choke" develops as the vegetable matures. When the *fond* of a mature artichoke is reached, the choke is lifted aside with the fork. The *fond* is then cut and eaten with the fork. Artichoke bottoms filled with sauce or stuffing are served as a vegetable with a main course, as a separate course, or as an item on an antipasto platter. Canned or frozen artichoke hearts are served whole or split as a vegetable or added to a salad.

## ARTISTS

This word is often used for people skilled in any of the fine arts, though most commonly it refers to those who practice one of the graphic arts. People who would not dream of asking a doctor or lawyer for free consultation—or a garage mechanic for free service—all too often put a heavy demand on an artist's free time and generosity by asking for a sketch, layout, design for a bookplate or weathervane, or a recital in exchange for supper.

See CELEBRITIES.

**ASHTRAYS.**    See MEALS AND THEIR SERVICE; SMOKING; TABLE MANNERS.

## ASPARAGUS

Asparagus may be served as a first course, as a separate salad or vegetable course, or on the plate with the main course. In all cases, it should be well drained before serving. When asparagus is offered on a serving platter, a sauce is usually offered in a separate dish. Some authorities say that, except at a formal dinner, the lower part of the stalk may be picked up in the fingers and pulled through the teeth to extract the softer substance from the woody fiber

of one driver, nothing is gained by giving him an outraged bawling out. It should always be remembered that no one plans a collision deliberately—and that it nearly always takes two less than alert drivers to make one accident. Needless to say, it is irresponsible beyond any excuse to drive a car that is not sufficiently insured to cover both injury to people and damage to the property of others.

**BORROWING.** It is not necessary to replace gasoline used during a brief run in a borrowed car, but the least expected of a borrower who takes a car any appreciable distance is to return it with the tank filled to the same level or with more fuel than when he started; as tidy as when he picked it up—and promptly at the agreed time. A borrower is obligated to report to the owner any accident involving the car while it was in his possession, and to pay for damage not covered by insurance, just as he would be in the case of any other borrowed item.

**CAR POOLS.** Anyone breaking the unwritten but nonetheless exact rules governing the behavior of members of a car pool is likely to find himself suddenly back at his own wheel. Ready or not, the car-pool member is expected to bound out of his house at the first honk or be waiting at the appointed pickup place; to be punctual in arriving at the meeting place for the return trip; and only in an emergency to ask his fellows to wait while he stops for any time-consuming errand.

**CHAUFFEURS.** *See* CHAUFFEURS.

**DRIVERS.** Being behind the wheel of a car in no way exempts a person from the basic rules of good behavior anywhere—in spite of considerable evidence to the contrary. A driver is expected to treat his passengers as if they were guests under his roof, and to give another driver the same courtesy as if both were on foot.

He does not leave the window beside him open without making sure it is not creating an uncomfortable draft for his passengers. He avoids jackrabbit starts, unnecessarily abrupt stops, and swinging into curves at a speed that throws his passengers off balance. He restrains that impulse to lean on the horn in a traffic jam when the noise can do no good except as a release for his own irritation, at the expense of everyone within earshot. He touches his horn lightly, taking care not to startle and perhaps confuse other drivers—or pedestrians—with unnecessary blasts of noise. He does not yell uncomplimentary comments at other drivers or at pedestrians, and spares his passengers the boredom of listening to a stream of complaints about everyone else on the road. He takes care not to roar through puddles and fling a spray of water on pedestrians or cars. He does not wait for a passenger to ask for a comfort-station stop, but anticipates such a need. He observes speed limits and all other traffic laws. And he obeys the behavior rules following.

**ENTERING AND LEAVING.** As a general rule, a man opens the door for a woman and helps her in before taking his place; he gets out first, offers her his hand, and closes the door after her. Common sense suspends these rules if it is not both safe and reasonably comfortable to follow them. If there is heavy traffic, mud, or any other hazard on his side of the car, a male driver properly says, "I'd better get in from your side," and enters first. When leaving a car under the same circumstances, he follows her out. Passengers in the rear of a car or taxi follow much the same rule. On a one-way street, if the woman is on the curb side at a stop in heavy traffic, a man climbs past her if the car is sufficiently roomy; if there is little or no extra knee room and it is neither safe nor sensible for him to get out on the street side and walk around to open the door, a woman should take the initiative and get out first. The standard rules are observed on any formal occasion, but an able-bodied pair correctly ignore them on many informal occasions—when getting in and out for supermarket shopping, for example.

The old rule that a woman must always be seated at the right of a male companion in the back seat of any vehicle is an absurdity today, as well as an impossibly awkward rule to follow in any car much less roomy than a limousine. In horse-and-buggy days, the seat on the right automatically put a woman on the curb side and so gave her maximum protection from the mud, water, or pebbles that might be tossed by the wheels of passing carriages. Modern one-way streets make the old rule meaningless. Whoever enters the back seat of a car or taxi first should take the far seat.

If two men and one woman are sharing the back seat, one man usually gets in first and the woman sits between her two male companions. If two women and one man share the rear seat, the man enters last and sits on the right, though if the car is roomy he may sit in the middle if he likes.

When two married couples going to or from some social festivity share a car, they assort themselves in any convenient way. Unless one couple is picking the other up and so is already seated in the front, they generally switch partners, but there is nothing rigid about this rule. Any arrangement that is most practical and pleasant is correct.

When stopping briefly in traffic to pick up a woman passenger, a male driver does not leave the wheel to help her in, but under all usual circumstances he does get out if he is parked. And when it is practical, a man in the rear seat of a car or taxi gets out and helps a woman in, even if there is a doorman to do so.

**HITCHHIKERS.** In some states, hitchhiking is against the law. Whether it is lawful or not, there is only one rule of safety, sense, and good behavior about hitchhiking for children: DON'T. Hundreds of thousands of youngsters thumb rides safely every day—but never a year passes without its series of tragic abuses of little hitchhikers. Responsible parents have no choice except to forbid hitchhiking, and drivers should help them by refusing to stop for children.

The only sensible choice for women and teen-age drivers is to ignore the appeal of all hitchhikers. It is difficult for a good-hearted driver to skim past a weary, anxious, adult hitchhiker, but it is better to let grown men or couples be the good Samaritans in this case—and they should remember that they have legal responsibilities to any passenger, friend or stranger.

A driver bound for a distant destination wisely evades answering the direct question "How far are you going?" Otherwise, he may find it awkward to get rid of a tiresome or otherwise undesirable hitchhiker before the end of his journey. If a hitchhiker does not give his name and destination when entering a car, the driver should ask for that information. Though a driver is not obligated to give his own name in return, he usually gives his last name as a routine courtesy, but does best to volunteer no other personal information.

**LIGHTS.** A series of cars with lights on in the daytime are moving as a convoy. This signal is customarily used when cars are going as a unit to a cemetery, as a request to other motorists to cede the right of way. Other motorists should give any convoy the right of way, and should never cut into the line of such a unit except in an extreme emergency.

**LITTERING.** It is against the law in all but a very few communities to toss any kind of litter onto a public thoroughfare. It also is indefensibly bad manners to add so much as an empty cigarette package to the unsightly clutter of discarded papers, boxes, cans, bottles, and tissues that line all too many sidewalks, throughways, and country roads. It is extremely dangerous to throw a burning cigarette stub out of a car even if passing through a desert where there is no chance of starting a roadside fire. The wind can easily sweep the stub into the back seat or into a passing or following car. It is equally risky to flip ashes out of a car window, since the wind can tear off the burning tip of the cigarette.

**PARKING.** The most elementary consideration for others calls for parking so that the allotted space for another car is not blocked. Don't put a car in the middle of two parking spaces between driveways, for example, leaving room for no more than a bike fore and aft. Don't leave a bumper jammed against that of another car. Leave equal clearance between the car in front and the one at the rear so that both drivers can pull out without a struggle. It is fair enough to release the hand brake and move a thoughtlessly parked car a few inches if there is a real need, but it is never fair to leave a car in any position that will be a problem to its driver. Bumping and nudging a car that is in gear or has one wheel turned against a curb can cause real damage.

Particular care should be taken not to nudge motorcycles, motor scooters, and bicycles when parking near them. Very little pressure will knock them over, and a fall can crack off starter or brake pedal, throw the front wheel out of line, or do other serious damage. Moving a motorcycle or scooter that occupies a metered parking space to a place between meters is dishonest. Not only will the delicate small vehicle be exposed to damage when adjacent cars leave; its owner may be fined for illegal parking on a metered street.

Few things stir a driver to quicker or more justified rage than the parking thief who whips into the space for which he is obviously waiting.

**PASSENGERS.** No passenger can go far wrong if he treats the driver's car as if it were part of his dwelling. Using the car floor as an ashtray or wastebasket is just as rude as it would be to discard trash on the floor in the driver's house. Passengers are not privileged to turn on or adjust a radio without permission, nor to adjust windows without making sure the change causes no discomfort to others. The rules of safety as well as manners demand avoidance of anything that will distract, rattle, or handicap the driver. He must not be expected to take a hand off the wheel to light a cigarette, help with a wrap, or control a romping child or a frisking dog. A passenger sitting beside the driver should attempt to relax. "Helping" to control the car by pressing the floorboards as if they were the brakes only makes the driver nervous. Leaning forward at an intersection to see if the way is clear blocks the driver's vision when he is trying to see. A mistake common to many passengers who do not drive is pointing to a sign on the left that calls for a right turn; always point in the direction the driver should take. And do as little back-seat driving as humanly possible.

**PEDESTRIANS.** Drivers are obligated to respect the rights of pedestrians. In turn, pedestrians should give drivers a fighting chance to do so—by remembering that it takes a few feet or even yards for the best driver to bring his car to a stop. Watch the traffic—not only the traffic lights. Stop and look before leaving the sidewalk; and on a road without sidewalks, walk facing the oncoming traffic.

**SIRENS.** Behavior in response to a siren is not a matter of etiquette. It is a matter of law. But it is so important that it is included here anyway. All cars must pull over to the extreme right. Drivers may then proceed with caution, but must never cross an intersection until they are certain that the vehicle sounding the siren will not be blocked or delayed. Pedestrians must also clear the streets.

**TIPPING.** Garage mechanics usually are not tipped, though if one works overtime in an emergency or gives other special service, a tip is in order in recognition of kindness beyond the requirements of duty.

It is not necessary or customary to tip the attendant in most parking lots and garages. The attendant in a parking lot or garage used regularly is usually given a dollar from time to time, and is remembered with a tip at Christmas.

Any special service such as keeping a car dusted and swept out deserves a tip.

Parking attendants who pick up and deliver cars at the door of a hotel, restaurant, nightclub, or residence are tipped. A doorman who watches a double-parked car or one in a limited-time zone also is tipped.

Gas-station attendants are never tipped for regular service, but either the words or manner of a client should say "Thank you," and a direct order such as "Clean the windshield" certainly should always be accompanied by a spoken or implied "please."

## AVOCADOS

An avocado, when stuffed with salad, is served peeled. Half of an avocado with only salad dressing in its seed cavity is served in its shell. In this case, the left hand steadies the avocado as a bite-size piece is cut out with either spoon or fork, though a fork is more commonly used. A peeled avocado is cut and eaten with a fork.

**AWARDS.**   *See* DECORATIONS, MEDALS, ORDERS.

# B

## BABIES

Not everyone welcomes an invitation to hold a new baby. Proud mothers find this hard to believe, and sometimes throw visitors into a panic by handing over a baby without warning. On the other hand, mothers have their problems with friends who reach out to pick up or kiss a baby without invitation. "Hands off" is the standard rule when meeting a new baby.

**GIFTS.** It is customary for close relatives and intimate friends of the parents to give a present to the baby either before or shortly after its arrival—and it is a good idea to take along some little toy to any older child to let him know that he has not lost the spotlight completely.

Babies grow so fast and usually are so well supplied with everything they will need in their first months that it is best to choose things suitable for a one-year-old, or something else for use in the future—from a piggy bank to a bond.

By tradition pink is for girls and blue for boys but a gift in a pastel shade of any color is appropriate and white is always safe.

**SHOWERS.** What is commonly called a "stork shower" is given several months before the baby is due, since its purpose is to supply part of the layette. If a baby dies shortly after birth, shower presents are not returned. If there is hope for another child, they are saved for it. Otherwise, they are passed along, in due time, to some other baby.

*See* ADOPTIONS; BIRTH ANNOUNCEMENTS; BIRTH CERTIFICATES; BRIT MILAH; CHRISTENING AND BAPTISM.

## BABY CARRIAGES

There is no heavy labor involved in pushing a baby carriage even when it is loaded with hefty twins. A modern buggy rolls on its ball bearings at the touch of a finger. Just the same, pushing a baby carriage is not woman's work when husband and wife are together unless he has an armful of parcels. If he strolls with empty hands while his wife shoves the carriage, he puts her in the symbolic position of a beast of burden. Illogically, this rule does not hold if a male acquaintance happens to join a mother for a few blocks when she is out for a walk with her baby in its buggy. He helps her with the carriage at curbs and steps, but he is not obligated to make himself look like part of a cozy family unit by pushing the carriage along a sidewalk.

## BABY-SITTERS

A baby-sitter is a specialist, not a maid of all work, and should not be expected to fill in her time with household chores while her charges are asleep. The sitter who is asked to wash the dinner dishes, for example, is within her rights to explain politely that she does not consider such extra services part of her job. Special arrangements can be made with a sitter, of course, but the employer who wants a sitter to do housework should offer to pay her at a houseworker's rate, which is commonly higher than a young sitter's fee.

The baby-sitter left in charge of a child and a house is in a position of extreme trust. Under no circumstances should she abuse that trust by exploring closets, peeking into drawers, trying on clothes, or questioning a child in her care about intimate family matters. And if she has any manners at all, she will not help herself to candy, raid the refrigerator, or invite a friend to keep her company without specific permission. On the other hand, parents who have not forgotten their own teens will be properly sympathetic to the insatiable appetite of those years, and, in common compassion, provide enough snacks to sustain the sitter through the evening.

Much trouble and confusion can be avoided if the duties and privileges of a sitter are clearly explained to her—and also if her authority is clearly explained to her charges, so that they are not inspired to give her a runaround, as a form of indoor sport, as soon as their parents leave. Under all circumstances, the employers should leave a telephone number at which they can be reached in an emergency or, if this is not possible, the number of a neighbor or relative who will be at home and prepared to respond if help is needed.

If the return of the parents is delayed much past the agreed hour, they should not fail to telephone to a young sitter so that she, in turn, can let her own parents know she will be late.

The responsibility of the employers does not end with payment of a young sitter's fee. They must make certain that a neighborhood girl (or boy) gets safely home any time after dark and most especially in the late evening. If the baby-sitter's parents are not standing by to pick her up, the employer should drive or walk a young girl to her door, or keep watch while she runs across lawns to her own house. The same consideration is due an older baby-sitter—modified, of course, according to her age, the neighborhood, and the hour.

**TIPPING.** There are exceptions, but as a general rule a baby-sitter is treated as a professional and is not tipped. A sitter who has been put to unexpected trouble or who has given service beyond the call of duty usually is given a little extra money or some kind of present, however.

## BACHELOR DINNER. *See* WEDDINGS.

## BACHELORS

Many young single men are not equipped to return dinner invitations in their own quarters, and cannot afford to entertain sizable groups at a restaurant or theater. So, as a general rule, very young bachelors are exempted from the obligation to return entertainment more or less in kind. A bachelor is obligated to pay his way by other means, however, though some hostesses, hard-pressed for extra men, feel that the bachelor who condescends to be a guest has evened the score—and too many young men seem to agree.

The least a bachelor can do is telephone or send a note of thanks to a hostess a day or so after a party. Many young men neglect this courtesy, feeling (mistakenly) that such an expression of thanks must be accompanied by a return invitation, especially if the hostess is single. Unless a young man has had a dreadful time and is determined not to accept another invitation to that house, he does best not to disappear into silence—for selfish reasons, if for no other. Follow-up thanks will endear him to any hostess and is almost certain to produce other invitations for him. A bachelor or any other guest need not turn up with a gift in hand every time he accepts an invitation to a meal. But he makes it clear that he is not a freeloader if he takes or sends a book, a bottle, some candy, or flowers to a hostess after he has enjoyed a series of her parties.

A bachelor can also pay his way by helping to make a party run smoothly. The single man who holds himself ready to help at a bar is a blessing, though he should take care not to appoint himself a deputy host in the home of a single woman and so give the impression of more intimacy than is a fact—or than should be advertised. For the same reason, he should not stay on alone with his hostess after her other guests leave.

A bachelor is not obligated to see his dinner partner home, but the least he can do is to see an unaccompanied woman to a taxi or to her car if she leaves at the same time. If he is driving, he gains the thanks of his hostess if he offers to ferry other guests who lack transportation, though he certainly need not go miles out of his way to get them home. If for his own good reasons he wants to avoid such courtesies, he contrives not to leave with guests who might be a problem to him.

**DATES.** The general rule is that a host and hostess are included in the first invitation to someone introduced under their roof. A bachelor need not follow this rule completely. He should include them if he entertains a couple, unless the host and hostess are very much senior to them and to him, but he is entirely free to make a date with a single woman without including the host or hostess who introduced them, if he wants to.

See also DATES.

**ENTERTAINING AT HOME.** There are no lifted eyebrows today if a bachelor stirs up dinner in his own apartment for a woman friend, but a single man does not ask a girl to visit his apartment without giving her a fair chance to accept or refuse if no one else is to be there. If he asks her to dinner and does not mention other guests, a good, graceful answer is "Who else is coming?"— if she wants to make clear that she would rather not go to his place unchaperoned. A bachelor does not ask a young woman to visit his apartment alone late at night unless he does not care about her reputation—or suspects that she does not care about it either. For the same reason, he does not suggest that she stay on after other guests leave, and she makes a point of not doing so.

It is more tactful of the young bachelor host to ask a married woman to sit opposite him at table than to put a young unmarried woman in the hostess's place, unless he wants to suggest the far-off sound of wedding bells, or unless he assigns the head of his table so matter-of-factly that there is no overtone of "playing house."

With a few common-sense exceptions, it is the bachelor's duty to see that no woman guest leaves his place alone late at night. He arranges for another guest to drop her at her door, puts her in a taxi, or takes her home himself. If she has come in her own car, he puts her safely in it. However, if she is leaving earlier than other guests, all he need do is see her as far as his door or to the door of the elevator. It is not necessary for him to abandon his other guests while he finds her a taxi, for example.

**THANKING THE BACHELOR.** Women thank any host, married or single, for a pleasant time when leaving his party or at the end of a date. In return, the host thanks a woman for being his guest.

An old-fashioned rule of etiquette decreed that a woman should never write or telephone thanks to a single man following a party at which he was the host (excepting only a house party, which always requires a bread-and-butter letter). Today's good, though not required, practice is a note or a telephone call of appreciation to a single man from a woman guest.

## BACON

Very crisp bacon, which would shatter into bits if cut, may be picked up in the fingers. If it is not cooked to crispness, it is cut with a knife and eaten with a fork.

## BADGES

Name badges serve a practical purpose at very large business gatherings and at some clubs or other semisocial gatherings that bring many strangers together. They are not appropriate at a strictly social event. A name badge should be big enough so that the name can be read easily, but an oversized badge is neither attractive nor dignified. Many people dislike wearing name badges when passing through the lobby or corridors of a hotel—from one meeting of a convention to another, for example—and so the most practical badges are those that may be easily detached and slipped into a pocket or handbag. Badges that fasten on with pins rather than clips are easier for women to use.

The "badges" for ushers at weddings, balls, and other social events are small but distinctive boutonnieres, never name badges.

## BADMINTON

Within about the last twenty years, badminton has become a full-fledged international competitive sport, though many people still think of it as a casual backyard game. Increasingly, clubs and schools are installing permanent outdoor courts, and many also have gymnasium floors marked for indoor play. Official badminton tournaments are always played indoors in this country.

Behavior rules for players and spectators are the same as for tennis (*which see*).

CLOTHES. In national championship play and in most tournaments, the white clothes suitable for formal tennis competition are correct. For informal play, color is of no importance, and any simple, comfortable clothing that permits freedom of movement is suitable. Women wear either shorts or slacks. Special badminton shoes are available, but most people find that sneakers are a satisfactory substitute. Woolen socks serve as an additional cushion for the feet. A lightweight jacket or sweater is sometimes needed for indoor play, since indoor courts are often kept quite cool.

## BALLS AND DANCES

Today, the word "ball" is used almost exclusively to mean a very large official or subscription dance, though it can be applied correctly to a very large formal private dance. It should be noted, however, that an invitation to even the largest and most spectacular *private* dance does not read "to a ball"; the only correct phrase is "to a dance." "Ball" is correctly used only in an invitation to public or official entertainments like inaugural balls, charity balls, or other subscription balls.

The basic rules for behavior are the same whether the party is called a ball, assembly, cotillion, dance, prom, or hop, but there are variations in certain of the procedures depending on the size, character, and location of the event.

ARRIVING. At an informal party—dancing to records at someone's house, for example—the guests are expected to arrive very close to the time specified in the invitation. At a ball or large dance, public or private, guests are privileged to turn up when they like. The usual limit of delay is about an hour after the starting time.

If an admittance card has been issued, the guest should carry it. Anyone who has mislaid or forgotten to bring his card can send a message in to the hostess or a committee member asking for clearance, but that causes awkward delay for him at the entrance, and certainly will not endear him to whoever has to drop other duties to identify him.

If there is a receiving line of any kind—host and hostess, committee members, chaperones—the guests go through it as soon as they have left their wraps in the place provided. It is never correct to bypass a receiving line; those who do so also risk being suspected of party crashing. If there is no receiving line or if it has disbanded, a guest at a big private party finds an occasion to speak with the host and hostess as soon as possible—certainly before supper. If the hostess is dancing, a single man might cut in. A couple might start dancing and make a point of speaking with her in passing, and also make their arrival known to the host in the same or any other convenient way. At a subscription ball, guests need not look up members of the sponsoring committee (if the receiving line has disbanded) unless they have personal reasons for doing so. At a small party, the host and hostess will be alert to welcome arriving guests, but if they are not immediately available, a guest finds them without delay. A housemother at a sorority, for example, or any other chaperone in a similar capacity occupies the position of official hostess and is treated accordingly.

The procedures for teen-age dances at school and elsewhere are given under CHAPERONS.

**CLOTHES.** An invitation should indicate the kind of dress expected. A formal engraved invitation calls for Black Tie unless other dress is specifically stated. A woman wearing long gloves keeps them on, but she tucks them in at the wrist when she takes refreshment while standing near a buffet, and takes them off completely if she is seated at a table for supper. At a dance in someone's house, a handbag can be left with wraps or put down in any convenient place in the room cleared for dancing. Elsewhere, a woman carries her small evening bag with her when she is dancing, if she likes.

**CRASHING.** There is only one rule: Don't.

How to deal with the misguided people who break the rule is discussed under PARTY CRASHERS.

**DANCE CARDS.** The little tickets or folders known as dance cards or dance programs are completely out of fashion today at private dances, though of course not incorrect. They are sometimes supplied at college and other dances.

**DANCING MANNERS.** Definite rules that cannot properly be broken govern the manners of dancers on all occasions, from the most informal teen-age hop to the ball of the year.

**Asking for a Dance, Accepting, Refusing.** A man does not use the old-fashioned dancing-school bow when asking for a dance, but only the small bow that accompanies any formal greeting. Or, less formally, a smile and gesture of inquiry can serve equally well. Something like "May I have this dance?" is the standard formula, but it is more often shortened to "Dance?" than elaborated· to "May I have the honor of this dance?" which sounds stilted under ordinary circumstances.

In accepting, all a woman needs to do is smile, and rise if she is seated. She always smiles in farewell to the man who is sitting beside her or is with her.

A woman may refuse an invitation to dance if she wishes to, but she is expected to say something that will take the sting out of a flat refusal: "I'm not free for this one—maybe later?" or "I'm sorry. I have to make a telephone call" (in which case she is obligated at least to seem to go and make the call).

"I'm sitting this one out" is also a good excuse for not dancing; but if she is sitting with a group, the ordinary gracious procedure is to ask the man she has turned down to join the group, unless he is obviously tipsy or in some other way out of line. By the rules, a woman cannot refuse to dance with one man and then immediately accept the invitation of another, since that would be a pointed insult.

There are no firm rules about which partner precedes the other on and off the dance floor. If it is simplest and easiest for a woman to precede a man, she does so. If they have to make their way through a throng, he goes first to break the trail. If they must walk across the floor at the end of the dance, her partner walks on her left or leads the way through a crowd.

The one unbreakable rule is that a man never leaves his partner to make her way alone from the floor. If she was sitting with a group, he takes her back to it; or steers her to a group of friends at the refreshment table and then slips away, but he must not leave her stranded. This can take some fast footwork if he has the next dance booked, and so his partner is expected to help him out by any method she can find—pointing out her next partner, joining a group of friends, and so on.

A man always thanks a woman, directly or by implication, for dancing with him. She does not thank him in so many words for asking her, but she is expected to give even the partner with two left feet an acknowledging smile, and she can certainly say something like "That was fun" if she wants to let him know that she really enjoyed dancing with him.

**Cutting In.** No more than a touch on the shoulder of a woman's partner is needed, though "Cut, please" or "May I?" or any similar words may be added. Under all ordinary circumstances, a request to cut cannot be refused. The woman must say, or smile, a farewell to her old partner and step off amiably with her new one. She is supposed to show neither special relief nor regret about the switch. By the rules, her first partner cannot cut back immediately, but must wait until another man has cut in or until the music stops and starts again. This rule does not hold for double cutting in which two men exchange partners. They can switch back after a short time if they like.

**Duty Dances.** A man's first duty is to the woman he takes to a dance. He is expected to keep an eye on her during the evening, see that she is not stuck or stranded, and it is taken for granted that he will have at the very least the first and last dance with her and will sit with her at supper.

A man must always ask his hostess, her daughters, and a woman guest of honor to dance. At a sizable party, this may mean no more than a few steps after cutting in, but he must make a point of seeking at least a turn with them—if he is dancing at all.

If a man has been a guest at one of the small dinner parties so often given before a group goes on to a ball, he must ask his dinner hostess and the women who were at his right and left to dance. Under most circumstances, he dances with all the women who were at the preliminary dinner.

At a public ball or other subscription dance, if a host has signed up for a whole table, he dances first with the woman seated at his right (provided, of course, that his group arrives together and is seated at the same time). Any man who is a guest at such a table must ask each woman in the party to dance unless for some reason he is not dancing at all. At public balls, a man is not obligated to dance with anyone outside his own party. For example, he need not ask the official hostesses or members of the receiving committee to dance.

**Special Problems.** Either a man or woman can suggest leaving the floor in the middle of a dance, and it is certainly better to do so than to stumble around with a poor partner. Any pretext will do, from a frank "This is too fast for me," to more evasive excuses like "The floor is too crowded for fun" or "Let's have some punch."

Getting stuck is everybody's nightmare. It can happen to the most attractive people—for any number of reasons, especially at a dance where the music never stops. The important thing is for all hands, including the stuck couple, to observe standard rescue measures. It is the duty of the host and the ushers (if any) to cut in on a man who has been dancing overly long with one partner. A man can make a discreet signal to a friend in the stag line. A woman should always find some way to release her partner if no one cuts in after an obviously too long time, rather than cling for dance after dance to a partner who, by the rule, cannot leave her stranded. She can suggest stopping to talk with acquaintances so that her partner can move away in due course, without leaving her alone; or suggest going to the punch table, where there is always a good chance to become involved with a group. All else failing, she is duty-bound to ask to be taken to the dressing room on the pretext of wanting to fix her shoe, makeup, or whatever; and to trust to her host and hostess to provide another partner when she reappears.

**INTRODUCTIONS.** The roof is the introduction at the average private dance, just as it is at a private cocktail party, though the host and hostess take pains to see that each newcomer is introduced to at least a few of their other guests. The situation is different at balls and large formal dances. At these, a man must be introduced before he can properly ask for a dance, and so he seeks out his host, hostess, an usher, or a member of the floor committee and asks to be presented, rather than making a self-introduction. An usher, being a deputy host, may ask a girl he does not know to dance and also may introduce two people whom he does not know to each other.

**INVITATIONS.** Extra invitations can be requested under a number of circumstances (for a houseguest, for example), but generally an invitation for an extra woman is not requested without careful thought because the problem of most hostesses is to find enough men to go around. Extra men are a different matter. They are always welcome, since the aim at any dance is to have one or more extra men for each ten women. There is only one definite prohibition: Never request an invitation for a couple or an individual already known to the hostess. She may well have left them off her list for some good reason. The most a mutual friend can do is drop a hint and leave it to the hostess to follow through if she has left someone out by an oversight or mischance.

*See* INVITATIONS for correct formal and informal invitations and replies.

**LEAVING.** The signal that the dance is over is given by the orchestra. At either a prearranged time or at a signal from the host, the orchestra gives a musical hint—"Good Night, Ladies," "Seeing Nellie Home,' "Home, Sweet Home," and so on. The guests take a final turn, say good night, and take themselves off.

At any private dance, saying good-bye to one's host and hostess is just as obligatory as greeting them on arrival. A guest says his farewell before finding his wraps if he is leaving before the last dance.

At a small informal dance at home, the host or hostess sees a guest to the door. At a large party where there is an employee to see guests out and summon or get their cars, the host and hostess remain with their other guests.

At a subscription dance, it is not necessary or expected that guests look up members of the committee. If there has been a receiving line, it does not reassemble for farewells.

The hostess always makes every effort to see that a woman does not leave unaccompanied. She asks a man or a couple to give a woman who arrived alone a lift, or at least sees that someone puts her in a cab. And one of the duties of the good male guest who has come alone is to ask his hostess if he can be of help in seeing an unescorted woman home. The hostess shows due mercy by picking a girl for him who lives within reasonable distance of his route.

**ORCHESTRA AND ENTERTAINERS.** *See* ENTERTAINERS.

**PATRONS AND PATRONESSES.** Anyone who accepts an invitation to be listed as a patron or patroness of a charity ball is generally expected to take a number of extra tickets, if not a whole table. Otherwise, patrons have no special duties except to their own guests.

For the forms of invitation and the reply card that includes a line granting permission to use the patron's name in publicity releases, *see* "To Be a Patron" under INVITATIONS, FORMAL.

**RECEIVING LINES.** At a subscription dance, a receiving line can be set up in any way that the sponsoring committee chooses—or there may be no line at all.

At a small or informal dance, it is not customary to have a receiving line as such, unless one makes it easier for guests to identify chaperons (at a school dance, for instance) or if there is a special guest of honor, as at a dance for a debutante. Instead, the host and hostess may start dancing, but they remain very near the entrance at the beginning of the party so that they can welcome each guest on arrival.

At a formal dance, there usually is an announcer, and the hostess stands next to him at the entrance to the ballroom; the host stands nearby until most of the guests have arrived.

A receiving line breaks up in from half an hour to an hour, depending on the number of guests. It does not reassemble at the end of the party.

*See* RECEIVING LINES for details.

**REFRESHMENTS.** Punch or some similar thirst-quencher is always made available throughout the evening. Champagne, of course, is the most festive of drinks that can be served throughout a dance, but in any case there should also be a nonalcoholic punch for those who are genuinely thirsty rather than in need of a stimulant.

Supper can be anything from doughnuts and pop to a three-course meal, depending on the character of the dance. At a party for young people, supper is sometimes served as early as ten o'clock. At a formal dance, supper generally begins anywhere from midnight to one o'clock. At some balls, supper is served at formally set tables by waiters. At most private dances, however, it is served buffet style. The guests help themselves and then find places to sit at tables set up in appropriate places. At a big party, supper is not announced and all guests do not eat it at one time. Usually, the music and dancing continue during supper, and the guests stop to eat whenever they like.

If dancing goes on until close to dawn, a breakfast of coffee, chocolate, scrambled eggs, or other suitable foods is often offered in addition to supper.

**TEA DANCES.** An invitation to a tea dance always states both the opening and closing hours, four or four thirty to seven being the most popular. Guests need not arrive on the dot unless they want to, but they are expected to leave promptly, especially if the party is at a hotel or club. The procedures are in general just like those at a formal tea (*see* TEAS), except that there is space for dancing.

Refreshments are available throughout the party. Usually only tea, little tea sandwiches, cookies, and perhaps cake are served, though sometimes coffee and chocolate are added to the list. Almost always a cold fruit-juice punch is also available. If the party is at home the tea table is set up in the dining room and manned by pourers, and guests go to it for refreshments. At a hotel, there may be a certain amount of table service, but more often guests go to a buffet and help themselves.

**TIPPING.** At a private dance at home, even if a caterer's staff is on hand to check coats and park cars, there should be no tipping. A good host should make sure that tips, if offered, are refused because any services given by the staff should be as much a part of his hospitality as the refreshments.

The same rule applies at a private party at a club or hotel if the host is able to reserve the needed spaces. However, in some circumstances, it is not possible for a host to arrange exclusive use of a checkroom and washrooms for his party, and his guests therefore have to do their own tipping.

At a public ball or subscription dance, the price of the ticket generally includes a tip for the waiter if table service is given, and this fact is noted on the invitation to buy a ticket. It is customary, though, to tip the checkroom and washroom attendants, and to tip the waiter if any extra service is requested.

**USHERS.** At a private dance they are called "ushers." At a subscription dance they are called the "floor committee." By either name, this group of single men is essential to the success of a large dance. Ushers serve as deputy hosts, and their duty is to help in every way to make the party go happily and smoothly—mainly by dancing with the girls who do not have a rush of partners, cutting in on any stuck couples, inspiring the stags to dance by promising to rescue them on signal, and making introductions.

It is an honor to be asked to serve as an usher. A man cannot refuse unless he refuses the invitation to the party as well, though the duty is a mixed blessing. For one thing, ushers cannot act with the freedom of stags, who are privileged to drift in and out of several parties if they have multiple invitations for the same evening. Ushers arrive at the beginning of a dance, put on their identifying boutonnieres, and prepare to think of duty before pleasure until the party is over. They are expected to have some fun, of course, and can devote themselves to special friends when they have things under control—but, otherwise, the wallflowers are their portion.

**BANANAS.** *See* FRUITS.

# BANKS

As in all dealings with those who serve the public, some courteous recognition is due the human being behind the cashier's wicket—even if no more than a smile.

**CASHING CHECKS.** Everyone runs out of cash once in a while. In an emergency, it is entirely reasonable to ask a friend or a regularly patronized merchant to cash a check, but the chronic casher of small checks quickly wears out his welcome. The cashing of a check is a favor that, at best, may demand an unplanned and time-wasting trip to the bank. Some neighborhood markets offer the cashing of checks as a standard service, but as a general rule it is an imposition to use a local merchant regularly as a banker.

A store can be expected to accept a stranger's check for the exact amount of a reasonably small purchase if good identification such as a driver's license or a credit card is offered. Of course, such cards are merely identification of the buyer as a person. The signature on a driver's license, for example, does not prove ownership of a car—or enough money in the bank to buy one. It is therefore not sensible to be offended when a merchant refuses to accept a check in payment for a valuable item unless the merchandise is to be delivered after the check has cleared.

**ENDORSING CHECKS.** A check must be endorsed exactly as written. If a check with some minor error in spelling is received—Marie Smith instead of Mary Smith, for example—it need not be returned for correction, but is endorsed Marie Smith with Mary Smith added below.

Checks sent for deposit to a bank by mail or messenger are correctly endorsed as follows:

Pay to [name of the bank]
for deposit only
Mary Smith

**PAYEE'S NAME AND TITLE.** A check is not correctly written with "Mr.," "Miss," "Mrs.," or any other title preceding the name of the payee, with two exceptions. A check in payment for a doctor's professional services may be written to Dr. John Smith (or John Smith, M.D. or D.D.S., etc.), since such canceled checks may be needed to prove a deduction to an income tax auditor. The title "Dr." (or degree initials following his name) is not correctly used on a check written for any other purpose—the repayment of a loan or the purchase of property, for example. A check is made out to Mrs. John Smith only when her given name is unknown and it would be inconvenient or delaying to discover it.

**POSTDATED CHECKS.** A postdated check is not a promise to pay in the sense that an I.O.U. is. It is an explicit order to a bank to pay on a specified date. Sometimes the simplest and best arrangement for the repayment of a loan is to write a postdated check, though this has its hazards. There is always the possibility that an expected deposit may be delayed, with the result that the check will be returned marked "Insufficient Funds," and cause embarrassment to the person who deposited it in good faith and issued checks against it. When written acknowledgment of a debt is needed, it is better to write an I.O.U. than a postdated check if there is the slightest possibility that the check will not be good on the date specified.

**SIGNATURES ON CHECKS.** Any signature may be set up for a bank account, though it is poor taste to use "Mr.," "Miss," or any other title as part of a bank signature—with the exception of "Mrs.," which is correctly used on occasion. For example, a married couple may find it practical to sign a joint account "John Brown" and "Mrs. John Brown" to avoid confusion if the wife has a separate account in the same bank for which she uses the more usual form: Mary Greene Brown (without "Mrs.," however, when signing her first name).

**STOPPING PAYMENT OF A CHECK.** If a check is lost or stolen, the person who wrote it should be notified at once. He, in turn, gets in touch with his bank immediately, reports the check number, amount, date, and the payee's name, and requests that payment be stopped. He then can issue another check for the same amount but with a new number and different date. As a general rule, it is not wise to stop payment on a check (other than a lost or stolen one) unless actual provable fraud is involved. The issuer may be subject to suit if he stops payment because he suspects that he has been cheated but cannot prove it. A buyer also may be subject to suit if he stops payment on a check for merchandise that proves to be faulty—or just because he has changed his mind about making the purchase. In all but unusual circumstances it is safer, as well as more courteous, to go through the routine of returning the item and getting a replacement or refund.

## BANNS

Banns are a proclamation in a house of worship, on three successive Sundays or holy days before a marriage, of the intention to wed. Their purpose is to give anyone who knows of any reason that the marriage should not take place a chance to protest. In many faiths it is not the custom to proclaim banns.

## BANQUETS

By dictionary definition, a banquet is "a sumptuous entertainment of food and drink, now usually a ceremonial or a state feast, followed by speeches." A strictly social dinner party, no matter how big or elaborate, is not properly spoken of as a banquet. We use the word today only for a public or semipublic dinner given as a fund-raising event, for publicity purposes, in honor of a person or persons, or in celebration of some event.

**ARRIVING.** Men check their hats and coats before entering the dining room. Women also usually check their coats, though they keep a stole or short jacket if it may be needed for warmth. Usually members of a receiving committee stay near the entrance to accept tickets or admittance cards, to assign seats if there are no seating charts, and to hand out printed material about the organization, unless this is already in place on the tables.

If the dining room is open, guests may go in and take their seats. If guests are directed to a reception room adjoining the dining room for predinner drinks, the opening of the dining-room doors is a signal that they are expected to find their places promptly. At a very small banquet, everyone waits behind his chair for the signal of the presiding officer, and then all sit at the same time. At any big public or semipublic dinner, guests seat themselves as soon as they find their places, and do not wait for the guest of honor and others at the speakers' table to be seated.

Strangers seated together at small tables or adjacent at long tables introduce themselves. A group of acquaintances should not ignore strangers at the same table or exclude them entirely from conversation during the meal. Self-introductions are made after new arrivals are seated. Men do not rise when strangers join them at a table. If everyone at a table is a guest of one host, men follow the standard rule and rise for any woman who joins the table. Those who arrive late should not expect to be served courses they have missed. Waiters and chefs have to observe a tight schedule, especially when speeches are to be broadcast, and as a general rule should not be asked to give special service.

**CLOTHES.** At many big banquets, especially those open to anyone who buys a ticket, men may wear either dinner jackets or dark suits, even if "Black Tie" is specified on the invitation. Women usually wear cocktail or dinner dresses rather than evening gowns, unless "White Tie" is specified.

It is correct for the chairman and all others at the speakers' table to wear dinner jackets even if "Informal" has been specified on the invitation, and to wear tailcoats when "Black Tie" has been specified, if everyone invited to sit at the speakers' table is informed of such a plan.

**DRINKS.** At some banquets, drinks may be ordered at the table. At others, thirsty guests are dismayed to learn, too late, that the waiters are not equipped to give this service. At some club banquets, it is the custom for a host to bring a bottle to his table, ask for setups, and serve his guests himself. On other occasions this would be a mistake. Better make sure in advance.

**GUESTS OF HONOR.** Anyone who will be seated at the speakers' table is obligated to arrive promptly at the agreed time. Often, a small reception for the guest of honor is given before a banquet by the officers of the organization. The dinner committee, program committee, and any special guests (always including all those who will be seated at the speakers' table) should be invited. Such a reception usually is held in a private room near the banquet room. It may be formal, with a receiving line (*which see*), or as informal as a cocktail party. Sometimes invitations are given verbally. Sometimes cards of admission are issued. This small reception serves two practical functions: (1) it ensures introductions of key people to each other, and (2) it brings together all those who will be at the speakers' table, so that when dinner is announced they can enter and take their places without delay or confusion.

**INTERRUPTIONS.** The only permissible interruptions of any speaker are a spontaneous burst of applause and the request "Louder, please." Any question from the floor that interrupts a speaker and any loud comment that comes under the classification of heckling are taboo. If a speaker is interrupted, it is the duty of the presiding officer to come to the rescue and ask that all questions be held until later.

**INVITATIONS.** There is some latitude in the wording of invitations to a public banquet, though in general they follow the rules for formal dinner invitations (*see* INVITATIONS). Banquet invitations, however, should include the purpose of the banquet, the speakers' names, the price of tickets, and should specify the kind of dress that is expected. A reply card and return envelope usually are enclosed.

A standard form:

> I  will / will not  be able to attend the Annual Awards Dinner
>
> of The Society of Citizens on Saturday, April fourteenth.
>
> Please reserve . . . tickets at $12.50 each.
>
> > a table for eight . . .
>
> > a table for ten   . . .
>
> Check enclosed for $ . . .
>
> (Name) . . . . . . . . . . . .
>
> (Address) . . . . . . . . . . .

Many people who do not intend to go to a fund-raising banquet buy tickets as a contribution to a charity. In this instance, the fact that a purchaser will not attend should be noted on the reply card so that his seats can be re-sold or assigned to others.

An admittance card for each place reserved is generally mailed soon after an acceptance and check are received. Since the admittance card serves as a ticket, it is troublesome for everyone if it is misplaced or forgotten. Some busy member of the door committee then has to check the records and issue a duplicate. The host who has invited guests to share his table may send admittance cards to them in advance, leave a card in each guest's name at the entrance, or keep all the cards for his party and turn them in himself at the proper time.

**LEAVING.** The usual procedure is for guests to stay in their places at table until the chairman brings a banquet to a formal close. Guests may then look up friends, go to say a word to the speakers, or move out to retrieve their wraps. Anyone who has to leave early should go between speeches, never during a speech. At some time before speeches start, he explains his intention to his dinner companions. Then, when the time comes, he need only nod a farewell and depart as inconspicuously as possible. If someone at the speakers' table must leave before the last speech is made, the chairman usually makes an explanation for him when introducing him, or at another appropriate time.

**MENU CARDS.** Menu cards vary enormously. They may be elaborate souvenir items of many pages or a single sheet of cardboard that does no more than list the food and drink.

Simple menu cards may be printed with no decoration, or merely with the emblem of the organization. Occasionally, they are engraved. They may be in French, as is the custom in many large hotels, or in English. Simple menu cards often are displayed in small racks. Sometimes one is set above each place plate, or one card may be set between each two places. On occasion, there is only one menu card at each table.

A double menu card is one that has a single fold. The front usually carries identification of the event and the date. Inside, the wine list is on the left of the fold, the list of foods on the right. Such a card is put at each place in any convenient position, as is a more elaborate menu card. The banquet service at some hotels includes the printing of menu cards of standard design.

**PAGING.** A doctor or other guest who is likely to be sought during the course of a banquet should leave name and table number at the telephone desk and with the headwaiter also, because a guest is never paged during a banquet. If it is absolutely necessary to reach someone because of a serious emergency, the caller is obligated to indicate the nature of the emergency when he asks that a message be handed to the chairman. The chairman can then use his discretion. If the chairman cannot direct the page boy to the guest, he makes a brief announcement, usually between speeches, such as, "Is Mrs. John Jones here? She is wanted on the telephone." The page waits to see if someone responds, then leads the way to the nearest telephone.

**PLACE CARDS.** If place cards are used, they match the menu card in style, and therefore are best ordered at the same time. They may be white or colored, plain or decorated with an emblem or initials. Names may be typed or hand-written. Even if place cards are not used on other tables, they are needed at the speakers' table to prevent any error or confusion in seating the honor guests according to plan. Any plain white cards may be used for this purpose.

See PLACE CARDS for details.

**PROGRAM.** At a well-run public meal of any kind, the speakers' table is served each course a little in advance of those at the other tables. While those at the head table are finishing dessert, microphones and a stand for notes are put in place before the chairman. The business session usually starts after all tables have been cleared except for the coffee cups, but if time presses, the chairman may begin it as soon as tables on the floor have been served dessert and coffee. In this case, guests finish eating dessert during the opening remarks, but all conversation should cease when the chairman, toastmaster, or whoever is presiding stands and calls for attention. All service ceases, too, and waiters leave the floor unless, by explicit request, they finish serving and clearing during the preliminary remarks.

If there is an invocation and also a salute to the flag, the invocation is given first. Everyone stands during both of these ceremonies.

The presiding officer usually makes an opening statement concerning the purpose of the gathering or about the organization sponsoring it. At this time he may introduce a toastmaster and also those guests at the speakers' table who will not be introduced later as speakers. Especially distinguished guests seated at other tables usually are introduced at this time, too. They acknowledge the introduction by standing and bowing, though if time is short, the chairman may ask them not to do so. In this case, they bow from their seats. A short round of applause after each introduction is customary. No guest introduced under these circumstances speaks unless specifically called upon by the chairman. Announcements, the reading of telegrams and reports, and other such routine business matters are completed before the main speakers are introduced. Such organization business should be held to the minimum. It is inconsiderate to guests to let it drag on. One of the reasons that guest speakers so often break the rules of good manners and arrive late is their understandable desire to avoid the boredom of lengthy reports of no interest to outsiders.

If there is a fixed microphone, or if a speaker needs a lectern for his notes, the presiding officer steps aside and lets the speaker have his place. If the speaker's remarks are to be brief, the chairman remains standing several paces behind him as he speaks. Otherwise he sits in the chair vacated by the speaker. The chairman thanks each speaker at the conclusion of his address. The audience applauds each speaker when he is introduced and again after he finishes.

The principal speaker usually is the last on the program. An audience is not obligated to rise except for the President of the United States, though it is customary to rise for a governor and a mayor and any other extremely distinguished speaker.

The chairman closes the evening with a brief speech of thanks to all speakers.

**SEATING.** Working out a seating chart is a thankless task. It should be taken for granted that the seating committee has done its best with a difficult problem. Complaints about location are best skipped, since they seldom mend matters and only injure the festive spirits of others.

If there are place cards, early comers are not privileged to switch them from table to table. If one or two guests at a table notice that their presence is separating or splitting a group of friends, they show ordinary social awareness by offering to exchange places, but it is not customary to ask flatly for this favor. The suggestion should come from those who will move away.

If neither place cards nor a seating chart is used, a guest may take any seat, even if a table is partly occupied, but it is usual to ask those already seated if they are holding the empty places for friends. A chair tilted against the table is a sign that the place is reserved, and it must be respected.

Seating charts are run off at the latest possible time. Names are arranged alphabetically, with the table number following. Standards holding large numbers above the tables make seating and the location of friends easier. They are usually removed before the speeches start.

**SPEAKERS' TABLE.** This may be a separate table, but the head of a horseshoe table also is given this classification. Often, officers and honor guests are seated behind a long, narrow table on a dais so that all other guests will have a clear view of them. No one at the speakers' table should be seated with his back to the main part of the room.

The ranking officer of the group sits at the center of the speakers' table (though he may relinquish his place later to a toastmaster). To his right is the most honored speaker or guest. To his left is the guest or speaker next most distinguished. This may put a man between two men, or a woman between two women. Social rules of seating are not observed at a public banquet, though effort is made to alternate men and women when possible. The wife of a speaker is seated at the speakers' table if there is room. She is usually placed beside some officer toward one end of the table rather than to the immediate left of the official host. If there is not enough room for her at the head table, she is seated at the table of a member of the organization, as a special guest there.

**TABLE-HOPPING.** One of the purposes of any big gathering is to give friends who do not see one another frequently a chance to meet. But any table-hopping that delays service of the meal should be avoided, and it is the worst of manners to circulate or to chat during a speech. As a general rule, a man does not leave a woman companion in order to table-hop unless she is comfortably surrounded with acquaintances at their table.

**TALKING.** One of the purposes of any big gathering is to give friends who do not see each other frequently a chance to meet. But any extended conversation while the speaker has the floor is taboo, and so is table-hopping. No matter how dull, verbose, and repetitious a speaker may be, banquet guests have no choice but to endure their term as a captive audience in polite silence.

**TIPPING.** A tip for the waiter usually is included in the price of a banquet ticket. If tips are not included in the price of admission the waiters will make the matter clear by passing a salver to each man at the table before the speeches begin. The usual tip is about 10 percent. A dollar per person is usual for meals between eight and twelve dollars. If a host has filled a table, he takes care of tips for the whole party. Women are not asked for tips when men are at the table, but a single woman should make a point of paying her share when at a table of strangers.

Coatroom attendants may have been tipped in advance by the dinner committee, but the best plan for the banquet guest is to offer a tip even if the usual saucer with coins is not displayed as a hint. It will be refused if other arrangements have been made.

**TOASTS.** At a public or semipublic dinner, toasts are proposed at the end of the meal or with dessert.

The presiding officer or a toastmaster proposes the first toast, which traditionally is to the guest of honor or—if there is none—to the main speaker. Under certain circumstances, the first toast is made to someone who is not present. For example, the first toast properly would be to the President of the United States at a public dinner sponsored by his political party. In this case, the guest of honor or main speaker is toasted second, and other toasts may follow. Toasts are proposed only by those seated at the speakers' table—never by any member of the general audience. Even those at the speakers' table must gain the toastmaster's attention and permission before proposing a toast.

## BAPTISM

The words "baptism" and "christening" often are used interchangeably. By strict definition, only "baptism" applies to the religious ceremony in which water is used to symbolize dedication of a person to Christ. An object is never baptized. A ship, for example, is christened. A building or statue is dedicated. Most Christian faiths practice baptism, though some do not use water in naming or other dedicating ceremonies.

*See* CHRISTENING AND BAPTISM for details. *See* BRIT MILAH for Jewish naming ceremonies.

## BAR MITZVAH AND BAT MITZVAH

Bar Mitzvah is an important religious ceremony in the life of a boy of the Jewish faith. It marks the time when he becomes recognized as an adult member of the Jewish congregation. The Bar Mitzvah service generally is followed by a social celebration.

The religious ceremony is held traditionally as a part of the morning service in a temple or synagogue on the first Sabbath (Saturday) after the boy's thirteenth birthday according to the Jewish calendar. Close friends of other faiths often are invited. No special rules govern them beyond those of standard good behavior in all houses of worship. They should follow the congregation in standing and sitting, and, of course, refrain from all comment during the service. Invited guests join the congregation when, directly after the religious service, they gather briefly in the social rooms of the synagogue or at home to congratulate the Bar Mitzvah boy and his family.

Later on—either during the same day or in the evening or on the following day—a reception may be held in the social rooms of the synagogue or Jewish community center, at home, or at some other location. This may be a family celebration or a very large party. Again, all guests congratulate the young man and his family as well. If invited to either the religious ceremony or a reception elsewhere, or both, it is customary to give the young man a present.

It should be noted that if the Bar Mitzvah has been held in an Orthodox or Conservative synagogue, there can be no smoking or dancing at a following reception until after sundown. Guests of other faiths should observe these rules, most especially during a reception at a synagogue. Always, when in doubt, follow the example of members of the boy's family.

**BAT MITZVAH.** This religious ceremony for girls of the Jewish faith is the equivalent of the Bar Mitzvah for boys, though it is not nearly so widely celebrated. It came into use only within the last half-century, in order to allow women a greater place in religious life. The Bat Mitzvah ceremony is observed only by Conservative and Reform congregations, not by Orthodox families. The service is usually held on the first Friday evening or Saturday morning after the girl's thirteenth birthday according to the Jewish calendar. Conduct of the guests at the synagogue and the party thereafter is governed by the rules given under Bar Mitzvah.

## BARBECUES

Barbecue is a contraction of the French *barbe à queue,* which originally meant the cooking of a whole animal ("from beard to tail") out of doors in a pit or on a spit. By today's use, any meal with one or more main items—from hot dogs to a turkey—cooked outdoors on an open fire is called a barbecue.

Barbecues are informal meals, but guests still are bound by the standard rules of table manners. Unless a hostess instructs her guests to choose their own places, they wait for her directions as to seating, and in a small gathering for her signal to start eating. The ban against picking up chicken and chops in the fingers is often lifted, but again it is best to follow the lead of the hostess before feasting from the fist, Middle Ages style. Even at the most informal barbecue, flower beds should never be used as a kitchen midden. Small bones tossed away in a garden attract ants and may send a pet to a hospital for a painful and expensive stay.

At almost any big, informal meal, a certain amount of help from guests is welcomed by the chief cooks and bottle-washers. Not by the barbecue chef! A guest who rearranges the fire or presumes to touch the food on it, unless specifically requested to do so, or ventures any advice, commits the unforgivable sin. The barbecue chef is a sensitive creative artist. He must be allowed to burn, undercook, or otherwise complete his masterpiece without interference.

## BARBERSHOPS

In a barbershop, the tip depends on how many employees are involved in the service. In most shops, 15 to 20 percent is customary for one barber, with an additional fifteen or twenty-five cents to a checkroom attendant, if there is one. If a manicurist, shoeshine boy, and other specialists are used, each is tipped separately, and the overall tip runs from 20 to 25 percent. An owner or manager who works only at the appointment desk has professional standing and is not tipped, but the owner who works along with his employees is offered a tip and given a chance to accept or refuse, as he wishes.

## BARS

As a general rule, drinking equipment and supplies that are kept in a living room are housed in some piece of furniture that conceals them when they are not in use. Lacking this, unless drinks are served by an employee, some kind of bar is needed in or near the living room so that host or hostess does not have to make repeated trips to the kitchen for refills. A side table or a shelf makes a good temporary bar without lending a saloon-like look to family quarters. No matter what arrangement is used, a guest does not properly assume that a display of bottles is an invitation to mix his own drinks, except at sizable and informal cocktail parties.

**IN PUBLIC PLACES.** Anyone entertaining in a public place is required by the rules to be on hand slightly before the appointed hour. A host or hostess may order a drink while waiting at a bar or a table for a guest. The standard procedure for the early guest is to wait for the host or hostess before ordering, but there is nothing rigid about this rule. It is correct for a guest who is extremely early to order a drink, especially if it is awkward to occupy a seat at a crowded bar without doing so, or if he knows that his host does not take a drink before a meal. A tip always is left for the bartender even if unfinished drinks are sent to the table and the charges for them are added to the meal check. A patron himself does not carry his unfinished drink from the bar to a table—in restaurants with any pretensions to good service, a waiter makes the transfer.

**WOMEN IN BARS.** Not too long ago, no "nice" woman alone took a place at a bar. Today, a woman alone may order a drink at a very wide variety of bars without a second thought. At lunch or dinner, a woman who is meeting someone in a restaurant or who is waiting for a single table often takes a place at the bar and orders a drink. A woman alone or two women together are often seen in neighborhood taverns where the atmosphere is more that of a club than of a saloon, or at the "dating bars" recently so popular with post-college single men and women. Customs vary widely in different communities, however. It is not reasonable for a woman drinking alone at a bar to be insulted if a stranger starts a conversation. She has asked for it by picking the wrong bar.

## BATH MATS

A bathroom rug and a bath mat often are enough alike in size to confuse the houseguest. Both serve to keep the floor clean and dry when someone steps, dripping, from a tub or shower. A rug is part of the permanent furnishing of the room, however, and the bather should protect it with a bath mat, if one is provided.

A rug, no matter how damp, is left on the floor to dry. A bath mat always is put back on the side of the tub or on the towel rack where it was found.

## BATHROOMS AND WASHROOMS

The single most important rule about a bathroom or washroom is this: Each user must leave it in at least as good order as he found it. Only a spoiled child or an irresponsible adult leaves a basin messy, a tub ringed, or a toilet seat splashed.

**BATHROOMS.** Needless to say, a bathroom door must be locked as well as closed when the room is in use if there is the slightest possibility that someone may enter. A bathroom door is generally kept closed at all times, though at a party the location of the room is sometimes indicated by leaving the door slightly ajar so that guests can find it without asking. A guest leaves the door in this position upon departure, never wide open. Even the noisiest toilet must be flushed. Men do not properly leave the seat raised.

Guest towels are not an ornament. They are there to be used. Under no circumstances is the corner of a bath towel a good substitute, though a surprising number of guests create a confusing laundry problem for their bewildered hostesses by this curious "saving" of pretty little hand towels. After use, a guest towel is returned to the rack but not folded so carefully that it appears unused.

It is the duty of a host or hostess to offer the use of the bathroom, or at least indicate its location clearly, to a guest who arrives after a long walk or other enterprise that may have kept him away from a toilet. It is interesting to note that in some circles the word "bathroom" is going the way of "toilet," which in its time was the fashionably genteel substitute for "privy." Some people now avoid both in favor of "little girls' room," "little boys' room," "the john," and "the powder room," among an extensive list. There is nothing wrong with such substitutes, though most of them strike some adults as a bit cute. For that reason they are best not used to an employee or a stranger when asking directions.

"Lavabo" is not a synonym for "bathroom." It means "washbowl," rather than a room with toilet facilities. "Lavatory," as most commonly used, means a place where things are washed. It is preferred in England to "bathroom" but has a rather pretentious sound in this country when applied to a home bathroom, though it is used fairly often instead of "washroom" in office buildings.

**WASHROOMS.** Some people ask for "the bathroom" in a public place when they want a toilet. However, "washroom," "ladies' room," and "men's room" are the standard terms for toilet facilities in office buildings, hotels, restaurants, and other public places. In theaters, for some reason, "lounge" is the term commonly used. "Rest room" is usually reserved for facilities in department stores, depots, and stations. "Comfort station" is generally used only for facilities in parks, gas stations, and similar public places. But all these distinctions are quite unimportant.

See HOUSEGUESTS; also Washrooms in the Index.

## BEACHES AND POOLS

The outstandingly important rule of conduct at any beach or pool, public or private, is: Don't clown with the lifeguard. He is on duty to guard lives— not to play games.

The whistle of a lifeguard directing a swimmer to shore must be obeyed immediately. There are no exceptions. From his tower or post of vantage he can see danger that a swimmer cannot. If a complaint about his behavior is in order, don't embroil him in an argument while he is on duty. Take it up with him later or report the matter to the proper authorities.

**BEACHES.** More or less anything goes at a beach within the limits of the following common-sense reservations:

Some people go to a public beach to make new friends. Some go to get away from those they already have. Therefore, if a group has established itself well away from others, newcomers take the hint and do not choose a base right under their noses. Children are going to run and romp, but it can be hoped that they will do their racing and shrieking at a reasonable distance from somnolent sunbathers.

On a crowded beach, avoid personal remarks about neighboring groups and, especially, flip remarks about any profession or occupation. Even a whisper can be carried a long way by the wind, and admirals, barbers, and dog-catchers look alike in bathing suits.

If someone is in difficulty in the water, don't take for granted that the lifeguard has noticed. Shout for him or take direct action—though only a strong swimmer who is also thoroughly familiar with lifesaving techniques should go to the assistance of someone far from shore. Too often lifeguards have to struggle back with an impetuous rescuer as well as the original victim.

All evidence to the contrary, everyone is obligated to leave a beach in no worse shape than he found it—not littered with the jetsam of a picnic or a ring of cigarette stubs. Burn, carry away, or bury discarded cans, bottles, cartons, paper napkins, and tissues. In the interests of safety, never throw bottles or cans into the water. Bury them above the high-water mark if there are no trash receptacles. Grind every cigarette stub out and bury it, and douse all other fires and bury the ashes—both to keep the beach beautiful and to guard against the always present possibility of fire. Long after picnickers have departed, the wind can fan one ember to life, fling sparks to a great distance, and perhaps start a disastrous conflagration in the underbrush bordering a beach.

**CLOTHES.** Today, almost anything goes in the cut and style of bathing suits —so far as the law in public places and the by-laws of private clubs are concerned. The choice between the classic maillot and the skirted dressmaker suit, and the two scraps of cloth that constitute the bikini is no longer a matter of good and bad taste in most areas—if all are equally becoming. As one wit puts it: "The word 'bikini' is either a common noun or a very common abbreviation, depending on who is wearing it."

**CLUBS.** Behavior at a private beach or swimming club is both more formal and, in some ways, less formal than at a public facility. The precincts themselves are an introduction. A member does not join a group of strangers or slight acquaintances, however, without specific invitation, and no group is under obligation to include a stranger.

Unless there is an attendant assigned to return chairs and other club gear to their proper places, members are expected to do so when finished with them. Otherwise, the standard rules for behavior at a public beach are followed.

**POOLS.** More than one generous owner of a private pool finds that he has put himself in the unwilling position of bath-house attendant, pool cleaner, and laundryman for more people than he planned. Unless a host specifically tells guests invited to use his pool not to bother with bringing towels, they should bring their own. And if a host supplies towels, guests are expected to hang them up, not leave them in soggy heaps at poolside or in a dressing room. Greaseless suntan lotions are by far the better choice because oily ones add very considerably to the owner's pool-cleaning problems. Needless to say, anyone suffering from a contagious malady—from athlete's foot to yaws— should not use a pool, public or private.

## BEAUTY SHOPS

Tips in beauty shops depend on how many operators are involved in the service. In most shops, 15 to 20 percent is customary if one operator does a shampoo, set, and manicure, for example, with an additional fifteen or twenty-five cents to the dressing-room attendant. If several operators are involved, the overall tip usually runs from 20 to 25 percent.

Tips may be left at the desk when the bill is paid. More often, they are handed to the operator or dropped into an apron or shirt pocket, always with spoken thanks.

An owner or a manager who works only at the appointment desk has professional standing, and is not tipped. The owner or manager who works along with the staff should be offered a tip and given the chance to accept or refuse.

Some beauty shops insist that employees speak of each other by title and first name: "Miss Rose is ready for you" or "Mr. John will be right with you." The client does not use such forms of address. She says, "My appointment is with John," and says, "Thank you, John," when he has finished. Under no circumstances is the client's use of an operator's first name an invitation for the operator to call her by her first name in return.

The basic rule for both clients and employees is: Avoid all gossip and personal remarks about others. There is no guarantee that the stranger in the next chair or booth is not a relative or friend of the person under discussion. Every hairdresser has some rude, captious clients. But he picked his trade, and enduring difficult patrons in discreet silence is part of it. Don't trust or encourage an operator who makes fun of or passes along gossip about any other client. If he is indiscreet about one patron, there is no reason to suppose that he will spare others.

## BEDS

A properly trained maid follows a standard procedure when turning down a bed. She removes the spread completely and puts it, folded neatly, on a chair, shelf, or in a blanket box, leaving the blanket cover (if there is one) on the bed. If the bed is to be occupied by one person, she turns the blanket cover, blankets, and sheet back together in a triangle. A bed for two persons is turned down with a triangle on each side or with a straight horizontal fold.

For an afternoon nap, the spread is removed but the bed usually is not turned down completely. The blanket cover is left in place with the pillows on top of it. The guest lies on top of the blanket cover, and pulls up an extra blanket or light throw, which has been left across the foot of the bed. In a house with a big staff, the beds are usually turned down by a maid while the guests are at dinner. In a house with a limited staff, or none, a guest turns down his own bed, though the hostess sometimes helps on the first night of a visit. When turning down their own beds, guests should fold the spread neatly to prevent wrinkles. A very light spread may be left across the foot of the bed, but no spread should be left fully covering the bed during the night.

Guests staying for more than one night in a house with a small staff, or none, are expected to make their own beds reasonably early in the morning. Guests leaving early in the morning leave their beds spread open neatly to air. A male guest leaving late in the day spreads up his bed so that the room will look tidy. A woman guest asks the hostess for clean linen and makes the bed for her. Many hostesses refuse this offer, since all guests are not adept at bed-making. If her offer is declined, the woman guest strips the bed of used sheets and leaves them neatly folded on a chair or on top of the spread, which she puts back into place.

## BEDTIME

The hostess, not the houseguest, makes the first move to call it a day. Quite often a hostess will excuse herself and leave her husband and their male guests to continue talk or a game, but as a general rule a woman guest follows the lead of her hostess and starts for bed when she does.

*See* HOUSEGUESTS.

## BEER AND ALE

Beer and ale are often served in ordinary water tumblers, but the standard containers are a tall straight glass holding about 12 ounces, a Pilsener glass, which is also tall but tapers to a point above a pedestal foot, and a beer stein or mug. The first two are generally used at the table, though steins are popular on casual occasions, especially in summer; the heavy glass or pottery keeps the beer chilled and the handle protects it against the warmth of the hand.

In restaurants, the waiter opens bottled beer at the table and, if the glass is too small to hold the full serving, he leaves the bottle on the table. At home, beer usually is served from a sideboard, or filled glasses are brought in from the kitchen, and bottles are not left on the table.

Beer is served chilled to some degree. Most people in this country prefer quite cold beer. A big head of foam is the sign of an inept server. A half-empty glass or a boiling head that overflows the brim can be avoided by pouring beer slowly down the side of a tilted glass.

No explanation need be given when refusing beer—certainly not such startling confidences as "It bloats me" or "It gives me the burps."

## BEGGARS

Anyone who asks for money on the street is in trouble of some kind. Many people would rather be a soft touch for the professional panhandler than risk refusing aid to even one unfortunate person in temporary need. Others refuse all beggars by policy. That is their privilege. But a shake of the head or "I'm sorry" does just as well as any of the brusque variants of "Beat it!"—a callous brushoff that dismays most women when they hear a male companion use it.

## BELCHING

In case of this unhappy surprise, the only thing to do is say, "Excuse me," and try to suppress the next one. Any explanation of digestive troubles is best skipped. If a guest is obviously in continuing difficulty, the host or hostess should ask, "Can I get you something?" Otherwise, the less notice taken, the better.

**BELLBOYS.** *See* HOTELS AND MOTELS.

## BENEFITS

An invitation to attend any fund-raising event should specify that it is a benefit and explain its purpose. It is not cricket to ask guests to a tea, for example, and let them discover after arrival that the occasion is a fund-raising raffle.

People who do not plan to attend a fund-raising luncheon, banquet, ball, or performance sometimes buy tickets as a contribution to the charity. In this case, unless the tickets are to be passed along as a gift, the fact that the purchaser will not attend should be noted on the reply card. Otherwise, places that could be resold are held for him, and go to waste.

At a benefit theater party, patrons are obligated to arrive on time out of consideration for the actors and the rest of the audience, and to behave as they would at any regular performance.

Working out seating charts for any kind of benefit is a thankless task. Obviously, every patron cannot be given a ringside table or seats front and center. Take it for granted that choice places are allocated in the order in which reservations are received, with certain exceptions made honorably for good reasons. A complaint can seldom mend matters. It usually serves only to ruffle the feelings of the seating committee, who are doing their best to make the benefit a success.

**BERRIES.** *See* FRUITS.

**BEST MAN.** *See* WEDDINGS.

## BETROTHALS

Engaged couples of any faith may speak of each other as "my betrothed," even though no formal betrothal ceremony is celebrated.

A formal betrothal is a religious ceremony that is relatively rare in this country, except in the Greek Orthodox and Roman Catholic faiths. It is usually held in church before an invited gathering, not a regular congregation. (A Greek Orthodox betrothal service may also be held at home.) Betrothal promises are exchanged. These are solemn vows, but not as binding as wedding vows. A betrothal may be broken, just as an engagement to marry may be. In the Catholic faith, a formal betrothal is known as a "canonical engagement."

## BETTING

Betting on any uncertain outcome, from the results of a race to the possibility of rain, is a game in that it is subject to its own rigid rules of sportsmanship, and so it is dealt with under GAMES.

**BIKINIS.** *See* BEACHES and POOLS.

## BILLIARDS

Billiards is a game that demands intense concentration. The major restrictions governing the behavior of both players and spectators are aimed at protecting the player from distraction and the delicate equipment from mishandling. The following rules apply to both pocket billiards (pool) and billiards:

1. Don't talk, move around, squeak chalk on a cue, or in any other way divert the attention of a player when he is lining up a shot or about to shoot.
2. Don't show impatience with the player who takes his time to line up a shot in several different ways. Making careful decisions is part of the game.
3. If an opponent is about to make an error—play the wrong ball, for example —warn him before he shoots. Don't keep quiet and then call a foul and exact the penalty.
4. Each player should be meticulously honest about calling his own fouls. But a courteous player will not call another player's fouls unless asked to judge.
5. Handle the equipment carefully. Don't lean on a cue or leave one where it is likely to fall. Don't set a drink on the table rim, rest a cigarette there, or smoke while shooting and risk scarring the finish or burning the cloth. The player who damages the felt is obligated to pay for the repair—and the cost will be considerable—but assuming the expense does not compensate the owner for the temporary inconvenience of being unable to use the table.
6. Keep at least one foot on the floor when shooting. When not shooting, don't use the table edge as a seat or a backstop for lounging.

## BIRTH ANNOUNCEMENTS

In some cities, reporters pick up the news of a birth as part of their regular routine, when a doctor files a birth certificate. In others, they do not. In either case, parents who want to share their good news through the press have a choice: They can insert a paid notice in the Vital Statistics columns; or they can send a release to the society editor, who is privileged to cut and rewrite it, but who runs it without charge if space permits.

Copy for a paid notice usually is confined to the essential facts—date and place of birth, sex of the child, and parents' name. A look at local papers will show the local custom in wording and type of information. A release sent to a society editor commonly includes more facts about family and business connections than a paid insertion.

**ANNOUNCEMENT CARDS.** A formal announcement card is really two cards: a tiny white card engraved with the baby's name and date of birth, tied with a ribbon to a card 3 by 4 inches. The cards and ribbon may be white, but more popular are cards with narrow borders in color (blue for a boy, pink for a girl) and a ribbon to match.

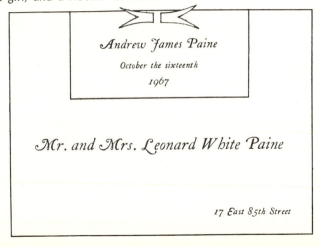

*Andrew James Paine*

*October the sixteenth*

*1967*

*Mr. and Mrs. Leonard White Paine*

*17 East 85th Street*

(The city and state can be added under the street address; if so, the Zip Code number is used.)

Printed birth announcement cards with spaces to be filled in by hand are often used. On these, the parents' names are written Mary and John Smith, never Mr. and Mrs. John Smith.

Some families take pleasure in designing their own announcements. A hotel man may fill in a replica of a registration card. A writer may choose to announce "Volume Two of the Smith Family Saga, titled Ann Brown Smith." A chemist may announce a new "alloy." An actor may send what looks like a theater ticket with the date of the "opening performance," and so on. Such announcements are a matter of personal taste, but since they are in no sense formal, they usually are sent to a fairly limited circle of intimates.

Either engraved or printed announcements are sent as soon as can be managed, usually within two weeks. If they cannot be mailed within a month, they are better forgotten.

## BIRTH CERTIFICATES

By law, the doctor is required to fill out a birth certificate giving the name of the parents and sex of the baby, and to file it with the proper city or county bureau. If a name has not been chosen for the baby, the birth certificate will read "Baby" Jones. This can be amended later when the child is given a name, but by far the best procedure is to be prepared with a choice of names for a boy or girl so that the baby's full name can be registered immediately on this civil document, which may be needed on many occasions in later life.

## BIRTHDAYS

Nearly every child thinks his birthday is *the* red-letter day of the year. Most adults also expect (and enjoy) some kind of celebration on their birthdays, and many feel forlorn or are actually hurt if friends let the occasion go unnoticed. However, as they grow older, some people very much prefer that the day be ignored (except by intimates), since any big celebration inevitably causes speculation about their age. It is easy to spot the adult who has such qualms. If the answer to "When is your birthday?" is anything as evasive as "It's months away," drop the matter.

No birthday party is complete without the traditional cake with its crown of candles. Children's cakes carry one candle for each year and an extra one "to grow on," but only at a family gathering is a candle for each year put on an adult's cake unless a special milestone such as a fiftieth or seventy-fifth birthday is being celebrated. A candle for each person present and one extra, or one candle for the past year and one to grow on, is the standard substitute.

When the lighted cake is borne in, all except the honor guest sing "Happy Birthday." At the end of the song he makes a silent wish, takes a deep breath, and blows out the candles. If all of them are extinguished in one blow, his wish will positively come true within the year, as everyone knows. He then makes the first cut as part of the magic, and keeps the first piece, even if he continues to cut and serve the cake. However, the hostess usually takes over the task of removing the candles and serving after the first cut has been made.

If the invitation makes it clear that the party is to celebrate a birthday, each guest is expected to bring some little present. Anyone who cannot accept the invitation is not obligated to send one.

**PARTIES FOR CHILDREN.** To all children past babyhood, a birthday party is a dazzling celebration. However, a party for a child under three is meaningless to the birthday child, and often too much of a challenge to any participant—not forgetting the mother faced with a houseful of pre-kindergartners already overstimulated by anticipation. All parties are best kept small until a child is about four, and even then his mother had better enlist a number of steel-nerved friends to stand by as shock troops and help control the merrymaking.

No one can possibly predict the course of a children's party or anticipate to what degree the excitement will inspire both host and guests to show off. It is a good idea to stage a rehearsal of "how it's going to be," shortly before the party starts. If the young host or hostess has been coached to greet each guest, and if each guest knows he is expected to say "Happy Birthday" and hand over his present, the well-known arrival panic is less likely to set in—and the guests may even be sufficiently impressed by their own worldly grace to remember to say good-bye on leaving.

**Entertainment.** Organized games or other entertainment is a necessity except for toddlers. Otherwise, in a matter of minutes, the party will break up into scuffling and romping. Traditional party games like Pin-the-Tail-on-the-Donkey and Musical Chairs are the best choices because they involve the entire group, and shyer children are drawn out of their corners before they know it. The winner gets a special prize, of course, but crises are avoided if everybody gets some kind of prize for effort if not for skill and luck.

Paid clowns and other entertainers are a joy to children and a boon to mothers. Very little children have a brief span of attention, however, and the important thing is not to overorganize entertainment or plan any that keeps children sitting still for a long time.

**Food.** Ice cream and cake are essential, but since small children usually are not able to eat a regular meal after a birthday party, more substantial food often is served as well. It should be simple and easily handled. Large bibs for very small guests and large napkins for older ones help preserve party clothes, if not the floor and furniture. Since most of the guests will have their minds firmly fixed on food, it should not be too long in coming, though a party is no place to urge food on a child who does not want to eat. The combination of food and excitement can lead to disaster.

**Gifts.** Each guest brings a present, and it is a very good idea for his mother to make it clear to the small donor that his package is a gift. More than one youngster has been known to refuse to let anyone else play with "his" present, and has gone home wailing because what he thought was his very own possession was left behind. Any mother experienced in giving children's parties makes sure that each guest goes home with some little trophy or souvenir as a fair exchange for the gift he brought.

**Invitations.** The birthday child usually takes keen interest in his invitations —sometimes to the point of issuing them to all he meets. Even if a child has reached what should be an age of discretion, his verbal invitation, unless given in the presence of his mother and the prospective guest's mother also, should not be regarded as official. A telephone call from mother to mother, if not a written invitation, must confirm it.

**Parents.** Not infrequently, the mother of the birthday child is dismayed to find herself with two parties on her hands—an extra, unplanned one for the mothers of the invited guests. The mother (or nurse) of a toddler is expected to stay for the duration, but the mother of an older child does not remain unless specifically invited to do so. The tactful way to avoid confusion on this point is to state clearly in the invitation when the guests are to be called for. In all mercy, parents calling for children should be prompt and should leave with dispatch. If many parents are invited to stay throughout the party, they should be seated in another room, if possible. A blight of self-consciousness falls on many children, who would otherwise behave well, simply because Mother is there.

**Time.** There is no problem with late arrivals at a children's party. Most of the guests will arrive early unless forcibly restrained. Three to five in the afternoon is generally considered the most suitable time—after naps and with leeway for busy mothers to get home in time to prepare dinner after picking up the celebrants.

## BIRTHSTONES

In ancient times, gems were thought to be related to the planets, and each stone was believed to have its own attributes and a particular influence on man. We have a carry-over of that belief: many people today believe that the wearing of a birthstone brings good luck. The following list shows the traditional birthstone for each month:

| | |
|---|---|
| January | Garnet |
| February | Amethyst |
| March | Aquamarine or Bloodstone |
| April | Diamond |
| May | Emerald |
| June | Pearl, Alexandrite, or Moonstone |
| July | Ruby |
| August | Peridot or Sardonyx |
| September | Sapphire |
| October | Opal or Tourmaline |
| November | Topaz |
| December | Turquoise or Zircon |

## BISCUITS

Both "the biscuits" and "the biscuit" are correct plurals.
　　*See* BREAD.

## BISHOPS.　*See* FORMS OF ADDRESS (Clergy).

## BLACK TIE, WHITE TIE

"Dinner coat," "dinner jacket," and "Black Tie" are the standard terms for a man's formal dinner suit. "Tuxedo" and "Tux" are also widely used, and if all one's friends say "Tux," it is affected to avoid it pointedly. "Tuxedo" is not properly substituted for "Black Tie" on an invitation, however.

"White Tie" or "Tails" is the standard term for a man's full-dress evening suit. "White tie and tails" is redundant, since a white tie is worn only with an evening tailcoat. "White Tie" (not "Tails" or "Formal") is used on an invitation to indicate that full evening dress is expected.

As a general rule, boys do not wear dinner jackets much before they are fifteen, or tailcoats before they are about eighteen.

Evening clothes are not worn on the first or last nights of a voyage, generally not on Sunday night, and never before six in the evening except by waiters. This last rule is impossible to observe strictly, of course. It is proper for a man to drop in at a cocktail party dressed for the evening, if he is going on to an early dinner.

These rules are the same abroad with one exception that does not concern the average tourist. An American wears full evening dress when being received on certain formal daytime occasions by a head of state—but anyone so honored will be briefed in all details by the United States Embassy.
　　*See* CLOTHES; INVITATIONS; WEDDINGS.

## BLESSING

A blessing is the invocation of God's favor on a person or thing. A blessing may be given by anyone. It may be spoken without gesture, or with the right hand raised, or accompanied by the sign of the cross. People of any faith may give a blessing to those of another.

In a house of worship, the response of the congregation is a murmured

"Amen." Elsewhere, the response to an individual giving a blessing is "Thank you" or "Amen." It is a grave discourtesy to ignore a blessing. What is being given is best wishes under highest auspices. Acceptance of a blessing in no way indicates acceptance of another's faith, only of his good intent.

**BLESSING OF FOOD.** "Grace" and "blessing" are used interchangeably for the short prayer preceding meals. Both are correct, but the former is in wider use.

See GRACE.

**THE BLIND.** *See* THE HANDICAPPED.

**BLIND DATES.** *See* DATES.

## BOASTING

> "A bore is a fellow who opens his mouth
> and puts his feats in it."—*Henry Ford*

Boasting is done in many ways. All of them usually defeat their purpose, which is to impress others favorably. One of the most useful lessons young people can learn is that the really distinguished let others tell of their achievements, the really rich do not talk about their wealth, and the really prominent do not drop names.

## BOATING

Each year more families by the thousands are turning to the water for recreation. There are now some eight million privately owned boats—and few owners go out alone. According to conservative estimate, more than forty million people enjoy the sport of boating, which today is the largest participant sport in this country.

The special rules for good behavior afloat are more than mere politeness or traditional customs. They are based on the safety of the craft and everyone concerned with it.

**CAPTAIN AND CREW.** The captain is responsible for the safety of all aboard. What he says is the law, and must be obeyed.

The captain and mate of a chartered fishing boat have professional standing and are treated more or less as members of the party. Though one of them may prepare lunch, both are invited to share it with their patrons, and any refreshments brought aboard are offered to them. However, they do expect and will accept tips, just as professional guides will. By today's custom, they usually are addressed by a first name or nickname, but they address a mature client by title unless otherwise instructed.

On a privately owned boat big enough to need a paid captain and crew, the captain is addressed as "Captain Smith." A mate and chief engineer are addressed as "Mr. Smith." Other crew members are addressed by last name only or, following the lead of the owner, by first name or nickname. The captain of a big boat is never tipped, but a steward and anyone else who gives direct service to an overnight guest is tipped at the end of a cruise just as a staff member would be after a weekend in a large country place.

**CLOTHES.** For nearly any kind of run aboard an owner-operated boat, a guest needs sturdy functional clothes, including a sweater or windbreaker no matter how hot the weather may be ashore. Whether for an afternoon's sail or a weekend cruise, flat shoes with rope or nonslip rubber soles are a necessity. Leather soles are slippery and dangerous. High heels are hazardous to the wearer and also dismay the owner because they scar his treasured deck.

Clothes similar to those worn for the same kind of party in town may be expected for a lunch, dinner, or dance aboard a big boat with a paid crew. When in doubt, ask the host or hostess. For a cruise of several days, clothes like those for a weekend in the country will be needed. This may mean a sports jacket for dinner, Black Tie—or just a change of dungarees; but a properly worded invitation will tell the guest what is expected.

Only members of a yacht club wear yachting jackets. These are similar to a naval officer's, except that the stripes on the sleeves are black, not gold. They are worn with a cap with white or dark blue top and a black visor bearing the club insignia, and with white or gray flannel trousers. Nonmembers do not properly wear any imitation of such gear, and women especially do best to avoid any jaunty Jack Tar getups.

**GOING ABOARD.** The owner always does what is most comfortable and safest for his guests, but the general rule is that he goes aboard first and steps ashore last.

**GUESTS.** The main duty of a guest is not to get hurt or otherwise become a hazard. This means wearing clothes that will afford protection against painful wind- and sunburn; getting permission of the operator before going over the side for a swim; staying clear of boom and lines; never changing position in a very small boat without warning; asking permission before lighting a cigarette if the owner is not smoking; never lighting a cigarette or the galley stove while the engine is being started; never throwing overboard anything that will not sink readily. Boating is an active sport, and a guest should volunteer to do a fair share of the work and the cleaning up. A guest usually brings or sends a boat present in any circumstances where, ashore, he might give a house present.

## BOATS AND SHIPS

By dictionary definition, a boat is any small open craft propelled by sail, oar, pole, paddle, or motor, and a ship is a large craft in which people and goods are transported under cover. However, only the most ignorant of landlubbers speaks of certain specific very large vessels as "ships."

Say "boat" when referring to a launch, cutter, dinghy, gig, gondola, sampan, punt, skiff, rowboat; to a scow, ferry, excursion steamer, and cabin cruiser; and to any sailing craft (except passenger and freight carriers built before steam—the great Yankee Clippers and the small open sailing vessels that brought the Vikings here are both called "ships"). It is safe to call any craft used for sport or pleasure a "boat." Even the largest of yachts is never called a "ship."

Freighters, tankers, cruise ships, and liners are "ships." It is safe to call all Navy vessels, including submarines, "ships," with the exception of lifeboats and small craft used for harbor transport, such as cutters and gigs, which are "boats."

*See* TRAVEL.

## BONES

Bones are not taken up in the fingers except at the most informal meals, such as picnics, if the standard rule is followed. An exception is made at table only for the very small joints of tiny game birds and the smaller joints of frogs' legs. These may be held by one end while the meat is nibbled, or a very small joint may be put in the mouth with the fork and the bone returned to the plate on the fork or with the fingers. The tiny bits of bone that may have been left by the butcher's cleaver or fishbones inadvertently put into the mouth with the fork, are taken out of the mouth in the fingertips.

The paper frills sometimes served on the bone ends of chops and crown roasts are decorations only, not an invitation to pick the piece up in the fingers.

## BON VOYAGE GIFTS AND PARTIES.    *See* TRAVEL.

## BOOKS

It is curious how often the ethics as well as the manners of otherwise meticulously honest and considerate people break down completely where books are concerned. Familiar to everyone is the person who will spend a nickel to return a dime borrowed for a telephone call, but who keeps a borrowed book on permanent loan with seemingly no sense of guilt. These people deserve firm treatment. There is no reason to reward the irresponsible by making them a present of what they borrow. And there is no reason to continue to operate as a free circulating library for those who handle books carelessly.

Only in very rare circumstances is a borrower justified in passing along a book to a friend without the permission of the owner.

The borrower is always responsible for returning a book in as good shape as when it was trusted to his care—clean, unmarked by weather, pencil, or spilled food or drink; the binding uncracked; the dust jacket untorn. Leaving a book open and face down can cause permanent damage, and turning down the corner of a page is an abominable practice. So is using a dust jacket as a place marker.

If a borrowed book is lost or seriously damaged, a fresh copy (with an explanation and apology) must be returned if the book was a new one. If it was old or is out of print, an offer to replace it with some other book is in order.

All these rules hold to a considerable degree for paperbacks, which inevitably show wear and tear rather quickly. Many people regard paperbacks as expendable, but it should be remembered that many of them go out of print in a short time and are impossible to replace. Therefore, they are not exempt from the rules for return.

The sentimental value of a gift book is often enhanced if it carries an inscription from the donor—but if there is a chance that the copy might be a duplicate, or that the recipient might prefer another book, enclose a card instead so that the book can be exchanged.

*See also* GUEST BOOKS AND REGISTERS.

## BORES

> "Generally speaking, bores are
> generally speaking."—*Guyan Lewis*

It is the sad truth that everyone is a bore to someone. It is only sensible to escape from a bore, but only decently kind to do it politely. No one is a bore on purpose.

Voltaire's opinion is worth remembering: "The secret of being a bore is to tell everything."

## BORROWING

All of us have to borrow something once in a while. It is impossible to find a person who has not needed to borrow an umbrella, a tire wrench, or taxi fare. The borrowing of books, chairs, teacups, card tables, and countless other items is a sensible, comfortable way of life for millions of neighbors. "Neither a borrower nor a lender be" is not a rule. It is a quotation that continues, "For loan oft loses both itself and friend." No one can deny the truth of the second line, but only the stingy who value possessions more than people make a policy of following the recommendation of the first line. Borrowing, however, is governed by strict rules.

A borrower is obligated to return an article promptly in as good condition as he found it, or to replace it if it is lost or damaged. Unless fully prepared to take this responsibility, it is better not to borrow. Under very few circumstances should a borrowed article be passed along on loan to a third person without the specific permission of the owner.

It is always difficult to refuse a direct request to lend something, and therefore the would-be borrower does best to open negotiations with a broad hint.

For example, a hostess in need of many extra cups for a big tea might report to a neighbor that she has to make a tiresome trip across town to borrow what she needs. This gives the neighbor a chance to offer her own china, but it also saves her from having to refuse flatly if it does not suit her to lend her things.

It is no service to lend extremely valuable or irreplaceable objects. It is far better to answer a request with "Those cups were my great-grandmother's— so I know you wouldn't want to be responsible for them." Or, if freely offering to lend a delicate piece of equipment or expensive breakables, it is only kind to let the borrower know just how much of a responsibility is being so generously offered.

With few exceptions, the person asked to lend articles for a party must be invited to the party. A good neighbor may be asked to lend equipment needed for a business party, or some such gathering as a tea for the parents of the graduating class of P.S. 42, without being asked to attend, since it is quite obvious that she does not qualify as part of the group. Otherwise, if her possessions come to the party, she must be invited.

Equipment borrowed for a party should be returned the day after, unless a later date is specifically arranged. Usually, borrowed articles are returned with a small gift.

**DAMAGE.** If a borrowed article is damaged or lost, the borrower is expected to replace it, not to offer its value in cash. Before a replacement is ordered, however, the owner should be notified of the mishap. Rather than a duplicate, he may prefer a different model or color. Exact replacement of a borrowed article is not always possible, of course. When a duplicate cannot be found, the borrower's best course is to send something similar of equal value that can be exchanged.

**MONEY.** Small amounts may be borrowed casually and returned with equal casualness at next meeting, or by mail if more convenient, though an occasional dime for a telephone call or a postage stamp need not be returned.

It is difficult to make strict rules. Many circumstances can justify a man's borrowing a sizable sum from a woman, and vice versa. In general, however, a man turns to his men friends first, and a woman to her woman friends.

**BOUILLON.** *See* SOUPS.

**BOUQUETS.** *See* FLOWERS.

**BOUTONNIERES.** *See* FLOWERS.

## BOW TIES

The most important rule about bow ties is that they must be hand-tied. The too perfect ready-made tie is for waiters and theater ushers. Both ends of a bow tie should be hidden by the loops, producing a two-winged rather than a four-winged butterfly.
*See* CLOTHES.

## BOWLING

Within a relatively few years, bowling has become one of the most popular sports. In spite of the informal atmosphere in most lanes,* there is nothing catch-as-catch-can about the rules of play. The following nine-point code of etiquette, prepared by the American Bowling Congress and reprinted here with their permission, is accepted by bowlers everywhere:

1. Be prepared to take your regular turn on the lanes. Remember, the player to the right has the right of way.
2. Take your time, but don't waste everybody else's by useless posing or **delay.**

* Note: The preferred term today is "lanes" rather than "alleys."

3. Stay on your own approach and step back off the approach after making each delivery.
4. Don't use another player's ball without his permission.
5. Good bowling requires concentration. When an opponent is set to bowl, give him the courtesy of making his shot without interference. Save the kidding for the players' bench or locker room.
6. Be ready to bowl as soon as it is your turn, but be sure you wait until the pinsetting machine has completed its cycle and the sweep bar is raised.
7. Getting the ball out on the lane is necessary, but "lofting" is bad for your game and the lane.
8. Play to win the game, but to be a gracious loser if you are on the short end of the count at the end of the game.

**CLOTHES.** There is one all-important rule: Players must wear special shoes with the right sole of rubber and the left sole of leather. Some lanes allow sneakers, but most ban them. Correct shoes can be rented at most lanes.

Men find slacks and sports shirt a comfortable costume. Many women do too, but the Women's International Bowling Congress forbids slacks at the national tournament and requires contestants to wear sports dresses, or blouses and skirts or culottes. Although the Congress has no control over the dress of women bowlers in general, it discourages the wearing of any garment that calls attention to the anatomy—stretch pants, leotards, tight slacks, or very brief shorts, for example.

**TIPPING.** Today, virtually all lanes are equipped with an automatic pin-setting device, and so there is no pinboy to be tipped. At a refreshment counter in a bowling center a tip is not customarily expected in most parts of the country, though the waiter or waitress who gives table service does expect a tip. The guest at a private club that has bowling facilities either leaves the tipping to his host or asks his host about the club custom.

# BOWS

A slight bow is a standard part of a formal exchange of greetings. A man bows by bending slightly from the waist, avoiding both the abrupt military bow and the deep bow of the headwaiter. A slight inclination of a woman's head and a very slight inclination of her body serve as a bow.

**CHILDREN.** All children have to be taught that words of greeting are not enough and that a courteous little bow must accompany them. Boys bow as do their elders. Little girls sometimes curtsy instead.

**PERFORMERS.** Applause after a speech is acknowledged by a slightly deeper bow than called for in other circumstances, but not the very deep bow customarily given by a performer in response to applause. The bow of the stage performer accepting applause is a delightful performance in itself—the actor knows how it should be done, and the rest of us do not need to.

**BOYS.** *See* CHILDREN AND MANNERS; CLOTHES.

# BRACELETS

Bracelets that rattle or clank can be an irritating distraction. For that reason, they are inappropriate in church, at a concert, and in most offices. Bracelets may be worn over gloves but generally are seen over only the long evening gloves that reach above the elbow.

# BRANDY

Brandy is a strong spirit that can be distilled from many different substances. The word "brandy" alone on a label indicates that the contents were distilled from grapes. If another base was used, the brandy is usually so labeled: Apricot

Brandy, Blackberry Brandy, and so on.
  *See* WHISKIES AND OTHER SPIRITS.

## BRAVO AND BRAVA

Some opera buffs demonstrate their knowledge of Italian by shouting "Brava!" for a woman and "Bravi!" for more than one person, but "Bravo!" is correct as a compliment to a man, woman, or an entire cast.

## BREAD

Bread, hot or cold, is passed at the table in a basket or tray, with one exception—hard rolls may be in place on the butter plates before guests sit down. Biscuits and other hot breads are kept warm by lining the tray with a folded napkin.

If a butter plate is not provided, bread or hard rolls are put on the tablecloth, but sticky rolls are put on the edge of the dinner plate.

Butter is not put directly on bread with the butter-serving knife or pick. It is first put on the butter plate or the side of the main plate. A whole slice of bread is not buttered at once. Hot rolls and biscuits may be split and buttered as soon as served, but one piece at a time is broken off for eating. Tiny biscuits that can be eaten in two bites need not be broken.

Bread should not be used to push food onto a fork or held in the fingers to sop gravy. A bite-size piece of bread may be broken off, put on the dinner plate, and then eaten with the fork after it has absorbed that last delicious mouthful of sauce.

Small delicate rolls, such as Parker House, or small hard rolls are usually served at dinner rather than sliced bread. Big onion rolls, buns, and sticky rolls of any kind are reserved for casual family-style meals.

Bread is not served with soup (unless it is a hearty soup forming an important part of an informal meal); crackers, croutons, or Melba toast is offered instead.

Bread and butter and butter plates are removed from the table before dessert is served, but at an informal meal where fruit and cheese are the dessert, they may be left on. Some people prefer bread to crackers with cheese, and some like butter with it.

## BREAD-AND-BUTTER LETTERS

Today, a telephone call sometimes replaces the bread-and-butter letter of follow-up thanks that, by the rules, must be sent to one's hostess after an overnight visit. But a personal note, written within five days, is still the first choice. A bread-and-butter letter is addressed to the hostess, not to a couple jointly, and should be written by the wife of the visiting couple. If a child has been an overnight guest without his parents, the child writes to the hostess, and his mother does also, if the child is very young.

A visiting card with some such handwritten message as "Thank you for the wonderful time" can serve as a substitute for a letter, but it is rather less thoughtful than a little note unless flowers (or another gift) are sent with the card.

A commercial greeting card of thanks is not correctly substituted for a bread-and-butter note.

## BREAKAGE.  *See* DAMAGE.

## BREAKFASTS

A meal served to a wedding party in the morning or as late as one o'clock is called a "wedding breakfast," never a "wedding luncheon," even though the hour and menu are both typical of lunch.

*See* WEDDINGS. For other breakfasts, see MEALS AND THEIR SERVICE.

## BRIDEGROOMS

"Groom" and "bridegroom" are used interchangeably for a man on his wedding day and for a few days before and after.

*See* WEDDINGS.

## BRIDES

"Bride" is used of a woman on her wedding day. Before that she is technically a "bride-to-be," though she is referred to as "the bride" during rehearsals and parties immediately before the wedding, and usually during the honeymoon. After that, she becomes a "recent bride."

*See* WEDDINGS.

## BRIDGE. *See* GAMES.

## BRIT MILAH

Brit Milah is the name of the ceremony at which a Jewish baby boy is circumcised, named, and dedicated to the Jewish way of life, on the eighth day after his birth unless the doctor recommends that the ceremony be postponed. The ceremony is held at home or, more often today, at the hospital. Many hospitals have a room set aside for the ceremony.

The naming ceremony for Jewish baby girls has no special name. In Orthodox and Conservative congregations, the baby's father attends the first service that he can following her birth, to read a portion of the Law, and after having done this he names the little girl. In some Reform congregations, the rabbi announces the little girl's birth and her name, and gives her his blessing, at a regular service on either the first Friday evening or Saturday morning after her birth.

Friends of other faiths should not feel neglected if not asked to attend a Brit Milah or a naming ceremony for a little girl. Few if any friends are customarily invited. Since the ceremonies follow birth within a week and the mother is still convalescent, there is no celebration similar to a christening party.

Jewish children do not have godparents who undertake special responsibilities as do godparents in Christian faiths.

## BRUNCHES. *See* MEALS AND THEIR SERVICE.

## BUFFETS. *See* MEALS AND THEIR SERVICE.

## BUSES

In some communities, passengers are developing the habit of queuing up at bus stops, boarding in order of their arrival in line, and sparing themselves the jostling and shoving of those people who always have to get on first as a sort of game. If there is no queue, an unaccompanied man stands aside for women, but if several couples are getting on it is simpler for everyone, including the harassed driver, if each woman is followed immediately by her escort.

It used to be the rule that no able-bodied man kept a seat in a public conveyance if a woman was standing. This rule no longer holds. A man keeps his seat in a crowded bus unless an old person, a handicapped one, or a mother with a very small child needs it. Young women, boys, and girls also are expected to surrender a seat under such circumstances.

When leaving a bus, the man makes his way to the exit first, gets off first, turns and helps a woman companion down the steps. The same rule holds for a young man or woman accompanying an older person of the same sex.

Passengers make life easier for themselves and everyone else if they move to the rear; use the rear door for exit; apologize for jostling even if the driver's lurching stop was to blame; hold a child young enough to ride free if a paying passenger must otherwise stand; do not treat a public conveyance as a waste-basket—and take no offense at the notoriously bad manners of the average bus jockey. Things are uncomfortable enough on a crowded bus without starting a war with the driver.

## BUSINESS MANNERS

Anyone in doubt about a matter of business behavior cannot go wrong by following the standard rules for good social conduct. At worst, he will be ex-posed as a beginner (but a mannerly one) in the working world. The marked differences between good social and business behavior concern, very largely, two relationships:

1. That of men and women to each other. (A woman who has a job cor-rectly behaves, and expects to be treated, as just another worker—not as a "lady"—with certain explicit exceptions.)

2. That of older and younger workers to each other. (Relative rank governs their behavior, not relative age.)

Details are given below, along with other major differences in business and social etiquette.

**CALLERS.** As a general practice, anyone making a call or receiving a caller on business premises observes the same rules that govern a guest and a host anywhere. The following rules relate to visitors other than fellow staff members.

The occupant of a private office rises to greet and to say good-bye to a caller under all ordinary circumstances. If there is more than one place to sit, the caller does not choose any seat he pleases without giving the host a chance to indicate a specific position. He takes the place indicated by the host, who may have a good reason for his selection.

It should not be necessary to say (but it is!) that the caller who lets his eyes wander over exposed correspondence is out of bounds. So is a host who wastes a caller's time by carrying on an extended telephone conversation, most espe-cially a personal one, except in an emergency.

All behavior during a business call is governed by the simple truth that someone is paying for the time of both parties. A caller is expected to arrive at the exact time of an appointment, and the person he is seeing is expected to be ready for him. But human nature and modern traffic being what they are, punctuality is not always possible. The visitor who discovers he will be late telephones, if possible, and gives the host a chance to rearrange his schedule. If a visitor must be asked to wait in a reception room for more than a short time, a message of apology and an estimate of the delay should be relayed to him.

The rule says that a caller makes the move to end a visit, but this rule is observed in only the most general sense in business. If the caller misses the polite signals that time has run out, or ignores them, the host correctly ends the interview, and the caller must accept amiably and without delay any state-ment like, "I wish we could continue, but I have another appointment." The caller says good-bye to secretary and receptionist as he goes out.

When members of his family drop in at the office of any employee who does not have executive status, he should see to it that the interruption is a brief one. He may want to show off his children to his friends and introduce his wife to the boss, but he makes a bad impression—and so does his family—if he permits the visit to last more than a few minutes.

Visits of relatives and friends with an executive are also best kept within reasonable time limits, particularly when they are unexpected, and a drop-in visitor should not be offended by frequent interruptions or by being shunted to a reception area while the executive receives a business caller or attends to any other business matter.

**CLOTHES.** There is such an enormous range in the clothing appropriate to different places of business that only the general rule can be given here. Although there is plenty of latitude for personal taste, business clothes are nonetheless uniform in the sense that good judgment calls for reasonable conformity in appearance with one's fellow workers. Business clothes should never be so extreme in style, fabric, or cost that they make the wearer stand out among others at his place of business as conspicuously overdressed or underdressed. Obviously, a real estate salesman does not dress as if going to work in a city bank if his days are spent showing country property, nor does the young account executive affect tweedy sports jackets if the rest of the staff wears standard suits.

Both the woman executive and the telepone girl who arrive at nine in the morning in a costume suitable only for an engagement after work are out of line. Bracelets that clank or rattle are no more suitable in a business office than they are at a theater or concert because their noise can be a distraction to anyone within earshot. Jewelry suitable for daytime street wear is the best choice.

**CONFERENCES.** When executives or a departmental staff hold a formal conference, the executive who called the meeting usually opens it and controls the discussion. He brings the conference to a close unless, of course, it was assembled at the instigation of a superior officer who is present.

**CONVENTIONS.** When businessmen gather at conventions, they often wear name badges that identify them personally, as well as show the organization or company with which they are affiliated and sometimes their rank or position. A man's name appears on a badge without title. For example:

> George S. Brown
> Purchasing Agent
> XYZ Cosmetic Company

A married woman employee's name may appear with "Mrs." if that is the way she is known in business: Mrs. Helen Smith. A single woman's name appears without "Miss."

Small name badges are preferred to large ones because they can easily be slipped into pocket or handbag while going to or from meetings. They are not properly worn on the street or anywhere outside convention get-togethers.

Conventions of any sort have their social aspects, and often a holiday spirit prevails at after-hours events. This is one of the attractions of a convention so long as party behavior is kept within bounds and each delegate remembers that his conduct reflects on the firm he represents and on the place he lives—after hours as well as during the formal business proceedings.

**DOORS.** A business host taking a visitor into his office opens the door and ushers him in, just as he would in his private dwelling. A caller not connected with the firm, when leaving, is shown to the door of a private office by his host, and a caller of great distinction is seen to the outer office door or to the elevator. (See "Rising" below.) Otherwise, common sense and practicality govern precedence. As a general rule, relative rank dictates the order among the staff, not sex or age, but this is a matter about which there can be no one rule that applies to all circumstances.

When several executives are entering or leaving a conference, the juniors in grade of both sexes and of any age normally stand aside and let those of higher rank enter or leave first, and a secretary very often stands aside for her chief, or follows rather than precedes him during a walk through a plant or a big office. On the other hand, many businessmen habitually open a door for any woman, and nothing is lost by this routine social courtesy.

The closed door of a private office should be respected as faithfully as a closed door in a private dwelling; no one should open it without knocking—even the boss—unless clearly established office policy has dispensed with this standard courtesy.

**EATING.** Just as binding in an office as elsewhere is the general rule: Don't eat in front of any visitor without offering to share some portion of the refreshment. Anyone with food spread out on his desk sets it aside when a caller is admitted, or at least does not continue to eat without an explanation and apology. A caller with his wits about him will say, "Please go ahead," if he sees a half-finished meal courteously ignored. Good business sense will then dictate following or ignoring that instruction. A junior executive would certainly ignore it during a brief visit from the president of his firm, but under any circumstances an excuse is called for before going ahead with a meal that is palpably impossible or absurd to share.

**Coffee Breaks.** A midmorning cup of coffee is so thoroughly established a custom in many offices that a coffee wagon is permitted to make the rounds rather than have employees take time to brew their own or make a trip outside. But the break is only a "break"; it should not be a major interruption of the day's work.

**ELEVATORS.** When men and women who are strangers enter an elevator in a place of business, the same manners hold as when strangers board a bus or other public conveyance. If only a few women are waiting, a man lets them board first; if there is a crowd, those nearest the entrance enter in any order that causes the least delay. The same rule holds for a crowd of men and women from the same department who are using an elevator in a rush hour—first come, first served. A man does not take his hat off in an elevator in a business building.

**EMPLOYEE'S OBLIGATIONS.** Anyone who accepts a salary assumes certain duties and responsibilities as well. When he takes a wage he becomes a part of a business, and his behavior during working hours reflects directly on the firm's standing. The employee who has personal contact with outsiders speaks, in effect, for the company. An impatient answer, rudeness, or incompetence becomes, in the public eye, a fault or shortcoming of the firm.

The behavior of an employee in his private life can also reflect on the firm for which he works. Even on purely social occasions, his poor conduct can make others wonder what sort of firm would hire him. And the executive who is involved in scandal of sufficient proportions to be recounted in the newspapers is expected to offer his resignation if his personal problem becomes a problem to his firm also.

Employees of all ranks owe their employer loyalty. No honorable employee passes along inside information to family and friends. The employee who thinks his boss is impossible is better off seeking a new job than broadcasting his views to other people, either fellow workers or outsiders. Similarly, disapproval of a firm's policies should not be discussed with outsiders. An employee who feels out of step with his outfit and everyone in it will certainly be happier and more productive elsewhere.

Although many employers take an interest in the well-being of their employees outside the shop or office, an employee should be wary about burdening his chief with his personal problems and should avoid the not uncommon tendency to make a father image out of the boss.

**EMPLOYER'S OBLIGATIONS.** No considerate employer behaves as if his employees were machines. Family crises or serious personal trouble certainly should be given consideration and understanding, but an employer cannot overlook tardiness, absenteeism, or poor performance indefinitely. In most circumstances, an employer gives a staff member a second chance, though he is by no standards expected to provide third, fourth, and fifth chances.

By virtue of running a firm or being an executive in one, an employer has certain privileges. These carry their price. Having the final say in making decisions means that he also must accept responsibility for their outcome. If he makes a poor decision based on the advice of an employee, the responsibility for the decision is still his.

No matter how much overtime an employer or ambitious executive willingly puts in himself, he cannot expect his employees to be similarly dedicated. (See "Overtime," below.) When an employee does on occasion voluntarily put in extra time or effort special thanks or other recognition is due.

In a firm with hundreds of employees, the owner and the top executives naturally do not know the names of all their people or even of a fraction of them. In small organizations, on the other hand, the employer who fails to use the names of his employees is breaking the rules of business etiquette. Employees are individuals, not standardized "manpower units."

**ENTERTAINING.** Some of the rules governing business entertaining are markedly different from those for social entertaining. For example, an expense-account lunch or other entertainment need not be returned, though a guest thanks his host for it when they are ready to go their separate ways. One of the conventions of the business lunch is that the guest is supposed to wait for the host to introduce the matter they are meeting to discuss. If a host shows signs of going on at length about matters of general or his own personal interest, the guest is correct to plunge in, particularly if his time is limited.

Entertaining the out-of-town business acquaintance, especially one accompanied by his wife, can present problems, as long-suffering wives of executives well know. Here, again, social and business rules are different. If a business host can give some acceptable excuse for the absence of his wife, it is entirely correct for him to entertain a couple without her, but the excuse had better be a good one or business relations may be damaged instead of improved.

Neither host nor guest follows up business entertainment on the social level except with some caution. As a general rule, the person who accepts business entertainment is never obligated to return it on the social level; a business lunch is not repaid by an invitation to dine with the family at home, for example.

Warm personal friendships can develop between business acquaintances and their families, of course. And people who have (or would like to have) business dealings with each other sometimes meet, by calculation or accident, under social circumstances. It is not incorrect to take business advantage of a social gathering if the rules are observed. A host certainly can touch briefly on a business problem to a guest in his house, but ambushing a guest who has accepted a social invitation in good faith is taboo. And the guest who behaves like a Trojan horse—accepts an invitation, and then turns the social occasion into a business conference—is unlikely to receive a second invitation.

Within a staff, a junior in rank does not make the first move to social contact by asking his chief home to dinner.

**Expense Accounts.** The rules governing the use of expense accounts vary from company to company, but the rules governing behavior when entertaining or being entertained at a firm's expense do not.

1. Neither host nor guest emphasizes that the lunch, dinner, or other entertainment will be charged to a firm. Though that fact is clearly understood, it is ignored.
2. The business guest behaves like a social guest, and follows the lead of the

host in choice of restaurant and menu. He does not order the most extravagantly expensive items unless the host suggests them. He does not suggest going on to a series of nightclubs at the expense of the host's company after being entertained at dinner or the theater, or in any other way forget that the expenditure is at the discretion of his host—even though not out of his own pocket. The guest who virtually demands additional entertainment puts himself in the host's role, and should expect to pay the tab out of his own purse or his own expense account.

3. The padding of an expense account is a matter of honesty, not of manners, but it is a real breach of the rules of business etiquette to claim falsely to have entertained anyone and to list his name on one's expense account. The least the expense-account padder can do is not involve anyone else in his financial juggling.

4. The use of an expense account to entertain a personal friend is also a matter of personal honesty, not of etiquette. But it is inexcusable to say, "I'll take the check—it can go on my expense account," because that statement not only puts a friend in the position of a willing freeloader but gives him no chance to object without sounding moralistic about the host's own willingness to freeload.

5. A man should not feel any reluctance about accepting expense-account entertainment from a woman, though many men cannot resist grabbing the check when they see a woman reach into her purse for cash. The woman who entertains on an expense account does best to carry a credit card or to establish charge accounts at convenient restaurants so that she need only sign a check for tips as well as meals.

6. Some few executives are not expected to turn in detailed accountings of expenditures for business entertaining, but most expense accounts have to be submitted to someone for okay. Every care should be taken not to put that person on the spot. A chief too often has to choose between approving an expense account as submitted, or seeming to question its honesty by asking for receipts or more detail. It should be remembered that the person who approves an expense account becomes responsible for it—a department head to the employer; the employer, in turn, to income-tax authorities. No one who turns in a legitimate expense account should feel embarrassed at a request for explanation, but everyone is spared trouble if easily available receipts are attached.

**FIRING.**   See "Hiring, Firing, Resigning," below.

**GIFTS.** With a few exceptions, the general rules listed under GIFTS are just as valid in business as in social relationships. The most important single rule about any gift is that it must be acknowledged, whether or not it was paid for by an expense account. Following are the special rules governing gifts between business associates:

**From the Employer.** If an employer gives presents at Christmastime, all that is customary in return is spoken thanks or a short note of appreciation. A woman executive can give a woman on her staff something as personal as lingerie, if she likes. But a male executive (unless he is a manufacturer of the item) does not correctly give a major article of clothing to any woman outside his family. Accessories like a handbag, luggage, perfume, and so on are always correct as business presents.

**To the Employer.** At Christmastime, presents to the employer are usually best skipped. Let him be Santa Claus. There are many exceptions, of course, especially in small offices where employer and staff members of long standing are on close terms. On nearly all occasions, however, an employee does best to think twice before giving the boss a present. When in doubt, a gag present or a greeting card is generally a better choice than anything of real value, even on his birthday. Cuff links, ties, and other items for personal use are not correct. The same rules hold for junior staff members to their department heads and other executives.

If the office or department is small and the whole staff is on close terms with the employer or chief, a joint present from the staff is appropriate on a special occasion. A cigarette case or box, a watch or some other item that can be engraved, or something for his business use, such as a briefcase or luggage, is a good choice.

If an employer or department head is about to be married, his staff as a whole may chip in for a wedding present even if they do not know his fiancée. They follow the standard rule—select a present for joint use, and send it to his fiancée before the wedding or to the couple jointly after the wedding. It is not appropriate for an individual staff member to send a wedding present unless asked to the wedding.

**To the Employer's Family.** Presents are generally not sent to an employer's wife or family unless there is some degree of social as well as business relationship. For example, if an employee spends the weekend working at the employer's house, he does not properly send a house present—only the bread-and-butter letter due from any houseguest. On the other hand, the employee asked for the weekend follows the usual social rules if no office business is involved. He takes along a small present like flowers or candy for his hostess, or sends it within a few days, but does not ask the chief to tote it home.

When there is a death in the employer's immediate family, the staff customarily expresses sympathy by sending flowers jointly or by a contribution to a charity. Unless the funeral is announced as private, it is usual for employees close to the executive (but only those) to attend.

If the employer's daughter is being married, a gift from the entire staff is not usual—unless the entire staff is asked to the wedding and reception. But there is no fixed rule about all these matters except that a staff member avoids any present that would make a boss feel uncomfortably obligated.

**Outsiders' Gifts.** It is the long-established custom of some firms to send Christmas presents to employees in other firms with whom they do business. If such presents are relatively low in cost they are given and accepted openly as no more than a routine token of appreciation for pleasant dealings during the past year. A present expensive enough to approach '"payola" for a past—or a hoped-for—special favor is a sticky matter, admittedly hard to handle because it is hard to know where to draw the line. If in doubt about the propriety of accepting what seems to be a rather too overwhelming present, the best thing is to get the whole matter into the open by reporting it to one's chief, and leave the decision to him. The actual refusal, when one seems best, can be handled gracefully if warm thanks for the generous intent accompany the explanation that accepting gifts is against the policy of one's firm.

**GROOMING.** Employees are expected to arrive in the morning ready to go to work. Getting to the office on time and then spending twenty minutes on a hairdo is being twenty minutes late. Using an electric razor in an office in the presence of anyone, or making extensive repairs to makeup, is as out of line as cleaning fingernails or using a toothpick in public.

**HIRING, FIRING, AND RESIGNING.**

**Hiring.** An employer sometimes forgets that he is just as much an applicant for the services of a prospective employee as the worker is an applicant for the job, and that he too is bound by specific rules of conduct during an interview.

Under most circumstances, an employer rises to greet an applicant at the beginning of the interview and also when he terminates it. This is standard procedure when the interview is held in a private office and always when the applicant has professional standing. And even the youngest messenger boy is asked to be seated during the interview if the employer is seated. An employer may ask the otherwise taboo question "How old are you?" because that information has direct bearing on a company's insurance and retirement plans, but he should not ask it in the presence of others, and any records containing such personal information should not be kept in open office files.

The prospective employee, in turn, is privileged to ask questions about all aspects of the job, and is entitled to complete answers. The employer should volunteer all facts about working conditions that might be considered drawbacks. In the long run, an explicit explanation of both drawbacks and privileges saves everyone time and trouble.

**Firing.** Dismissing an employee for whatever cause is a miserable task. The important thing to remember is that there are almost always two sides to any dissatisfaction, and that the employer himself shares some part of the blame for hiring an incompetent or unsuitable person in the first place. A fair-minded employer tries to send such an employee away with any reasonable face-saving excuse to be repeated at home—or to the next employer. The employee does best to accept whatever excuse is given and at least leave behind him a good impression of his personal behavior in a trying situation.

Fair notice is only fair play. If it seems best to ask an employee to leave the premises without delay after dismissal, payment in lieu of notice is the standard alternative.

**Resigning.** There comes a time in nearly every working life when the words "I quit!"—followed by a soul-satisfying summary of the reasons—are the most tempting words in the language. This is a good moment to count to ten. After a spectacular exit, anyone feels like a fool if he has to go back to clean out his desk.

**ILLNESS.** A specific number of days of sick leave without loss of pay is standard in most offices. This provision is meant to serve as a protection for the worker in an emergency, not as extra vacation time or as an excuse to take time off for any other reason. Rules about colds vary from office to office. Many employers prefer a sneezing employee to an absent one. When is doubt, ask for the office rule.

**INTRODUCTIONS.** *See* INTRODUCTIONS for the marked differences between business and social introductions.

**INVITATIONS.** The general rules governing social invitations are followed almost exactly in the giving and the answering of business invitations.

An invitation with R.S.V.P. on it must be answered promptly, and a fill-in reply card should be marked and returned promptly too. If the card says only "I will attend," it may be ignored if the recipient will not be attending.

An invitation that need not be acknowledged is the come-one, come-all variety, which serves more as an announcement of an event than as an actual invitation. In this category are "invitations" to attend exhibits, take a tour of a plant, attend a stockholders' meeting, etc.

*See* INVITATIONS for standard forms.

**JOB AND POSITION.** The more important an executive is, the more likely he is to speak of his "job" rather than his "position." Today, no one makes a distinction between these two words, though "job" was once commonly used to refer to untrained labor rather than white-collar work. "Situation" is used rather more widely in connection with domestic work than either "job" or "position."

**LETTERS.** *See* CORRESPONDENCE, BUSINESS.

**NAMES AND TITLES.** There are several marked differences between the correct social and business uses of names.

**First Names.** In some business circles, it is the custom to use first names on first meeting. For anyone to object to this practice by a new acquaintance of about equal rank and age is stuffy, but a newcomer to a firm is always best advised to let the old-timers take the lead.

In social life the woman makes the first move to use first names. In business the employer (or chief), no matter of which sex, makes the first move. An executive's use of a staff member's first name is not necessarily an invitation to use his first name in return. Many senior executives call younger ones by their first names, fully expecting to remain "Mr. Jones" or "Miss Green" to them.

There are variations of these rules, of course. For example, the great Walt Disney was addressed as "Walt" by everyone on his huge staff—janitors to vice-presidents—but it should be remembered that Mr. Disney himself, not his employees, established this custom.

**Giving One's Name.** Common sense is the best guide to the correct forms when identifying and introducing one's self in business circumstances, once the distinct differences in the rules for men and women are understood.

A good general rule to follow is: Do not use a first name in any casual or one-time use when a first name has no bearing. For example, a secretary who needs to identify herself says something like "This is Miss Smith of Mr. Jones's office"—not "Mary Smith." And a man who needs to identify himself on the telephone in relation to his function with a firm says, "Complaint Department, Brown speaking"—not "John Brown." As a second choice he may say, "Mr. Brown, Complaint Department," because the self-applied "Mr." that is incorrect in social circumstances is acceptable in some business circumstances.

"Mr. Brown calling Mr. Green" is widely used to secretaries and receptionists, but better choices by far are any variants of the following. "My name is Brown. Mr. Jones is expecting me," or "I'm John Brown of Standard Products," or "Brown of Standard Products returning Mr. Green's call," or "John Brown to see Miss White"—all of which avoid the slightly pompous and self-important "Mr. Brown." And a man never speaks respectfully of himself as "Mr. John Brown" to anyone. When his first name is needed to distinguish him from other Mr. Browns, he drops the title "Mr."

Women correctly use a title and last name on many business occasions, since "Miss" or "Mrs." is properly part of an identification. "Mrs. [or Miss] Brown calling to see Mr. Green" is the usual and correct form for a woman giving her name to a receptionist or secretary, and to all others, when she is identifying rather than introducing herself. However, a woman executive often identifies herself to a secretary by her first and last name without title (Mary Brown), which is equally correct and decidedly less pompous. A woman may correctly identify or introduce herself as "Mrs. Paul White" if she uses her husband's name in any business connection. Otherwise, she uses "Mrs. White" or "Mary White"—never "Mrs. Mary White."

*See also* TELEPHONE MANNERS.

**Of a Husband or Wife.** Explicit rules govern the use of "Mr.," "Mrs.," "my husband," "my wife," and the first name of one's spouse in business relationships. The following rules apply to women as well as men.

To his employees, fellow workers, and business associates, a man uses "my wife"; to intimates with whom he is on a first-name basis, he can use either "my wife" or her first name. "Mrs. Jones" is not correct.

A business friend who has not met a man's wife correctly says either, "Is Mrs. Jones in town?" or, "Is your wife in town?" Friends on a first-name basis with the husband use "your wife" (neither "Mrs. Jones" nor her first name) if they have not met her, but a secretary or switchboard operator says, "Mrs. Jones is calling," not, "It's your wife."

**Substitutes for Names.** "Dear" is a term of personal affection. It is unbusinesslike when used indiscriminately in an office by the staff, and absurd when used by or to strangers as a substitute for an unknown last name.

**OFFICE PARTIES.** A staff picnic, dinner, dance, or other festivity is, in a way, a command performance. Lacking some very good excuse, every staff member is expected to put in an appearance and contribute to the success of the party.

Office parties are a time to forget rank and formality to a degree—but only to a degree. All staff members have equal status as guests of the company, and the boss's secretary who will dance only with executives and refuses the invitation of the mailroom boy is breaking the first rule of office-party behavior. No one need dance, enter games or races, or join in any other activity that will put him at a disadvantage or embarrass him later, so long as he is not stuffy or superior in refusing.

**OVERTIME.** Common sense calls for meeting an occasional emergency in business with the same generosity demanded in social circumstances—and the same appreciation in return. But, even in those firms where overtime is automatically paid for, an employer is not privileged to demand it as a right, at the last minute. He is expected to give due notice so that the worker asked to stay late can adjust his personal plans. If overtime is not paid for, the least an employer can do is arrange for the employee to have time off during a subsequent working day to even the debt.

The executive who, at the end of the day, loads a secretary with dictation that must be ready for his signature when the office opens in the morning deserves the trouble he undoubtedly will have in keeping competent help. On the other hand, the clock-watching employee who is coated, hatted, and ready to whiz out of the door on the dot of closing hour is actually leaving ahead of time.

**PROMOTIONS.** A business promotion is never officially announced in the press by the person promoted. The officers of a firm tell the news within the company, and send out the press release.

When two or more people are in line for the same job, it is only basic consideration to inform the loser before the news is made public.

**REFERENCES.** A messenger boy or service employee generally prefers a written reference. The employee on a higher job level, rather than present written references, usually refers a prospective employer to his earlier employers.

The whole system of references breaks down if they are not honestly worded. To endorse someone as reliable who has been irresponsible is completely unfair to a prospective employer and is an irresponsible act in itself. But where no major matter (dishonesty, for instance) is involved, a former employer gives emphasis to the employee's virtues and does not dwell on minor reasons for dissatisfaction that would be of no moment to another employer or in a different job.

**RISING.** All rules for rising are amended by practical considerations. As a general thing, anyone receiving a caller not connected with the firm rises in greeting and in farewell. This rule is always observed by the occupant of a private office.

An executive does not rise when receiving a junior staff member or every time his own secretary comes in. To do so would be obviously absurd, since he might do nothing but pop up and down all day. He does get to his feet when welcoming a new employee to the staff, and rises to shake hands when a staff member of whatever rank comes in to say his formal good-bye on leaving the firm. In many companies, an executive rises when receiving a staff member of equal or higher rank who enters his office, though this is seldom the practice in offices where informality is the rule.

A secretary stationed outside her chief's office does not rise for him or his callers under most circumstances, but a junior staff member usually rises when a senior executive stops at his desk to talk.

Women in a business office are, as already mentioned, treated as fellow workers and not accorded all the courtesies expected in a social relationship. An executive does not rise, for instance, when a woman employee (even a much older woman) enters his office on a routine errand. If, on the other hand, she has asked to speak to him about some special matter and her visit to his office is in the nature of an appointment, an executive treats her in much the same way as he would any caller—rises, offers her a chair, and rises when she leaves. Here, again, practical considerations and the degree of formality customary in a particular firm are guiding factors.

**SALARIES.** Today, "wages" is generally used only for the earnings of unskilled workers, and even so, "salary" is the preferred term for all regularly employed people. Each person's salary is his own business. If someone mentions his own salary as a heavy hint for information, there is no need to satisfy his curiosity. Unless salary checks are handed directly to each individual by the comptroller, paymaster, manager, or some other person who already knows the amount, they should be enclosed in sealed envelopes.

**SECRETARIES.** One thing is sure—automation is no threat to the good secretary. No machine can supply the judgment and tact demanded of this combination front-line-of-defense and backstop. In all usual business circumstances, a secretary inevitably learns a good bit about her chief's personal as well as business relationships. One of her prime responsibilities is to keep all such matters to herself, even though they may not seem to be confidential. Her chief has the right to tell his own news when and how he chooses. Whenever in doubt, her best rule is: Don't volunteer information, no matter how minor it may seem. For example, if someone asks, "Is he free for lunch?" the correct answer is "I'll ask him to call you" or "He has that time checked off. Shall I ask him to call?" She does not volunteer where or with whom he has a lunch date, particularly to an outsider. This leaves him free to rearrange his schedule, should he want to, without revealing that he is breaking a prior date.

Common sense amends the rule about giving details of his business engagements, of course, but other staff members should take care not to put a secretary in a difficult position by asking questions out of idle curiosity or asking one that should be asked directly of her chief, if at all.

See also TELEPHONE MANNERS and, for rules concerning the secretary traveling with her boss, HOTELS AND MOTELS.

**SMOKING.** The absence of ashtrays in a reception room or office can be taken as evidence that smoking is not wanted or perhaps permitted. Even if there are ashtrays in a private office, the caller generally waits for his host to light a cigarette or to offer him one. By the same token, a visitor does not enter a private office carrying a lighted cigarette or cigar.

**TELEPHONE.**   See TELEPHONE MANNERS.

# BUTLERS

The male member of a couple who are the only employees is sometimes spoken of as a butler, but "houseman" is the technically correct term in this case because "butler" is reserved for the ranking male employee on a large staff.

For details of duties and dress, see HOUSEHOLD EMPLOYEES.

## BUTTER

Elaborate service calls for butter in balls or curls, but the average hostess has more pressing demands on her time than the rolling of butter balls; she quite correctly serves pats of butter cut from a stick and attractively arranged. (A whole stick of butter is not put on the table except at informal meals.) Curls and balls of butter are brought to the table in a small bowl of water and ice, and pats often are also. A butter pick or small fork is the standard implement for serving butter offered in ice water. The usual broad-blade butter knife is more efficient for butter on a dish.

Butter is not put directly on a food with the serving implement. It is first put on the butter plate or, if there is none, on the side of the main plate.

**Melted Butter Sauces.** Liquid butter is served in a sauceboat and is spooned or poured directly over any food it accompanies. Tiny individual bowls of melted butter are served on the plate with an artichoke if artichoke plates with wells for sauce are not used. A small individual bowl on its own underplate carries the melted butter served with steamed clams, often also with broiled lobsters.

**Whipped Butter.** The standard service of whipped butter is in a chilled crock, not in balls, since it is too light to work.

**BUTTER KNIVES.** The correct position of the butter knife is on the butter plate, not beside it. After use, the knife is returned to the butter plate, not propped with its handle on the table. The butter knife is not used to butter anything on the main plate with one exception—to transfer butter from the butter plate to an ear of corn on the main plate. The dinner fork is used to put butter on rice, baked potato, or any other food on the main plate.

**BUTTER PLATES.** At the most formal dinners in the past, butter plates were not provided. This is another custom that is being amended to suit today's changing needs and eating habits. At big dinners and banquets at hotels, butter plates and butter knives are now customarily used. And it is now not considered incorrect to use butter plates as part of a formal dinner place setting—but without butter knives, since butter is still not offered at a completely formal private dinner. The tiny dishes known as "butter chips" are not used except in restaurants.

The butter plate is set at the left of the place setting, just above the forks. The butter knife is put on, not beside, it.

Butter plates are removed before dessert is served.

Butter plates need not match the other plates being used so long as they are harmonious in style. A pottery butter plate of a solid color is effective with a decorated pottery main plate, for example, and fine glass and china combine to good effect.

Celery, olives, radishes, and tiny whole pickles to be eaten from the fingers are put on the butter plate, but chopped pickles, chutney, cranberry sauce, and other condiments offered as accompaniments to meats are put on the main plate. Honey, jam, jelly, or preserves meant to be eaten on biscuits or toast are put on the butter plate. Honey is poured directly on hot cakes or waffles, however.

# C

**CABINET OFFICERS.**   *See* FORMS OF ADDRESS (Government).

## CABS

"Taxi" and "cab" are used interchangeably but "taxi" *(which see)* is in widest use in this country.

**CADETS.**   *See* FORMS OF ADDRESS (Armed Services).

**CAFE AU LAIT, etc.**   *See* COFFEE.

## CAFETERIAS

A single patron should not expect to occupy a table alone in a cafeteria. Tipping customs vary widely. In many localities it is now quite usual to leave about ten cents per person for the busboy who clears the tables.

## CAKES

A cake with a soft or sticky icing is served on a plate and eaten with a fork. A firm, dry, pound cake or fruitcake is passed on a platter when offered with another dessert. It is put on the edge of the dessert plate, as are cookies, not on the tablecloth.

**CALLING CARDS.**   *See* VISITING CARDS.

## CALLS

*"The social ramble ain't restful."—Leroy "Satchel" Paige*

The formal call, complete with visiting card, is virtually unknown today except in very limited official circles. However, there are still formalities that govern all visits, even the most casual.

**ARRIVING AND LEAVING.** A host or hostess always rises to greet and to say good-bye to a caller. Under formal circumstances a caller, man or woman, who is seated before the host or hostess appears, rises to be greeted. A male guest always rises, but common sense amends the general rule for women. For example, if the man of the house puts in an appearance while his wife is entertaining a group of her friends, the whole circle of visiting women does not rise as if his entrance were accompanied by the first strains of our national anthem.

Since the visitor makes the first move to end a social call, the host and hostess are a captive audience to a point. Of course, if a call drags on beyond reason and convenience, the rule has to be ignored and the visitor eased on his way with any believable excuse that can be invented.

In all but special cases, a host or hostess sees a caller to the front door and, in an apartment house, very often to the elevator. Unless a host has duties to other guests, he usually sees a woman caller comfortably into her car.

As a general rule, a caller leaves shortly after another visitor arrives, unless pressed to stay on.

**AT HOME.** "Not at home" does not necessarily mean that someone is literally away from the house. "At home" is widely used to mean "free to" see a caller or to answer the telephone. When an unexpected caller arrives, the polite response from a well-trained maid is "I'll see if she is at home." If for any reason her mistress does not wish to be disturbed, the correct answer to a stranger is: "I'm sorry that she is not at home. Will you leave a message?"

Some explanation usually is given to a friend—for example: "She is so sorry that she is not at home. She is taking a sunbath, and can't ask you to wait because she is going out as soon as she dresses." Any such personal message originates with the employer, of course.

Children, especially, need to be taught not to volunteer personal information such as: "She's not at home. She's right in the middle of dyeing her hair," or to bring back the inhospitable report "She's busy," which carries the implication "She's too busy to see *you*."

See INVITATIONS for the use of "At Home" on formal bids to a dance; WEDDINGS for "At Home" cards sent with announcements.

**BUSINESS.**   *See* BUSINESS MANNERS.

**CASUAL.**  In cities, even the closest of friends generally do not drop by even briefly without first telephoning, but in many suburban communities it is the everyday custom for acquaintances to turn up without warning for a short visit. If an unexpected caller arrives at an inconvenient time, all that is required of a host or hostess is a frank excuse—"I wish I could ask you in, but we're just sitting down to dinner" or ". . . getting ready for the income tax man," or whatever. The caller who knows the rules leaves without delay, and certainly without any such countersuggestion as "I'll just wait until you're free."

**CONDOLENCE.**  The condolence call today is a matter of practical and imaginative friendship, not one of the standard social requirements that it once was. Even so, the rules governing the call of condolence and sympathy have changed drastically. Today, only the closest of friends who are certain that their presence will be of solace, or that they are otherwise actually needed, pay an unannounced call on a bereaved family, most especially before a funeral. A good neighbor can ring the bell, of course, and offer help if there is any chance that it is needed, but that is no more than a thoughtful act of sympathy and in no sense a formal call. By today's firm rule, anyone calling on a recently bereaved person should telephone to set an explicit time. And, as a general rule, a telephone call of condolence should be kept reasonably brief. The same holds for a visit of sympathy. Too often, condolence calls become an added heavy burden to those already suffering the heavy emotional strain of great sorrow.

See FUNERALS for the customs concerning calls at a mortuary before a funeral.

**FORMAL.**  The following rules for the now almost unknown, strictly formal social calls will be mainly of use only in a few official circles or to people moving in very formal circles abroad:

A strictly formal call is generally paid in the afternoon after four o'clock. It usually lasts about fifteen minutes. Because it is so brief, it is not customary to offer refreshments to the caller, though of course a drink or tea may be. The caller usually refuses.

It is customary to dress with some care even if the call is no more than leaving a visiting card at the door without asking to be admitted. A woman wears a hat and gloves. A man wears a street suit. He leaves his hat, topcoat, and gloves in the hall. A woman keeps on her hat and gloves.

A husband and wife sometimes pay a formal call together, but very often the wife does the honors for the family and calls alone on the lady of the house (and if she is leaving her own card, leaves one or more of her husband's, by the rules following).

**Cards.**  "Visiting card" and "calling card" are equally correct. It should be noted that a visiting card is not a necessity when making a formal call. All that the caller need do is ignore the lack and simply state his name at the door. However, the rules are explicit if cards are used.

Different numbers of cards are left depending on the circumstances. The important thing is to have one's cards ready at the appropriate time. There is nothing graceful (or formal) about rummaging through a card case and laboriously counting out the required number when it is time to hand them over or leave them.

The marital status of the caller, as well as the hostess, controls the number of cards to be left. A married woman calling on a single woman (unmarried, widowed, or divorced) leaves either a "Mr. and Mrs." card or one of her own and one of her husband's.

A married woman calling on a married woman leaves a "Mr. and Mrs." card and an extra one of her husband's, or one of her cards and two of her husband's. (This combination is based on the rule that a woman does not pay a *formal* social call on a man, and so, with either alternative, the indication is that *she* has called on the lady of the house, and that her husband has, technically, called on the lady of the house and on her husband as well.)

A card is never handed to the person on whom a formal call is being made. If the hostess herself answers the door, the visitor states her name, and she leaves the required number of cards on the hall table or any other convenient place when she takes her leave. If a servant answers the door, the visitor states her name and asks for the person on whom she is calling. If the servant produces a card tray, she puts her personal card on it. If she is leaving other cards, she lays them in any convenient place in the hall as she departs. If the servant who answers the door says, "I am sorry, madam, but Mrs. Jones is not in," the caller then hands over the appropriate number of cards, and by this act has, technically, made a formal call.

Envelopes are never used with cards that are left in person. Exceptions to this rule are made only if cards are left at the desk of an apartment house or hotel. In this case, an envelope is needed to protect them, and to carry the name of the recipient.

In certain circles, and under certain circumstances, the following initials that stand for French terms are written on the lower-left-hand corner of cards left at the door. Capitals may be used, but are not usual:

p.c.—stands for *pour condoléance* (to express sympathy)

p.f.—stands for *pour féliciter* (to congratulate)

p.p.c.—stands for *pour prendre congé* (to take leave, meaning that the caller is leaving town)

p.r.—stands for *pour remercier* (to thank)

**MILITARY.** Customs vary according to the wishes of the commanding officer. It is best, therefore, for an officer to check with the base adjutant or executive officer immediately upon arriving at a new post to find out what is expected. If the commanding officer is of the old school, he will expect a formal call within twenty-four hours; so it is best to look into the matter right away. An officer paying a formal call wears his uniform. His wife wears hat and gloves. (Children do not accompany their parents.)

**NEW NEIGHBORS.** A newcomer to a neighborhood must wait for the neighbors to make the first call. This friendly gesture usually is a fairly casual dropping-by for a self-introduction and a brief chat—in other words, a cordial identification of one's self combined with a scouting trip to see just how the newcomers will best fit into the life of the community. If the call has any degree of formality about it, it should be returned within about ten days.

It is not customary for neighbors in apartment houses to call on a new tenant.

**PARTY CALLS.** The custom of paying a call of thanks after a dinner or other entertainment is completely a thing of the past. Under many circumstances, a guest will telephone to a hostess to thank her for a pleasant time, or will write her a little note (this is expected in the South), but an actual call is not made.

**RETURNING CALLS.** A formal call should be returned within about ten days. Calls of condolence are not returned. A recovered patient need not return calls made during his illness, since these are—in a way—condolence calls.

## CAMPERS

Whether a camper pitches a tent, parks a trailer, or rents a cabin at a public campsite, moors a canoe, tethers a horse, or arrives on foot for a stop deep in a roadless area, he is a houseguest of the land. As a good guest, he is obligated to respect the rights of all others in his vicinity and of those who will come later, hoping to enjoy the outdoors in their turn. The following basic rules will help him fulfill this obligation:

First of all, start out well equipped with all the necessities; other campers, though willing to share supplies and gear in a time of need, are not to be looked upon as handy traveling commissaries.

Don't camp on posted land without getting permission.

In a wilderness area where there is the whole outdoors for a campsite, don't choose one closely adjacent to another camping party unless invited to (others have a right to privacy and solitude, if they prefer them).

Don't build a fire so closely upwind of a fellow camper that its smoke will be an annoyance or discomfort to him.

Don't leave a campfire untended. Even on a seemingly safe shore, never leave a fire to burn out by itself—the wind can carry sparks an unbelievable distance. Before leaving a fire, douse it with water, scatter the ashes, and douse them again to make sure that no single small ember is left smoldering.

Say a friendly hello to camping neighbors, but never assume that love of the outdoors is a substitute for a social introduction—or for a credit reference.

Keep voices and radios low, especially at night. Sound carries farther and much more clearly in open country than in a city, and at a heavily patronized campsite one noisy group can spoil the pleasure of most of its neighbors.

Leave the land unlittered and undespoiled. Don't leave damp garbage and other trash half burned. Dig a trench and bury cans and all other discards that cannot be completely consumed by fire. In addition to being unsightly, such refuse attracts hordes of ants and rodents and other small animals. For the same reason, don't throw dishwater on the ground near an established campsite; ants and other insects love it.

Ask for help—and give it promptly—in an emergency.

## CANAPES

Canapés can be crackers or small bits of bread or toast spread with some spicy mixture, or small boats of puff paste with a hot filling. "Canapé" also means a larger piece of fried toast on which a food is served at table, but as commonly used in this country it refers to any of the bite-size appetizers served before dinner or at a cocktail party, including the tiny croquettes eaten with toothpicks, and the vegetables, shrimps, or bits of meat or fish to be dipped into sauces.

Canapé toothpicks are not returned to the serving plate after use, but are dropped into any convenient ashtray.

**CANCELLATIONS.**  *See* APPOINTMENTS and separate listings such as DATES; ENGAGEMENTS TO WED; INVITATIONS; WEDDINGS.

## CANDLES

When candles are part of a table decoration, the rules say that they must be lighted. Unlighted candles or empty candelabra at lunch make the center-piece look left over from last night's dinner. For the same reason, candelabra are not used on the table at a tea unless the curtains are drawn and the candles are lighted. Candles for a dining table should be either very short or very tall so that the flame is below or above the eye level of the seated guests.

It is not correct to light cigarettes from candles on the table—no argument.

Snuffing out the candles is best left to the hostess. She can have nothing but hard thoughts for the "helpful" volunteer who blows them out for her, and leaves smoking wicks that fill the room with their pungent smell—if not splashes of wax on the table.

**CANDLEHOLDERS.** Pottery, china, glass, crystal, silver, or any other material that is in keeping with the rest of the service is appropriate for table candleholders. They should be evenly spaced—a candelabrum in the center of the table, or two flanking a centerpiece; or one or two pairs of candlesticks grouped or lined up in the center, or set at equal distances from the center-piece.

## CANDY

Candy taken to a child is best presented through his mother in order to give her a chance to control when and how much of it will be eaten. Otherwise, a gift box of candy is opened and passed around at an appropriate time during the donor's visit.

Candy is picked up in its paper frill when it is offered in a bonbon dish, but the frill is usually left behind when a box of candy is offered, unless the candy is sticky or not to be eaten immediately.

Small dishes of bonbons or mints are often set on a table near the center-piece before a meal is announced, though they are not passed from guest to guest until after dessert.

**CANES.** *See* CLOTHES.

## CANONICAL ENGAGEMENT

This is the term used in the Roman Catholic faith for the formal ceremony of Betrothal (*which see*).

**CANONS.** *See* FORMS OF ADDRESS (Clergy).

**CANTALOUPES.** *See* FRUITS.

**CANTORS.** *See* FORMS OF ADDRESS (Clergy).

**CAPTAINS.** *See* BOATING; FORMS OF ADDRESS (Armed Services).

**CARD GAMES.** *See* GAMES.

**CARD PARTIES.** *See* "Cards" under GAMES; *also see* STAG PARTIES.

**CARDINALS.** *See* FORMS OF ADDRESS (Clergy).

## CARDS

**ADMITTANCE CARDS.** A card of admission serves as an entrance ticket. Such a card is issued only for very large balls, banquets, receptions, weddings, or other sizable gatherings where it is necessary to guard against party crashers. An admittance card may be enclosed with an invitation or sent after an acceptance has been received. Any specialist in formally engraved stationery has samples of the correct forms for different events.

### AT HOME CARDS.

*See* INVITATIONS for the use of "At Home" on formal bids to a dance; WEDDINGS for "At Home" cards sent with announcements.

**BLANK CARDS.** Most florists have the good taste to supply plain blank cards for the use of customers who do not have personal cards available. Unfortunately, many other merchants have the deplorable taste to supply "blank" cards that carry the name or monogram of the firm. If a card of this kind is the only one available, send it and don't worry—it is the shop that is at fault, not the patron.

As a general rule, "Mr.," "Mrs.," "Miss," or any other title is not signed on a blank card. Exceptions are correctly made to this general rule under the circumstances noted below:

Good form for Miss (or Mrs.) Brown, with or without a message:

> love____
> Mary Jane Brown

Good form for Mr. Brown, with or without a message:

> John Charles Brown—

Good form for Mrs. Brown, with or without a message, if she has a relative with the same first name or if other confusion might result:

> with sympathy—
> Mrs. John Charles Brown.

Good form for a couple sending a gift to someone they know slightly or not at all—a wedding present to the daughter of a business friend, for example:

BEST WISHES —
Mr. & Mrs. John Charles Brown

Good form for an intimate friend:

BEST WISHES —
BOB C. B.

Good form for Mr. and Mrs. Brown, with or without a message:

CONGRATULATIONS —
John AND Mary Brown

Poor form because of the possibility of confusion, except
for someone with an unusual first name:

**CALLING CARDS.**   *See* VISITING CARDS.
**CHANGE OF ADDRESS CARDS.**   *See* ADDRESSES.
**CHRISTMAS CARDS.**   *See* CHRISTMAS.
**CHURCH CARDS.**   A church card enclosed with a wedding invitation
means that the church will be closed to the general public shortly before and
during the ceremony. Anyone who receives a church card should be sure to
take it to the wedding, since it serves as an admittance ticket. Church cards are
needed only for weddings at houses of worship where many sightseers or
communicants are customarily present or when the prominence of the wedding party and guests might attract great numbers of curious strangers. A
church card is engraved on plain stock in the same style as the invitation.
    A standard form:

> *Please present this card at*
>
> *St. George's Church*
>
> *Wednesday, the tenth of June*

    (*Note:* No time is given, since that is specified in the invitation. The abbreviations
"St." may be used, though "Saint" is correct in the invitation.)

**CORRESPONDENCE CARDS.**   *See* CORRESPONDENCE.
**FOLD-OVERS OR INFORMALS.**
    *See* VISITING CARDS (Social) for the uses of these small double cards, which are
slightly larger than social visiting cards and often engraved from the same plate.

**GREETING CARDS.** Printed cards carrying good wishes for recovery from illness, for birthdays, other anniversaries, and special occasions, are widely used and are a pleasant and correct form of communication, with only a few exceptions. Such printed messages should never be used to express sympathy after a death or thanks for entertainment.

Otherwise, these printed, decorated cards are useful and entirely proper for invitations and for many announcements and congratulations. If in doubt, check the rules under separate listings.

**GUEST CARDS.** Members of many clubs are entitled to extend the use of the premises to nonmembers by issuing guest cards, which entitle the holder to most of the privileges of membership, but not all, for a specified number of days or weeks.

For the responsibilities of a guest-card holder, *see* CLUBS.

**PEW CARDS.** The purpose of a pew card is to ensure a preferred place in a house of worship on any occasion when a great many guests are invited to a ceremony, though these cards are mainly used for extremely large weddings.

*See* WEDDINGS.

**PLACE CARDS.** *See* MEALS AND THEIR SERVICE; PLACE CARDS.

**PLANE AND TRAIN CARDS.** These are used only if a plane has been chartered or a special car on a train has been reserved by a host for a group of guests. For a lesser number of guests, the host sends along standard tickets. A train or plane card is enclosed with an invitation and, of course, requires a prompt answer. These cards serve as tickets, and so they may be printed even if enclosed in an engraved invitation. Two usual forms are:

---

A special car will be attached to the train leaving Pennsylvania Station for Princeton Junction at 2:15 P.M. Another will be attached to the train leaving Princeton Junction at 9:30 P.M.

PLEASE SHOW THIS CARD TO THE CONDUCTOR.

R.S.V.P.

Guests for the flight
to Chicago
are requested to be at the
American Airlines Terminal
Kennedy International Airport
on October tenth at 10:00 A.M.
The return flight will leave
the same evening at 10:30 P.M.
from the American Airlines Terminal
Chicago-O'Hare International Airport.

PLEASE PRESENT THIS CARD.

R.S.V.P.

---

**POSTCARDS.**   *See* CORRESPONDENCE (Social).

**RECEPTION CARDS.**   These are useful when only a limited number of the guests invited to attend an event are also invited to a reception preceding or following it. The reception card is enclosed with the invitation to the event—a wedding, ship launching, banquet, and so on. When a reception card is received, a prompt acceptance or refusal is required.

**REMINDER CARDS.**   Only those who frequently entertain large numbers of guests have any use for formal engraved reminder cards. Far better for this purpose in most circles is a calling card or fold-over—or a brief note. A reminder card (or note) is sent when an invitation to be relayed by a servant or a child has been given on the telephone, or at some meeting when the guest obviously does not have a datebook at hand and so might forget accepting the invitation or be confused about time and place. A reminder card is not sent if a written acceptance has been received.

The formal reminder card, about 4 inches by 5 inches in size is mailed in a matching envelope. It is partially engraved, with spaces left blank to be filled in by hand. There are several variants in wording, all correct. Following is one widely used:

*To remind you that*

*Mr. and Mrs. John Brian Smith*

*expect you for*

*on*

*at              o'clock*

*10 West Avenue*

A standard form on a visiting card or a fold-over:

To Remind —

Dinner — Friday — June 6

*Mr. and Mrs. John Brian Smith*

AT  8  o'clock

10 West Avenue

**REPLY CARDS.** With few exceptions, it is not correct to enclose a response card with an invitation to a strictly social event. (*See* INVITATIONS.) Response cards are useful and entirely correct with an invitation to a business event and also to such charitable events as fund-raising balls or theater parties, no matter how "social" their sponsorship. If a response card is received in an invitation marked R.S.V.P., it must be returned promptly with its blank spaces properly marked for acceptance or regrets.

**TRAIN CARDS.**   *See* "Plane and Train Cards," above.

**VISITING CARDS.**   *See* VISITING CARDS.

## CAREER WOMAN

"Career girl" is generally used to mean a young unmarried woman with professional training or with ambitions to make her mark in business or a profession. "Career woman" applies to both married and unmarried women who win distinction in any career.

**CARS.**   *See* AUTOMOBILES.

## CARVING

Carving is an art. Either master it or give up serving roasts (to guests, anyway) unless the carving can be properly done before the meat is brought to the table. The choicest cut, cooked to perfection, will be markedly less tender and appetizing if incorrectly sliced; and few sights at table are more painful than the struggle of an inept carver with a turkey, ham, leg of lamb, or other large piece of meat.

By tradition, carving is man's work, but there is no rule that bans carving by a hostess, and there is no reason why she should not carve at the table if she is adept and the host is not. A woman entertaining alone should certainly not ask a male guest to carve unless she is sure that he is both willing and competent. There is no guarantee that a man can carve just because he has reached voting age, though, for reasons unknown, many men act as if the lack of carving experience is somehow shameful, and when asked to take on the task, cannot bring themselves to admit their incompetence.

Carving is not hard to master, but good intentions and blind courage are not enough. The rules are worth study because the performance of a deft carver is an appetizer in itself—and carving one of the most delightful ceremonies of dining at home. Of major importance are a sharp knife of correct size and shape, and plenty of room to work in. A carver is hopelessly handicapped by a knife too long, too short, or dull; by a platter so small or crowded with garnishings that he cannot maneuver the meat without littering the cloth; and by lack of elbow room because other dishes are set too close by.

The carver's aim is to provide neat slices of uniform size—thick or thin, depending on the cut of meat and the method by which it is cooked. Even with a sharp knife of exactly the right type, the task is easier if a roast is allowed to "season" in a warm place for about twenty minutes after it is cooked.

A medium-size roast or bird can be handled with a standard carving set that consists of a knife with a blade eight to nine inches long and a fork with a hand guard. The standard steak set is more convenient for small roasts and birds as well as for steaks. For large roasts and birds, the roast-meat slicer, which has a long straight blade, and a carver's helper with its two widely spread tines are more efficient.

The carving tools are placed on the table to the carver's right: the fork (tines down) nearest to him, then the knife, then the steel if one is provided. The gravy boat is to the right of the tools, and vegetable dishes are also on the carver's right if he is to serve each plate fully. A small stack of plates is put directly in front of the carver, between him and the roast. For a big group, the stack of plates is put to the carver's left, and he sets one at a time in front of him when ready to serve it.

A carver sits or stands, whichever he finds more convenient. The usual procedure is to carve approximately enough for all at the table before starting to put meat on the plates. This procedure enables the carver to divide the choice portions equally and to give each diner his preference of rare or well-done, light or dark cuts. If the platter is not big enough to accommodate the slices as they are cut, a supplementary platter is provided, set to the carver's left. It is also correct to carve and at once serve a single portion, but this method does not always give the carver latitude to provide balanced servings according to each diner's preference.

Also of major importance is the correct placement of the roast before the carver. A ham, leg of lamb, or unboned shoulder is put on the table with the shank to the carver's right if he is right-handed. A stuffed bird is put before the carver with its legs to the right or left, depending on the number to be served at the first round. If he will need to carve only one side, the legs are to the right because this position will give him easy access to the stuffing. If he will need to carve both sides for the initial round of servings, he will have to reverse the bird, and so he starts with the legs to his left.

Skewers and trussing strings are removed before a roast is brought to the table, with the exception of a boned and rolled roast, which may lose its shape if all the strings are removed in the kitchen. The carver cuts the strings on it as he needs to, one at a time.

At a formal meal, serving platters are not put on the table. The meat is always carved in the kitchen, and the sliced meat is offered to each diner in turn.

When the host carves at table, he may add gravy and vegetables to the plates; or he may serve the meat only and pass each plate to the hostess for the addition of vegetables; or the vegetable dishes may be passed from guest to guest. If there is a maid, she may stand at the host's left and take each fully served plate to the guest for whom it is intended; or the host may pass plates served with meat down each side of the table, and the maid may offer the vegetable dishes to each diner individually after the plates are in place.

"Cut meat across the grain" is the standard rule. If meat is cut with the grain, the long fibers give the slices a stringy texture. Steaks are the exception. They are cut straight down or at a slight slant.

The final rule applies to guests: Coaching from the sidelines is taboo. No matter how obvious a carver's mistakes, his butchery of a beautiful roast must be watched in silence. There will be no temptation to coach, of course, if the inexperienced carver has taken a few minutes to look up the rules.

The following diagrams* and instructions are for the cuts that most often present a challenge to a carver.

---

* Meat diagrams courtesy of the National Live Stock and Meat Board.

## ROLLED RIB ROAST

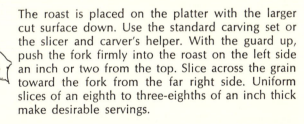

The roast is placed on the platter with the larger cut surface down. Use the standard carving set or the slicer and carver's helper. With the guard up, push the fork firmly into the roast on the left side an inch or two from the top. Slice across the grain toward the fork from the far right side. Uniform slices of an eighth to three-eighths of an inch thick make desirable servings.

As each slice is carved, lift it to the side of the platter or to another hot serving platter. Remove each cord only as it is approached in making slices. Sever it with the tip of the blade, loosen it with the fork, and allow it to drop to the platter.

## OTHER ROLLED ROASTS

Because of the difficulty of carving shoulder and rump cuts, they are often boned and rolled at the market. All are sliced across the face in the same way as the rolled rib, but since many of them make a long roll, carving is easier with the roast lying horizontally on the platter. The slices are cut straight down.

## STANDING RIB ROAST OF BEEF

Place the roast on the platter with the largest end down to form a solid base. Insert the fork between the two top ribs. Starting on the fat side, carve across the grain to the rib bone.

Use the tip of the knife to cut along the rib bone to loosen the slice. Keep close to the bone to make the largest servings possible.

Slide the knife back under the slice and, steadying the slice with the fork, lift it to the side of the platter. If the platter is small, place the slices on another heated plate or platter set close by.

## CROWN ROAST OF LAMB

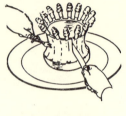

Remove any garnish in the center of the roast that will interfere with the carving. Steady the roast by inserting the fork firmly between the ribs. Start carving at one of the two ends where the ribs are tied together.

Cut down between the ribs, allowing one or more ribs for each serving. Using the fork to steady it, lift the slice on the knife blade to the platter. Dressing can be cut and served with the slices.

## BLADE POT ROAST OF BEEF

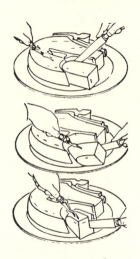

Put the pot roast on the platter with the rib and back bones away from the carver. It is best to separate the muscles at the seams and along the bones.

Remove the first section to be carved by cutting between the muscle and the bone. Set it up on edge.

With the fork holding the meat firmly, carve across the grain. Continue carving the rest of the roast, following this pattern.

## PORTERHOUSE STEAK

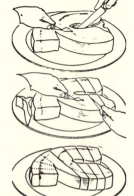

After inserting the fork at the left to hold the steak, cut closely around the bone. Lift the bone to the side of the platter where it will not interfere with the carving.

With the fork firmly holding the tenderloin, cut across the full width of the steak, making wedge-shaped slices (wider at the far side). Each wedge will include a portion of the tenderloin and of the top loin.

Serve the flank end last if additional servings are needed. (A board that fits the platter will protect the cutting edge of the knife.)

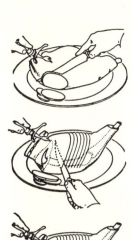

## LEG OF LAMB

Place the roast on the platter with the shank to the carver's right and the tip section on the near side. From this, remove two or three slices lengthwise, to form a flat base.

Turn the roast so that it rests on this base. Starting at the shank end, make slices perpendicular to the leg bone, as shown in the illustration.

After reaching the aitch bone, loosen the slices by cutting under them, following the top of the leg bone. Remove slices to the platter and then serve.

## BAKED HAM

Place the ham on the platter with the decorated side up and the shank to the carver's right. Remove several slices from the thin side to form a solid base.

Turn the ham on the base. Starting at the shank end, remove a small wedge; then carve perpendicular to the leg bone as shown.

Release the slices by cutting under them and along the leg bone, starting at the shank end. For additional servings, turn the ham over to its original position. Again, make slices to the bone, release, and serve.

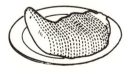

## BEEF TONGUE

Trim excess tissue and cartilage from the large end of the tongue, and also peel off the skin, in the kitchen. To get thin, even, parallel slices, start carving from the tip.

## LOIN ROAST OF PORK

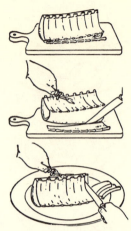

Have butcher saw the backbone free from the ribs for easier carving. The saw cut should not cut into the meaty center.

Before bringing the roast to the table, remove the backbone by cutting close along the bone, taking care to cut away as little meat as possible. Place the roast so that the bone side faces the carver.

Insert the fork in the top of the roast. Slice downward, cutting close along each side of a rib bone. One slice will contain the bone; the next will be boneless.

## TURKEY

*(The same procedure is used for small birds
except that the legs are not sliced.)*

The first step is to remove the entire leg—drumstick and thigh. Hold the drumstick firmly and pull it away from the body. At the same time, cut through the skin between the body and the leg. The entire leg will now pull free from the body.

Press the leg farther away from the body to snap the connecting joint. If necessary, sever the joint with the knife point. Follow the body contour carefully with the knife to cut off the dark meat.

Put the severed leg on a separate plate and cut through the connecting joint to remove the thigh. The two pieces may now be individually sliced. Tilt the drumstick at a convenient angle and slice toward the plate, as shown. To slice the thigh, hold it firmly with the fork. Cut even slices parallel to the bone and arrange neatly on the plate. (Repeat the process with the other leg.)

To slice the breast, place the knife parallel and as close to the wing as possible. Make a deep vertical cut into the breast, cutting right to the bone. This is the base cut at which all additional cuts will stop.

After the base cut, start halfway up the side of the breast and slice downward, ending at the base cut. Start each new slice slightly higher up on the breast. Keep the slices thin and even, and slice only as needed.

# CATERERS

Some caterers specialize in large parties, but many catering firms will supply anything from a few boxes of cocktail canapés to all the equipment, refreshment, and staff needed for a party of any size or kind.

As in arranging for any other services, it is only sensible to place an order long enough in advance to give a caterer time to supplement his standard equipment and staff, if necessary. The stock equipment of a big catering firm includes china, glassware, silver, linen, tables, chairs, and portable bars and buffets. The caterer also can provide and set up a tent or marquee complete with a dance floor and lights; supply flowers and other decorations, as well as all refreshments, including extras from cigars and cigarettes to bonbons; and send a correctly uniformed staff to park cars, check wraps, serve food and drinks, and clean up. If the catering firm is small, it is best to select from the menus the caterer suggests, since he is aware of the limitations of his kitchen and equipment.

**CHARGES.** Unless some other arrangement is made at the time the order is placed, the caterer is paid at the end of the party. Charges vary from a flat fee to sliding scales based on an hourly charge for his staff, the number of guests above a guaranteed minimum, and the amount of liquor consumed. Very frequently a caterer brings a large supply of bottles, and charges only for those that are opened.

**STAFF.** The caterer's staff for a large party usually includes a captain or supervisor who directs and coordinates all the services provided. The host channels all major instructions through this majordomo just as he would through his own butler. Otherwise, a caterer's staff is treated by both host and guests just as servants regularly employed by the host would be.

**TIPPING.** A caterer's staff is tipped by the host at about the rate customary in a good restaurant. If the caterer has supplied a large staff, the most convenient tipping method is to add 15 percent of his total charge to the bill and let him distribute the tips. If only one barman and perhaps two or three waitresses are concerned, a sum to be divided among them may be handed to the individual who presents the bill, or they may be thanked and tipped individually. It is never necessary for guests to tip the catering staff.

## CATS.  *See* PETS.

## CATSUP

This popular condiment is served at table in its original bottle only at casual meals. Otherwise, it is served in a small bowl. Catsup is put on the main plate, not the butter plate, and beside rather than on top of the food it complements.

## CAUDLE

A mixture of milk and honey was the traditional drink for breaking the fast that preceded baptism in early Christian days. Later, this was replaced by a mixture that included ale or wine, and was known as "caudle." Today, "caudle" means hot eggnog, though the word is seldom used, and then only in connection with a party following a christening.

## CAVIAR

Caviar is salted sturgeon roe. It is available in various qualities, sizes, and colors, and is served in different ways according to the particular grade as well as according to the occasion. Russia and Iran are the world's major producers of caviar.

**COLORS AND SIZE.** Color ranges from gray to black, and has no bearing on the quality of the caviar. Similarly, the size of the berry (egg) is no measure of quality. Although the largest egg, produced by the huge Beluga sturgeon, commands the highest prices, many connoisseurs prefer caviar made from the smaller roe of smaller sturgeons. The Ossetrina sturgeon produces a medium-sized egg, and the Sevruga yields a small size.

**Red "Caviar."** Though everyone calls it caviar, the popular, delicious, and less expensive red roe is not true caviar because it is made from the eggs of the salmon, not the sturgeon. It is heavily salted and can be kept on open shelves, since it does not need refrigeration, though it is refrigerated once the jar is opened.

**QUALITY.** Caviar comes whole, pressed, and compressed. The handling the roe has received, the methods used to preserve it (icing, salting, and pasteurizing), and the amount of salt added determine the quality and price.

All caviar is prepared with some salt. What is known as "fresh" caviar is the best and most expensive. A very little salt is added for flavor, but not nearly enough to preserve it. Fresh caviar, even when sealed, must be kept under controlled refrigeration. Freezing causes the eggs to break, and ruins the quality.

**"Malosol,"** most often seen in connection with Beluga, is the Russian word for "little salt." It is not a brand name, but signifies that only one part salt has been added to forty-one parts of caviar.

In the highest grade of caviar each berry is whole, not crushed, and coated with its own fat. Because of all these factors, it is quite possible for a carefully handled small-egg caviar to be of higher quality than a Beluga that has received poor treatment. The only sure test for good caviar is that it have no fishy odor. A high grade of fresh caviar costs fifty dollars or more a pound in this country.

Pressed and compressed caviars are usually prepared from the very small Beluga eggs and from larger eggs that have been damaged. They often have an excellent flavor, but because they are less attractive to look at, their cost is approximately a third that of the whole-berry caviar.

Pasteurized caviar is less expensive than the fresh. The berries used are small and are packed with more salt than is the fresh. The sealed jar does not have to be kept under refrigeration.

Imitation caviars made of the dyed eggs of lumpfish, whitefish, and other fishes less expensive than sturgeon are tasty, have a flavor of their own, but cannot pretend to be the real thing.

**SERVING.** The best-quality caviar is served with plain toast or black bread and without butter or garnishes. The traditional accompaniments to caviar of other grades are lemon wedges, finely chopped egg white, egg yolk, and onion or chives.

Caviar is usually served ice-cold, either directly from the refrigerator or embedded in ice if it is to be left standing for any extended time, as at a buffet; it can be served already spread on toast or black bread as a canapé.

## CELEBRITIES

"A celebrity is a person who works hard all his life to become well known, then wears
  dark glasses to avoid being recognized."—*Fred Allen, Treadmill to Oblivion*

Anyone who has gained distinction in any field is not public property just because his achievements have given much pleasure to the public, though all too often the admirers of notables act as if the opposite were true. It is extraordinary how many friends and acquaintances, as well as total strangers, take it for granted that the talent and spare time of a professional in any of the arts should be available for the asking.

In a way, this is the fault of the celebrities themselves. People of the entertainment world, in particular, always have been extravagantly generous in giving performances without charge for charitable enterprises. When asking a star to appear at a benefit, it should be remembered that a valuable commodity is begged as a gift—and also that no one famous person can possibly say Yes to everyone who wants to exploit him for a special cause, no matter how worthy the cause may be. A refusal should be accepted with awareness of this fact. An acceptance deserves warm thanks at the conclusion of the performance and also a follow-up letter of gratitude—both not infrequently forgotten.

The same consideration is required of the personal friends of professionals on all levels. It is taking advantage, since a refusal is all but impossible, to ask a professional musician to a party and then expect him to sing for his supper—unless, of course, the hostess is completely certain that he would be hurt rather than happy if not invited to perform—admittedly, a delicate matter. To a marked degree, part of the artistic temperament is enjoyment of the spotlight and pleasure in giving pleasure. All anyone can safely do is proceed with caution. This is especially necessary when dealing with professionals in the nonperforming arts. It is remarkable how many people will ask a decorator, landscape architect, or commercial artist to spend half a day "knocking off" a sketch as an unpaid personal favor, though it would be just as logical to ask a doctor to devote the same amount of time to giving a free checkup. When in doubt, wait for anyone of special talent to volunteer his advice or services—and also any information about his earnings. All too often, people who would not dream of asking a businessman what his salary or annual income is do not hesitate to ask a writer what he made from his last book, or a musician, actor, or other artist about financial matters that only the income tax examiner has a right to know.

It is never correct to ask any stranger who makes his living by writing to give the very considerable present of his time (and skill) by submitting a manuscript to him for criticism. Nor is it sensible. Nearly all successful authors are bedeviled by accusations of plagiarism. For that reason, their own common sense as well as the advice of their literary agents, lawyers, and publishers tells them to return unread any manuscripts from strangers—an annoying chore if it demands a special trip to the post office.

People who are under the seemingly widespread misapprehension that authors have an unlimited supply of free copies of their works do not endear themselves either. An author usually is supplied by his publisher with no more than ten complimentary copies. It is true that he can buy additional copies at a discount, but even close friends should think twice about asking this favor, which, at best, demands more time than the relatively small saving in money justifies.

**FAN MAIL.** Favorable fan mail is highly prized by many celebrities, especially those in the entertainment and sports fields. A great flood of admiring letters can affect the terms of a contract quite emphatically. A note of appreciation and admiration is always welcome to a celebrity provided that it does not include a request for any special favor. Stars under contract to big studios and networks may have access to the facilities of the company for aid in answering fan mail, but an independent star or a player of less than star stature can find it a real financial burden to answer fan mail with anything more than a form letter or some other standard release.

**FANS.** It is widely recognized that a brief phase of star worship is to be expected in most teen-agers and that it may have real value if fixation on their idols leads youngsters to set higher standards of appearance and behavior for themselves. Even shrieking, squealing, and fainting in the aisles is more silly than serious, though such interruptions chill the blood of serious artists, who much prefer not to share the spotlight with members of an audience more intent on showing off than on the show. However, there is no excuse for the conduct of fans who lurk around hotels, stage doors, and sports arenas braced to grab off a button if they cannot beg an autograph. The actual manhandling that some stars endure is a serious reflection on the parents of their admirers, who have failed to teach (or make sure that their children observe) the most rudimentary rules of decent behavior.

Anyone can be forgiven a stare somewhat more marked than ordinarily polite when a world-famous figure is spotted on the street, in a shop, restaurant, theater, or other public place. And there is nothing amiss in a stranger's approaching briefly to say a complimentary word, provided that the time and place are suitable. But to interrupt a celebrity who is in conversation with friends to ask for an autograph or for any other purpose is much more likely to bore than flatter; and under all circumstances "Hands off!" is the unbreakable rule.

## CELERY

Fresh celery may be on the table in its own dish when guests sit down, and may be passed by them, or it may be brought in and passed by a maid. One or two stalks are taken with the fingers and put on the butter plate or, if there is none, on the side of the main plate.

Salt may be sprinkled along a whole stalk from the shaker. If salt is served in an open dish, some of it is put on the butter plate or the edge of the dinner plate, never on the tablecloth. The celery is then dipped into it.

## CEMETERIES.  *See* FUNERALS.

## CENTERPIECES

The best centerpieces are low enough so that guests can look over them rather than have to peer through or around a jungle-like thicket. Candles should be either quite tall or very short so that they are above or below eye level; if used, they are always lighted. Centerpieces should be evenly balanced along the length of the table so that each side matches.

There is no limit to the objects and materials that can serve as centerpieces, and the hostess who varies her table decorations usually wins compliments out of all proportion to the time involved in finding novel combinations of flowers, fruits, vegetables, figurines, and so on. Handsome old-fashioned epergnes carrying bottles of seasonings and condiments are amusing on a small table, though not practical for use on a long one.

On a very small table, a main dish of food often takes the place of a centerpiece, but this usually is not practical when more than four are seated. In general, a main part of the meal is best not used as the centerpiece, since this leaves the table in disarray or empty during the last course. Fruit is the exception. A spread of fruit is a beautiful and practical centerpiece if fruit and cheese are the dessert course.

## CHAIRMAN

"Chairman" is the title given to a person of either sex presiding at a meeting (never "chairlady" or "chairwoman"). In direct address, say "Mr. Chairman" or "Madam Chairman" (not "Miss" or "Mrs." Chairman).

## CHAIRS

It is a sound guess that the inventor of the very first straight chair tilted it on its back legs and found comfort in using it as a rocker. People have always used straight chairs in this fashion, and always will. There is nothing wrong with doing so under certain informal circumstances, but it is a breach of the rules on a formal occasion.

Tilting one's chair back at the table after finishing a meal is never correct. It is the privilege of the head of the house to break this rule under his own roof at a family meal if he wants to set a bad example to his little ones, but a guest should never tilt back any chair unless the host or hostess first sets the example—and most especially a chair that has legs and back of delicate size.

Deciding how best to save both a fragile chair and a heavyweight guest who courts disaster by tilting it has turned many a hostess gray before her time. This is a case where it is better to risk hurting the guest's feelings by correcting his manners than to remain silent in the precarious hope that neither he nor his dignity will be seriously injured when he finds himself on the floor among the splinters. The most sensible procedure is to invite him to change to another chair with some such explanation as "That chair looks sturdy, but I really must have it fixed before someone gets hurt."

A little imagination is all a man needs to understand the only good way to help a woman with her chair at the table. He pulls it out, and as the woman starts to sit he slides it smoothly into place, being careful not to strike her knees and throw her off balance, or to move it so slowly that she has the apprehensive feeling she may be sitting on air in the next second. He reverses the procedure when helping a woman out of her chair. As she starts to rise, he slides the chair back far enough so that it clears her knees and she can stand up freely.

**CHAMBERMAIDS.**  *See* HOTELS AND MOTELS; HOUSEHOLD EMPLOYEES.

**CHAMPAGNE.**  *See* WINES.

## CHAPERONS

The presence of a chaperon is still a standard requirement at certain teen-age gatherings, but otherwise the chaperon has all but vanished. Today, young unmarried women can go unchaperoned almost anywhere they please provided that they use the wits they were born with in observing the customs that protect them from gossip—for example, the rule that a girl does not stay on in a man's apartment late at night after his other guests leave. By today's custom, a mixed group of unmarried friends is sufficient chaperonage in almost all circumstances, and a girl of college age causes no raised eyebrows when she goes with a young man for a weekend to some such place as a ski lodge if several other girls and their dates are in the party.

Teen-agers, too, enjoy more latitude than they did in the past. It would be absurd to forbid a girl old enough to baby-sit to go alone to the movies, a skating rink, or other public place with a boy; but, under all ordinary circumstances, she should not ask him to join her under her own or any other private roof unless a responsible grown-up is present. Parents who observe the rules do not allow teen-agers, boys or girls, to go to a party unless it is properly chaperoned—no argument about this convention. They also make a point of calling for a girl after a party if some other adult is not seeing her safely home. Proper chaperonage at a teen-agers' party does not mean that parents need to be present to watch every move. All that is required and usual is for parents to be on the premises and look in every half-hour or so to make sure that nothing is getting out of hand—that party-crashers (*which see*) have not slipped in the back way, for example. However, at a school or club party, the chaperons stay on duty and in sight continuously.

Manners to the chaperons at school dances vary in different communities. At most schools, the principal and a few men and women teachers, as well as some mothers and fathers, turn out as chaperons but do not generally form a receiving line or otherwise act as official hosts and hostesses. The youngsters make a point of speaking at some time during the party with any of the chaperons they know, but are not obligated to say good night in addition, as they would to the chaperon at a private party.

At a private party, it is routine procedure for the parents to be on hand to greet the young guests as they arrive, and all guests must say good night—by the standard rules, and also so that the chaperon (who, after all, is responsible for them) will know when and with whom they leave.

**CHAPLAINS.**   *See* FORMS OF ADDRESS (Armed Services).

## CHARGE ACCOUNTS

In a number of ways, charge accounts are better business practice than paying for all purchases in cash. They make shopping by telephone easier. The monthly bills are an orderly record of expenditures and of the sales taxes that may be deducted from state and federal income taxes. Most importantly, charge accounts paid promptly produce a good credit rating, which may be useful in many ways.

Bills usually are due within ten days of the mailing date. A few days' delay in payment does not affect one's credit rating. When a bill is very large, a partial payment nearly always will maintain an account in good order.

Charge accounts frequently are set up to be signed in the same way merchandise and statements will be addressed, to avoid confusion. This is one of the few cases where a woman may sign "Mrs. Henry Brown," if it suits her best to have the account set up under that name. However, a man never signs a charge account "Mr."

## CHARITIES

"Money giving is a very good criterion, in a way, of a person's mental health. Generous people are rarely mentally ill people."—*Dr. Karl Menninger*

About ten billion dollars are raised annually by organized charities to fight disease, feed the hungry, promote scientific research, provide scholarships, train the handicapped, care for the mentally ill, aid when disaster strikes an area, and make possible other services of enormous benefit, directly and indirectly, to all of us. There is no telling how many more billions are collected by the countless unorganized charities. But, in spite of the good work done by charitable organizations, the multiciplicity of their appeals and some of the methods used by fund-raisers can try both the patience and the purse of the most generous citizen.

No individual can possibly respond to every appeal directed to him. Each person must make his own choice, just as he must decide for himself how much he cares to contribute. These are not matters of etiquette. But what are matters of etiquette are the manner in which a donor gives or refuses and also the manners and methods used by fund-raisers.

The solicitors who ring doorbells, man collection booths, collect contributions in offices, sell raffle tickets, and otherwise assist in fund-raising are largely unselfish volunteers whose task is far from an easy one. They are not panhandling for themselves. It is inexcusable to dismiss them brusquely or to brush past them impatiently. The contribution of a smile and "Sorry" is a requirement, though a contribution of money is not. If the solicitor is a personal acquaintance, no purpose is served by an irritated lecture on what a nuisance constant appeals are getting to be. A few words of explanation can convey the same meaning far better: "I'd like to help, but we've decided to concentrate this year on the Workshop of the Children [or whatever]."

Such an explanation should be accepted without argument by the fund-raiser. In some communities, competition among volunteer fund-raisers to bring in the largest sum has become so intense a game that unfair business or social pressure is often put on a solicitor's friends, neighbors, or associates to give beyond their means. A solicitor should remember that "charity" is not a tax rightfully due. Charity is a gift, and the choice of when, where, and how much to give lies with the donor.

A stranger soliciting funds door-to-door should be asked to show his credentials if he does not show them when he identifies himself. The collectors who offer money boxes or raffle tickets on the street also should be able to produce credentials, if asked. A bona fide solicitor not only has credentials but is quite willing to show them, and also to give an official receipt for each contribution—though it would be absurd to demand one for every quarter dropped into a collection box.

The methods of some professional fund-raisers have aroused a good deal of justified criticism in recent years. Really irritating to many people is the technique of sending "gifts" by mail—in the calculating hope that the recipient will feel ashamed to keep the gadget, especially one stamped with his name, without sending a check. If it is true that the Lord loveth a cheerful giver, it should follow that the Lord loveth not tricky direct-mail dodges that tempt the donor to take His name in vain.

A donor can be reasonably sure that his money will be used to good advantage if he gives to a tax-exempt organization. Tax-exempt status is not granted unless an organization fulfills certain requirements, which include submitting to state or federal authority a yearly audit of its books by a certified public accountant. However, it should be remembered that a great many splendid causes whose funds are impeccably managed do not have tax-exempt status, which requires the expense of incorporation, among other things. "Investigate—then invest" is as good a rule for money donated to a charity as for that spent for stocks.

## CHAUFFEURS

A chauffeur is usually called by his last name, without "Mr.," by employers and guests (including children), though his complete first name is sometimes used. A nickname or diminutive is not strictly formal practice.

**DRESS.** If any special uniform or house livery is used, the employer supplies them. The old-fashioned formal livery of breeches, puttees, and coat with standing collar is very seldom seen today.

The usual dress of a chauffeur of either a private or hired car is a black or very dark gray double-breasted suit, white shirt, black four-in-hand, black shoes, socks, and gloves. In winter a plain double-breasted overcoat with standard dark buttons is worn with it. But the headgear remains the traditional chauffeur's cap.

**DUTIES.** Today, except in extremely large and busy households, a chauffeur takes on extra duties such as those of a houseman or gardener. If the car is kept in a private garage, the chauffeur is expected to wash it. By arrangement at the time of employment, he is on call during certain hours seven days a week, or may have regular days off.

**HIRED CARS.** Manners of and to the chauffeur are exactly the same as described below. The employer is expected to leave the driver of a car hired for the day time to get lunch or dinner, and give him the money to pay for these meals. The usual tip for the driver of a hired car is 20 percent of the bill. This may be given to the man in cash, or added when the patron signs the bill or timecard submitted by the chauffeur supplied by a rental agency if arrangements have been made to charge the costs.

**MANNERS.** Unless there is a footman or doorman on duty to assist passengers into the car, the chauffeur stands ready to open the door, after touching his cap. If he has not already been given instructions, he waits at the door for the passenger's orders, or, if these are not given, says, "Where to ———?" adding "Sir," "Madam," or the name of the passenger if it is known to him.

At the end of a trip, he gets out, opens the door, and touches his cap as the passenger leaves. The passenger never treats him as part of the car, but always nods or says, "Thank you," when leaving.

The chauffeur does not get out when there is a doorman on duty, especially when traffic is heavy, unless he is driving someone who is in need of special help from car to doorway. In this case, if his arm is needed, he holds his forearm parallel with the ground, palm turned in, so that the hand of the passenger can rest on top of the steady surface as on a railing.

Since a chauffeur's hours can be extremely long, considerate employers let him know as much in advance as possible when he will be needed and when he will be free, so that he can plan his time off.

**SEATING.** Owners or guests who have known a chauffeur for many years often choose the informality of sitting in front with him for a chat between station and house. Otherwise, seating in the back seat of a chauffeur-driven car is the same as in any other.

**TIPPING.** The general rule is that servants are not tipped unless a guest has made an overnight stay. A guest who is run across town after lunch, for example, merely says, "Thank you, Smith." He is not expected to tip, and never tips if the owner is in the car. However, when the chauffeur has made a long run into town from the country, especially if late at night, a tip is in order. This can be anywhere from one to five dollars, depending on the hour, distance, size of the party, and weather. The chauffeur who meets a guest at a train and helps with luggage is not tipped on arrival, but is given one or two dollars, generally when the guest leaves, depending on the length of the stay and the amount of service given. The same is expected if a chauffeur washes a guest's car or runs any special errands. Tips are best not given in view of host and hostess, but are slipped to the chauffeur while he is handling luggage or at another appropriate time.

**TRAVELING.** In either a private or hired car, the employer is responsible for costs of a chauffeur's lodging and food while on a trip.

# CHEATING

Like lying, cheating is a matter of morals, not etiquette—except for the problem of how best to deal with a suspected or discovered cheat. The painful alternatives are discussed in general under LYING and specifically as to procedures under GAMES.

# CHECK GRABBERS

Chronic check grabbers are almost as tiresome—though not quite—as chronic check dodgers. The Lord or Lady Bountiful who fights for every tab, tip, and taxi fare overemphasizes his ability to pay, and puts his companions in the poor-relations bracket. The check dodger reverses these roles, with equal lack of judgment.

# CHECKING

Checkroom attendants are always tipped except in clubs where the house rules prohibit tips. At public dinners, checkroom tips may or may not be included in the price of admission, though tips for the waiters most generally are. When in doubt, offer a tip. It will be courteously rejected if not allowed or if already paid. There is no need to tip lavishly. Checkroom attendants are almost without exception on a straight salary, and all tips go to the management, not to the poor little working girl. The service is not free, however, and she will be in trouble if customers skip tips entirely.

**RESTAURANTS AND NIGHTCLUBS.** A man checks his hat and coat immediately after entering. A woman usually wears her coat to the table, but is free to check it if she wishes. If she does, the man accompanying her helps her off with her coat before removing and checking his own. When leaving, he asks for her wrap first, and helps her on with it before putting on his own. A woman may stand beside a man in a long lineup at a checkroom, or at the edge of the crowd while he reclaims their wraps.

**THEATERS.** A woman seldom checks her coat unless it is rain-drenched. A man certainly is far more comfortable and appears more graceful if he checks his topcoat and hat, though many men prefer not to do so because of the slight delay reclaiming them causes after the show ends. Of course the nonchecker must balance the bundled-up coat on his lap during the performance, and his hat also, unless there is a rack for it under the seat or he chooses to put it on the floor beneath the seat. For reasons unknown, men do not generally do the logical thing and sit on a coat spread back over the top of the seat, as women so sensibly do.

## CHECKS.    *See* BANKS.

## CHEESE

Cheese in one form or another can make its appearance at any course from canapés to dessert, and many people enjoy the taste of sharp cheese after a sweet dessert. Cheese served with salad is put on the salad plate, not the butter plate, and eaten with the salad fork. A favorite dessert with many people is cheese and fresh fruit. Firm cheeses are eaten with the fruit fork, if there is one. If only a fruit knife is provided, firm cheese is picked up in the fingers; soft, runny cheeses or very pungent ones are spread on a cracker with the fruit knife.

## CHERRIES.    *See* FRUITS.

## CHEWING GUM

Etiquette authorities who ban the use of chewing gum are in much the same position as King Canute when he commanded the tide to stop—though the fact remains that the chewing of gum has a very limited place in public if the rules are observed. Many people find that gum helps to ward off car sickness. Gum is a great aid in relieving pressure on the eardrums during a sudden change of altitude. Dieters find artificially sweetened gum a substitute for snacks, and gum is also a help to people trying to break the smoking habit. However, gum-chewing is taboo in all routinely formal business and social circumstances. And it should not be necessary to say (though it is) that wads of gum should not be discarded on the street.

## CHICKEN

Picking up a piece of chicken in the fingers is strictly for informal occasions. Otherwise, unless the hostess sets the example, the guest manages as best he can with knife and fork, and leaves those tempting bits of meat that cling to the bones.

*See* CARVING.

## CHILDREN AND MANNERS

"A child should always say what's true
And speak when he is spoken to,
And behave mannerly at table;
At least as far as he is able."
—*Robert Louis Stevenson, "The Whole Duty of Children"*

Basic good manners for children are the same as basic good manners for adults. This section could end with that sentence if only the rules for children were under consideration. But the manners of children spring directly from the manners of the grown-ups in their lives. As Dr. Benjamin Spock puts it in discussing good manners for the very young, "Probably the most important step is foi a child to grow up in a family whose members are considerate of each other. Then he absorbs kindliness. He wants to say 'Thank you' because the rest of the family say it and mean it."*

The main procedures that a little child needs to learn first and fast are not too much of a challenge. A baby will build "please" and "thank you" into his speech as he learns to talk if those words are said to him as consistently as they should be said to an adult. And any three-year-old can master the following rules if the grown-ups in his life give him half a chance by constant example:

1. Answer nicely when spoken to.
2. Say "hello" and "good-bye" politely.
3. Stand up for visitors.
4. Don't start to eat first at the table.
5. Don't interrupt in a noisy or insistent fashion.

It is a rare child of four who cannot remember the exact time of his favorite television program, and so even a prekindergartner is certainly quite able (with perhaps a few secret signals from his parents) to add the following to his basic social graces:

6. Eat with reasonable silence and tidiness.
7. Chew with the lips closed.
8. Make a simple introduction correctly.
9. Don't contradict a grown-up flatly.
10. Say "Excuse me" (once in a while).
11. Don't interrupt (quite so much).

### GUIDELINES FOR PARENTS

1. Give a child a fair chance. Most lapses in manners come because a child is taken by surprise and does not know what is expected of him, or because he is required to stay still and silent for a totally unreasonable length of time. It is unrealistic to expect children not to show off. The trick is to outguess them— open the way for them to show off how polite (rather than how outrageous) they can be—and it is an easy one because children would rather be right than wrong. Before a visitor arrives or before a child is called on to meet any other considerable behavior challenge, jog his memory with a briefing of "how it will be . . ." And then trust to luck that the visitor will not confuse the issue by breaking the very rules the child is struggling to observe.

2. Don't break the rules when coaching a child. Certainly there are plenty of times when a child needs to be firmly corrected or stopped—right now and no nonsense about it—because it is just as ill-advised to be permissive about bad manners as about running into the street. There are some things all of us have to learn, and the sooner we do, the easier and safer life is for everyone. Coaching is a different matter.

With children as with adults, compliments and encouragement get better results than nagging criticism. It is much more effective to give a child a smile of approval for a good try that did not quite come off than to belittle his effort by heckling for perfection, most especially in the presence of others. The mother who orders, "Johnny, you know standing up is not enough. Go shake hands properly and say 'How do you do, Mrs. Smith,' " is not setting a shining example of considerate behavior. She is embarrassing the child in public; she is giving an order when a friendly suggestion would serve better; and by demonstrating to her visitor what an assiduous disciplinarian she is, she herself is certainly showing off.

*Baby and Child Care. Pocket Books, Inc., 1965.

3. Save punishment for privacy. It often is necessary to correct small children in public, but actual punishment (from a scolding to a spanking) in the presence of a guest is usually as much of a punishment to the visitor as to the child. If things get out of hand, remove the child, suppress him, or divert him —but deal with the actual punishment after guests have gone.

4. Be as consistently courteous to a child as nature and self-control will allow. Manners are taught by example. A child cannot be expected to remember his manners on special occasions unless he is on the receiving end of considerate behavior in his everyday life.

**TEEN-AGERS.** As far as manners go, teen-agers are grown-ups, and therefore are expected to observe all the rules that govern the behavior of men and women. The very few procedures that are slightly different for boys and girls are explained in detail where any sensible young person would expect to find them —under the specific topical headings, along with the standard rules for the adults that they will soon be. See INTRODUCTIONS, for example, for the explicit exceptions that are correctly made when boys and girls are being introduced and are themselves making introductions.

See Children in Index for complete list of references to children and their manners.

**GEORGE WASHINGTON'S RULES OF ETIQUETTE.** When George Washington was in his fifteenth year, he evidently decided that no one could be sure of all the rules of good behavior without some formal reference work to consult. So he compiled his own. In an elaborately careful hand he wrote a list headed "Rules of Civility & Decent Behaviour in Company and Conversation" in one of his school copybooks, now preserved in the library of Congress.

For many years it was assumed that his 110 rules had been composed as well as written down by Washington, but research eventually revealed that his maxims were based (though rephrased and amended to fit his time) on an etiquette book printed in London in 1640, nearly a century before he was born, a book based on a still earlier treatise on manners published in France.

Many details of our manners have changed since young George wrote down his rules. But just as valid today as in Colonial Virginia are the common sense, the concern for the comfort and pleasure of others, and the respect for the dignity of all men on which his maxims—and good manners in any time—are based.

Any child who follows the spirit of George Washington's "don't's," quaint as they sound, will make the right choice in an emergency. About all his rules need for use today is the same amount of rephrasing and adapting the boy George gave to the rules handed along to him. The first rule, for example, could well mean "Don't interrupt the conversation of grown-ups by turning the television up loud." Try taking it from there.

(Mice nibbled the edge of some of the pages in the copybook and destroyed a small number of words. A guess at what the lost words might have been is shown in brackets. Otherwise, except for a few minor changes in punctuation to make his meaning clearer, and changing to a modern S the old-fashioned one that looks like today's F, the following rules are printed as George Washington wrote them, with mistakes in spelling untouched.)

1st   Every Action done in Company, ought to be with Some Sign of Respect, to those that are Present.

2^d    When in Company, put not your Hands to any Part of the Body, not usualy Discovered.

3^d    Shew Nothing to your Freind that may affright him.

4    In the Presence of Others Sing not to yourself with a humming Noise, nor Drum with your Fingers or Feet.

5^th    If You Cough, Sneeze, Sigh, or Yawn, do it not Loud but Privately; and Speak not in your Yawning, but put Your handkercheif or Hand before your face and turn aside.

6^th    Sleep not when others Speak, Sit not when others stand, Speak not when you Should hold your Peace, walk not on when others Stop.

7^th    Put not off your Cloths in the presence of Others, nor go out your Chamber half Drest.

8^th    At Play and at Fire its Good manners to Give Place to the last Commer, and affect not to Speak Louder than Ordinary.

9^th    Spit not in the Fire, nor Stoop low before it neither Put your Hands into the Flames to warm them, nor Set your Feet upon the Fire especially if there be meat before it.

10^th    When you Sit down, Keep your Feet firm and Even, without putting one on the other or Crossing them.

11^th    Shift not yourself in the Sight of others nor Gnaw your nails.

12^th    Shake not the head, Feet, or Legs rowl not the Eys lift not one eyebrow higher than the other wry not the mouth, and bedew no mans face with your Spittle, by appr[oaching too nea]r him [when] you Speak.

13^th    Kill no Vermin as Fleas, lice ticks &c in the Sight of Others, if you See any filth or thick Spittle put your foot Dexteriously upon it if it be upon the Cloths of your Companions, Put it off privately, and if it be upon your own Cloths return Thanks to him who puts it off.

14^th    Turn not your Back to others especially in Speaking, Jog not the Table or Desk on which Another reads or writes, lean not upon any one.

15^th    Keep your Nails clean and Short, also your Hands and Teeth Clean yet without Shewing any great Concern for them.

16^th    Do not Puff up the Cheeks, Loll not out the tongue rub the Hands, or beard, thrust out the lips, or bite them or keep the Lips too open or too Close.

17^th    Be no Flatterer, neither Play with any that delights not to be Play'd Withal.

18^th    Read no Letters, Books, or Papers in Company but when there is a Necessity for the doing of it you must ask leave: come not near the Books or Writings of Another so as to read them unless desired or give your opinion of them unask'd also look not nigh when another is writing a Letter.

19^th    let your Countenance be pleasant but in Serious Matters Somewhat grave.

20^th    The Gestures of the Body must be Suited to the discourse you are upon.

21^st    Reproach none for the Infirmaties of Nature, nor Delight to Put them that have in mind thereof.

22^d    Shew not yourself glad at the Misfortune of another though he were your enemy.

23^d    When you see a Crime punished, you may be inwardly Pleased; but always shew Pity to the Suffering Offender.

[24^th    Laugh not too loud or] too much at any Publick [event.]

25^th    Superfluous Complements and all Affectation of Ceremonie are to be avoided, yet where due they are not to be Neglected.

26^th    In Pulling off your Hat to Persons of Distinction, as Noblemen, Justices, Churchmen, &c make a Reverence, bowing more or less according to the Custom of the Better Bred, and Quality of the Person. Amongst your equals expect not always that they Should begin with you first, but to Pull off the Hat when there is no need is Affectation, in the Manner of Saluting and resaluting in words keep to the most usual Custom.

27th  Tis ill manners to bid one more eminent than yourself be covered as well as not to do it to whom it's due Likewise he that makes too much haste to Put on his hat does not well, yet he ought to Put it on at the first, or at most the Second time of being ask'd; now what is herein Spoken, of Qualification in behaviour in Saluting, ought also to be observed in taking of Place, and Sitting down for ceremonies without Bounds is troublesome.

28th  If any one come to Speak to you while you are are Sitting Stand up tho he be your Inferiour, and when you Present Seats let it be to every one according to his Degree.

29th  When you meet with one of Greater Quality than yourself, Stop, and retire especially if it be at a Door or any Straight place to give way for him to Pass.

30th  In walking the highest Place in most Countrys Seems to be on the right hand therefore Place yourself on the left of him whom you desire to Honour: but if three walk together the mid[dle] Place is the most Honourable the wall is usually given to the most worthy if two walk together.

31st  If any one far Surpassess others, either in age, Estate, or Merit [but] would give Place to a meaner than hims[elf] the one ought not to except it, S[o the lesser one should refuse the courtesie unless he is offered] it above once or twice.

32d  To one that is your equal, or not much inferior you are to give the cheif Place in your Lodging and he to who 'tis offered ought at the first to refuse it but at the Second to accept though not without acknowledging his own unworthiness.

33d  They that are in Dignity or in office have in all places Preceedency but whilst they are Young they ought to respect those that are their equals in Birth or other Qualitys, though they have no Publick charge.

34th  It is good Manners to prefer them to whom we Speak befo[re] ourselves especially if they be above us with whom in no Sort we ought to begin.

35th  Let your Discourse with Men of Business be Short and Comprehensive.

36th  Artificers & Persons of low Degree ought not to use many ceremonies to Lords, or Others of high Degree but Respect and highly Honour them, and those of high Degree ought to treat them with affibility & Courtesie, without Arrogancy.

37th  In Speaking of men of Quality do not lean nor Look them full in the Face, nor approach too near them at lest Keep a full Pace from them.

38th  In visiting the Sick, do not Presently play the Physicion if you be not knowing therein.

39th  In writing or Speaking, give to every Person his due Title According to his Degree & the Custom of the Place.

40th  Strive not with your Superiers in argument, but always Submit your Judgment to others with Modesty.

41st  Undertake not to Teach your equal in the art himself Professes; it Savours of arrogancy.

[42d  To each let thy manner and] Courtesie be proper to the Dignity of his place [for it is absurd to ac]t ye same with a Clown and a Prince.

43d  Do not express Joy before one sick or in pain for that contrary Passion will aggravate his Misery.

44th  When a man does all he can though it Succeeds not well blame not him that did it.

45th  Being to advise or reprehend any one, consider whether it ought to be in publick or in Private; presently, or at Some other time in what terms to do it & in reproving Shew no Sign of Cholar but do it with all Sweetness and Mildness.

46th  Take all Admonitions thankfully in what Time or Place Soever given but afterwards not being culpable take a Time [&] Place convenient to let him know it that gave them.

[4]7th   Mock not nor Jest at anything of Importance break [n]o Jest that are Sharp Biting and if you Deliver any thing witty and Pleasent abtain from Laughing thereat yourself.

48th   Wherein you reprove Another be unblameable yourself; for example is more prevalent than Precepts.

[4]9   Use no Reproachfull Language against any one neither Curse nor Revile.

[5]0th   Be not hasty to believe flying Reports to the Disparag[e]ment of any.

51st   Wear not your Cloths, foul, unript or Dusty but See they be Brush'd once every day at least and take heed tha[t] you approach not to any uncleaness.

52d   In your Apparel be Modest and endeavour to accomodate Nature, rather than to procure Admiration keep to the Fashio[n] of your equals Such as are Civil and orderly with respect to Times and Places.

53d   Run not in the Streets, neither go too slowly nor with Mouth open go not Shaking yʳ Arms [go] not upon the Toes, nor in a Dancing [fashion].

54th   Play not the Peacock, looking every where about you, to See if you be well Deck't, if your Shoes fit well if your Stokings Sit neatly, and Cloths handsomely.

55th   Eat not in the Streets, nor in yᵉ House, out of Season.

56th   Associate yourself with Men of good Quality if you Esteem your own Reputation; for 'tis better to be alone than in bad Company.

57th   In walking up and Down in a House, only with One in Compan[y] if he be Greater than yourself, at the first give him the Right hand and Stop not till he does and be not the first that turns, and when you do turn let it be with your face towards him, if he be a Man of Great Quality, walk not with him Cheek by Joul but Somewhat behind him; but yet in Such a Manner that he may easily Speak to you.

58th   Let your Conversation be without Malice or Envy, for 'tis a Sig[n o]f a Tractable and Commendable Nature: And in all Causes of Passion [ad]mit Reason to Govern.

59th   Never express anything unbecoming, nor Act agˢᵗ yᵉ Rules Mora[l] before your inferiours.

60th   Be not immodest in urging your Friends to Discover a Secret.

61st   Utter not base and frivilous things amongst grave and Learn'd Men nor very Difficult Questians or Subjects, among the Ignorant or things hard to be believed, Stuff not your Discourse with Sentences amongst your Betters nor Equals.

62d   Speak not of doleful Things in a Time of Mirth or at the Table; Speak not of Melancholy Things as Death and Wounds, and if others Mention them Change if you can the Discourse tell not your Dreams, but to your intimate Friend.

63d   A Man ought not to value himself of his Atchievements, or rare Qua[lities, of his rich]es Virtue or Kindred.

64th   Break not a Jest where none take pleasure in mirth Laugh not aloud, nor at all without Occasion, deride no mans Misfortune, tho' there seem to be Some cause.

65th   Speak not injurious words neither in Jest nor Earnest Scoff at none although they give Occasion.

66th   Be not froward but friendly and Courteous; the first to Salute hear and answer & be not Pensive when it's a time to Converse.

67th   Detract not from others neither be excessive in Commanding.

68th   Go not thither, where you know not, whether you Shall be Welcome or not. Give not Advice whth[out] being Ask'd & when desired do it briefly.

[6]9   If two contend together take not the part of either unconstrained; and be not obstinate in your own Opinion, in Things indiferent be of the Major Side.

70th   Reprehend not the imperfections of others for that belongs to Parents Masters and Superiours.

71st   Gaze not on the marks or blemishes of Others and ask not how they came. What you may Speak in Secret to your Friend deliver not before others.

72d   Speak not in an unknown Tongue in Company but in your own Language and that as those of Quality do and not as ye Vulgar; Sublime matters treat Seriously.

73d   Think before you Speak pronounce not imperfectly nor bring ou[t] your Words too hastily but orderly & distinctly.

74th   When Another Speaks be attentive your Self and disturb not the Audience if any hesitate in his Words help him not nor Prompt him without desired, Interrupt him not, nor Answer him till his Speech be ended.

75th   In the midst of Discourse ask [not what has been said] but if you Perceive any Stop because of [your arrival ask him] to Proceed: If a Person of Quality comes in while your Conversing it's handsome to Repeat what was said before.

76th   While you are talking, Point not with your Finger at him of Whom you Discourse nor Approach too near him to whom you talk especially to his face.

77th   Treat with men at fit Times about Business & Whisper not in the Company of Others.

78th   Make no Comparisons and if any of the Company be Commended for any brave act of Vertue, commend not another for the Same.

79th   Be not apt to relate News if you know not the truth thereof. In Discoursing of things you Have heard Name not your Author always A Secret Discover not.

80th   Be not Tedious in Discourse or in reading unless you find the Company pleased therewith.

81st   Be not Curious to Know the Affairs of Others neither approach those that Speak in Private.

82d   Undertake not what you cannot Perform but be Carefull to keep your Promise.

83d   When you deliver a matter do it without Passion & with Discretion, howev[er] mean ye Person be you do it too.

84th   When your Superiors talk to any Body hearken not neither Speak nor Laugh.

85th   In Company of these of Higher Quality than yourself Speak not till you are ask'd a Question then Stand upright put of your Hat & Answer in few words.

86th   In Disputes, be not So Desireous to Overcome as not to give Liberty to each one to deliver his Opinion and Submit to ye Judgment of ye Major Part especially if they are Judges of the Dispute.

[87th   Behave yourself] as becomes a Man Grave Settled and attentive [Contra]dict not at every turn what others Say.

88th   Be not tedious in Discourse, make not many Digressions, nor rep[eat] often the Same manner of Discourse.

89th   Speak not Evil of the absent for it is unjust.

90   Being Set at meat Scratch not neither Spit Cough or blow your Nose except there's a Necessity for it.

91st   Make no Shew of taking great Delight in your Victuals, Feed not with Greediness; cut your Bread with a Knife, lean not on the Table neither find fault with what you Eat.

92   Take no Salt or cut Bread with your Knife Greasy.

93   Entertaining any one at table it is decent to present him wt meat, Undertake not to help others undesired by ye Master.

[9]4th   If you Soak bread in the Sauce let it be no more than what you [pu]t in your Mouth at a time and blow not your broth at Table [Le]t Stay till Cools of it Self.

[95]th   Put not your meat to your Mouth with your Knife in your hand neither Spit

forth the Stones of any fruit Pye upon a Dish nor Cast anything under the table.

[9]6   It's unbecoming to Stoop much to ones Meat Keep your Fingers clean, when foul wipe them on a Corner of your Table Napkin.

[97]th   Put not another bit into your Mouth til the former be Swallowed let not your Morsels be too big for the Gowls.

98th   Drink not nor talk with your mouth full neither Gaze about you while you are Drinking.

99th   Drink not too leisurely nor yet too hastily. Before and after Drinking wipe your Lips breath not then or Ever with too Great a Noise, for its uncivil.

100   Cleanse not your teeth with the Table Cloth Napkin Fork or Knife but if O thers do it let it be done wt a Pick Tooth.

101st   Rince not your Mouth in the Presence of Others.

102d   It is out of use to call upon the Company often to Eat nor need you Drink to others every Time you Drink.

103d   In Company of your Betters be no[t faster in eating] than they are lay not your Arm but o[nly your hand upon the table].

104th   It belongs to ye Chiefest in Company to unfold his Napkin and fall to Meat first, But he ought then to Begin in time & to Dispatch with Dexterity that ye Slowest may have time allowed him.

[1]05th   Be not Angry at Table whatever happens & if you have reason to be so, Shew it not but [put] on a Chearfull Countenance especially if there be Strangers for Good Humour makes one Dish of Meat a Feast.

[1]06th   Set not yourself at ye upper of ye Table but if it be your Due or that ye Master of ye house will have it So, Contend not, least you Should Trouble ye Company.

107th   If others talk at Table be attentive but talk not with Meat in your Mouth.

108th   When you Speak of God or his Atributes, let it be Seriously & [with] Reverence. Honour & Obey your Natural Parents altho they be Poor.

109th   Let your Recreations be Manfull not Sinfull.

110th   Labour to keep alive in your Breast that Little Spark of Celestial fire Called Conscience.

## CHINA

The word "china" is used to mean any kind of dishes for the table, just as "silver" is used as a generic term for eating implements of any metal. Technically, though, the only true china (also called fine china and porcelain) is made from a fine, light base and is thin, hard, and almost translucent. Pottery (also called earthenware and faïence) is opaque and much thicker. Stoneware is something between porcelain and pottery.

The day is past when a full set of matching china was considered essential for a dinner party. Indeed, many people today feel that dishes of the same pattern for all courses indicate lack of imagination. However, indiscriminate mixtures of patterns, styles, and textures make a table look like the salvage from a series of dish-washing disasters. It is best not to combine fine china and pottery at the same course, though some pieces of stoneware go well with either pottery or china. The general rule calls for the dishes for each course to match in general style and of course to go well with the table covering, centerpiece, and glassware. Otherwise, dishes of different colors and designs can be mixed freely to very attractive effect.

*See* MEALS AND THEIR SERVICE.

**CHOKING.**   *See* COUGHING AND CHOKING.

## CHOPS

Chop bones are not correctly taken up in the fingers to be gnawed or nibbled at the table. Bite-size pieces of meat are cut off the chop, and any meat that cannot be detached is left.

## CHRISTENING AND BAPTISM

The words "baptism" and "christening" often are used interchangeably. By strict definition, only "baptism" applies to the religious ceremony in which water is used to symbolize the dedication of a person to Christ. An object is never baptized. A ship, for example, is christened. A building or statue is dedicated. Most Christian faiths practice baptism, though some do not use water in naming or other dedicating ceremonies. Rituals and rules vary widely. Because ritual procedures are explained to the principals by the clergyman, they are not dealt with in this section, which is for the guidance of those not familiar with customs in faiths other than their own.

*Note:* There is no exact parallel between Christian and Jewish naming ceremonies. *See* BRIT MILAH.

### AGE OF THE CHILD.

**Catholic.** Baptism is not delayed more than two weeks after birth except for grave cause, and most usually is performed on the second Sunday after birth, always in church except for an infant in danger of death.

**Protestant.** Baptism is usually held within a month or two of birth, but may be put off for many months or even years.

### ATTENDANTS.

**Catholic.** Only the father and the godparents are required to accompany the child, though of course the mother goes to the church if she feels well enough.

**Protestant.** It is traditional for both father and mother to attend. It is required for godparents to attend.

*See* "Godparents" below for attendance by proxy.

### CLOTHES

**Adults.** Parents, godparents, and guests dress as they would for a High Mass or a communion service. Women wear hats and modestly cut dresses with sleeves, or suits. Men wear equally conservative clothes.

**The Baby.** A long christening robe, though charming, is not a requirement, and modern parents generally do not go to the expense of an elaborate new robe if an heirloom christening dress is not available. Any dainty white dress of fine linen, unstarched organdie, lawn, or soft washable silk is suitable, but materials like chiffon, taffeta, satin, and velvet are not. White is the usual color. The baby's bonnet and coat usually are white also, but may be of any color since they are removed before the ceremony. If there is a chance that the baby will be chilled during the ceremony, a white blanket is used over the dress.

**FEES OR DONATIONS.** No fee is required, but one is customary. This is paid by the child's parents, not by the godparents. The amount is decided by the circumstances of the parents. It is not discussed with the clergyman. From five to fifty dollars or more, usually in bills, is put in a plain white envelope if it is to be handed to the clergyman after the ceremony. Or a check may be mailed with the note of appreciation that always should be sent.

**GIFTS.** Godparents always give a christening present to the baby. Traditionally, this is something that the child will use and pass on as an heirloom, though it need not be. Silver mugs, porringers, prayer books, and crosses are the classic choices, usually inscribed somewhat as follows:

> Mary Jane Brown
> April 10, 1965
> with love from her godmother
> Alice York Smith

It is a good idea for godparents to check with each other so that there is no duplication.

A present may be sent in advance or taken to the party following the ceremony, but is best not given at the church because there the parents usually have their hands full of the baby and his gear. Gifts may be addressed to the child, or addressed to the mother with a card inside to the child. Godparents usually remember the child on his birthday each year, and on holidays.

Relatives and close friends who are invited to the ceremony and to the party following it are not required to send or take a present if the christening follows birth very closely and if a present welcoming the baby has already been sent.

**GODPARENTS.** The primary function of a godparent is to ensure the Christian upbringing of the child. Godparents usually are chosen from among friends about the age of the parents, since, to greater or lesser degree according to the particular faith, a godparent promises to undertake certain specific duties if the parents should die before the child is grown. Therefore, it is not sensible to ask friends to serve who are very much senior to the parents.

Close friends are generally chosen as godparents rather than relatives, the theory being that relatives will stand by the child anyway in case of need, but there is no rule that a relative may not be asked to serve as a godparent. It is extremely bad taste to ask a stranger, a slight acquaintance, or anyone who is only a business acquaintance to serve as a godparent. No one can be appointed a godparent without his specific consent.

A godparent is not required to be present at the baptismal or naming ceremony. If it is impossible for him to attend, a proxy is chosen by the child's parents. As a courtesy, the godparent is asked to approve this choice, and he also must send a written consent to be shown to the officiating clergyman. All that the proxy does is stand in the place of the actual godparent during the ceremony and make the responses in his name. The proxy undertakes no obligation whatsoever to the child. A baptismal present is not required from the proxy, though one is usual.

Following are the major rules concerning godparents in the Catholic faith and in most Protestant denominations:

**Catholic.** Church law requires that there must be one godparent as a baptismal sponsor. This may be either a man or a woman. No more than two godparents are permitted. If there are two, one must be a man, the other a woman. Godparents must be Catholics in good standing. Catholics are forbidden to act as godparents for a child of another faith. A Catholic who is asked to be a godparent may refuse the honor and, indeed, is required to do so if for any reason he is unable to assume the full obligation of the relationship, which involves much more responsibility than in most cases is required of godparents by Protestant faiths.

**Protestant.** Some Protestant faiths do not require godparents. In others they are customary. In still others, they are required.

There may be two godparents, one of each sex, but the usual number is three—two godmothers and one godfather for a girl, two godfathers and one godmother for a boy. There may be more. Godparents of a Protestant child usually are of the same denomination as the parents, though they may be of another if they are willing to make whatever promises the service calls for.

A Protestant asked to be a godparent must accept this honor. It is the greatest rudeness to make an excuse. Therefore careful thought and perhaps unofficial inquiry should be made before asking any Protestant to be a godparent.

**GUESTS AT CEREMONY AND PARTY.** Only relatives and very close friends are asked. The officiating clergyman and his wife must be invited to a party, though they are not obligated to accept.

**Catholics.** Although Catholics cannot participate as sponsors, they are allowed to attend the naming ceremonies of other faiths and they may invite friends of other faiths to attend their baptismal ceremonies.

**Protestants.** None of the major Protestant denominations forbid members to attend the religious ceremonies of other faiths as guests, and so they may be asked to both a baptismal ceremony and the party afterward.

**INVITATIONS.** Invitations are given in any informal manner—in person or by telephone or note.

An invitation to any kind of christening party must be answered. The invitation to the ceremony at church need not be, though anyone close enough to the parents to be invited would certainly feel obligated to explain his absence. It is entirely correct to accept only half of the invitation—to the party, for example, but not the service at church.

**PARTIES.** A christening party is similar to an informal reception or luncheon following a wedding. It is usually held at the baby's home or the home of a relative or friend.

A cake is always served, and some kind of festive drink—usually a non-alcoholic fruit punch, sherry, champagne, or eggnog. We seldom hear of a caudle cup today. A mixture of milk and honey was the traditional drink for breaking the fast that preceded baptism in early Christian days. Later, it was replaced by a mixture that included wine or ale. Today "caudle" means hot eggnog. Whiskey and soda or other such drinks may be served to guests who do not enjoy wine or eggnog, but always in moderation, since a cocktail-party mood is inappropriate following this formal religious ceremony.

The cake usually is white and may have the baby's initials decorating it as a symbol that the guests are accepting the baby's hospitality and are its friends.

The godfather proposes the first toast, always to the baby. The baby may appear briefly at the party, but more often is retired to solitude for a well-earned nap.

**PHOTOGRAPHS.** Most churches allow one photographer to take pictures during a baptism, though permission should be obtained from the clergyman. The photographer may be a guest or a professional. If a professional is hired, he should dress as the guests do and, needless to say, should be as inconspicuous as possible.

**PLACE AND HOUR.** Church baptisms (with the exceptions noted below) usually are held during or immediately after a regular service. The congregation stays for the ceremony since it is the welcome of a new Christian to the community of the church.

**Catholic.** Church law requires a Catholic baptism to be performed in church except when the infant is threatened with death. The usual time is Sunday afternoon. The ceremony rarely is celebrated before the congregation, but is held in the baptistry with only relatives and friends in attendance.

**Episcopal.** The rules call for baptism in a church except in case of illness. The ceremony usually is performed before the congregation at the Sunday-morning service.

**Protestant** (other than Episcopal). Baptisms at home are permitted, though the ceremony usually is held in church during or following a regular service.

A baptism at home may be held at any convenient hour. If the clergyman is to wear vestments, he will need a private room for robing. Decorations in the room where the ceremony is held usually are confined to flowers in vases rather than banked. The main requirement is a small table, usually covered with a white cloth, to hold the font. Any bowl of silver, crystal, or china, provided that it does not look like a finger bowl or a punch bowl, can serve as a font.

The parents receive the guests as they would at any other reception at home. The godparents, the baby, and the clergyman do not appear until all the guests have assembled. The clergyman enters first, followed by the godmother carrying the baby, and then the other godparents enter.

## CHRISTMAS

Anyone whose behavior is governed by the true spirit of Christmas—good will toward all men—cannot go far wrong during the holiday season. But since the celebration of Christmas touches the business and social lives of people of all faiths from Thanksgiving, when decorations appear in shops, to well after New Year's Day, it is best to know and observe certain firmly established customs.

**CARDS.** It is correct to send a card of the season's greetings to anyone, but some Christmas messages are not appropriate for everyone. It is far better to write a note to someone recently bereaved than to dispatch a card with one of the standard messages that incorporate words like "joyous" or "merry." It is equally thoughtless to send a card with a religious illustration to a non-Christian friend, though it is entirely correct to send a message of good wishes for the holiday season and the new year.

Religious themes are not suitable for illustration on business cards, with few exceptions, and, needless to say, any direct advertising on a card sent by a firm is in poor taste.

Over three billion cards—roughly, fifteen for every man, woman, and child —jam the mailboxes each year in this country alone. Once started, a Christmas-card list tends to grow. When a personal list swells to several hundred names, it is obvious that this basically delightful custom is out of bounds and that cards are being exchanged with virtual strangers "because they always send us one."

A Christmas card does not require an answer, and there is no obligation to send a card in return for each one received. It is customary, however, to thank the sender verbally if occasion offers the chance.

**Cost.** Christmas cards have a brief life, which is sad, because many truly distinguished ones get no more than a glance before they are put in a heap to be thrown away after the holidays are over. For that reason, many people feel that extremely expensive cards are a waste of money. Cards bought from a museum, church, UNICEF, or other nonprofit organizations are an excellent way to combine greetings and support for a good cause, and in this case expensive ones are in perfect taste.

**Ink.** Any brilliant color is correct except on cards with a soberly religious theme.

**Names.** The rules about addressing Christmas cards are fairly exact. The rules for signing or imprinting names on the cards are less so.

A title is always used before a name on an envelope.

A return address (*see below*) is standard.

A card sent to the home address of a married friend (business or personal) is properly addressed to "Mr. and Mrs." even though the sender knows only one of the couple.

A card to a business friend can be sent to his residence, but by first choice it goes to his office. If sent to his office, it is addressed to him only, unless the sender has met his wife. The same rule applies to a married woman in business.

The name of a wife (or husband) is not properly imprinted on a business card unless the couple are joint owners of a firm. Instead, John Smith, for example, sends cards carrying only his name to his list of business friends, and orders another set carrying the name of his wife also, to send to their personal friends.

It is quite usual to address an envelope to "Mr. and Mrs. John Smith and Family." However, since envelopes are likely to be thrown away, the standard and certainly warmer form is to address the envelope "Mr. and Mrs. John Smith" and add an appropriate message on the card: "Love to Polly and Teddy, too" or "To all of you from all of us," and so on.

Usually, only one card is sent to two friends who share the same roof. Both names are written on the envelope, one under the other. The older person's name generally goes on the first line, though if they are about the same age the name of the sender's closer friend goes first. Or the envelope can be addressed to the closer friend, and a handwritten message to both added on the card.

The sender signs his name on a Christmas card in the same way as on a letter. Therefore "Mr." or "Miss" or "Mrs." does not correctly precede a signature, though a card from an elderly couple to a much younger or a casual acquaintance can be signed "Mr. and Mrs.," followed by the husband's full name.

When adding one's name by hand, it is always best to sign both the first and last name even to intimates unless an unusual first name or an added message identifies the sender beyond all doubt. One of the minor irritants of the gladsome season is the card signed, with regal simplicity, "Bob," "Ann," or some other widely shared first name that leaves the recipient baffled as to which of several friends may have sent it.

A combination of first and last names, without titles, is correct for a single man or woman when the signature is imprinted below the greeting, and many married couples prefer the less formal "Mary and John Smith" to "Mr. and Mrs. John Smith." It is a minor point, very widely ignored, but the rules say that if a title is used, the name should precede the greeting. "Colonel and Mrs. John Smith send best wishes for the holiday season," for example.

There is no definite rule about the order in which the first names of a couple are handwritten or imprinted. When a card is signed, the person who writes both names usually puts the other's name first. A wife, for example, signs "John and Mary Smith." Some people advocate the same sequence when the names are printed, reasoning that it is logical to put the husband's name first, following the standard sequence of Mr. and Mrs. on a joint visiting card. Equally correct and popular, however, is "Mary and John Smith."

The father's name is always given first, whether written or printed, if children's names are added. "John, Mary, Anne and Timmy Smith" is one usual form. Another is "John and Mary Smith" on one line, followed by the names of the children on another line. "John and Mary Smith and Family" and "Mr. and Mrs. John Smith and Family" are not correct, but "The Smiths," followed on the next line by all the first names of the family, is.

**Opening.** It is only sensible to open cards as soon as they arrive instead of saving them to be opened on Christmas Day, since sometimes a Christmas card also carries an invitation to a party or other message that calls for an immediate answer.

**Postage.** Use first-class postage. A tucked-in flap and second-class postage give a card the unfortunate aspect of cheap advertising.

**Postcards.** Though less formal than a card in a sealed envelope, postcards with a suitable illustration are entirely correct for Christmas greetings.

**Return Addresses.** Some people feel that a return address is a tacit bid for a card in return, and so should not be used. This is not true. Any letter worth sending deserves a return address, and it is a real kindness to put one on a message to anyone who is not in frequent touch by mail, may not be sure of the sender's address, or may be put to some trouble to find it. By first choice, a return address is written or typed on the front, not the flap, of the envelope. Printed stickers may be used, but the appearance of the envelope is more attractive if the return address matches the main address in style.

**Seals.** Christmas seals were invented by a Danish postal clerk, who designed some stamplike stickers and sold them to raise money for a hospital for tubercular children. His idea spread rapidly all over the world. The first Christmas seals in this country were issued in 1907, also to promote funds to fight tuberculosis. Seals are now distributed by many nonprofit organizations and are widely used on the backs of cards and other mail, especially at Christmastime.

**Time to Mail.** It is correct to mail cards carrying the season's greetings any time after the first of December. Whenever possible, they should be mailed in time to be delivered by December 20.

**Typing.** It is not incorrect to type the address on a social card, though typing gives a decidedly less formal and personal overtone, and usually is reserved for business cards.

**DECORATIONS.** Christmas decorations go up in shops before the first of December, but houses are dressed with the traditional evergreen boughs and wreaths of holly only a few days before Christmas, and many people save this pleasant task for Christmas Eve. The poinsettia is now the standard Christmas plant. It is a traditional custom in some families to burn a tall candle in a window, a symbolic lighting of the way for the Holy Family wandering in search of shelter on the first Christmas Eve. No Christmas party is complete without its bunch of mistletoe. Everyone knows that any girl who can be lured under its waxy white fruit is fair target for a kiss.

Trees on lawns are strung with lights during the week before Christmas, but if long-established custom is observed, a tree indoors is not decorated until Christmas Eve—late at night if the job is trusted to Santa Claus.

Many people take decorations down before New Year's Day, but others leave them in place until Twelfth Night.

**DRINKS.** The traditional drinks served to callers on Christmas Day are eggnog and hot buttered rum. Eggnog, which is made of cream, sugar, eggs, and rum, is a little too sweet and hearty to please many people today, and so highballs and cocktails are usually served instead or are offered as alternatives to eggnog, and spiced unfermented cider or fruit punch is provided as a substitute for young people and teetotalers.

**FOOD.** Fish, either hot or cold, is a traditional dish for supper on Christmas Eve. Some families do not consider Christmas dinner complete without a suckling pig or a roast goose, but most Americans today celebrate with a roast turkey, and the standard combination at a buffet meal on Christmas is hot turkey and cold ham. Plum pudding with hard sauce and light and dark fruitcake are traditional desserts, with star- or tree-shaped cookies in addition for the children.

**GIFTS.** The exchange of presents at this time of the year was a custom long before the Christian Era. Primitive tribes observed the winter solstice, which falls about December 22, by feasting and gift-giving Early Romans exchanged lavish presents during the days of Saturnalia, which celebrated the return of the sun after the shortest day of the year. Within Jewish families, Hannukah (Festival of Lights), which also falls near the winter solstice, is a time of gift-giving.

December 25 has a special significance to Christians, but it is now the custom of many people of other faiths to observe the day as a nonreligious national holiday by giving and accepting gifts and good wishes as tokens of entirely personal friendship, affection, and esteem.

Since most gift-giving at Christmastime is reciprocal, it is best to think twice before giving an expensive present to a friend who cannot afford an equal expenditure but who might feel obligated to make one anyway. The best presents are those that fill a need, that have some element of novelty or surprise, and that show real thought in selection. Millions of dollars are misspent each year on gadgets of little or no use. When in doubt about the recipient's needs and taste, send a book or other gift that can be exchanged.

**Acknowledging.** All gifts, including those sent by business firms, should be acknowledged. Thanks in person or by telephone are enough, but if they cannot be expressed promptly, a note is required.

**Business.** The giving of Christmas presents to business acquaintances is governed by special rules given in detail under BUSINESS MANNERS. In brief, the rules are these:

An employer with a small staff usually gives a bonus or other gift to each employee. In a large office, factory, or other place of business, an executive (other than the owner) usually gives a present only to members of the staff who work closely with him.

An employee usually does not give the employer or his immediate chief a present in return. Spoken thanks or a note of appreciation is all that is expected or required.

In many circles it is the custom for firms to send gifts to employees of other firms, and when such presents are relatively low in cost they are given and accepted openly as what they are meant to be—an expression of appreciation for pleasant business dealings during the year. Money, however, or a present so expensive that it assumes the aspect of a payoff or bribe, is in poor taste, since it is awkward for everyone concerned when an unduly handsome present must be refused.

All presents should be acknowledged with spoken thanks or in a note.

**Mailing.** In compassion for the overburdened postman, gifts should be mailed as early in December as possible and, needless to say, must be securely wrapped and carry a return address. Gifts sent overseas must be chosen with care because certain items may require the recipient to pay high import duty.

**Money.** As a general rule, money—especially in cash—is not an appropriate present for a personal friend. Money may properly be given to a member of the family and to children and young people with whom one is on a familiar footing, but the best rule is: When in doubt, don't.

Gifts of cash are usually given only to people in certain service positions—building employees, household employees, and men who make regular deliveries, among others. Bills for them are better slipped into a Christmas card than handed over without ceremony. Bills to others also seem less like a tip if slipped into one of the special money envelopes available at banks and stationery stores, or into a greeting card built to hold a folded bill.

A check is a somewhat more formal way to give money than is cash, and is always a better choice if a substantial amount is involved.

Gift certificates are a graceful way to give a present of money when the situation warrants. They come in almost any denomination from five dollars up, and usually are attractively packaged by the store that sells them. Care should be taken to match the store and the recipient's needs or taste, however. For example, a gift certificate from an expensive specialty shop may be more of a problem than a pleasure to someone whose budget is restricted.

Stocks or bonds are often chosen instead of a check when a really substantial sum is given to a member of the family or to an employee of long standing. Except when given to a child, such presents should have no restrictions; it should be the privilege of the recipient to sell them when he chooses.

**Opening.** When presents are opened is a matter of custom and sentiment. Some people open them as soon as delivered to get an idea of how much to spend on a gift in return, to see if the gift may not be useful for a Christmas party—or to satisfy irresistible curiosity. It is traditional in many families to open gifts on Christmas Eve. Others brace themselves for the wakening of the children before dawn to see what Santa has left. A present brought by a guest on Christmas Day usually is opened during his visit, though the hostess who is busy with guests coming and going during an open house or other party quite properly puts all such gifts aside to be opened later.

**Passing Along.** If people did not pass along impossible or useless presents, much of the storage space in the house would soon be permanently devoted to them. But make sure that a recognizable present is not passed along to someone in the donor's circle, and don't perpetuate the crime by passing along a problem present to a friend. Get it out of circulation by donating it to a white-elephant sale.

**Returning to a Shop.** It is absurd to keep a gift that is the wrong size or color, or in any other way unsuitable, if it can be exchanged. For this reason, it is important not to put any but an obviously nonexchangeable gift into a box that came from a store where it was *not* bought, and also to make every effort to get those Christmas gloves, slippers, and lingerie in the right size. If an item is to be exchanged, it is only common decency to make the exchange promptly, before merchants have taken inventory and post-Christmas sales are in full swing.

**GREETINGS.** Christmas is a time for the exchange of spoken good wishes to friends and strangers as well. A certain amount of caution is needed in the choice of words, however, in some circumstances. To a non-Christian friend, the appropriate words are something like, "I hope you have a fine holiday." The same rule is best followed with strangers—salespeople, for example—if in any doubt as to their religion. "Merry," "joyous," and "happy" are words often carelessly used to the recently bereaved, for whom the day is almost certain to be filled with memories that will make it less than joyous. "I'll be thinking of you on Christmas" is one of many possible substitutes that are more considerate.

**GUESTS.** By tradition, any guest who knocks at the door must be made welcome on Christmas Day. The custom is observed in memory of the wanderings of the Holy Family in search of shelter. For this reason, think twice before making a Christmas call unless sure that it is the custom of a family to hold open house; and, under all circumstances, make a drop-in visit brief. More than one hostess with her hands full preparing for a big gathering in the evening has been drained of the last vestige of Christmas spirit by the unexpected afternoon caller, already finished with Christmas dinner, who stays and stays and stays.

**PARTIES.** It is the custom in some families to entertain friends on Christmas Eve and to reserve Christmas Day for a family gathering. Christmas Eve parties generally start after dinner, with guests dropping in whenever it suits them before a supper served around midnight. Since Christmas Eve is traditionally the time to trim the tree, guests often are invited to help, though a tree trimmed with so much assistance is not likely to be a striking aesthetic success. It is customary for each guest to bring a gift to a Christmas Eve party and for a package to be under the tree for everyone present.

A family dinner on Christmas usually is served any time in the afternoon after one o'clock. Many people make a point of asking one or two strangers to the community or friends without families of their own to join the family group. Such a guest brings a present if one has not been sent in advance. The meal is the main event. Guests often leave about an hour after it is finished, especially if there are small children in the family who have had the household up at dawn.

An open house during the day or evening is a custom in some families. Eggnog, hot or cold punch, and hot buttered rum are traditional drinks, but highballs, soft drinks, and coffee usually are also provided. Food may be anything from cookies and fruitcake to an elaborate buffet, according to the time of day. Guests are not expected to bring gifts, though of course they may, if they choose.

Office parties held on Christmas Eve all too often delay Santa Claus on his appointed rounds. They are far better scheduled a day or so earlier—and many firms now wisely put the money into bonuses instead.

**SANTA CLAUS.** Some modern parents believe that a child's faith in them will be irrevocably damaged when he discovers that he has been tricked into belief in Santa Claus. Others feel that a child deprived of a chance to whisk a letter up the chimney to Santa has been deprived of one of the happiest of childhood experiences. In either case, the rule for all children is the same. Those who have lost the faith or never had it, are bound not to blab the sad truth to the True Believers. The main responsibility of adults is to guard a youngster against the blind belief that Santa will bring every good child his heart's desire. Remember the sad disillusion of the little girl who, when asked by a department store Santa, "What do you want?" answered with all confidence in his magic power, "I want to be a boy."

**THREE KINGS' DAY.** Epiphany, also known as Three Kings' Day, falls on January 6. It is supposedly the date of the baptism of the Christ Child, and also the day on which the three kings, guided by the star, arrived in Bethlehem with their gifts. In Spain and in Cuba, Puerto Rico, Mexico, and other Latin American countries, Christmas is celebrated only as a solemn religious holiday, and Three Kings' Day is the big one for the exchange of gifts.

**TWELFTH NIGHT.** The eve of Epiphany is the twelfth night from Christmas, counting Christmas as the first. It marks the end of the Christmas season. Many people leave Christmas decorations in place until this date, January 5.

## CHURCHES

The first rule for attending any scheduled church service is: Be on time. Anyone who arrives after a service has started must enter as unobtrusively as possible and wait for an appropriate moment to take a seat, preferably one in the rear. If pews in the back are not occupied, it is correct to slip into one during a prayer, for example, but otherwise latecomers remain standing until a prayer is finished. Anyone who expects to leave before the end of a service usually chooses a rear seat so that his departure will not be noticed by the major portion of the congregation.

If ushers are on duty, a stranger to the church waits to be seated by one of them before taking any but a rear seat. In many churches, by custom certain pews are reserved for the use of regular attendants, and there are still quite a number of churches where members may pay a rent that entitles them to occupy the same pew each Sunday. When a church is more crowded than normal, as is usual at Christmas and Easter services, the family that rents a pew but does not occupy all the space in it often permits the ushers to seat others with them. However, if there are no ushers, strangers who arrive early for a service do not properly seat themselves in choice front pews except by invitation.

**CLOTHES.** Anyone attending a regular service is expected to wear clothing of reasonably restrained cut. In almost all houses of worship, it is customary for a woman to wear some kind of head covering as a token of respect, though today many clergymen feel that the act of reverent attendance is far more important than what a woman may or may not have on her head. When in doubt, a woman entering a church strange to her can always use a scarf as a substitute for a hat, but in this country clergymen of all faiths are beginning to decry the use of a handkerchief or facial tissue as conspicuous, unnecessary, and not too dignified a makeshift.

In a church with a coatroom, a man usually checks his topcoat, hat, and gloves before entering for a service. Otherwise, a man or woman folds a coat and puts it on the seat (or if the church is crowded, holds it in the lap) but does not drape it over the back of the pew. A woman usually leaves her gloves on except when taking communion or in very hot weather, though there is no firm rule.

**COMMUNION.** In many Protestant churches, anyone who has been baptized may partake of communion even though he is not confirmed in that branch of the Christian faith, but it is not correct for a non-Catholic to participate in a Catholic communion service.

**DONATIONS.** When a husband and wife attend church together, he usually puts a single donation in the collection as the family's contribution. When an unmarried couple attend church together, each makes his own contribution. It is customary for sightseers to leave a donation in the poor box.

**PHOTOGRAPHS.** It is never correct to take a picture of a service without gaining permission of the officiating clergyman.

**VISITORS AND SIGHTSEERS.** People of all faiths are welcome to attend services in any church. All that is required of them is respectful behavior. The visitor who attends a service in a church of another faith is not required to join in rituals contrary to the custom of his own faith. He need not kneel, cross himself, or join in responses, for example, though he should bow his head when others kneel to pray and in other ways conduct himself with reverence.

The sightseer who enters a church while a regular service is being held must not walk around, no matter how quietly, to look at the stained glass, carvings, and other decorations, but must stand still, sit in a pew, or leave. If a private ceremony is being held either at the main altar or in a side chapel, outsiders keep their distance and avoid intruding. When no service is in progress, a sightseer is still obligated to conduct himself reverently, quietly, and decorously and to refrain from making comments that can be overheard.

Sightseers are privileged to dress more informally than they would if attending a service, and it is entirely correct for a tourist to enter a church in any kind of reasonably informal clothes. It is no longer required of women tourists to cover their heads in many churches, but to do so in those churches where this is the custom is a sign of respect that is always appreciated by regular communicants. As noted above, it is customary for a sightseer to leave a donation in the poor box.

*See also* GUIDES; SYNAGOGUES AND TEMPLES.

# CIGARETTE GIRLS

An attendant at a tobacco counter is not tipped, but the girl who brings a tray of cigarettes to a table in a restaurant or nightclub is tipped, even though the charge per pack is usually well above the standard price.

**CIGARETTES AND CIGARS.** *See* SMOKING.

# CLAMBAKES

For this completely informal festivity, many of the usual rules for eating at table are suspended. Chicken may be picked up in the fingers, bread dunked in sauce, raw oysters or clams slurped from the half shell. Public clambakes are popular as fund-raising events in many areas. They are put on by professionals, or members of the sponsoring organization do the main part of the work. Patrons usually are expected to serve themselves and to dump shells, corncobs, and napkins in trash baskets and otherwise help to keep the tables and surrounding area attractive.

## CLAMS

Two species of clams are most popular: the soft (long-neck) clam and the rounder hard (short-neck) clam, which is also known as the quahaug. Because quahaugs have a stronger flavor than soft clams, and also can reach a size unmanageable in one bite, they are usually chopped or ground for cooking. Cherrystone clams are tiny quahaugs, and are delicious raw.

**CHOWDER.** This hearty stew is served in a soup plate or bowl, since soups served in bouillon cups should be thin enough to drink.

**COCKTAILS.** The clams must be small enough to be eaten in one bite. They are served in their sauce, usually in a stemmed food-cocktail glass, and are eaten with an oyster fork.

**FRIED.** Fried clams may be cut in two if very large. Any sauce served with them is put on the main plate, not the butter plate. They are eaten with a standard-size fork.

**HALF-SHELL.** Well-chilled raw clams are served as a first course. In some restaurants they are served on a bed of cracked ice, but usually are served without ice at home. A tiny glass of sauce may be on each plate, or only a wedge of lemon. The shell is steadied with the fingers of the left hand while the clam is detached with an oyster fork. The clam is eaten whole, never cut, and the shell is not used as a spoon and raised to the mouth. Only in restaurants or in informal service at home are condiments such as Tabasco sauce and horseradish put on the table or offered on a tray.

**STEAMED.** The hot shells are served on a big plate with a side dish of melted butter, a cup of hot clam broth, and a wedge of lemon. If a shell is not fully open, it is taken in the fingers and opened. A tightly closed shell indicates that the clam should not have been cooked. Leave it. The neck of the clam is taken in the fingers, and the clam is dipped first into the hot broth to remove any particles of sand, then into the melted butter into which the lemon has been squeezed. The whole clam is put into the mouth, and, with the fingers still holding the neck, the meat is pulled off. The neck is then discarded. Plates for empty shells may be provided for each person, or one large plate may be placed between two diners. Broth remaining in the cup is usually sipped. Finger bowls (*which see*) are a necessity after steamed clams.

**STUFFED.** Ground clams in a sauce are baked and served hot as a first course. They are eaten with an oyster fork.

## CLEANING WOMAN

Many people say cleaning "lady" rather than cleaning "woman." The matter is of no importance, and whichever is the local custom is the better choice. However, "woman" is in no sense belittling, and since "career woman," "businesswoman," and "clubwoman" are positively preferred to "career lady," and so on, "cleaning woman" is the logical choice.

*See also* PART-TIME WORKERS.

## CLERGYMEN

Anyone may seek counsel from a clergyman even though not a member of his congregation, but clergymen have many demands on their time and it is taking advantage to drop in for a talk without an appointment.

**CALLS FROM CLERGYMEN.** In some communities it is the custom for a clergyman to make calls on members of his congregation without prior notice. If a clergyman arrives at a time when it is totally inconvenient to see him, it is entirely proper to behave as to any other unexpected visitor, and courteously regret that he cannot be asked in.

**FEES.** See separate listings, such as CHRISTENING AND BAPTISM; FUNER-ALS; WEDDINGS, for occasions when clergymen receive fees for their services, and when and how these are given.

**FORMS OF ADDRESS.**
For the use of "Reverend" and other titles, *see* FORMS OF ADDRESS (Clergy).

**INTRODUCTIONS.** An exception is made to the rule that men always are introduced to women in the case of clergymen of the rank of bishop and higher. Women are introduced to them, and women rise for such introductions.

## CLOSETS AND DRAWERS

As a general rule, a guest does not open a closet or drawer without asking permission. It is inexcusable to peek into a medicine cabinet, slide open a desk drawer, or examine any other storage space out of curiosity. But often it is more sensible and considerate to open a medicine cabinet, for example, when in need of an aspirin, than to upset a hostess by admitting to a headache, or take her away from pressing duties to other guests to supply minor first aid.

## CLOTHES

We wear clothes first of all for comfort—and that includes the all-important comfort of self-confidence that comes from being suitably as well as becomingly clad. As far as manners go, suitability comes before all other considerations. Therefore, no matter what the current fad or fashion, certain rules about good taste in clothes do not change:

1. Choose clothes appropriate to the time, place, and occasion in their style, fabric, and degree of formality.
2. If in doubt, be slightly underdressed rather than conspicuously overdressed.
3. Choose clothes that fit comfortably. The girdle that needs tugging, the collar that requires constant shrugging into place, the belt that has to be hitched, or any garment that demands repeated adjustment is tasteless and never will be anything else.
4. Adapt extreme fashions to age and figure. Fads come and go. Keeping up with them is fun only if they do not make the wearer an object of fun—stretch pants, for example, on a woman long overdue for a reducing diet.
5. Observe the traditions concerning dress on special occasions. At a wedding, funeral, or other religious service in a house of worship, follow the custom of the congregation; and elsewhere follow to a reasonable extent the custom of the community as to character and formality of dress.

*Note:* Specialized information about correct clothing appears in many places throughout this book. For active sportswear, *see* separate listings from BADMINTON to SKIING; for special events, *see* other separate listings from BANQUETS to WEDDINGS. For rules of behavior involving clothes (when a glove is removed for a handshake, for example), *see* such headings as CHECKING; COATS; GLOVES; HATS; RESTAURANTS; THEATERS; and so on.

Following are the rules of current good taste that apply across the board to clothes for children, men, and women.

**BOYS.** To a very large degree, the customs in his community should govern the style of a boy's play and school clothes. In his earlier years, a boy has a strong need to conform to a group. He is put at a disadvantage with his fellows if he is required to wear clothes markedly different—shorts, for example, if his schoolmates wear long pants, or a suit if dungarees and a windbreaker are the local school uniform. This does not mean that a boy should be indulged in following any weird fad that comes along if it is in blatantly poor taste. All of us are judged by our appearance, and it is never too early for youngsters to learn that being conspicuous at any cost is poor taste in clothes as in everything else.

Much the same general rules apply to boys' clothes as to men's, though boys do not correctly wear a dinner jacket much before the age of fifteen or tails before eighteen.

For parties and other formal occasions, the standard dress for a boy is a dark-blue suit, black shoes, white shirt, plain socks of dark blue or gray, a tie of solid color or of several colors in a quiet small pattern, and a white handkerchief. If gloves are required at dancing school, little boys wear white cotton (not chamois or doeskin); on other occasions, they wear functional gloves or mittens of leather or wool or other fabrics. In summer, for dress-up occasions, boys wear cotton or other lightweight suits in colors suitable for men.

**Jewelry.** Under the age of fourteen, boys generally do not wear any jewelry except perhaps a simple gold or silver collar pin or tie clip. Their wristwatches are silver or stainless steel rather than gold, and by first choice worn on a leather strap or woven band rather than a metal bracelet. After age fourteen, some boys wear rings, either signets or rings set with plain dark stones—never imitation rubies, emeralds, or stones cut in flashing facets. Boys do not wear double cuffs on their shirts, and so they have no need for cuff links.

**GIRLS.** In spite of the available wide variety, in cut and fabric, of clothes for girls of all ages, good taste denies them the styles, materials, and accessories that make them look like miniature matrons—no *femme fatale* black sequin sheaths for high school dances, for example; no fancy, fragile fabrics for school, or clothes that are markedly more handsome and elaborate than those of their classmates. Otherwise, they and their mothers can indulge themselves to the limit in bright, becoming colors and current fashion fads suitable to the time, place, and occasion.

Little girls wear short white or pastel-colored gloves of cotton or nylon (not white or tinted kid ones) for dress-up occasions, summer and winter. At other times, they wear serviceable gloves or mittens of leather, wool, or other fabric.

**Jewelry.** Little girls under five usually do not wear jewelry except on dress-up occasions, and then something delicate and small, like a necklace of tiny seed pearls or a thin gold chain and small locket, is the most attractive. In their early teens, girls do not correctly wear any extremely valuable jewelry and never diamonds or rhinestones. Current taste bans earrings before about age sixteen. However, there is a vast choice of necklaces, bracelets, and pins that little and big girls can wear in good taste to satisfy their natural interest in ornaments—provided only that a teen-ager does not look as if she had raided her mother's jewel box. As a general rule, girls wear costume jewelry (if any) to school—little scatter pins of enamel on their sweaters, for instance, if that is the current fashion, and simple sturdy wristwatches with cloth or leather straps. Girls in their teens save smaller watches on metal bracelets or ribbon bands for dress-up occasions.

**MEN.** The rules about men's clothes are far more exact than those governing correct dress for women because a man's formal dress is virtually a uniform. Year by year, men's everyday clothes become more comfortable and colorful, but such changes are largely in minor details. Men of conservative taste observe the following general rules as if they were Articles of the Constitution.

**Ascots.** An informal ascot is a wide soft piece of silk of any color. It is cut so that it can be folded over itself, not knotted. The ascots we see most frequently are worn inside the open neck of a casual or sports shirt much as a scarf would be. They are coming into increasing favor for occasions that are a bit too dressy for an unadorned throat but that do not demand a tie. A stickpin is not worn with such ascots.

A formal ascot is a standard part of only two costumes. A white piqué stock is worn with formal riding clothes. A silk ascot (of silver gray, dark gray, very fine stripes producing a gray effect, or black) is worn only with a cutaway and a wing collar, and is held in place with a stickpin. An ascot is the standard neckware at a formal daytime wedding, but is generally not worn today on any other occasion, and an ascot is never correct at a funeral.

**Belts and Suspenders.** Whether they are called "suspenders," "braces," or "galluses," there is one unbreakable rule: A man does not appear in shirt sleeves when wearing them. Suspenders are always worn with formal day and evening clothes and are first choice with many men for regular daytime town clothes, especially a suit with a vest. All trousers hang better if supported by suspenders. However, they are never correctly worn with sports jacket and slacks or shorts.

Suspenders of any color may be worn with a regular suit. White ones are standard with full evening dress. White, black with a white edge, or black ones are worn with a dinner jacket. White, gray, or black and white ones are correct with formal day clothes.

**Boutonnieres.** Fashions change in the wearing of flowers with dress clothes —in some seasons a boutonniere is usual, in others not the style. It is customary for male members of a wedding party to wear flowers, but otherwise a boutonniere is optional, except that one is never worn to a funeral or with a decoration. A fake flower is often worn by a floorwalker as a badge of office; otherwise, better no flower at all than an imitation one.

**Everyday.** A man's business controls to a large degree what he appropriately wears in the daytime. A real-estate salesman in a suburban community may feel and look best in a sports jacket and slacks, and shoes with heavy rubber soles if he is doing much walking around country property. But the standard business costume, summer or winter, in the average office is a suit of conservative color and cut, with or without a matching vest (or sometimes a contrasting waistcoat), a white shirt (or, more usually today, one in a fairly light color, patterned or plain), reasonably restrained tie, belt or suspenders, smooth leather oxfords (brown or black) with leather soles, socks of an inconspicuous color, a white linen or colored silk handkerchief. There are many variations, of course, in all these details, but unless a man has a very large wardrobe, he does best to stay within the limits of the basic conservative fashion in choosing his business clothes.

After six, if a man is going to dinner or a party in street clothes, he wears a dark suit, matching vest (if any), white shirt, and much the same accessories as in the daytime. Black shoes are the first choice, but brown shoes are now increasingly seen on less formal occasions in the evening.

Unless a man has a sizable wardrobe, he is wise to choose a topcoat that will look well with his street clothes both day and evening, rather than a burly tweed or a very dressily cut coat. The range in fabric and color between these extremes is quite large—from a well-cut gabardine, for instance, to a dark cashmere—but the cut should be simple.

**Formal Day.** Very few men outside certain government and diplomatic circles have any need for the cutaway (or slightly less formal sack coat) and striped trousers sometimes called formal "morning" dress, though they are correct for any formal occasion before six o'clock in the evening, and are the standard costume for male members of the wedding party at a daytime wedding.

There are some few correct variations, but no one can go wrong in following these conservative components:

1. Boutonniere: Optional and never worn to a funeral; usually a white or dark red carnation; never artificial.
2. Coat: A cutaway of black or oxford gray with plain peaked lapels.
3. Collar: Wing or starched fold-over (note "Tie" below).
4. Gloves: Gray doeskin finish.
5. Handkerchief: Fine white linen; white initial.
6. Hat: Black silk top hat.
7. Scarf: White or gray silk.
8. Shirt: White neckband. Pleated or plain bosom. Double cuffs or starched single cuffs.
9. Shoes: Black calf oxfords with a plain toe cap.
10. Socks: Black or dark gray; silk, lisle, or light wool.
11. Spats: Optional—seldom seen today, and never worn to a funeral. In winter, gray woolen fabric. In summer, gray or white linen to match waistcoat.
12. Stick or umbrella: Optional. Black.
13. Studs and cuff links: Matching; gold or gray pearl or enamel.
14. Suspenders: White, black and white, or gray.
15. Tie: An ascot or four-in-hand, gray or black, plain or with a restrained pattern or stripe. Either an ascot or a four-in-hand can be worn with wing collar, but an ascot is not worn with a fold-over collar. (A black four-in-hand with a fold-over collar is correct at a funeral—never a wing collar, a gray tie, or an ascot.)
16. Topcoat: Midnight blue, black, or dark gray; with or without a velvet collar.
17. Trousers: Striped, black and gray or black and white; cuffless.
18. Waistcoat: Double-breasted. In winter, usually gray fine wool, though it can match the cutaway. In summer, gray or white linen.
19. Watch: A pocket watch; key chain across the waistcoat or to a side pocket. By today's custom, a wristwatch is also correct.

**Formal Day, Variations.** Very often chosen for weddings and similar ceremonies is this slightly less formal daytime costume, which is the same in all details as the cutaway with these exceptions:

1. Collar: Starched fold-over.
2. Coat: Single-breasted sack coat, black or oxford gray.
3. Hat: Black or gray Homburg (usual choice) or soft black felt or black derby.
4. Spats: None.
5. Tie: Black or gray silk four-in-hand.
6. Waistcoat: Double-breasted; usually pearl gray, but it can match the material of the coat.

**Formal Evening, Black Tie.** If an invitation reads "White Tie" or "Decorations," a man is expected to wear full evening dress, but otherwise what is variously known as a dinner suit, dinner clothes, dinner jacket, Black Tie, or tuxedo will see a man through almost any formal evening event with complete adequacy. (Though "tux" and "tuxedo" are very widely used, quite a number of people make a point of using one of the other terms above. This is not a matter of great importance, but it should be noted that Black Tie, not Tuxedo, is the correct term for use on formal invitations to indicate that a dinner suit rather than a street suit or White Tie is expected.) Very often at formal public events in big cities—the opening of the opera, for example—there will be a goodly show of men in full evening dress, but there will be many more in dinner jackets, and entirely correct they will be. And at formal dances today, a dinner suit rather than tails is the standard dress in many parts of the country.

The first choice in a city, summer and winter, is the black or midnight-blue dinner suit. At resorts, in the suburbs, and on shipboard, a white dinner jacket with black trousers is more often worn in warm weather. However, there is increasingly more latitude of choice in color and in the accessories correct with dinner clothes, and today soft shirts with attached collars, instead of the less comfortable stiff shirtfront and hard collar, are the general rule.

Black Tie is not correctly worn before six in the evening, on Sunday night, or on shipboard on the first and last nights of a voyage.

1. Boutonniere: Optional; white but usually a dark-red carnation; never artificial.
2. Coat: Black or midnight blue; usually single-breasted with shawl or peaked lapels faced with satin or dull silk. In summer, a white coat of the same cut may be worn, and on less formal occasions a dinner jacket of some other color, plain or madras, but always with black trousers.
3. Collar: Today, usually a soft attached fold-over, but a wing collar is also correct.
4. Gloves: Gray chamois or buckskin; frequently none.
5. Handkerchief: The same as with full evening dress.
6. Hat: Optional. In winter, black Homburg, or black or dark gray soft felt. In summer, white Panama or Milan.
7. Scarf: Same as for full evening dress.
8. Shirt: White; soft plain or pleated bosom and double cuffs; or starched bosom, plain starched cuffs with a wing collar.
9. Shoes: Black patent-leather oxfords or highly polished smooth calf, or plain patent-leather pumps.
10. Socks: Same as full evening dress.
11. Studs and cuff links: Same as for full evening dress; also correct are smoky gray or black enamel studs and gold cuff links, plain or set with enamel to match the studs, or dark onyx, etc.
12. Suspenders: Black, black with a white edge, or white.
13. Tie: Black bow, hand tied; or the same color as the cummerbund.
14. Topcoat: The same as for full evening dress.
15. Trousers: Black or midnight blue to match the jacket, with a single stripe of satin or braid; cuffless.
16. Waistcoat or cummerbund: The most conventional choices are a waistcoat in the material of the jacket or of black silk; single or double-breasted. Or a black silk cummerbund, though cummerbunds in maroon are also popular.
17. Watch: Either a wristwatch or pocket watch.

**Formal Evening, White Tie.** Full evening dress, also known as "White Tie" or "tails," is governed by strict conventions, and very little latitude is allowed. Tails are not correctly worn before six in the evening, on Sunday night, or in summer.

1. Boutonniere: Optional. Usually a white carnation or small gardenia; never artificial and never worn with a decoration.
2. Coat: Black or midnight-blue tailcoat with peaked lapels faced with satin or a dull silk.
3. Collar: Wing.
4. Gloves: White buckskin or kid.
5. Handkerchief: Fine white linen; an initial or monogram (if any) in white, gray, or black only.
6. Hat: Silk hat, opera hat, black Homburg—or no hat.
7. Scarf: White silk; initial (if any) white, gray, or black only.
8. Shirt: White; bosom and single cuffs stiffly starched.
9. Shoes: Black patent leather; pumps or oxfords.

10. Socks: Black silk.
11. Studs and cuff links: White pearl or mother-of-pearl; cuff links to match or of white gold or platinum.
12. Suspenders: White.
13. Tie: White piqué bow, hand tied.
14. Topcoat: Black, midnight blue, or oxford gray; velvet collar optional; double-breasted, or single-breasted with fly front. An evening cape is also correct.
15. Trousers: The same material as the coat; cuffless. A single stripe of satin or braid.
16. Waistcoat: White piqué; single- or double-breasted.
17. Watch: Pocket watch worn in the watch pocket of the trousers with a chain to the side pocket; or, less formal but correct, a wristwatch.

**Hats.** Today, many men wear hats only in the most inclement weather, and better no hat at all than one that is strikingly inappropriate by standard taste— a stitched tweed, for example, with a dressy overcoat, attractive as this headgear is with more casual clothes. A gray fedora goes with anything except full evening dress or a cutaway, and is always a safe choice. A Homburg is more dressy than a fedora or other soft felt, though also correct with a conservative business suit. Caps and berets are for open cars and for sports, not for city streets. A derby is correct with a business suit, but these hard hats are so seldom worn today that they are somewhat conspicuous.

**Jewelry.** By today's fashion, men of conservative taste do not wear diamonds, star sapphires, or other precious stones or brilliantly colored semiprecious ones. What jewelry they do wear is functional (except for rings), simple, and masculine-looking in design—collar pins and tie clips of gold or silver without stones, and cuff links to match or set with plainly cut dark stones like onyx or sardonyx.

A man's wedding ring is generally a heavy plain gold band. He wears it on the ring finger of his left hand, and usually does not wear any other ring if he wears a wedding band.

The first choice among other rings with most men is a signet or an emblem ring like those designating membership in a school or college class or an organization—in other words, a ring that has some special meaning. Also in good taste are rings set with masculine-looking semiprecious stones. A man usually wears such a ring on the little finger, though a signet ring may be worn on the ring finger of either hand.

A man's wristwatch is plain and sturdy-looking. Many men prefer woven bands or straps of leather, especially with business and sports clothes, though a heavy metal bracelet is first choice with others.

A slim pocket watch of gold, silver, or platinum was once standard equipment with formal evening dress, but this custom is changing. Today, a wristwatch is far more frequently seen with Black Tie than a pocket watch, and quite often with White Tie.

A pocket watch is usually worn with a chain. In the daytime, the watch chain is worn across the waistcoat (not threaded through a buttonhole), with the watch in one lower pocket and a good-luck charm or other weight in the other pocket rather than attached to the middle of the chain. A watch chain is never worn across the waistcoat with evening dress, however. The watch is carried in the change pocket of the trousers, with the chain anchored in the side pocket. Modern watch chains are slim, of plain design, and are not set with stones.

**Suspenders.** *See* "Belts and Suspenders" above.

**Sticks.** It is a minor point, but "stick" rather than "cane" is today's first choice—perhaps because "cane" has the overtone of disability rather than dash. A walking stick is an optional accessory with formal clothes. A dress stick is made of black or extremely dark wood, and is lighter and slenderer than the standard walking stick.

Sticks carried in the country are sturdy, of light or dark wood, with a right-angled or crook handle of comfortable size to be grasped to support one's weight over rough ground or to push aside heavy brush. The heavily carved, brilliantly painted, excessively knobby sticks made for tourists by the inventive natives of far places are best left abroad.

**Ties.** The rules for the color and style of the ties worn with formal day and evening dress are explicit. With other suits there is wide latitude, though neckwear should always complement the shirt and suit—not stand out as a striking, attention-getting item, except perhaps on St. Patrick's Day. A four-in-hand is the most popular cut, but bow ties are equally correct with street clothes—provided they are hand-tied. The too-perfect readymade tie is for waiters and theater ushers. Both ends of a correctly tied bow tie are usually all but covered by the loops, producing a two-winged rather than a four-winged butterfly.

**Topcoats.** A man's dress topcoat to be worn with formal day or evening clothes is black, midnight blue, or gray-black; straight-cut with set-in sleeves; with or without a velvet collar. It may be single- or double-breasted, though a single-breasted one is more practical, since it also can be worn with a conservative daytime suit of smooth fine fabric.

For regular daytime wear, a topcoat can be single- or double-breasted, and if it is not of tweedy fabric or pronounced pattern, can also be worn with a dinner jacket, especially if the fabric is dark cashmere or a similar material. Many men find a coat of gabardine, camel's hair, or other soft wool useful for both day and evening wear, and others let a well-cut, light or dark cloth raincoat take them almost anywhere.

Heavy tweed topcoats are mainly for daytime wear, preferably with sports and country clothes.

**Umbrellas.** A man's umbrella is always black, of silk or nylon, and has a crook handle. Colored umbrellas belong on the musical comedy stage or in the hands of doormen. When not in use, an umbrella looks best if kept tightly furled, but most men do not bother to use the cover.

**Vests and Waistcoats.** "Vest" means the matching waistcoat of a street suit, but "waistcoat" is the correct word for the single- or double-breasted garment worn with formal day and evening clothes whether it matches the coat in color or not, and also for a garment that is different in color or material from the suit it is worn with.

**WOMEN.** Different parts of the country observe somewhat different clothes conventions, but the following guidelines are observed everywhere by the woman who knows that the primary demand of good taste is clothes suitable to the time and occasion, her figure and her age.

Fads in fashion enjoy so wide a swing that practically anything goes for the housewife in her own house and garden. But the young wife who wants to keep up with the Joneses on the right side of the tracks does not look as if she were dressed (or undressed) for a Miss America contest when she goes to the supermarket. And the girl who wants to make her mark in a business career avoids the far-out extremes of a fashion fad until after hours.

**Afternoon.** An afternoon or cocktail dress differs from a dinner dress only in that it is always street length. According to the occasion and time of year, a cocktail costume can be an elegantly simple dress touched up with lovely jewelry, a dressy suit, or a low-cut dress of anything from cotton to velvet.

However, a cocktail dress certainly is not limited to afternoon wear. Frequently a cocktail dress or suit is the best choice for dinner in a restaurant, for the theater and other evening events. A hat may or may not be worn with such a dress.

**Evening.** What is generally called a dinner dress can be either long or short, depending on the current fashion. It can be of any fabric—all the way from cotton or wool to velvet, brocade, lace, or chiffon. It may be sleeveless, fairly covered up, or have long sleeves, but it is not completely off the shoulders. Though often more vivid in color and trimming than a cocktail dress, a dinner dress is less extreme in cut than the formal evening or ball gown, which is long, usually cut quite low front and back, is sleeveless and often strapless, and can be made of any handsome material.

A dinner dress is appropriate at a gathering at which men wear dark suits rather than evening clothes. It also is the first choice for most occasions where men are in Black Tie. The true ball gown is saved for much more elaborate events—a formal dance, the opera, an opening night at the theater, and other occasions where men are in either full evening dress or Black Tie.

Long gloves usually are worn with a ball gown. A hat is not worn with either a dinner dress or a ball gown.

**Furs.** Fur stoles are now worn the year around—even in summer if the nights are at all chill, as they are in San Francisco, for instance, which is noted for its well-dressed women.

*See also* FURS.

**Gloves.** Gloves are a standard part of any formal or semiformal costume. They may be of any color or material that is currently in fashion and suitable to the time of year, though of course delicate kid or suede gloves are not worn with rough-and-ready coats and suits. Even in warm weather a woman usually wears cotton or nylon gloves to church, on city streets, and to any dress-up event whether she is wearing a hat or not.

**Hats.** A hat is a standard part of a costume worn to any kind of official daytime ceremony, to a formal reception, lunch, or tea. However, by today's custom, a woman may go hatless wherever she pleases except to a service in a house of worship. In some faiths, hats are not an absolute requirement at a religious service, but the well-dressed woman wears one as a matter of taste, since a head covering is considered a mark of respect. The only exception to this rule is for evening (but not daytime) weddings in some faiths and in certain parts of the country, where guests customarily go without hats if the wedding is to be followed by an elaborate reception with dancing.

**Jewelry.** Styles vary with the years—in jewelry as in everything else. Before Chanel popularized the wearing of pearls with her sweaters and suits, it was considered unthinkably bad taste to wear those gems with street clothes. Today, a pearl necklace is appropriate any time and anywhere and with anything except shorts, bathing suits, and other costumes for active sports. But it is still not today's custom to wear diamonds (or rhinestones) or any extremely valuable jewelry—with the exception of an engagement ring—with business or informal clothes.

Multiple bracelets and noisy bracelets are out of place in an office, at a theater, concert, church, or other place where their clinking can distract the attention of anyone nearby.

Bracelets may be worn over long gloves, but are not generally worn on the outside of street gloves.

Everyone wears costume jewelry today, and it is fun to be able to change these frank fakes when the fashion changes. The rules are the same as for real stones—it is just as inappropriate to wear a rhinestone bracelet as a diamond one to the laundromat.

Long, dangling earrings are not for daytime, or for young girls at any time. Other earrings are appropriate at any time of day or evening, except with active sports clothes like tennis dresses, bathing suits, and riding clothes. Earrings worn to work or with street clothes should be discreet in size and brilliance.

Women customarily wear rings on the little finger or the ring finger of either hand, though any ring worn on the ring finger of the left hand signifies an engagement to wed. Occasionally, rings with very large stones are worn on the middle finger, but today this custom is considered an affectation, though a harmless one.

Most women have only one watch, mounted on a reasonably conservative metal bracelet, and wear it on all occasions. A watch with a ribbon or leather band is nonetheless always more appropriate and attractive for active sports, especially field sports like hunting and fishing. Diamond-studded watches are not suitable with sports costumes or in an office, and are best saved for late-afternoon and evening events. Even a very handsome jewel-studded bracelet watch is not worn with an elaborate ball gown unless the watch face is concealed or a hidden part of the bracelet. Watches are not worn over gloves.

## CLUBS

A striking evidence of how our lives are changing is the rapid and continuing increase in both town- and country-club memberships. The average family has more money and more leisure time than ever before, but living quarters are getting markedly smaller and so are the ranks of domestic workers. Therefore, each year a growing number of prosperous families find a club with a good dining room, a pool, golf course, tennis courts, and other recreational facilities the most practical and pleasant place to entertain friends of all ages—from nonathletic cardplayers to members of the wading-pool set.

**APPLICATIONS FOR MEMBERSHIP.** Anyone may apply directly in person or by mail for membership in a municipal club that is operated for the benefit of the whole community, but a completely different procedure is followed at clubs that are private organizations. Anyone who wants to become a member must wait for a formal invitation to join. About the most that a hopeful outsider can do, without hurting his chances, is drop a hint to a member, but in good taste he cannot ask a member in so many words to propose him for membership. It is not necessarily a social snub if an invitation to join a club is not readily extended to a newcomer in a neighborhood. Membership in most clubs is limited by their by-laws to a number that can be comfortably accommodated on the premises, and many of the older clubs have a long waiting list of well-sponsored eligible applicants.

Members are elected by some variant of the following standard procedure. Usually several members are required as sponsors. They formally propose the name and explain the qualifications of the prospective member to the proper committee. Members of the board or of the membership committee sometimes will interview the proposed member, but in any case must approve him. After that, the membership at large usually is given a chance to vote on the application. A wise sponsor always makes some discreet inquiries before he actually submits an application, to make sure that the prospective member qualifies and also that, for personal reasons, he will not be blackballed—an eventuality that can only be a great embarrassment to everyone concerned. If for any reason an applicant is turned down, a sponsor must give him the best face-saving explanation he can find. All the applicant can do is accept the explanation without argument, thank his sponsors for their efforts, and drop the matter—for the time, at least.

**GUESTS.** A member provides for a guest's comfort and entertainment much as he would at home. A host or hostess either meets a guest in the lobby or instructs the guest to ask to be shown to the bar, dining room, or elsewhere, making sure in this case that the doorman has the guest's name and will admit him readily.

The guest is in exactly the same position he would be in his host's home.

He does not order refreshments or offer to pay for them; he does not criticize food or service or take charge of the party, any more than he would under his host's own roof.

**Guest Cards.** In some clubs, members can extend temporary membership privileges to out-of-town friends by means of a guest card. The holder of such a card is not welcome to walk in on membership or committee meetings. Otherwise, he is privileged to use all club facilities freely, though he is expected to observe the house rules with special care, since his member-friend is held responsible for his conduct. The holder of a guest card is expected to pay for all his expenses for food, drink, and tips, as well as for his room, in a residential club. At a club where the display of cash is banned and members sign chits for all food and services, the guest makes arrangements with the manager to sign his own name. If that is not according to club custom, he will be asked to sign his host's name followed by his own. In either case, he should settle his account directly with the club before departure, just as he would at a hotel—not wait for a bill to be sent to his sponsor and then settle with him. The holder of a guest card may entertain other friends—members and nonmembers—at the club, but it is an unwritten law that he does not treat the member who provided the guest card, there; he takes him elsewhere when returning hospitality.

**MEETINGS.** The standard work on parliamentary procedures at all kinds of meetings is *Robert's Rules of Order*, available at any public library and at most bookstores.

Even if a meeting is conducted without strict regard to the formal rules, certain formalities are observed for the sake of efficiency if not plain everyday politeness.

If one person is presiding, all others are required to gain recognition from the chairman before speaking. Properly, only the chairman is privileged to interrupt a speaker so recognized. In all usual circumstances, it is very poor manners to break in on anyone who has the floor. Arguments, corrections, rebuttals, and all other comments should be suppressed until a speaker—no matter how misguided—has finished. Otherwise, a free-for-all results, and no one has a chance to complete a point.

At a membership meeting, a visitor generally does not join a discussion unless specifically asked to do so.

A main obligation for members attending a board or committee meeting is to arrive promptly and not to leave before the scheduled business is completed, except in a real emergency. The all too well known member who chronically turns up late and then blithely asks for a summary of the discussion to that point shows an infuriating indifference to the value of everyone else's time.

"Chairman" is the title given to a person of either sex presiding at a meeting. "Chairlady" or "Chairwoman" is not used. The proper address in speaking directly to a chairman is "Mr. Chairman" or "Madame Chairman" (not "Miss" or "Mrs. Chairman").

See also BANQUETS for conduct during public meetings.

**MEMBERS.** A club member is expected to act with a little more formality than he might at home, but otherwise the premises are treated as an extension of a member's own roof. In most clubs members speak without introduction, though newer members naturally go slowly and do not take for granted that they are welcome to join all individual groups. A new member usually has no serious problem, since it is the duty of a sponsor to introduce him, explain the customs not covered in the by-laws, and otherwise see that he is comfortably launched.

Some clubs have several classes of memberships with varying initiation fees and dues. An honorary member has all privileges but does not pay either initiation or dues.

**RESIGNING.** When a member resigns from a club, he is expected to write a formal letter, suitable to be filed, to the president or other appropriate officer. A verbal resignation is not according to the rules.

**TIPPING.** Some clubs ban tipping but add a service charge to food and drink bills, or to the monthly statement, so that a member need not hand out small change any more than he would at home. In others, many small expenses may be on a pay-as-you-go basis, and tips are expected by members of the service staff. As a general rule, a guest leaves all tipping to his host, though in some athletic and country clubs it is customary for a guest to tip his own caddy, locker-room attendant, and so on. If in doubt, make the offer and then be guided by the response of the host.

See also FRATERNITIES AND SORORITIES.

# COATS

A man helps a woman into and out of her topcoat, but she does not help him with his unless he has some disability and really needs her assistance. Men (except those in service positions) generally do not help other men into their coats.

Helping a woman put on a coat is no courtesy at all unless it is done properly. To start with, the man holds the coat so that it hangs evenly from the collar, with the armholes at a convenient distance between the woman's waist and shoulders, making it possible for her to slip her hands easily into the sleeves without fumbling or doing a back bend. Once her hands are in the armholes, he lifts the coat gently and steadily to her shoulders and she settles it in place for herself.

For unknown reasons, a man does not sit on his coat spread back over a chair in a restaurant or a seat in the theater. In a restaurant, he checks it or puts it on a spare chair; in a theater, if he does not check it he holds it bundled in his lap.

A man does not take off his suit coat if he is wearing suspenders, and if he takes off his jacket he also takes off his vest if he is wearing one. The rules call for men to wear jackets in public places like restaurants and theaters, and this is sensible enough, since these places are air-conditioned in the main. However, the custom that condemns men to sweltering under two or more layers of clothing in many other places when the weather is blistering is rapidly and mercifully dying out. In countless cities today, men are beginning to appear on the street in crisp fresh shirts without jackets. On very hot days it is absurd for a man to wear a jacket in his office, and any hostess worthy of the name insists that men guests take off their coats on arrival when the weather is uncomfortably hot.

See also CHECKING; FURS.

# COATS OF ARMS.    See HERALDIC DEVICES.

# COCKTAIL PARTIES

One of the outstanding virtues of the cocktail party is that it makes hospitality at home possible for a group much too large to be accommodated in most houses for a meal. But the outstanding hazard of a good, well-planned cocktail party is its very success. Enlivened by pleasant company, guests all too often stay on and on until the desperate hostess is driven by hunger to throwing together a sketchy dinner of some sort for the diehards who have ignored the rules.

**ARRIVING AND LEAVING.** The rules for arriving and leaving are the same for business and social cocktail parties. Guests show up at the opening hour if they like, or any time thereafter until twenty minutes (at the latest) before the closing hour. Dismaying to any hostess who has issued invitations from five to seven, for example, is the inexperienced guest who considers seven the dead-line for arrival rather than departure. A party does not rate as a success if all guests clear out on the dot, but guests are expected to leave not too long after the specified closing time.

**CLOTHES.** Cocktail parties allow a wide range of choice in clothes. Quite correct are the guests who drop by in street clothes after a day at work. So are the guests who arrive dressed quite elaborately for a dinner party if one is on their schedule as their next stop.

If a woman guest is wearing a hat, she keeps it on. She leaves her handbag with her wraps or keeps it with her, but she takes off her gloves before taking any refreshment. A hostess does not wear a hat unless her party is at a hotel, club, or similar "public" place. A guest does not circulate to say good-bye after putting on his or her wraps—unless the hostess has asked for aid in dislodging lingerers who have lost track of the time, in which case a conspicuous departure serves as a good graceful hint to others.

**GUEST OF HONOR.** A guest of honor usually sends flowers to the hostess before or after the party, is on hand to receive with the hostess at the opening hour, and stays until the closing hour. Each guest is obligated to say a few words to the guest of honor at some time during the party, making a self-introduction if that is the easy and practical thing to do. At a small party, each guest says good-bye to the guest of honor. At a very large party, that is not customary or necessary.

**GUESTS.** One of the main purposes of a cocktail party is to give a sizable number of people a chance to meet, and so the first duty of each guest is to remain mobile to some degree and be ready to move easily from one group to another. A blight to any party is the guest who settles down for a long confab with one or a few old friends. So is the lone lady who plants herself in a seat on arrival and, by refusing to budge, becomes a problem to her hostess as well as to anyone unwary enough to be trapped beside her. Unhappy experience with such homesteaders is the origin of the rule generally observed by veterans of big afternoon gatherings: "Never sit down at a cocktail party."

A guest finds the host and hostess immediately after arrival, and, by the rules, must seek them out to say good-bye. There is no need to write or tele-phone thanks afterward, but it is a pleasant courtesy often observed after a small party.

**HOST AND HOSTESS.** If the hostess does not answer the door herself, she stays near the entrance of the living room to welcome her guests and make introductions. At a very small party, she or the host sees each guest to the door. At a very large party, host and hostess do not desert their other guests to see each departing one out. It is the rule that host and hostess spend at least a little time with each guest. Otherwise, their main duties are to act as trouble-shooters in seeing that no one is at a disadvantage—left alone, or stuck too long with one person or group.

**INTRODUCTIONS.** At a small party—and early in a big one—each guest is introduced to all others on arrival. After that, the roof is an introduction, and strangers identify themselves to each other. With the exception of shaking hands with the host and hostess, who offer a hand to each guest in welcome, women do not generally shake hands—an obvious impracticality for someone holding a glass, cocktail napkin, and perhaps a purse and cigarette. Men need make no point of shaking hands with each other.

**INVITATIONS.** Bids to a cocktail party are given by telephone, note, visit-ing card, or the practical and popular little printed fill-in invitations available in card shops. Whether an invitation is spoken or written, the single most im-portant item is the explicit statement of the length of the party. An invitation for cocktails from six to eight, for example, clearly means that guests are not expected for dinner. But a hostess who says, "Can you come for cocktails at six?" has no one but herself to blame if some of her guests take it as an invitation for the evening. When issuing a verbal invitation, a good way to make doubly sure that there is no confusion about the length of the event is something like, "Come as early as you can because we have a dinner date right after . . ." If guests are expected to stay on indefinitely, the invitation should make that entirely clear by specifying "Cocktails-Buffet" and the starting time—which of course is a different party entirely from the regular cocktail party.

An invitation to a business cocktail party does not require an answer unless it carries R.S.V.P. But an invitation to any private party with or without a request for a reply must be answered.

**REFRESHMENTS.** Since most people have marked preferences among liquors, it is customary to stock a bar with gin and whiskey (in most circles, both Scotch and bourbon) as a minimum selection, in addition to sherry for those who do not care for hard liquor, and always a few bottles of soft drinks for the teetotalers. Often, martinis and perhaps another mixed drink like a daiquiri are offered, but water, soda, and suitable glasses for long drinks should be available for the many people who prefer them to the more lethal cocktail.

Food ranges from a few strategically placed bowls of nuts to elaborate hot canapés (if the hostess has help in the kitchen), but the standard cocktail food is a selection of small items that can be picked up in the fingers or on a toothpick and eaten in one or two bites. Of major importance to a smoothly running party is keeping the platters of food circulating if they are not so placed that guests in all parts of the room can readily help themselves to canapés, tiny sandwiches, shrimps, cubes of cheese, and other items speared with toothpicks or the popular self-service dips and spreads.

**SERVICE.** The most important rule about the service of drinks is: Don't slug a drink or otherwise betray a guest into taking more alcohol than he realizes. The host who circulates with a martini pitcher hospitably filling half-empty glasses will not be remembered kindly by the guest who gets one too many because he has not been able to keep accurate count. And neither is it fair play to mix a gin and tonic, for example, with three ounces of liquor instead of the regulation two.

A table covered with a cloth to absorb any spillage is the standard temporary bar for a large party. It should be set up in any place where the guests who inevitably collect around it will not block traffic to and from the front door. Everything needed—ice, bottle opener, knife, lemon peel, bar towel, glasses, mixers, and liquor—should be on the table so that the bartender need not be constantly on the run to the kitchen for supplies.

For a party run without professional help, the hostess usually concentrates on welcoming the guests and passing canapés, leaving the bar to the host. A single woman usually asks a male guest to man her bar at the start of a party, but takes care not to keep any one guest occupied as barman for the duration. After the first round of drinks at an informal cocktail party, guests are usually expected to return to the bar and mix drinks for themselves. A man ready for another drink properly asks a woman with whom he is chatting if he can bring her one, but her best bet, at many times, is to move along with him as a graceful way to change the pattern of any group that has been too long isolated from circulation.

At a very large party, one or more waiters are usually detailed to circulate with trays of drinks. A guest takes his choice or puts an empty glass on the tray and asks for a special drink if the waiter does not have a replacement. Most furniture today is alcohol-proof, but a guest takes care to use coasters if they are provided, and under any circumstances never uses a book or magazine as a coaster. Even if waiters are on hand, a guest is always privileged to make his way to the bar to set down an empty glass or to get a refill.

**SIZE.** There are only two really good sizes for a cocktail party. A successful one has to be small enough so that all guests can be seated or so large that only a relatively few guests can find seats at any one time. Parties of these two sizes are entirely different in character, but the party that falls between them in size has the disadvantages of both and the pleasant qualities of neither.

## COCKTAILS

Cocktails are designed to whet the appetite, and for that reason are not served except shortly before a meal.

Cocktails are sipped, not tossed off as a short drink of straight liquor may be. An onion, cherry, or olive, unspeared by a pick, is not generally picked up in the fingers, though no one has been drummed out of house or bar yet for doing so. A pick of ivory or metal is put back in the glass; a toothpick may be left in the glass or discarded in an ashtray.

Sometimes only one kind of cocktail is offered, especially if a fancy or unusual one has been chosen as an especially suitable introduction to the food and wines following. However, the experienced hostess knows that nearly everyone has marked preferences among hard liquors, and so she offers a choice of predinner drinks.

Except in a restaurant, "What will you have to drink?" puts a guest in an embarrassing position, since he may find himself asking for something not on hand. Instead, some such question as, "Will you have a martini—or a Scotch or bourbon?" lets the guest know what is available, and if he hesitates the host can suggest the soft drink that should always be available for guests who do not take alcoholic drinks. If a host with an impressively well-stocked bar should say, "What can I get you?" a guest is free to ask for rye, vodka, rum, a whiskey sour, or some other usual choice, but unless he wants to put his host on the spot, he does not challenge him to produce a complicated cocktail that demands ingredients not generally at hand in a bar at home—a Pink Lady, for example, which requires applejack, grenadine, and white of egg in addition to gin.

In a small group, it is customary for guests to wait until all present are served and the host or hostess lifts a glass for the first sip. In a large group, the first guests served do not wait.

Anyone who does not take alcohol should make no point of his abstinence when cocktails are served. A guest accepts any nonalcoholic substitute that is offered rather than remain conspicuously empty-handed; and a host fills a glass for himself with cider, soda, or whatever he likes, without comment about its contents.

**SERVING.** One round of cocktails is mixed at a time, since they grow weak and watery very quickly if allowed to stand with ice in a pitcher or shaker. The most usual and pleasant way to prepare premeal drinks is at a bar in view of the guests. Such a "bar" usually is no more than a tray of bottles, ice, glasses, and whatever else is needed, set on any convenient side table or shelf, though the easy availability of the makings is most definitely not an open invitation to a guest to help himself.

A host usually takes charge of serving drinks, but there is no reason for a hostess not to do so. A woman entertaining alone often asks one of her male guests to take over this duty for her. Any guest may ask a host if he would like help at the bar, but it is never the privilege of a guest to preempt a host's place and hospitably press refills on other guests. The old rule "Never do the honors in another's home" is especially well worth remembering in this connection.

Cocktails are not served at a dining table except in a restaurant. Guests whose drinks are unfinished when dinner is announced do not carry them to the dining table unless specifically instructed to do so.

It is customary to serve some kind of salty finger food with cocktails—little canapés, hot or cold; cubes of cheese or sausage, speared with picks; shrimps or fresh vegetables with a dip; or perhaps no more than salted nuts. With any such food, napkins are needed and small paper ones are today's standard practical choice.

For other details, *see* BARS; MEALS AND THEIR SERVICE; RESTAURANTS.

## COFFEE

Coffee did not begin to move into its place as the most popular American beverage until after the Boston Tea Party, but today it ranks at the top of the list, and no formal meal is complete without it.

Until the late seventeenth century, coffee was seldom made at home. In both Europe and this country, it was mainly available in coffeehouses, many of which became noted as meeting places for people who wanted to engage in literary and political discussions. These early coffeehouses are considered to be the forerunners of the modern club. Today, coffeehouses are coming back into popularity in many big cities, and perhaps this renaissance has inspired the present interest in serving at home different varieties of coffee made by techniques new to most of us. Among the many examples are the thick, sweet, extremely strong Turkish coffee, espresso, and *cappucino,* which is a combination of coffee, chocolate, and steaming milk. These and other delicious variants of the standard American coffee have brought with them an increased interest in both exotic imported coffees and the special equipment and cups suitable for them.

Decaffeinated coffees are popular with many people and have a rightful place in every pantry, but no good hostess serves decaffeinated coffee without also offering her guests the strong, hot, freshly made real coffee that is an extremely important part of most meals to most people.

**SERVICE.** Coffee is served informally in anything from paper cups to the finest china, and from fifty-cup electric urns to heirloom silver. Formal service of after-dinner coffee, however, demands a coffee service and cups of special character and size.

The standard coffee cup is somewhat taller and less saucer-shaped than a teacup, but in most households coffee cups and teacups are used interchangeably. For everyday purposes, far more important than the shape of the cup and the style of the pot is the brew itself, which should be strong and scalding hot. A feeble, lukewarm infusion is worse than no coffee at all.

**After Dinner.** The literal meaning of "demitasse" is "half-cup." This pretty equipment, also called "after-dinner coffee cups," is used only for coffee served after a meal. Demitasse cups are usually a matching set, but some people use a trayful of unmatched cups to charming effect. Demitasse spoons are an essential with these cups. In formal service, the tray, coffeepot, sugar bowl, and cream pitcher are usually silver.

Demitasses may be used after any dinner, and are correct after a strictly formal lunch, though coffee is served in standard cups with or after informal lunches.

Coffee in small cups may be served at table after the dessert dishes are removed, but far more generally after-dinner coffee is served in the living room or elsewhere away from the table.

Traditionally, coffee served in demitasses is taken black, with or without sugar. However, "correct" or not, cream should be provided because a guest who enjoys cream in his coffee should certainly have it, no matter what the size of the cup.

If the hostess pours at the table, a tray with the coffee service and the little cups is set beside her. She asks each guest how he likes his coffee, and adds cream and sugar to order. If a guest takes sugar or cream, she also puts a demitasse spoon on the saucer before the filled cup is passed along the table. If the hostess pours in the living room (far the more usual procedure), she follows the same routine. No strict order of service need be observed, but in a small group seated away from the dining table it is most practical—and therefore correct—to serve first those seated farthest from the hostess if cups are passed along from guest to guest. If the group is scattered through a bigger room, the guests come up for their own cups, or perhaps the host delivers them as they are poured. For a large group, it is more efficient and pleasant if a maid or the hostess moves around the room with a sizable tray bearing the filled cups, with their spoons in place on the saucers, and the cream and sugar.

It is entirely correct to offer granulated sugar because for many people a lump of sugar is far too much sweetening.

**At the Table.** There is only one important rule about the service of coffee—in cups of any size—at the table. The server should never risk an accident by reaching between two diners with a hot pot in hand to fill or refill a cup. The only correct and safe procedure is to pick up the cup and saucer from the right of a diner, fill it, and then put it back in place.

At all informal meals, coffee may be served in whatever way suits the hostess best. A maid may pass a tray of filled cups, or the hostess may pour from her place at the table. If the hostess pours, she adds a teaspoon to the saucer before passing a cup along. She may add cream and sugar to order, or they may be passed along after the cups are in place. Or empty cups may be on the table at each place—with the teaspoon on the saucer (not on the cloth with the other silver); and a maid or the hostess then goes around the table to fill the cups.

**Café au Lait.** This standard breakfast drink in France is a combination of hot milk and strong black coffee in very nearly equal parts. The classic serving procedure is to pour the two into the cup at the same time, holding the coffeepot in one hand and the container of hot milk in the other.

**Café con Leche.** The same drink, Spanish version.

**Café Diable.** This is black coffee seasoned with spices and citrus peel and flamed with brandy. It can be served in demitasses if the special diable cups are not available.

**Iced Coffee.** Iced coffee or iced tea is often served throughout an informal meal—in a tall straight-sided glass holding about fourteen ounces. A small underplate is not a requirement, but one certainly is useful because otherwise what to do with the long-handled iced-tea spoon is a problem. If there is an underplate, the spoon is put on it after the iced drink is stirred. If there is no underplate, there is nothing to do but leave the spoon in the glass and hold it (with the index finger) to the far side when taking a sip. The spoon is never laid on the cloth or mat or the butter plate, or propped against the dinner plate.

The iced coffee or tea glass is set to the right of the water glass, or in its place if water is not also served. At the beginning of the meal, the correct position for the spoon is on the side with the knives, to the extreme right.

Iced coffee may be poured before guests sit down, or the glasses may be filled with ice and the liquid added later. Some people like to pour freshly brewed, hot coffee over packed ice cubes. Cold coffee is usually poured from a pitcher.

Many hostesses choose powdered sugar for cold drinks, since it dissolves more quickly than granulated sugar, but either is correct. Cream, of course, is offered.

**TRAYS.** A tray carrying a coffee service or a collection of filled cups, cream, and sugar is not covered by a cloth in formal service.

**COFFEE BREAKS.**   *See* BUSINESS MANNERS.

## COFFEES

Growing in popularity with women in many communities are parties held in the morning, usually between ten and noon. This festivity is known as "a coffee party" or simply as "a coffee." It can be as large or small, formal or informal, as its afternoon counterpart, a tea. The virtue of a coffee lies in its hour—more convenient for many women than teatime, when the children are out of school, there is dinner to be cooked, and perhaps a commuting husband to be met at the train.

Refreshments served at a coffee range from simple sweet buns, doughnuts, or coffee cake to an elaborate variety of sandwiches and other substantial finger foods, as well as sweet breads and cakes. Otherwise, the procedures for the hostess and guests are the same as those for teas (*which see*).

**COGNAC.**   *See* WHISKIES AND OTHER SPIRITS.

## COLDS

The common cold is a social disaster and a business blight. Since a cure for colds has so far baffled science, the only thing the victims can do is endure their misery as inconspicuously as possible and give some thought to the protection of others.

Anyone in the early stages of a cold, when sneezing threatens to spread the infection, has certain clear obligations. Under no circumstances is it excusable to pay a call on a sick person (except another cold sufferer). The prospective guest who comes down with a heavy cold just before a party should notify the hostess, especially if there are young children in the house. She may prefer to have him renig rather than risk infecting her family and other guests. A person with an extremely heavy cold should also give a dentist, beauty shop operator, or anyone else who comes in close personal contact with a client or patient a chance to postpone the appointment.

There are no hard-and-fast rules for employees suffering from a cold. Some employers much prefer an absent employee to a sneezing one. Others operate on the theory that once an employee is in the grip of a cold it is already too late to fend off the infection of fellow workers, and so they expect the victim to show up on schedule.

If a cold sufferer cannot manage to recover in solitude, the least he can do is to suppress the sounds and others evidences of his malady as much as possible. Sneezing cannot be soundless, though resounding explosions certainly can be suppressed. No apology for a sneeze is necessary beyond one murmured or signaled "Sorry," but good sense demands the covering of mouth and nose during a sneeze. Saying "Gesundheit" or "God bless you" once, if at all, to a sneezer is enough. Forcing an already breathless sneezer to repetitions of "Thank you" during a paroxysm is a silly form of sport. Clearing the throat, particularly when accompanied by spitting into a tissue, belongs strictly out of hearing and sight. So does an uninhibited blast to clear the nose, though it certainly is better to give one vigorous blow when it is needed than to avoid it by sniffling and snuffling. An adequate supply of tissues is far better than the repeated use of a damp, rumpled handkerchief.

# COLLEGE WEEKENDS

Many customs vary widely from campus to campus, but certain of the problems of the weekend visitor to a college are the same everywhere.

**CHAPERONAGE.** Some colleges require parental permission before a girl may leave her own campus for a weekend visit, and under most circumstances it is routine for a girl to get parental permission before accepting any such invitation. If a man follows the rule and spells out acceptable plans for housing his date when he issues his invitation (see *below*), that should be the end of the chaperonage problems for both of them. With this basic requirement taken care of, there is no reason for a girl not to join the thousands of others who fill the trains and planes on all big-game and other special weekends.

**CLOTHES.** Too much gear is just as bad as too little, and the issuer of the invitation is responsible for telling the visitor how to avoid both extremes. Once the invitation is accepted, be specific about major events so that the guest knows what to dress for. If, for example, the plan is to go directly from the train to a faculty reception, a girl who is adequately briefed can arrive in a suitable dress or suit, and a man in a suit instead of a windbreaker and slacks.

For most weekends, a girl needs one dancing dress, one dress appropriate for dinner, tea, or cocktail parties, and one or two daytime outfits, depending on what spectator or participating sports events are planned. A wide variety of dress will be seen at any college weekend, but as on other social occasions, noticeably flashy and extreme clothes are a poor gamble; it is better to be a bit underdressed than emphatically overdressed.

A man visiting at a woman's college probably will need his dinner jacket, a suit for later afternoon and dinner parties, slacks and a sports jacket for daytime.

If the one issuing the invitation has left a first-time visitor to the campus in doubt about what clothes will be appropriate, the guest should not hesitate to ask, "Will I need a dancing dress [Black Tie]?" Better be frank in admitting ignorance of the customs at that particular school than turn up with all the wrong things.

**EXPENSES.** A special understanding about expenses can be reached between old friends, of course, but in all other cases the following procedures are taken for granted: The guest pays for transportation to and from the visited campus. The person who issued the invitation pays for all other major expenses.

If the guest is to stay at a hotel, the host (or hostess) makes a reservation and pays for the room in advance. The guest, however, leaves a tip for the chambermaid and takes care of other minor tips that may be necessary. An exception is made at the Service schools like West Point and Annapolis, where it is the custom for a girl to pay her hotel charges as well. The host (or hostess) also buys tickets in advance, whenever possible, for all the weekend activities.

A girl has a slight advantage over a man when it comes to incidental expenses. If she is the guest, the man pays for all meals except possibly breakfast, if it is not included in the hotel rate and if he is not joining her for it. If the man is the guest, he pays for taxis, any snacks or drinks that he and his date may pick up, and at least offers to pay for any admissions that his hostess has not been able to pay for in advance—movie tickets, for example. A hostess usually plans for her guest to take meals at her sorority or another place where she can make advance arrangements to pay the charges. But if the man suggests any change of plan or any special entertainment, he picks up the tab.

If a guest has been housed with personal friends of the student host or hostess, some small house present is customary just as it would be from any houseguest to a weekend hostess. If an entire fraternity or sorority house has been turned over to guests for the weekend, it is usual though not necessary for all guests to chip in and leave one community present for the house.

**INTRODUCTIONS.** In general, the standard rules given under INTRODUC-
TIONS are followed. However, a girl visiting a man's school is introduced to
faculty members: "Dr. Smith, this is my guest, Miss Brown." When parents visit
a school, faculty members ((except in receiving lines) are introduced to the
student's mother: "Mother, this is Dr. Smith." The father is introduced to the
faculty member: "Dr. Smith, this is my father."

**INVITATIONS.** The success or failure of a weekend often depends on how
carefully the invitation is handled. An invitation, especially one for any of the
big-game or other special weekends, is best given as much as three or four
(and not less than two) weeks in advance. A belated or last-minute bid may seem
to imply that the recipient is a second—or third or fourth—choice. Whether an
invitation is given in person, by telephone, or by mail, exact dates should be
mentioned when the subject is first brought up. The invitation should be
answered promptly, of course. If it is accepted, specific details should follow,
including information about where the guest will stay, and a fairly complete
rundown of the planned activities so that the guest will have a clear idea of
what clothes to bring. Transportation schedules should be given, and definite
instructions about where and when the guest will be met. Girls, in particular,
feel more comfortable and have more fun on the way if arrangements are made
for them to meet other girls bound for the same campus on the same train
or plane.

**MANNERS IN GENERAL.** The rules governing a houseguest anywhere will
see the weekending college student through nicely, with a few added precautions. If his hostess is bound by curfew laws at her school, a man is obligated
to see that she is back in her quarters at the prescribed time, and otherwise
make it easy for her to observe the rules at her school. For example, if drinking
is banned, he does best not to embarrass her by sneaking a bottle onto her
campus or, under any circumstances, by making her feel like a wet blanket if
she refuses a drink. Host or hostess and guest alike must remember that a date
is a date. A guest does not make separate or independent plans with other
friends. He goes along, with good grace, with whatever plans his date has made.
Host (or hostess), in turn, devotes full attention to the guest and adapts the
plans as far as possible to the guest's comfort and pleasure.

**THANKS.** As after any overnight stay, the guest must send a bread-and-
butter note of thanks. And if a guest has stayed in the house of a faculty member or with personal friends of the host or hostess, a letter of thanks to the
lady of the house is also required. So is a note to a housemother if she has
given assistance in an emergency or otherwise been especially helpful. Thank-
you presents are not obligatory, but a male guest, especially, often sends his
hostess a little token in acknowledgment of an especially good time, though
he chooses nothing personal or expensive.

**COLOGNE.** Cologne is the lightest in strength of the bottled fragrances. *See*
PERFUME.

**COLONELS.** *See* FORMS OF ADDRESS (Armed Services).

**COMFORT STATIONS.** *See* BATHROOMS AND WASHROOMS.

**COMMANDERS.** *See* FORMS OF ADDRESS (Armed Services).

**COMMENCEMENTS.** *See* GRADUATIONS AND COMMENCEMENTS.

## COMMUNION

Visitors of another faith who find themselves in a church during a communion service need not leave, but they must conduct themselves with complete reverence in token of respect for the solemn meaning this service has for the communicants. A tourist who has entered to inspect the church must not move around during any service, but must take a seat, stand still, or leave inconspicuously by the nearest exit.

In many Protestant churches, anyone who has been baptized is welcome to partake of communion even though he is not confirmed in that branch of the Christian faith. It is not correct for a non-Catholic to participate in a Catholic communion service, however.

**COMPANY PARTIES.** *See* BUSINESS MANNERS.

## COMPLIMENTS

A sincere compliment is one of the most valuable lifts to the spirit that one person can give another. But, as with all presents, there are certain taboos to be observed if compliments are to rate the neat definition "the applause that refreshes."

Children are rightly warned never to make personal remarks of any kind, since all too often out of the mouths of the little ones come such paralyzing questions as "Why does that lady have white roots to her hair?" After childhood, however, the blanket ban against personal remarks certainly does not extend to compliments, if they are given by the rules, because the intent of a compliment is recognition of some personal distinction—in appearance, behavior, or performance.

Sincerity and a reasonable degree of truth are the keynotes of any good compliment, and brevity is the best safeguard against the unintentional kickback that ruins so many well-meant words of praise. "You look marvelous!" has no meaning if used to all comers as an habitual substitute for "Hello." Equally empty are such outright fibs as "Never saw you looking better" to the shaky convalescent who knows he never looked worse. And "How do you keep so young?" is no compliment at all to a much older acquaintance who wants no emphasis put on relative ages.

Of damaged value, too, are the compliments that deal a glancing blow. "That's a wonderful haircut" is a fine thing to hear, but an addition like "It makes you look so much smarter" is in the same unfortunate category as "I've always loved that dress on you"—too easily translated by the sensitive into "You've been looking like a charity case."

"Comparisons are odious" is never truer than of compliments that ricochet off an innocent bystander, leaving a gratuitous nick in his self-esteem. "You have the prettiest hands I ever saw" is the sort of personal remark better saved for another time if it will make someone else within earshot feel like sitting on her great sturdy paws. Otherwise, compliments are among the best and the most lastingly remembered gifts, and the more we have of them, the brighter life is for everyone.

Accepting compliments gracefully is just as much an art as giving them effectively. Always safe is the appreciative "Thank you" that any gift deserves. So is a deserved compliment in return. But protests like "Oh, you say that to everybody," or any other belittlement or contradiction, can only inspire the compliment-giver to uncomplimentary regrets for his kind words.

## CONCERTS

"Painters paint on canvas. We paint our tone pictures on silence. Only you can supply that."—*Leopold Stokowski* (giving one of his milder reproofs to a noisy audience)

"Concert" is the generic term that covers all musical performances other than theatrical ones. A recital is a concert given by one or two soloists. A musicale is a concert given under private auspices—a social entertainment, to some degree, with music as its chief feature.

The rules for behavior at concerts are the same as those given in detail under theaters, with the following additions and exceptions:

**APPLAUSE.** The conductor and the soloists are applauded each time they make an entrance or exit. Often the concertmaster of a symphony orchestra is applauded on his first entrance. Otherwise, applause is appropriate only at the end of a selection. It is not given following each of a group of related but separate selections offered as a unit even though there is a marked moment of silence between them, or between the movements of a symphony or any other large, integrated musical work. When in doubt, do not applaud until a conductor turns and faces the audience, or, if a soloist pauses briefly, wait for the lead of others in the audience before starting to applaud.

In this country, it is not our custom to boo, no matter how poor a performance may be. Instead, American audiences give only desultory applause. However, good manners in this country do call for at least a show of clapping hands from patrons in the front rows when bows are being taken. Music patrons are notably more vociferous in applause than are theater patrons, and cries of "Bravo," and so on, are occasionally heard. They are correct, if somewhat conspicuous.

**Sacred Music.** When sacred music is performed in a house of worship, it is *never* applauded even if given as a concert and not as part of a religious service.

Even if performed in an auditorium or concert hall, major sacred works like the *Messiah* and the Bach B minor Mass and *St. Matthew Passion* are not applauded during or after the performance. The first entrance of the conductor, the orchestra, and the choir may be applauded, though frequently this applause, too, is omitted.

Sometimes when such organizations as the Bach Aria Group give a concert, the soloists and the chorus are applauded after single numbers and at the end of the performance. And it is correct to applaud a sacred work that is interspersed among secular pieces in a recital.

**ENCORES.** A symphony orchestra practically never gives an encore, and so the audience evidences its pleasure by prolonged applause without actually shouting "Encore." At informal concerts and in small halls an ensemble may occasionally give an encore at the end of the program, but it is not usual to request an encore before that time. Soloists quite frequently will respond to the call for an encore before the intermission. As a general rule, the flattering demand for encores is saved for the end of a recital. On extremely rare occasions an artist will respond to insistent calls of "Encore" (or "Bis," which means the same) immediately following an exceptionally brilliant rendition of a number, but it is considered better musical manners for the audience not to interrupt the program in this fashion. At a proper time for encores, the performer usually offers a number or numbers of his own choice, though the audience may call for a repetition of any short item or something else in his repertoire.

**ENTERING AND SEATING.** Every effort should be made to be seated before a concert begins. At a private concert or recital, guests who arrive late wait for the end of a number before finding seats unless they can slip into a back row. At public concerts, frequently the doors are closed before the first number begins, and patrons who are late are made to cool their laggard heels until it is finished.

**FLOWERS.** As a general rule, flowers are not sent to a male soloist in the United States, though quite frequently a European artist making a concert appearance in this country will receive some bouquets from friends who know the customs in his native country.

When a great star gives a concert, flowers may or may not be presented over the footlights. That decision is made by the artist or her manager, who may direct that bouquets be delivered to her dressing room instead.

At smaller recitals, and especially when a woman artist is making her professional debut, it is the pretty custom to accept flowers over the footlights.

Flowers delivered to a concert hall are taken out of their boxes and wrappings under supervision of the head usher or some other employee of the house, who sees to it that the card of the donor is attached to the bouquet. Usually, just before the intermission, ushers bear the flowers down the aisles (though, at the discretion of the artist, delivery in this fashion may be made at the end of the concert). If there are great quantities of flowers, the ushers or backstage attendants help to place them attractively. Baskets are banked at the sides of the stage. Sheaves and smaller bouquets are left on the piano (unless the artist is a pianist) when she makes her exit at intermission, and the flowers remain in place during the second half of the recital. Since the piano is open during a piano recital, sheaves of flowers are carried off at intermission.

**LEAVING.** It is considered a marked rudeness to both performers and fellow patrons to leave during a number. Anyone who needs or wishes to leave before the end of a concert waits for the end of a piece or slips out quickly and quietly between the movements of a long composition.

## CONDIMENTS AND RELISHES

In general, the word "seasonings" is used for substances added during cooking to heighten the flavor of a food, and "condiments" is used for the many highly flavored items served separately as an accompaniment to, rather than a part of, a cooked dish. Catsup, mustard, chutney, Worcestershire, and other bottled sauces, and horseradish, capers, chopped pickles, and tart jellies are classed as condiments. The word "relishes" is widely used to cover all condiments, as well as other less highly flavored side dishes—radishes, spring onions, olives, celery sticks, and whole pickles, for example.

Condiments and relishes are one of the great pleasures of the table and are an important part of any festive meal except the most formal. Usually, they are in place on the table before guests are seated. After the main-course plates are in place, guests pass the condiment dishes along and each helps himself, or a maid may bring in one or several and offer them to each diner individually.

Condiment dishes—bowls or compotes—may be of silver, china, cut glass, crystal, or pottery, as long as they match the rest of the dinner service in general style.

Condiments are not served in the bottles in which they are bought except under the most informal circumstances. Worcestershire sauce is served in a plain, small decanter, and catsup in a bowl. For entirely informal meals such as cookouts, condiment bottles may be put on the outdoor tables.

All condiments are put on the main plate, not the butter plate, and beside the other foods, not on top of them. Olives, whole pickles, and the fresh vegetables that rate as relishes are put on the butter plate.

Condiment and relish dishes are removed before dessert is served.

## CONDOLENCES

At no time are brevity and restraint more valuable than in speaking words of sympathy to someone who has suffered a major sorrow. It is much kinder to show sympathy in practical ways than add to the emotional strains of a bereaved person by dwelling at length on the loss and its details. A very few words, like "I'm so sorry," or no more than a handclasp is easier on everyone than a long speech or a series of questions.

A call of condolence should be short (see FUNERALS for details), and the bereaved person is not expected to return it.

A message of condolence should be sent as promptly as possible. The easiest to write—and read—are the shortest and simplest. All that is really needed is something like "I am thinking of you with tenderest sympathy." Such a message sent promptly is nearly always far more solacing than a long letter much delayed. A letter of condolence should be handwritten unless it is from someone who is writing in a business capacity as a representative of a firm. It is never correct to express sympathy by sending a commercially printed "greeting" card.

A message of condolence, whether flowers or a note, should be answered in due course. Again, all that is required in most cases is a line or so saying something like "Thank you for your kind message."

**CONFIDENCES.**  *See* SECRETS.

## CONFIRMATIONS

A confirmation is an important milestone, but unlike some other religious ceremonies, it is not usually followed by any social celebration beyond perhaps a small gathering for a family meal honoring the event. Parents, grandparents, and godparents (if any) customarily give a child a confirmation present, and of course anyone else who has the kindly impulse may send a present or a note or printed card of congratulation. Presents are usually something of a religious nature or something suitable to wear to church, rather than toys, candy, or other frivolous secular items. It is not usual to invite friends of other faiths to a confirmation ceremony unless there is some special reason to do so.

## CONGRATULATIONS

Congratulations are in order for any happy event, always provided that one person's good fortune is not due entirely to another's ill luck. A man may be fulsomely congratulated on his great luck in winning a sweepstakes prize—but certainly not on a promotion that came to him automatically because his chief suffered an accident, for example.

The timing and manner of giving and receiving congratulations depend on the feelings of others who may be involved. Traditionally, the loser in a game of any kind congratulates the winner on his skill, never on his good luck. But the winner accepts the congratulations only by commiserating with the loser on his bad luck. Unrestrained joyous congratulations to the winner are thoughtless within the hearing of the loser, most especially if a prize or promotion is involved. Good sportsmanship requires the loser to hide his disappointment as best he can and to offer his congratulations to the winner promptly and gallantly, without making excuses for his failure.

Custom bans the use of the word "congratulations" under certain specific circumstances. It is never correct to say "Congratulations" to a woman on the occasion of her engagement or marriage, since the word implies that she has achieved success after a long, hard campaign. Even though that may be the fact, the fiction is maintained that it is the man who has wooed and at last won. It is correct to say "Congratulations" to him, but the proper words for the bride are "Best wishes for your happiness." Her parents are not congratulated in so many words either—that might seem to imply that by luck and persistent effort they have finally succeeded in finding her a husband.

**CONGRESSMEN.**  *See* FORMS OF ADDRESS (Government).

**CONSOMME.**  *See* SOUPS.

**CONTRADICTIONS.**  *See* CHILDREN AND MANNERS; CONVERSATION.

**CONVENTIONS.**  *See* BUSINESS MANNERS.

## CONVERSATION

*"For good or ill, your conversation is your advertisement. Every time you open your mouth you let men look into your mind."—Bruce Barton*

Conversation, according to Webster, is "oral exchange of sentiments, observations, opinions, ideas." By this definition, "You said it!" in answer to "Hot enough for you?" rates as a conversation, and so does a name-calling quarrel.

Good conversation is a different matter—fenced in as it is with special restrictions. Some subjects are banned at certain times and places—the cost of food and the details of illnesses at the table, for example. Other subjects, dealt with below under "Dangerous Topics," are safe among intimates but are real booby traps in general conversation. Our conventions forbid certain direct questions. We have well-established ground rules about interruptions. And overriding all other aspects of good conversation is the vast difference between "talking to" and "talking with," neatly stated by one kindergartener: "Talking is when you do all of it. Conversation is when you listen in between."

**Rules in General.** Everyday conversation is largely an exchange of experiences and reactions. Since the rules for "listening in between" can be applied across the board, from jokes to the discussion of a philosophical concept, no one who observes the following guidelines can go far wrong:

Suit the length of a story to the occasion. Don't launch into a long one if a series of interruptions is inevitable—to a hostess, for example, when she is trying to answer the doorbell, make introductions, and get dinner on the table all at the same time.

Don't make a group a captive audience by repeating a story from the beginning for the benefit of one newcomer or by telling a long tale that can be of interest to only the few members of a group familiar with the person or event.

Don't "draw out" anyone by insisting that he tell a story if he shows reluctance to do so. He may have a good reason for refusing at that particular time in that particular company.

Think twice before making a flippant reference to death, funerals, a physical handicap, or subnormal mentality. There is always the possibility that a careless wisecrack will add to the burden of someone touched by a tragedy he keeps to himself.

Consider everyone within earshot—servants, bystanders, and companions—and if there is a shadow of doubt about the suitability of a topic, skip it.

"Are you old enough to hear a dirty story?" is a question asked only by those old enough to know better because there is no good answer—No is stuffy, Yes endorses off-color humor, and silence gives consent.

Checking the acceptability of a story with a question like "'Is anyone here a Christian Scientist?" is always ill-advised. That query not only reveals the speaker as willing to make sport of members of a special group behind their backs; it leaves him no graceful way out if someone says, "*I* am."

Many stories dealing with race, color, or creed are funny and harmless in themselves. However, the person in step with our changing manners is increasingly wary about jokes concerning Mandy and Mose, Izzy and Abe, the two preachers, and so on. In today's world, gags that carry national, racial, or religious prejudice are out of style, if nothing else. There is one exception. A Scotsman, for example, can tell as stinging a joke as he likes about the fabled thriftiness of his fellow countrymen, since by implication he is telling the joke on himself.

Also, think twice about telling an anecdote, no matter how amusing, that shows up someone as inept or idiotic—especially someone who is present. Leave the hilarious tales of others' mistakes and mischances for them to tell on themselves.

Avoid the meaningless command "Stop me if you're heard this." No one will. And don't be in a hurry to say Yes when someone asks, "Have you heard the one about . . .?" Unless the story is out of line in the present company, let the teller and other listeners have their fun. Especially, don't kill the point by bursting in with the tag line before the speaker can say it.

Resist the impulse to interrupt. Ambrose Bierce went to the heart of this matter with his definition of a bore: "A person who talks when you wish him to listen." When there must be a choice, let the other person be the bore.

And don't forget that possibly the most engaging words in our language are "What do *you* think?"

**CONTRADICTIONS AND CORRECTIONS.** On rather rare occasions, it is the clear responsibility of someone sure of a fact to contradict a misstatement that could be troublemaking later if allowed to go unchallenged, though corrections in front of others are always risky to a degree. The trick is to put the speaker straight by some face-saving words. "That's not true!" may be true, but it is all wrong if it turns a discussion into a quarrel or brings it to a stiff stop. And it does not take a psychiatrist to tell what is wrong with the eager correcter of inconsequential details ("No, dear! She spilled her *tea*, not her *coffee*"). Equally suspect is the person who must gain status by cutting others down to size—the walking reference shelf, ever ready to correct pronunciation, grammar, fact, and manners under the guise of helpfulness. It is certainly sensible, if it will save a friend future embarrassment, to slip in a casual correction of a mispronounced place name, for example. But, in the main such interruptions show up the speaker as correct—except in manners, imagination, and good conversational sense.

**DANGEROUS TOPICS.** No topic is dangerous in itself in its proper time and place. And no topic is dangerous so long as everyone involved in a conversation knows how to stay on the right side of the line that differentiates discussion and argument. Therefore, such strictures as "Never discuss politics or religion" are valid only for (and with) those who can see only one side of a question and who feel that a difference of opinion is an all-out assault on their taste, judgment, sense, or logic—though any subject more controversial than the weather is potentially dangerous with these touchy souls, anyway.

Certain subjects have rightly earned the label "dangerous," however, because it takes luck as well as diplomacy to deal with them deftly enough to avoid their inherent hazards.

**Advice.** Oscar Wilde's opinion is worth remembering when that impulse to say "If I were you . . ." turns up: "It is always a silly thing to give advice, but to give good advice is absolutely fatal."

**Age.** In some primitive cultures, the tribesman who neglects to ask the stranger "How old are you?" shows himself sadly lacking in social polish. But in our world, the whole subject of age is better avoided in general conversation. Too many people are sensitive, for one reason or another, about their years, and are acutely uncomfortable if the age of any other adult is discussed.

**Gossip.** There is a narrow margin for error between genuine interest in other people and their problems and gossip for its own sake. The gossip who blabs all he knows or passes along all he hears is, in a backhanded way, as egocentric as the person who can talk only of himself. He is playing a subtle, dual game—showing himself superior to his audience by having a juicy piece of inside information, and superior to the subject of the gossip as well, if the item has an edge of malice.

It is not easy to deal with indiscreet gossip without sounding pompous. About the only good way to deflate a rumor-monger is an offhand "Don't tell me you believe *that*!" or "How do you *know?*" It is interesting how often the gossip who claims, "I know it for a fact because one of my best friends actually saw . . ." will be unable to produce the name of that friend.

"Can you keep a secret?" is a fair warning of danger if the speaker is passing along any secret but one of his own. His question makes it apparent that he, for one, cannot—and had better not be trusted with any confidence in return.

**Money.** Money talks—no doubt of it; but it is generally wiser to let it speak for itself in its own eloquent silence and skip all price-tag discussion unless the emphasis is kept strictly on consumer problems in general. There are countless money matters, from rising taxes to bargain sales, that can be freely discussed, but direct questions about costs or income are almost invariably out of line. "Is Bobby on a scholarship?" "What rent do you pay?" "How much was your bonus?" and so on fully deserve no answer at all or any other frank snub.

**Politics and Religion.** Discussion of these absorbing topics is safe for those who remember Bernard Baruch's statement of belief about freedom of speech: "Every man has a right to his own opinion, but no man has a right to be wrong in his facts"—and also the Articles of our Constitution that guarantee every citizen the right to worship and vote as he pleases.

**INTERRUPTIONS.** There is a fine line between the interrupting questions of the truly interested listener and the compulsive interruptions of people who cannot bear to stay out of the conversational spotlight even briefly. Those in the first category keep conversation alive. Those in the second reduce talk to fragmented chitchat.

"I know I'm interrupting, but . . ." is generally no excuse for breaking in except when it is necessary to add a point that is valid at that time and no other, or when the speaker needs to be steered away from dangerous ground. An interruption that completely changes the subject is something to pay attention to, however. It may be the work of a conversational featherhead. Or it may be the protective hint of a social lifesaver, aware that the talk is taking an embarrassing turn.

The most important thing about a necessary interruption is its timing. Nothing is more disconcerting to a speaker just about to end a story with the tag line that gives it its point than the hostess who rushes away to answer a bell on its first ring. The speaker with his wits about him finishes fast or comes to a pause. But the listener owes him the split second he needs to do so.

**PERSONAL REMARKS.**  *See* COMPLIMENTS.

**QUESTIONS AND ANSWERS.** Widely promoted as an unmatched way to win friends is the attitude expressed in the magic words "Now let's talk about *you.*" Most people need little if any encouragement in that direction, provided that they are not made to feel cross-examined by a rapid fire of direct questions.

"Do you mind if I ask a personal question?" is an empty query. All it does is emphasize that the speaker knows he is invading forbidden territory and is willing to risk trespassing anyway. It also is not a fair question because there is no polite way to say No, and therefore evading an answer is doubly awkward. A more subtle way to ask a forbidden question is to volunteer a parallel fact— "I'm making two hundred a week," or "I'll be thirty-seven on my next birthday," for example. However, such confidences are no more than probing personal questions in flimsy disguise, and anyone who wants to is privileged to say "Really?"—and let it go at that. There is no law of manners that says a direct and unduly personal question need be answered, either. Depending on whether the question was thoughtlessly or deliberately indiscreet, the answer can be anything from "I'll leave you guessing," to silence—with silence and an accompanying smile or shrug to take off the sting probably being the most useful, adaptable of meaning, and impeccable way to deal with the problem question.

A nosy question about a third person's concerns is harder to sidetrack. If "I don't know" is obviously untrue, something like "Why don't you ask him yourself?"—though a snub—is a lesser evil than talking out of turn. In this connection, Calvin Coolidge's statement of policy is worth remembering; "You don't have to explain what you don't say."

As a general rule, a flat Yes or No is taboo, especially in answers to and from children, employees, salespeople, and strangers. By the rules of courtesy, something needs to be added—a name or a few words, as in "I'm sorry, no," or "Yes, I did." Children pick up this elementary rule of good conversational manners quickly if their parents observe it when speaking to them. An employee also falls easily into the habit of giving what she gets and answering by the same polite formula.

**SPEECH AND VOCABULARY.** Words and the way they are pronounced quickly reveal far more than their actual meaning. There are linguistic experts who can spot the home town of a speaker after hearing him say a few sentences. Social as well as general geographical background is almost as readily revealed to any listener.

One of the great charms of American speech is the difference in regional accents and certain local expressions and turns of phrase. Except for those who are training for careers in radio, television, the movies, or the stage, there is no point whatever in remodeling a regional accent or vocabulary drastically. There is, however, every reason to try for distinct pronunciation, modulated tone of voice, and the choice of words that represents the best of local use.

Self-betterment is one of the strongest of American drives. A desire to improve their financial, social, or political status brought the ancestors of all of us here, whether they came long ago, complete with vast grants of land, or yesterday, with little more than they could carry. We are all equal in that. Therefore, it is in the best American tradition to improve one's speech by weeding out the so-called "problem" words that, among other tremendous trifles of behavior, label a speaker as unaware of today's best customs.

Leading the list are the words that reveal the speaker as trying too hard, in one way or another, to impress the listener with his refinement. These include overly delicate, "genteel" words and phrases like "in the family way" and "in an interesting condition" instead of "pregnant" or "having a baby"; "expectorate" instead of "spit"; "lavatory" for a bathroom at home; and the pretentious or otherwise affected word instead of a familiar short one—"purchase" and "acquire" for "buy"; "reside at" instead of "live at" "ascertain" instead of "find out"; "launder" instead of "wash"; "desire to" instead of "want to"; "made her acquaintance" instead of "met"; and such gobbledygook as "finalize an undertaking" instead of "finish a job."

Some clichés are useful as a sort of verbal shorthand, but the overuse of phrases that have become hackneyed, or meaningless so far as their once-apt reference is concerned, puts them also on the "problem" list. Put it this way: "Getting down to brass tacks about clichés, anyone is apt to get a cold shoulder unless he runs like a rabbit to avoid them like the plague." The same applies to the overuse of the slang words that are a delightful part of a living, growing language. One slang word can often serve as a vivid, amusing substitute for a stuffy long description, but as in all other matters of behavior, too far out is *out*.

There is another whole group of words that are just plain wrong—not in themselves, but by our conventions—when they are used in certain specific connections. These include words popularized by inventive merchants—"drapes" instead of "curtains," and "hosiery" instead of "stockings—" as well as the words that can unintentionally injure the feelings of a listener if misused. The difference between "lady" and "woman" is one example. The wrong choice can imply that a woman is no lady.

See LADY AND WOMAN.

For other examples, see Problem Words in the Index.

## COOKIES

When served at the table, or at tea when a plate is provided, cookies are taken from the serving platter and put first on the plate, not directly into the mouth. Small cookies are eaten in one or two bites. Big cookies at table are broken and eaten in small pieces rather than in a series of bites from the whole cookie.

Cookies are put on the edge of a dessert plate, not on the tablecloth, when served with ice cream or a similar dessert.

## CORN

Corn on the cob is taken from the serving platter in the fingers unless tongs are provided, and put on the main plate, not the butter plate. If small silver or pottery handles are used, they are best inserted in the kitchen rather than at table. Fixing them firmly into a steaming ear of corn is all but impossible without the aid of a napkin, and the table napkin is not properly used for this purpose.

Butter is put on the butter plate. The butter knife is used to spread it on the ear. The dinner knife is used only if butter plate and knife are not provided. A whole ear is not buttered at one time, since this almost guarantees a buttery chin.

An ear of corn may be broken in two or left in one piece. The corn is lifted in both hands, and nibbles usually are taken down the length of the ear because it is easier to control the dripping of butter by this method.

Cobs are left on the main plate, not put on a butter plate. When second helpings are offered, a discard dish for cobs is almost a necessity. It may be passed by a maid or from guest to guest.

Anyone who finds corn on the cob too difficult to eat is privileged to cut it off at the table.

Creamed corn is often served in side dishes at so-called home-style restaurants and at informal family meals.

**CORRECTIONS.**  See CHILDREN AND MANNERS; CONVERSATION.

## CORRESPONDENCE

The rules concerning *formal* social communications such as engraved invitations are explicit and should be followed exactly. They are given in detail under IN-VITATIONS. The rules relating to all other social correspondence—from Christmas cards to telegrams—are also standardized, though many variations are usual and allowable. Following are the major guidelines for personal notes and letters.

(*Note:* See also CORRESPONDENCE, BUSINESS, following, for certain procedures standard in business letters that also are the first choice in personal mail—the lengthy list of official abbreviations of the names of states, for example.)

### ADDRESSES ON ENVELOPES

**Abbreviations.** Contractions like "St.," "Blvd.," and "Ave." and of state names like "Conn." and "Ill." are always wrong in formal correspondence. Though not the best choice in the day-to-day run of personal letters and notes, they are risky rather than wrong, and are widely used. However, when possible without crowding a line, write such words out fully. Otherwise, make sure that an abbreviation is not so carelessly scribbled that the postman cannot tell if a letter is to go to Mass. or Miss., N.J. or N.Y.

**Names and Titles.** It is extremely poor form to omit the title of a girl or adult on an envelope and direct a letter to Margaret Brown or John Jones. A title of some kind must be used on all mail except to a boy.

"Master" is correctly used to a boy under twelve, though many people today consider it a bit stilted. His name without a title is equally correct and more often used. If the rules are strictly followed, a boy's name is written without "Mr." until he is eighteen—but so many people compliment boys of high school age by promoting them to "Mr." in correspondence that this rule can be broken without a second thought. *See* NAMES for the use of "Junior," "Senior," "Second," and so on.

A girl rates "Miss" on her mail from the day she is born. It is a real mistake to omit her title on any mail addressed to her.

"Messrs." is an abbreviation of the French *Messieurs,* and means "Misters." It is correctly used on personal letters only to brothers, not to a father and son. (Only in a business letter is it correctly used to a father and son and to unrelated men.) The envelope may be addressed "The Messrs. Brown," "Messrs. Brown," or "Messrs. John and Charles Brown." "Messrs." is rarely used today. It is far more usual, when a communication is addressed jointly to two men who live under the same roof, to write each name on a separate line, with the name of the older one first:

Mr. John Brown
Mr. Charles Brown

"Esq." (always abbreviated) is correct though seldom used in this country as a substitute for "Mr." (John Jones, Esq.) except to lawyers. It is never used with any other title preceding the name, or in a signature.

A professional title is used before a name in personal correspondence (Dr. John Jones). John Jones, M.D., is restricted to business correspondence. *See* FORMS OF ADDRESS for the rules governing the use of military, governmental, and other titles.

By the standard rules, mail is never correctly addressed to a widow, divorcée, or married woman with "Mrs." and her given name (Mrs. Mary Brown). However, this is a rule that is changing with great rapidity. *See* NAMES.

It is customary to address a letter written jointly to a married couple to the wife, but equally correct to address such a letter to "Mr. and Mrs. George Brown," which guarantees that the husband will feel free to open the letter if his wife is out of town.

Using a nickname or diminutive on an envelope is not correct in formal correspondence—an engraved invitation, for example—but otherwise is a matter of the writer's choice.

**Punctuation.** It is today's fashion to omit commas at the end of lines and to use punctuation within a line only if needed for clarity. A period is used after any abbreviation.

**Return Addresses.** A return address should be used on all mail, formal and informal. On personal letter paper, the standard place for a printed return address is the flap of the envelope. It is not incorrect to write the return address on the flap. But that placement adds considerably to the troubles of the postman when a letter must be returned to the sender, and so, by first choice, the return address is written at the upper left on the face of the envelope.

Clearly written abbreviations are correct in return addresses, and city, state, and zip code are properly written on the same line.

It is not necessary to use a name in a return address if the sender does not care to identify himself on the outside of a letter. An address alone can be used, or initials, or an apartment number. Sometimes used, though quite informal, is the last name only: Jones (handwritten, not printed).

"Mr." is not used before a man's name in a return address, written or printed, but if the return address is printed, a military or other professional title is correctly used. A woman's name is preceded by "Miss" or "Mrs."

Tiny printed stickers carrying the return address are a convenience, and many people use them on all run-of-the-desk mail, but they are not the best choice on formal engraved announcements and invitations.

**Standard Forms.** Any arrangement that looks attractive, does not crowd the envelope, and leaves plenty of empty space for a forwarding address, should it be needed, is correct, but the following, typed or handwritten, are the most usual ones:

```
R. J. Jones
130 Montgomery St.
Chester, Pa. 00000
```

```
                    Mr. George Greene
                     210 Ridge Road
                       Westchester
                       Ohio 00000
```

```
Mrs. M. S. Smith
16 Fifth Avenue
New York, N.Y. 00000
```

```
                    Mrs. Henry Stanton
                    2714 Brooke Boulevard
                    Andersonville, Utah 00000
```

**BASIC LETTER FORMS.** The form of a social letter depends to some degree on the shape and size of the paper and what imprinting there may be on the first sheet.

**Address and Date.** The writer's address should be placed somewhere on a letter itself, unless the letter is to someone who knows the address so well that to give it would be an absurdity. A printed address can be spaced and placed in any way at the top of the first sheet. The usual place for a handwritten address is at the upper right of the first sheet with the date on a separate line below it, but either or both can be put on the last page. The important thing is to give the date somewhere—and clearly. There is no rule banning the use of only the day—"Tuesday," for example—but that is usually a poor choice. If the postmark is smudged and the letter must be forwarded or is otherwise delayed in reaching its destination, the recipient may be completely baffled as to which Tuesday is indicated. The best choices are "March 12" or "Jan. 4, 1967" (abbreviations of months are correct in personal notes and letters). To be avoided is the form 2/5/67 because, at some later date, who can be positive whether the letter was written on the second of May or the fifth of February?

**Openings and Closings.** The standard opening salutation of a personal letter is "Dear George" or "Dear Mr. Smith." The use of "My" before the salutation has a special meaning. Though logic indicates that the reverse should be true, the fact remains that "My dear Mr. Smith" is both more formal and stiffer than "Dear Mr. Smith." Therefore, "My" should be used only to a stranger or someone with whom the acquaintanceship is both slight and on an extremely formal level. "My dear John" is not correct, since the formal, distant "My" combined with a first name is a contradiction in itself. "My darling John" is a different matter, of course.

There is a good deal of latitude in the choice of the complimentary closing for a personal letter. All of the following are common, according to the degree of intimacy intended: "Sincerely," "Yours sincerely," "Very sincerely yours," "Affectionately," "Devotedly," "With love," "Dearest love," and so on. "Faithfully," "Gratefully," and "Most appreciatively" are useful when applicable, and "As always" can be either fraught with tender meaning or sound forgivingly patient, depending on the content of the letter.

It is a minor point, but if the rules are followed, any variant of "Very truly yours" is reserved for business correspondence.

"Cordially" is correct, though it sounds a bit patronizing to some people, and it is not appropriately used from a younger to a much older person.

"Respectfully" is to be avoided, since it is correct only in a very few cases. A *formal* letter to the President of the United States or to an extremely high-ranking member of the clergy is signed "Respectfully" (see FORMS OF ADDRESS for details), but an informal personal note (an invitation, for example) to such dignitaries is closed with the standard "Very sincerely yours" or some other appropriate closing. Otherwise, "Respectfully" is used only by a domestic employee to an employer or a tradesman to a customer—and today it is considered a little old-fashioned in even these cases.

**Punctuation.** In a typewritten letter, the salutation in personal mail is followed by a comma (not a colon, semicolon, or dash). In a handwritten letter, either a comma or a dash is correct.

**Sequence of Pages.** This is a matter of little importance, the only necessity being to number the pages if there would be confusion as to the sequence.

**Signatures.** A title is never written before a letter signature. A married woman signs all her letters, whether to the principal of a school, a department store, or a social acquaintance, with "Mary Smith" or "Mary Brown Smith." If she needs to make her marital status clear or indicate the way an answer should be addressed, she adds in parentheses under her signature (Mrs. Robert Smith). A man or an unmarried woman with a name given to both girls and boys (Shirley, Leslie, and so on) adds in parentheses (Mr.) or (Miss) before the signature, if needed. Otherwise, a signature can be anything from a single initial to a nickname, depending on the circumstances, but it should be handwritten, never typed.

**GREETING CARDS.** Printed cards carrying good wishes for birthdays and other special occasions are widely used and are a correct shortcut to the communication of congratulations and other happy messages. However, printed messages to express sympathy after a death or thanks for entertainment are not correct. In these cases, any kind of message—handwritten, typed, or spoken—is better than a printed sentiment.

*See* CHRISTMAS for the correct use of names on envelopes and the sequence of names in signatures for all cards of holiday greetings.

**HANDWRITING AND TYPING.** One custom in personal correspondence has changed very rapidly in recent years. Today, virtually all social letters may be typed—and a splendid thing this is for all concerned, including the postman.

Handwriting is still required—no argument—in a formal answer to a formal third-person invitation. It also must be used for all messages written on social calling cards and engraved fold-over cards, and is decidedly the first choice for brief notes of invitation and the answers to them. It is still customary today, but not absolutely obligatory, to use handwriting in notes of apology and particularly of condolence. But far, far more important than the form of such letters is the prompt dispatching of them.

Handwriting that is first of all legible and then attractively placed on both paper and envelope is a major requirement in social correspondence. A scrawl difficult to read indicates a careless haste that is, in itself, a small breach of good manners. Handwriting that is individual in character is an asset, but such childish affections as enormous capitals, exaggeratedly long loops, and circles instead of dots and periods are best discouraged in the very young before they become a habit.

**INK.** Following the development of felt-nibbed pens, brilliant inks emerged as high fashion for personal correspondence. Today the use of bright papers and inks is a matter of personal style and is no longer banned as either childish or too flashy for good taste. The conservative choice is still toward muted shades of letter paper and darker shades of ink, but there is no longer anything utterly "wrong" about rainbow colors in personal letters. Black and blue-black ink are still correct for formal invitations and announcements—but in our changing world, this may well change too.

**INVITATIONS.** The special rules governing the style and format of formal and informal invitations are given in detail in the extensive separate section INVITATIONS.

**LETTERS (Special Problems and Forms).**

**Anonymous.** An anonymous letter that contains any kind of disturbing news or comment is not only bad taste; it is the work of a coward—or psychopath. Anyone who wants to call names should be willing to identify himself with a signature and take the consequences.

**Bread and Butter.** In some parts of the country, it is customary to write (or telephone) thanks to the hostess after any meal. This is a pleasant courtesy but not a standard requirement. By the rules, a guest's thanks on departure are sufficient.

After an overnight visit, however, some kind of written message of thanks must be sent as soon as possible. Five days is the limit of delay before sending a "bread-and-butter" letter, if the rules are followed. This kind of letter may be either handwritten or typed. It is written to the hostess, not to the couple jointly, and should be written by the wife of a visiting couple. If a child has been an overnight guest without his parents, the child writes to his hostess. His mother does also if the child is very young, and usually does as a courtesy after a teen-ager has been a houseguest. A commercially printed card of thanks is not correct.

A letter is not necessary, of course, if a card with "Thank you for a wonderful time" written on it is sent promptly with flowers or some other thank-you present.

**Condolence.** Long letters of sympathy to people who have suffered a great loss are hard to write, but a brief note is actually all that is needed—if it is sent promptly. A message that says no more than "All my thoughts are with you in deepest sympathy" nearly always serves far better than a longer one—no matter how beautifully written—that is long delayed. A note of condolence is best handwritten; commercially printed cards are not correct.

**Dangerous Mail.** All letters have a built-in hazard. Often, a writer knows so well what he means to say that he does not notice that his words have a second meaning, quite different from his intent, which can lead to a misunderstanding. This is the reason love letters so often sound indiscreet—they inadvertently imply more intimacy than is the fact. Since any letter can fall into the wrong hands, the good old rule is worth remembering: Write nothing that if read by a third person would damage the reputation of a woman—or of anyone else, for that matter.

A letter dashed off in anger is also dangerous. Write it, by all means. But wait a day or so before mailing it. For one thing, an apology or explanation may be in the mail. In any case, harsh words on paper can never be recalled, and they can make it hard to arrive at the working social armistice that may well be necessary later on.

**Introduction.** It is correct to ask for a letter of business introduction, but it is never correct to ask in so many words for a letter of social introduction. It is also incorrect, in most cases, to give a slight acquaintance a letter of social introduction to a close friend because a letter of introduction implies two things most definitely: a social endorsement of the person introduced, and a positive request (which cannot politely be ignored) to entertain or otherwise sponsor the person introduced.

When a letter is given directly to the person being introduced, it is handed over in an unsealed envelope, which the recipient should seal immediately. He does not correctly read the enclosed letter before sealing the envelope. The writer then should telephone or write to his other friend to explain that a note of introduction will be presented, and give further details that may be necessary or useful.

Very often, this order is reversed. The person making the introduction writes first to an out-of-town friend to explain that So-and-So is arriving in his locality and to suggest that it would be pleasant for everyone if a meeting could be arranged. This gives the recipient a chance to say that he is leaving on a holiday or to dodge the obligation in some other fashion—or to answer that it will be a pleasure to meet the visitor. In the latter case, a letter of introduction is then sent (unsealed) to the person who will present it, along with a covering note giving him any necessary or pertinent details.

Letters of introduction impulsively pressed on a traveler can sometimes be a burden instead of a benefit—particularly if his visit in another city will be brief and busy. When this is the case, the traveler need feel under no obligation to present the letter, though the standard polite procedure is to take time for a telephone call, explain the pressures on his time, and express regrets that a meeting cannot be arranged.

The person given a letter of introduction generally does not hand it over directly to the addressee—unless it is obviously inconvenient to do otherwise. The usual procedure is for the bearer to telephone and let plans for a meeting develop during the conversation, or mail the letter of introduction shortly after arrival, with a covering note saying that a telephone call will follow.

Under all circumstances, anyone who is given a letter of introduction is expected to make some kind of report to the writer—even if it is no more than, "My visit was cut short and I didn't have a chance to see your friends."

**Reference.** The writer of a letter of reference has a dual responsibility: to be kind and fair to the employee to whom it is given; and not to mislead any prospective employer to whom it will be shown. Examples of how this delicate balance can be maintained are given under HOUSEHOLD EMPLOYEES.

**MEMOS.** It is quite common practice to sign messages left for domestic employees, the milkman, and others in similar positions with "Mrs. [or Mr. or Miss] Smith"; but if the standard rule is followed, a title is not used. Instead, both a man and woman uses one or more initials with the last name (M. J. Brown) or initials only (M. J. B.).

**PERSONAL.** A social letter sent to a business address is properly marked "Personal" as an indication to a secretary that it is not to be opened with the general run of office mail, and of course a letter so marked should never be opened by anyone except the addressee. However, it is a breach of etiquette to mark a letter sent to a home address "Personal," since this would give the insulting implication that members of the addressee's family were suspected of opening private mail.

**POSTAGE.** All social letters are sent first class or by airmail—no exceptions.

**POSTCARDS.** The same rules as for writing a name and address on a letter are followed. Outside of this, a postcard is completely informal. Anything goes, so long as the message will not embarrass the recipient if read by the postman, maid, or anyone else who may happen on it. No salutation is necessary, though one may be used of course. It is a good idea to date a postcard because postmarks are so frequently smudged or undecipherable. A postcard need not be signed if there will be no possible doubt as to the identity of the sender, but it is usually best to add some identifying name or initials. Too many travelers baffle their friends with "Wish you were here" messages signed only with an initial or "Ann," "Bill," or some other common name.

**READING OTHERS' MAIL.** A letter is the private property of the person to whom it is addressed; and opening someone else's letter or reading an opened one is just as much an invasion of privacy as opening the door of a private room without knocking.

**SEALING WAX.** Sealing wax is out of style because it is hard enough today to find time to answer letters—let alone to decorate them in this fashion.

**SEALS AND STICKERS.** The stamplike seals and stickers distributed by charitable organizations during fund-raising campaigns can be used to seal the flap of an envelope, but should not be stuck on the front. They are correctly used on any mail except formal announcements and invitations.

**STATIONERY.** Every detail of a letter reflects the writer's personality, and nothing speaks more emphatically or quickly than attractive—or unattractive—writing paper. Recently there has been a big change in the long-established rules of good taste in personal correspondence. Gone is the day when the only "correct" paper was white, off-white, and palid tints of gray, buff, and washed-out blue, with even pale green suspect and pink considered impossible. The best way to come to a decision about personal writing paper is to look at the sample books that any good stationer has on display. They show a wide range of lovely colors imprinted with vivid inks. They are expensive, and not for the conservative, but they are in good taste today if they suit the individuality of the user. Single sheets are the most popular today for both men and women for all general correspondence.

**Children.** Notepaper of their very own sometimes make it a bit easier to persuade children to write those thank-you notes that everyone has to learn to send. Almost anything goes in letter paper for very little children. It can be a pastel color and decorated with printed designs, an initial, first name or nickname. The babyishly tiny sizes are not a good choice, though, because it is hard for someone learning to write to confine his royal scrawl to doll-size paper.

**Correspondence Cards.** A correspondence card is not to be confused with the personal postcard. It is a piece of heavy paper or board that fits an envelope measuring about four by six inches or, for men, somewhat larger. It is popular with men for short notes, and is especially useful for invitations. If the name and address are engraved or printed on it, it can be used exactly as a visiting card or fold-over informal is used for invitations and replies—and of course is a more comfortable size for those and other messages.

Correspondence cards can be white or tinted, plain or decorated with a colored border, a monogram, heraldic device, or a little map showing the route to a country place. A name alone, or name, telephone number, and address are often used. The most conservative and formal correspondence cards are white or off-white engraved in black, but colored borders can be used even on these.

If the address is engraved or imprinted it is put in the upper right corner, not below the name as it would be on a visiting card or informal.

A standard form:

---

MU 8-6454                                45 EAST 52ND STREET


                 MR. AND MRS. TONY SMITH BELL

---

**Family Paper.** Many families today order one paper suitable for the use of all members of the household, including guests. Such paper carries only the address and perhaps the telephone number. When an address is used, it is today's custom to include city, state, and zip code. Printing can be set up in an attractive fashion along the top edge—or even run along one side as a border. The paper may be either a single or double fold that, folded once, fits an envelope somewhere close to four by six inches. Printing and paper can be any color, so long as they are not too extreme or too feminine for some members of the family. The envelopes are usually not lined unless the paper is airmail weight, though they may be.

**Men.** As a general rule, a man's personal writing paper is a single sheet a bit longer and wider than a woman's, though many men prefer a sheet that, folded once, fits its envelope, rather than the longer sheet that takes two folds. If a man's writing paper is printed or engraved, "Mr." never precedes his name. White, off-white, gray, and buff are the conservative choices, with printing in any fairly dark color. However, the break-through to color that men started some time ago with their pink shirts has now reached their letter paper. Pink paper is certainly not recommended, but men of taste now use papers in muted —or quite bright—shades of many colors, if they like, and there is a trend to vivid linings for envelopes. As a general rule, envelopes for a man's use are not lined unless they are airmail weight and lining is needed to conceal the message inside.

**Women.** Women whose personal correspondence is heavy find it practical to have two sizes of letter paper available—standard letter size that, folded once, fits an envelope in the general area of four by six inches, and, for shorter messages, a supply of double-fold notepaper that fits an envelope about four by five inches. There is quite a wide range in the size and shape of a woman's paper, and many women choose letter sheets that, folded once, fit a squarish envelope that can also be used for notepaper. Most popular today for both men and women are letter papers in single rather than double-fold sheets.

A woman can choose any color for paper and ink that pleases her, though the conservative choice for run-of-the-desk correspondence to Grandmother as well as the department store is white, off-white, gray, muted blue, or another light shade. However, today there is no limit to the bright shades of paper and ink, both for imprinting and writing, that a woman can use, if she fancies a striking and individual extension of her personality through the mail. Her latitude of choice is as wide as her choice of color in clothes—entirely a matter of what is most useful, becoming, and suitable.

Deckled edges are not popular today, and scalloped, metallic, or other fancy borders are to be avoided, though many lovely (and expensive) papers come with a narrow border of white or a deeper shade of color, and with lined envelopes.

For personal use, a woman's letter paper correctly carries her initials, a monogram, or her address—or it can be plain. On the envelope, she very often uses her initials or an apartment number rather than her full name, though she can use that if she likes. If she does, it is preceded by "Miss" or "Mrs." By the rules, a woman's name is imprinted only on a letter sheet that she uses mainly for business or professional use, but this rule is widely ignored because it is convenient to have the name spelled out properly on the top of the letter sheet. In this case, the first choice on the business or professional letter paper of a single woman is her name without "Miss." A married woman can also correctly use her given and last name without "Mrs." on her business or professional letter paper, but if she uses "Mrs.," her husband's name (not her given name) follows.

**TELEGRAMS.** All social telegrams are signed without a title, just as a letter would be. However, a woman signs a business telegram—a request for hotel reservations, for example—as she would a hotel register with "Miss" or "Mrs." Otherwise, a social telegram is worded much as a brief note would be.

**VISITING CARDS.** Visiting cards and engraved fold-over cards can be used instead of notepaper for invitations, their replies, and other brief messages. By Post Office ruling, they may not be mailed in envelopes less than $2^3/_4$ inches by 4 inches in size.

*See* VISITING CARDS for illustrations.

**ZIP CODE.** A zip code is part of every address, and should be used in addressing all mail, formal and informal.

# CORRESPONDENCE, BUSINESS

It would be hard to find the housewife, taxpayer, or student who does not have to dispatch a number of business letters each year. Collected here are the major rules that will make it easy for them, as well as for any other typist who is not a specialist in the business field, to produce business correspondence that will not look as if it was turned out by loving hands at home.

**ABBREVIATIONS IN ADDRESSES.** The following rules govern the use of abbreviations wherever an address is used in either business or personal correspondence—on an envelope, a letterhead, in a letter, and in all printed or engraved announcements and invitations:

**Cities.** Do not abbreviate the name of a city in either business or social correspondence. There are no exceptions. Do not use "City" instead of the full name of a city, to indicate that a letter is to be delivered within the city where it was posted.

| Right | Wrong |
|-------|-------|
| Chicago | Chi. |
| Las Vegas | Vegas |
| Los Angeles | L.A. |
| New York | N.Y. |
| Philadelphia | Phila. |
| San Francisco | S.F., Frisco |

**Countries.** Do not abbreviate the name of a country in either business or social correspondence, with two exceptions: U.S.A. (not U.S.) is correct for the United States of America. U.S.S.R. is correct for Union of Soviet Socialist Republics (not Russia).

| Right | Wrong |
|-------|-------|
| Mexico | Mex. |

*Note:* Capitalize the name of a country on an envelope: ITALY, but not in a letter: Italy.

**Names (Firms and People).** The name of a corporation, organization, or firm should be typed exactly as shown on its letterhead. Some firms use the ampersand (&) for "and," for example. Some spell out "Corporation" and others use "Corp." Such variants should be carefully noted and used.

Do not abbreviate the name of a person in either the inside or outside address, even if the man himself customarily signs Wm., Chas., Robt., Jas., and so on.

**Numbers.** Use figures for all house, building, and room numbers except '"One," which should be spelled out: One Main Street (not 1 Main Street). Do not use the number sign (#) or the abbreviation "No." in any part of an address: Room 210 (never Room #210 or Room No. 210).

Always spell out a street (avenue, boulevard, and so on) that has a numerical name—up to and including "Tenth"; First Avenue (not 1st); Second Street (not 2nd).

Rapidly gaining the widest acceptance is the typing of a numerically named street without "d," "nd," "rd," "st," or "th" following the number: 72 Street (instead of 72nd Street). Both forms are correct for business mail, but "72 Street" is not used on social letters. When addressing an envelope by hand, it is only common sense to avoid the chance of confusion by underlining "nd," "rd," "st," and "th" and putting them a bit above the line in this fashion: $72^{nd}$.

**States.** The name of a state is never correctly abbreviated on the envelope or in the body of a *formal* announcement or invitation, but abbreviations are very widely used in the general run of both business and personal letters. If an abbreviation is used, choose the official one, below *(United States Government Correspondence Manual)*. Note that a period always follows such abbreviation:

| | Official Abbreviation | Wrong |
|-------|-------|-------|
| Alabama | Ala. | Al. |
| Alaska | Alas. | Aka. |
| Arizona | Ariz. | Ari. |
| Arkansas | Ark. | Arka. |
| California | Calif. | Cal. |

|  | *Official Abbreviation* | *Wrong* |
|---|---|---|
| Colorado | Colo. | Col. |
| Connecticut | Conn. | Con. |
| Delaware | Del. | Dela. |
| District of Columbia | D.C. (preferred to spelling out) | |
| Florida | Fla. | Flo. |
| Georgia | Ga. | Geo. |
| Hawaii | (none) | Ha. |
| Idaho | (none) | Id. |
| Illinois | Ill. | Illi. |
| Indiana | Ind. | Inda. |
| Iowa | (none) | Io., Ia. |
| Kansas | Kans. | Kan. |
| Kentucky | Ky. | Ken. |
| Louisiana | La. | Lou., Lsa. |
| Maine | (none) | Ma., Me. |
| Maryland | Md. | Mld. |
| Massachusetts | Mass. | Massa. |
| Michigan | Mich. | Micha. |
| Minnesota | Minn. | Min., Minna. |
| Mississippi | Miss. | Mis., Missi. |
| Missouri | Mo. | Mis. |
| Montana | Mont. | Mon. |
| Nebraska | Nebr. | Neb. |
| Nevada | Nev. | Neva. |
| New Hampshire | N.H. | N. Hamp. |
| New Jersey | N.J. | N. Jer. |
| New Mexico | N.M. | N. Mex. |
| New York | N.Y. | N. York |
| North Carolina | N.C. | N. Car. |
| North Dakota | N.D. | N. Dak. |
| Ohio | (none) | O. |
| Oklahoma | Okla. | Ok., Okl., Oka. |
| Oregon | Oreg. | Ore. |
| Pennsylvania | Pa. | Pen., Penn., Penna. |
| Puerto Rico | P.R. | |
| Rhode Island | R.I. | Rd. Is. |
| South Carolina | S.C. | S. Car. |
| South Dakota | S.D. | S. Dak. |
| Tennessee | Tenn. | Ten. |
| Texas | Tex. | Txs. |
| Utah | (none) | Ut. |
| Vermont | Vt. | Ver. |
| Virginia | Va. | Vir., Virg. |
| Washington | Wash. | Was. |
| West Virginia | W. Va. | W. Virg. |
| Wisconsin | Wis. | Wisc. |
| Wyoming | Wyo. | Wy. |

**Streets, and so on.** Abbreviations are never correct in any formal invitation or announcement, and are not first choice on other mail, though widely used.

| *Always Right* | *Second Choice* |
|---|---|
| Avenue | Ave. |

| *Always Right* | *Second Choice* |
|---|---|
| Boulevard | Blvd. |
| Place | Pl. |
| Street | St. |
| Terrace | Ter. |
| General Delivery | Gen. Del. |

The following abbreviations, however, are correct:

R.D. (Rural Delivery)
R.F.D. (Rural Free Delivery)
R.R. (Rural Route)

Note that these abbreviations should be followed immediately by a numeral (R.D. 4); do not use *No.* or the number sign (#) before the numeral. (The same rule holds in giving a box number: Box 212.)

East, West, North, and South are written in full, as first choice: East Main Street (not E. Main Street). But when an area direction such as Northwest, Southeast, and so on, follows a street address, an abbreviation is correct: 200 Quebec Street, N.W.

**Titles.** By first choice, write military and religious titles in full unless to do so would crowd a line.

**ATTENTION LINE.** A business letter addressed to a firm sometimes bears an attention line containing the name of a particular person who is familiar with the matter discussed in the letter or who is the individual the writer believes most capable of dealing with the matter. Such a letter is not a personal communication for the individual named in the attention line—in his absence, it can be opened by someone else and the matter dealt with. An attention line is typed (underlined) on the extreme lower left of the envelope. In the letter it is typed, again underlined, two spaces below the address and the same distance above the salutation, which is "Dear Sirs" or "Gentlemen," since the letter is basically to the company. "Attention" is not abbreviated, and a title is used with either initials and the last name or with the full name:

Attention Mr. Henry Y. Brown

**CARBON COPY NOTATIONS.** It is customary, though not obligatory, to let the addressee know that a carbon copy of a letter addressed to him has been sent to someone else by adding a notation at the end of the letter. The notation is typed, flush right, below any other notations and begins "'Copy to" (or C.C.) followed by the name of the person who is to receive the carbon.

When the writer does not want the addressee to know that a carbon has been sent elsewhere, the notation is put only on the file copy, to keep the office records straight. In this case, it is known as a "blind copy notation."

**CHRISTMAS CARDS.** *See* CHRISTMAS for correct signatures.

**CLOSINGS.** The practice of preceding the complimentary close with stereotyped phrases ("Hoping to hear from you soon" or "With kindest regards, I am" or "With all good wishes, I beg to remain") has pretty much passed out of fashion in this country, though such phrases are considered routine courtesy in letters to and from firms overseas.

The following forms are the most commonly used in business:

Yours very truly,
Very truly yours,
Sincerely yours,
Very sincerely yours,
Cordially yours,

**CONFIDENTIAL.** One of the more irritating (and least successful) of the dodges of direct-mail advertisers is to mark an envelope CONFIDENTIAL or PERSONAL in order to attract special attention.

"Confidential" is correctly used when a business matter is for some reason restricted from general circulation, and so it is prominently placed, capitalized and underscored to attract attention. On the envelope it is placed above the name of the addressee. On the letter it is centered below the main address but above the salutation. "Personal" is obviously needed on the envelope only.

**DATES.** The date on a dictated letter should be the date of the dictation— not the date the letter was transcribed.

The date is typed on a line by itself. On occasion, the date is placed at the end of a letter on the lower left, but the standard position is at the top, centered or flush with either the right or left margin, at least two lines beneath the letterhead so that is stands out distinctly. An abbreviation for the month is not formal business style; and figures for both month and day (6/3/60) are not used because of the obvious possibility of confusion—6/3 can be interpreted as either June 3 or March 6. (10 June 1967 is standard European usage but is not generally used except by the Armed Services in this country.)

**DICTATED.** "Dictated but not read" is a rudeness both to the person to whom the letter is addressed and to the secretary who types it. The secretary's initials, handwritten under the name she has signed for the writer, clearly reveal to the recipient that the writer was not available to sign (and therefore to read) the letter himself.

*See* "Signatures" below.

On dictated letters, the initials of the writer, followed by those of the secretary, are placed flush with the left-hand margin, usually on the same line as the last line of the signature. MBS:KP is the most widely used form.

**ENCLOSURE LINE.** When something is enclosed with a letter, it is customary to type "Enclosure" flush with the left-hand margin below the identification initials. If more than one item is enclosed, the number is added: Enclosures 3. In the case of important documents, the enclosures are identified:

Enclosures 2
Copy of Affidavit
Cert. Check $16,842

**ENCLOSURE OF COINS.** Loose coins in a letter can interfere with the canceling process. If coins are sent by mail, they should be taped to a card big enough to hold them away from the cancellation area.

**ENVELOPES.** The address on both business and social letters should start about halfway down from the top of the envelope. It should be approximately centered so that space is left on each side for any notation the postman may need to make.

A title is always used before the name of the addressee on any letter, business or social.

The city, state, and zip code can be on one line or two, whichever looks better. But the name of a foreign country should be typed on a separate line— not "Rome, Italy," for example, on the same line.

Each succeeding line of the main address may be indented, but common business practice today is to type them flush to the left (since this saves the typist's time). The lines of the return address are always typed flush to the left.

"Mr." is never used with a man's name in the return address. If a woman's first name is spelled out, it is correctly preceded by "Miss" or "Mrs.," but this is a minor matter in business mail, and many women ignore this rule and follow the standard form for men.

The preferred place for the return address is on the face of a business envelope, not the flap.

A zip-code number is a standard part of every address, business and social, and should be used in both main and return addresses.

*See* "Names and Titles" following.

**FOLDING AND INSERTING A LETTER.** To avoid having a letter cut when the envelope flap is slit, a single-fold sheet is inserted fold first (and correctly with the top half of the letter nearest the front of the envelope). When using a sheet that requires two folds, see that it does not completely fill the envelope. The correct procedure is to fold the bottom edge up first—about a third the length of the sheet, and then fold the top edge downward to within about half an inch of the first fold. Insert the final fold first, and settle the letter well down in the envelope so that when the flap is slit the letter knife will not engage the top fold and cut the letter too.

**INKS.** Blue-black ink is the standard conservative choice for signatures on business letters.

**INVITATIONS.**  *See* INVITATIONS.

**LEGAL OWNERSHIP.** The person to whom a letter is written is the legal owner of the actual letter, but the legal right to print it remains with the writer.

**LETTERS (Forms).** The inside address should reproduce the address on the envelope for the good reason that this gives a complete record on the carbon of the full name, title (if any) in the firm and address, and so can save time and possible confusion later. The city, state, and zip code usually are typed on the same line for the sake of appearance and compactness. A couple of lines below, the salutation "Dear Mr. Jones" or whatever is suitable follows.

Paragraphs should be separated by a space to make the letter easier to read. Each paragraph can begin with an indentation, or can start flush with the left-hand margin. The latter is known as "block" style.

*See also* "Punctuation" below.

There are many variations, but following is a popular and standard form for use on a printed letterhead:

March 26, 1968

Name and Title
Name of Firm
Street Address
City, State, and Zip Code

Salutation:

It is difficult to give hard-and-fast rules about spacing.  The choice of a style depends on several factors.  Among them are the arrangement of the letter-head, the size and shape of the stationery, and the size of the typewriter type.

It is important to keep in mind the appearance of the letter as a whole, and to arrange the typing so that the margins frame it attractively.

In style, this letter is known as "semiblock" because all lines except the complimentary close, signature, and title of the writer are typed flush on the left.

                              Complimentary Close

                              Name (handwritten)
                              Typed Name of the Writer
                              Official Title of the Writer
MBS:KP
Any Notation Lines


Following is a standard form if a letter is written on blank paper instead of a letterhead:


                              492 King Avenue South
                              Westford, Tenn. 00000
                              September 12, 1968

Name and Title
Name of Firm
Street Address
City, State and Zip Code

Salutation:


**LETTERS (SPECIAL PROBLEMS).** Among the dozens of kinds of letters written daily in the business world, certain types require particular mention because of the special problems they present.

**Introductions.** It is not correct to ask directly for a letter of social introduction, but asking for a letter of business introduction is common and proper practice. Good judgment controls the request, however, because a letter of introduction obligates the person receiving it to take some action, and so puts the writer in his debt to some degree. Under all ordinary circumstances, a request for a letter of introduction is not refused, but if complying with such a request is in any way uncomfortable, all that is needed is some kind of explanation—perhaps: "I'm sorry, but my acquaintanceship with him is so slight that a letter of introduction from someone else would serve your purpose much better."

The major rules governing business letters of introduction are as follows:

1. Make the reason for the introduction specific so that the recipient knows what is expected of him.
2. Do not seal the letter before giving it to the person to be introduced. He, however, seals it immediately without reading it unless instructed to do so. As a general rule, the holder of a letter (or card) of introduction mails it to the addressee with a covering letter of his own explaining where he may be reached or making arrangements to telephone for an appointment. This procedure is more businesslike than presenting the letter in person, since it gives the addressee a chance to estimate, before the interview, what is expected of him.

It is also a customary courtesy for the writer of a letter that is to be handed to the person being introduced to telephone or write without delay to the addressee, to prepare him for the call and perhaps explain the reason for the introduction in more detail.

3. Frequently, it is more convenient for the writer to send a letter of introduction directly to the addressee. If this is done, the writer always informs the person being introduced that the promised letter has actually been sent—often by sending him a carbon copy.

4. The one unbreakable rule concerns the thanks that must be sent to the writer by the subject of the letter after it has been delivered. Whether or not the letter has been useful is beside the point. The person introduced must report the results (or lack of them) and thank the writer for at least a good try in his behalf; and he must also send a note to the person to whom he was introduced, thanking him for his time even though the interview was unproductive.

**Recommendations.** Almost everyone holding an executive position in the business world sooner or later is asked to write a letter of recommendation. Sometimes a departing employee asks for such a letter to take with him for use as a general reference. Or a prospective employer writes the former employer for information about an applicant's character and his performance in his previous position.

The letter written for an employee to take with him upon departure is sometimes addressed "To Whom It May Concern," but it may be a statement of fact without that salutation.

A letter of recommendation should be dated, contain the full name of the employee, state what position he held and how well he filled it, the length of his employment, and the reasons for his leaving. His salary or wages should not be mentioned; if an employee has a chance to better himself financially, he should be allowed that opportunity.

The other basic essential in a letter of recommendation is fairness to both the employee and a prospective employer. On the one hand, a fellow human being's chances of rewarding work are at stake, and minor matters of dissatisfaction are best given only by implication rather than directly stated in any general letter of reference—there is always the possibility that what was a real drawback to one employer may be of no consequence to another. On the other hand, a prospective employer's time, money, and business reputation may be at a risk, and so it is unfair to write a letter that gives a false impression of an employee's competence and reliability.

Following are samples of two general letters of reference showing two degrees of endorsement:

Date

Charles Smith has been with this firm as an assistant bookkeeper for the past three years. He is leaving of his own volition because there is no chance here for the advancement for which he is qualified. We see him go with regret. Our best wishes and our complete endorsement of him as a pleasant, conscientious, efficient, and reliable staff member go with him.

(The above is an unqualified recommendation in a brief form.)

Date

Charles Smith has served as assistant bookkeeper with this firm for the past fourteen months. His work has been superior, and we have found him consistently prompt, reliable, and conscientious. I shall be glad to help him by answering any questions a prospective employer may care to ask.

(This is a qualified recommendation because it omits the reason Mr. Smith's employment is terminated, and so indicates there was some minor dissatisfaction that the writer feels is best—and more fairly—discussed in answer to a query from a prospective employer, rather than explained in detail in a general letter of reference.)

**Refusals.** For most people, almost any kind of letter is easier to write than one refusing to grant a requested favor. Here are the general rules that make such a letter easier to write—and to receive:

1. Of first importance is to ignore that impulse to put off an unpleasant task. Procrastination only compounds the difficulty by keeping the person who requested the favor on tenterhooks. Send the bad news promptly, but with appropriate regrets.
2. Make the letter detailed enough to show the recipient that his request has been seriously and fairly considered.
3. Explain the company regulations or other reasons that make the refusal necessary.
4. Suggest, if possible, another solution.

**NAMES AND TITLES.** Both on the envelope and inside the letter in the main address, "Mr.," "Mrs.," "Miss," or some other title of formal address must be used. The title that indicates the addressee's position or office in the firm is added after his name—on the same line or the next one, whichever will look best, depending on the length of the addressee's name and title and of the firm's name. But "Treasurer," "Comptroller," or any similar business title is never used before a name in place of "Mr.," for example. And of course the business title is not added after the name unless the name of the firm also follows.

**Esquire.** *See* ESQUIRE.

**Excellency and Honorable.** *See* FORMS OF ADDRESS (Government).

**Junior, Second, Third,** and so on. These designations are part of a name, and must always be used on an envelope and in an inside address. A salutation line, however, reads "Dear Mr. Brown"—never "Dear Mr. Brown, Jr."

In business correspondence, "Jr." is always abbreviated. So are "2nd" and "3rd," or the Roman numerals II and III may be used instead.

*See* NAMES for further details.

**Mesdames and Messrs.** In addressing mail to two or more women jointly, "Mesdames" (or its abbreviation "Mmes.") can be used if any one of the women is married. If the women are not married, "Misses" is correct. However, much more usual today on an envelope and in the major inside address is to use some variant of "Mrs. John Hayes and Miss Ruth Carl," or simply to write one name below the other.

"Messrs." (the abbreviation of "Messieurs") can be used before the names of two or more men on a business letter, though on a social letter it is correct only to brothers.

Neither "Mesdames" nor "Messrs." is correctly used if "Inc.," "Co.," or a similar designation follows the name. (Wrong, for example, is "Messrs. Brown and Black, Inc.")

**Miss.** "Miss" has long been used as a courtesy title in the theater, regardless of an actress's marital status, and "Miss" is now widely used in the business world to acknowledge a woman's professional status even if she is married and the mother of six. If a woman signs business mail "Mary Smith," it is never a mistake to address the answer to "Miss Mary Smith" unless she has indicated that she prefers "Mrs." by having her name typed "(Mrs.) Mary Smith" below the space for her signature.

**Names.** In business, many people prefer to use one or more initials instead of one or more given names spelled in full. All business mail, including formal business invitations, should be addressed according to an individual's preference, which is clearly indicated by the way his name is typed below his signature. If a man's name is typed H. W. A. Black, that is the way business mail to him should be addressed. On the other hand, it is not incorrect (though second choice) to address mail with initials of first names even though the writer customarily spells them out. Abbreviations like "Jas.," "Chas.," and so on are never correct, even though a man may use a short form in scribbling his signature.

See also "Salutations" below.

**PUNCTUATION.** The punctuation on an envelope should match the style used in the enclosed letter. Increasingly used today is what is called "open" punctuation. In this style, punctuation marks are omitted after the date, after the name and each line of the address, after the complimentary close, and after each line of the signature (see sample letter, above). The "closed" style uses punctuation after such lines—a period or comma as needed.

The correct punctuation after any salutation in a business letter is a colon —not a semicolon, comma, or dash.

**SALUTATIONS.** When a company is being addressed rather than any individual in it, the following salutations are used:

Dear Sirs:
Gentlemen:
Messrs:

Or, if the firm is composed of women:

Ladies:
Mesdames:

(Illogically enough, though "Dear Sirs" is correct, "Dear Gentlemen," "Dear Messrs.," "Dear Ladies," and "Dear Mesdames" are not.)

When an individual is addressed, the following (given in their relative order of formality) are correct:

| | | | |
|---|---|---|---|
| Dear Mr. Black: | | Dear Mrs. (Miss) Black: | |
| Dear Sir: | | Dear Madam: | |
| My dear Mr. Black: | } very { | My dear Mrs. (Miss) Black: | |
| Sir: | } formal { | Madam: | |

("Dear Miss" and "Dear Mrs." without a name is not correct. Neither is "Dear Dr.," "Dear Colonel," or any other title not followed by a last name.)

**SIGNATURES.** The signature on a business letter has two parts—the handwritten name and the typed lines, if any, near it.

The writer's name is typed under the space left for his signature exactly as he wants return mail addressed to him, not necessarily as he will sign. A man may scribble "Robt. Chas. Smith," "R. C. Smith," or "Bob," but the typed name should read "Robert Charles Smith" if that is the way his name appears on his business cards. (When the writer's name is imprinted on the letterhead, his typed name is often omitted below his signature.)

When a man is writing for his company, the title of the firm, if used in the signature, is typed in capital letters first. A space is left for the handwritten name. Then comes the typed name (preceded by "By" if he has no official title). Otherwise, his title in the company is given on the last line, and "By" is omitted.

```
                              Very truly yours,
                              GOURMET FOOD PROCESSORS

                              By Robert C. Smith
```

When a secretary signs a letter for her chief, she puts her initials below his name; and in this case she should also sign the file copy to show that the letter was dictated but not read:

Very truly yours,

Henry B. Smith (<u>handwritten</u>)
M.J.

Henry B. Smith
Treasurer

When a secretary—or someone else—writes a letter in behalf of her chief, she makes it clear that she is speaking for him by signing her own name. There are many variants of form, but this is a good example:

Very truly yours,

GOURMET FOOD PROCESSORS
John Smith, Treasurer

Susan Lane (<u>handwritten</u>)

By Susan Lane
Secretary to Mr. Smith

**STATIONERY.** Cheap stationery can be a false economy. The appearance of the paper and the way it feels in the hand hint at the degree of prosperity of the company. And even a skilled typist is hampered by cheap paper, which takes erasure badly.

Both envelopes and second or continuation sheets should be of the same quality paper as the letterhead. (Some firms have the company name—and sometimes also the address—repeated on the continuation sheet in small letters at the top left.)

**TELEPHONE NUMBERS.** Prefixes are printed or typed in full on a business letterhead: PLaza 0-0000, rather than PL 0-0000.

**ZIP-CODE NUMBERS.** In all correspondence, business and social, a zip-code number is a necessary part of an address. It is placed after the state, and is not set off by a comma or followed by a period.

**CORSAGES.**  *See* FLOWERS.

**COSMETICS.**  *See* MAKEUP.

## COUGHING AND CHOKING

One of the unhappiest accidents at table is a conspicuous choking fit. If a bit of food that goes down the wrong way cannot be dealt with quickly, the best procedure is to slip away from the table and deal with the paroxysm in private. Only the man on her left rises, or half rises, when a woman leaves the table in this emergency and when she returns.

Choking usually is damaging only to the makeup and emotions, and the less notice taken of it, the better. However, it can sometimes be extremely dangerous. Unless a guest returns promptly, either host or hostess should investigate in case first-aid techniques are required.

A spasm of coughing at a theater, church, or in some other such gathering can be disconcerting to a speaker or performer, as well as irritatingly distracting to the rest of the audience. Out of consideration for others, anyone caught in a momentarily uncontrollable siege of coughing should seek a dressing room. As a general rule, the cougher's companion does not go out with him unless it is obvious that he needs help.

## COUNTRY CLUBS.    See CLUBS.

## CRABS

There are more than a thousand species of crab. The blue, or common, crab of the Atlantic and Gulf coasts, the Morro crab of the Pacific, and the giant king crab are the most widely known of the hard-shell crabs. The meat of a hard-shell crab usually is extracted from the shell before it is served, but occasionally cracked crab claws or cracked segments of king crab legs are brought to the table. They are eaten with an oyster fork, and, as with steamed or boiled whole lobsters, a finger bowl of warm water with a slice of lemon floating in it is almost a necessity.

Soft-shell crabs are not a different species. They are hard-shell crabs at a special period in their growth. A crab's shell does not grow or expand. When it gets tight, the crab sheds it and emerges covered with a soft skin that soon hardens into another shell. Crabs caught while the skin is still thin and papery are a great delicacy. The center containing the stomach is cut out before they are sautéed or deep-fried. Soft-shell crabs are cut with either the fork or the knife, and pieces of both skin and meat are put into the mouth. The skin usually is thin and tender enough to eat, but if any tough residue is left it is taken out in the fingertips and put on the side of the plate.

Oyster crabs are minute baby crabs. They often are scooped up with whitebait, and are also found in mussels and oysters. They too are a great delicacy, either raw or cooked.

## CRACKERS

Crackers, including oyster crackers, are picked up in the fingers from the serving basket or tray and put on the butter plate or, if there is none, on the table-cloth. Large crackers are broken and the small pieces eaten separately, as bread is. Small crackers are eaten in two or more bites without breaking. Oyster crackers may be dropped whole, a few at a time, into the soup or may be eaten one at a time from the fingers, but the rules say that, properly, no cracker is broken and crumbled into the soup.

## CRANBERRY SAUCE

This classic accompaniment to turkey is also often served with chicken. It is put on the main plate, not the butter plate. A dish of cranberry sauce may be on the table before guests sit down or it may be passed by a maid after the main course is served.

## CREAM

Whole milk, condensed milk, half-and-half, as well as real cream are all called "cream" when offered with coffee. Many people enjoy milk in tea but do not care for the rich taste of cream, and so tea experts are careful to say "milk" if that is what is in the jug, and specify "cream" if either cream or half-and-half is served.

## CREDIT CARDS

The modern credit-card system of charging the goods and services of many different firms to one account dates back only to 1950, but the fact that several million people today carry such cards is evidence of the convenience they offer at relatively small cost.

The member of a credit-card "club" pays a small yearly fee. Then, instead of paying as he goes or settling numerous charge accounts on a monthly basis, he can charge to one account such diverse things as car rentals and clothes, flowers and furniture, gasoline and gifts, travel fares, hotel and motel expenses, meals, tips, and even money. (Some credit-card companies offer their clients the privilege of cashing small personal checks.) At the end of the month, the client receives an itemized statement that he pays with a single check, directly to the credit-card company.

The credit-card system is of obvious advantage to people who have heavy day-to-day expenses but dislike carrying a sizable amount of cash. Businessmen who do any great amount of expense-account entertaining find the system practical. The itemized monthly statement is a permanent record useful in income tax and other accounting procedures, and it also saves the business host the awkwardness of asking for a receipt after entertaining in a restaurant on his company's money. A credit card is especially useful to a woman who is entertaining a man on either the business or social level, since she can pay for both a meal and a tip by signing rather than by the display of cash that makes so many male guests feel uncomfortable. It should be remembered, though, that if a tip is charged, a percentage of it goes to the credit-card company along with the standard percentage paid on all charges by the firms that honor the cards.

Identification of the holder of a credit card is supplied by his signature on the card. Since signatures are not difficult to fake, anyone who loses his card needs to protect himself by immediately notifying the credit-card company by wire or telephone, and then in writing. (Insurance can be taken out against the risk of a lost card and against forgery, but the holder remains responsible for taking proper care of the card and for prompt notification of the issuer if the card is lost.)

**CRESTS.**   *See* HERALDIC DEVICES.

## CRITICISM

Good, honest, reasonably open-minded criticism of a public policy, entertainment, or performance is a sign of an alert mind. Criticism of work carelessly or incompetently done can be both necessary and constructive. But the habitual criticism of individuals on a personal and social level nearly always is a sign of a gnawing self-dissatisfaction—a curious backhanded demand for recognition of one's own superiority, deserved or not. As Will Durant puts it, "To speak ill of others is a dishonest way of praising ourselves."

Probably one of the most inaccurate statements ever to win wide use is the childhood retort "Sticks and stones will break my bones, but names will never hurt me." Little repeated jabs of criticism can work like the drops of water that wear away a stone. They break up romances, ruin friendships, and damage careers. It is tiresome to be forever Pollyanna, the Glad Girl, accentuating the positive to a neurotic degree. But the person who emphasizes only the freckle on a lovely face and only the minor idiocies that all of us occasionally commit is even more wearing in the long run.

The atmosphere of mind that leads to constant belittlement of others is hard to combat because the sad truth is that the comment with the slight sting is likely to be far more entertaining, memorable, and quotable than the one without its acid. But the person incapable of resisting the amusingly caustic personal comment, no matter how unfair it is, should be regarded by friend and foe alike as dangerous to some degree.

Giving the constructive criticism that so often is a real kindness is a delicate matter well worth a second thought before speaking impulsively. The instinctive response to criticism of one's self is to retaliate in kind, and anyone planning to dish it out better be prepared to follow Harry Truman's advice: "If you can't take the heat, get out of the kitchen."

Accepting criticism gracefully—even criticism considerately given with a mollifying balance of praise—is never easy. If the criticism is unjust, a defense of one's self is certainly called for. If there is truth in the criticism, the most disarming reply is "Thank you for telling me"—without further comment.

## CROUSTADES

A croustade is a piece of French-fried bread on which other foods are served. It is always taken from a serving platter along with its topping. The croustade need not be eaten, but it is not left on the platter.

## CROUTONS

Croutons are tiny dice-shaped pieces of bread, dried, buttered and dried, toasted, or deep-fried. When served with soup they are offered with a serving spoon. A helping is put directly on top of the soup, not on the butter plate or tablecloth as oyster crackers would be.

**CRUISES.**  *See* BOATS AND SHIPS; TRAVEL.

## CRUMBING THE TABLE

Crumbing the table before dessert is a routine of quite formal service only. The table is first cleared of plates, condiment dishes, and salt and pepper containers. The server then brushes each place lightly from the left, using a folded napkin and a tray or plate. Place cards, if any, are taken off at this time.

If a meal is served by one maid who is also the cook, she does not correctly crumb the table, since she has enough to do without trying to ring this grace note too. And a hostess who is herself the cook and server never crumbs the table.

**CUPS AND SAUCERS.**  *See* COFFEE; MEALS AND THEIR SERVICE; SOUPS; TABLE MANNERS; TEAS.

## CURLERS

One of the more curious daytime sights in some suburban streets is girls with their hair skinned up in curlers, not infrequently in full view of the beaux they intend to dazzle with the resulting hairdo during the evening. By any standards, this is poor sense as well as poor taste. The same goes for curlers worn under a scarf in public. Even when covered, curlers belong at home.

## CURTSIES

If all a little girl's classmates are taught to curtsy, it is sensible for her to do so too, even when away from her school. However, it is a hardship on a child if she is the only one in her group who is required to curtsy. Though the curtsy is a pretty formality when not overdone, the child who makes a bob every time she says, "Yes, ma'am," or "No, sir," to an adult may well be suspected of showing off with more energy than sense. Many parents take a dim view of the curtsy, since such a habit learned in early childhood is hard to break, and a big girl looks absurd making a curtsy. Age eleven is considered about the limit for it.

Women are expected to curtsy when being presented to royalty. There is no question that American women should do so when being presented at any court. Under this circumstance, the court curtsy is no more than routine politeness in observance of customs of the host's roof. Women also curtsy when being presented to royalty visiting this country, though the deep court curtsy is not appropriate. The more sophisticated American woman makes a slight, slow bob when being presented to visiting royalty, but she is equally correct if she makes a formal bow.

## CUSTOMERS

Because salespeople are ruled by the dictum "The customer is always right," the obligation on the customer to be right is double.

*See* SHOPPING, for details of a good customer's behavior.

## CUTTING

The deliberate cut, done by looking through an acquaintance as if he were not there, is a deadly insult. It is inexcusable for one guest to cut another under the roof of their host. In this case, the only procedure for enemies so bitter that they cannot bear to speak is to avoid a direct meeting if possible. Otherwise, at least an unsmiling nod is required of each as recognition of the other's presence.

*See* BALLS AND DANCES for rules about cutting in; TABLE MANNERS for cutting food.

# D

## DAMAGE

Everyone concerned with accidental breakage or other damage is in an unhappy spot, and the best anyone can do is to put himself in the other person's place. The guest or borrower responsible for the mishap is expected to do all he can, within reason, to repair or replace the damaged article; and the only understanding thing the unfortunate owner can do is to minimize his natural distress as much as possible.

The person who has broken an article does not generally offer cash on the spot to pay for its replacement or repair. If a duplicate is easily available, his routine procedure is to tell the owner that he will find and send a replacement—and do so promptly. If the broken article is unique and duplication is impossible, some token replacement is called for. In such case, either an article that serves the same purpose or something entirely different can be sent with a note of regret.

Serious damage to furniture presents a different problem. Burned upholstery, for example, demands the services of a specialist. The person responsible should insist on paying for the repair, but it is only reasonable to ask the owner to choose his own repair service, take care of the details, and, when the bill is received, to forward it.

The same procedure is followed when someone's clothing is seriously damaged. The person responsible for a bad burn or stain, for example, asks the victim to take the garment to a cleaner or reweaver and to forward the bill. Many people who have suffered such accidental damage to clothing feel awkward about accepting payment and insist (whether it is true or not) that the garment can be readily restored at home. In this event, the person responsible cannot do much except express his regret and then send flowers, a book, or some other small item as a tangible token of it.

The above rules do not hold when an employee breaks or damages something. An employee asked to dust, wash, or otherwise handle fragile or expensive objects should be warned of their value, but in case of accidental damage it is not fair for the owner to subtract the cost of repair or replacement from a servant's wages. The owner assumes the risk of damage when he asks an employee to deal with his possessions.

See APOLOGIES AND EXCUSES.

**DANCES.**  See BALLS AND DANCES.

## DARES

It is an unwritten law of sportsmanship that no one issues a dare unless prepared to take the risk himself. This rule goes double for women and girls who put men in a spot by daring them to attempt something that quite obviously they would not or could not do themselves. It is a demonstration of simple good sense to refuse a dare to any foolhardy action. No one should hesitate to refuse a dare, no matter who issues it, that involves the risk of danger or indignity.

## DATEBOOKS

No matter how carelessly it is displayed, a datebook must be regarded as a completely personal possession, and a guest does not open one under any usual circumstances.

A secretary who has access to her employer's datebook takes care to keep the information it contains reasonably confidential. If a caller asks, "Is he free for lunch?" she quite properly says, "He has that time checked off," but that is as far as she goes. She does not volunteer where or with whom his lunch date may be, and so leaves him free to rearrange his schedule if he should want to, without revealing that he is breaking a prior date to make one with the caller.

**DATES.**  See FRUITS.

## DATES

"Date," in its meanings of "appointment" and "the person with whom one has an appointment," and "dating" in all its variety of meanings from "going steady" to serious courting, are fairly new and extremely useful words that started as teen-age slang but have won a solid place in the everyday language of all ages. Whether a date is made by a youngster or an adult, the conventions are the same.

The most important single rule about making a date is: Be specific. Suggest a definite diversion or a choice of several—the movies, a ball game, a meal. Always inept are such vague invitations as "How about a date Saturday night?" —most especially if followed by no more than "I'll pick you up at eight," which leaves a girl in total doubt about what to wear.

Even more inept, after the girl accepts, is "'What would you like to do?" which puts both in a hopeless position. Unless she knows her host and his tastes very well, she has to risk suggesting something that may well bore him or be too expensive for him—and he is stuck with her choice, like it or not. When a date is for a meal, "Where do you want to eat" can be a paralyzing question if the girl has no idea whether a coffee shop or the town's most expensive steak house is the more suited to her host's preference and pocketbook.

As a general rule, dates originate with men. A girl can evade this restriction by asking a man to her house or by supplying tickets herself to a show or sports event. However, even if she buys the tickets herself, the usual formula is one of the comfortable social fibs like "I've been given tickets to the Saturday game. Would you like to go with me?" because the convention still holds that the man is the pursuer and makes the first move.

Once made, a date should be honored as any other promise should be—within all reasonable limits. Of course, any engagement can be broken in a real emergency—illness or an honest business or personal demand on the same time—but an invitation from another, more interesting, person is never a legitimate excuse for canceling a prior date.

When it is necessary to break a date, it should be done as promptly as possible, and an explanation is always called for. It is inconsiderate, to put it in the mildest terms, to break a date at the last minute if there is any way to avoid doing so. The person who breaks the date is obligated, after making the explanation and an apology, to suggest another specific time if this is at all feasible.

Both parties to a date are expected to be prompt. No one likes to be kept waiting—a girl for the man who chronically turns up late; a man for a girl who forever needs twenty more minutes to get ready. When a delay of more than fifteen minutes is unavoidable, telephone and say so if the person can be reached by telephone.

By the rules, a man calls for a woman at her office or house. This custom is quite often—and sensibly—honored in the breach. If time is extremely short, it is reasonable to suggest meeting at a restaurant for dinner before going on to a movie that starts at eight o'clock, for example.

There are exceptions to all these rules, but generally it is considered far too offhand for a man to park, honk, and lounge in his car waiting for his date to run out. Certainly, if she lives on a heavy-traffic street, he can arrange to pick her up in front of her place, but under usual circumstances he goes to her door. And the conventional routine for her is to ask him in for a few words with her parents or housemates or, if she lives alone, while she gets her wraps on.

The man is responsible for virtually all expenditures during a date unless a Dutch treat has been agreed upon. If his girl meets him away from her house, he does not reimburse her for her cab or carfare. And she is expected to have small change for a tip to a washroom attendant. Otherwise, the man pays for transportation, food, and entertainment, and provides her brand of cigarettes if she runs out. She, in turn, is careful not to take advantage of his vulnerable position as total provider by suggesting extra expenditures or ordering the most expensive items on the menu unless he first suggests the black caviar and golden pheasant.

A woman does not suggest going on somewhere else after a dinner or theater date. The man suggests any such further entertainment, but it is her privilege to refuse if she wants to end the evening then. A woman makes the first move to bring a date to a close under all usual circumstances. However, if a man wants to make the evening an early one, all he need do is to say so when making the date so that his guest is prepared to cooperate—which she will do if she is worth dating in the first place.

At the end of a date, and most especially at night, a man is expected to see his girl safely home. If for some good reason he is putting her in a cab instead of seeing her to her door, he asks the driver what the fare will probably be and pays him, including a tip. He does not hand the cab fare to his guest, but always gives it directly to the driver. And he should telephone after she has had time to get home, to make sure that she is safely there. The general procedure is to see a girl to the door of her house, then make certain she has her keys and is safely inside before he leaves. If she lives in an apartment that has a doorman, her date sees her inside the street door; otherwise, to the elevator and puts her in it.

A man does not invite himself in for a nightcap—unless he is deliberately testing his date's conventionality. And if she says, "No, it's too late," he has no right to be offended or insistent. She is behaving according to the standard rules.

The good-night kiss is a matter entirely open to negotiation, but at the end of a date, even if it has been a bore, a woman thanks a man in any words she can find for at least trying to give her a good time. And, even if the man is determined never to make another date with her, he thanks her for "the pleasure of her company," though those actual words would sound somewhat stilted from most people today. Both seduously avoid the always awkward question "When will I see you again?"—which makes a woman sound over-eager and a man both overconfident and passive.

In any case, at any time during a date, a woman has four words at her command that more than even the inequality of strength, weight, and stamina between strong man and frail woman in the war of the sexes: "I have a head-ache." Those simple little words are a blockbuster of an excuse that brooks no argument. The only thing a man can do is take the lady home.

**BLIND DATES.** Needless to say, only a really foolish girl makes a blind date with a stranger who calls her telephone number by mistake.

If a blind date arranged through or by friends is accepted, the obligations are exactly the same as for a date made with any friend. If stuck with the bore of the world, a man is expected to see that she gets safely home and to thank her for her company, even though he is lying in his teeth. The girl is expected to be equally polite, though she can feign the useful headache and cut the evening short.

**DUTCH TREATS.** Today, when so many women have salaries equal to those of men, it is only practical and sensible for a woman to pay her own way in many circumstances. But, whether two people or a group are con-cerned, certain conventions need to be observed to make a Dutch treat grace-ful and easy.

It is of the greatest importance to make clear from the start that the oc-casion is on a Dutch-treat basis. Suggesting the splitting of a check after it is presented to someone who has been graciously operating as a host or hostess can only make that person feel awkward, unthanked, and faintly belittled.

It is annoyingly bad taste for either a man or woman to suggest or allow a change in an agreement to share expenses. One person in a group, for instance, should not suddenly decide to be Lord or Lady Bountiful and insist on picking up the check. Very often, though a man and woman have agreed to "go Dutch," he still feels impelled to go through the motions of offering to pay, but she should not agree—not if she wants to originate a date with him again.

A woman generally takes the lead in suggesting, "Let's go Dutch," since most men are reluctant to make that suggestion to a woman. She certainly should do so if she originates any plan involving a sizable expenditure. How-ever, out of respect for a man's customary touchy pride in money matters, she makes no public display of giving bills directly to him. In a restaurant, she either tells the waiter "separate checks" and gives her own order, or she allows the man to go through the motions of a host and relay her order to the waiter, then hands over enough to cover her share of the bill in an inconspicuous fashion before they leave the table. If there will be a number of separate tabs for transportation, food, and admissions, she can either give the man enough to cover her share at the beginning of their date or settle up matter-of-factly toward the end of it. A man who has agreed to a Dutch-treat date is required to be equally matter-of-fact about giving an accounting and accepting payment.

**THE DEAF.**   *See* THE HANDICAPPED.

# DEANS

The senior member in length of service (not in age) in any group is given the honorary title of "Dean." It is used only in speaking about him—"John Jones is the dean of City Hall reporters" or "Henry Brown is dean of foreign ambassadors"—never as a written title.

See also FORMS OF ADDRESS (Academic, Clergy).

# DEATH

Jokes or flippant remarks about undertakers, funerals, coffins, graveyards, the last words of the dying, or about any other matter related to death are made within the hearing of a stranger or slight acquaintance only by the thoughtless. Too often such jokes give added, unnecessary distress to a casual friend who is keeping a sorrow to himself. Even to intimates they are risky. No one can know all of another person's memories.

It is bad taste to celebrate in any way the death of an enemy or of a despised political figure. Death comes to all. The fact of death calls for respect even if none is felt for the deceased.

See FUNERALS.

# DEBUTS

Originally, a coming-out party served as a formal notification that a girl had reached marriageable age and was ready to meet the "right" young men. The custom developed in the days when a girl finished her education by the age of eighteen and, in upper- and upper-middle-class circles, could look forward to no other career than marriage. Today, though we still have a far from classless society, labels like "upper-middle class" are used only by sociologists; and it is fashionable for girls from even the most privileged financial backgrounds to busy themselves with some kind of job if they do not go on to college. Therefore, debuts now have a completely different emphasis.

Making a bow at one of the famous annual assemblies, cotillions, and balls is an important status symbol in certain very limited circles. However, hundreds of parents, as a matter of affection and pride, give a party that says in effect, "Here is our darling daughter, eighteen years old and socially of age." In any case, for a party to rate as a debut rather than as a birthday party, friends of the parents as well as of the debutante must be invited. Following is the general range of formality in coming-out parties:

1.  A ball honoring one girl (obviously possible only for parents of great wealth and a very large social circle).
2.  A very large formal tea dance honoring one girl.
3.  A ball at which a number of girls make their debuts jointly.
4.  A comparatively small lunch, tea, or dinner party at which one of several girls are the honored guests.

**AGE.** A debut usually is held when a girl is about seventeen or eighteen—after she graduates from high school or during her first year in college. Many families prefer to wait until a daughter is twenty-one, and then give a coming-of-age party in her honor. Though such a festivity may be very elaborate, it rates as a birthday party, not as a debut.

**CLOTHES.** When girls make their debuts in a group, their costumes, though different, are traditionally all white. Long dresses and long white gloves are standard. The cut, fabric, and trimmings of the dresses vary markedly in different parts of the country. In some cities, very elaborate and handsome materials are favored; in other, simpler dresses are customary. At balls where a curtsy is part of the ceremony, fairly full skirts are usually worn because a deep curtsy is defeated by a narrow sheath and, of course, is absurd-looking in an extremely short skirt.

If the dance honors only one girl, a dress in a pastel shade or a white dress with touches of color is sometimes chosen instead of the traditional all-white costume.

It should be noted that a girl never wears a pure white costume to the debut of a friend—unless, of course, they are making their bows at the same party or on the same evening (one at a dinner and the other at a dance, with each girl appearing at both events).

The "trousseau" for a girl who is swept into the big whirl of her debutante season can easily run to an investment larger than that for a bride because she will need a number of dancing dresses as well as pretty costumes for day-time parties. Since debut ball dresses are often quite expensive, it is the practical and charming custom in many families to order extra material for long sleeves and perhaps a train so that the white coming-out dress can serve later as a wedding gown.

For a debut at lunch or a tea dance, a debutante wears either a white or pastel-colored costume suitable to the time of day. The debutante's mother wears any color she chooses to except black.

At some balls White Tie is usual for all the men, but in many localities Black Tie is increasingly favored.

**DANCING.** Traditionally, the debutante has the first dance with her father and then dances with her special escorts while her father takes his next turns with her mother, grandmother, or other close relatives.

**ESCORTS.** It is customary for each girl to invite two or more special escorts, and for her family to provide their tickets if the dance is on a subscription basis. Under any circumstances, the aim of anyone sponsoring a debut dance is to provide several stags for each girl present. Invitations are handled in various fashions. In some cases, each girl is asked to submit the names of her chosen escorts, and then invitations are sent to them. In others, the committee or a social bureau hired to manage all the details has a long list of young men between the ages of eighteen and about twenty-one, and invitations are sent to them directly.

**FLOWERS.** A debutante carries a bouquet while standing in a receiving line or when being presented at a mass debut—usually the bouquet provided by her parents, though as a matter of sentiment she may alternate several of her bouquets at different times while in the receiving line.

In many localities it is customary for close relatives and friends to send flowers, especially to a private coming-out party. These may be baskets or large or small bouquets, and they usually are banked behind the debutante in the receiving line. The cards of the donors are, of course, removed.

**GIFTS.** Very close friends and relatives usually send a present as well as flowers to celebrate a girl's debut. Anything that might be chosen for a birthday present is appropriate.

**GROUP DEBUTS.** The big dances at which several or many girls make a joint debut are by far the most popular of the formal coming-out parties today. The debutantes have more fun because the main event produces many new friends and also numerous smaller parties to which they will be invited. By pooling expenses and responsibilities, the parents are spared a great deal of individual effort and can afford far handsomer decorations and a more distinguished orchestra than possible for many of them otherwise.

Mass debuts fall into two main divisions: the private dances that are sponsored by a group of parents who get together as co-hosts and divide expenses, which in any case can range from considerable to staggering; and the many famous annual cotillions, assemblies, and balls that are sponsored by clubs, associations, or other special groups. The latter are run by committees, who invite a limited number of girls to make their formal bow under the sponsorship of the club or group. Many such annual balls are also benefits for a charity. There is a charge for all tickets. In addition, the father of each debutante makes what is usually a quite sizable donation (which, of course, is tax deductible) to the charity.

The procedures are well established at the various big annual balls. At some group debuts, the debutantes go through intricate cotillions that require rehearsal under the direction of a choreographer or dancing master and that are as pretty as a stage production. Sometimes a promenade around the floor, with each debutante on the arm of her father, replaces a cotillion or precedes it. Sometimes each girl moves to a central position accompanied by two young escorts, makes her curtsy, and then joins a receiving line with the other debutantes before the traditional first dance with her father. The variations are almost endless, and any routine that a group chooses to lend drama to the presentation is correct—after all, it is a party, not a presentation at court.

Very frequently, before a group debutante ball, the individual sets of parents each give a small dinner with their daughter as the guest of honor, or sometimes they honor her at a supper (really a breakfast) after the ball ends at three or four in the morning.

Otherwise, the rules governing any other ball or dance are observed, with the exception that at least two, if not more, young men are invited for each debutante present.

**INVITATIONS.** The word "debut" does not appear in the invitation. Instead, the invitation is to lunch, tea, a dance, and so on, with the debutante's name listed as a joint hostess with the name or names of whoever is giving the party; or the invitation may specify that the party is in her honor. And the word "ball" is not used on the invitation to a private dance, no matter how large and lavish it may be. Otherwise, the general rules governing all invitations (given in detail under INVITATIONS, FORMAL are observed).

Following are the most often used forms of invitation for debut parties.

**Afternoon.** The father's name does not usually appear on a formal invitation to a tea or tea dance, even though he will be present. The most formal invitations use the "At Home" form:

Mrs. Henry York Brown

Miss Mary Ann Brown

will be at home

Friday, the second of January

from four until seven o'clock

The Plaza Hotel

R.S.V.P.                                                       Dancing
800 Fifth Avenue
New York 00000

**Dances.** The father's name appears on an invitation to an evening party. The "At Home" form may be used; or the invitation may be phrased "at a dance" with the debutante's name listed under that of her parents or following "in honour of":

Mr. and Mrs. Henry York Brown

Miss Mary Ann Brown

request the pleasure of

the company of

*Mr. and Mrs. George Towne Jones* [handwritten]

at a dance

on Saturday, the eighteenth of December

at ten o'clock

The Country Club

R.S.V.P.
10 Main Street
Tulane, Nevada 00000

The following is also correct when the party is given by the debutante's **parents**, but it is always used if someone other than her parents is giving the **party.** If a relative or godparent is giving the party, the relationship is added.

Mrs. and Mrs. John Wilbert Martin

request the pleasure of

the company of

*Mr. Ronald Bank Smith* [handwritten]

at a dance in honor of their niece

Miss Mary Ann Brown

*etc.*

**Group Debuts.** The committees of the various annual assemblies, cotillions, and balls have their established forms. Any appropriate variation of the rules given for "Multiple Hosts" under INVITATIONS is used when several parents are the co-hosts for a joint debut for their daughters.

**RECEIVING LINES.** At a group debut, the committee in charge sets up the receiving line in any way it finds most practical and pleasant. At a private party, usually only the debutante and her mother stand in line, with the mother nearest the entrance so that she is the first to welcome the guests and then make the introduction of her daughter, if necessary. The girl's father usually does not stand in line but stays nearby to welcome guests and introduce them to one another. The receiving line breaks up after about an hour at most parties or as soon as all guests have arrived. (Details are given under RECEIVING LINES.)

Sometimes close girl friends of a debutante are asked to "receive" with her. This is no more than a pretty honor. They do not stand in line, as bridesmaids do, though they usually are seated at supper at a special table with the debutante and a special set of escorts.

**TEAS.** The procedure is the same as for any large tea or reception. The girl's father sometimes stands third in the receiving line, but usually lets his wife and daughter take care of that honor.

**TIME OF YEAR.** The usual months for debut parties are June, September, late November (during the Thanksgiving holidays), and late December and early January (during the Christmas holidays). The midwinter period is by far the most popular.

## DECANTERS

Many people prefer to serve wine of a good year and from a fine vintner in its original bottle. Others like to serve wine from a handsome decanter. Both ways are correct for some wines. But champagnes and other sparkling wines, which lose effervescence quickly, are never decanted; they are served directly from the bottle as soon as it is opened. White wines and rosés, which should be served well chilled, are usually not decanted unless bought in bulk containers. If decanted, the decanter should also be chilled.

A decanter of water or wine may be put on the table, without a stopper, and passed from guest to guest at informal meals, but wines at a formal meal are not put on the table; they are poured by the waiter from the original bottles.

Hard liquors, liqueurs, and fortified wines like sherry, port, and Madeira may be left in decanters with tight tops indefinitely. Stoppers are left in the decanters if such drinks are brought on a tray for after-dinner service in the living room, for example. Liqueur decanters are decidedly smaller than the standard size used for whiskey, rum, and other hard liquors.

Labels of silver, enamel, or china hung around the necks of decanters are an attractive and useful aid to identification when there is a large selection. They are never used for decanters of wine served during a meal, but may be used for decanted cocktail wines such as dry sherry, for after-dinner wines such as sweet sherry, and for all hard liquors and liqueurs.

## DECORATIONS, MEDALS, ORDERS

The words "orders," "medals," "decorations," and "citations" all refer to honors granted in official recognition of outstanding military or civilian performance or achievement. There is understandable confusion about these words, as well as about which medals and other symbols of honor may be worn—and which are never worn.

"Decorations" is correctly applied to all badges of honor meant to be worn. This includes medals, jeweled and enameled medallions, rosettes, lapel ribbons, and buttons, pins, and other devices.

The range of medals is enormous. Tons of them are awarded yearly by schools, churches, and other organizations to the winners of everything from athletic contests to spelling bees. Medals of this sort are meant to be treasured but not worn, except perhaps on the day awarded. A good general rule is that only the medals awarded by the President, Congress, and the Armed Services are worn.

A citation is the formal statement of the achievements of a person receiving an academic honor (such as an honorary doctoral degree); it is also a specific reference in a military dispatch to meritorious performance of duty. Military citations sometimes (not always) are accompanied by a medal or other emblem that rates as a decoration and may be worn.

An order is an honor conferred by foreign states. The United States government does not grant orders.

See "Foreign Decorations," below.

**AMERICAN DECORATIONS: ARMED FORCES.** George Washington established our first official decoration on August 7, 1782, when he issued an order for a medal honoring military merit. It probably was the first medal in history available to enlisted men as well as officers, and the following portion of the directive creating this honor has special meaning today to countless American families:

> The General, ever desirous to cherish a virtuous ambition in his soldiers, as well as to foster and encourage every species of military merit, directs that, whenever any singularly meritorious action is performed, the author of it shall be permitted to wear on his facings, over his left breast, the figure of a heart in purple cloth or silk, edged with narrow lace or binding. Not only instances of unusual gallantry, but also of extraordinary fidelity, and essential service in any way, shall meet with a due reward.

> Men who have merited this distinction to be suffered to pass all guards and sentinels which offcers are permitted to do. The road to glory in a patriot army and a free country, is thus opened to all. This order is also to have retrospect to the earlier stages of the war, and to be considered as a permanent one.

Contrary to Washington's intent, the honor did not become a permanent one. Other medals and honors replaced it and it was forgotten until, in 1932, it was revived as the Medal of the Purple Heart—now awarded for wounds or death suffered in action. (*Note:* Membership in the Order of the Purple Heart is not granted by the government; only the medal is. The Order is a society of the people who have been awarded the Purple Heart, as is the organization formed by people who have been awarded the Medal of Honor. This accounts for some of the confusion about the meaning of American "orders.")

Today, the highest honors among the many decorations awarded to Service personnel are the Medals of Honor—usually called "Congressional Medals," since they are given in the name of Congress—conferred in recognition of "conspicuous gallantry and intrepidity at the risk of life, above and beyond the call of duty . . ." There are two of these medals, one for the Army and Air Force, one for the Navy, Marine Corps, and Coast Guard.

Distinguished Service Crosses and Medals are given by the different Services in recognition of exceptionally meritorious service or extraordinary heroism. Other awards of particular distinction, in addition to the Purple Heart, are the Legion of Merit, the Bronze Star Medal, the Silver Star, and the Air Medal. Each branch of the Service also confers special medals for heroism "under conditions other than those of conflict with an armed enemy," as well as Commendation Medals, Campaign Medals (for service in a particular theater of war), and Good Conduct Medals—to name the major ones.

**AMERICAN DECORATIONS: CIVILIAN.** The Presidential Medal of Freedom is the highest honor a President can bestow on a civilian. It was established by President Kennedy on July 4, 1963, and is granted to civilians in all fields of endeavor including federal service. It can be worn in one of three ways: a small lapel ribbon attached over the edge of the lapel is correct with street clothes, dinner jacket, or full evening dress; the medal itself can be worn on a ribbon around the neck by both men and women in evening dress (either Black or White Tie); the third is a wide ribbon worn over the right shoulder (by both men and women) with a large badge on the left hip—but this one is worn only on state occasions and with full evening dress.

The Army and Navy also give awards to civilians, and almost all the military decorations can *under exceptional conditions* be given to civilians. For example, Charles Lindbergh received the Medal of Honor for his solo flight across the Atlantic. Army and Navy medals specifically designed for civilians are awarded only to Army and Navy civilian personnel. These are the Distinguished Civilian Service Award, the Superior Civilian Service Award (lapel emblem, no medal), and the Meritorious Civilian Service Award (lapel emblem, no medal).

The Treasury Department awards decorations to civilians for lifesaving. The Silver Lifesaving Medal and the Gold Lifesaving Medal are worn on the left lapel or over the heart.

The National Security Medal was established by Executive Order in January, 1953. It is awarded to persons, including the Armed Forces of the United States, for distinguished achievement or outstanding contributions in the field of intelligence relating to the national security. It is an oval medal surmounted by an eagle and is worn on the left lapel or over the heart.

**FOREIGN DECORATIONS.** Most foreign countries grant awards to citizens of other countries for distinguished service (both military and civil) to the state. A number of Americans are entitled to wear the ribbon of the French Legion of Honor, and many Americans have been honored by the Croix de Guerre.

American civilians may wear foreign decorations when they please, but members of our Armed Services may not wear a foreign decoration (except by special Act of Congress) until they are civilians again.

**Orders.** This word for certain foreign decorations goes back to medieval times when it was the custom to grant knighthood in return for military services. When a man was knighted, he was admitted to the "order" of the monarch or lord who granted it—King Arthur's legendary "Order of the Round Table," for example. In former times, the order of knighthood was usually accompanied by a grant of land or other reward, and the right to use the title "Sir." Today, knighthood and its accompanying title, "Sir," are awarded by Denmark, England, and Spain, among other countries, as an honor in recognition of outstanding achievement or service to the state, but with no accompanying lands.

Americans may accept this outstanding honor with certain limitations. They may accept membership in the order, and may wear the decoration accompanying it, but do not use the accompanying title "Sir," abroad or at home, because Americans are not permitted by our Constitution to accept a foreign title except by special permission of Congress.

**WHEN AND HOW WORN.** "Decorations" on an invitation (usually on the lower right-hand corner) means the same as "White Tie"—it indicates that the occasion is one of great formality and that anyone entitled to wear decorations is expected to wear one (or all) of them.

Even if "Decorations" does not appear on an invitation, the wearing of decorations is customary on many occasions.

The wearing of decorations by men in uniform is governed by special regulations. Decorations are worn by American citizens in civilian dress in the following order:

American Decorations
American Service Medals
Foreign Decorations
Foreign Service Medals

**American Decorations.** These are the awards made to individuals for acts of meritorious achievement, valorous conduct, and so on. They are worn in the order of their importance, not the order in which bestowed. An American citizen who possesses many decorations usually wears only the most important, though he may wear all if he chooses. However, if he wears any foreign decoration, he must also wear an American one if he possesses it, and always above any foreign decoration, regardless of relative importance or date of bestowal.

**American Service Medals.** These are medals authorized collectively for those in the Services who participate in an expanded campaign, incident, invasion, action, and so on.

**Foreign Decorations.** These are worn by Americans in the order of their bestowal (except that decorations from the same foreign country are grouped), rather than in the order of their relative importance. For example, a man or woman who has two French decorations, one granted before and one after a British decoration was awarded, would wear both French decorations above the British one. There is one exception to this rule. An American abroad who is attending a social or official function honoring a foreigner wears the decoration granted to him by the honored guest's country above other foreign decorations. And, if being presented formally in court to a reigning monarch or to a head of state, a decoration of the ruler's country is worn above other foreign decorations. In neither case, however, is a foreign decoration worn above an American decoration.

**With Civilian Evening Dress.** If a person wishes, he can wear all the decorations he has received, but the general custom is to wear only those awarded for individual service and valor, and sometimes only the highest. For example, a person who has the Medal of Honor or the Medal of Freedom may choose to wear only that one decoration. These two American decorations are the only ones that are worn around the neck on a ribbon with Black Tie or full evening dress (never with street clothes in this form). A medal worn around the neck is reserved for state occasions of great formality. These and other American decorations are usually worn in miniature on the left lapel or above the left pocket by men, and on the left breast by women. If several are worn, the highest is put at the upper right (from the wearer's own viewpoint) of his left lapel. Additional ones are arranged in one or more rows toward the wearer's own left, in the order explained above.

A boutonniere or corsage is never worn at the same time as a medal or decoration.

**With Other Civilian Clothing.** With any clothing other than full dress, one decoration is usually all that is worn—the one most suitable to the particular ceremonial occasion. If two are worn, the higher-ranking one is worn above the other.

The miniature worn will be one of the three types proper with either Black Tie or street clothes. These are ribbons to be pinned on, reproductions in enamel for the buttonhole, and thin ribbons worn so that they run from the buttonhole to the edge of the lapel and fasten on the reverse side.

**DEGREES.**   For the correct use of abbreviations of academic degrees on visiting cards and elsewhere, *see* Degrees in the Index.

## DEMITASSES

Demitasses, also called "after-dinner coffee cups," are used only for coffee served after a meal. They are not properly used for coffee served with dessert. They may be used at the table after the dessert dishes are removed, but this is not common practice. The standard procedure is to serve after-dinner coffee in the living room or elsewhere away from the dining table. Demitasses may be used after any dinner, but are not used after a lunch unless it is a strictly formal one. Standard tea or coffee cups are used at all other lunches. *Café diable* may be served in demitasses if the special *diable* cups are not available.

*See* COFFEE for details of service.

**DENTISTS.**  *See* DOCTORS.

**DESSERT.**  *See* MEALS AND THEIR SERVICE.

## DIETS

Anyone on a rigidly limited diet, such as a salt-free one, can only refuse most dinner invitations unless willing to break his regimen. It is not fair to treat a hostess as a short-order cook and expect her to produce special food for one guest when she has her hands full preparing for a big party.

The guest who must avoid certain foods can mention the matter when asked to a family dinner with close friends, but allergies (*which see*) or other dietary difficulties or religious food restrictions are generally not mentioned when accepting an invitation to a big party because that would be a tacit demand for specially prepared food if not a change in a planned menu. In most cases, mention of food restrictions is also skipped after a guest reaches the table since it is then too late for the hostess to do anything about a replacement without some trouble. Instead, a good guest quietly passes up a problem food, or takes a token helping and leaves it untouched on his plate.

Many religious groups observe certain restrictions and taboos related to food and drink. Moslems, for example, do not eat shellfish or pork and do not take alcoholic drinks. Catholics have days of complete or partial abstinence from meat. Some of these vary in date from one calendar year to another. Therefore, a hostess planning to entertain guests likely to observe restrictions of this sort is well advised either to ask the guests about them in advance or to offer a menu that provides choices acceptable in most circumstances. Such a menu might include both a roast and a meatless main dish. Usually, a buffet that includes a choice among meat, fish, and cheese or egg dishes offers some main dish that will be acceptable to almost everyone.

## DINNER CLOTHES

"Dinner clothes" means Black Tie for men and an evening dress less elaborate than a ball gown for women. "We are dressing" is another way to indicate the same degree of formality in dress.

## DINNERS

"Dinner" is a catchall word that can mean any meal at the end of the day. It may mean a banquet, a meal served buffet style, a backyard barbecue, or a family gathering complete with the baby in his high chair. Occasionally "supper" is used by a hostess who wants to emphasize that her evening meal will be a very simple one. Otherwise, "supper" is generally used today to mean a light meal nearer midnight than six o'clock.

*See* MEALS AND THEIR SERVICE.

**DIPLOMATS.**  *See* FORMS OF ADDRESS (Diplomatic).

## DIRECTORS

"Director" is not used as a title preceding a name, in writing or in speech. It is correct to address a business letter in either of the following ways, the choice depending on the length of the individual's name and the organization name:

Mr. William Fry Smithington
Director, The City Symphony
*or*
Mr. Ray Ford, Director
The City Recreational Bureau

It is never correct to address a letter "Director John Smith," or to begin one "Dear Director Smith," or to introduce a man as "Director Smith."

**DISHES.**   *See* CHINA; MEALS AND THEIR SERVICE.

## DIVORCES AND SEPARATIONS

We live in a society in which some long-established customs give women certain advantages and put what is sometimes an unfair burden on men. Nowhere are these inequities more evident than in a number of the traditions concerning the breakup of a marriage.

Convention calls for the wife to bring the suit for divorce, no matter who is the injured or dissatisfied party. It is nearly always cause for gossip and speculation, if not scandal, when a husband brings suit. Therefore, though it may cause both husband and wife real inconvenience, a man usually does not institute the divorce action unless his wife has behaved so outrageously that he feels he must demand custody of the children and cannot come to an agreement with her out of court, or unless he is determined to have a divorce and his wife flatly refuses to bring suit (or is unable to do so because of special circumstances).

This means that countless honorable, well-behaved, responsible men must submit to embarrassing and false public charges of inflicting mental anguish, committing assault, battery, and other brutalities or even crimes, to satisfy the legal requirements for divorce in some of our states.

Even if such charges are true, a divorce court is not the place to air them. A divorce is a private matter. Whenever possible, it should be the aim of both parties to reach a private agreement and not make public in court any details of personal resentments, division of property, support of children, alimony, and other such matters. "Incompatibility" is the commonest charge in the states where this decently inexplicit reason is legal grounds for divorce. However, some states grant divorces only if a grave charge such as adultery or insanity can be proved. This, of course, means that there is one law for the rich and another for the poor, since people who can afford to do so establish residence in a state where public embarrassment need not be added to the private sorrow, expense, and trouble that accompany any divorce.

**ANNOUNCEMENTS.**   It is not correct to send formal engraved announcements of a divorce, and it is not customary to make any announcement in the press. Instead, relatives and friends are notified in any informal fashion—verbally or by personal letters—and the word is allowed to spread in that fashion. Announcements are sent to newspapers only if the divorce is in some way newsworthy enough to bring queries from reporters. In this case, such questions are forestalled by a press release that confines itself to the basic facts, such as the date of the divorce and new addresses.

If a press announcement is made, it comes from the woman. If an inquiry from the press is directed to the man, he refers the reporter to his wife's lawyer for a statement, or, if it makes matters easier for her, he may issue a statement in an impersonal form such as:

> Mrs. Henry York Brown is leaving next week to establish residence in Reno, Nevada, and to institute divorce proceedings. A private separation agreement has been reached.

**BEHAVIOR.**   It is obvious that some major dissatisfaction must have preceded any divorce and that the period following even the friendliest divorce is one of major dislocation and adjustment for the principals and also for their families and friends. Never is silence more golden than at this time.

A divorce is public acknowledgment of a failure. The natural impulse of both parties is to justify the action by shifting the blame to the other, but trouble is only doubled by personal confidences that force friends to take sides. Certain close relatives and very intimate friends may deserve to know some details, but even with them a degree of reserve is best in the long run. Any divorced person who pours out a long tally of grievances to all listeners or who makes a career of long-suffering endurance and self-pity is a bore to acquaintances and, sooner or later, a burden to friends.

Friends need to be equally discreet about comments. The announcement of a divorce is never an excuse for "sympathetic" frankness of opinion like "Now I can say it—I never could see how you put up with . . ." or "All I can say is I'm glad because . . ." Sharply critical comments about a divorced spouse can only reflect on the judgment of the person who chose the wrong partner in the first place, and are as tactless as direct questions about what really caused a divorce.

Friends are forced to take sides to some extent in even the friendliest of divorces, since it is awkward for a recently divorced couple to meet at a social event, especially a small one. If the divorce has left bitter feelings, the principals usually make it clear that they want to avoid all chance meetings. On some occasions, this can pose an insoluble problem to their friends. For example, it might be unthinkable to ask one and not the other to a wedding reception under certain circumstances. In this situation, the only thing to do is to issue the invitations and leave it to each of the divorced couple to inquire if the other has accepted, and then to accept or refuse. If by any mischance a divorced couple find a face-to-face meeting unavoidable at a party, they must at least exchange nods in greeting. It is inexcusably rude to cut anyone under another's roof.

**DIVORCE, DIVORCEE.** A divorced man is a divorcé. His former wife is a divorcée. The words are no more than a description of marital status. They have nothing to do with the question of which person brought the divorce action. A divorced person never properly uses "widow" or "widower" to describe marital status. Those words are used only for the survivor of a marriage ended by death, and the same rule holds for "late."

"Former" husband or wife is the correct word to use for a divorced spouse, and very wide use has made "ex-husband" or "ex-wife" equally acceptable. It is a minor matter, but "my ex," or "your ex" is not. "Ex" is not a title, and is not correctly used by itself.

**GIFTS.** Wedding presents are not returned, even if a divorce takes place after a marriage of only a few weeks or months. It is the convention that all wedding presents become the property of the woman, though no woman of taste and responsibility would keep such a wedding present as heirloom silver given by her former husband's family—unless there are children. Such things may be returned to the donor, but usually are left in the former husband's possession.

**INTERLOCUTORY DECREES.** In some states the law requires a definite period between the time a judge grants a provisional divorce (known as an interlocutory decree of divorce) and the time final divorce papers are issued. A divorce is not legally in effect during this period.

**NAME OF A DIVORCEE.** Since a divorce is not final when an interlocutory decree is granted, a woman remains Mrs. Henry York Brown, for example, during the required waiting period. When final divorce papers are issued, she has a choice of surnames. She may petition the court to restore legally her maiden name and become Miss Mary Greene again, or she drops her former husband's given names, substitutes her maiden name for them, and becomes Mrs. Greene Brown. If her maiden name does not go well with her former husband's last name, she may use another family surname. For example, if her maiden name was also Brown, she could avoid the absurdity of "Mrs. Brown Brown" by using the maiden name of her mother or a grandmother and become Mrs. Maitland Brown. If her maiden name was Frank, Alexander, John, or something comparable, she might also prefer to use some other family name to avoid the impression that she divorced one Mr. Brown and then married another. There is still another choice for a woman who divorces a second husband. If she had children by the first husband and not by the second, she may choose to take back her first husband's last name.

Until quite recently, it was a major breach of etiquette to introduce, address, or refer to a widow, a divorcée, or a happily married woman, for that matter, as "Mrs. Mary Brown," but all rules of etiquette are based on what is most practical and sensible for everyone concerned, and therefore are changed or modified by changing times. The rule that a woman's first name is never preceded by "Mrs." is widely ignored today by both married and divorced women in business and the professions.

This change has come about for several good reasons. For one, "Miss" is widely used as a business title, regardless of a woman's marital status. A divorcée without children very often chooses to avoid the whole issue, even if she has not taken back her maiden name, by using Miss Mary Brown in both her business and social life after divorcing Mr. Henry York Brown. This can cause confusion if she has children, and so many divorcées prefer to challenge the traditional rule and use Mrs. Mary Brown on all business occasions, and reserve the use of Mrs. Greene Brown for social connections. But this, in turn, causes confusion on occasions when business and social activities overlap. Therefore, more and more, we find divorcées using "Mrs." with a first name in all social as well as business circumstances. Though the combination is still not in accord with traditional rules, both its practicality and its extremely wide use, especially for women who achieve any degree of distinction in a career, are giving it increasing status.

Whatever decision is made about a name and title, banks, stores where there are charge accounts, and the post office should be informed of the change of name to avoid confusion with a possible second wife of the divorced husband. If the former wife has legally resumed her maiden name, her passport and Social Security records need changing also.

See NAMES for rules concerning legal change of name.

**RINGS.** There is no firm rule concerning this matter. A divorcée may continue to wear her wedding and engagement rings if she chooses, but it is becoming quite usual for her to remove her wedding ring, even if she has children. If she does remove that ring, she usually makes her status doubly clear by wearing her engagement ring on her right hand, or has it fitted to the little finger of her left hand. In any case, it is usual to have the setting redesigned. A man who has worn a wedding ring removes it after his divorce.

**SEPARATIONS.** Formal engraved announcements of a separation are never correct. Relatives and others concerned are told the news in any convenient informal way—in person or by letter or telephone.

**Legal Separation.** A legal separation is not a divorce. A wife continues to wear her wedding ring and to use her husband's name, Mrs. Henry York Brown. A legal separation may be no more than a document of agreement, signed by husband and wife before witnesses, concerning division of property, custody of children, and other matters.

Whenever possible, a private agreement should be reached before a petition for legal separation is taken to court, so that although the action will be a matter of court record, the details of the agreement will not need to be exposed in public. An actual suit for legal separation is brought only if the parties concerned are in such a state of warfare that they must leave the terms of settlement to the decision of a judge.

**Trial Separation.** A trial separation often precedes a legal separation or a divorce. Since this is an experiment made in hope of reconciliation, the fact of separation is best kept as much of a secret as possible. Either husband or wife makes some reasonable excuse for absence, such as an extended visit or trip. This conceals the fact that a trial separation is in effect and makes it possible to patch up difficulties without advertising the fact that there has been a rift. If neither husband nor wife can get away from town, it is usually the husband who leaves home and moves to a club or hotel. There is no rule that he must be the one to move out, however. This is a matter to be decided individually.

## DOCTOR

"Dr." can be used as a title instead of "Mr.," "Mrs.," or "Miss" by anyone who has been granted a doctoral degree in any one of scores of subjects from Business Administration to Zoology. However, it is not the general practice outside the fields of medicine, education, and religion to use "Dr." as a form of address. The custom followed by lawyers provides a good example. A professor of law is properly addressed as "Dr." on campus and in social life; but a practicing lawyer is not addressed by his title in the courtroom or anywhere else.

For the use of "Professor," "Dean," and other academic titles, see FORMS OF ADDRESS (Academic).

## DOCTORS

Good manners to the men and women in the healing profession—the general practitioner, the surgeon, the dentist, the eye doctor, and others in the field—are based on giving them all reasonable protection against the built-in hazards of their calling, which everyone admits is not a life of ease, peace, and comfort, but a day-in and day-out dealing with distress, anxiety, pain, and—inevitably—tragedy.

**APPOINTMENTS.** Even though doctors are notorious for running behind schedule at their offices, a patient should keep his appointment on the dot. This one-sided obligation is entirely fair because an emergency always has first claim on a doctor's time, no matter how much non-emergency patients are inconvenienced. If a patient's time is also under heavy demand, the sensible procedure is to telephone the doctor's office before showing up, and if he is running late, adjust plans accordingly.

An office appointment with a doctor, particularly with a dentist or other specialist who is able to keep on schedule, is an agreement to pay for a specific amount of his time and skill. Therefore, when an appointment must be broken, it is important to do so as far in advance as possible. And it is only reasonable to expect to be billed for a forgotten appointment or one broken at the last moment.

**CHANGING DOCTORS.** A patient who feels in need of a second opinion can properly ask his regular doctor to bring in a consultant or specialist. But a patient who for any reason decides to change a doctor who has been his regular man for any length of time should give him an explanation—for practical reasons, if no other. The new man may need to consult the old about the details of the patient's medical history, for one thing. The medical records that a doctor maintains in his office are his property, not that of the patient. It is common practice for a doctor to send such records to a colleague, but he does not give them to the patient, and the patient should not expect him to do so.

**ETHICS.** Trusting one's doctor with all information pertinent to an ailment is only ordinary common sense. However, though emotional stress does have a physical effect, the patient should resist the temptation to use the doctor as a wailing wall—unless he is a psychiatrist. No matter how embarrassing a fact may be, it is better to tell the doctor honestly and fully about it if it is pertinent to the malady he is treating, rather than suppress facts that might aid him in diagnosis and treatment. A doctor's ethics, embodied in the Hippocratic Oath, are high. Among other things, he has sworn not to pass along any privileged information confided by a patient.

Ethics in medical matters is not a one-way street. The patient is also bound by rules. He is out of line if he tries to pump the doctor for information about other patients or (except in an emergency) to trap him for professional advice at a party or other entirely social occasion.

**FEES.** When illness strikes, first aid takes precedence over financial considerations, and the doctor accepts this as one of the obligations and hazards of his calling. Nevertheless, if a patient is not able to pay for a doctor's services promptly, he is obligated to say so, and to make a definite arrangement about payment in installments—before an operation, for example, rather than after it. And everyone is protected if the cost of treatment is discussed in advance—frankly and in detail—with the doctor.

**GIFTS.** Many people, grateful for a doctor's kindness and skill, want to show their appreciation in some tangible way, but only in special circumstances is a present in addition to his fee either called for or expected. Appreciation is best shown by paying his bills promptly, by being on time for appointments, and by using decent restraint in calling him outside office hours except in an emergency.

**HOME VISITS.** Unless by prior arrangement, the doctor should not be asked to examine other members of the household when he has been called to treat one person, though an exception may be made in an emergency. It is not considerate to ask him to take a look at Junior's throat and see if his tonsils should come out next year, when the call is being made to see about Sister's measles. The doctor usually is on a tight schedule, and may not have time to run through routine examination of the whole family. If he is asked to do so, he is within his rights to charge for each person examined.

A patient should be ready to see the doctor without delay when he arrives, even though the doctor himself may be late in arriving.

**OFFICE NURSES.** A doctor's office nurse is addressed as "Miss" or "Mrs." or, if her name is unknown to the patient, as "Nurse." She is usually much too busy to be expected to serve as a conversational sparring partner for a patient waiting for the doctor. And, though often very knowledgeable, she is not a doctor and should not be blamed if she very properly refuses to give medical advice or information.

**TELEPHONE CALLS.** Calls to the doctor should be confined to his office hours except in emergencies. A patient asking for advice over the telephone should have pencil and paper handy, his list of questions ready, and make the call as brief and businesslike as possible. When calling a doctor at his home, remember that he does not have his records at hand, and be prepared to provide a quick summary of the facts he may need. Many doctors maintain an answering service with which they check at frequent intervals when out of the office. When a doctor is asked to return a patient's call, someone should be at home, ready to answer when he telephones.

**DOGS.**  *See* PETS.

## DOILIES

A service tray should always be left bare, whether it is a small one for a single glass or a large one for carrying a coffee or tea service or passing cocktails. Foods to be taken in the fingers, such as tea sandwiches or cookies, small cakes or petits fours, may be served on a platter that is covered with a doily, which may be of linen, lace, or lace paper.

Doilies are not needed under finger bowls, and many hostesses think that they just clutter up the service. If they are used, they must be of linen or lace, never of paper.

Doilies of linen may be used in the basket or on a small platter under oyster crackers, croutons, small rolls, and other breads, though a folded napkin often is used.

## DOORMEN

The patron of a theater, restaurant, or shop and the resident of an apartment house or hotel need not tip the doorman for opening the door of a car when it pulls up or of a cab already waiting. He should however, be tipped a quarter if he makes some special effort to get a cab, helps with luggage, or parks a car. And the permanent resident of a hotel or apartment house usually makes it a habit to tip his doorman on a fairly regular basis. A passerby who joins regular patrons of an establishment when they are waiting for cabs is expected to hand over a tip, and must do so if he asks the doorman to signal a cab.

A nightclub doorman is generally tipped for opening a car door for a departing patron.

## DOORS

Good manners are really very simple. All anyone needs is a firm grasp of *why* we developed a particular custom in order to know when a rule applies and when it does not. It is hard to find a better example than the rules about getting through doors.

In all usual circumstances, a man opens a door for a woman and lets her enter first. He is acting out his symbolic role as protector—against the wild beasts pursuing them to the cave, or from the strain of pushing aside a slab of wood heavy enough to keep out robbers. From these practical beginnings came two gallant conventions: Opening a door (even one as lightweight as a screen door) is a symbol of respect; so is standing aside to let another person go through a door first (even when the "door" is an open arch). This is why, today, the host (or hostess) invites a guest to precede him into his house, and in public places a younger person stands aside for an older one of the same sex.

However, these conventions are abandoned instantly whenever they are obviously empty of sense. A host or hostess enters a pitch-black dwelling first in order to find lights; a man goes first through the heavy doors on trains in order to manage them efficiently; he also goes first through the exit door of a bus to be in a position to help his woman companion down the steps.

Common sense also governs the actual opening of a door. All things being equal, a man resents it when a woman masterfully reaches for every doorknob and thwarts him in his instinctive gesture; but a woman who stands before a door and pointedly waits, seemingly handless as a hen, shows about as little social sense as one. And when a man's arms are full of bundles, a sensible woman opens and holds a door for him without hesitation.

## DRINKS

One rule holds on all occasions when an additional drink is offered. The correct words are something like "Will you have some wine?"—never "some more" wine. And any variant of "Let me get you a drink"—not "another drink" —is the standard correct form.

Drinking and eating are touched on in many places in this book, since these two activities are part of so many of the occasions when people get together.

See separate listings from BEER AND ALE to WINES, and see also Drinks in the Index for page references within other listings to alcoholic and non-alcoholic drinks.

**DRIVING.**   See AUTOMOBILES.

**DRUNKENNESS.**   See INTOXICATION.

## DUNKING

The dipping of toast, doughnuts, cookies, rolls, or any other breads or cakes into beverages or soups is in questionable taste for an obvious reason—the process nearly always leaves an unappetizing residue of crumbs or grease in the cup, and the soggy, dripping piece of food itself is not the most pleasant sight. If done at all, dunking is best saved for a meal in solitude.

**DUTCH TREATS**   See DATES.

# E

**EASTER.**   See HOLIDAYS.

## EATING

The rule is simple and positive: Don't eat in front of any caller without offering to share at least some portion of the meal, if no more than a cup of coffee. It is then up to the visitor to accept or refuse. This rule is just as binding in an office as elsewhere. If it is necessary to admit a caller when lunch is spread out on a desk, offer some part of it or set it aside until he leaves—though a caller with his wits about him will say, "Please go ahead," if he sees a half-finished lunch courteously ignored. Good business sense will dictate whether to accept or refuse the suggestion. A junior executive would certainly ignore it during a brief visit from the president of the company. Under any circumstances, an apology is necessary before going ahead with a meal that is obviously impossible or absurd to share.

See also BUSINESS MANNERS; TABLE MANNERS.

## ELBOWS

There is nothing wrong with putting one or both elbows on a dining table between courses, or when leaning forward in conversation, but only if an implement, cup, glass, or piece of food is not in either hand. As a general rule, players keep their elbows off the table during a card game.

## ELEVATORS

The suspicion grows that a great many elevator passengers play a little game called "Do It the Hard Way." Otherwise, why would a crowd waiting to board an elevator completely block the door and cause a time-wasting scrimmage for the passengers who are trying to get out? Why do so many passengers aimed for the topmost floors achieve the same result by taking a firm stand, front and center in the car, instead of moving to the rear or sides? Why do so many passengers in the front row act as if they had homesteaders' rights and refuse to step out temporarily to make exit easy for others? And why do so many passengers ignore a basic rule of physics (the sum of the parts cannot be greater than the whole) and jam ruthlessly into an already jammed elevator in the belief that there always is room for one more?

Common-sense behavior and good manners are identical in an elevator. A man obeys the standard rule about doors and lets a woman precede him, unless this courtesy would inconvenience others. If an elevator is packed and a man is blocking his companion's way, it is absurd for him to force her to squeeze past him. He steps out first without waste of time, and stands waiting for her to follow.

**APARTMENT HOUSES.** Manners are slightly more formal in apartment-house elevators than in those in public buildings. An apartment-house elevator is treated as part of each tenant's residence, but the following rules are correctly ignored when it is obviously awkward or delaying to observe them.

A man allows any woman to enter and exit first (with the exceptions below). A teen-age boy stands aside for all elders and for girls. A teen-age girl gives precedence to any woman. Everyone stands aside for the very old or infirm. When nonresidents of the same sex and about the same age approach an elevator, the one nearer the entrance waves the other ahead if both cannot step in simultaneously, but only if this can be done casually and without delay. An elaborate "After you," and "No, after you," exchange is unnecessary.

**Host and Hostess.** A hostess accompanied by a male guest enters her elevator first. If accompanied by several couples, she waves them in ahead, though one man in her party stands aside until she is aboard. A hostess always shows a female guest into her elevator first, even if the guest is a teen-ager and the hostess is elderly. A hostess precedes a guest out of an elevator and leads the way to her door. A host lets a guest leave his elevator first, or if it is more convenient, steps out first and stands aside until the guest joins him.

When a guest leaves an apartment, the hostess stands in her door, if the elevator entrance is in sight, until the guest enters it. She need not accompany a guest to an elevator that is around a corner, but often does so. A host takes a woman guest to the elevator, rings for it, and waits until she is aboard. These rules are suspended if either host or hostess has duties to other guests at a big party, or if there is a maid to see guests out. A maid does not follow the above rules, however.

**HATS.** A man who properly wears his hat when moving through the aisles of a department store often takes it off unnecessarily when he enters the elevator. A store elevator is considered as much of a public corridor as the aisles. A man does not take off his hat when entering an elevator in a store, station, office building, or any other public structure of similar character. It is customary, however, for a man to take off his hat when sharing an apart-ment elevator or hotel elevator with any woman. Common sense dictates ignor-ing this general rule if he has his arms full of bundles, or if the elevator is so crowded that it would be awkward for everyone if he followed the rule.

**OPERATORS.** In an apartment house, a resident is required to nod, smile, or give some other greeting to the operator when entering and when leaving the elevator. It is conspicuously rude to ignore the presence of any employee of the building, or to give the floor number curtly or as an order to the operator. "Please" must be added unless the tone of voice or a smile takes the place of that word. Elevator operators who go to any special trouble to get a taxi, help with luggage, or perform other unusual service are tipped at the time unless a tenant tips on a monthly basis.

**PUBLIC BUILDINGS.** In busy elevators, the same manners hold as when strangers board a bus or other conveyance. A waiting crowd stands aside to let passengers off. If only a few passengers are boarding (or leaving), men let women go first. When a sizable group is waiting, those nearest the door get on in whatever order is most practical and expeditious. However, a man stands aside for any woman acquaintance. For this reason, a young woman employee with her wits about her will drift toward another car in the rush hour if her employer or chief is also waiting. Otherwise he might feel obligated to let her board first, and so be left behind himself.

**SELF-SERVICE.** All standard rules are observed except that it is often sensible and therefore correct for a man to step out first and hold one of those quick-action doors that nip closed without warning. The passenger nearest the control panel pushes the button for another passenger if it is awkward for a newcomer to reach it.

**SMOKING IN.** Lighted cigarettes and cigars should not be carried into a crowded elevator because of the obvious danger of burning someone who may be unexpectedly forced against the smoker.

**ELOPEMENTS.** *See* WEDDINGS.

**EMPLOYEES, EMPLOYERS.** *See* BUSINESS MANNERS; HOUSEHOLD EMPLOYEES.

**ENGAGEMENTS.** *See* APPOINTMENTS; BUSINESS MANNERS; DATES; PUNCTUALITY.

## ENGAGEMENTS TO WED

**ANNOUNCEMENTS.** The two most important rules concerning the announcement of an engagement are:

1. It is not correct to send an engraved or printed notice similiar to a wedding announcement.
2. Any *formal* announcement must come from the bride or her connections. If she has no close relatives, the announcement may be made by a godparent or guardian, or she may send it herself to the press. Under no circumstances is it correct for the news to be announced at a party given by her fiancé or any member of his family.

**Formal.** A formal announcement is made by sending a release to the society editor of a newspaper (*see* "Press" below) or by telling the news at a party. Frequently both methods are used. If so, the press notice is scheduled for printing the day following the party, never in advance of it.

The closest relatives of the engaged couple are always told the news before a formal announcement is made, and if the engagement will be a disconcerting surprise to a friend (a still hopeful sweetheart, for example), it is only considerate to break the news in advance rather than let it be read or heard without warning.

**Informal.** After closest relatives have been informed, the news is spread in whatever way is convenient. The bride-to-be wears her engagement ring on the third finger of her left hand—an indication in itself of her engagement—and tells her friends. The man tells his. The parents of both pass the word along to theirs. (For a paid press notice in Vital Statistics columns, *see* "Press" below.)

**At Parties.** Even though the purpose of the announcement party is an open secret, it is not mentioned in the invitations. Sometimes the announcement is made to guests as they arrive. At a small gathering, the bride-to-be may make the announcement herself by displaying her ring to each guest on first greeting. At a large gathering, there may be a receiving line with the mother of the girl, the mother of the man, the girl, and her fiancé receiving in that order, the announcement being made by the girl's mother as guests go through the line. After greeting a guest, she makes an introduction (if necessary) to the young man's mother and makes the announcement by also identifying her as "Mary Ann's future mother-in-law." The fiancé's mother then makes any necessary introductions to her future daughter-in-law. The girl, in turn, introduces her fiancé to the guests who do not know him. The fathers usually do not stand in the receiving line, though the young man's father sometimes stands in the third place if he is unknown to most of the guests.

Very often the announcement is not made until all guests have assembled and can join in a toast proposed by the girl's father or, if he is not present, by a close relative. At a cocktail party or reception, he chooses any appropriate time. If the announcement is made at a meal, the toast may be proposed after all glasses are filled for the first time, or later. The girl's father rises, calls for attention, says a few words, and lifts his glass. He may make a formal statement such as: "I have the honor and pleasure to announce the engagement of our daughter, Mary Ann, to John Jones Smith, and to propose a toast to their happiness in their marriage." Or he may say something as simple as "To Mary and John. Happiness together." When he raises his glass, everyone present— with the exception of the engaged couple—rises and drinks. Glasses need not be drained and are never broken, as sometimes is done after the toast to the bride-to-be at the groom's bachelor dinner. Traditionally, the toast is made with champagne, though any beverage will serve. Teetotalers need not actually drink, but it is a marked discourtesy not to raise a glass to the lips in token that the toast is being shared. As the others take their seats, the young man rises and says a few words of thanks for himself and his fiancée for the good wishes. Then the engaged couple are free to lift their glasses.

**Press.** Any kind of paid press announcement of an engagement is not correct if the standard rules are strictly observed. However, this is one of the rules of etiquette that is fast being changed. Because there is not room in the society columns of big-city newspapers for separate reports of all engagements, it is the growing custom to make a press announcement by paid insertion in the Vital Statistics columns. Though this method has not yet reached complete acceptance, there is no reason to disapprove it if there is no other way to inform the whole community of an important family event.

The separate items on a society page are printed without charge, of course. In order to achieve such an announcement, a release is sent to the newspaper at least three or four days in advance of the desired date of publication. It should be typed, double-spaced, and addressed to the society editor. At the top of the page, the name, address, and telephone number of the person sending the release should be given, to aid a reporter who may want to call for additional information. The release date should be prominently placed, especially if the announcement is sent to more than one newspaper. A picture of the bride-to-be usually is sent with a release, and to avoid confusion her name should be written on the back of it. It is not customary to ask a newspaper to return a photograph, even if it is not used. Neither is it customary to send a picture of the fiancé. If he is of special importance, the newspaper will use a picture of him from its files, or make a request for one. The society editor usually rewrites a release, but an announcement always has a better chance of being used if one of the two following standard forms is followed:

## STANDARD FORM I

Release Date:
Name [of person sending the release]:
Address:
Telephone Number:

Mr. and Mrs. Henry York Brown of 10 Main Street announce the engagement of their daughter, Mary Ann, to Mr. John Jones Smith, son of Mr. and Mrs. William Barkeley Smith of Phoenix, Arizona. Miss Brown is a senior at Town College. Mr. Smith is a graduate of City College, and is associated with the law firm of Greene, Scott and Black. The marriage will take place late in June.

## STANDARD FORM II

[This is known as the impersonal form. It is correct under all circumstances, and is the first choice when relationships are complicated by divorce.]

Release date, etc., as shown above.

Announcement is made of the engagement of Miss Mary Ann Brown, daughter of Mrs. George Steven Tower and of Mr. Henry York Brown, to Mr. John Jones Smith, son of Mrs. Maitland Smith and Mr. William Barkeley Smith. . . .

Some newspapers provide a helpful service—an engagement form that will be sent on request. The following is typical, and gives a good idea of the details that may be added to the sample releases above:

## ENGAGEMENT FORM
Please fill out and return to Society Editor

Full name of Bride-Elect _____ Phone _____
Residence of Bride-Elect _____
Parents _____
Parents' Residence _____
College & Prep Schools _____
Social Affiliations _____
Family Connections _____
Full name of Bridegroom-Elect _____
Residence of Bridegroom-Elect _____
Parents _____
Parents' Residence _____
College & Schools _____
Affiliations _____
Family Connections _____
Date of Wedding _____
How Engagement is Announced _____
Release date: _____
Signature of Bride-Elect or one of her parents _____

(Use reverse side for additional information)

# STANDARD FORMS: SPECIAL CIRCUMSTANCES

**1. Adoption.** No mention of an adoption is made if the engaged person's name is legally the same as that of the adoptive parents. An explanation is given if the adopted person's name has not been changed, and also if a bachelor or a single woman is announcing the engagement of an adopted daughter:

> Miss Janice Towne Green announces the engagement of her adopted daughter, Joyce June Greene . . .

**2. Deceased Parent or Parents.** The names of both parents, whether living or dead, are given in the announcement, but "the late" must be used before the name of a deceased parent.

*If both of the girl's parents are dead* and the announcement is made by a relative or guardian, the relationship is specified. If the relative issuing the announcement is married, the name of his (her) spouse is also used:

> Mr. and Mrs. John Stone Greene announce the engagement of her niece, Miss Mary Ann Brown . . . Miss Brown is the daughter of the late Mr. and Mrs. Henry York Brown. [Note that "Miss" is used if it is necessary to give the last as well as the first name of the girl.]

*If one parent is dead and the other has not remarried:*

> Mr. Henry York Brown announces the engagement of his daughter, Mary Ann . . . Miss Brown is also the daughter of the late Mrs. Brown.

*If the father is dead and the mother is remarried:*

> Mr. and Mrs. George Steven Tower announce the engagement of her daughter, Miss Mary Ann Brown . . . Miss Brown is also the daughter of the late Henry York Brown.

*If the mother is dead and the father is remarried:*

> Mr. and Mrs. Henry York Brown announce the engagement of his daughter, Mary Ann . . .

In this case, the use of "his daughter" indicates that her mother is dead and that he has married again, and is sufficient.

**3. Divorce.** If either of the engaged couple has been divorced, a formal announcement usually is not made in the press. This rule can be ignored if the bride-to-be is marrying for the first time. (It is poor taste to make an announcement of any kind if either of the couple is waiting for a final decree of divorce.)

*If the bride-to-be is a very young divorcée:*

> Mr. and Mrs. Henry York Brown announce the engagement of their daughter, Mary Ann Smith . . . Mrs. Smith's marriage to Mr. John Jones Smith was terminated by divorce last year.

*If the bride-to-be is a mature divorcée,* the standard impersonal form is usually used:

> Announcement is made of the engagement of Mrs. Brown
> Smith, daughter of the late Mr. and Mrs. Henry York Brown . . .
> The marriage of Mrs. Smith, the former Mary Ann Brown, to
> Mr. John Jones Smith was terminated by divorce.

### If the fiancé is divorced:

No mention is made of his former marriage and divorce in an announcement sent to a newspaper, though the editor is privileged to add that information if it is of news value.

### If the parents are divorced:

The girl's mother usually issues the announcement. Only in a special circumstance is it made by her father—if she has made her home with him for many years and if her mother lives at a great distance, for example. No matter who makes the announcement, both parents are mentioned. If one parent lives in another city it is customary to include that fact. The standard impersonal form is by far the most useful and usual. Other standard forms are:

> Mrs. Greene Brown [never Mrs. Elizabeth Brown]
> announces the engagement of her daughter, Mary Ann . . . Miss
> Brown is also the daughter of Mr. Henry York Brown of
> Washington, D.C.

### If a divorced mother has remarried:

> Mr. and Mrs. George Steven Tower announce the engage-
> ment of Mrs. Tower's daughter, Miss Mary Ann Brown . . . Miss
> Brown is also the daughter of Mr. Henry York Brown of this city.

**4. Legally Changed Names.** Unless a whole family has changed its name legally, it is necessary to make some explanation of a statement that otherwise would look like an error:

> Mr. and Mrs. Henry York Brown announce the engagement
> of their daughter, Mary Ann, to Mr. John Paul Scott, son of Mr.
> and Mrs. Jan Paulus Scatowski. Mr. Scott changed his name
> legally after the publication of his first novel . . .

**5. Legally Separated Parents.** No mention is made of a separation, legal or otherwise, and the standard "Mr. and Mrs. Henry York Brown announce" form is used, or, more often, the standard impersonal form.

**6. Self-Announcement.** If the bride has no close relatives, she sends the announcement in her own name but uses the standard impersonal form.

**7. Widows.** The engagement of a widow usually is not announced in the press, though it is entirely correct to send a release to the society editor. In such case, a mention of her late husband is always made.

*A very young widow's engagement is announced by her parents:*

> Mr. and Mrs. Henry York Brown announce the engage-
> ment of their daughter, Mrs. John Jones Smith . . . Mrs. Smith
> is the widow of the late Mr. Smith and before her marriage was
> Miss Mary Ann Brown.

*An older widow's engagement* announcement usually is not issued by her relatives. She issues it herself in the standard impersonal form:

> Announcement is made of the engagement of Mrs. John
> Jones Smith . . . Mrs. Smith, before her marriage to the late Mr.
> Smith, was Miss Mary Ann Brown. She is the daughter of Mrs.
> Henry York Brown and the late Mr. Brown . . .

**BEHAVIOR OF AN ENGAGED COUPLE.** As a general rule, dates with other beaux come to an end once an engagement is announced, and a hostess does not ask one of an engaged couple to a party without the other, except under unusual circumstances, if both are in town.

A man who respects himself naturally takes care not to put his future wife in a situation that could cause gossip. If the rules are observed, a girl does not make an overnight motor trip alone with her fiancé, for example, or spend the night under the same roof unchaperoned.

**BETROTHALS.** Engaged couples of any faith may speak of each other as "my betrothed"—though that term sounds absurdly stilted today unless used in referring to a formal betrothal ceremony. A formal betrothal is a religious ceremony that is relatively rare in this country except in the Greek Orthodox and Roman Catholic faiths. It usually is held in church before an invited gathering, not a regular congregation, though a Greek Orthodox betrothal service may be held at home. Betrothal promises are solemn vows, though not as binding as wedding vows, since a betrothal may be broken just as a formally announced engagement may be. In the Catholic faith, a formal betrothal is known as a "canonical engagement."

**BREACH OF PROMISE.** A suit for damages due to a breach of promise to wed implies that some injury has been suffered beyond the emotional hurt caused by a change of mind. This is a legal matter, not one of etiquette, since it is part of an action already outside the bounds of good behavior.

**BROKEN.** At best, a broken engagement causes some embarrassment to the families concerned as well as to the couple and their friends, but far better to break an engagement than to stick to it if in doubt about one's feelings.

If an engagement has been announced in the press, an announcement of its cancellation should be sent to the same newspapers. The standard form contains the explanation "by mutual consent," whether this is entirely true or not. And no matter which of the couple breaks the engagement, the girl's family announces the cancellation. Either of the following is sufficient:

> Mr. and Mrs. Henry York Brown announce that the
> engagement of their daughter, Mary Ann, to Mr. John Jones
> Smith has been broken by mutual consent.

*or*

> The engagement of Miss Mary Ann Brown and Mr. John
> Jones Smith has been broken by mutual consent.

Closest members of both families and intimate friends should be told the news before any announcement is sent to the press. If the rules are followed, the man does not give any explanation to anyone. In addition, the code of a gentleman requires him to indicate that the engagement was terminated by the girl's decision—even if just the opposite was the fact. The most dignified explanation for both to give, best for everyone in the long run, is, "We decided together that it just wouldn't work out," with no further details.

Legally, a ring given as an engagement present is the property of the girl.

The rules of good behavior say that the ring should be returned, no matter who breaks the engagement. So should any valuable presents given by the man or his family, and most especially any heirlooms or other family treasures. If the engagement is ended by the death of her fiancé, the girl should offer to return an heirloom ring to his family. A new ring remains in her possession, without question.

Engagement or wedding presents given to the couple jointly are returned, with a note from the girl. A brief message is all that is required in most cases:

> Dear Joyce,
>
> Since John and I have broken our engagement, I am returning the silver tray that you and Bill so kindly sent us.
>
> Love,
>
> Mary Ann

**CALLS.**   *See* "Parents," below.

**CONFERENCE WITH THE GIRL'S FATHER.**   The day is long past when a proper young man was required to ask permission from a girl's father before proposing marriage to her. However, any young man mature enough for marriage will realize that his fiancée's parents deserve to be told of his prospects, plans, and financial status. If he wants to get off to a good start as a new member of the family, he explains such details to her father as soon as possible after being accepted—unless his circumstances are so well known that an accounting would be an absurdity. Such a conference usually is between the two men only, though if this seems stuffy there is no reason to exclude the girl and her mother.

**CONGRATULATIONS.**   The word "congratulations" is used only to a fiancé. "Best wishes for happiness" is one of the many substitutes when speaking to a fiancée. Otherwise, the implication would be that she is the winner in a long, hard pursuit of a reluctant quarry. Her parents may be congratulated on the addition of such a fine young man to the family, but "Congratulations!" without such qualification implies that they had a tough time finding someone else to support their daughter.

**GIFTS.**   The man's traditional engagement present is a ring, though any other item of jewelry is correct. The bride-to-be usually gives him something in return that will be of permanent personal use such as a watch or cuff links. The girl's parents often give a present to the young couple jointly—a check or some item that both will enjoy in their life together. The man's parents may do the same, or may welcome the bride-to-be to their family by giving her something for her personal use, usually jewelry. Such presents are a charming token of approval, but are not obligatory. Engagement presents are not customary from friends.

Before the wedding, a man does not properly give his fiancée very valuable or very personal presents with the exception of the engagement ring. He may give her a handbag, gloves, and other small items for personal use, but not a coat, suit, or lingerie, or anything so expensive as a car.

**LENGTH.**   The standard rule is that an engagement is formally announced no more than six months, and no less than six weeks, before the wedding. This relates only to the formal announcement, of course. Many young couples have an understanding that lasts for several years. Once their plans are told to their parents and friends, they properly speak of themselves as engaged. In this case, the girl need not wait for the formal announcement, but wears her engagement ring or her fiancé's fraternity pin.

**LOVE LETTERS.** Engaged people naturally write to each other in tender terms, but they should take care not to put anything on paper that might be construed as unduly intimate if read by a third person. The rules say that a man must not show an intimate love letter to anyone. It is a good rule for women to follow, also. When an engagement is broken, the rules say that love letters must be returned to the writer.

**MOURNING.** An engagement may be announced in the press very shortly after the death of a close relative, but if either family is in mourning a big announcement party is not appropriate.

**PARENTS.** Both families are told the news as close to the same time as possible, the girl's parents first, however, if the happy pair makes joint calls on the telephone or in person to announce their engagement. If they tell the news separately, the man's mother telephones or writes without delay to her future daughter-in-law, and includes a message of welcome from the whole family. The girl's mother also telephones or writes to her future son-in-law without delay. If the families are intimate, there is a spontaneous outbreak of telephone calls and of family get-togethers with no special protocol observed. By the rules, however, it is the duty of the man's parents to make the first formal move—a call in person on the girl's parents, which they arrange to return promptly. If calls are not possible, the parents exchange letters. These rules are followed, with slight changes, by divorced and remarried parents. For example, if the parents of the young man are divorced and both remarried, his mother writes to the girl and her family, including the good wishes of her son's stepfather with those of the rest of the family, and the stepfather accompanies her in her formal call to the girl's parents. The young man's father also writes to the girl and her parents, includes the good wishes of his current wife, and takes her with him when he makes his call. The stepmother also writes separately to the girl, since good sense calls for behavior that emphasizes step*mother* rather than *step*mother.

**RING.** The tangible token of engagement to marry is a ring worn on the third finger of the left hand. An engagement ring may be worn as soon as it is given, though if there is to be a formal announcement party it usually is not worn before that day. An engagement ring need not be the traditional diamond. Any stone is appropriate. Presumably, an engagement ring is to be worn for life, and so it should be of a size and style to go with any costume without being unduly ostentatious. A diamond solitaire of fairly moderate size and simple setting is a better choice, especially for a young bride-to-be, than a great flashing stone in a bejeweled setting that would look absurd in the morning at a supermarket.

A man may select the engagement ring by himself, but the usual procedure is for his fiancée to aid in the choice. Unless the sky is the limit, he makes a first stop alone, gives the jeweler his price limit, and makes a preliminary selection, leaving the final decision to his sweetheart. There is no rule that an engagement ring must be new. An heirloom stone—given a modern setting, if this is the girl's wish—can serve with added sentimental value. Such a family treasure must be given first to the man, however—never directly by his parents to his fiancée, if it is to count as an engagement ring.

A girl may set up a joint fund with her fiancé to save for other expenses, but no part of her money should be spent for either the engagement or the wedding ring. Any girl worthy of a ring will accept the smallest stone happily rather than make this breach of sentiment and taste.

**SHOWERS.** There is a definite distinction between an engagement shower and a bridal shower. A bridal shower is given to help a couple with the furnishing of their first home together. Only items for their joint use or service are appropriate. The groom and other men may attend. An engagement shower is confined to personal items for the bride's trousseau. Men, including the groom, are not invited. If an engagement shower is given, it should be held shortly after the engagement is announced so that the bride can avoid duplication in buying items for her trousseau. Otherwise, the rules for showers given under WEDDINGS are followed.

## ENTERTAINERS

We are considering here the obligations of the hostess to an entertainer who appears for a fee at a private social gathering, not manners in general to celebrities (*which see*), or behavior to entertainers in nightclubs, at concerts, or in theaters, which is covered in those separate categories.

The range of talented people available for paid appearances is wide—from the magician for a children's party, to a full dance band, a noted lecturer, a distinguished soloist, a famous theatrical personality or group—and the range of procedures for dealing with them is equally wide, depending on the distinction of the performer and his own wishes, as well as the character of the gathering.

**CELEBRITIES.** Even if appearing for a fee, a lecturer, singer, or other star performer is often treated in all ways as the guest of honor: He may arrive at the beginning of a party, stand with or near the hostess so that all guests may be introduced as they arrive, and stay until the end of the party.

Many artists, however, prefer not to join a party before a performance. If the artist feels this way, or if the hostess herself prefers to present the entertainer just before his performance, he is greeted with the ceremony due a special guest, and shown to a private room where he can wait comfortably. If someone else has admitted him, his host and hostess make a point of greeting him shortly after his arrival and making sure that he has been offered refreshments and anything else he may need. When the time comes for his appearance, either the host or hostess escorts him from his retreat and makes some kind of formal introduction to present him to the gathering. At the conclusion of his performance, the hostess goes up to thank him and to introduce any guests who come up to speak with him. If refreshments follow a private lecture or musicale, for example, the entertainers are always invited to remain and may accept or not, according to their own wishes and schedule.

**OTHER PAID ENTERTAINERS.** The entertainers who are not expected to join the party as guests should also be given the consideration due any visitor of professional standing. For example, a clown engaged to perform at a children's party may be smuggled in the back way if he is in costume and his appearance is to be a surprise; but, if possible, he is shown a private waiting room rather than asked to cool his heels in the kitchen, is greeted by the hostess or other person in charge of arrangements, and offered anything he may need for his comfort.

The procedures are much the same for musicians engaged to play throughout a party, from a single accordionist to a dance band. A band, for instance, is shown to the dressing room assigned to the group and also given a chance to inspect the place where they will play if they do not take their positions before the first guests arrive. The host and hostess make a point of greeting the leader shortly after his arrival, just as they would any other guest, and also arrange for refreshments to be served to the group in some suitable room (not the kitchen) at appropriate times.

**PAYMENT.** All entertainers should be thanked by the host and hostess before their departure. Unless an entertainer has been engaged through a bureau and some other specific arrangement has been made for the payment of his fee, it is handed over before his departure, whether he has joined the party as a guest or not. Entertainers of all degrees are professionals, and so tips are not in order except in some few cases. A singing waiter, for example, can be tipped, but not a soloist.

## ENTERTAINMENT

Accepting entertainment on the social level calls for some return, though not necessarily in kind. Many single people and young couples who are valued guests at parties given by older or more prosperous friends are not equipped to return entertainment on anything approaching the same scale. It is absurd to attempt to keep up with the Joneses, but the Joneses will certainly mark off as a freeloader an acquaintance who makes no return whatever. Returning entertainment is not a matter of matching expenditures. It is the sharing of the best one has, no matter how elaborate or simple that may be. It is entirely sensible to return a picnic for an elaborate dinner in a restaurant, or a date at the movies for a theater party, but there is seldom an excuse for staying permanently on the receiving end of entertainment—or a chance, for that matter. Sooner or later, anyone who does not pay his way loses the chance to do so.
  *See* Entertaining in the Index.

## ENTREE

The literal translation of the French *entrée* is "entry." In the days when formal dinners of six or seven courses were customary, *entrée* meant the course served after the fish and before the meat as an entry, or introduction, to the main course. Today, especially in restaurants, "entrée" usually means the main course. The word also is used to mean a figurative open door: "He has entrée to the best circles."

## ESCALATORS

"Escalator" is a trademarked name. Technically, an escalator is one particular manufacturer's moving stairway, though the word is widely used by the general public to mean any moving stairs. On a wide moving stairway, a man and woman step on side by side. On a narrow one, a man lets his companion step on first. A younger person stands aside for an older. Otherwise, all comers take their turn as they do in any queue in a public place.

## ESQUIRE

Only the abbreviation "Esq." is used in any written form of address. In this country "Esq." is almost never used in business correspondence (except to lawyers) and is rarely used for social correspondence. "Esq." is a substitute for "Mr.," and so it is never used in addition to "Mr.," "The Honorable," "Mayor," "General," or any other title. Nor is it engraved on a calling card or written as part of a signature. It is just as incorrect for a man to sign a hotel register "John Jones, Esq." as it would be to sign "Mr. John Jones."

**ESTATE.**  *See* HOUSE AND HOME.

## EUROPEAN PLAN

At a hotel or resort, "European Plan" means that the meals are not included in the quoted price for the room. Waiters and others who give direct service are tipped at the time it is given.

## EX

"Ex" combined with a title is never used when speaking directly to the person concerned. "The Ex-President [Ambassador, Mayor, etc.]" is correct when speaking about a former President, but the prefix is not included when addressing him directly. In such case, either "Mr. President" or "Mr. Smith" is correct.

Since "ex" is merely a prefix that qualifies status, it is not correctly used by itself as a noun, though "my Ex" and so on has fairly wide use as a substitute for "former husband (wife)." "Ex-husband" always means one removed by divorce, not by death.

## EXCELLENCY

It is not the American custom to use "Excellency" as a form of address for American officials. (*Note:* In some few states, the governor is addressed as "His Excellency," but our State Department uses "The Honorable" in addressing mail to all governors, and so "The Honorable" is always correct.) In this country, "Excellency" is correctly used only in referring to and addressing by mail a foreign ambassador, cabinet officer, or other foreign high official. A person once entitled to be called "His Excellency" continues to be so referred to and addressed by mail after he leaves office.

*See* FORMS OF ADDRESS (Foreign).

## EXCUSES.    *See* APOLOGIES AND EXCUSES.

## EXHIBITS.    *See* MUSEUMS, ART GALLERIES, AND EXHIBITS.

## EXPENSE ACCOUNTS.    *See* BUSINESS MANNERS.

# F

## FANS

Most teen-agers go through a phase of star worship. This can be expected and even welcomed if the star sets a high standard of behavior and the youngster follows it. It is the behavior of fans who are more interested in being noticed themselves at any cost, than in complimenting their favorites, that turns parents, police, and performers gray before their time.

*See* CELEBRITIES.

## FAREWELL PARTIES

Anyone can give a farewell party. One neighbor may give a party for a family about to move away; several friends may join forces to give a party; or the departing family may give one. Members of a staff may join to give another staff member, from office boy to chief, a send-off, or an executive may show his regard for the staff he is leaving by giving them a party before his departure.

In business, a farewell party is generally held on the day of departure. In private life, the convenience and pleasure of all who are concerned govern the time. Under most circumstances, a big party on the eve of a trip adds to problems of departure, and so the usual choice is several days in advance.

As a general rule, a guest is not expected to take a present to the guest of honor. Very often, though, each person invited to a farewell party is asked to chip in a small sum toward one substantial memento of the occasion from the entire group.

*See:* TRAVEL (Bon Voyage Parties).

## FATHER'S DAY

Father's Day is the third Sunday in June.
*See* MOTHER'S DAY.

## FEET

Feet belong on the floor or near it, not on furniture, on the facing seat of a train, against the front seat of a car, or twisted around the rungs of a chair. Feet also belong in shoes, with few exceptions. On an overnight plane, train, or bus trip, a passenger may take his shoes off if he wants to. Elsewhere, women are the decidedly privileged sex. A woman slips her heels out of her shoes or even takes them off in the dark of a theater if she wants to risk an embarrassing search for one inadvertently kicked several rows away. No such relief is permitted a man. Even at the family fireside, Daddy is frowned on as hopelessly uncouth if he does not cover his stockinged feet with slippers.

## FEMALE AND FEMININE

When filling in any questionnaire with a blank for sex, "female" is the right word, not "feminine." "Female" may be used as a noun: "The dog is a female"; or as an adjective: "of the female sex." "Feminine" always is an adjective, but is used only to describe a quality or a manner, not a sex. "Female cat" (not "feminine cat") and "female help" (not "feminine help") are correct. This rule applies to "male" and "masculine" also.

## FIGHTS.   *See* QUARRELS.

## FIGS.   *See* FRUITS.

## FINGER BOWLS

Finger bowls are a necessity after foods that leave the fingers oily, sticky, stained, or strongly scented. So it is better not to serve whole steamed lobsters, for example, unless prepared to supply finger bowls afterward.

Finger bowls are more of a grace note than a necessity at the end of a formal meal. They can be brought in with the dessert service or after the final course.

If a finger bowl is brought in on an underplate that also carries a fork to the left and a spoon or knife to the right of the finger bowl, it is a clear signal that dessert is to be served on the underplate. The guest first puts the dessert silver on the cloth to the right and left of the underplate. Then he lifts the finger bowl and doily (if there is one) together, and sets them to the left in about the position occupied earlier by a butterplate. He does not use the finger bowl until after he has finished dessert. If there is any variation of this service, such as a small glass plate between the finger bowl and the dessert plate, wait for the hostess to make the move, and follow her example.

If a finger bowl is brought in without implements, it is a signal that the meal is finished and the finger bowl is not to be moved from its underplate.

A doily is not necessary between the finger bowl and its underplate, but if one is used, it must be of linen or lace, never of paper. The finger bowl served at the end of a meal is filled about half-full or a little more with cool (not iced) water. Flower petals may be floating on the water, but never a slice of lemon. The finger bowl served during a meal, after a greasy or sticky food that was handled with the fingers, contains warm (not hot) water and a slice of lemon. This finger bowl is removed before the next course is served, of course, not set aside by the diner, who, in any case, dips only the tips of his fingers into the water.

## FIRES

Good manners call for resisting the temptation, seemingly shared by all, to play with fires. The good guest never adds fuel or rearranges any already burning in a fireplace in the presence of his host unless asked to do so, and leaves a barbecue fire strictly in charge of the cook.

Behavior when a siren is heard nearby is not a matter of etiquette. It is a matter of law, but is so important that it is included here anyway. All cars must pull over to the extreme right. They may proceed with caution within a block, but must never cross an intersection until there is complete certainty that the vehicle sounding a siren will not be blocked or slowed. Pedestrians also must clear the streets.

## FIRING AN EMPLOYEE.   *See* BUSINESS MANNERS; HOUSEHOLD EMPLOYEES.

## FISH

Smelt and other small fishes often are served whole, though they should be cleaned before cooking. Only the minute whitebait is popped into the pan without cleaning. Whether brought to the table with head and tail, or without them, a whole fish is dealt with in the same manner. The fork (or knife and fork) is used to detach bite-size pieces from the upper side. When the spine has been exposed, the fish is turned over and the other side eaten. The meat may be removed from both sides of a smelt, and the spine set to one side of the plate, but larger fish are not boned completely before eating, except by a waiter, who puts the spine on a separate plate and removes it. Fishbones are taken out of the mouth with fingertips, not a fork. They are put on the side of the dinner plate, not on the butter plate.

*See* separate listings for the various shellfish.

## FLAG OF THE UNITED STATES

Federal laws govern the handling and display of our national flag to ensure its proper use as the symbol of the nation. Custom and tradition have established other rules. The Armed Services have precise regulations concerning the display of the flag. The use of the flag by all other citizens is governed by Public Law 623, approved by the Seventy-seventh Congress in 1942, and later amended.

**ADVERTISING.** Only the United States Government may use the flag in display advertising. No person, agency, or company may do so, nor may any advertisement, sign, or pennant be attached to the flagpole or standard carrying the flag. A federal law prohibits registering a trademark that consists of, or comprises among other things, "the flag, coat-of-arms or other insignia of the United States, or any simulation thereof."

**CARRYING.** Do not carry the flag flat or horizontally, but always aloft and free. Keep it from becoming soiled. Do not allow the flag to touch the ground or floor, or to brush against other objects.

**DECORATION.** The flag must not be printed, embroidered, or otherwise used as a decoration on any clothing, furniture, cushions, boxes, stationery, paper napkins, or tablecloths. Nor should it be used to cover a piece of furniture, including a speakers' table. It must not be looped or draped as decoration on a wall, ceiling, or any other surface.

**DEFACING THE FLAG.** No lettering or writing may be placed on the flag.

**DIPPING.** The flag must not be dipped to any person or thing, with one exception: Navy vessels, upon receiving a salute of this type from a vessel registered by a nation formally recognized by the United States, must return the compliment. Aside from this, only such flags as regimental colors, state flags, and organizational or institutional flags are dipped as a signal or honor.

**DISPLAY.** Following are the major regulations governing display of the national emblem:

**Automobiles.** The flag may be attached to a staff fixed on the radiator cap or the right end of the front bumper in line with the right fender. It should clear the radiator hood. The flag should not be hung, draped, or displayed in any other fashion on a car.

**Boats and Ships.** The flag is displayed only from a staff. It is never hung flat or draped, and it must never trail in the water. No other flag should be flown above it except the church pennant (a dark blue cross on a white background), when used during church services conducted at sea by naval chaplains.

**Church.** When a flag is displayed in a church it should always occupy the position of honor. If it is in the chancel it should be placed at the clergyman's right as he faces the congregation. Any other flag also displayed in the chancel should be placed at the clergyman's left. If the flag is to occupy a place in the body of the church, it should be placed at the right of the congregation as they face the chancel. If another flag is also displayed, it should be placed on the left of the congregation.

**Grouped Flags**

1. When a number of flags of states or cities or pennants of societies are grouped and displayed from separate staffs along with our national flag, and can be viewed from all sides, our national emblem should be at the center or at the highest point of the group. If, however, the flag is displayed from a staff along a wall, it should be placed to the flag's own right (the observer's left), with state and other flags to the left. This rule also applies to the display of our national flag in a bracket from a wall.

2. When displayed with another flag against a wall from crossed staffs, the flag of the United States should be on the right, the flag's own right, and its staff should be in front of the staff of the other flag.

3. When the flags of two or more nations are displayed, they should be flown from separate staffs of the same height, and the flags should be of approximately equal size. International usage forbids the display of the flag of one nation above that of another nation in time of peace. (Only the United Nations flag at UN Headquarters may be flown above the Stars and Stripes.) Our national flag is displayed to the left of the others from the observer's viewpoint. In this country, it is the first to be raised and the last to be lowered. When American and foreign flags are hung against a wall, our national flag is again at the left of the others as seen from the audience, and the union is always at the upper left.

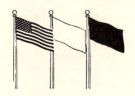

4. When flags of states or cities or pennants of societies are flown on the same halyard with the national emblem, the latter should always be at the peak.

**Half-staff.** Flags must never be flown at half-staff or half-mast without official decree. Since the flag of the United States symbolizes the nation, it is displayed at half-mast or dressed with crepe only to indicate official national mourning. It is against the law for a family or business organization to show personal loss in this manner. When flown at half-staff, the flag should be hoisted to the peak for an instant and then lowered to the half-mast position, which is halfway between the top and the bottom of the staff. Before lowering the flag for the day it should be raised again to the peak.

**Horizontal Staff.** When the flag is displayed from a staff projecting horizontally or at an angle from a windowsill, balcony, or the front of a building, the union of the flag should go all the way to the peak of the staff unless the flag is at half-mast.

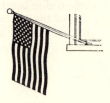

**Night Display.** Although there is no law forbidding display of the flag at night, it is customary to display it in the open only from sunrise to sunset. When an exception is made at a *public* building or monument, it is ordinarily authorized by a presidential proclamation or public law, or continued because of a long-standing tradition. However, a private citizen may display the flag at night on special occasions, when it is desired to produce a patriotic effect, without special permission to do so.

**Parades.** In a parade the flag is carried aloft on a staff not horizontally. When one other flag is carried, the national flag is at the right of the marching column. When two or more flags are carried, the national flag is in position in front of the other flags in the center line. The flag should not be attached to the sides of, or displayed on, a float in any way except on a staff. See "Funerals," below, for the use of the flag in funeral processions.

**Public Auditoriums.** When a flag is displayed in a public auditorium, it should always occupy the position of honor. If it is on the platform it should be placed on the speaker's right. If the flag is displayed from a staff elsewhere than on the platform, it should be at the right of the audience. Any other flag so displayed at the same time should be placed on the left of the audience.

**Sidewalks.** When suspended from a rope between a house and a pole at the edge of a sidewalk, the flag should be hoisted outward from the building toward the pole, union first.

**Street.** When displayed over the middle of the street, the flag should be suspended vertically with the union to the north in an east-west street or with the union to the east in a north-south street.

**United Nations Headquarters.** The United Nations flag is flown above the Stars and Stripes at United Nations Headquarters.

**Walls and Windows.** When the flag is displayed, either horizontally or vertically, on a wall or in a window, it should be displayed flat, never draped, and should fall as freely as if it were staffed. The union must be uppermost and to the flag's own right—that is, to the observer's left.

**DISTRESS.** The flag must never be flown with the union down except as a signal of serious distress.

**FLAG DAY.** Flags are displayed on June 14 to commemorate the adoption, on that date in 1777, of the Stars and Stripes as the United States flag. It is not a legal holiday except in Pennsylvania.

**FRINGE.** Fringe is not considered part of the flag. It is used as enrichment only on flags that are carried or used for display purposes. Fringe is not used on flags flown from halyards or fixed flagstaffs.

**FUNERALS**

1. The flag is carried in a funeral procession only by official decree. It is not carried at half-mast but flown from the top of a staff with a black crepe bowknot, with or without two streamers of black ribbon, tied at the point of the staff. Black crepe is not used on the flagstaff except by order of the President of the United States.

2. The flag is used only on the caskets of members of the Armed Services, or former members with honorable discharges. When the flag is used to cover a casket, it should be placed so that the union is over the left shoulder of the deceased. Flowers are not placed on the flag. It must be removed before cremation or before the coffin is lowered into the grave, and must not be allowed to touch the ground during this procedure. The casket should be carried foot first.

3. Flags are provided for burial services of military personnel and most veterans. If a person dies while on active duty, his own Service furnishes the flag used to drape his coffin. The flag for the funeral of a veteran is furnished by the Veterans Administration, Washington, D.C., and may be procured from the nearest post office by executing properly Veterans Administration Form 2008. In filling out the application, the person signing for the flag must state whether he is the next of kin, or if another relative, must give kinship. The flag is presented to the next of kin at the proper time during the burial service. If there is no relative, or one cannot be located, the flag may be presented, on request, to a close friend or associate of the deceased veteran. Otherwise, the flag must be returned to the Veterans Administration in the franked container provided for that purpose. Postmasters require proof of honorable discharge before issuing the flag. Flags are issued promptly upon proper evidence.

**MEMORIAL DAY.** On Memorial Day, May 30, the flag is displayed at half-mast from sunrise until noon in honor of dead American servicemen, and at full staff from noon until sunset. Flags that are placed on graves for Memorial Day should be removed the next day. It is disrespectful to our national emblem to allow them to remain until they become soiled and torn.

**OBLIGATIONS.** Every citizen is obligated to see that no disrespect is shown to the flag of the United States of America.

**PLEDGE TO THE FLAG.** The correct pledge of allegiance to the flag is as follows: "I pledge allegiance to the flag of the United States of America, and to the Republic for which it stands, one nation under God, indivisible, with liberty and justice for all." During the pledge, everyone should stand. A man in civilian dress holds his hat over his heart. A woman, or a man without a hat, holds the right hand over the heart. Anyone in uniform holds the military hand salute. If there is to be an invocation as well as the Pledge of Allegiance at the opening of procedures, the invocation is given first.

**RAISING AND LOWERING.** The flag should be raised and lowered by hand. Do not raise the flag while it is furled, nor tie it with bunting or ribbons after it is raised. Unfurl, then raise quickly. Lower it slowly and with dignity, never allowing it to touch the ground.

**SALUTING.** During the ceremony of hoisting or lowering the flag, or when the flag is passing in a parade or in a review, all American citizens present should stand and face the flag. A man in civilian dress salutes by holding his hat over his heart. A woman, or a man without a hat, holds the right hand over the heart. Anyone in uniform holds the military hand salute. Aliens should stand at attention. The salute to the flag in a moving column should be given at the moment the flag passes.

**STATUES OR MONUMENTS.** If the flag is used in connection with the unveiling of a statue or monument, it should be a distinctive feature of the ceremony but never a covering for the statue.

**WHEN FLOWN.** The flag may be flown any day out of doors, from sunrise to sunset, but should not be raised while it is raining, and should be lowered if rain starts. Weather permitting, special care should be taken to see that the flag is flown on the following days:

New Year's Day, January 1
Inauguration Day, January 20
Lincoln's Birthday, February 12
Washington's Birthday, February 22
Easter Sunday (variable)
Mother's Day, second Sunday in May
Armed Forces Day, third Saturday in May
Memorial Day, May 30 (flag is half-staff until noon, then full staff until sunset)
Flag Day, June 14
Independence Day, July 4
Labor Day, first Monday in September
Constitution and Citizenship Day, September 17
Columbus Day, October 12
Veterans Day, November 11
Thanksgiving Day, fourth Thursday of November
Christmas Day, December 25

The flag should also be flown on any special days proclaimed by the President of the United States, on the birthdays of states (dates of admission), and on state holidays.

**WORN OR DAMAGED.** When the flag is in such condition that it is no longer a fitting emblem for display, it should not be cast aside or used in any way that might be viewed as disrespectful to the national colors, but should be destroyed as a whole—privately, preferably by burning or by some other method in harmony with the respect we owe to the emblem representing our country.

**WRAPPING.** The flag must not be used as a receptacle for receiving, carrying, or delivering anything. Never place upon the flag, or attach to it, any mark, insignia, letter, word, figure, design, picture, or drawing of any nature.

## FLOWERS

Flowers are one of the best gifts in token of love, thanks, sympathy, or apology. There are certain occasions, however, when it is a breach of the rules to send flowers or to wear them. And there are other occasions where flowers are inappropriate presents, not as a matter of taste but of common sense. See "When Inappropriate," below.

**ARTIFICIAL.** The imperishability of artificial flowers is one of their appeals. But even though they do not wither, they still need care. Few sights are more tiresome than the same bunch of imitation flowers blooming week after week (or month) in the same vase in the same place. And few sights are more dismal than artificial flowers darkened by time and neglect, with telltale layers of dust in their hearts. Dust or wash such flowers regularly, and rearrange or temporarily retire a bouquet occasionally—it should not be a permanent fixture.

**BOUQUETS.** Any bunch of cut flowers, from an armful of three-foot gladiolas with a ribbon to a handful of dandelions, in or out of a vase, can be called a bouquet. Very small bouquets arranged to be carried sometimes are called nosegays, but a bride's bouquet, even if small, is always termed her "bouquet."

In acknowledging a bouquet delivered by a florist, send thanks for "the yellow roses" or "the tulips and daffodils," rather than for "the bouquet," so that the donor will know his order was correctly filled and his gift not confused by the recipient with other bouquets sent on the same occasion.

**BOUTONNIERES.** A flower worn on a man's lapel gets the name "boutonniere" from the French word for buttonhole. Any small flower is suitable. A red or white carnation is most often seen today, with white being the more formal. A red carnation is the customary choice with a dinner jacket, and white with a tailcoat, though it should be noted that it is equally correct not to wear a flower with formal clothes—and better none than an artificial one, which is appropriate only as a badge for a floorwalker on duty. A boutonniere is never worn with a medal or decoration, or to a funeral.

**CORSAGES.** A corsage is an arrangement of a flower or flowers and leaves or other trimmings meant to be worn rather than carried. It may be worn on either shoulder or pinned to a belt, purse, or anywhere else the wearer chooses. Usually a corsage is worn on the right shoulder for dancing. It may be pinned with the stems up or down, whichever looks best. Many people choose to remove the florist's decorations except for the foil protecting the stems, and a corsage worn with a suit always looks best if tinsel or satin bows are removed. Since a corsage is crushed if a wrap is worn over it, it is unpinned before a coat or stole is put on. It can then be pinned to the wrap or carried in the hand (not in its box) until the time comes to put it back on the dress.

Fashions in the wearing of flowers change, as do all other styles. At one time, a man felt obligated to take or send a corsage to the woman he was taking to a formal dance, and a woman without a corsage felt conspicuous and neglected. Then, in certain circles and localities, it became the style not to wear flowers with evening dresses, and the gift of a corsage became a real problem rather than a pleasure to the recipient. Even when flowers with evening dresses are out of fashion, it is customary to provide flowers to be worn by the women guests of honor at a reception and by the woman speaker at a lecture and other such events. In all cases, it is best—if at all convenient—to send a corsage in advance rather than present it at the last minute, since most women need a little time and a mirror to place a corsage to best advantage. Flowers of emphatic color can also be a problem, and it is always best to ask what color dress a woman is wearing before ordering a brilliant purple orchid or glowing red camellias, for example. A woman wearing a decoration or medal does not wear a flower also and it is never appropriate to wear a flower to a funeral.

It is a matter of no great moment, but though "corsage" is properly used in writing about an arrangement to be pinned on, by today's custom "flower (or flowers)" rather than "corsage" is first choice when speaking.

**DRIED.** Arrangements of dried flowers, grasses, and seed pods are delightful decorations, but the same rules hold as for artificial flowers—keep them dusted, and don't make them as permanent an installation as the curtains.

**WHEN INAPPROPRIATE.** Flowers are traditional symbols of joy and congratulation to members of the Jewish faith. They should not be sent to an Orthodox or Conservative funeral service or to the home of the bereaved, though it is now quite common practice for members of Reform congregations to send and accept flowers as tokens of sympathy. Flowers are not displayed in some Catholic and Episcopal churches during a funeral service. When in doubt, ask the undertaking establishment for guidance.

A flower should never be worn by anyone attending a funeral service.

It is best to think twice before arriving at a big party with an armful of flowers for the hostess. The thought is charming, but dealing with such a gift at that time may be something of a problem for her.

**FOOTMEN.**  *See* HOUSEHOLD EMPLOYEES.

## FOREIGNERS

In general, foreigners have somewhat more formal manners than we have in this country. It is always safest and best to deal with a stranger of another land, either here or in his own country, with rather more formality than might be used to a stranger or casual acquaintance of United States citizenship. Nothing is lost and much good will may be gained. It should never be taken for granted that a foreigner not able to speak English does not understand it. Such slighting words as "wop," "greaser," "frog," "Hunky," "spik," and "Chink" are in bad taste used to a foreigner and in questionable taste even if none is present. And it should be remembered that "Chinaman" is considered slighting by the Chinese. Say "a Chinese man" or, "He is Chinese."

## FORKS

It is correct to lift food on a fork held in either the left hand (European style) or the right hand (American style) provided that the rules given under TABLE MANNERS are followed.

## FORMAL, INFORMAL, SEMIFORMAL

The words "formal" and "informal" as used in this and other etiquette books have exact meanings, and it is easy to become confused unless the arbitrary distinction between them is clearly understood.

"Formal" when applied to clothes, invitations, meals, parties, service, and so on is restricted to the meaning "on the completely ceremonious level in all details," and so it covers an extremely limited field.

"Informal" is used to describe all events and procedures (no matter how large or elaborate or impressive or expensive) that vary in any way from the above definition of "formal." "Informal" in this sense never means "entirely lacking in formality." It denotes only some lesser *degree* of formality than the strictly formal. For example, an elaborate wedding with scores of guests and a full complement of bridesmaids and ushers is not technically "formal" unless the men in the wedding party wear the cutaways and striped trousers that are the formal daytime costume for men or, after 6:00 P.M., evening clothes.

"Semiformal" is sometimes used to describe events (especially weddings) that very nearly rate the term "formal" except in a few details, but it is essentially a vague and confusing term. Most people avoid it because it demands more explanation than it is worth, and its use is limited. There is no such thing as a "semiformal invitation," for instance. An invitation is either formal (expressed in certain explicit third-person forms) or it is informal. "Semiformal" is not generally a substitute for "informal." For example, a "formal engagement" means that some kind of general announcement has been made of a couple's intention to marry; and an "informal engagement" means that parents and close friends know that marriage is planned but that a date for the wedding is not set.

"Formal" in such uses as "I'm wearing a formal" is still in transition, but it is making its way fast because it is short and because its meaning, "a formal evening dress," is clear. However, in some circles people would rather stay home than say, "I'm wearing a formal," or, "We're going formal." These purists choose instead some variant of the standard "We're dressing."

## FORMS OF ADDRESS

There is quite a bit of latitude in certain of the correct forms of address to the people who hold special positions or ranks or titles, depending on how intimate a friend the writer or speaker may be. And there are also correct variants of some of the forms given in the following charts. However, chosen for this section are the forms that are always proper and correct and that are also the usual first choices in today's practice.

The names "John Jones Smith" and "Mary Brown Smith" are used throughout this section to indicate when at least a person's first name should be spelled out (and when to spell out the middle name would also be correct).

### ACADEMIC

1. "Dr." can be used as a title instead of "Mr.," "Miss," or "Mrs." by anyone who has been granted a doctoral degree by a college or university in any one of scores of subjects from Architecture to Zoology.

   However, it is not the general practice outside the fields of education, religion, and medicine for those with doctoral degrees to use "Dr." as a title. A practicing lawyer, for example, who holds a doctorate forgets his academic title, and uses "Mr."

   In scholastic circles it is always best to address anyone who has a doctoral degree as "Dr." When in doubt, use "Dr." also in social circumstances, though some educators make no great point of being called "Dr." away from the academic community. The choice is entirely a matter of individual preference.

2. "President," "Professor," "Dean," "Instructor," "Principal," "Teacher," and so on, are titles denoting the position an educator holds on the staff of an educational institution. These titles are not correctly used preceding a name, as is "Dr.," in social circumstances. See the charts for their limited use in business.

3. Honorary degrees are conferred by colleges and universities in recognition of outstanding achievement. Such a degree is a notable honor, but it is not the general custom for the holder of

| PERSON | ENVELOPES | BUSINESS LETTER |
|---|---|---|
| President, college or university, **with doctoral degree**<br><br>See Note 2. | **Business:**<br>Dr. John Jones Smith<br>   (**or** John Jones Smith, Ph.D.)<br>President, (Name of institution)<br>Street address<br>City, State   00000<br><br>**Social:**<br>Dr. John Jones Smith<br>Address<br>Dr. and Mrs. John Jones Smith<br>Address | Dear Dr. Smith:<br>   Very truly yours,<br>   Sincerely yours, |
| President, college or university, **without doctoral degree**<br><br>See Note 2. | As above, with "Mr." instead of "Dr." | As above, with "Mr." instead of "Dr." |
| President (woman), **with doctoral degree**<br><br>See Notes 2 and 5. | **Business:**<br>Dr. Mary Brown Smith<br>   (**or** Mary Brown Smith, Ph.D.)<br>President, (Name of institution)<br>Address<br><br>**Social:**<br>Dr. Mary Brown Smith (**single**)<br>Mrs. John Jones Smith (**married**)<br>Mr. and Mrs. John Jones Smith<br>Address | Dear Dr. Smith:<br>   Very truly yours,<br>   Sincerely yours, |

In formal invitations, the middle as well as the first name should be spelled out, but in business and everyday correspondence it is also correct to drop the middle name or to use an initial.

This section deals with written and spoken address to people in special professional categories, to foreign officials and foreigners with titles.

The correct forms of address for all the rest of us, in day-to-day as well as special circumstances, are dealt with under BUSINESS MANNERS; CORRESPONDENCE; DOMESTIC EMPLOYEES; INTRODUCTIONS; INVITATIONS; NAMES; TELEPHONE MANNERS; and other separate listings.

an honorary degree to use the title or be addressed "Dr.," though he uses the appropriate initials after his name under certain circumstances—when identified as a lecturer on a printed program, for example. In such use, "Hon." is also used: Hon. Ph.D.

4. The form "John Jones Smith, Ph.D." is correctly used in a business letter only, or on a business visiting card. ("Dr. John Jones Smith," without initials, is the correct social form.)

If a person holds degrees in two or more different fields, the initials denoting all of them may be used: Ph.D., LL.D., D.D.

"Ph.D.' is used throughout this sec-

tion to represent the use of any abbreviation denoting a doctoral degree.

5. An unmarried woman educator with a doctoral degree is addressed "Dr. Mary Ann Brown" in both social and business letters. A married woman who holds a doctorate is addressed "Dr. Mary Brown Smith" in professional connections, but socially she drops the "Dr." and is addressed "Mrs. John Jones Smith."

6. "Very truly yours," by tradition, is correct on business but not on social mail. It is the standard form for a business letter; but the trend today is to use "Sincerely yours," which is also correct and is considered less stiff by some people.

| SOCIAL LETTER | IN CONVERSATION | INTRODUCTIONS | ABBREV. |
|---|---|---|---|
| My dear Dr. Smith, **(very formal)** Dear Dr. Smith, Sincerely yours, | To and **about:** Dr. Smith (or, sometimes in the scholastic community, "President Smith.") | **Individual:** Dr. Smith **Presentation to an audience:** Dr. John Jones Smith, President of———— | Do not use "Pres." |
| As above, with "Mr." instead of "Dr." | As above, with "Mr." instead of "Dr." | As above, with "Mr." instead of "Dr." **or** President John Jones Smith of ———— College | None |
| **Single:** My dear Dr. Smith, **(very formal)** Dear Dr. Smith **Married:** Use "Mrs." instead of "Dr." Sincerely yours, | To and **About:** **Single:** As for a male president with a doctoral degree **Married:** On campus: "Dr. Smith" Socially elsewhere: either "Dr. Smith" or "Mrs. Smith," depending on circumstances | **Individual (single):** Dr. Smith **Individual (married):** On campus: "Dr. Smith" Socially elsewhere: either "Dr. Smith" or "Mrs. Smith," depending on circumstances **Presentation to an audience:** Dr. Mary Brown Smith, President of ———— | None |

| PERSON | ENVELOPES | BUSINESS LETTER |
|---|---|---|
| President (woman), **without doctoral degree**<br><br>See Notes 2 and 5. | **Business:**<br>Miss [Mrs.] Mary Brown Smith<br>    (**or** Mary Brown Smith, Ph.D.)<br>President, (Name of institution)<br>Address<br><br>**Social:**<br>Miss Mary Brown Smith<br>Mrs. John Jones Smith<br>Address | Dear Miss [Mrs.]<br>    Smith:<br>    Very truly yours,<br>    Sincerely yours, |
| Dean **with doctoral degree** "Dean" is generally used on campus but not in social life.<br><br>See Note 2. | **Business:**<br>Dr. John Jones Smith<br>    (**or** John Jones Smith, Ph.D.)<br>Dean, School of———<br>University of———<br>Address<br><br>**Social:**<br>Dr. John Jones Smith<br>Address<br>Dr. and Mrs. John Jones Smith<br>Address | Dear Dr. Smith:<br>    Very truly yours,<br>    Sincerely yours, |
| Dean **without doctoral degree**<br><br>See Note 2. | As above, with "Mr." instead of "Dr." | Dear Dean Smith:<br>    Very truly yours,<br>    Sincerely yours, |
| Dean (woman)<br><br>See Notes 2 and 5. | The same rules as for men | |
| Professor **with doctoral degree**<br><br>See Note 2. | **Business:**<br>Professor John Jones Smith<br>Dr. John Jones Smith<br>John Jones Smith, Ph.D.<br>Department of———<br>Name of institution<br>Address<br><br>**Social:**<br>Dr. John Jones Smith<br>Address<br>Dr. and Mrs. John Jones Smith<br>Address | Dear Dr. Smith:<br>    Very truly yours,<br>    Sincerely yours, |
| Professor **without doctoral degree**<br><br>See Note 2. | **Business:**<br>Professor John Jones Smith<br>Department of———<br>Name of institution<br>Address<br><br>**Social:**<br>Mr. John Jones Smith<br>Address<br>Mr. and Mrs. John Jones Smith<br>Address | Dear Professor Smith:<br>Dear Mr. Smith:<br>    Very truly yours,<br>    Sincerely yours, |

| SOCIAL LETTER | IN CONVERSATION | INTRODUCTIONS | ABBREV. |
|---|---|---|---|
| As above, with "Miss" or "Mrs." instead of "Dr." | **To:**<br>Miss [Mrs.] Smith<br><br>**About:**<br>Miss [Mrs.] Smith (or, sometimes in the scholastic community, "President Smith") | **Individual:**<br>Miss [Mrs.] Smith<br><br>**Presentation to an audience:**<br>Mary Brown Smith, President of ——— | None |
| My dear Dr. Smith, **(very formal)**<br>Dear Dr. Smith,<br>Sincerely yours, | **To:** Dr. Smith<br><br>**About:** Dr. Smith (On campus, "Dean Smith" can be used in both cases above, but "Dr." or "Mr." is used in social life.) | **Individual:**<br>Dr. Smith<br>Mr. Smith<br><br>**Presentation to an audience:**<br>Dr. John Jones Smith, Dean of the School of ———, University of ——— | None |
| My dear Mr. Smith, **(very formal)**<br>Dear Mr. Smith<br>Sincerely yours, | **To:**<br>Mr. Smith (On campus, either "Mr. Smith" or "Dean" Smith)<br><br>**About:**<br>Mr. Smith (Or, on campus, "Dean Smith") "Dean" is not used outside the scholastic community in social circumstances. | **Individual:**<br>Mr. Smith<br><br>**Presentation to an audience:**<br>John Jones Smith, Dean of the School of ———, (name of institution) | None |
| My dear Dr. Smith, **(very formal)**<br>Dear Dr. Smith,<br>Sincerely yours, | **To** and **About:**<br>Dr. Smith (On campus, either "Dr. Smith" or "Professor Smith") | **Individual:**<br>Dr. Smith (or, on campus, "Professor Smith")<br><br>**Presentation to an audience:**<br>Professor John Jones Smith of the Department of ———, Name of the institution | Do not use "Prof." |
| As above, with "Mr." instead of "Dr." | **To** and **About:**<br>Mr. Smith (or, on campus, "Professor Smith") | As above, with "Mr." instead of "Dr." | None |

| PERSON | ENVELOPES | BUSINESS LETTER |
|---|---|---|
| Professor (woman)<br><br>See Notes 2 and 5. | | |
| Associate Professor<br>Assistant Professor<br>  These titles are not used be-<br>  fore a name. Use "Mr.,"<br>  "Miss," "Mrs.," or if he has<br>  a doctoral degree, "Dr." | **Business:**<br>Mr. John Jones Smith<br>Associate [or Assistant] Professor<br>Department of——<br>Name of institution<br>Address<br><br>**Social:**<br>Mr. John Jones Smith<br>Address<br>Mr. and Mrs. John Jones Smith<br>Address | Dear Mr. Smith:<br>Very truly yours,<br>Sincerely yours, |
| Instructor<br><br>See Notes 2 and 5. | Follow the pattern of<br>  Associate Professor | |
| Principal<br><br>See Notes 2 and 5. | **Business:**<br>Mr. John Jones Smith<br>Principal, Name of institution<br>Address<br><br>**Social:**<br>Mr. John Jones Smith<br>Address<br>Mr. and Mrs. John Jones Smith<br>Address | Dear Mr. Smith:<br>Very truly yours,<br>Sincerely yours, |
| Teacher<br><br>See Notes 2 and 5. | **Business:**<br>Mr. John Jones Smith<br>Name of department (**optional**)<br>Name of school<br>Address<br><br>**Social:**<br>As for Principal | As above |
| Coach<br><br>See Notes 2 and 5. | As above | As above |

## THE ARMED SERVICES

It must be emphasized that the information in this section is for the guidance of civilians, since forms of address within the Armed Services are different, in some uses, from the forms that civilians use when writing or speaking to military personnel.

The whole matter of correct forms of military address strikes the civilian, at first glance, as complicated beyond all hope of understanding. It is not, really. As a general thing, a civilian will choose the right form if he follows the standard social guidelines for correspondence and introductions, and substitutes rank for "Mr." There are a number of exceptions, noted in detail in the charts, and—in general—in the points following.

1. **Spoken Address.** There is a marked difference among the services in how titles are used when speaking directly to or introducing certain junior officers and noncommissioned personnel.

   (a) **In the Army, Air Force, and Marine Corps:**
   All generals are "General" in spoken address (not "Brigadier General," for example).
   All colonels are "Colonel."
   All lieutenants are "Lieutenant."
   All warrant officers are "Mister."
   All cadets are "Mister."
   All sergeants are "Sergeant."
   A corporal is "Corporal."
   Privates, all grades, are "Private."

| SOCIAL LETTER | IN CONVERSATION | INTRODUCTIONS | ABBREV. |
|---|---|---|---|
| | | | None |
| My dear Mr. Smith, (**very formal**) Dear Mr. Smith Sincerely yours, | **To** and **About:** Mr. Smith | **Individual:** Mr. Smith<br><br>**Presentation to an audience:** John Jones Smith, Associate [Assistant] Professor in the Department of ———, Name of the institution | None acceptable |
| | | | None |
| My dear Mr. Smith, (**very formal**) Dear Mr. Smith Sincerely yours, | **To** and **About:** Mr. Smith | **Individual:** Mr. Smith<br><br>**Presentation to an audience:** Mr. John Jones Smith, Principal of the ——— School | None |
| As above | As above | **Individual:** Mr. Smith<br><br>**Presentation to an audience:** Mr. John Jones Smith, of the ——— Department, Name of school | None |
| As above | As above | "Coach" may be used preceding the name in a public presentation, but not as a title otherwise. | |

There are no corporals or privates in the Air Force. In that service, a man below the rank of staff sergeant is "Airman" in spoken address.

**(b) In the Navy and Coast Guard:**

All admirals are "Admiral" in spoken address (not "Rear Admiral" or "Vice Admiral").
A commodore is "Commodore."
A captain is "Captain."
A commander is "Commander."

For personnel below the rank of commander, the correct forms of spoken address vary sharply from the customs in the Army, Air Force, and Marine Corps. Officers through the rank of lieutenant commander, and warrant officers, are introduced by title and last name, but thereafter addressed "Mr." ("This is Lieutenant Commander Smith. Mr. Smith is on the 'Helena.'" The correct answer to this introduction is "How do you do, Mr. Smith?")

A lieutenant commander is always "Lieutenant Commander" (not "Commander").

In **civilian** circumstances, officers through the rank of lieutenant commander, and warrant officers, may be spoken to as "Mr.," although they are normally introduced by their rank.

Navy midshipmen and Coast Guard cadets are both "Mr." (A look at the charts will make these and other standard forms clear.)

(c) In prolonged conversation, it is correct to drop an officer's last name and speak to him directly by his title only. As a general rule, however, in social life it is best to avoid overuse of "Admiral," "Colonel," "Chief," and so on.

2. **Written Address.** On a big base, post, or carrier, there may be several men of the same or similar name and rank but of different services—Colonel J. J. Smith of the Army and Lieutenant Colonel J. J. Smith of the Air Force, for example. Therefore, when writing to a member of the Armed Services **at his duty post,** it is important to follow the rules that have been developed to avoid confusion and delay. On the envelope, put a man's complete rank, written out or abbreviated, before his full name, and put the initials of his service after his name.

Each member of the Armed Services has his own service number. It is also

**Army, Air Force, Marine Corps:** *Note: Change USA (U.S. Army) to USAF (U.S. Air*

| PERSON | ENVELOPES | BUSINESS LETTER |
|---|---|---|
| General | **Business:**<br>General John Jones Smith, USA<br>Address<br><br>**Social:**<br>General John Jones Smith<br>Address<br><br>General and Mrs. John Jones Smith<br>Address<br><br>See Note 2. | Dear General Smith:<br>Very truly yours,<br>Sincerely yours, |
| Lieutenant General<br>Major General<br>Brigadier General | **Business:**<br>Lieutenant General John Jones<br>Smith, USA<br>Address<br><br>**Social:**<br>See Note 2. | Dear General Smith:<br>Very truly yours,<br>Sincerely yours, |
| Colonel | **Business:**<br>Colonel John Jones Smith, USA<br>Address<br><br>**Social:**<br>See Note 2a. | Dear Colonel Smith:<br>Very truly yours,<br>Sincerely yours, |
| Lieutenant Colonel | **Business:**<br>Lieutenant Colonel John Jones<br>Smith, USA<br>Address<br>See Note 2b.<br><br>**Social:** See Note 2a. | Dear Colonel Smith:<br>Very truly yours,<br>Sincerely yours, |
| Major | **Business:**<br>Major John Jones Smith, USA<br>Address<br><br>**Social:** See Note 2a. | Dear Major Smith:<br>Very truly yours,<br>Sincerely yours, |
| Captain | **Business:**<br>Captain John Jones Smith, USA<br>Address<br><br>**Social:** See Note 2a. | Dear Captain Smith:<br>Very truly yours,<br>Sincerely yours, |

correct to use that number on mail going to a duty post, though such numbers are not used (outside official service mail) on letters going to a home address.

(a) Note, however, that it is not necessary or customary to use a man's service initials after his name on social letters if he lives off a base. In that case, his home address makes them obviously unnecessary. And service initials are never correctly used on an envelope addressed jointly to a man and his wife (Admiral and Mrs. John Jones Smith).

(b) As a general rule, it is best to follow the most formal practice and spell out in full a man's rank or rating. It is not incorrect to abbreviate certain titles, however, when to spell them in full would crowd an envelope beyond reason. (See the charts for approved abbreviations correct for social use.)

3. **Service Initials:**
USA—U.S. Army
USAF—U.S. Air Force
USCG—U.S. Coast Guard
USMC—U.S. Marine Corps
USN—U.S. Navy

*Force) or USMC (U.S. Marine Corps), where appropriate.*

| SOCIAL LETTER | IN CONVERSATION | INTRODUCTIONS | ABBREV. |
|---|---|---|---|
| My dear General Smith, (very formal)<br>Dear General Smith, Sincerely yours, | To and About:<br>General Smith<br><br>See Note 1c. | Individual:<br>General Smith<br>Presentation to an audience:<br>General John Jones Smith, his service and command | None acceptable |
| As above<br>(Note that "Lieutenant," "Major," and "Brigadier" are not used in the salutation of a letter —only on the envelope.) | To and About:<br>General Smith<br><br>See Note 1c. | Individual:<br>General Smith<br><br>Presentation to an audience:<br>Lieutenant General John Jones Smith, his service, and duty if applicable. (After the first statement of his rank, he is referred to as "General.") | Lt. General<br>Maj. Gen.<br>Brig. Gen.<br>Also acceptable:<br>Lt. Gen.<br>Maj. Gen.<br>Brig. Gen. |
| My dear Colonel Smith, (very formal)<br>Dear Colonel Smith, Sincerely yours, | To and About:<br>Colonel Smith<br><br>See Note 1c. | Individual:<br>Colonel Smith<br><br>Presentation to an audience:<br>Colonel John Jones Smith, and his branch of service | Avoid "Col." |
| My dear Colonel Smith, (very formal)<br>Dear Colonel Smith, Sincerely yours, | To and About:<br>Colonel Smith<br><br>See Note 1c. | As for Lieutenant General | Lt. Colonel<br>Also acceptable:<br>Lt. Col. |
| My dear Major Smith, (very formal)<br>Dear Major Smith, Sincerely yours, | To and About:<br>Major Smith<br><br>See Note 1c. | Individual:<br>Major Smith<br><br>Presentation to an audience:<br>Major John Jones Smith, and his branch of service | None acceptable |
| My dear Captain Smith, (very formal)<br>Dear Captain Smith, Sincerely yours, | To and About:<br>Captain Smith<br><br>See Note 1c. | As above | Avoid "Capt." |

| PERSON | ENVELOPES | BUSINESS LETTER |
|---|---|---|
| Lieutenants<br>"First" and "Second" are grade distinctions that are ignored by civilians in both written and spoken address. | **Business:**<br>Lieutenant John Jones Smith, USA<br>Address<br><br>**Social:**<br>See Note **2a.** | Dear Lieutenant<br>Smith:<br>Very truly yours,<br>Sincerely yours, |
| Chief Warrant Officer<br>Warrant Officer<br>In social address, spoken, and in the written salutation of a letter, all Warrant Officers are "Mr." | **Business:**<br>CWO John Jones Smith, USA<br>WO John Jones Smith, USA<br>Address<br><br>**Social:** By first choice, spell out his full rank, but on informal mail his rank can be abbreviated.<br><br>See Note **2a.** | Dear Mr. Smith:<br>Very truly yours,<br>Sincerely yours, |
| Cadets (Army and Air Force)<br>The Marine Corps has no academic facility similar to those of the Army, Air Force, and Navy, and so has no Cadet or Midshipmen Corps.<br><br>Note: Air Force Cadets are no longer addressed "Air Cadet." | **Business** and **Social:**<br>Cadet John Jones Smith<br>U.S. Military Academy<br>West Point, New York   10996<br><br>Cadet John Jones Smith<br>U.S. Air Force Academy<br>Colorado   80840 | Dear Cadet Smith:<br>Very truly yours,<br>Sincerely yours, |
| Sergeant Major<br>His full title is always used to a sergeant of this rank. | **Business:**<br>Sergeant Major John Jones Smith, USA<br>Address<br><br>**Social:**<br><br>See Note **2a.** | Dear Sergeant<br>Major Smith:<br>Very truly yours,<br>Sincerely yours, |
| Chief Master Sergeant<br>First Sergeant<br>Master Sergeant<br>Sergeant First Class<br>Platoon Sergeant<br>**Technical** Sergeant<br>**Staff** Sergeant<br>**Sergeant** | **Business:**<br>Full rank (usually abbrev.), followed by full name and service initials<br>Address<br><br>**Social:**<br><br>See Note **2a.** | Dear Sergeant Smith:<br>Very truly yours,<br>Sincerely yours, |
| Corporal (Army and Marine Corps)<br>There is no rank of Corporal in the Air Force. | **Business:**<br>Corporal John Jones Smith, USA<br>Address<br><br>**Social:** See Note **2a.** | Dear Corporal Smith:<br>Very truly yours,<br>Sincerely yours, |
| Airmen<br>First, Second, Third Class | **Business:**<br>Airman First Class John Jones Smith, USAF<br>Address<br><br>**Social:** See Note **2a.** | Dear Airman Smith:<br>Very truly yours,<br>Sincerely yours, |
| Private, First Class | **Business:**<br>Private First Class John Jones Smith, USA<br>Address<br><br>**Social:** See Note **2a.** | Dear Private Smith:<br>Very truly yours,<br>Sincerely yours, |
| Private | **Business:**<br>Private John Jones Smith, USA<br>Address<br><br>**Social:** See Note **2a.** | As above |

| SOCIAL LETTER | IN CONVERSATION | INTRODUCTIONS | ABBREV. |
|---|---|---|---|
| My dear Lieutenant Smith, **(very formal)** Dear Lieutenant Smith, Sincerely yours, | **To** and **About:** Lieutenant Smith See Note **1c.** | As above | Avoid "Lieut." |
| My dear Mr. Smith, **(very formal)** Dear Mr. Smith, Sincerely yours, | **To** and **About:** Mr. Smith | **Individual:** Mr. Smith **Presentation to an audience:** Chief Warrant Officer [or Warrant Officer] John Jones Smith, his service and station, etc., if applicable. (After the first statement of his rank, he is referred to as "Mr. Smith.") | CWO WO |
| My dear Mr. Smith, **(very formal)** Dear Mr. Smith, Sincerely yours, | **To:** Mr. Smith **About:** Cadet Smith | **Individual:** Mr. Smith **Presentation to an audience:** Cadet Smith of the U.S. Army (or Air Force) | None |
| My dear Sergeant Major Smith, **(very formal)** Dear Sergeant Major Smith, Sincerely yours, | **To** and **About:** Sergeant Major Smith See Note **2c.** | **Individual:** Sergeant Major Smith **Presentation to an audience:** Full rank, full name, and service | Sgt. Major |
| My dear Sergeant Smith, **(very formal)** Dear Sergeant Smith, Sincerely yours, | **To** and **About:** Sergeant Smith See Note **2c.** | **Individual:** Sergeant Smith **Presentation to an audience:** Full rank, full name, and service | Sgt. Avoid in social use. |
| My dear Corporal Smith, **(very formal)** Dear Corporal Smith, Sincerely yours, | **To** and **About:** Corporal Smith See Note **2c.** | As above | None in social use. |
| My dear Airman Smith, **(very formal)** Dear Airman Smith, Sincerely yours, | **To** and **About:** Airman Smith | As above | Avoid in social use. A1C A2C A3C |
| My dear Private Smith, **(very formal)** Dear Private Smith, Sincerely yours, | **To** and **About:** Private Smith | As above | PFC |
| As above | As above | As above | PVT. |

## Chaplains (All Faiths)

All chaplains are commissioned officers.

A chaplain is always introduced by his rank—"This is Captain [or General, Commander, etc.] Smith"—but his status is then made clear by some such words as "Chaplain Smith is stationed at . . ." After being introduced by rank, he is then spoken to and referred to as "Chaplain Smith,"

though Roman Catholic and some Episcopal chaplains are thereafter addressed and referred to as "Father Smith." Jewish chaplains, after introduction by rank, are then "Rabbi Smith."

Envelopes are addressed to a chaplain by the following formula:

## Medical Officers and Nurses

All doctors are commissioned officers, and all mail is addressed to them by rank:

Captain John Jones Smith, USN

If the envelope is addressed to Captain and Mrs. John Jones Smith, the service initials are dropped.

In the Army, Air Force, and Marine Corps, in letter salutations and in direct speech, all doctors are customarily addressed by military rank—not as "Dr."

In the Navy and Coast Guard, the rules for the forms of address to other officers

## Navy, Coast Guard   Note: Change USN to USCG, where appropriate.

| PERSON | ENVELOPES | BUSINESS LETTER |
|---|---|---|
| Admiral | **Business:**<br>Admiral John Jones Smith, USN<br>Address<br><br>**Social:**<br><br>See Note 2a. | Dear Admiral Smith:<br>Very truly yours,<br>Sincerely yours, |
| Vice Admiral<br>Rear Admiral | **Business:**<br>Vice Admiral John Jones Smith, USN<br>(Rear Admiral John Jones Smith, USN)<br>Address<br><br>**Social:**<br><br>See Note 2a. | Dear Admiral Smith:<br>Very truly yours,<br>Sincerely yours,<br><br>(Note that "Vice" and "Rear" are not used in the **salutation** of this letter—only on the envelope.) |
| Commodore<br>This is not an active rank except in wartime. However, many retired officers hold this rank. | **Business:**<br>Commodore John Jones Smith, USN<br>Address<br><br>**Social:**<br><br>See Note 2a. | Dear Commodore Smith:<br>Very truly yours,<br>Sincerely yours, |
| Captain | **Business:**<br>Captain John Jones Smith, USN<br>Address<br><br>**Social:**<br><br>See Note 2a. | Dear Captain Smith:<br>Very truly yours,<br>Sincerely yours, |
| Commander | **Business:**<br>Commander John Jones Smith, USN<br>Address<br><br>**Social:**<br><br>See Note 2a. | Dear Commander Smith:<br>Very truly yours,<br>Sincerely yours, |

Chaplain (Major) John Jones Smith, USA
Address

A letter addressed jointly to a married
chaplain and his wife should read:

Chaplain (Major) and Mrs. John Jones
    Smith
Address

His military rank is not used in the salutation of a letter. Instead, the correct
salutation is:

Dear Chaplain Smith,
    (**or,** when appropriate)

Dear Father Smith,

Dear Rabbi Smith,

---

are followed, except that "Dr." is used
instead of "Mr." where applicable. This
means that in direct speech and in the
salutations of letters, doctors of the rank
of commander and higher are addressed
by rank, but lieutenant commanders, lieu-

tenants, and ensigns are "Dr." (See the
chart following.)

All nurses are commissioned officers, and
in all services they are properly addressed
by military title and last name.

---

| SOCIAL LETTER | IN CONVERSATION | INTRODUCTIONS | ABBREV. |
|---|---|---|---|
| My dear Admiral Smith, **(very formal)** Dear Admiral Smith, Sincerely yours, | **To** and **About:** Admiral Smith  See Note 1c. | **Individual:** Admiral Smith  **Presentation to an audience:** Admiral John Jones Smith, his service, and his command | None acceptable in civilian mail. |
| My dear Vice [Rear] Admiral Smith, **(very formal)** Dear Vice [Rear] Admiral Smith, Sincerely yours, | **To** and **About** Admiral Smith  See Note 1c. | **Individual:** Vice [Rear] Admiral Smith  **Presentation to an audience:** Vice [Rear] Admiral John Jones Smith, his service and duty, if applicable. (After the first statement of his rank, he is referred to as "Admiral.") | Vice Adm. and Rr. Adm. can be used but are best avoided. |
| My dear Commodore Smith, **(very formal)** Dear Commodore Smith, Sincerely yours, | **To** and **About:** Commodore Smith  See Note 1c. | **Individual:** Commodore Smith  **Presentation to an audience:** Commodore John Jones Smith, his service, and duty station or status | None |
| My dear Captain Smith, **(very formal)** Dear Captain Smith, Sincerely yours, | **To** and **About:** Captain Smith  See Note 1c. | **Individual:** Captain Smith  **Presentation to an audience:** Captain John Jones Smith, his service, and his duty station | None acceptable |
| My dear Commander Smith, **(very formal)** Dear Commander Smith, Sincerely yours, | **To** and **About:** Commander Smith  See Note 1c. | **Individual:** Commander Smith  **Presentation to an audience:** Commander John Jones Smith, his service, and his duty station | None acceptable |

| PERSON | ENVELOPES | BUSINESS LETTER |
|---|---|---|
| Lieutenant Commander | Use his full title on all envelopes<br>**Business:**<br>Lieutenant Commander John Jones<br>Smith, USN<br>Address<br><br>See Note 2b.<br><br>**Social:**<br><br>See Note 2a. | Dear Mr. Smith:<br>Very truly yours,<br>Sincerely yours, |
| Lieutenant | **Business:**<br>Lieutenant John Jones Smith, USN<br>Address<br><br>**Social:**<br><br>See Note 2a. | Dear Mr. Smith:<br>Very truly yours,<br>Sincerely yours, |
| Lieutenant, Junior Grade | **Business:**<br>Lieutenant (jg) John Jones Smith, USN<br>Address<br><br>**Social:** As above, or<br>Lieutenant (jg) and Mrs. John Jones Smith<br>Address<br><br>See Note 2a. | Dear Mr. Smith:<br>Very truly yours,<br>Sincerely yours, |
| Ensign | **Business:**<br>Ensign John Jones Smith, USN<br>Address<br><br>**Social:**<br><br>See Note 2a. | Dear Mr. Smith:<br>Very truly yours,<br>Sincerely yours, |
| Chief Warrant Officer<br>A warrant officer is a man who has won his commission in his specialty. There are many of these: Boatswain, Carpenter, Photographer, Yeoman, etc. He is addressed "Chief Warrant Officer," instead of by his specialty, however. | **Business:**<br>Chief Warrant Officer John Jones<br>Smith, USN<br>Address<br><br>See Note 2b.<br><br>**Social:**<br><br>See Note 2a. | Dear Chief Warrant<br>Officer Smith:<br>Very truly yours,<br>Sincerely yours, |
| Warrant Officer | As above, without "Chief" | As above without<br>"Chief" |
| Midshipman (Navy) | Midshipman John Jones Smith<br>U.S Naval Academy<br>Annapolis, Maryland   21402 | Dear Midshipman<br>Smith:<br>Very truly yours,<br>Sincerely yours, |
| Cadet (Coast Guard) | Cadet John Jones Smith<br>U.S. Coast Guard Academy<br>New London, Connecticut   06320 | Dear Cadet Smith:<br>Very truly yours,<br>Sincerely yours, |
| Chief Petty Officer | **Business:**<br>Chief Petty Officer John Jones Smith, USN<br>Address<br><br>See Note 2b.<br><br>**Social:** See Note 2a. | Dear Chief Petty<br>Officer Smith:<br>Very truly yours,<br>Sincerely yours, |

| SOCIAL LETTER | IN CONVERSATION | INTRODUCTIONS | ABBREV. |
|---|---|---|---|
| My dear Lieutenant Commander Smith, **(very formal)** Dear Lieutenant Commander Smith, Sincerely yours, | **To** and **About:** Mr. Smith (unless his rank is applicable) | **Individual:** Lieutenant Commander Smith  **Presentation to an audience:** Lieutenant Commander John Jones Smith, his service, and duty station. (After the first mention of his rank, he is referred to as "Mr. Smith.") | "Lt. Commander" is permissible. |
| My dear Lieutenant Smith, **(very formal)** Dear Lieutenant Smith, Sincerely yours, | As above | As above, without "Commander" | "Lt." and "Lieut." are best avoided. |
| My dear Lieutenant (jg) Smith, **(very formal)** Dear Lieutenant (jg) Smith, Sincerely yours, | As above | **Individual:** Lieutenant junior grade Smith  **Presentation to an audience:** Lieutenant junior grade John Jones Smith, his service, and his duty station. (After the first mention of his rank, he is referred to as "Mr. Smith.") | As above |
| My dear Ensign Smith, **(very formal)** Dear Ensign Smith, Sincerely yours, | As above | **Individual:** Ensign Smith  **Presentation to an audience:** Ensign John Jones Smith, his service, and duty station. (After the first mention of his rank, he is referred to as "Mr. Smith.") | None |
| My dear Chief Warrant Officer Smith, **(very formal)** Dear Chief Warrant Officer Smith Sincerely yours, | **To** and **About:** Mr. Smith (unless his rank is applicable) | **Individual:** Chief Warrant Officer Smith  **Presentation to an audience:** Chief Warrant Officer John Jones Smith, his service and duty station; and thereafter "Mr. Smith" | Avoid when possible CWO. |
| As above without "Chief" | **To** and **About:** Mr. Smith (unless his rank is applicable) | As above, without "Chief" | Avoid WO. |
| My dear Midshipman Smith, **(very formal)** Dear Midshipman Smith, Sincerely yours,  My dear Cadet Smith, **etc.** | **To** and **About:** Mr. Smith (unless his rank is applicable) | **Individual:** Midshipman Smith  **Presentation to an audience:** Midshipman [Cadet] John Jones Smith, and his service. Thereafter, he is referred to as "Mr." | None |
| My dear Chief Smith, **(very formal)** Dear Chief Smith, Sincerely yours. | **To** and **About:** Chief Smith | **Individual:** Chief Smith  **Presentation to an audience:** Chief Petty Officer John Jones Smith, his service and duty station | Avoid CPO. |

| PERSON | ENVELOPES | BUSINESS LETTER |
|---|---|---|
| Petty Officers<br>First, Second, and Third Class | **Business:**<br>Petty Officer First Class John Jones<br>    Smith, USN<br>    Address<br><br>**Social:** As above, or<br>    Petty Officer First Class<br>    and Mrs. John Jones Smith<br>    Address<br><br>See Note **2a**. | Dear Petty Officer<br>  Smith:<br>Very truly yours,<br>Sincerely yours, |
| Seaman | **Business:**<br>Seaman (general rate) John Jones<br>    Smith, USN<br>    Address<br><br>**Social:** As above, or<br>    Seaman and Mrs. John Jones Smith<br>    Address<br><br>See Note **2a**. | Dear Seaman Smith:<br>Very truly yours,<br>Sincerely yours, |

## Retired Personnel

An officer who retires after twenty years of professional military service is entitled to continue to use his rank, and most officers are inclined to do so.

It is not incorrect for social acquaintances to address mail to a retired officer

## Women

The forms of address for women officers and noncommissioned personnel are exactly the same as for men except that "Mrs." or "Miss" is substituted where "Mr." is found in the charts.

In general, insignia for women are the same as those for men, though in some cases are somewhat smaller.

There are several formulas for addressing joint mail to a servicewoman and her husband. If he is also in military service, a formal invitation or announcement is addressed to them jointly by *his* rank even if his wife outranks him: Major and Mrs. John Jones Smith.

## THE CLERGY

There are proper variants of some of the forms in the following charts, but the ones given below are the most widely used and are always correct when addressing members of the clergy.

1. "Reverend" is an adjective. It is never correctly used by itself as "Sir" in speech and "Dear Sir" in writing can be. ("Yes, Reverend," "Ask the Reverend," and "Dear Reverend" are wrong.)

   When spoken or written, "Reverend" should be followed by both a first and last name, or by a title and last name. (Correct uses include "The Reverend John Smith," "The Reverend Dr. Smith,"

   "The Reverend Mr. Smith"—but "Reverend Smith" is wrong.)

   "Reverend Sir" is a correct and extremely formal salutation generally reserved for the opening of an official or business letter. Otherwise, the salutation on a letter should use the clergyman's ecclesiastical title ("Dear Bishop Smith," for example), or "Dear Dr. Smith" if he has a doctoral degree, or "Dear Mr. Smith." A look at the charts will make clear the preferred uses for clergymen of various titles and faiths.

   "The Most Reverend," "The Right Reverend," and "The Very Reverend"

| SOCIAL LETTER | IN CONVERSATION | INTRODUCTIONS | ABBREV. |
|---|---|---|---|
| My dear Petty Officer Smith, (very formal) Dear Petty Officer Smith, Sincerely yours, | **To** and **About:** Petty Officer Smith | **Individual:** Petty Officer Smith<br><br>**Presentation to an audience:** Petty Officer First Class John Jones Smith, his service, and duty station | None |
| My dear Seaman Smith, (very formal) Dear Seaman Smith, Sincerely yours, | **To** and **About:** Seaman Smith | **Individual:** Seaman Smith<br><br>**Presentation to an audience:** Seaman John Jones Smith, his service, and duty post | None |

by the official formula of the services: Colonel John Jones Smith, USMC (Ret). However, the customary and by far the better form for civilians is to omit the service initials and (Ret) after the name.

If he is a civilian, her rank is ignored when addressing them jointly, and the envelope should read: Mr. and Mrs. John Jones Smith.

However, if the woman in service is being invited in her *official* capacity, one invitation can be addressed to her by her rank (Colonel Mary Brown Smith), and a separate invitation can be addressed to her husband; or the envelope can be addressed:

Colonel Mary Brown Smith
and Mr. Smith
Address

are forms reserved for use to clergymen of specified high rank. (See the charts.)

"The" is always used on an envelope preceding "Reverend." Any title incorporating "Reverend" can be written on the same line with the name: The Reverend John Smith. Also correct, if the full title and a long name would crowd one line, is:

The Reverend
Dr. John Jones Smith
(or John Jones Smith, D.D.)
Address

"Reverend" is best spelled out, when possible, but "Rev." and "Rt. Rev." and "V. Rev." are not incorrect.

2. Initials following the name of a clergyman may stand for an academic degree (D.D.; LL.D.; Ph.D., for examples); or may stand for his membership in an Order of his church (S.J., for example, if a Catholic clergyman is a Jesuit, or S.S.J.E. if he is a Cowley father in the Episcopal Church).

   (a) The initials standing for a doctoral degree are never used in addition to "Dr." Correct forms are "Dr. John Smith" or "John Smith, D.D."—but never "Dr. John Smith,

D.D." If a clergyman has several doctoral degrees, all of them may be used after his name (but no more than three are correct).

Initials denoting a doctoral degree are generally reserved for use on an official or business letter, but they need not be used at all. It is not customary to use them on a social letter, and they are never used on an envelope addressed jointly to a clergyman and his wife.

(b) The initials denoting membership in an Order of a church are governed by different rules from those denoting a doctoral degree because they do not stand for any specific title or position. All they indicate

is that the individual has taken the vows of some special branch (Order) of the church. Such initials obviously can be used correctly after any title (Archbishop, Canon, Father, Sister, etc.). However, they are not an essential part of an address, and can be omitted. They are customarily used on official or business envelopes rather than on social letters.

3. "Respectfully" is one of the correct and customary signatures on a business letter to members of the clergy of the rank of Bishop and above, but it is not a required form, by the standard rules of etiquette, except in a few cases. See

## Catholic (Greek Orthodox)

Just as the Pope holds the highest office in the Roman Catholic Church, the Patriarchs hold the highest offices in the various Orthodox branches of the Catholic religion.

There are four Greek Orthodox Patriarchs. Each is the head of his own patriarchate. The four Patriarchs are of equal importance, but the Patriarch of Constan-

tinople is given the honorary title of "First Among Equals" because his is the oldest patriarchate.

The Patriarch of Constantinople does not have the administrative power of the Pope, since his ecclesiastical jurisdiction is confined to his own partriarchate and the churches under it. He is, however,

| PERSON | ENVELOPES | BUSINESS LETTER |
|---|---|---|
| The Patriarch of Constantinople | His Holiness James<br>The Ecumenical Patriarch of<br>  Constantinople<br>Istanbul<br>Turkey | All letters follow this form:<br>  Your Holiness:<br>    Respectfully yours, |
| The Patriarchs of Alexandria<br>  Antioch, and Jerusalem | His Beatitude James<br>The Patriarch of (Place)<br>City<br>Country | Your Beatitude:<br>  Respectfully yours, |
| The Archbishops of Cyprus and<br>  Athens | His Beatitude James<br>The Archbishop of (Place)<br>City<br>Country | Your Beatitude:<br>  Respectfully yours,<br>  Very truly yours,<br>  Sincerely yours, |
| Archbishop (in the U.S.) | The Most Reverend James<br>Archbishop of the Greek Orthodox Arch-<br>  diocese of North and South America<br>Address | Your Eminence:<br>  Respectfully yours,<br>  Very truly yours,<br>  Sincerely yours, |

the charts for the occasions when "Very truly yours" and "Sincerely yours" are also correct. "Very truly yours" is the traditional closing for a business letter, but the trend today is to use "Sincerely yours," which is considered less stiff by some.

4. As a general rule, both men and women are introduced **to** clergymen of the rank of Bishop and higher as a mark of respect to their office. Otherwise, the standard rules given under INTRODUCTIONS are followed.

5. It is customary to use a clergyman's title and last name when speaking to him directly: Bishop Smith, Canon Smith, Rabbi Smith, and so on. However, in prolonged conversation, either "Sir" or his title is correctly used alone. Note, however, that although a Catholic or an Episcopalian properly says "Father" ("Mother," "Brother," "Sister") to someone of his own faith, people outside the faith usually do not use the title alone; they say "Father John" or "Father Smith" and so on.

6. Depending on the customs of his Order, and sometimes his own preference, a clergyman with the title "Father" is addressed "Father (first name)" or "Father (last name)." The same rule holds for Mothers and Sisters.

generally recognized as the spiritual leader of World Orthodoxy.

There is one Greek Orthodox archbishop in the United States. He is the Archbishop of the Archdiocese of North and South America.

Clergymen in the Greek Orthodox Church are celibate, with the exception of certain priests and deacons.

As elsewhere throughout the entire FORMS OF ADDRESS section, "John Jones Smith" is used to indicate that either a first and last name, or a first, middle, and last name, are correctly used. In the charts below, "James" is used to indicate that the clergyman's ecclesiastical name is used alone.

| SOCIAL LETTER | IN CONVERSATION | INTRODUCTIONS | ABBREV. |
|---|---|---|---|
| | **To:**<br>Your Holiness | All visitors would be presented **to** a Patriarch. | None |
| | **About:**<br>His Holiness **or**<br>The Patriarch of<br>Constantinople<br>Patriarch James | **Presentation to an audience:**<br>His Holiness James,<br>the Ecumenical Patriarch of<br>Constantinople | |
| | **To:**<br>Your Beatitude | His Beatitude James,<br>the patriarch of (Place) | None |
| | **About:**<br>His Beatitude **or**<br>His Beatitude James | | |
| | **To** and **About:**<br>As above | His Beatitude James,<br>the Archbishop of (Place) | None |
| My dear Archbishop<br>James,<br>**(very formal)**<br>Dear Archbishop,<br>James,<br>Sincerely yours, | **To:**<br>Your Eminence<br><br>**About:**<br>His Eminence | **Individual:**<br>His Eminence, Archbishop James<br><br>**Presentation to an audience:**<br>His Eminence James,<br>the Archbishop of (Place) | None |

| PERSON | ENVELOPES | BUSINESS LETTER |
|---|---|---|
| Metropolitan<br>(A metropolitan is a bishop who is the head of an ecclesiastical province.) | The Most Reverend James<br>Metropolitan of (Place)<br>Address | As above |
| Bishop of a Diocese | The Right Reverend James<br>**or**<br>His Grace James<br>Bishop of (Place)<br>Address | Your Grace:<br>Respectfully yours,<br>Very truly yours,<br>Sincerely yours, |
| Archimandrite<br>(a celibate priest eligible to become a Bishop) | The Very Reverend John Jones Smith<br>(Title and/or Church, if any)<br>Address | Reverend Sir:  **or**<br>Dear Father John:<br>Very truly yours,<br>Sincerely yours, |
| Priest and Deacon<br>(non-celibate) | The Reverend John Jones Smith<br>(Church)<br>Address<br><br>The Reverend and Mrs. John Jones Smith | Reverend Sir:<br>Very truly yours,<br>Sincerely yours, |

## Catholic  (Roman)

| | | |
|---|---|---|
| The Pope | His Holiness<br>Pope (Name and Roman numeral)<br>Vatican City<br>Italy | **All** letters correctly follow this form:<br>Your Holiness:  **or**<br>Most Holy Father:<br>Respectfully yours, |
| Apostolic Delegate<br>(An Apostolic Delegate is usually an Archbishop or a Bishop.) | His Excellency<br>The Most Reverend John Jones Smith<br>The Apostolic Delegate<br>Address<br><br>See Note 2**b.** | All letters correctly follow this form:<br>Your Excellency: **or**<br>Most Reverend Sir:<br>Respectfully yours,<br>**or**<br>Sincerely yours, |
| Cardinal | His Eminence<br>John Cardinal Smith<br>Archbishop of (Archdiocese)*<br>Address<br>*(If he is also an Archbishop, as is usually the case.)<br><br>See Note 2**b.** | Your Eminence:<br>Respectfully yours,<br>Very truly yours,<br>Sincerely yours, |

| SOCIAL LETTER | IN CONVERSATION | INTRODUCTIONS | ABBREV. |
|---|---|---|---|
| My dear Metropolitan James **(very formal)** Dear Metropolitan James, Sincerely yours, | **To:** Your Eminence **About:** His Eminence **or** Metropolitan James | **Individual:** Metropolitan James **Presentation to an audience:** His Eminence James, the Metropolitan of (Place) | None |
| Your Grace, **(very formal)** Dear Bishop James, Sincerely yours, | **To:** Your Grace **About:** His Grace Bishop James | **Individual:** Bishop James **Presentation to an audience:** His Grace James, the Bishop of (Place) | None |
| My dear Father John, **(very formal)** Dear Father John, Sincerely yours, | **To:** Your Reverence **or** Father John **About:** His Reverence **or** Father (First name) **or** Father (Last name) | **Individual:** Father (First name) **or** Father (Last name) **Presentation to an audience:** The Very Reverend John Jones Smith, and his position | Very Rev. V. Rev. |
| My dear Father Smith, **(very formal)** Dear Father John, Sincerely yours, | **To and About:** Father Smith | **Individual:** Father Smith **Presentation to an audience:** The Reverend (Full name) and his church | Avoid "Rev." |
| (**or**, more usual for Catholics) Your Holiness' most humble servant, | **To:** Your Holiness **or** Most Holy Father **About:** The Pope His Holiness The Holy Father Pope (Name) | The Pope is never introduced **to** anyone. All who meet him are presented **to** him. | None |
| | **To:** Your Excellency **or** Sir **About:** His Excellency **or** The Apostolic Delegate | **Individual:** The Apostolic Delegate **Presentation to an audience:** His Excellency Archbishop [Bishop] John Jones Smith, the Apostolic Delegate to ——— See Note 4. | None |
| My dear Cardinal Smith, **(very formal)** Dear Cardinal Smith, Sincerely yours, | **To:** Your Eminence **or** Sir **About:** His Eminence **or** Cardinal Smith | **Individual:** His Eminence Cardinal Smith Cardinal Smith **Presentation to an audience:** His Eminence, John Cardinal Smith, Archbishop of ——— See Note 4. | None |

| PERSON | ENVELOPES | BUSINESS LETTER |
|---|---|---|
| Archbishop | The Most Reverend John Jones Smith<br>Archbishop of (Archdiocese)<br>Address<br><br>See Note 1. | Your Excellency:  **or**<br>Most Reverend Sir:<br>Respectfully yours,<br>Very truly yours,<br>Sincerely yours, |
| Bishop | The Most Reverend John Jones Smith<br>Bishop of (Diocese)<br>Address<br><br>See Notes 1 and 2**b**. | Your Excellency:  **or**<br>Most Reverend Sir:<br>Respectfully yours,<br>Very truly yours,<br>Sincerely yours, |
| Abbot | The Right Reverend John Jones Smith<br>Abbot of (Name of abbey)<br>Address<br><br>See Notes 1 and 2**b**. | Right Reverend Abbot:<br>**or**<br>Dear Father Abbot:<br>Very truly yours,<br>Sincerely yours, |
| Monsignor<br>(If he is a<br>Papal Chamberlain,<br>the form is "The<br>Very Reverend." | The Right Reverend<br>Monsignor John Jones Smith<br>Address<br><br>See Notes 1 and 2 **b**. | Dear Monsignor<br>Smith:<br>Respectfully yours,<br>Very truly yours,<br>Sincerely yours, |
| Priest<br><br>See Note 6. | The Reverend John Jones Smith<br>Address<br><br>See Notes 1 and 2 **b**. | Reverend Sir:  **or**<br>Dear Father Smith:<br>Very truly yours,<br>Sincerely yours, |
| Brother | Brother John Jones Smith<br>Address<br><br>See Note 2**b**. | Dear Brother John:<br>Very truly yours,<br>Sincerely yours, |
| Lay Brother | As above | |
| Mother Superior<br><br>(Note: Today most religious<br>communities are beginning to<br>use the family name in<br>addition to the religious name.) | The Reverend Mother Superior<br>(Name of institution)<br>Address<br>**or**<br>The Reverend Mother Mary Brown<br>Mother Superior, Convent of———<br>Address<br><br>See Note 2**b**. | Dear Reverend<br>Mother:  **or**<br>Dear Mother Superior:<br>Very truly yours,<br>Sincerely yours, |
| Sister<br><br>As above. | Sister (Name)<br>(Name of institution)<br>Address<br><br>See Note 2**b**. | Dear Sister Mary:<br>Very truly yours,<br>Sincerely yours, |

| SOCIAL LETTER | IN CONVERSATION | INTRODUCTIONS | ABBREV. |
|---|---|---|---|
| My dear Arch-<br>bishop Smith,<br>**(very formal)**<br>Dear Archbishop<br>Smith,<br>Sincerely yours, | **To:**<br>Your Excellency **or**<br>Archbishop Smith<br>See Note 5.<br><br>**About:**<br>Archbishop Smith | **Individual:**<br>His Excellency Archbishop Smith<br>Archbishop Smith<br><br>**Presentation to an audience:**<br>His Excellency Archbishop John<br>Jones Smith of (Archdiocese)<br><br>See Note 4. | None |
| My dear Bishop<br>Smith,<br>**(very formal)**<br>Dear Bishop Smith,<br>Sincerely yours, | **To:**<br>Your Excellency **or**<br>Bishop Smith<br>See Note 5.<br><br>**About:**<br>Bishop Smith | **Individual:**<br>His Excellency Bishop Smith<br>Bishop Smith<br><br>**Presentation to an audience:**<br>His Excellency Bishop John Jones<br>Smith of (Diocese)<br><br>See Note 4. | None |
| My dear Father<br>Smith,<br>**(very formal)**<br>Dear Father Smith,<br>Sincerely yours, | **To:**<br>Abbot Smith **or**<br>Father Abbot<br><br>**About:**<br>Abbot Smith | **Individual:**<br>Abbot Smith<br><br>**Presentation to an audience:**<br>The Right Reverend John Jones<br>Smith, Abbot of (abbey) | None |
| My dear Monsignor<br>Smith,<br>**(very formal)**<br>Dear Monsignor<br>Smith,<br>Sincerely yours, | **To** and **About:**<br>Monsignor Smith<br><br>See Note 5. | **Individual:**<br>Monsignor Smith<br><br>**Presentation to an audience:**<br>The Right Reverend Monsignor John<br>Jones Smith, and his Order,<br>position, locality, etc. | None |
| My dear Father<br>Smith,<br>**(very formal)**<br>Dear Father Smith,<br>Sincerely yours, | **To:** A Catholic says<br>either "Father" or<br>"Father Smith."<br>Others say, "Father<br>Smith."<br><br>**About:**<br>Father Smith<br><br>See Note 5. | **Individual:**<br>Father Smith<br><br>**Presentation to an audience:**<br>Father John Jones Smith, his<br>Order (if he belongs to one),<br>parish, etc. | None |
| My dear Brother<br>John,<br>**(very formal)**<br>Dear Brother John,<br>Sincerely yours, | **To** and **About:**<br>Brother John<br><br>See Note 5. | **Individual:**<br>Brother John<br><br>**Presentation to an audience:**<br>Brother John of (Name of his<br>Order) | None |
| My dear Mother<br>Superior,<br>**(very formal)**<br>Dear Mother<br>Superior,<br>Dear Mother Mary,<br>Sincerely yours, | **To:**<br>Reverend Mother **or**<br>Mother Mary<br><br>See Note 5.<br><br>**About:**<br>Mother Superior<br>Mary<br>**or**<br>Mother Mary | **Individual:**<br>Reverend Mother Mary,<br>and add last name if used<br><br>**Presentation to an audience:**<br>Reverend Mother Mary,<br>and add last name if used,<br>her Order, and Convent | None |
| My dear Sister Mary,<br>**(very formal)**<br>Dear Sister Mary,<br>Sincerely yours, | **To** and **About:**<br>Sister Mary<br><br>See Note 5. | **Individual:**<br>Sister Mary, and add<br>last name if used<br><br>**Presentation to an audience:**<br>Sister Mary, and add<br>last name if<br>used, and her<br>Order, institution,<br>etc. | None |

| PERSON | ENVELOPES | BUSINESS LETTER |
| --- | --- | --- |
| Lay Sister | As above | |

Chaplains
  See "The Armed Services" above.

## Catholic (Russian Orthodox)

There is only one Russian Orthodox Patriarch, the Patriarch of Moscow. In the Russian Orthodox Church, a metropolitan outranks an archbishop, but both have the same form of address. There are three Russian Orthodox metropolitans in the United States.

There are no major Russian Orthodox monasteries in this country. There are, however, thirteen small monasteries.

| PERSON | ENVELOPES | BUSINESS LETTER |
| --- | --- | --- |
| The Patriarch of Moscow | His Holiness James<br>Patriarch of Moscow<br>Moscow<br>U.S.S.R. | Your Holiness:<br>  Respectfully yours, |
| Metropolitan, in the U.S. | The Most Reverend James<br>Metropolitan of (Place)<br>Address | Your Eminence:<br>  Respectfully yours,<br>  Very truly yours,<br>  Sincerely yours, |
| Archbishop | As above, with "Archbishop"<br>  instead of "Metropolitan." | |
| Vicar Bishop | The Right Reverend James<br>Bishop of (Place)<br>Address | Your Grace:<br>  Respectfully yours,<br>  Very truly yours,<br>  Sincerely yours, |
| Archimandrite | The Very Reverend John Jones Smith<br>Archimandrite of (Place)<br>Address | Reverend Sir:<br>  Very truly yours,<br>  Sincerely yours, |
| Proto Priest<br>  His rank is the same as<br>  that of the Archimandrite,<br>  but the Archimandrite is<br>  a celibate priest. | As above, with the addition:<br>The Very Reverend and<br>  Mrs. John Jones Smith<br>Address | Reverend Sir:<br>  Very truly yours,<br>  Sincerely yours, |
| Priest and Deacon | The Reverend John Jones Smith<br>Address<br><br>The Reverend and Mrs. John Jones Smith<br>Address | Reverend Sir:<br>  Very truly yours,<br>  Sincerely yours, |

As in the case of the Greek Orthodox Church, the tendency is to address Russian Orthodox priests as "Father (First name)."

As throughout this entire section, "John Jones Smith" is used to indicate that either a first and last name, or a first, middle, and last name, are correctly used.

In the charts below, "James" is used to indicate that a clergyman's ecclesiastical name is used alone.

| SOCIAL LETTER | IN CONVERSATION | INTRODUCTIONS | ABBREV. |
|---|---|---|---|
| | **To:**<br>Your Holiness | Visitors are presented **to**<br>a Patriarch. | None |
| | **About:**<br>His Holiness,<br>Patriarch James | **Presentation to an audience:**<br>His Holiness James,<br>the patriarch of Moscow | |
| My dear Metro-<br>politan James,<br>**(very formal)**<br>Dear Metropolitan<br>James,<br>Sincerely yours, | **To:**<br>Your Eminence<br><br>**About:**<br>His Eminence **or**<br>Metropolitan James | **Individual:**<br>Metropolitan James<br><br>**Presentation to an audience:**<br>His Eminence James,<br>the Metropolitan of (Place) | None |
| My dear Bishop<br>James,<br>**(very formal)**<br>Dear Bishop James,<br>Sincerely yours, | **To:**<br>Your Grace<br><br>**About:**<br>Bishop James | **Individual:**<br>Bishop James<br><br>**Presentation to an audience:**<br>His Grace, Bishop James<br>of (Place) | None |
| My dear Father<br>Smith,<br>**(very formal)**<br>Dear Father Smith,<br>Sincerely yours, | **To:**<br>Your Reverence **or**<br>Father Smith | **Individual:**<br>Archimandrite Smith<br><br>**Presentation to an audience:**<br>The Very Reverend John Jones<br>Smith, Archimandrite of ——— | None |
| My dear Father<br>Smith,<br>**(very formal)**<br>Dear Father Smith,<br>Sincerely yours, | As above | **Individual:**<br>Father Smith<br><br>**Presentation to an audience:**<br>The Very Reverend John James<br>Smith, his position, location, etc. | None |
| My dear Father<br>Smith,<br>**(very formal)**<br>Dear Father Smith,<br>**or**<br>Dear Father John,<br>Sincerely yours, | **To and About:**<br>Father Smith | **Individual:**<br>Father Smith<br><br>**Presentation to an audience:**<br>The Reverend John Jones Smith,<br>his title and church | None |

## Jewish

| PERSON | ENVELOPES | BUSINESS LETTER |
|---|---|---|
| Rabbi (with or without doctoral degree) The title "Rabbi" is preferred even if he holds a doctoral degree. Only when a rabbi holds a position other than as leader of a congregation, such as a teaching post, is he addressed "Dr." See also "Chaplains" under "Armed Services." | **Business:** Rabbi John Jones Smith Temple or Synagogue Street address City, State   00000 **Social:** Rabbi John Jones Smith Address Rabbi and Mrs. John Jones Smith Address | Dear Rabbi Smith: Very truly yours, Sincerely yours, |
| Cantor "Mr." is not a correct form of address to a Cantor. | **Business:** Cantor John Jones Smith Temple or Synagogue Address **Social:** Cantor John Jones Smith Address Cantor and Mrs. John Jones Smith Address | Dear Cantor Smith: Very truly yours, Sincerely yours, |

## Protestant

| PERSON | ENVELOPES | BUSINESS LETTER |
|---|---|---|
| Clergyman **with doctoral degree** (These forms are correct for all faiths that do not use special titles like Bishop, Canon, etc.) | **Business:** The Reverend John Jones Smith, D.D. (**or** The Reverend Dr. John Jones Smith) Name of church Address **Social:** The Reverend Dr. John Jones Smith Address The Reverend Dr. John Jones Smith and Mrs. Smith Address See Notes 1 and 2 **a.** | Dear Dr. Smith: Very truly yours, Sincerely yours, |
| Clergyman **without doctoral degree** | **Business:** The Reverend John Jones Smith Name of church Address **Social:** The Reverend John Jones Smith Address The Reverend and Mrs. John Jones Smith Address See Notes 1 and 2 **a.** | Dear Mr. Smith: Very truly yours, Sincerely yours, |

## Protestant—The Church of Christ Scientist

What is often called the "Christian Science Church" has no ordained clergy. Practitioners and Readers are addressed "Mr.," "Miss," or "Mrs."— not "Reverend."

| SOCIAL LETTER | IN CONVERSATION | INTRODUCTIONS | ABBREV. |
|---|---|---|---|
| My dear Rabbi Smith, **(very formal)** Dear Rabbi Smith, Sincerely yours, | **To** and **About:** Rabbi Smith | **Individual:** Rabbi Smith<br><br>**Presentation to an audience:** Rabbi John Jones Smith of (Name of his temple or synagogue) | None |
| My dear Cantor Smith, **(very formal)** Dear Cantor Smith, Sincerely yours, | **To** and **About:** Cantor Smith | **Individual:** Cantor Smith<br><br>**Presentation to an audience:** Cantor John Jones Smith of (Name of his temple or synagogue) | None |
| My dear Dr. Smith, **(very formal)** Dear Dr. Smith, Sincerely yours, | **To** and **About:** Dr. Smith | **Individual:** The Reverend Dr. Smith<br><br>**Presentation to an audience:** The Reverend Dr. John Jones Smith, his title or position, and the name of his church | None |
| My dear Mr. Smith, **(very formal)** Dear Mr. Smith, Sincerely yours, | **To** and **About:** Mr. Smith | **Individual:** The Reverend Mr. Smith<br><br>**Presentation to an audience:** The Reverend John Jones Smith, his title or position, and the name of his church | None |

## Protestant—The Church of Jesus Christ of Latter-day Saints (Mormons)

| PERSON | ENVELOPES | BUSINESS LETTER |
|---|---|---|
| President of the Church | **Business:**<br>President John Jones Smith<br>Church of Jesus Christ of Latter-day<br>Saints<br>Salt Lake City, Utah<br><br>**Social:**<br>President John Jones Smith<br>Address<br><br>President and Mrs. John Jones Smith<br>Address | Dear President Smith:<br>Very truly yours,<br>Sincerely yours, |
| First and Second Counselors of<br>the First Presidency<br>President of the Council of the<br>Twelve Apostles<br>President of a Stake (a division<br>similar to a diocese) | **Business:**<br>All are addressed as "President," with<br>"The First Presidency" or "The Council<br>of the Twelve Apostles," etc., on a<br>separate line after the name, before<br>the appropriate address.<br><br>**Social:**<br>Same as for the "President." | Dear President Smith:<br>Very truly yours,<br>Sincerely yours,<br>. |
| Patriarch | Follow exactly the same pattern as for<br>"President," with "Patriarch" sub-<br>stituted. | |
| Members, Council of the Twelve<br>Apostles<br>Assistants to the above Members<br>First Council of the Seventy | Address them as "Elder," and otherwise<br>follow exactly the pattern specified<br>under First and Second Counselors<br>of the First Presidency. | |
| A Presiding Bishop<br>His First and Second Counselors<br>The Bishop of a Ward | Address them as "Bishop," and otherwise<br>follow the pattern specified under<br>First and Second Counselors of the<br>First Presidency. | |

## Protestant—Episcopal

| Presiding Bishop | **Business:**<br>The Right Reverend John Jones<br>Smith, D.D.*<br>Presiding Bishop of the Protestant<br>Episcopal Church in the United States<br>of America<br>Address<br><br>*See Note 2.<br><br>**Social:**<br>The Right Reverend John Jones Smith<br>Address<br><br>The Presiding Bishop and Mrs. Smith<br>(**or** The Right Reverend and Mrs.<br>John Jones Smith)<br>Address<br><br>See Notes 1 and 2. | Right Reverend Sir:<br>**or**<br>Dear Bishop Smith:<br>Respectfully yours,<br>Very truly yours,<br>Sincerely yours, |

| SOCIAL LETTER | IN CONVERSATION | INTRODUCTIONS | ABBREV. |
|---|---|---|---|
| My dear President Smith, **(very formal)** Dear President Smith, Sincerely yours, | **To** and **About**: President Smith  See Note 5. | **Individual**: President Smith  **Presentation to an audience**: President John Jones Smith of the Church of Jesus Christ of Latter-day Saints | Avoid "Pres." |
| My dear President Smith, **(very formal)** Dear President Smith, Sincerely yours, | **To** and **About**: President Smith  See Note 5. | As above, with appropriate qual- ification added (of the Council of the Twelve Apostles, for example). | Avoid "Pres." |
| | | | None |
| | | | None |
| | | | None |
| My dear Bishop Smith, **(very formal)** Dear Bishop Smith, Sincerely yours, | **To** and **About**: Bishop Smith  See Note 5. | **Individual**: Bishop Smith  **Presentation to an audience**: The Right Reverend John Jones Smith, Presiding Bishop of the Protestant Episcopal Church in the United States of America | None |

| PERSON | ENVELOPES | BUSINESS LETTER |
|---|---|---|
| Bishop | **Business:**<br>The Right Reverend John Jones<br>   Smith, D.D.<br>Bishop of (Diocese)<br>Address<br> **or** <br>The Right Reverend<br>The Bishop of (Diocese)<br>(No name)<br>Address<br><br>**Social:**<br>The Right Reverend John Jones Smith<br> **or** <br>The Right Reverend and Mrs. John<br>   Jones Smith<br>Address<br> **or** <br>The Bishop of ——— and Mrs. Smith<br>Address<br><br>See Notes 1 and 2. | Right Reverend Sir:<br>Dear Bishop Smith:<br>   Respectfully yours,<br>   Very truly yours,<br>   Sincerely yours, |
| Archdeacon | **Business:**<br>The Venerable John Jones Smith, D.D.<br>Archdeacon of (Diocese or a named<br>   portion thereof)<br>Address<br><br>**Social:**<br>The Venerable and Mrs. John Jones Smith<br>Address<br><br>See Notes 1 and 2. | Dear Archdeacon<br>   Smith:<br>   Very truly yours,<br>   Sincerely yours, |
| Dean | **Business:**<br>The Very Reverend John Jones<br>   Smith, D.D.<br>Dean of (Name of church)<br>Address<br><br>**Social:**<br>The Very Reverend John Jones Smith<br>Address<br><br>The Very Reverend and<br>   Mrs. John Jones Smith<br>Address<br><br>See Notes 1, 2, and 5. | Dear Dean Smith:<br>   Very truly yours,<br>   Sincerely yours, |
| Canon | **Business:**<br>The Reverend Canon John Jones<br>   Smith, D.D.<br>Address<br><br>**Social:**<br>The Reverend Canon<br>   John Jones Smith<br>Address<br><br>The Reverend Canon and Mrs. John<br>   Jones Smith<br>Address<br><br>See Notes 1 and 2. | Dear Canon Smith:<br>   Very truly yours,<br>   Sincerely yours, |
| Monastic Clergyman<br>   A monastic clergyman is one who<br>has taken the vows, including<br>that of celibacy, of an Order.<br>His full name or a first name<br>conferred by his Order is used,<br>depending on the Order. | The Reverend John Jones Smith, O.H.C.*<br>Address<br> **or** <br>The Reverend Father John, O.H.C.<br>Address<br><br>*See Note 2. | Dear Father Smith:<br>Dear Father John:<br>   Very truly yours,<br>   Sincerely yours, |

| SOCIAL LETTER | IN CONVERSATION | INTRODUCTIONS | ABBREV. |
|---|---|---|---|
| My dear Bishop Smith, **(very formal)** Dear Bishop Smith, Sincerely yours, | **To** and **About**: Bishop Smith  See Note 5. | **Individual**: Bishop Smith  **Presentation to an audience**: The Right Reverend John Jones Smith, the Bishop of (Diocese) | None |
| My dear Archdeacon Smith, **(very formal)** Dear Archdeacon Smith, Sincerely yours, | **To** and **About**: Archdeacon Smith  See Note 5. | **Individual**: Archdeacon Smith  **Presentation to an audience**: The Venerable John Jones Smith, Archdeacon of (Diocese or a named portion thereof) | None |
| My dear Mr. Dean, **(very formal)** Dear Mr. Dean, Sincerely yours, | **To** and **About**: Dean Smith  See Note 5. | **Individual**: Dean Smith  **Presentation to an audience**: The Very Reverend John Jones Smith, Dean of (Church) | None |
| My dear Canon Smith, **(very formal)** Dear Canon Smith, Sincerely yours, | **To** and **About**: Canon Smith **or** Dr. Smith  See Note 5. | **Individual**: Canon Smith  **Presentation to an audience**: The Reverend Canon John Jones Smith, and his church or position | None |
| My dear Father Smith, **(very** My dear Father John, **formal)** Dear Father Smith, Dear Father John, Sincerely yours, | **To** and **About**: Father Smith Father John  See Note 5. | **Individual**: Father Smith Father John  **Presentation to an audience**: The Reverend Father John Jones Smith of the Order of ——— (or his first name only, depending on his Order) | None |

| PERSON | ENVELOPES | BUSINESS LETTER |
|---|---|---|
| **Secular Clergyman**<br>One who has not taken the vows of an order and therefore may marry. The use of "Father" to him depends upon his personal preference and parish custom.<br><br>Included in this category are:<br>    Rectors<br>    Vicars | **Business**<br>The Reverend John Jones Smith, D.D.*<br>Address<br><br>    *See Note 2.<br><br>**Social:**<br>The Reverend John Jones Smith<br>Address<br><br>The Reverend and Mrs. John Jones Smith<br>Address<br><br>    See Notes 1 and 2. | Dear Dr. Smith:<br>Dear Mr. Smith:<br>Dear Father Smith:<br>    Very truly yours,<br>    Sincerely yours, |
| **Brother** | Follow the rules for a monastic clergyman, but omit "The Reverend" and use "Brother" instead of "Father." | |
| **Mother Superior**<br>She is addressed by her ecclesiastical name. | **Business:**<br>The Reverend Mother Superior<br>    (**or** Mother Superior Mary, O.S.A.*)<br>Address<br><br>    *See Note 2.<br><br>**Social:**<br>Mother Mary<br>Address<br><br>    See Notes 1 and 2. | Dear Reverend<br>  Mother:<br>    Very truly yours,<br>    Sincerely yours, |
| **Sister Superior** | **Business:**<br>Sister Superior Mary, S.J.B.*<br>Address<br><br>    *See Note 2.<br><br>**Social:**<br>Sister Superior Mary<br>Address | Dear Sister Mary:<br>    Very truly yours,<br>    Sincerely yours, |
| **Sister** | The same as for a Sister Superior without "Superior" | |

## Protestant—Methodist

| | | |
|---|---|---|
| **Bishop**<br>Note that a bishop in this faith is not "The Reverend," but that the title "Bishop" is used by itself. | **Business:**<br>Bishop John Jones Smith, D.D.<br>——— Area<br>Address<br><br>**Social:**<br>Bishop John Jones Smith<br>Address<br><br>Bishop and Mrs. John Jones Smith<br>Address<br><br>    See Note 2. | Dear Bishop Smith:<br>    Very truly yours,<br>    Sincerely yours, |
| **Minister** | Use the formulas given for clergymen at the beginning of the "Protestant" section. | |

| SOCIAL LETTER | IN CONVERSATION | INTRODUCTIONS | ABBREV. |
|---|---|---|---|
| My dear Dr. Smith, **(very formal)** Dear Dr. Smith, Sincerely yours, <br><br> In the above, "Mr." is used if he does not have a doctoral degree. "Father Smith" and "Father John" are also correct, depending on his preference and parish custom. | **To** and **About:** Dr. Smith Mr. Smith Father Smith Father John <br><br> See Note 5. | **Individual:** Dr. Smith Mr. Smith Father Smith Father John <br><br> **Presentation to an audience:** The Reverend John Jones Smith and his church or position (with any of the variants above that are suitable) | None |
| My dear Reverend Mother, **(very formal)** Dear Mother Mary, Sincerely yours, | **To:** Mother Mary Reverend Mother <br><br> **About:** The Reverend Mother Mother Mary <br><br> See Note 5. | **Individual:** Mother Mary <br><br> **Presentation to an audience:** The Reverend Mother Mary, Superior of the Order of —— | None |
| My dear Sister Mary, **(very formal)** Dear Sister Mary, Sincerely yours, | **To** and **About:** Sister Mary <br><br> See Note 5. | **Individual:** Sister Mary <br><br> **Presentation to an audience:** Sister Mary, Superior of the Order of —— | None |
| My dear Bishop Smith, **(very formal)** Dear Bishop Smith, Sincerely yours, | **To** and **About:** Bishop Smith <br><br> See Note 5. | **Individual:** Bishop Smith <br><br> **Presentation to an audience:** Dr. John Jones Smith, Bishop of —— Area **or** Bishop John Jones Smith of —— Area | None |

## THE COURTS

1. It is not customary to address any member of the judiciary as "Your Honor" or to refer to him as "His Honor" except in court.

2. For details about the use of "Honorable" and "The Honorable," see Note 1 under "Government" in this section.

3. Follow the rules below for unmarried

| PERSON | ENVELOPES | BUSINESS LETTER |
|---|---|---|
| The Chief Justice<br>Supreme Court of the U.S.<br><br>See Note 4. | **Business**:<br>The Chief Justice of the United States<br>The Supreme Court of the United States<br>Washington, D.C.   20543<br><br>The Honorable John Jones Smith<br>Chief Justice of the United States<br>The Supreme Court of the United States<br>Washington, D.C.   20543<br><br>**Social**:<br>The Honorable<br>John Jones Smith<br>Address<br><br>The Chief Justice and Mrs. Smith<br>Address | Dear Mr. Chief<br>Justice:<br>Very truly yours,<br>Sincerely yours, |
| Associate Justice<br>Supreme Court of the U.S.<br><br>See Note 4. | **Business**:<br>Mr. Justice Smith<br>The Supreme Court of the United States<br>Washington, D.C.   20543<br><br>The Honorable John Jones Smith<br>Associate Justice<br>The Supreme Court of the United States<br>**etc.**<br><br>**Social**:<br>Mr. Justice Smith<br>Address<br><br>Mr. Justice Smith and Mrs. Smith<br>Address | Dear Mr. Justice:<br>Very truly yours,<br>Sincerely yours, |
| Judge of other courts, including:<br>U.S. Court of Appeals<br>U.S. Court of Claims<br>U.S. District Courts<br>State Courts<br>City Courts<br><br>See Notes 1, 3, and 4. | **Business**:<br>The Honorable<br>John Jones Smith<br>Judge, (Name of court)<br>Address<br><br>Judge John Jones Smith<br>Name of the court<br>Address<br><br>**Social**:<br>The Honorable<br>John Jones Smith<br>Address<br><br>The Honorable John Jones Smith<br>  and Mrs. Smith<br>Address | Dear Judge Smith:<br>Very truly yours,<br>Sincerely yours, |
| Magistrate | **Business**:<br>Mr. John Jones Smith<br>Magistrate<br>Name of court<br>Address<br><br>**Social**:<br>Mr. John Jones Smith<br>Address<br><br>Mr. and Mrs. John Jones Smith<br>Address | Dear Sir:<br>Dear Mr. Smith:<br>Very truly yours,<br>Sincerely yours, |

Women Judges and Magistrates

See Note 3.

women judges. In social circumstances, however, use "Mrs." and her husband's name, instead of "Judge," in addressing a married woman judge.

4. Retired justices and judges continue to be addressed by their titles and "The Honorable."

| SOCIAL LETTER | IN CONVERSATION | INTRODUCTIONS | ABBREV. |
|---|---|---|---|
| My dear Mr. Chief Justice, **(very formal)** Dear Mr. Chief Justice, Sincerely yours, | **To:** Mr. Chief Justice<br><br>**About:** The Chief Justice | **Individual:** The Chief Justice<br><br>**Presentation to an audience:** The Honorable John Jones Smith, the Chief Justice of the Supreme Court of the United States | None |
| My dear Mr. Justice, **(very formal)** Dear Mr. Justice, Sincerely yours, | **To:** Mr. Justice<br><br>**About:** Justice Smith | **Individual:** Mr. Justice Smith<br><br>**Presentation to an audience:** The Honorable John Jones Smith, Associate Justice of the Supreme Court of the United States | None |
| My dear Judge Smith, **(very formal)** Dear Judge Smith, Sincerely yours, | **To** and **About:** Judge Smith<br><br>(In prolonged conversation, "Judge" alone) | **Individual:** Judge Smith<br><br>**Presentation to an audience:** The Honorable John Jones Smith, Judge of the (full name of the court) | None |
| My dear Mr. Smith, **(very formal)** Dear Mr. Smith, Sincerely yours, | **To** and **About:** Mr. Smith | **Individual:** Mr. Smith<br><br>**Presentation to an audience:** Mr. John Jones Smith, Magistrate of ——— | None |

## DIPLOMATIC

1. For the use and placement of "Honorable" and "The Honorable," see Note 1 under "Government" in this section.

2. American diplomats are not addressed "Excellency," which is correctly used only in addressing a foreign ambassador (and certain other high officials, and former high officials, of other countries).

3. Our State Department approves the use of "American Ambassador" and "American Embassy" in certain circumstances, but gives "The Ambassador (Embassy) of the United States of America" as first choice, most especially in Latin American countries.

Spell out "United States of America" whenever possible without crowding a line (though the abbreviation "U.S.A." is not incorrect). However, note that "United States" should not be used alone; if the rules are followed, "United States of America" is used.

4. A woman serving as an ambassador is addressed exactly as a male ambassador should be, with "Madam" substituted for "Mr."

| PERSON | ENVELOPES | BUSINESS LETTER |
|---|---|---|
| U.S. Ambassador<br><br>See Notes 3 and 4. | **Business**:<br>The Honorable<br>John Jones Smith [Mary Brown Smith]<br>Ambassador of the United States<br>of America<br><br>(**or** American Ambassador)<br>City, Country<br><br>(In this use, it is not necessary to<br>add "The American Embassy" or a<br>street address.)<br><br>**Social**:<br>The Honorable<br>The Ambassador of the United States<br>of America<br>(**or** The American Ambassador)<br>The American Embassy<br>City, Country<br><br>The Honorable<br>The Ambassador of the United States<br>of America<br>(**or** The American Ambassador)<br>and Mrs. Smith<br>Address | Dear Mr. [Madam]<br>Ambassador:<br>Very truly yours,<br>Sincerely yours, |
| U.S. Ambassador<br>**with military rank** | Instead of "Honorable" use<br>(Full rank) John Jones Smith<br>Ambassador of the<br>United States of America<br>etc. | Dear Mr. Ambassador·<br>Very truly yours,<br>Sincerely yours, |
| U.S. Ambassador<br>**away from his post** | The Honorable<br>John Jones Smith<br>and Mrs. Smith<br>Address | Dear Mr. Ambassador:<br>Very truly yours,<br>Sincerely yours, |
| U.S. Consul General<br>U.S. Consul<br>U.S. Chargé d'Affaires | John Jones Smith, Esq.   **or**<br>Mr. John Jones Smith<br>and as for "Ambassador," with<br>"Consul," etc., substituted<br>for "Ambassador" | Dear Mr. Smith:<br>Very truly yours,<br>Sincerely yours, |

The wife of an ambassador is an "ambassadress," but that title is so seldom used that it is best forgotten.

5. The wife of an ambassador from an English-speaking country is addressed "Mrs." (unless he has a personal title, in which case she is, of course, "Lady" or whatever title is appropriate; **see** "Foreign" in this section). If the ambassador has a royal title, for example, an envelope to him would be addressed by this formula:

His Royal Highness
The Duke of _____

Ambassador of _____
Address

If the ambassador has a nonroyal title, an example of the correct form (depending on his title) is:

His Excellency
Lord _____
Ambassador of _____

His Excellency
The Ambassador of _____
and Lady _____

See "Foreign" charts below.

| SOCIAL LETTER | IN CONVERSATION | INTRODUCTIONS | ABBREV. |
|---|---|---|---|
| My dear Mr. [Madam] Ambassador, **(very formal)** Dear Mr. [Madam] Ambassador, Sincerely yours, | **To:** Mr. [Madam] Ambassador **or** in prolonged conversation, Mr. [Miss, Mrs.] Smith  **About:** The Ambassador Ambassador Smith | **Individual:** Ambassador Smith  **Presentation to an audience:** The Honorable John Jones Smith, Ambassador of the United States of America to ——— **Or, in this country:** Our Ambassador to ——— | None |
| My dear Mr. Ambassador, My dear Admiral [General] Smith, **(very formal)** Dear Mr. Ambassador, Dear Admiral [General] Smith, Sincerely yours, | **To:** Mr. Ambassador **or** (according to circumstances and his preference) Admiral [General] Smith  **About:** As above | **Individual:** Ambassador Smith  **Presentation to an audience:** Admiral [General] Smith, Ambassador, etc. | None |
| As above | As above | As above | None |
| My dear Mr. Smith, **(very formal)** Dear Mr. Smith, Sincerely yours, | **To and About:** Mr. Smith | **Individual:** Mr. Smith  **Presentation to an audience:** Mr. John Jones Smith, his position, post, etc. | None |

| PERSON | ENVELOPES | BUSINESS LETTER |
|---|---|---|
| Foreign Ambassador in the U.S. (For a woman ambassador, use "Her" Excellency.)<br><br>See Note 5 above, and also Note 1 under "United Nations, following. | **Business**:<br>His Excellency<br>John Jones Smith (no prefix unless he has some such title as "Dr.," "Sir," "Count," etc.)<br>Ambassador of ——<br>Local address<br><br>**Social**:<br>His Excellency<br>John Jones Smith<br>Ambassador of ——<br>Local address<br><br>His Excellency<br>The Ambassador of ——<br>  and Mrs. Smith | Excellency:<br>Very truly yours,<br>Sincerely yours, |
| Foreign Ambassador **with a title**<br><br>See Note 5 | | |
| Foreign Ministers | As for Ambassadors, with "Minister" instead | |
| Foreign Chargé d'Affaires in the United States | **Business**:<br>Mr. John Jones Smith<br>Chargé d'Affaires of (Country)<br>Business address<br><br>**Social**:<br>Mr. John Jones Smith<br>Home address | Dear Mr. Chargé d'Affaires:<br>Dear Mr. Smith:<br>Very truly yours,<br>Sincerely yours, |

# FOREIGN

This section is for the guidance of the countless thousands of Americans who today have occasion to speak or write on a nondiplomatic level to foreigners with titles —the Americans who are traveling for business or pleasure, and the Americans who have reason to meet distinguished visitors to our country.

In many instances, our own government officials use more ceremonial forms of address than those given in the charts below.

## Foreign (any country)

| PERSON | ENVELOPES | BUSINESS LETTER |
|---|---|---|
| A King (The same rule governs forms of address to his Queen or to a reigning Queen.) | His Majesty<br>King (name and Roman numeral)<br>City and Country | Your Majesty:<br>Respectfully yours, |
| A Reigning Prince (nonroyal) | His Serene Highness<br>Prince (name and Roman numeral, if any)<br>City and Country | Your Serene Highness:<br>Respectfully yours, |

| SOCIAL LETTER | IN CONVERSATION | INTRODUCTIONS | ABBREV. |
|---|---|---|---|
| My dear Mr. [Madam] Ambassador, **(very formal)** Dear Mr. [Madam] Ambassador, Sincerely yours, | **To:** Mr. [Madam] Ambassador **or** Your Excellency **About:** The (Norwegian) Ambassador **or** His title (Mr., Sir, Count, etc.) and Name | **Individual:** Mr. (**or** Dr., Sir, Count, etc.) Smith **or** Ambassador Smith <br><br>**Presentation to an audience:** His Excellency, John Jones Smith, the ——— Ambassador | None |
| | | | As above |
| | | | As above |
| My dear Mr. Smith, **(very formal)** Dear Mr. Smith, Sincerely yours, | **To:** Mr. Smith (or his personal title) **About:** The ——— Chargé d'Affaires Mr. Smith | **Individual:** Mr. Smith (or personal title) <br><br>**Presentation to an audience:** Mr. John Jones Smith, Chargé d'Affaires, post and country | None |

And customs vary among the different countries, of course. However, there are certain forms of address that can be widely applied.

Chosen for this section are the simplest of the correct forms that an American can follow with confidence when he is in doubt about how to address royalty, heads of state, other high officials, and foreigners with personal titles.

| SOCIAL LETTER | IN CONVERSATION | INTRODUCTIONS | ABBREV. |
|---|---|---|---|
| Dear King (Name), Sincerely yours, (This form is extremely informal and is properly used only by persons of intimate social acquaintance with a sovereign or other member of a royal family.) | **To:** Your Majesty Sir (in prolonged conversation) **About:** His Majesty The King King (name) | All who meet a King are presented **to** him. | None |
| Dear Prince ———, and as above | **To:** Your Highness Sir (in prolonged conversation) **About:** Prince ——— | As above | None |

| PERSON | ENVELOPES | BUSINESS LETTER |
|---|---|---|
| A President | His Excellency<br>(Full name, preceded by Mr., Dr.,<br>  General, or other title)<br>President of (Country)<br>Address | Your Excellency:<br>Respectfully yours, |
| Various high officials | Follow the rule for a President (above),<br>except for British officials, who use<br>"The Right Honorable" instead of<br>"Excellency." **See also** "Diplomatic"<br>and "United Nations" charts. | |

## Foreign (British)

1. Special rules govern the forms of address to members of the royal family and all other titled personages. The Queen is never addressed **in speech** by any other words than "Your Majesty" or "Ma'am." That is all there is to remember—never "Your Highness," "Queen Elizabeth," or "Queen." All other members of the royal family—the Queen Mother, Prince Philip; and Princes, Princesses, Royal Dukes and Duchesses—are addressed in person "Your Highness" or "Sir" or "Ma'am."

   (a) Only those who are on close terms should address a letter directly to any member of the royal family. Instead, the correct procedure is to direct a letter to the secretary of the person concerned.

2. In England, there are seven degrees of nonroyal rank that carry a title. In the order of importance, they are:

   Duke (Duchess)
   Marquess (Marchioness)
   Earl (Countess)
   Viscount (Viscountess)
   Baron (Baroness)
   Baronet (Lady)
   Knight (Lady)

   The first five are noblemen. They are known as Peers. Their titles are hereditary. They have the inherited right to sit in the House of Lords.

   Baronets and Knights are not noblemen or Peers. The title "Baronet" descends from father to son. The title "Knight" is an honor bestowed for life only, and is not inherited.

3. All Peers have a family name (Smith is used in this section as on all other charts) as well as their titles, though sometimes a title and a family name are the same in the lower brackets: John Jones Smith could be Baron Smith, for example.

   Almost all Peers of the rank of Duke, Marquess, and Earl have a number of lesser titles also. For example, John Smith, The Duke of Claridgeshire, may also be The Marquess of Montshire, The Earl of Whitnoy, and The Viscount Haliford because he inherits all titles granted to his forebears (except that of Knight).

   (a) The eldest son of a Peer takes the family title next highest to that of his father, and **his** eldest son takes the third highest title. For example, the eldest son of The Marquess of Montshire would be Earl of Whitnoy (note —no "The"), and his eldest son would be Viscount Haliford. In each case, the wife takes the corresponding title.

   The younger sons of a Peer do not take such family titles. See the charts for the titles they do take.

4. "The" preceding a title has several special meanings. When "The" precedes the title "Princess," for example, it means that she is the daughter of a Sovereign. All other Princesses are addressed without the "The."

   A Peer in his own right uses "The" before his title. Let us say he is The Marquess of Montshire. "The" in this case signifies that "Marquess" is the highest title in his direct line. If "The" is omitted, it signifies two things: that his father is living and also that his father has a higher title.

5. In spoken address, of paramount importance are certain forms of address that should **not** be used. Under social

| SOCIAL LETTER | IN CONVERSATION | INTRODUCTIONS | ABBREV. |
|---|---|---|---|
| Dear Mr. President,<br>Sincerely yours, | **To:**<br>Mr. President **or**<br>Sir<br><br>**About:**<br>President (Last<br>name)<br>The President<br>of (Country) | All individuals are properly<br>introduced **to** a head of state.<br><br>**Presentation to an audience:**<br>His Excellency (Dr., General,<br>etc., if he has a special personal<br>title), his full name, President<br>of (Country) | None |

circumstances, it is never correct to say "Your Grace," "Your Lordship," "Your Ladyship," "My Lord," or "My Lady." These forms of address are correctly used only by tradesmen, servants, and those in service or business positions who have no social acquaintance with the person addressed.

6. It is correct for an American to use most of our own standard forms in addressing envelopes and in the salutation and closing on letters. However, it is well to be aware of certain definite differences between correct British and American forms.

   In England, the envelope of a formal invitation is addressed to the wife only (not, as is our custom, to "Mr. and Mrs."), though of course the names of both are written in the body of a formal invitation, and Christmas cards are jointly addressed.

   The stiffly formal American salutation is "My dear Mr. Smith," but just the opposite ("Dear Mr. Smith") is the distant and formal form in England. And, as a completely minor point, we write "Sincerely yours," and the British prefer the reverse sequence: "Yours sincerely."

7. "H.R.H." is a correct and frequently used abbreviation for His (Her) Royal Highness. It is used on an envelope, not on the letter itself.

   In this country, we spell out "Honorable" as first choice. By British custom, "Honourable" (note the British spelling) is abbreviated: Hon. or Hon<u>ble</u>, and it is customary to use "The" before it. "Honourable" is used on the envelope—not within a letter.

   Englishmen in England are not correctly addressed "Your Excellency," though British ambassadors and certain other high officials like the Governor General of Canada are correctly addressed "Excellency" when they are abroad. Use "The Right Honorable" when writing to a Privy Councillor, Prime Minister, Lord Mayor, and other high officials in England. **See also** "Diplomatic" and "United Nations" charts.

8. Initials following a name can indicate membership in an Order (K.G., for example, means that the individual is a Knight of The Most Noble Order of the Garter—a very high honor); or can stand for a Decoration or Honor; or initials can stand for an academic degree or for membership in an association; M.P. stands for Member of Parliament. Such initials are written after a name as occasion demands. If in doubt, it is no error to omit them. If they are used, they are put on the same line as the name.

9. "Esq." is preferred in England to "Mr." (especially on a letter to a friend) on an envelope to any British gentleman who does not have a title. Only in extremely formal correspondence, such as a formal invitation, is "Esquire" spelled out. As in the United States, "Mr.," "Dr.," "Hon.," and so on are not used before a name when "Esq." follows it. But, contrary to our custom, letters denoting a doctoral degree are correctly used: John Smith, Esq. M.D. This rule covers all professional men without titles—lawyers, writers, editors, painters, musicians, and so on, as well as members of the House of Commons; in the latter case, the correct address is John Jones Smith, Esq. M.P.

| PERSON | ENVELOPES | BUSINESS LETTER |
|---|---|---|
| The Queen<br><br>See Note 1. | Her Majesty<br>   The Queen<br>     Buckingham Palace<br>     London  S W I<br><br>     (England is added only on<br>     a letter sent from abroad.) | Madam:<br>   Respectfully yours, |
| Prince Philip<br>  (The Queen and Prince<br>  Philip are never properly<br>  addressed jointly in writing.)<br><br>    See Note 1. | His Royal Highness<br>   The Prince Philip<br>     The Duke of Edinburgh<br>     Address | Sir:<br>   Respectfully yours, |
| A Royal Prince or Princess<br><br>See Notes 1 and 5. | His [Her] Royal Highness<br>   The Prince [Princess] | Sir:<br>Madam:<br>   Respectfully yours, |
| A Royal Duke or Duchess<br><br>See Notes 1 and 5. | His [Her] Royal Highness<br>   The Duke [Duchess] of ———<br>     Address | Sir:<br>Madam:<br>   Respectfully yours, |
| The Duke and Duchess of Windsor<br>  They are addressed as above,<br>except that "Her Grace" instead<br>of "Her Royal Highness" is used<br>to the Duchess, following the<br>rules for a non-Royal Duchess<br>given below. When the names<br>are written jointly, the form is:<br>  His Royal Highness, The Duke<br>  of Windsor and Her Grace,<br>  the Duchess of Windsor | | |

## FOREIGN (British Titled Personages—non-Royal)

| PERSON | ENVELOPES | BUSINESS LETTER |
|---|---|---|
| Duke<br>  (A Duke's title is always taken<br>    from a place.)<br><br>    See Notes 2 and 5. | **Business**:<br>  His Grace<br>    The Duke of Claridgeshire<br>      Address<br><br>**Social**:<br>  The<br>    Duke of Claridgeshire<br>      Address<br>  The<br>    Duke and Duchess of Claridgeshire<br>      Address | My Lord Duke:<br>   Yours sincerely, |

| SOCIAL LETTER | IN CONVERSATION | INTRODUCTIONS | ABBREV. |
|---|---|---|---|
| Madam,<br>(Only someone who is an intimate social acquaintance would address a letter directly to her.)<br>Sincerely yours, | **To:**<br>Your Majesty<br>Ma'am (in prolonged conversation)<br><br>**About:**<br>Her Majesty, the Queen | All visitors are presented **to** the Queen. | None except H.R.H.<br><br>See Note 7. |
| Sir,<br>(as above)<br>Sincerely yours, | **To:**<br>Your Royal Highness<br>Sir<br><br>**About:**<br>His Royal Highness Prince Philip | All visitors are presented **to** Prince Philip. | As above |
| Sir,<br>Madam,<br>(as above)<br>Sincerely yours, | As above | As above | As above |
| Dear Duke,<br>Dear Duchess,<br>Sincerely yours, | **To:**<br>Your Royal Highness **or** Sir [Ma'am]<br><br>**About:**<br>His [Her] Royal Highness<br>The Duke [Duchess] of ——— | As above | As above |

| SOCIAL LETTER | IN CONVERSATION | INTRODUCTIONS | ABBREV. |
|---|---|---|---|
| Dear Duke<br>of Claridgeshire,<br>(an acquaintance)<br>Dear Duke,<br>(a friend)<br>Yours sincerely, | **To:**<br>Duke<br>**About:**<br>The Duke<br>The Duke of Claridgeshire | The Duke of Claridgeshire | None |

| PERSON | ENVELOPES | BUSINESS LETTER |
|---|---|---|
| Duchess | As above | Madam:<br>Yours sincerely, |
| Sons and Daughters of a Duke<br>  Eldest son and his wife:<br>    See Note 3a.<br>  A younger son takes the title<br>    "Lord" with his given and<br>    family names. The wife of a<br>    younger son uses "Lady"<br>    preceding his given and<br>    family name. | The<br>  Lord John Jones Smith<br>  Address<br><br><br>The<br>  Lady John Jones Smith | Sir:<br>  Yours sincerely, |
|   Daughter of a Duke: She takes<br>    the title "Lady" with her<br>    given and family names. | The<br>  Lady Mary Smith<br>  Address | Madam:<br>  Yours sincerely, |
| Marquess and Marchioness<br>  (Some Peers of this rank prefer<br>  the spelling "Marquis." The<br>  title of a Marquess is nearly<br>  always taken from a place.)<br><br>  See Note 5. | **Business**:<br>  The Most Hon.<br>    The Marquess [Marchioness]<br>      of Montshire<br>    Address<br><br>**Social**:<br>  The<br>    Marquess [Marchioness] of Montshire | Sir:<br>  Yours sincerely,<br><br>Madam:<br>  Yours sincerely, |
| Sons and Daughters of a Marquess<br>  The eldest son and his wife:<br><br>  See Note 3a.<br><br>  The younger sons and their wives:<br>    exactly as for the younger<br>    sons of a Duke.<br>  The daughters: As for the<br>    daughters of a Duke. | | |
| Earl and Countess<br><br>See Notes 4, 5, and 7. | **Business**:<br>  The Right Hon.<br>    The Earl [Countess] of Whitnoy<br>    Address<br><br>**Social**:<br>  The<br>    Earl [Countess] of Whitnoy<br>    Address | My Lord:<br>Madam:<br>  Yours sincerely, |
| Sons and Daughters of an Earl<br>  The eldest son and his wife:<br><br>  See Note 3a.<br><br>  A younger son of an Earl,<br>    and his wife, take the title<br>    "Honorable."<br><br>  The daughter of an Earl has the<br>    title "Lady"—exactly as for<br>    the daughter of a Duke. | The Hon.<br>  John Jones Smith<br><br>The Hon.<br>  Mrs. John Jones Smith | Sir:<br>Madam:<br>  Yours sincerely, |

| SOCIAL LETTER | IN CONVERSATION | INTRODUCTIONS | ABBREV. |
|---|---|---|---|
| Dear Duchess<br>of Claridgeshire,<br>(an acquaintance)<br>Dear Duchess,<br>(a friend)<br>Yours sincerely, | **To**:<br>Duchess<br><br>**About**:<br>The Duchess<br>The Duchess<br>of Claridgeshire | The Duchess of Claridgeshire | None |
| Dear Lord John<br>Smith,<br>(acquaintance)<br>Dear Lord John,<br>(friend) | **To** and **About**:<br>Lord John Smith **or**<br>Lord John | Lord John Smith | None |
| Dear Lady John<br>Smith,  **or**<br>Dear Lady John,<br>Yours sincerely, | Lady John Smith **or**<br>Lady John<br>(But never Lady<br>Smith) | Lady John Smith | |
| Dear Lady Mary<br>Smith,<br>Dear Lady Mary,<br>Yours sincerely, | **To** and **About**:<br>Lady Mary<br>Lady Mary Smith | Lady Mary Smith | |
| Dear Lord<br>Montshire,<br>Dear Lady<br>Montshire,<br>Yours sincerely, | **To**:<br>Lord Montshire<br>Lady Montshire<br>**About**:<br>The Marquess<br>[Marchioness]<br>of Montshire<br>Lord [Lady]<br>Montshire | The Marquess [Marchioness] of<br>Montshire (**formal**)<br>Lord [Lady] Montshire (**less<br>formal**) | None |
| Dear Lord Whitnoy,<br>Dear Lady Whitnoy,<br>Yours sincerely, | **To**:<br>Lord Whitnoy<br>Lady Whitnoy<br>**About**:<br>The Earl [Countess]<br>of Whitnoy<br>Lord [Lady]<br>Whitnoy | The Earl [Countess] of Whitnoy<br>Lord [Lady] Whitnoy (**less<br>formal**) | None |
| Dear Mr. Smith,<br>Dear Mrs. Smith,<br>Yours sincerely, | **To** and **About**:<br>Mr. Smith<br>Mrs. Smith | Mr. Smith<br>Mrs. Smith | None<br>except<br>for<br>Note 7. |

| PERSON | ENVELOPES | BUSINESS LETTER |
|---|---|---|
| Viscount and Viscountess | **Business**:<br>The Right Hon.<br>   The Viscount [Viscountess] Haliford<br>   Address<br><br>**Social**:<br>The<br>   Viscount [Viscountess] Haliford | Sir:<br>Madam:<br>   Yours sincerely, |

**Sons and Daughters of a Viscount**
All the sons and daughters of a Viscount have the same title:
"Honourable"—since below the rank of Earl the eldest son does
not use one of his father's lesser titles.

| | | |
|---|---|---|
| **Baron and Baroness**<br>A Baron is addressed "Lord,"<br>never "Baron," and his wife<br>(unless a Baroness in her own<br>right) is addressed "Lady." | **Business**:<br>The Right Hon.<br>   Lord [Lady] Smith<br>   Address<br><br>**Social**:<br>The<br>   Lord [Lady] Smith<br>   Address | Sir:<br>Madam:<br>   Yours sincerely, |
| **Baroness (in her own right)**<br>She takes the title "Baroness,"<br>but may also be addressed<br>"Lady." | **Business**:<br>The Right Hon.<br>   The Baroness Smith<br>   Address<br><br>**Social**:<br>The<br>   Baroness Smith    **or**<br>The<br>   Lady Smith | Madam:<br>   Yours sincerely, |

**Sons and Daughters of a Baron**
They all take the title
"Honourable," as for the
children of a Viscount.

| | | |
|---|---|---|
| **Baronet**<br>**Wife of a Baronet**<br>**Sons and Daughters of a Baronet**<br>They have no titles, and are<br>addressed "Mr." or "Miss." | Sir John Smith, Bart.<br>Lady Smith | Sir:<br>Madam:<br>   Yours sincerely, |
| **Knight**<br>His wife takes the title<br>"Lady" with his surname<br>only. See Wife of a<br>Baronet, above. | Sir John Smith, K.B.E.<br>   (or other suitable initials<br>   of his Order, if any) | Sir:<br>   Yours sincerely, |
| **Dame**<br>This title is an honor conferred<br>for life. It is similar to knight-<br>hood except that the husband<br>of a Dame does not share his<br>wife's distinctions or assume the<br>title "Sir." | Dame Mary Smith, D.B.E.<br>   (or if she has a higher title,<br>   it is used, with "D.B.E." after<br>   her name) | Madam:<br>   Yours sincerely, |

## FOREIGN (British—various nontitled personages) See Notes 7 and 9.

## FOREIGN (Spanish)

The main matter of importance in writing or speaking to Spanish and Latin-American citizens is understanding their use of names. Señor Juan Gómez y Gon-zález should be addressed "Señor Juan Gómez" because the position of "Gómez" indicates that it is his father's name, and the "y González" means "and González"

| SOCIAL LETTER | IN CONVERSATION | INTRODUCTIONS | ABBREV. |
|---|---|---|---|
| Dear Lord Haliford, Dear Lady Haliford, Yours sincerely, | **To:** Lord [Lady] Haliford **About:** Viscount [Viscountess] Haliford **or** Lord [Lady] Haliford | Viscount [Viscountess] Haliford Lord [Lady] Haliford (**less formal**) | None except for Note 7. |
| | | | As above |
| Dear Lord Smith, Dear Lady Smith, Yours sincerely, | **To and About:** Lord [Lady] Smith | Lord [Lady] Smith | As above |
| Dear Baroness Smith, **or** Dear Lady Smith, Yours sincerely, | **To:** Lady Smith **About:** Baroness Smith **or** Lady Smith | Baroness Smith Lady Smith (**less formal**) | As above |
| | | | As above |
| Dear Sir John, Dear Lady Smith Yours sincerely, | **To:** Sir John **About:** Sir John Smith **To and About:** Lady Smith | Sir John Smith Lady Smith | As above |
| Dear Sir John, Yours sincerely, | **To:** Sir John **About:** Sir John Smith | Sir John Smith | |
| Dear Dame Mary, Yours sincerely, | **To:** Dame Mary (or, if she prefers, ''Miss'' or ''Mrs. Smith'') **About:** Dame Mary Smith **or** Dame Mary | Dame Mary Smith (unless she has a higher title) | |

(his mother's name).

His wife, the former Juanita Ibáñez y Blanco, is Señora Juanita Ibáñez de Gómez. It is customary to address an envelope to her in that fashion. The greeting in a letter to her should be ''Dear Señora de Gómez'' —never ''Dear Señora Gómez.''

## GOVERNMENT

There are correct variants of some of the forms given in this section, but selected are the forms that are always correct and are in widest use.

1. **Honorable** and **The Honorable.** The questions most often asked about the use of these two titles are: Which one is correct? Where does one put "Honorable" on an envelope? Here are the rules:

Use "The Honorable," always, when only a person's title (not his name) follows, as it should on some formal letters to certain high officials. (Details are in the charts.)

For example:

The Honorable
The Governor of New York
Address

Except for the rule above, either "The Honorable," on a line by itself, or "Honorable," on the same line with the name, is correct.

"The Honorable" on a line by itself is traditional and most formal, and is used on mail going from the office of our Secretary of State in these forms:

The Honorable
John Jones Smith
Address

The Honorable
John Jones Smith
and Mrs. Smith
Address

However, the trend today is toward simplification, and all other departments in Washington now approve and use the following slight modifications when writing to anyone who rates the title "Honorable" (though the White House retains the "The" when using the following compact forms):

Honorable John Jones Smith
Address

Honorable and Mrs. John Jones Smith
Address

Private citizens who only occasionally need to write to the dignitaries who are correctly addressed "Honorable" usually choose the slightly more ceremonial form (with "The Honorable" on a separate line), but the choice is entirely a matter of individual preference and convenience. The shorter, more compact form is certainly recommended for any large mailings of typed letters.

2. Do not combine "Honorable" in any form with another title, such as "Mrs.," "Dr.," "Senator," "Mayor," "Judge," or with the initials of an academic degree. ("The Honorable Dr. John Jones Smith" and "Honorable John Jones Smith, Ph.D." are both wrong.)

3. Spell out a name preceded by "Honorable." ("Honorable J. J. Smith" is completely wrong.)

4. Spell "Honorable" in full as first choice, though the abbreviation "Hon." is not incorrect.

5. Do not use "Honorable" in the opening salutation of a letter. ("Honorable

---

## Federal Government

These charts are arranged for ease of reference, and are **not** according to the sequence of precedence. See the separate entry WASHINGTON for a list showing correct precedence.

| PERSON | ENVELOPES | BUSINESS LETTER |
|---|---|---|
| The President | **Business:** <br> The President <br> The White House <br> Washington, D.C.  20500 <br><br> **Social:** <br> As above,        **or** <br> The President <br> and Mrs. Smith <br> The White House <br> Washington, D.C.  20500 | Sir:    **or** <br> Mr. President: <br> **(formal, official)** <br> Dear Mr. President: <br> **(private individual)** <br> Respectfully, <br> **(formal, official)** <br> Faithfully yours, <br> **(less formal, official)** <br> Respectfully yours, <br> **(private individual)** |

Sir," "Dear Honorable Smith," and "My dear Honorable" are wrong.)

6. A person entitled to be addressed "Honorable" never himself uses that title on his letter paper, as part of his signature, or in any other way.

7. "The Honorable" is used in an introduction only if the full name follows. ("May I present the Honorable Smith?" is wrong.)

8. "The Right Honorable" is largely a British form, and is not used to an American citizen.

9. Anyone who has won the right to the title "Honorable" (by virtue of being elected or appointed to high office) maintains the right to be so addressed for life.

   The list of people entitled to this form of address is quite extensive. It includes mayors, governors, and other high state officials, senators and representatives (both state and federal), cabinet officers, ambassadors, special assistants to the President, and our representatives to international organizations, among others, many of whom are listed in the following charts.

10. Official and business mail is, of course, sent to the office address. In Washington, it is also customary and correct to send invitations and other social letters to an official's office, since they can usually be handled more efficiently there than at his home address.

11. There are three ways to address a for-

mal invitation or announcement to a woman offcial and her husband.

On strictly social mail, use her husband's title, if he has one—even if she outranks him. Otherwise address the envelope to "Mr. and Mrs. John Jones Smith." If the woman is being asked to an official event in her official capacity, two separate invitations can be sent: one to her, addressed by title and the other to her husband. Or the following form can be used:

> The Honorable
> The Secretary of Labor
>   and Mr. Smith
> Address

12. "Very truly yours," by tradition, is correct on business but not on social mail. It is the standard form for a business letter, but the trend today is to use "Sincerely yours," which is also correct on a business letter and is considered less stiff by some people.

13. As a very general rule, the officials of a state government are not addressed by title in social life. Except when he is on duty in the state capital, a state senator, for example, is usually addressed "Mr. Smith," though it is not incorrect to use "Senator." The reason, of course, is to avoid confusion between state and federal government officials of the same rank.

14. "Excellency" is correctly used to foreign ambassadors and other foreign high officials, but it is not our custom to address an American citizen as "Excellency."

| SOCIAL LETTER | IN CONVERSATION | INTRODUCTIONS | ABBREV. |
|---|---|---|---|
| My dear Mr. President, **(very formal)** Dear Mr. President,* **(formal)** Sincerely yours, | **To:** Mr. President **or** Sir ("Mr. Smith" is not correct) **About:** The President **or** Mr. Smith | **Individual:** Everyone is presented **to the** President, and his name is not spoken. The form is "Mr. President, may I present . . ." **Presentation to an audience:** The President of the United States (no name) | Never "Pres." |

*By the rules of protocol, the President is never correctly addressed "Dear Mr. Smith," and people familiar with Washington rules avoid it—though a great many others use this form, and it is a sound guess that the President himself does not give the mistake a second thought.

| PERSON | ENVELOPES | BUSINESS LETTER |
|---|---|---|
| The President's Wife | Mrs. Smith<br>The White House<br>Washington, D.C.   20500<br><br>**Note**: Above is the form approved by the State Department, and the first choice in diplomatic circles. Less formal, but also correct and very widely used, is the following:<br>Mrs. John Jones Smith<br>The White House | Dear Mrs. Smith:<br>Very truly yours,<br>Sincerely yours, |
| A Former President<br>He should be addressed as "The Honorable," though if he holds a permanent military rank (General Eisenhower), his rank is used instead. He is never addressed directly nor introduced as "Mr. Ex-President." | **Business:**<br>The Honorable<br>John Jones Smith<br>Address<br><br>**Social:**<br>The Honorable<br>John Jones Smith<br>Address<br><br>The Honorable<br>John Jones Smith<br>and Mrs. Smith<br>Address | Dear Mr. Smith:<br>Very truly yours,<br>Sincerely yours, |
| Special Assistant to the President<br>Anyone appointed to the office of Special Assistant (the President's Press Secretary, for example) is entitled to be addressed "Honorable." However, special military aides to the President are addressed by military rank. | **Business:**<br>The Honorable<br>John Jones Smith<br>Special Assistant to the President<br>The White House<br>Washington, D.C.   20500<br><br>**Social:**<br>The Honorable<br>John Jones Smith<br>Address<br><br>The Honorable<br>John Jones Smith<br>and Mrs. Smith<br>Address | Dear Mr. Smith:<br>Very truly yours,<br>Sincerely yours, |
| Special Assistant (woman) | As for a man, except that a joint invitation is addressed simply:<br><br>Mr. and Mrs. John Jones Smith<br>Address | |
| Secretary to the President | Same as for a Special Assistant to the President | |
| The Vice President<br>See Note 10. | **Business:**<br>The Vice President<br>United States Senate<br>Washington, D.C.   20510<br><br>**Social:**<br>The Vice President<br>Address<br><br>The Vice President<br>and Mrs. Smith<br>Address | Sir:<br>Mr. Vice President:<br>**(formal, official)**<br>Dear Mr. Vice President<br>**(private individuals)**<br>Very truly yours,<br>Sincerely yours, |

| SOCIAL LETTER | IN CONVERSATION | INTRODUCTIONS | ABBREV. |
|---|---|---|---|
| My dear Mrs. Smith,<br>**(very formal)**<br>Dear Mrs. Smith,<br>Sincerely yours, | **To:** Mrs. Smith<br><br>**About:** Mrs. Smith | **Individual:**<br>Everyone is introduced **to** the wife of the President. The form is "Mrs. Smith, may I present . . ."<br><br>**Presentation to an audience:**<br>Mrs. John Jones Smith | |
| My dear Mr. Smith,<br>**(very formal)**<br>Dear Mr. Smith,<br>Sincerely yours, | **To:**<br>Mr. Smith **or**<br>Sir<br><br>**About:**<br>Mr. Smith<br><br>**Note:** It is quite customary in conversation to continue to use "Mr. President" to a former President. | **Individual:**<br>Mr. Smith<br><br>**Presentation to an audience:**<br>The Honorable John Jones Smith | |
| My dear Mr. Smith,<br>**(very formal)**<br>Dear Mr. Smith,<br>Sincerely yours, | **To and About:**<br>Mr. Smith | Follow standard rules. | None |
| | | | None |
| My dear Mr.<br>Vice President,<br>**(very formal)**<br>Dear Mr.<br>Vice President<br>(See note above under President.)<br>Sincerely yours, | **To:**<br>Mr. Vice President<br><br>**About:**<br>The Vice President<br>**or**<br>Mr. Smith | **Individual:**<br>Mr. Vice President<br>Generally, everyone is introduced **to** the Vice President, and his name is not spoken.<br><br>**Presentation to an audience:**<br>The Vice President of the United States | None |

| PERSON | ENVELOPES | BUSINESS LETTER |
|---|---|---|
| The Cabinet is composed of the following members. All are addressed "Secretary" with the exception of the Attorney General and the Postmaster General.<br>   Secretary of State<br>   Secretary of the Treasury<br>   Secretary of Defense<br>   The Attorney General<br>   The Postmaster General<br>   Secretary of the Interior<br>   Secretary of Agriculture<br>   Secretary of Commerce<br>   Secretary of Labor<br>   Secretary of Health, Education,<br>      and Welfare<br>   Secretary of Housing and<br>      Urban Development<br>   Secretary of Transportation<br><br>   See Notes 1 and 10. | **Business, Official:**<br>   The Honorable<br>   The Secretary of (Department)<br>   The Department of ———<br>   Washington, D.C.   00000<br><br>**Social:**<br>   The Honorable<br>   John Jones Smith<br>   Address<br><br>   The Honorable<br>   The Secretary of (Department)<br>      and Mrs. Smith<br>   Department of ———<br>   (or home address)<br>   Washington, D.C.   00000<br><br>      (For a woman Secretary: As above,<br>      except that a joint invitation is<br>      addressed by the rules in Note 11.) | Dear Mr. Secretary:<br>Dear Madam Secretary:<br>   Very truly yours,<br>   Sincerely yours, |
| The Attorney General | **Business:**<br>   The Honorable<br>   The Attorney General<br>   The Department of Justice<br>   Washington, D.C.   20530<br><br>**Social:**<br>   The Honorable<br>   John Jones Smith<br>   Address<br><br>   The Honorable<br>   The Attorney General<br>      and Mrs. Smith<br>   Department of Justice<br>   (or home address) | Dear Mr. Attorney<br>   General:<br>   Very truly yours,<br>   Sincerely yours, |
| The Postmaster General | Same as for the Attorney General, with Postmaster General and | |
| Under Secretary<br>   (The same form is followed<br>   for a Deputy Secretary or<br>   an Assistant Secretary of<br>   a Department.)<br><br>   Note: Below the rank of<br>   Secretary, officials of<br>   government departments should<br>   be addressed by name—**not**<br>   "Mr. Under Secretary,"<br>   and so on. | **Business:**<br>   The Honorable<br>   John Jones Smith<br>   Under Secretary of (Department)<br>   Address<br><br>**Social:**<br>   The Honorable<br>   John Jones Smith<br>   Address<br><br>   The Honorable<br>   John Jones Smith<br>      and Mrs. Smith<br>   Address | Dear Mr. Smith:<br>   Very truly yours,<br>   Sincerely yours, |
| Senator<br>Senator (woman)<br><br>   See Note 11. | **Business:**<br>   The Honorable<br>   John Jones Smith [Mary Brown Smith]<br>   United States Senate<br>   Washington, D.C.   20510<br><br>**or if away from Washington:**<br>   The Honorable<br>   John Jones Smith<br>   United States Senator<br>   Local address<br><br>**Social:**<br>   The Honorable<br>   John Jones Smith<br>   Home or office address<br><br>   The Honorable<br>   John Jones Smith<br>      and Mrs. Smith<br>   Home or office address | Dear Senator Smith:<br>   Very truly yours,<br>   Sincerely yours, |

| SOCIAL LETTER | IN CONVERSATION | INTRODUCTIONS | ABBREV. |
|---|---|---|---|
| My dear Mr. [Madam] Secretary, **(very formal)** Dear Mr. [Madam] Secretary, Dear Mr. [Miss, Mrs.] Smith, Sincerely yours, | **To:** Mr. Secretary **or** Mr. Smith **About:** The Secretary of State **or** Mr. Smith | **Individual:** The Secretary of State (Under formal circumstances, especially in Washington, a Cabinet member's title only is spoken. However, when circumstances warrant, "Mr. Smith" can be used.) **Presentation to an audience:** The Honorable John Jones Smith, the Secretary of State | Do not use "Sec." or any other abbreviation |
| My dear Mr. Attorney General, **(very formal)** Dear Mr. Attorney General, Sincerely yours, | **To:** Mr. Attorney General **or** Mr. Smith **About:** The Attorney General **or** Mr. Smith | **Individual:** The Attorney General (See note above.) **Presentation to an audience:** The Honorable John Jones Smith, the Attorney General | None acceptable |

Post Office Department, Washington, D.C. 20560    used where applicable.

| SOCIAL LETTER | IN CONVERSATION | INTRODUCTIONS | ABBREV. |
|---|---|---|---|
| Dear Mr. Smith, Sincerely yours, | **To and About:** Mr. Smith | **Individual:** Mr. Smith **Presentation to an audience:** The Honorable John Jones Smith, Under Secretary of the Department of ——— | None acceptable |
| My dear Senator Smith, **(very formal)** Dear Senator Smith, Sincerely yours, | **To:** Senator Smith Senator **About:** Senator Smith | **Individual:** Senator Smith **Presentation to an audience:** Senator John Jones Smith of (State) | None |

| PERSON | ENVELOPES | BUSINESS LETTER |
|---|---|---|
| The Speaker of the House of Representatives | **Business**:<br>The Honorable<br>John Jones Smith<br>Speaker of the House of<br>    Representatives<br>Washington, D.C.  20515<br><br>**Social**:<br>As above    **or**<br>The Honorable<br>John Jones Smith<br>Home or office address<br><br>The Honorable<br>The Speaker of the House of<br>    Representatives<br>    and Mrs. Smith<br>Address | Dear Mr. Speaker:<br>Very truly yours,<br>Sincerely yours, |
| Member of the House of Representatives<br><br>Note: It is now the correct practice to address a Representative as ''Congressman.'' ''Congresswoman'' is not incorrect, but the trend is to use ''Congressman'' as a title for both sexes, as the title ''Senator'' is used. | **Business**:<br>The Honorable<br>John Jones Smith<br>House of Representatives<br>Washington, D.C.  20515<br><br>**Social**:<br>The Honorable<br>John Jones Smith<br>Address<br><br>The Honorable<br>John Jones Smith<br>    and Mrs. Smith<br>Home or office address<br><br>**For a woman member**:<br>Mr. and Mrs. John Jones Smith<br>Address | Dear Mr. [Miss, Mrs.]<br>    Smith:<br>Very truly yours,<br>Sincerely yours, |

## State Government

| PERSON | ENVELOPES | BUSINESS LETTER |
|---|---|---|
| Governor | **Business**:<br>The Honorable<br>The Governor of ———<br>Official address<br>**or**<br>The Honorable<br>John Jones Smith<br>Governor of ———<br>Official address<br><br>**Social:** As above,  **or**<br>The Honorable<br>The Governor of ———<br>    and Mrs. Smith<br>Official or home address<br>**or**<br>The Honorable<br>John Jones Smith<br>    and Mrs. Smith<br>Address | Dear Governor Smith:<br>Very truly yours,<br>Sincerely yours, |
| Former Governor<br>A former Governor maintains the right to the title ''Governor'' in **spoken** address and as a salutation inside a letter, but **not** on the envelope. | **Business** and **Social**:<br>The Honorable<br>John Jones Smith<br>Address | As above |

| SOCIAL LETTER | IN CONVERSATION | INTRODUCTIONS | ABBREV. |
|---|---|---|---|
| My dear Mr. Smith, **(very formal)** Dear Mr. Smith, Sincerely yours, | **To:** Mr. Speaker Mr. Smith **About:** The Speaker Mr. Smith | **Individual:** The Speaker, **or** Mr. Smith—depending on circumstances. In Washington "The Speaker" is used, since everyone knows the name of the man who ranks next to the Vice President. **Presentation to an audience:** The Honorable John Jones Smith, Speaker of the House of Representatives | None |
| My dear Mr. Smith, **(very formal)** Dear Mr. Smith, Sincerely yours, | **To:** Mr. Smith **About:** Mr. Smith Representative Smith Congressman Smith | **Individual:** Mr. Smith, **or** Congressman (or Representative) Smith of (State) **Presentation to an audience:** The Honorable John Jones Smith, Congressman (or Representative) from the State of ——— **or** Congressman (or Representative) John Jones Smith of ——— | None |
| My dear Governor Smith, **(very formal)** Dear Governor Smith, Sincerely yours, | **To:** Governor Smith Governor **About:** Governor Smith The Governor | **Individual:** Governor Smith **Presentation to an audience:** **Within his state:** The Governor **Outside his state:** Governor Smith of (State) | None |
| As above, **or** Mr. Smith is also correct | **To** and **About:** Governor Smith Mr. Smith | **Individual:** Governor Smith **or,** depending on circumstances, Mr. Smith **Presentation to an audience:** The Honorable John Jones Smith, the former Governor of ——— | None |

| PERSON | ENVELOPES | BUSINESS LETTER |
|---|---|---|
| Lieutenant Governor | The same as for Governor, with "Lieutenant" added | Dear Mr. Smith:<br>Very truly yours,<br>Sincerely yours, |
| Secretary of State | The same formula as above | Dear Mr. Secretary: |
| Attorney General of a State | The same formula as above | Dear Mr. Attorney General: |
| Treasurer, Comptroller, or Auditor | The same formula as above | Dear Mr. Smith: |
| State Senator<br><br>See Note 13. | **Business**:<br>The Honorable<br>John Jones Smith<br>(Name of state) Senate<br>City, State    00000<br><br>**Social**: As above, or<br>The Honorable<br>John Jones Smith<br>Address<br><br>The Honorable<br>John Jones Smith<br>    and Mrs. Smith<br>Address | Dear Mr. Smith:<br>Very truly yours,<br>Sincerely yours, |
| State Representative, Assemblyman, or Delegate<br><br>Note: In some states, the lower house is known as the Assembly. In others, it is known as the House of Delegates. Nebraska has a one-house legislature, and all its members are Senators.<br><br>See Note 13. | **Business**:<br>The Honorable<br>John Jones Smith<br>(Name of State) House of Representatives<br>    (or Assembly or House of Delegates)<br>City, State    00000<br><br>**Social**: As above,  **or**<br>The Honorable<br>John Jones Smith<br>Address<br><br>The Honorable<br>John Jones Smith<br>    and Mrs. Smith<br>Address | Dear Mr. Smith:<br>Very truly yours,<br>Sincerely yours, |

## Town and City Government

| PERSON | ENVELOPES | BUSINESS LETTER |
|---|---|---|
| Mayor<br><br>Mayor (woman)<br><br>See Note 11. | **Business**:<br>The Honorable<br>John Jones Smith [Mary Brown Smith]<br>Mayor of (Name of city)<br>Street address of city hall<br>City, State    00000<br><br>**Social**: As above,  **or**<br>The Honorable<br>John Jones Smith<br>    and Mrs. Smith<br>Home or office address | Dear Mayor Smith:<br>Very truly yours,<br>Sincerely yours, |
| Former Mayor<br><br>See Notes 1 and 11 | **Business and Social**:<br>The Honorable<br>John Jones Smith<br>Address | Dear Mr. Smith:<br>Very truly yours,<br>Sincerely yours, |

| SOCIAL LETTER | IN CONVERSATION | INTRODUCTIONS | ABBREV. |
|---|---|---|---|
| My dear Mr. Smith, **(very formal)** Dear Mr. Smith, Sincerely yours, | **To:** Mr. Smith <br><br> **About:** The Lieutenant Governor **or** Mr. Smith | **Individual:** Lieutenant Governor Smith **or** Mr. Smith <br><br> **Presentation to an audience:** Lieutenant Governor John Jones Smith of (State) | None |
| As above | As above <br><br> See Note 13. | As above | None |
| As above | As above | As above | None |
| As above | As above | As above | None |
| My dear Mr. Smith, **(very formal)** Dear Mr. Smith, Sincerely yours, | **To** and **About:** Mr. Smith <br><br> See Note 13. | **Individual:** Mr. Smith <br><br> **Presentation to an audience:** The Honorable John Jones Smith, State Senator from (State) | None |
| My dear Mr. Smith, **(very formal)** Dear Mr. Smith, Sincerely yours, | As above <br><br> See Note 13. | The same formula as above | None |
| My dear Mayor Smith, **(very formal)** Dear Mayor Smith, Sincerely yours, | **To:** Mr. [Madam] Mayor **or** Mr. [Miss, Mrs.] Smith <br><br> **About:** The Mayor **or** Mayor Smith | **Individual:** Mayor Smith <br><br> **Presentation to an audience:** **In his own city:** The Mayor **Elsewhere:** The Honorable John Jones Smith, Mayor of the City of ——— | None |
| My dear Mr. Smith, **(very formal)** Dear Mr. Smith, Sincerely yours, | **To:** Mr. Smith (or, very often, the courtesy title "Mayor Smith") <br><br> **About:** Mr. Smith | **Individual:** Mr. Smith <br><br> **Presentation to an audience:** The Honorable John Jones Smith, the former Mayor of ——— | None |

## THE SALVATION ARMY

All ranks are open to women, including that of general.

Forms of address in the Salvation Army follow very closely those used in the Regular Army, though there are two striking exceptions. The wife of an officer uses her

| PERSON | ENVELOPES | BUSINESS LETTER |
|---|---|---|
| General | General John Jones Smith<br>Address<br>General and Mrs. John Jones Smith<br>Address | Dear General Smith:<br>Very truly yours,<br>Sincerely yours,<br>Dear Mrs. General<br>Smith: |
| His Wife | Mrs. General John Jones Smith<br>Address | |
| Commissioner | Commissioner John Jones Smith<br>Address<br>Commissioner and Mrs. John<br>Jones Smith<br>Address | Dear Commissioner<br>Smith:<br>Very truly yours,<br>Sincerely yours,<br>Dear Mrs. Com-<br>missioner Smith: |
| His Wife | Mrs. Commissioner John Jones Smith<br>Address | |
| Lieutenant Commissioner<br>Colonel<br>Lieutenant Colonel<br>Brigadier<br>Major<br>Captain<br>Lieutenant<br>Cadet | Follow the formula used for<br>Commissioner with appropriate<br>changes for rank. | |

## UNITED NATIONS

The United Nations is an organization of sovereign states. It functions through six principal branches:

The General Assembly
The Security Council
The Economic and Social Council
The Trusteeship Council
The International Court of Justice
The Secretariat

Each member nation is represented by a Mission to the United Nations. A Chief of Mission generally has the personal rank of Ambassador, though there are some few exceptions, and a Mission may be headed by a Representative.

Formal diplomatic forms of address for official governmental communication with all members of Missions to the United Nations are governed by special rules. However, the many private citizens who have occasion to speak with or write to a representative of any nation to the United Nations properly use the somewhat simplified forms in the chart below.

1. The United Nations hyphenates certain titles (Secretary-General, Under-Secretary), and our State Department does not. The United Nations uses "His Excellency Mr. (Name)," and our State

| PERSON | ENVELOPES | BUSINESS LETTER |
|---|---|---|
| The Secretary General<br><br>See Note 1. | His Excellency<br>John Jones Smith<br>Secretary-General of the United Nations<br>New York, N.Y.   10016<br><br>His Excellency<br>The Secretary-General of the United<br>  Nations and Madame (**or** Mrs.) Smith<br>Address<br><br>**See Note 2.** | Dear Mr. Secretary-<br>  General:<br>Very truly yours,<br>Sincerely yours, |

husband's rank on all occasions. For example, the wife of Major Smith is addressed directly and introduced as "Mrs. Major Smith." And, if she is an officer, she nonetheless assumes her husband's rank, even if she holds a higher one.

| SOCIAL LETTER | IN CONVERSATION | INTRODUCTIONS | ABBREV. |
|---|---|---|---|
| My dear General Smith, **(very formal)** Dear General Smith, Sincerely yours, My dear Mrs. General Smith, | **To** and **About:** General Smith See Note 5. Mrs. General Smith | **Individual:** General Smith His wife: Mrs. General Smith **Presentation to an audience:** General John Jones Smith, international leader of the Salvation Army | Avoid "Gen." |
| My dear Commissioner Smith, **(very formal)** Dear Commissioner Smith, Sincerely yours, My dear Mrs. Commissioner Smith, | **To** and **About:** Commissioner Smith See Note 5. Mrs. Commissioner Smith | **Individual:** Commissioner Smith His wife: Mrs. Commissioner Smith **Presentation to an audience:** Commissioner John Jones Smith, and his command | None |

Department does not use "Mr." following "Excellency." So far as the private citizen is concerned, these are entirely minor matters, and either form can be correctly used.

2. A representative from any nation is correctly addressed "Mr." (unless he has a personal title, in which case "Sir," "Lord," and so on, are used, according to the rules given in the "Foreign" charts). It is also correct to use "Señor," or whatever other title is customary in his own country, if he is known to prefer that. U Thant is a case in point. "U" means "Mr." in Burma.

The wife of a representative to the United Nations from any English-speaking country is addressed in speech and writing as "Mrs." All others are addressed as "Madame," but can also be addressed according to the custom of their own homelands—"Señora," and so on.

3. Avoid abbreviating whenever possible, though it is customary and correct to use "U.N." for United Nations; "U.S.A." for the United States of America; "The Hon." and "His Ex." when not to abbreviate would crowd an envelope beyond reason.

| SOCIAL LETTER | IN CONVERSATION | INTRODUCTIONS | ABBREV. |
|---|---|---|---|
| My dear Mr. Smith, **(very formal)** Dear Mr. Smith, Sincerely yours, | **To:** Mr. Secretary-General Mr. Smith **About:** The Secretary-General Mr. Smith | **Individual:** The Secretary-General of the United Nations **or** Mr. Smith **Presentation to an audience:** His Excellency, John Jones Smith, the Secretary-General of the United Nations | None acceptable |

| PERSON | ENVELOPES | BUSINESS LETTER |
| --- | --- | --- |
| An Under Secretary of the United Nations<br><br>See Note 1. | The Honorable<br>John Jones Smith<br>Under-Secretary for ———<br>United Nations<br>New York, N.Y.   10016<br><br>The Honorable<br>John Jones Smith<br>  and Madame (**or** Mrs.) Smith<br>Address<br><br>See Note 2. | Dear Mr. Smith:<br>Very truly yours,<br>Sincerely yours, |
| Representative to the U.N. (other than from the U.S.A.) **with personal rank of Ambassador** | His Excellency<br>John Jones Smith<br>Representative of (Country) to the<br>  United Nations<br>Address<br><br>His Excellency<br>The Representative of (Country)<br>  to the United Nations<br>  and Madame (**or** Mrs.) Smith<br>Address<br><br>See Note 2. | Dear Mr. Ambassador:<br>Very truly yours,<br>Sincerely yours, |
| U.S. Representative to the U.N. **with the personal rank of Ambassador** | As above, with "The Honorable" instead of "His Excellency." | As above |
| Representatives other than Ambassadors | Use the same form as for an Under-Secretary. | |

## FOWL

If standard rules are followed, pieces of chicken, turkey, and other birds are not picked up in the fingers except at completely informal meals. Meat is cut from the bones while a piece is anchored with the fork. An exception is made only for the very small joints of tiny game birds. These bones may be held by one end while the meat is detached in the mouth, or a very small joint such as a wing tip may be put into the mouth with the fork and, after being cleaned of meat, returned to the plate with the fork. The rule that any portion of something put into the mouth on a fork or spoon is taken out with the same implement is suspended in the case of the small shot sometimes found in game birds, and for small splinters of bone. These are taken out of the mouth with the fingertips.

*See also* CARVING.

## FOX HUNTING.   *See* RIDING.

## FRATERNITIES AND SORORITIES

Fraternities and sororities fall into two main categories: social societies open to college undergraduates; and professional societies whose members are drawn from a special field or profession and which, in the main, do not concern people still in school. In addition to these two major groups, which are concerned largely with the social life of their members, there are the honor or recognition societies whose members are chosen on the basis of their outstanding scholarship or other achievement. Fraternities and sororities are also known as "Greek letter societies," since they take their names from the initial Greek letters of the society's motto (usually known only to its initiates).

A student can belong to only one of the college Greek-letter societies. Pro-

| SOCIAL LETTER | IN CONVERSATION | INTRODUCTIONS | ABBREV. |
|---|---|---|---|
| My dear Mr. Smith, **(very formal)** Dear Mr. Smith Sincerely yours, | To and **About**: Mr. Smith | **Individual**: Mr. Smith <br><br> **Presentation to an audience**: The Honorable John Jones Smith, the Under-Secretary for ——— of the United Nations | None |
| My dear Mr. Ambassador, **(very formal)** Dear Mr. Ambassador, Sincerely yours, | To and **About**: Ambassador Smith | **Individual**: Ambassador Smith <br><br> **Presentation to an audience**: His Excellency, John Jones Smith, Ambassador of (Country) to the United Nations | None |
| As above | As above | As above, with "The Honorable" instead of "His Excellency." | |

fessional societies in the same field are also mutually exclusive, though a person may belong to a college society and a professional society and also accept the honor of membership in one of the recognition societies.

The first American college fraternity, Phi Beta Kappa, was organized on December 5, 1776, at William and Mary College in Williamsburg, Virginia. Since then, fraternities and sororities have gradually become a major feature of American college life. Phi Beta Kappa, originally a secret society, did not remain so. It was reorganized in 1883 as a scholarship honor society. The oldest, continuously active, social college fraternity is Kappa Alpha, founded at Union College, Schenectady, New York, in 1825. College sororities have nearly as long a history.

A majority of the college societies have their own chapter houses on campus in which members may (and sometimes are required to) live and eat, though at some colleges only upperclassmen are permitted to live in a chapter house.

**ADVANTAGES AND DISADVANTAGES.** Membership in a college Greek-letter society provides a busy, organized social background and a sense of belonging that is rewarding to many young people. Life in a chapter house demands a good deal of give-and-take, and so provides training in adjustment to a social group. Another great benefit is the fellowship and loyal interest of congenial "brothers" or "sisters," and their moral support with both curricular and extra-curricular problems.

On the other hand, the Independent (the student who does not join a fraternity, whether by choice or because he was not asked) often makes more diverse friendships than does the fraternity member, and often has a wider choice in the use of his time. Also, the student on a limited budget or who is earning part of his expenses may find that demands on his purse are somewhat less outside a fraternity.

In some colleges fraternities and sororities are banned. Many educators feel that the social life in a chapter house can distract a student's attention from academic pursuits, but the main complaint against Greek-letter societies has been that they practiced undemocratic discrimination against certain ethnic and other groups and that, even when such discrimination was not practiced, a failure to receive a bid (for whatever reason) assumed the proportions of a major personal tragedy in some cases, affecting not only a student's grades but his desire to pursue his education. Such criticism of college secret societies has changed them considerably in recent years. On some campuses, fraternities and sororities are charged to work things out among themselves so that membership in some one of them is available to any registered student. On other campuses where the so-called "Eating Clubs" long had the same exclusive character as Greek-letter societies elsewhere, the same rules have been established by the authorities. A formal invitation to join is still a necessity, however.

**BIDS.** An invitation to join a fraternity or sorority is called a bid, and a student must wait for a bid to be offered. A sure way *not* to get a bid is to make direct application for one. Receiving no bid is only as much of a tragedy as a young person chooses to make it.

The student who accepts a bid from a fraternity or sorority is obligated to be a loyal member. It is foolish to hold a feeling of resentment against any group that did not offer a bid. Most fraternities and sororities have membership limitations that prevent them from taking in more than a definite number of new members from each class. It frequently happens that they cannot take in everybody they would like as members. Also, at some colleges, an interfraternity or faculty committee is given the task of matching up, as far as possible, the "bid" list of the various groups with the students' preference lists.

**HIGH-SCHOOL FRATERNITIES.** Some high schools permit fraternities and sororities, but in general these organizations are not approved at the high-school level. One reason is the obvious immaturity of the membership. Another is the fact that nearly all high-school students live at home, and eat lunch in the school cafeteria, and so the high-school fraternity or sorority is little more than an exclusive social clique, though some such groups undertake projects that benefit their school or the community. There is little or no correlation between high-school and college fraternal organizations.

**PINS AND PINNING.** The badge of membership in a fraternity or sorority is a small pin bearing Greek letters or other distinctive symbols. A student customarily wears his pin during his college years. Graduates usually do not, though members of the professional fraternities and the honor organizations frequently wear a special watch charm as a badge of membership (like the much-prized Phi Beta Kappa key).

A romantic understanding of some degree is indicated when a girl wears a man's fraternity pin. Pins are not exchanged because a man never wears a sorority pin. A pin can take the place of a ring as an indication of an actual engagement, or it may mean no more than that she is admittedly his current best girl. When either party breaks off the relationship, the girl is obligated to return the pin. The girl who attempts to make a collection of pins to prove her popularity and the man who distributes duplicate pins are breaking the rules.

**RUSHING.** New members of a social college fraternity or sorority are chosen by the old members—never by petition or application of a would-be member. At most colleges a particular week each year is designated as rush week. During this period, an open house and various other parties are given by each fraternal group to help members decide to which students they want to issue bids and to give students an opportunity to decide which group they prefer. This can be a time of anxiety and tension for candidates. By far the best thing to do is behave naturally and let Fate take its course. As in every other social circumstance, the person who tries too hard to make a good impression or to play hard to get defeats his own purpose.

## FREIGHTERS

With the exception of scows and other open freight-carrying vessels, any freighter is called a ship, not a boat.

See TRAVEL.

## FRENCH ABBREVIATIONS.   *See* ABBREVIATIONS.

## FROG'S LEGS

If served in one piece, a frog's leg is severed at the joint with knife and fork. The meat may easily be cut away from the bone of the larger joint, and eaten with the fork. It also is correct to put the whole larger joint in the mouth and to remove the bone in the fingertips after it has been cleaned of meat. The smaller joint is picked up in the fingertips and held while the meat is detached.

## FRUITS

Fresh fruit for dessert may be on the table as a centerpiece when guests sit down, or a bowl of fruit may be put in the center of the table after it is cleared for dessert, or a platter of fruit may be passed by a maid or from guest to guest. In formal service of fruit as a dessert, a fruit knife and fork are brought in (flanking a finger bowl) on each fruit plate. Less formally, knife and fork are on the table at the beginning of the meal, set above the place plate, parallel with the table edge. In this country, frequently only a fruit knife is provided.

A dessert-size spoon is the standard implement for baked, stewed, or poached fruits, and for fresh fruit compotes, but a teaspoon is often used. A dessert spoon and a lunch-size fork are often provided with large fruits that have been cooked whole.

Fruit plates are seven to eight inches in diameter. Salad plates can be used instead. Diced fresh fruit and stewed fruit are served in bowls, usually of glass with matching underplate.

Cookies or cheese and crackers are classic accompaniments. Usually only one cheese is offered, but there may be a choice of several varieties on the cheese platter, which is passed after guests have helped themselves to fruit. A helping of cheese is put on the fruit plate, not directly on a cracker. Small amounts of cheese then may be put on a cracker with the fruit knife or picked up with the fruit fork. Sliced cheese is offered only on antipasto and cold-cut platters.

**APPLES.** When served at table, an apple is never held whole in the hand and eaten bite by bite, or peeled spirally. If both fruit fork and knife are provided, the apple is quartered, cored, peeled, and eaten with their aid, and the fruit is not touched with the fingers. Fruit is carved in this fashion quite commonly in Europe, less often in this country. If only a fruit knife is provided, slices not larger than two-bite size are cut, peeled, and eaten from the fingers.

**APRICOTS.** Raw apricots are picked up in the fingers and eaten in two or more bites. The stone is not put into the mouth.

Pickled or spiced apricots, served with a meat course, are put on the dinner plate, not the butter plate. They are cut and eaten with the fork, or knife and fork. The seed is not put into the mouth.

Stewed apricots are served in a small dish with an underplate. They are cut with a spoon and eaten in several bites. The stone is left in the dish. If tiny apricots are taken into the mouth whole, the seed is taken out with the spoon and put on the underplate.

**BANANAS.** When bananas are served whole at table, the skin should not be peeled partly down and the whole fruit, along with its dangling skin, raised to the mouth. This is acceptable procedure only at picnics. At table, the fruit may be partially peeled, or the entire skin may be removed and put on one side of the plate, but in both cases small pieces of banana are broken off and eaten from the fingers. If a fruit knife and fork are provided, small pieces of the banana may be cut and eaten with the fork in the European fashion.

**BERRIES.** Most formally, hulled berries are served in a small glass bowl set on a dessert plate. Informally, they are served in a bowl without an underplate. Berries may be put directly on the dessert plate if sour cream is offered instead of sweet cream. Powdered rather than granulated sugar is the usual choice.

Strawberries are the only berries served with their hulls on. They are served on a dessert plate, with powdered sugar only or with sugar and sour (not sweet) cream, and are eaten from the fingers. Individual containers of powdered sugar and sour cream may be in place on the plate, or sugar and sour cream may be passed. If they are passed, small helpings of each are put on the side of the plate, not on the fruit itself. Each strawberry is picked up by the hull, dipped into sugar or into sugar and sour cream, and eaten in one or two bites.

**CANTALOUPES.**   See "Melons," below.

**CHERRIES.** Fresh cherries are served with their stems. The stem is pulled off after the whole fruit is put into the mouth. The pit is taken out with the fingertips.

Stewed cherries are eaten with a spoon. The pits are removed from the mouth with the spoon and put on the edge of the underplate, not back in the bowl.

**DATES.** Dates are best eaten in two bites so that the stone need not be put into the mouth. If the stone is put into the mouth, it is taken out with the fingertips.

**FIGS**. Fresh figs are picked up in the fingers and eaten in several bites.

**GRAPEFRUIT.** Grapefruit may be peeled and split into segments, the membrane removed, and the segments served in a dessert bowl. Half a grapefruit is served on a dessert plate. Before grapefruit is brought to the table, the white core is usually removed, the segments cut free from the rind and from the membrane separating them, and very often sugar, honey, sherry, or a liqueur and a maraschino cherry added. In preparing grapefruit, care should be taken not to pierce the rind so that juice will not leak through to the plate. Unless the segments are properly cut, it is better not to cut them at all, though the segments should be divided if grapefruit is served hot. Grapefruit is eaten with a teaspoon or with a pointed grapefruit spoon. Seeds are taken out of the mouth with the spoon. The shell is not picked up and the juice squeezed from it.

**GRAPES.** A single grape should not be pulled from a bunch in a serving bowl. Small bunches are cut off with grape scissors, or broken off, and put on the dessert plate. Then individual grapes are pulled off. The entire small bunch should not be lifted and separate grapes nibbled off. Crisp grapes rather than those with pulpy flesh are the best choice to serve at table, since discarded skins and pulp are an unappetizing sight. In Europe, grapes are not washed before serving because this damages the bloom, and so small clusters are dipped into the finger bowl—or even the water glass—but that custom is not followed in this country.

**MANGOES.** This delicious fruit is so bursting with juice, so firmly attached to its seed, and leaves a stain so difficult to remove from linen, that it is far better to serve it peeled and sliced than whole. Sliced mango is eaten with a fork.

**MELONS.** A wedge of lemon is the classic accompaniment for all melons (except watermelon) served plain. Many people enjoy salt and black pepper on plain melons, so these are not cleared from the table before melon is served as dessert. All melon is best if served well chilled.

Melon served in balls often is marinated in honey or sugar, and perhaps also wine or a liqueur. Melon balls are served in a dessert bowl, or may be heaped in the half of a cantaloupe. They are eaten with a spoon.

Melons cut in halves or wedges or thick slices are served with the rind attached, on a dessert plate. They are eaten with a dessert spoon or with dessert knife and fork. Thin slices may be peeled and served on a dessert plate and eaten either with a spoon or with knife and fork.

Halves and wedges with a hollow are often heaped with sherbet, ice cream, berries, split green grapes, or other cut fruits.

Watermelon usually is served in such large wedges or slices that a dinner plate is needed. It is eaten with a fork or fork and knife. Seeds are cut away with the fork before a piece is put into the mouth. If a seed does get in the mouth it may be removed on the fork, though it is correct and much safer to remove these slippery bits in the fingertips.

**NECTARINES.** If both dessert knife and fork are served, big nectarines are carved and eaten with them. Small ones are picked up and eaten from the hand in several bites, as are plums. The seed is not put into the mouth.

**ORANGES.** An orange cut in half is eaten from the shell with a spoon, after removing any seeds with the tip of the spoon. If a seed gets into the mouth, it is taken out with the spoon. The shell is not picked up and squeezed to extract the remaining juice.

Whole oranges (other than Temple oranges, which can be peeled as easily as tangerines) are a poor choice for a dessert at table because they are difficult to handle gracefully, especially without a fruit knife. If they are served at table, the skin should be slit in quarters with the fruit knife and peeled back, the quarters remaining attached to the fruit like the petals of a flower. The fruit is then opened into its separate natural segments, which are eaten from the fingers. Seeds are removed in the fingertips. If no fruit knife is provided, the orange should be completely peeled by breaking off small bits of the skin. Peeling an orange spirally is a messy procedure requiring a sharp knife, and is best not done at table.

**PEACHES.** Fresh freestone peaches are a better choice than clingstones to serve at table, since the fuzz, juice, and firmly attached flesh of clingstones are too much of a challenge for graceful handling. Small peaches are cut in two, larger ones in small segments, and usually skinned (though they need not be), and eaten from the fingers or with a fruit fork. A whole peach is not held in the hand and eaten in a series of bites except at a picnic. Peach fuzz should not be polished off with the napkin.

Pickled peaches are put on the dinner plate, not the butter plate, and pieces are eaten with a fork.

Whole poached peaches in syrup are best handled with both fork and spoon.

**PEARS.** Fresh pears are quartered, cored, and then eaten from the fingers or with a fruit fork. They are usually peeled, but need not be. One quarter of a pear is prepared at a time, rather than peeling the whole fruit first. A whole pear is not held in the hand and eaten in a series of bites except at a picnic.

Whole poached pears, like peaches, are most easily handled with both fork and spoon.

Half of the huge, extremely juicy Comice pear, split lengthwise, is served in its skin with the core removed. It is eaten with a spoon, as half a cantaloupe is, leaving the skin whole.

**PERSIMMONS.** This fruit is so soft and juicy when fully ripe that it is comfortably handled only with dessert knife and fork or knife and spoon at table. The persimmon is put on the plate with the stem end down. The skin is slit from top to bottom in quarters, and bite-size pieces cut away from seed and skin. The skin may be eaten, but is usually not because it can pucker the mouth strongly even when the pulp is honey-sweet. Less often, persimmons are served with the tops cut off, and the flesh is then scooped out with a spoon. Or the skin may be slit and peeled back from the meat, like the petals of a flower, before the fruit is brought to table. It is then eaten with knife and fork.

**PINEAPPLES.** A wedge of unpeeled fresh pineapple to be served on its shell is first cored and the wedge cut free. A fruit knife and fork are needed unless the wedge is cut in bite-size pieces suitable to be eaten from a fork. Fresh pineapple cut up and marinated in sugar, honey, and perhaps a liqueur is eaten with a spoon, as is canned pineapple.

**PITS AND STONES.** The general rule is: Anything that goes into the mouth on a fork or spoon is taken out with the same implement; anything that goes in with the fingers comes out in the fingertips. Exceptions are made for small or slippery seeds more safely handled in the fingertips, but under no circumstances is the cupped palm of the hand used. Pits, seeds, and stones taken from the mouth are put on the underplate if cooked fruit has been served in a bowl.

**PLUMS.** Fresh plums are picked up in the fingers and eaten in several bites. The seed is not put into the mouth. The best choice for service at table is freestone plums, whether fresh or cooked.

**POMEGRANATES.** There is only one answer to the challenge of this fruit of the brilliant red flesh and myriad small seeds. Save it for eating in private. It does not belong in the fruit bowl at table except as decoration. A pomegranate is cut into wedges, a bite of both fruit and seeds is taken, and the seeds are removed in the hand—impossible to manage gracefully at table.

**PRUNES.** Big, plump, uncooked sun-dried prunes sometimes are added to a bowl of fresh fruit served as dessert. They are picked up in the fingers and eaten in several bites. The seed is not put into the mouth.

Stewed prunes are cut with the side of the spoon and the seed is left in the bowl. If a very small prune is put into the mouth whole, the seed is removed with the spoon and put on the side of the underplate.

**STRAWBERRIES.**  *See "Berries," above.*

**TANGERINES.** These are an excellent choice for a bowl of mixed fruits. The easily broken skin is peeled back. One segment of the fruit is broken off at a time and eaten from the fingers, usually in two bites. Seeds are returned to the plate in the fingertips.

**WATERMELONS.**  *See "Melons," above.*

# FUNERALS

Religious rules and community and family customs concerning funerals vary widely. In some faiths no deviation from established ritual is permitted. In other faiths there is wide latitude of choice. In some families a religious or a secular memorial service is held after a burial or cremation, instead of a funeral service. In other families neither a funeral nor memorial service is held. All decisions concerning a funeral are entirely a family matter. The only breach of good behavior is any criticism from those whose own customs or preference differs.

**ACKNOWLEDGMENTS.** Flowers, memorial donations to charity, mass cards, letters, and other expressions of condolence require acknowledgment. The briefest note will suffice, but, by the rule, it should be handwritten. This rule is correctly ignored in certain circumstances for practical reasons, and engraved or process-printed cards of "appreciation for your expression of sympathy" are sent instead. For example, such cards are a necessity when the family of a prominent person has received so many messages and tokens of sympathy that it is an impossibility to acknowledge them by personal notes. Even in this case, handwritten notes of acknowledgment should be sent to closest relatives and friends, to the clergyman who conducted the service, and to honorary pallbearers.

Notes of acknowledgment need not be written by the deceased person's closest relative; they may be written by some member of the family if this task is too demanding on the chief mourner or mourners. Any personal note or letter paper of quiet color is appropriate. Black-bordered paper is seldom seen today.

**ANNOUNCEMENTS.** A death is not announced by engraved or printed cards, though the printed program of a memorial service, with a brief handwritten message added, is a useful way to notify a distant friend who does not see local newspapers. Relatives and very close friends are notified of the death and of the time and place of the funeral by telephone, wire, or letter. These facts may be announced from a pulpit, at a school assembly, or at a similar gathering. In a business office, a memo may be circulated or an announcement may be made over a public address system. Otherwise, the information is given only through newspaper announcements (*which see,* in this section).

**ATTENDING FUNERALS.** Anyone may go to a funeral service if the printed notice states the time and place. Friends should make every effort to attend, since publication of that information indicates the family's wish for their presence. "'Funeral private" in the death notice means that only friends who have been given a specific invitation (usually made by telephone) are expected to go. Anyone invited under these circumstances must not refuse unless able to give an acceptable explanation.

Anyone attending a funeral should arrive in time to be seated at least ten minutes before the hour announced for the service, and should make no move to leave until the family has withdrawn after the service. Friends exchange nods or brief words of greeting, but otherwise restrict conversation until after the service. Those of other faiths follow the custom of the congregation as far as possible. They sit and stand and bow the head when others do. They need not cross themselves, however, or join in responses not customary in their own faith, or kneel, though they should at least lean forward with bowed head when others kneel.

**BURIAL.** A service at a grave is a matter of individual family choice, governed by varying local and religious customs. After funeral services held elsewhere, the family may leave for home, or may go to the cemetery accompanied by the clergyman, who conducts another, briefer ceremony there. Usually only closest relatives accompany the body to the cemetery or crematorium. Friends should inquire about the wishes of the family before following them to the cemetery without a specific invitation.

**CALLS.** In some circles, it is the custom for friends to call at the mortuary as a sign of sympathy and respect. Sometimes members of the family are there to receive calls, sometimes not. This is a matter to be decided by family and local custom. There is no rule governing such calls except that they should be brief and that callers should be dressed quietly and behave quietly. There is no obligation to pass by the coffin if it is open. If there is a register, it should be signed with first and last names, not a first name only. A married woman who was an intimate friend of the deceased but has slight or no acquaintanceship with the family signs formally: Mrs. John Lee Jones. If she is an intimate friend of the most closely bereaved relative, she signs: Mary Brown Jones. The same rule holds for a married couple calling together. One signs for both: either Mr. and Mrs. John Lee Jones or Mary and John Jones. Otherwise, Mr., Miss, and all other titles are omitted.

Calls before a funeral are made today only by closest friends, and almost never without first telephoning to make sure that a visit will be welcome. A neighbor, fellow member of an organization, or a friend may ring the bell and leave an offer to help with anyone who opens the door, but should not request to see the bereaved person. A formal call of condolence within a few days after a funeral is not obligatory today, and should not be made without telephoning to set a convenient time unless the customs of the family call for a different procedure. In other words, a condolence call is a matter of practical and imaginative friendship, and it is often more considerate to send a note of sympathy. Too often, condolence calls are an added heavy burden to those already under the heavy demands of shock and sorrow.

Orthodox and Conservative Jews observe a week of mourning after a funeral. The immediate relatives stay at home, and religious services are held morning and evening. It is customary for friends and neighbors to prepare the meal for the mourners returning from the cemetery, and for friends to call with gifts of food during the week of mourning, since the immediate family does no cooking during this period. As in the case of any condolence call, it is often wise to telephone to make sure the time of the proposed visit is appropriate and convenient.

### CATHOLIC FUNERALS.

**Coffin.** Closed during the funeral service, though it may be open during the Rosary service.

**Clothes.** Women attending should wear head coverings.

**Flowers.** Except for one spray or a pall of flowers, usually sent by the family, flowers are generally not admitted to the church. Whether permission for other flowers is granted depends on the pastor. Flowers may be sent to the bereaved family at home, to the mortuary for the Rosary, or to the church to accompany the body to the cemetery.

**Place.** Always in a church.

**Procedures.** On occasion, the coffin may be in place in front of the altar. Usually it is carried in after the congregation is seated. This processional is governed by established rules. It is led by altar boys and sometimes by the choir. The priest follows. After him walk the honorary pallbearers and ushers, if any. Then comes the coffin, followed by the immediate family, led by the chief mourner. Usually each woman walks with a man, but two women or two men may walk together. The recessional in which the coffin is carried out follows the same order.

**Seating.** The family sits on the right.

**Time.** A funeral mass nearly always is held in the morning, but in some dioceses it may be held in the evening.

**CHILDREN AT FUNERALS.** There is no rule that very young relatives of the deceased, even those most closely related, must attend a funeral. This is a matter to be decided by the family.

**CLOTHES WORN TO A FUNERAL.** Friends attending a funeral wear any quiet clothing suitable for a regular church service, but avoid light or bright colors, brilliant jewelry, and colored handkerchiefs. Women should wear hats. Men attending a Jewish funeral should follow the custom of the congregation about head coverings.

Members of the immediate family usually choose dark or black dresses and very dark suits. Children wear white or quiet colors. It is not today's custom, except in a very few families, to dress children in black or for adults to buy (or have clothes hastily dyed) black to wear at a funeral. The quietest, most appropriate clothes from the existing wardrobes are chosen, unless, as is rarely done today, the most closely bereaved will wear formal mourning for the traditional number of months (see MOURNING). A bereaved woman may choose to wear a black chiffon veil if she feels that its protection will be helpful.

**CLOTHING FOR BURIAL.** Unless a shroud is to be used, a suit for a man or a dress for a woman is usually chosen from the existing wardrobe. The choice of clothing, like many of the other details of the funeral, is entirely the province of the family. However, a dinner jacket, White Tie, or a décolleté evening gown is not considered appropriate by most clergymen.

**CREMATION.** Cremation is forbidden, except with special permission, by the Roman Catholic and Greek Orthodox faiths, and is contrary to Orthodox and Conservative Jewish tradition, though permitted in Reform congregations. If a funeral service is read in church, the family may go directly home or may accompany the body to the crematorium. If asked, the minister will go with them and conduct a second brief ceremony there, or there may be none, or the funeral director may be asked to read a prayer.

Most crematoriums have a nonsectarian chapel. The funeral service may be conducted there, with the family leaving at the end of the service. It is most unusual for the family to remain in the chapel or elsewhere at the crematorium while cremation is taking place, but, again, this is a matter of individual choice, though also dependent on the possibility of arranging proper solitude. The ashes may be dispersed, put in a columbarium, or buried. A few states have laws that forbid or restrict the scattering of ashes or placing them elsewhere than in a cemetery or columbarium. These laws are now being challenged as an invasion of civil liberties.

In some states there are no facilities for cremation.

*See* "Shipment of a Body" in this section.

**DEATH CERTIFICATE.** This is a document that, by law, must be filled out, signed, and filed with the proper civic authority, usually within twenty-four hours of death, by a doctor or other authorized person. In case a doctor has not been in attendance, the city or county medical examiner or coroner must sign it.

**DEATH NOTICES.**

*See* "NEWSPAPER ANNOUNCEMENTS AND OBITUARIES," in this section.

**DONATIONS TO CHARITY.**

*See* "MEMORIAL DONATIONS," in this section.

**THE DOOR.** The custom is not widely followed today, but if the family wishes to protect itself from the calls of salesmen or others who may not know that a death has occurred, ribbon-like or crepe streamers, or streamers and flowers, are displayed on the front door until after the funeral. White usually is used for a child or young person, black streamers and white or purple flowers for older people. The streamers and flowers should be removed by a friend or by a member of the funeral director's staff before the family returns from the funeral service.

**EULOGIES.** In some faiths, it is the custom for the clergyman to give a eulogy and for one or several more eulogies to follow his. In other faiths a eulogy is not customary, and in some none is permitted. Anyone requested to speak in eulogy should not refuse except for good reason such as illness or unavoidable absence from town.

**EXPENSES.** Increasingly, today, the custom endorsed by all religions is to avoid the expensive and ornate in all aspects of a funeral, no matter how large a number of mourners will attend, though this too is entirely a matter of the family's wishes. No one can make an error in taste in choosing the simplest of coffins.

Frequently there is no charge to members of the congregation for the use of a house of worship for a funeral. If charges are made for opening a church, the sexton or other regular employee submits a bill that includes the fee for the organist and so on. In many small communities, such duties are performed without pay by members of the congregation, but often the organist and others who assist in the service expect to be paid an established fee, though fees are not sent to personal friends who aid in these ways.

If the clergyman is a relative or intimate friend of the family, an honorarium is not offered to him, though a contribution may be made to the church or synagogue in his name. The amount of his fee is not discussed with the family's regular pastor. It is decided by the family, according to their financial circumstances. If there is doubt as to what is proper and customary, an officer of the congregation or the funeral director will provide advice. A funeral director is also prepared to arrange for the services of a clergyman when a family has no regular pastor and will include a proper honorarium for him in the bill, along with all the other charges due at the church and elsewhere. Otherwise, the family simply sends a check with a note of appreciation to the clergyman within a few days after the funeral. (*See* also "Newspaper Announcements and Obituaries" below.)

**FLAGS.** Explicit rules govern the display and other use of flags during a funeral and during a period of mourning. *See* FLAG OF THE UNITED STATES.

**FLOWERS.** When a funeral announcement includes the statement "Please omit flowers," the request must be observed. Some families feel that masses of flowers, which they will see briefly if at all, are a waste of money that might better have been devoted to a charity. Sometimes the request is printed to guide friends of other faiths who do not know that flowers are a symbol of joy and congratulations to Jews and that they are never appropriate as a token of sympathy to an Orthodox or Conservative Jewish family. A good many Reform congregations permit flowers, but inquiry should be made before flowers are sent.

**Display.** Flowers are not generally admitted to Catholic churches for display during a funeral (except for a spray or a pall of flowers to be placed on the coffin). In some localities it is still the custom to carry the floral pieces in a car in the procession to the church, and leave them outside during the service, after which they accompany the body to the cemetery. Flowers are displayed at a mortuary, and may be left in place during a Rosary service. Some Episcopal churches allow no more than one bouquet on the altar. In others, flowers may be banked near the coffin during the service. It is always appropriate to send flowers to the house of a bereaved Catholic or Protestant family before or after a funeral.

The card of the donor should be removed before funeral flowers are put on display anywhere. If flowers are sent to a mortuary, a staff member usually removes the card and makes a note on the back—"spray of red roses," for example—for the information of the family so that the note of acknowledgment can be specific rather than for "your flowers." If flowers are sent to a church, the sexton or a friend should be asked to make such notes when removing the cards.

It is not customary to display flowers conspicuously in a funeral procession. If they are to be taken to the cemetery, they are usually transferred in a closed car, by the undertaker, and are in place near the grave when the family arrives. When a great many flowers are sent to a funeral, a family sometimes prefers that not all of them be transferred to the cemetery, and directs that suitable floral arrangements (those in containers, not wreaths, pillows, or sprays) be sent to an old people's home or similar institution.

**Sending Flowers.** Flowers sent to mortuary or church are addressed:

The Funeral of Mr. Henry York Brown
Community Church
100 Main Street
Eastbrook, New York
Funeral at 3 P.M. Wednesday

A visiting card or a plain white card is enclosed. (See CARDS for correct signatures on blank cards.)

**GRAVESTONES AND GRAVE MARKERS.** A grave or a niche in a columbarium is marked with the name, and the dates of birth and death. Sometimes a family relationship such as "wife of" or "beloved wife of" is added, or an epitaph, or both. Mr., Mrs., Miss, or any other title is not used before a name. If a military title is used, it follows the name on a separate line. A funeral establishment usually is prepared to order a small temporary marker of bronze or other metal for placement on a grave at the time of burial. Otherwise, a stone or marker is put in place at some later date.

### JEWISH FUNERALS

**Coffin.** Public viewing of the body of the deceased is contrary to Jewish tradition, and so the coffin is always kept closed at Orthodox and Conservative funerals where the traditional rules are observed. The coffin is in place before the mourners assemble. (Custom varies in Reform congregations, though the coffin is customarily closed during the service.)

**Clothes.** Men are required to wear head covering during Orthodox and Conservative services. Men of Reform congregations do not wear hats during a religious ceremony. Married women in Orthodox congregations and all women in Conservative congregations wear head covering, and it is customary for women of Reform congregations to do so. Those of other faiths attending a Jewish funeral should follow the practice of the other mourners. An usher will supply a head covering at the door, if it is needed. It must not be refused.

**Flowers.** Flowers must not be sent to the home, funeral establishment, or funeral of a member of an Orthodox or Conservative congregation. Flowers are permitted by some Reform congregations, but it is best to inquire of the rabbi, at the mortuary, or of some member of the family before sending any flowers.

**Place.** Traditionally, Jewish funerals are not held in a synagogue, except on rare occasions for a person of unusual piety—or in localities where a funeral chapel is not available. Reform Jewish funerals may be held in the temple but far more often are held in the chapel of an authorized mortuary.

**Procedures.** Friends may say a few words of condolence to members of Reform families either before or after the service if they make themselves available. If the family enters from a side room just before the service and follows the coffin as it is carried out, as is the Orthodox and Conservative practice, no attempt should be made to speak with them. Generally, only members of the family and very close friends attend the ceremony following at the cemetery, and inquiry should be made of the family's wishes before doing so. At Reform funerals, an announcement is sometimes made that cars are available for those who want to go to the cemetery.

**Seating.** The family sits on the side nearest the door by which they enter, whether right or left of the main aisle.

**Time.** A funeral may be held in the morning or afternoon. Orthodox and Conservative funerals are held within twenty-four hours after death. In Reform congregations the funeral is held at the convenience of the family, usually one or two days after death.

**MASS CARDS.** A person of any faith may send a mass card (sometimes known as a "spiritual bouquet") in token of sympathy to a Catholic friend. A mass card is obtained by mail or by calling at any Catholic church and making a donation, in return for which a mass will be said for the repose of a soul. The mass card may be given to a member of the family, left at the Rosary, or may be mailed before or after the funeral.

**MEMORIAL DONATIONS.** Many people prefer to make a memorial donation to a charity instead of sending flowers to a funeral. The procedure is simple. A check is mailed to the chosen organization with a note giving the name and address of the bereaved person as well as the name and address of the donor. The organization sends an acknowledgment, mentioning the amount, to the donor. It also sends a notification to the designated relative that a donation has been received in memory of the deceased, giving the name of the donor but not the amount of the donation.

**MEMORIAL SERVICES.** Some families prefer to hold a memorial service instead of a funeral service. Sometimes a memorial service is held in addition to a funeral service that is limited to the immediate family. A memorial service usually follows burial or cremation within a few days, but may be held weeks or even months later, depending on the circumstances. It may be in church, at home, under the roof of some organization, or out of doors.

A memorial service may be conducted by a clergyman according to the formal ritual prescribed by certain faiths, or it may be a secular proceeding with friends of different faiths asked to speak, or there may be only music and a gathering of relatives and friends for silent meditation.

The family may or may not receive condolences in person after a memorial service, entirely according to their wishes. Flowers or memorial contributions may be sent, just as for a funeral, but always with the exceptions noted under "Flowers" in this section.

**MESSAGES OF CONDOLENCE.** A message of condolence is sent as promptly as possible. It may be a note, a telegram, or a line of sympathy written on a card enclosed with flowers, but a commercial card carrying a printed message of sympathy is not correct. A note of condolence nearly always is better than a telephone call. Too often someone in the first shock of sorrow must bear the unnecessary extra burden of emotional outbursts of sympathy from well-meaning friends. Especially before a funeral, telephone calls should be made to a bereaved family by only the most intimate friends. An executive, writing officially for his company, not as an individual, can correctly dictate a letter, but a dictated letter of condolence to a personal friend is never correct. On many occasions, a close friend sends a personally typed letter of condolence, and this is sensible if the letter is long and his handwriting is poor. However, if the rules are followed, a note of condolence is in longhand. A telegram of condolence follows the standard telegraphic form, and should be signed by both the first and last name if there is any chance of confusion with someone else of the same first name.

**MOURNING.** By today's custom, very few families go into formal mourning dress after a bereavement.

*See* MOURNING for details.

**MUSIC.** In most Protestant faiths there is wide latitude in the choice of music to be played before, after, and during the service, though the family should discuss the selections with the clergyman.

**Catholic.** Masses for the dead follow established rituals. A Low Mass is read. A High Mass and a Solemn Requiem Mass are chanted with prescribed music, and no variation is permitted.

**Jewish.** At Orthodox and Conservative funerals music is rarely approved. At Reform funerals music is usual. The choice of selections is at the discretion of the rabbi and the family.

**Protestant Episcopal.** Organ music before the service is customary.

**NEWSPAPER ANNOUNCEMENTS AND OBITUARIES.** There are two kinds of obituary notices possible in a newspaper—a paid notice in the Vital Statistics columns, and an obituary, for which there is no charge, printed at the discretion of the editor in the regular news columns.

**Paid Obituaries.** Contrary to the understanding of many people, all local newspapers do not automatically pick up the news for a Vital Statistics column when a doctor files a death certificate. Such death and funeral notices are printed at space rates. They usually are sent in by the undertaker after consultation with the person in charge of the funeral arrangements, and the charges are incorporated in the undertaker's bill. Or the information may be telephoned to a newspaper by a member of the family, in which case a bill is sent where specified. The printing of a death notice is not legally required, but is customary. A published notice is genuinely useful in virtually all cases since it is the best way to inform the community as a whole. The simplest standard form for a paid notice is:

> BROWN, Henry York—In this city on [date and year], husband of Mary Greene Brown, father of Mary Ann Jones, Jane Brown, and Henry Brown. Funeral at [place] at [time and date].

All facts that will spare the family telephone calls should be added—that the services will be private, that visits may be made to a mortuary, the time of a Rosary, a request that flowers be omitted, and the name of a specific charity to which memorial donations may be sent. A printed request, such as "Denver papers please copy," does not ensure reprinting. If it is important to notify other communities, the undertaker should be instructed to place and to pay for notices in out-of-town papers.

The age of the deceased is not usually given in a paid notice, though it may be, and sometimes it is useful in preventing confusion with someone of the same or a similar name. The printing of the home address is advisable, especially in large cities, for the same reason.

Forms vary widely in different communities. A glance at local papers is the best guide to local custom. Very frequently a business connection, details of military service, memberships, and any other connections that help to make identity unmistakable are included in the paid announcement. Such details serve two purposes. They may bring old friends of the family together and refresh strong bonds out of the past, and they give the obituary editor some idea of the items to be dealt with in fuller detail in the editorial section.

**Unpaid Obituaries.** There never is any charge for an obituary written by a newspaper reporter and printed anywhere in the news columns. A list of facts for this use may be sent or telephoned to a newspaper, but the writing of the news notice is left to a staff member. Under any circumstances, a member of the family or some authorized person should be prepared to answer questions that may be asked by a reporter. A copy of the paid death notice is sent to the desk of the obituary editor as a routine newspaper procedure. He then checks the newspaper's files to see if items have been collected for an obituary. If additional facts are needed, he gets in touch (almost always by telephone) with the family. Unless answers have been prepared, it always is best to ask a reporter to call back within the brief time needed to make an accurate list of the names of the close relatives and to collect other pertinent information. Otherwise, items of importance may be forgotten or dates and spellings may be given incorrectly.

**PALLBEARERS.** Frequently, by today's custom in large cities, pallbearers act only in an honorary capacity, since members of the undertaker's or the sexton's staff may do the actual carrying of the coffin. A relative or friend who serves as an usher may also be an honorary pallbearer.

The number of pallbearers is ordinarily between four and ten, though there is no rule that more may not be asked to serve. It is not correct to refuse this invitation unless some legitimate excuse can be given.

Pallbearers usually represent all major aspects of the deceased's life. Business associates, fellow members of various organizations, personal friends, and perhaps distant relatives may be asked to serve, though a member of the immediate family does not serve as a pallbearer. On occasion, the pallbearers are all chosen from a single group—a fraternal society, a regiment, or a school, for example. With few exceptions, men of other faiths may serve.

Honorary pallbearers precede a coffin that is carried into a house of worship. They walk slowly, two by two, and sit in the front row or rows opposite the family. If the coffin is to be carried out, they precede it, again marching slowly two by two. If the coffin is in place before the altar, the honorary pallbearers march slowly up the aisle in pairs and take their seats just before the family enters from the vestry. They precede the coffin down the aisle to the waiting hearse. They are expected to follow the family to the cemetery. A note of thanks from a member of the family must be sent to honorary pallbearers and to friends who act as actual pallbearers.

In no faith do women generally serve as actual or honorary pallbearers.

**PROCESSION TO CEMETERY.** Usually only members of the family go to the cemetery after funeral services have been held elsewhere. Friends follow only when specifically invited—unless continuing to the cemetery is the widely observed local custom.

Cars supplied by the funeral director are a convenience for members of the immediate family, since the chauffeurs can have them waiting in line behind the hearse outside the place of the service and the family can be seated without confusion or delay. If friends follow, they use their own cars unless invited to use cars provided by the family. All cars in the procession must observe traffic signals.

Cars move at dignified, moderate speed, though not markedly slower than normal traffic unless all other traffic along the route of the procession has been cleared. Bright lights are turned on to indicate to traffic officers and other drivers that the cars in the procession are moving as a unit and that other motorists should cede the right of way. When traffic has been cleared along the way for a funeral cortege, pedestrians come to a halt and men remove their hats when the hearse passes.

**PROTESTANT FUNERALS.**

**Clothes.** Women should wear head coverings.

**Coffin.** The coffin usually is in place at the altar before the mourners assemble. In the Episcopal faith, it is usually closed. In other faiths, it may be open or closed. If the coffin is open, it is the custom for those who wish to do so to file by for a last look. The coffin is generally closed before the service begins.

**Flowers.** In some Episcopal churches, the coffin is covered by a pall of cloth only, or by one spray, and other flowers sent to the church are not displayed there but are taken to the cemetery. In others, flowers are admitted to the church for display. In all other Protestant denominations, flowers may be displayed. It is appropriate to send flowers to the home of the bereaved, to the mortuary, or to the church.

**Place.** In church, at a mortuary, or at home.

**Procedures.** The family usually enters from the vestry after the congregation is assembled and just before the hour of the service, though if the coffin is carried in after the mourners are assembled, the processional and recessional follow the form given under "Catholic Funerals." At the end of the service, the family usually leaves through the vestry, though sometimes the honorary pallbearers and the family follow the coffin if it is carried out down the main aisle. In either case, all members of the congregation remain seated until the family has withdrawn. The family makes itself available to friends or leaves immediately, entirely according to their wishes.

**Seating.** At church or mortuary, the immediate family sits in the front row or rows to the right, facing the altar or lectern.

**Time.** A funeral may be held in either the morning or afternoon in most Protestant denominations. Family preference, community custom, and sometimes the convenience of the minister influence the day and time chosen. However, a service is less often scheduled for Sunday than for the other days of the week, and when Sunday is chosen, the time is almost always in the afternoon, no matter where the service is to be held. In some large cities, funerals are occasionally held in a mortuary at night, particularly when most of the deceased's friends are businessmen who would be unable to attend a daytime service, but this is far from common practice.

**REFRESHMENTS.** In some families it is the custom to receive callers at home before the funeral, and perhaps also to provide food and other refreshments. After a funeral to which many relatives and friends have come from some distance, either lunch or tea is sometimes served following the return from the cemetery. Usually a widow stays in some withdrawn room and sees only a very few of the guests there, though she does whatever will give her the greatest solace.

**ROSARIES.** A Rosary is a religious ceremony observed by Catholics on the evening preceding the day of a funeral. It usually is held in a room at the mortuary, but may be held wherever the body is lying. The coffin may be open or closed, according to the wishes of the family. A Rosary usually is attended by relatives and close friends, though if the time of the Rosary is publicly announced, acquaintances may attend. The service consists of prayers said by a priest. It is correct to say a few words of sympathy to members of the family and to converse quietly with other friends before and after the service. Flowers may be displayed at a Rosary, and friends often present mass cards to the family or leave them in a provided place.

**SEATING.** If there are no ushers, those attending a funeral service come in quietly, making every effort to be in place at least ten minutes before the designated time. The immediate family does not enter until just before the service begins. Traditionally, at Christian services, the right-hand front pew belongs to the family, and the left-hand front pew is for pallbearers and ushers. At Jewish funerals, the family sits on the side nearest the vestry.

**SHIPMENT OF A BODY.** Contrary to the belief of many people, there is no law that a body shipped by train or other common carrier must be accompanied by an escort (though Orthodox and Conservative Jewish tradition requires that a body be accompanied, and the practice is customary though not required by Reform Jews). What is a requirement in all localities is that a licensed funeral director must accompany the body to the local terminal or station, since local laws require that he sign papers relative to the shipment. The very widely held belief that a body must be accompanied by an escort is based on the fact that two first-class tickets must be purchased when a body is sent by rail. Whether an escort uses the second ticket or not depends entirely on the circumstances and the feelings of the family because the railroad company or Railway Express can serve as escort. If a relative or friend makes the journey, that person rides in regular passenger space, not with the body. Tickets are not required when a body is sent by plane or ship because charges are based on weight.

The undertaker is equipped to make all arrangements for shipment, as well as for someone of his profession to meet and assist any escort at the end of the journey, and for the services of a clergyman, if desired.

**USHERS.** At a large funeral it is a help to have ushers show people to seats. Some funeral directors are prepared to supply ushers from their staff. In big churches, the sexton usually has a staff available for such purposes. Or friends of the family can serve. Ushers walk down the aisle with those they are seating but do not offer an arm to a woman as they do at a wedding, or chat as they may do at a wedding.

Ushers may also act as pallbearers. If there are no pallbearers, the ushers may precede the casket down the aisle, or march down two by two and take their places in the front row across from the family just before the service is to begin.

There are no ushers as such at a funeral held in a mortuary, though members of the funeral director's staff are on hand to be of assistance if needed.

**VIGILS.** A vigil is entirely a matter of the wishes of a family, though sitting up in constant vigil during the days and nights before a funeral is not usual today. If there is a continuous vigil, arrangements should be made for enough relatives and friends to serve so that each watcher is relieved after a few hours.

**VIEWING THE BODY.** In some faiths, it is customary for the coffin to be left open at the mortuary, during a lying in state of a public figure, and perhaps during the funeral service. Those who wish to may pass by the coffin and view the body, but there is no obligation to do so unless aware that the action will give comfort to the bereaved.

## FURS

No matter how valuable a fur coat may be, the first and most important rule is: Wear it—don't let it wear you. At best, brushing aside a handsome fur coat to avoid sitting on it is a graceless gesture. Being oversolicitous in the care of a fur coat does not emphasize the rarity and preciousness of the fur—it merely implies that the owner is not accustomed to luxury.

In a theater, a woman treats a fur coat as she would a cloth one—she sits on it. She does the same in a restaurant, but if there is a spare chair handy, she lays the coat aside as she would any other. She does not fold it inside out with a great show of care, though a well-trained waiter will do this for her.

Insurance is the only real and sensible protection for valuable furs, but it is unwise to leave any valuable and easily portable possession—even an insured one—unguarded in a public place, since insurance is no protection against the inconvenience of loss. Usually a woman can safely leave her fur coat in a theater seat when she goes out during intermissions. On a train making stops, however, she is much wiser to carry it with her to the dining car than leave it unguarded in the open.

# G

**GAMBLING.**  *See* GAMES.

## GAMES

Each game has its own special regulations, but certain principles of sportsmanship and rules of behavior are common to all of them—from anagrams to tennis.

Whether the goal of a social game or contest is money or an award, good sportsmanship and good taste call for manners that emphasize the fun of the competition, not the prize itself. Of course each participant is expected to play his best—or to seem to. If for any reason he chooses to let an opponent win, it is poor taste to let the winner suspect that his victory was contrived, and poor sportsmanship to indicate that fact to anyone else.

When playing for money, a time or some other limit to the game should be set before play starts. Otherwise, it is the loser's duty to call a halt at a reasonable hour, since, by the rules, a winner does not make the first move to end the play.

The winner breaks all rules if he shows any special delight at the sum won; a loser, any real dismay at a sum lost. And the good loser also takes his defeat without making excuses for his poor showing. Mentioning a handicap—a headache, a blistered heel, or unfamiliar territory or equipment—in a way that sounds like an alibi does not change the score, only the loser's standing as a good sport. Under this rule, the loser always compliments the winner on his skill, never on his luck. In turn, the good winner avoids any criticism of the loser's technique, but instead sympathizes with him for his bad luck.

When invited to play with experts at any game, the beginner or the poor player does best to decline in the full understanding that polite companions are more or less obligated to extend the invitation and that they are depending on the social responsibility of players out of their class to refuse. Only if urged to play after making his companions fully aware that he is not in their class should an inexpert player accept such an invitation.

As a general rule, it is the host or hostess—not a guest—who properly suggests chess, Scrabble, cards, charades, croquet, or any other game, indoors or out, that involves more equipment or time than playing "Heads or Tails" with a flipped coin. This rule is broken constantly—and correctly—as long as the guest does it in a way that leaves the host free to follow or ignore the suggestion if it does not fit his plans for the occasion. But a guest is completely out of line if he takes over the host's place as master of ceremonies and enthusiastically organizes a game like charades that will involve everyone at a party for a considerable time, or promotes a table of cards like bridge that will exclude some of his fellow guests. (Incidentally, if some guests want to play a game and others do not, either the host or hostess usually stays out of the game.)

**BETTING AND GAMBLING.** A bet and a gamble both are the risking of something on the uncertain outcome of any matter—the flip of a card, a political contest, or a winning score—but there is a marked difference in the meaning of the two words as they are commonly used. Most of the people who find a game of cards no fun unless played for stakes do not consider themselves gamblers— and resent being so labeled—because to say that a person is a gambler implies that he risks money or safety more rashly than is reasonable by normal standards; and it also often implies that he customarily hazards high stakes on cards, dice, and other games of chance as a way of making a living or supplementing his income rather than as a social diversion. But, whether one is betting or gambling, the rules are the same.

By any code of honor, placing a wager on a sure thing is cheating. However, a refusal to bet on a sure thing can be a delicate matter in some cases. For example, if a person has been given inside knowledge but has been pledged not to reveal it, he cannot refuse to bet by saying frankly, "I can't take your bet because I know the matter is settled." Instead, he must try to evade the issue with a casual "I'm not in a betting mood" or some other offhand remark. Whenever a person shows himself reluctant to bet—for whatever reason—the matter should be dropped instantly. "Are you afraid to bet?" is the question of a bully. If asked, it should be ignored.

Any bet is a debt of honor and so takes precedence over routine obligations. By the rules, a money bet must be settled immediately after the outcome is decided. Neglecting to pay up promptly comes high on the list of social misdemeanors; and welshing on a bet is an unforgivable social sin. If the loser cannot settle at the end of a game, he must set a definite date for payment. A winner may suggest to a loser decidedly his junior that payment of a heavy loss be delayed until after the next session to give luck a chance to even the score, but a younger person does not make this suggestion to anyone markedly his senior. Any suggestion the loser makes about delaying payment must be accepted pleasantly and casually. It is an insult to say, "Forget it." A winner cannot properly make a direct demand for the delayed payment of a gambling debt if it is not met by the specified time. However, since "forgetting" to settle a bet is a prime social offense, such a loser is likely to be rather pointedly left out of subsequent games. It is a breach of manners for a winner to ask for an I.O.U., and customary for a social acquaintance to refuse an I.O.U. if the loser offers it.

The rules about setting stakes are explicit: Never suggest high stakes unless entirely certain that everyone in the game can afford a high loss. Agree readily if any player suggests lower stakes. If high stakes are planned, don't invite a guest to join a game before telling him what they are and giving him a graceful chance to refuse the invitation. When the stakes are too high for him, a guest should say so frankly, but in a way that leaves the others free to reduce the stakes or to go ahead without him if risking large sums is part of their fun.

Old-fashioned as it seems, there is still a marked inequality between the sexes when it comes to betting except for the agreed stakes in a card game. Otherwise (as a general rule), a woman avoids betting any sizable sum with a man because, though a man pays a loss to a woman winner without discomfort, a great many men feel less than comfortable when accepting any large amount of money from a woman loser. A good way around the situation is to wager something tangible—a book, a bottle, theater tickets, a home-cooked meal against one in a restaurant, and so on.

No one, man or woman, can accept extravagant odds—a dollar against a new car, for example—unless willing to admit being open to payoff in this far from subtle fashion.

A child can't be blamed for accepting a "bet" on a sure thing, but the adult who offers it should be. "I'll bet you a quarter you can't finish the dishes in fifteen minutes" is not an honest bet but a tricky bribe, and a child is quick to realize it. The laws of sportsmanship have no exceptions for age and sex. The sooner a child learns this, the better. If a child makes a bet with another child, he should be held to it and so taught that his word must be honored.
*See also* DARES.

**Casinos.** During play at roulette, twenty-one, baccarat, and chemin de fer, silence from players and spectators is the rule, except for the necessary comment in connection with the play. Anyone who wants to chatter had better withdraw to the bar—or join a dice game, where cries of encouragement, pleas to luck, and other comments are expected.

Customs in tipping vary in different clubs and casinos. It is not customary, especially during brief play, to tip the dealer, croupier, or other house players stationed at a table where stakes are low and the turnover of players is high— in one of the outer rooms in establishments in Las Vegas, Reno, and other towns where gambling is a wide-open tourist attraction, for example. However, gamblers are superstitious individuals, and it is quite common for a player who has had several wins in a row to give a chip or so to the employee in charge of the table as a magic offering to his luck. A loser does not tip.

A chip can be tossed to the dealer, croupier, and so on, but many of them prefer a tip in the form of an additional wager riding for them. For example, if a player is putting down five one-dollar chips for himself he puts another chip "in front of the line" and the extra chip rides for the dealer. The size of the tip depends on the size of the win and the generosity of the player. Some people do not tip at all, but house players generally depend on tips that will about equal the salary they get from the management.

In many casinos, pretty girls circulate with trays of drinks, dispensing whatever the customers want in the way of liquid refreshment while they are playing. There is no charge for these drinks, but a good tip is expected. In Nevada when silver dollars were used as chips, one was the customary tip. Now that they are out of circulation, the average tip is fifty cents or more in silver or a chip. Again, the size of the tip for a free drink depends on the luck of the player. A heavy winner may "tip his luck" by tossing five dollars' worth of chips on the drink tray, and a loser may settle for a quarter.

**CARDS.** The basic rules discussed throughout this section apply to all card games. In addition, cardplayers observe special conventions if they want to be asked back for another session.

Poker, bridge, or any other game of cards is a serious, engrossing sport to good players, but it is still a game—not an event that demands the hushed silence of a religious ceremony. On the other hand, freedom to concentrate is every player's due, and one fidgety, featherheaded chatterer who insists on making the game secondary to conversation can ruin a session for everyone else. When in doubt, save talk for another time; and don't hold up the play in any other unnecessary fashion.

Even if random talk is held to the conventional minimum, some mannerisms can be as distracting as wordy interruptions. Repeated sounds and gestures like humming, drumming the fingers, constantly rearranging the hand, and snapping the cards down on the table can be exasperating enough to throw another player off his game. So can any infraction of the standard rules of card courtesy: A dealer after shuffling should automatically offer the pack to the player at his right for cutting, for example; and a player never picks up his hand until the deal is complete.

Postmortems hold up the game. They are best skipped, anyway, since it is all but impossible to analyze the play without seeming to gloat over one's own skill or belittle that of another player. For the same reason, it is never by the rules to reproach one's partner for a play or bid by word or expression or to show any gleeful reaction to an opponent's mistake.

If there is any question about the rules of play, the host is privileged to decide the issue. In every case, the rules should be made explicitly clear before play starts. In games where a banker is necessary, it is taken for granted that the host will serve in that capacity unless he asks a guest to take over the duty for him.

Out of line is the player who cannot resist bobbing out of his chair at every opportunity to join nonplaying guests or see how things are going at other tables. The dummy is certainly privileged to get himself a drink, but as a general rule is expected to sit quietly and watch the play.

And as for kibitzing, there is only one safe procedure: Don't.

**Parties.** There are almost as many different kinds of card parties as there are players. They range from the impromptu get-together of two or more friends to the benefit card parties that are a favorite means of fund-raising in many organizations.

Millions of women belong to groups of four to a dozen or more players who meet on a regular basis in the afternoon for bridge, canasta, or gin rummy, each member acting as hostess in her turn and serving lunch before the session or refreshments after it. These parties frequently, though not always, are rather more relaxed in their demands on the players for concentration and relative silence than are the sessions at evening clubs made up of both men and women, stag parties, or the occasional dinner party with cards announced as the planned entertainment for all guests after the meal.

In every case, the invitation should be specific about certain details. If the play is for money stakes rather than prizes, the host or hostess must make that clear when issuing the invitation so that anyone who has a moral objection to playing for money can refuse. It also is essential, as noted above as a basic rule, to give a guest a graceful chance to refuse an invitation to play for uncomfortably high stakes.

Since the presence of a specific number of players may be essential to even out tables, an invitation to a card party should be answered with extra promptness so that the hostess will have time to ask other guests to take the places of those who regret. Anyone who is not a player is expected to turn down an invitation if bridge, poker, or any other specific game is stipulated as the main feature of the occasion. It is neither considerate nor correct for a person who does not play bridge, for example, to accept an invitation with the dismaying words, "I don't play but I'd love to come and watch."

The hostess collects her money winnings without question. If a hostess has provided prizes instead of stakes or in addition to them, she cedes any prize she wins to the guest with the score nearest hers. Things are a bit different at a benefit card party. If a hostess has bought a table and takes players along as her guests, she can feel free to keep the table prize if her score is the highest, since she has not supplied the prize herself.

No matter what or where the occasion, if cards are a planned part of the entertainment, the host and hostess are obligated to provide reasonably comfortable conditions for play as well as all needed cards, score pads, and so on. No one enjoys crouching over a low table, sitting at a standard table in a chair so low that he chins himself, playing at tables crowded together beyond reason, or enduring the handicap of lights placed so that they cast a glaring reflection from the cards.

*See also* STAG PARTIES.

**CHEATING.** Cheating is a matter of morals, and a cheater is already so far beyond the bounds of decent behavior that we can forget him—but unfortunately not the problems in behavior the cheater presents to others. How to behave when faced with cheating is a difficult and delicate matter. Each case involves its own painful decision, depending on the circumstances and the position of the person who spots a cheat—the unfortunate host who has sponsored him, the fellow guest, and the individual victim all have different responsibilities to themselves and to others.

There is no greater social insult than the charge of cheating, and so it is of the greatest importance, before taking any action, to be absolutely certain that a person has deliberately moved a ball, miscalled a shot, misdealt cards, or in any other way taken a cheat's unfair advantage, rather than made one of the honest, innocent mistakes that any player makes on occasion.

If the host detects the cheater, about all he can do in most circumstances is to terminate the game quickly. If any of his other guests has lost heavily to the cheater, the host is in a real spot. By the laws of hospitality, he is responsible because he has sponsored the cheat by inviting him. But once the moment of cheating is past, the fact may be impossible to prove; and an open accusation can lead to an extremely ugly and inconclusive scene, since the cheater is certainly going to deny furiously a charge that cannot be proved. The best way out for the host is to call all bets off if he can find any pretext for doing so, and then exclude the cheater from future sessions—using his own judgment about how much he can and should hint of his reasons to the others involved.

If another guest spots a cheater, his position is equally delicate. He cannot correctly make a disturbance under his host's roof, and so his only recourse is to make any excuse except his real one for terminating play. Under most circumstances, he owes it to his host to explain why he has done so—preferably the next day or after the cheater has left, so that he does not force the host to take action against a guest under his own roof. However, if the victim is a newcomer to a close circle of players, he had best keep his conclusions to himself and decline all further invitations to play with that group.

**SPORTS.** Manners for both players and spectators during games like golf and tennis are given under separate headings, as are the rules for sports like hunting, skiing, and so on, but these general rules always apply:

Don't ask to borrow equipment; wait for a fellow sportsman to volunteer the use of his racquet, bowling ball, golf clubs, skiis, and so on.

Don't give unsolicited suggestions or advice about how to improve his play to any individual—from the solitaire player on; wait until he asks for advice, criticism, or help.

Don't distract anyone in the middle of play or performance. Stay silent and motionless and at a reasonable distance when a pool player is preparing to shoot, when a golfer is addressing his ball, when a contestant in a track or field event is reading for his attempt, or at any other time when maximum concentration is demanded of a player or athlete.

Let applause fit the time, place, and sport. Cheers, boos, whistles, catcalls, and yells are a standard part of spectator participation and of the fun, to some people, at wrestling matches and prizefights. So is cheering, rhythmic stamping, and clapping at football games and certain other team sports— amateur or professional—and booing the umpire at a baseball game. As a general rule, however, applause belongs at the end of a play, turn, or whatever— not during it. Applause for a winning team or specific player can be as vociferous as a spectator cares to make it. But boos for a losing team or individual or for a mistake during play are unsporting and taboo.

Otherwise, the main duty of a spectator is to enjoy himself without interfering with others' doing likewise—by standing on the sidelines, for example, and blocking the view of those in the front row. And anyone who repeatedly blocks the view of the people behind him by leaping to his feet for a better view himself starts a chain reaction that deserves the outraged cries of "Down in front!"

## GARAGES

Garage mechanics usually are not tipped, though if one works overtime in an emergency or gives other special service, a tip is in order, in recognition of kindness beyond the requirements of duty.

It is not necessary or customary to tip the attendant in a temporary parking lot or garage. The attendant in a parking lot or garage used regularly usually is given a dollar from time to time, and is remembered with a tip at Christmas. Special service such as keeping a car dusted and swept out deserves a tip.

Parking attendants who deliver cars to the door of a hotel, restaurant, or residence are tipped. So are the men who park cars for nightclub patrons. A doorman who watches a double-parked car or one in a limited-time zone also is tipped.

## GARDEN PARTIES

A party in a garden can be as informal as a picnic in bathing suits beside a backyard pool, but an invitation that specifies "garden party" indicates a formal reception, tea, or cocktail party out of doors. Guests are not expected to turn up in casual clothes. Invitations, acceptances, clothes, and behavior are the same as for any formal afternoon event.

## GARLIC AND ONIONS

Garlic, like the onion, is the bulb of a plant belonging to the lily family. The garlic bulb is formed of many segments, each of which is called a "clove" or "bud." The whole bulb is called "a head" of garlic.

Garlic is used in seasoning meats and fish, vegetables, salads, soups, and pickles. The flavor of garlic is a delight to many people, but others find the pungent odor and strong taste extremely unpleasant, and still others are allergic to garlic, so it must be used with great discretion. Dishes flavored with garlic are not suited to formal meals or, in truth, to any but family meals unless the hostess knows her guests well enough to be sure that garlic will please all of them.

Since the odor of garlic lingers on the breath, it is inconsiderate of others, as well as indicative of a rash indifference to one's own effect on them, to eat a dish flavored with garlic before a business or social engagement, and most particularly before dancing, going to the theater, or playing cards.

All this applies to raw onions as well as to both raw and cooked garlic. Cooked onions lose the pungency that lingers on the breath and so are always safe to serve.

## GARNISHES

A garnishing on food is anything used to decorate a serving or platter, from sprigs of parsley to the elaborate flowers of glacé fruit sometimes seen on hams. When a host is serving, he usually puts a bit of any edible garnish on each plate. When a garnished platter is passed, a guest may take a bit of garnish so long as the general attractiveness of the dish is not disturbed.

Paper frills garnishing the tips of a crown roast or ends of chops are not an invitation to pick up the meat in the fingers. They are meant only to conceal charred ends.

## GAS STATIONS

One of the very best demonstrations of good American manners is given hundreds of thousands of times daily by the gas-station attendants who bound out to wipe windshields, check tires, and give information about routes, as well as sell gas and oil. There are dismal exceptions, but on most well-traveled routes gas-station employees are so consistently polite and helpful that the motoring public may well take their good manners as a high standard of behavior, and match it. Gas-station attendants are not tipped, but either the words or manner of a client should say, "Thank you." A direct order such as "Clean the windshield" certainly should not be given unaccompanied by a spoken or implied "please."

## GATE-CRASHERS.    *See* PARTY-CRASHERS.

## GENERALS.    *See* FORMS OF ADDRESS (Armed Services).

## GENTLEMAN AND MAN

The correct choice between "gentleman" and "man" is a tricky matter, just as is the choice between "lady" and "woman." The words can be used interchangeably in some circumstances, but not many, and so it is well worth getting a firm grasp on the guidelines because hurt feelings can result if the wrong one is chosen—or the speaker can give the wrong impression of his own status.

"Ladies and gentlemen" is the standard form of direct address to a group of men and women in either business or social life, and "gentlemen" to a group of men is correct under formal circumstances—"Sit down, gentlemen," for example. However, the same person, in speaking about associates or guests, would say, "There were ten men and only two women present."

**BUSINESS.** Salespeople and others who serve the public use "gentleman" as the standard word of reference that they expect themselves when they are customers, and say, "This gentleman is next," never correctly, "This man is next." In most other business circumstances, however, "gentleman" is used far less than "lady," since "man" does not carry the same onus "woman" does in many connections. A good deal depends on the character of the office and the formality of the relationship between an employer and his secretary. For example, in a staid law office, a secretary might say, "Two gentlemen to see you," in the unlikely case that she is not announcing them by name, or "The gentleman you are lunching with called." In many other offices, such use of "gentleman" might sound unnaturally stilted.

**SOCIAL USE.** The rule is more exact in social circumstances. The word "gentleman" is never used, except as noted below, when speaking to a social acquaintance about a social equal. For example, a wife describes her husband to a neighbor as "a thoughtful man," not "a thoughtful gentleman." A man says, "I sat beside a man," not, "beside another gentleman," and a man never refers to himself as a "gentleman" in any such sentence as "I am the gentleman who called last night." Only to maids, waiters, porters, doormen, domestic employees, and others in similar positions is such a remark as "I am waiting for that gentleman" correct from either a man or a woman.

There are only two exceptions to this rule. When speaking of a very old man it is proper to say, "He is such a wise old gentleman." A boy or a very young man may be complimented by "such a nice young gentleman." But "He is such a nice gentleman" without any other qualifying adjective indicates that the man referred to is a cut above the speaker socially, and is properly said only by a servant.

The rules call for a child to say, "May I take that gentleman to see my puppy?" rather than "that man," but it is absurd to make much of a point of this matter with small children. Just be thankful that a kindergartner is trying to help entertain a visitor, rather than take the shine off his hospitable suggestion by any correction at the time. If this use of "gentleman" sounds stilted, as it often does, the problem can be met in the case of older children by teaching them to remember to use the name and title of a visitor—a mannerly procedure they must learn sooner or later anyway. A child making a statement of fact properly says, "Man on the phone for you," or "That man is Bobby's uncle."

## GENTLEWOMAN

The word "gentlewoman" has all but completely dropped out of use, except on the floor of Congress, where such formal terms as "the gentlewoman from Oregon" and "the gentleman from Ohio" are still the accepted form.

## GIFTS

All presents have a double life. First, of course, a present is supposed to please the recipient; but it also speaks loud and clear of the donor's taste, judgment, and good sense. A donor is never justified in choosing (or passing along) a present that he himself considers in poor taste—unless he has been specifically informed that it is the heart's desire of the person he wants to please.

Whether it is delightful or dismaying, any present must be acknowledged in some fashion—by thanks in person, by a telephone call or note, depending on the circumstances.

**BABIES.** By tradition, pink is for girls, blue for boys, but any pastel shade is suitable for both, and white is always safe.

*See* BABIES for details.

**BON VOYAGE.** Nearly every good-bye present is better delivered in advance than pressed into the hands of the traveler at the moment of departure. A bulky or heavy item handed over at that time can be a nuisance to anyone leaving by train, plane, or bus, since his luggage may well have been checked through. Even if it is still available, there is little likelihood that it has room for a sizable last-minute addition. Only small, lightweight items for use during the first leg of the journey are entirely safe moment-of-departure presents. Heating pads and the electric coils for making instant coffee (with converter plugs for foreign use), passport cases, and travel books are excellent good-bye presents, but these certainly should be given in advance after making sure that a well-organized traveler has not already provided his own.

(See TRAVEL for details.)

**BOOKS.** The pleasure of a book is often enhanced if it carries a message from the donor. However, if there is any chance that the gift is a duplicate or a less than perfect choice in any other way, it is better to enclose a card than to inscribe the book and so make it impossible to exchange.

**BOXES.** Any box can be used to hold a gift if it is clearly only a container and will not be mistaken as an indication of the source of the present. More than one recipient of a piece of costume jewelry, for example, has been embarrassed by taking it back to Tiffany for cleaning or repair, and being told that only the box came from there.

**BROKEN OR DAMAGED.** Damage to a gift sent through the mail should be reported to the sender so that an insurance claim may be made. (In the event that the package was not insured, the donor is in an unhappy position because he has a clear obligation to supply a replacement.) If a gift is delivered in bad shape by a shop, the shop is responsible, and the recipient does whatever is simplest for all concerned. If the item is something unique, the damage must be reported to the donor so that he can make the complaint and arrange for another present. If the gift is a standard item, the recipient usually calls the shop, reports the damage, and arranges for a replacement without distressing the donor by mentioning the mishap.

**BUSINESS.**   See BUSINESS MANNERS for the special rules governing presents to and from an employer, and other details.

**CARDS.** A card or message of some kind should be enclosed with a gift not delivered in person. The name of the sender and the return address on the outside of a package are not enough. If a card is not enclosed, send a note advising the recipient that a gift is on its way.

**CHILDREN.** Make sure that any present to a child is not going to be a white elephant or worse to his parents. If in doubt about its suitability, ask the parents, not the child. Children are likely to take an inquiry as a promise, and more than one cloudburst of tears has followed the provisional gift of a kitten, for example, "if your mother will let you have it." For the most part, children live for the moment, but they have long memories where the promise of a present is concerned. It is never a kindness to promise a child a present "sometime." The limit of "sometime" to little children is tomorrow afternoon. Be prepared to put up or shut up.

A present of candy is best not handed directly to a child; it should be given to the mother so that she can control how much of it is eaten at one time—and choose the appropriate time. Noisemakers like drums or whistles are booby traps if given to a child at a time when he is struggling to be on his best behavior—seen but not heard. Potentially dangerous gifts like chemistry sets should be given only after prior consultation with the parents, and presents for babies should be nonpoisonous and scrupulously clean, since they are sure to end up in the child's mouth. Breakable, sharp, pointed, or abrasive toys can also be dangerous. Clothing that cannot be exchanged is a risky choice unless one is very sure of the mother's taste and the child's size.

**CHRISTMAS.**   See CHRISTMAS.

**EXCHANGING.** It is absurd to keep a gift that is the wrong color or in any other way undesirable or useless if it is practical to take it back for exchange, since it is only sensible to assume that the donor selected the gift in the hope of giving pleasure. Report frankly to the donor the reason for the exchange and how much pleasure the new item provides. Unfortunately, there is nothing to do about an item put together by loving hands, or the bargain picked up at a clearance sale months before, except to give as fulsome thanks for the thought as can be managed—and hide or pass along the problem gift.

**FOREIGN COUNTRIES.** Before sending any present abroad, make sure that it will not require the recipient to pay a heavy duty. High import taxes are levied on many items sent abroad, and more than one dismayed foreigner has found himself paying dearly for a "present."

**GIFT CERTIFICATES.** These are a good way to get around the taboo against giving money in bills as a present. Gift certificates usually are given to younger friends or junior members of a staff rather than to those equal in age and income, though of course there are exceptions.

**HOUSE PRESENTS.** Some gift is customary from a guest who stays overnight or longer. It may be given on arrival or sent within a few days after a visit.

**ILLNESS.** A series of small gifts and bouquets is a better choice than one spectacular flower arrangement for the patient making an extended stay in a hospital. Too often a hospital room looks like a flower shop during the first days and is meagerly supplied with flowers during the following weeks. Cologne, books, a small deck of cards for solitaire, and other items for practical use or to divert the bored patient, and plants rather than cut flowers usually are the most welcome tokens of sympathy and concern.

**INITIALS AND MONOGRAMS.** Unless the giver is positive that there will be no need to exchange an article, and also knows the style of marking chosen by the recipient, it is never a good idea to have a gift marked. Far better procedure is to send the gift unmarked, with the understanding that the shop will stamp, engrave, or embroider markings to match similar items. (*See* INITIALS AND MONOGRAMS; and WEDDINGS for details.)

**MEN TO WOMEN.** By the long-established rule, a man does not give a dress, coat, lingerie, or any other major or intimate item of wearing apparel to any woman except a member of his family. Accessories like handbags, gloves, umbrellas, handkerchiefs, and scarves are safer choices.

**MONEY.** Money is a welcome present to many people, but the rules about how to give it are fairly rigid. Only to very young children or people in service positions is money given in cash. A bonus to a business employee is given by check, not in bills. The same is true of any sizable sum given to members of a family—an anniversary or wedding present, for example. Gift certificates for smaller sums, and stocks or bonds for larger amounts, are also considered better choices than a gift in bills.

**TO NURSES.** Tips are not generally given to nurses of professional standing, but a gift is customary to a nurse who has been especially helpful, patient, and attentive during a long illness or stay in a hospital.

**OBLIGATORY.** The acceptance of certain invitations calls for a present. *See* separate listings such as BIRTHDAYS; HOUSEGUESTS; WEDDINGS; etc.

**OPENING.** As a general rule, all presents (except Christmas presents given ahead of time) should be opened when received, and most particularly those handed over in person by the donor.

If some guests have brought presents to a party and others have not, the packages should still be opened at some convenient time during the party —and the presentless guests comforted by some such remark as, "But nobody was supposed to know it was my birthday." There is no need for a guest to be embarrassed at not having brought a gift when there was no advance intimation that a gift would be appropriate.

**PRICE TAGS.** Care should be taken to remove price tags. At best, a price tag indicates haste and carelessness in wrapping. At worst, it emphasizes the money rather than the sentiment involved.

**REFUSING.** This is a delicate matter, but if accepting a gift is for any reason inappropriate, the gift should be refused with thanks for the thought and with some explanation. This matter comes up frequently in business, particularly with employees in purchasing offices and other positions where the acceptance of any handsome present may place them in a position difficult to explain. Warm thanks and a frank statement that accepting gifts is against company (or one's personal) policy is the only good procedure.

(*See* BUSINESS MANNERS.)

An expensive gift from a man to a girl or woman who is not a member of his immediate family or a close relative is—according to the old rule, and present usage also—poor taste in all ordinary circumstances. There is no need to be stuffy in refusing such a gift, however, and the refusal should emphasize the donor's generous impulse, not his mistake in taste.

**RETURNING.** The return of gifts after a quarrel means very bitter feelings. It is better to delay a little and give the matter second thought before ruining any chance of a reconciliation.

An engagement ring must be returned when an engagement is broken. If wedding presents already have arrived when marriage plans are canceled, they must be returned too. Heirlooms given to a bride by the groom's family usually go back to them after a divorce, if there are no children.

(*See* DIVORCES AND SEPARATIONS; ENGAGEMENTS TO WED; WEDDINGS.)

**RETURNING CONTAINERS.** When a gift of food is delivered in a casserole or bowl or on a platter, the container should be returned as promptly as reasonable, and it is the graceful convention that it must not go back empty—flowers from the garden or some small delicacy make an appropriate addition.

**SALESPEOPLE.** A gift to a salesperson is seldom called for, and a tip may well be regarded as an insult. However, if a shop employee goes to a great deal of trouble beyond the call of duty, a small token of appreciation like a box of candy may be given to him. In general, appropriately warm thanks are all that is expected.

**SENDING.** It is important for the buyer to get a receipt from a shop so that if there is delay or difficulty in delivering a gift, the sender can trace the package, as it is his responsibility to do. Gifts sent through the mail are best insured, since this automatically produces a receipt.

**THANKS.** Any gift not delivered in person calls for a note or telephone call acknowledging its arrival and expressing appreciation.

**WOMEN TO MEN.** As a general rule, women do not give articles of clothing to men outside the family, but this rule is broken all the time—and sensibly—by good friends. It is hard enough to find presents for men without putting a ban on scarves, sweaters, and other accessories.

**GIRLS.** *See* CHILDREN AND MANNERS; CLOTHES; and Children in the Index.

# GLASSES

Glasses come in traditional shapes for the service of all beverages, but very few households today have a need for—or a place to store—the full complement of specialized sizes and shapes. The average family that does quite a bit of entertaining can get along comfortably and in perfect taste with the following sets: water tumblers (which can double for milk, iced tea, highballs, and beer), water goblets, cocktail glasses (which can be used for sherry), Old-Fashioned glasses (for any drink on the rocks, and juices, too), all-purpose wineglasses (for both white and red wine), and liqueur glasses (also correct for brandy).

Two rules are of main importance: 1. Choose glasses that match the china in general style and quality. A delicate crystal goblet looks absurd with a pottery plate and a checked gingham cloth; and so does a heavy cast tumbler with fine china and linen. 2. Fill glasses to the proper levels indicated in the illustrations.

Glasses are made in a bewildering variety of quality and weight as well as of shape. An understanding of the following terms is useful when choosing glasses for daily use.

*Blown Glass.* Glasses so shaped can be either very fine or very cheap. They are shaped in three ways—mouth-blown and shaped without a mold; mouth-blown into a mold; or blown by machine into a mold and shaped by compressed air, as are light bulbs and inexpensive thin glasses.

*Crystal.* Rock crystal is a semiprecious stone, but "crystal" applied to glass means that is of a very fine quality and that it will ring with a bell-like tone when tapped.

*Cut Glass.* This term is applied to heavy crystal glass into which designs are deeply cut by an abrasive wheel. Though cut glass was manufactured in the United States as early as 1770, its peak period of popularity and perfection was not reached until the latter part of the nineteenth century. It is now coming back into style for use with fine china.

*Engraved Glass.* This glass is also cut on a wheel, but the design is very shallow. Both inexpensive glass and thin crystal are decorated by this means.

*Etched Glass.* The design or decoration on this glass is made by the action of acid. An etched decoration is more frosty-looking than one produced by engraving.

*Pressed Glass.* This glass is shaped by pressing molten glass into a mold; the term is generally applied to glass with a heavy raised or indented pattern. Antique pressed glass is widely sought by collectors. The most famous of such glass was made by the Boston and Sandwich Glass Company in the nineteenth century.

**HOW TO HOLD.** Tumblers are held near the base. Stemmed water goblets are held by the bottom of the bowl. So are wineglasses, except those carrying chilled wine, which are picked up by the stem so that the hand will not warm the wine. The bowl of a brandy snifter is cradled in one or both hands to warm the brandy and bring out its aroma and flavor.

**STANDARD SHAPES AND SIZES.** Glasses are divided into two main categories: tumblers (any glass without a stem or handle) and stemware. There are countless correct variations, but the shapes and sizes shown here are the most popular.

Unless otherwise indicated below, glasses are filled to within half an inch to an inch of the brim.

*Beer.* The capacity of the stein or mug ranges from 8 to 16 ounces. The pilsner glass holds about 10 ounces. Beer is also correctly served in a straight-side tumbler holding from 7 to 10 ounces.

*Brandy.* The balloon-shaped bowl and small opening of the brandy snifter hold in the aroma of the liquor. Snifters range in size from a total capacity of 6 to 25 ounces, but only about 2 ounces of brandy are correctly poured into a snifter at one time. Brandy is also correctly served in a liqueur glass.

*Cocktail.*   Both shapes range in total capacity from 3 to 4½ ounces. About 2 ounces is the usual serving.

*Cooler.*   This tall glass is for long drinks packed with ice. A popular size holds close to 16 ounces.

*Highball.*   A straight-side glass holding 10 to 12 ounces. A water glass of the same structure serves just as well.

*Iced Tea.*   The shape is optional. Any tall tumbler will do, though a capacity of about 12 ounces is the most popular size.

*Juice.*   This glass holds from 3 to 6 ounces. The shape is optional. An Old-Fashioned glass is often used instead.

*Liqueur.*   This tiny glass is also called "pony" and "cordial glass." Capacity ranges from 1 to 2 ounces.

*Old-Fashioned.*   The standard size has a total capacity of about 8 ounces, but the range is up to "doubles" of 16 ounces. They can be used for any drink on the rocks. Fill to within an inch of the top or ¾, full, depending on the size.

*Punch.*   Total capacity is usually 4 to 5 ounces. Fill it ⅔ full.

*Shot.*   For serving whiskey neat. Total capacity from about 1 to 3 ounces, with 1½ ounces the most popular size.

*Sour.* The stemmed glass holds about 4½ ounces; the Delmonico or straight-side holds 5 ounces. A cocktail or juice glass will serve just as well.

*Water.* The goblet is correct for formal lunches and dinners. At breakfast and away from the table, water is served in a straight-side tumbler. The usual total capacity is 10 ounces or a little more.

*Wine.* As a good general rule, fill a wineglass only about half full so that the aroma is caught in the upper part of the glass. There are several specific exceptions, though—champagne and sherry glasses are correctly filled to within about half an inch from the top, and it is also correct to fill any very small wineglass to the same level.

There is a wide range in the size of wineglasses, but today's trend is away from the very small ones for table wines, and the following are the most popular.

*All-purpose Wine.* Correct for either white or red wine. The bowl has straight sides and a total capacity of from 6 to 9 ounces. Fill it one-half or less full.

*Champagne.* The saucer-shape with a capacity of about 6 ounces is the most popular. This glass is also used for frozen daiquiris and champagne cocktails. Fill it to within about half an inch of the top. Champagne can also be served in a white-wine glass.

*Red Wine.* The classic bowl is slightly tulip shaped. Total capacity ranges from 8 to 10 ounces. Fill it about half full or less.

*Sherry.* The traditional shape is pointed. Total capacity from 2 to 3 ounces. Fill it to about half an inch from the top.

*White Wine.* The standard white wine glass *(left)* is somewhat smaller than the regular red wine glass, having a total capacity of from 5 to 8 ounces. The sides are straight. Fill it about half full, or less.

Only hock or Rhine wine is served in the glass shown at the right on the preceding page (though they can just as well be served in an ordinary wine-glass). Fill this glass to within half an inch of the brim.

## GLOVES

Even if a woman does not wear a hat, gloves are a standard part of her dress when she goes to a formal gathering such as a tea, reception, lunch, or dinner. Men have a wider latitude of choice, and as a general rule they wear gloves mainly for practical reasons—to protect the hands in bitter weather or when driving or playing a sport.

When gloves should be worn is of lesser importance by today's easygoing standards of dress than when, if they are worn, they must be taken off.

A man slips his right glove off for a handshake when he can do so quickly and easily. Otherwise, he shakes hands with his glove on without excuse or comment, never saying anything like "Pardon my glove." A man serving as an usher at a wedding, funeral, and so on does not remove his glove for a handshake.

A woman generally does not remove her right glove when shaking hands. Women standing in a receiving line keep their gloves on, and so do women going through a receiving line except when being presented to the President of the United States, the head of a foreign government, or a very high dignitary of the church. In these instances, they remove a short right glove or tuck the fingers of a long one in at the wrist.

A man standing in a receiving line does not wear gloves. A man going through a receiving line takes off his right glove if he has not left both gloves with his wraps.

Before a private audience with the Pope, both men and women are instructed to take off both gloves.

A man takes his gloves off as he enters a private dwelling unless he is sure that the door will be opened by an employee and a handshake will not be immediately required. Otherwise, he takes them off after entering and leaves them with his hat.

A woman keeps her gloves on when entering a private dwelling. She takes them off or leaves them on as she likes during a brief call or at a tea or reception, but always takes them off before taking refreshments. A woman wearing shoulder-length gloves with a formal evening dress takes them off completely at a dining table, but may tuck the fingers in at the wrist when taking food away from the dining table. Bracelets may be worn over gloves, but watches are not.

A woman does not properly put her gloves on a dining table at home or in a restaurant. She holds them in her lap, tucks them into her purse, or leaves them in any convenient place—just so long as she does not turn a man into a mobile checkroom by stowing them in his pocket.

Both men and women take off at least one glove when smoking under cover, and it is usual to do so on the street, except in winter weather, because nicotine quickly permeates a glove and leaves a strong, unpleasant odor, if not a discoloration.

Women and girls usually wear gloves to church the year around. Men generally wear gloves to church only in the winter. A woman leaves her gloves on or takes them off during the service, as she likes. A man takes his gloves off when he takes off his topcoat. Gloves must be removed before partaking of communion.

Children follow the rules that govern their elders.

See also CLOTHES; HAND-KISSING.

**GODPARENTS.**  See CHRISTENING AND BAPTISM.

# GOLF

"If you watch a game, it's fun.
If you play at it, it's recreation.
If you work at it, it's golf."—*Bob Hope*

Whether a golfer is playing on a public or private course, he is expected to observe the same rules concerning his fellow players and those who will follow.

Usually the rankest of greenhorns has somewhere picked up the information that a golfer is supposed to replace his divots, though doing so is only one of his responsibilities to the course. Everybody sends grass roots flying once in a while, but the beginner should be careful about where he makes wild practice swings that will scar the turf, particularly that of a putting green.

A fine putting green deserves the most respectful treatment, and no one is easily forgiven for leaving damaging traces of his passage over it—by flinging down his golf bag carelessly, using his club as a cane or crutch, or dragging the flagstick out instead of lifting it. Nor is anyone easily excused for plowing through a bunker and leaving deep footprints behind to make bad lies for following players. Needless to say, the course is no place to discard empty cigarette packages or other trash.

No one makes himself popular by arguing about the score, offering unsolicited advice, or postmorteming every hole. And the player who spends an eternity in the attempt to line up a shot from every angle both delays and annoys other players. So does the golfer who fails to allow faster players to play through. The regulation permitting only a five-minute search for a lost ball is another rule that should be carefully observed.

In tournament play, specific rules govern the order on the first tee, but in casual circumstances precedence is often decided by a flip of the coin, though a guest, an older player, or a woman is, in some situations, accorded the honor.

**CLOTHES.** As in many other sports, the main consideration is comfort and freedom of motion. Shorts and sport shirts are rapidly replacing the more formal golfing clothes on many courses, though some clubs do not approve of shorts for either men or women. The guest at a private club is wise to check on this matter with his host.

**Men's.** In summer weather, knee-length shorts and either a loose cotton sports shirt or the more close-fitting knitted shirt are most comfortable; in colder weather, slacks, sports shirt, and a sweater or loose jacket. Shoes should be rubber-soled (but not sneakers) or spiked—though spiked shoes are not worn into the clubhouse proper.

**Women's.** Bermuda shorts and a tailored shirt are suitable in summer on courses where shorts are permitted; otherwise, the standard shirtwaist-type golf dress is the usual outfit. For colder weather a wool skirt, a sweater over a shirt, and perhaps a loose jacket or windbreaker on top make a comfortable costume. Rubber-soled or spiked shoes are a necessity. Frilly or tight-fitting clothes, halter tops, high heels, toeless play shoes, and sneakers should be avoided.

**FEES AND TIPPING.** If a member of one golf club is the guest of a member of another club, there need not be any money problem. The guest can let his host pay all expenses, and in due course return the hospitality at his own club or in some other fashion. Under circumstances where the likelihood of being able to offer return hospitality is slim—if the guest is a visitor from a long way off, for instance—he offers to pay his own fees, but does not make a great issue of the matter if the host seems genuinely reluctant to have him do so. This is one of those situations that has to be played by ear.

A host pays a woman guest's fees just as a man always pays the expenses of a date—except under unusual circumstances.

At some clubs, tipping is prohibited. Where it is allowed, the rates vary regionally and according to the particular club, but a safe rule is to give the locker-room boy a dollar, and to give the caddie at least fifty cents a round in addition to the stated fee. If two players share a caddie, each tips as much as he would have for a separate caddie. At club tournaments a caddie's tip should be doubled or tripled. The caddie master is not tipped, nor is the golf pro, but in some circumstances it is permissible to send him a bottle at Christmas or to buy him a drink occasionally, depending on how well the player knows him and on the rules of the club where he works.

**SPECTATORS.** Golf is a game of concentration. During tournament play people in the gallery must remain out of the player's line of sight, stand still, and keep quiet when he is addressing the ball. Applause properly comes only after the shot is completed, and a request for a golfer's autograph is out of line before the round is completed.

### UNITED STATES GOLF ASSOCIATION RULES OF ETIQUETTE.

(Reprinted from the "Rules of Golf" by permission of the United States Golf Association. Copyright 1965, United States Golf Association.)

1. No one should move, talk or stand close to or directly behind the ball or the hole when a player is addressing the ball or making a stroke.
2. The player who has the honor should be allowed to play before his opponents or fellow-competitor tees his ball.
3. No player should play until the players in front are out of range.
4. In the interest of all, players should play without delay.
5. Players searching for a ball should allow other players coming up to pass them; they should signal to the players following them to pass, and should not continue their play until those players have passed and are out of range.
6. Before leaving a bunker, a player should carefully fill up all holes made by him therein.
7. Through the green, a player should ensure that any turf cut or displaced by him is replaced at once and pressed down, and that, after the players have holed out, any damage to the putting green made by the ball or the player is carefully repaired.
8. Players should ensure that, when dropping bags or the flagstick, no damage is done to the putting green, and that neither they nor their caddies damage the hole by standing close to the hole or in handling the flagstick. The flagstick should be properly replaced in the hole before the players leave the putting green.
9. When the play of a hole has been completed, players should immediately leave the putting green.

## GOOD-BYES

There are two major rules about saying good-bye that will see anyone through all social occasions in impeccable taste: (1) Do not leave without saying good-bye to the hostess. (2) Make it brief—say it and go, with no lingering at the door. There may be exceptions to the first rule, but it is hard to imagine a valid exception to the second.

**General Rules.** A visitor is supposed to make the first move toward ending a call, but life would be impossible if this rule were rigidly observed. If a visit lasts beyond reason or convenience and if courteous hints go unnoticed, it is entirely sensible and correct to get a caller on his way by some direct explanation—for example, "I have to get to the store," "I have an appointment at the beauty shop," or "I must meet John at six."

Anyone leaving a sizable party does not circulate to say good-bye after putting his wraps on—unless the hostess has appealed for aid in breaking up a gathering that is lasting too long. Instead, good-byes are said to a guest of honor, the host and hostess, and then a guest simply gets his wraps and slips out.

At a small gathering, either host or hostess sees a guest to the door. In an apartment, the host or hostess usually waits until the elevator comes if the entrance to it is in sight. A host takes a single woman guest to her car, or puts her in an elevator if she is leaving alone from a small gathering. At very large cocktail or other parties at home, or at receptions and dances in a club or hotel, the hostess accepts good-byes wherever the guest finds her, and need not go to the door. The same is true of the host. At enormous public or semipublic receptions or parties where the receiving line does not assemble for farewells, it is not necessary to say good-bye to host, hostess, or guest of honor.

A host always rises to say good-bye to any guest. So does a hostess, with few exceptions. The host, hostess, and any men at table rise if a woman guest must leave early, and either host or hostess shows the guest to the door, but only the host rises from a dining table to show a male guest to the door. Needless to say, leaving before a meal is finished is permissible only in an emergency. If the emergency is a serious one, the host and hostess break all rules in order to do whatever is practical to aid a distressed guest.

**IN BUSINESS.** Both men and women rise when saying good-bye to a caller in a private office, and often combine courtesy and speeding up the departure by going to the office door with the visitor.

**GUEST OF HONOR.** At a formal dinner party or other small, formal gathering, the rule is explicit: The guest of honor makes the first move to say good-bye, and all others stay until he does so, except in an emergency. This rule is widely ignored in everyday life. It is entirely correct for guests to explain that time is running out for their baby-sitter, that they must catch a train, or give any other good explanation for leaving before the guest of honor makes the move. At large receptions and parties, the guest of honor is obligated to stay to the end of the announced time, but others leave at any time that suits them.

**TELEPHONE.** The person who originates a telephone call makes the first move toward saying good-bye. This is another rule that can be observed generally, and broken with no more than a reasonable explanation if a hint does not get a long-winded caller off the line.

**GOSSIP.**  *See* CONVERSATION.

**GOVERNESSES.**  *See* HOUSEHOLD EMPLOYEES.

**GOVERNMENT OFFICIALS.**  *See* FORMS OF ADDRESS (Government).

# GRACE

"Blessings" and "grace" are used interchangeably in Christian households for the short prayer preceding meals, but "grace" is more widely used. It may be said with everyone at table standing behind his chair, or after all are seated. Nothing on the table, including the napkins, is touched until after the grace is finished. A guest realizes that a grace is to be said when he sees that the hostess does not unfold her napkin and is clearly waiting for quiet.

In Christian households, the head of the house may say grace, or members of the family, including children, may take turns at successive meals, or all may join in murmuring the words—perhaps of a familiar prayer. Quakers often start a meal with a silent blessing, joining hands or sitting with hands folded.

Guests may be asked to say grace, and it is the custom to ask a minister, elder, or other church official to do so if he is a guest. No matter what his belief, a guest is obligated to bow his head and maintain respectful silence during the saying of grace. Not to do so is an inexcusable discourtesy.

In observant Jewish households, blessings precede the meal and grace concludes it.

## GRADUATIONS AND COMMENCEMENTS

Both high school and college graduations usually are celebrated at a number of peripheral events—a dance, a parade, parties at various clubs, and so on— as well as by the actual graduation exercises at which speeches are made and diplomas presented. Families, of course, make a big point of being present, when possible, at the graduation exercises. Parents, dates, or both are often invited for the final day or so of the commencement-week celebration at a college.

Some schools provide announcements for the graduates to send out after the big event. If this is not the case, parents do not themselves order formal announcements, but tell the news by letter or in some other informal fashion. Even if announcements are available from the school, they should be sent only to relatives and close friends, as a general rule, because most people who receive an announcement feel obligated to send a present. However, all that is actually required is a note of congratulation, though it should be sent without much delay.

The invitations to attend a graduation are sometimes issued in the name of the principal and the faculty of the institution, sometimes in the name of the class itself. The graduate encloses a personal note, an engraved visiting card, or a blank card on which his name is written, with or without a message. Quite often an appropriate message turns the invitation into an announcement.

A limited number of places, depending on the size of the auditorium, is allotted to each graduate. Therefore, it is important to answer an invitation promptly so that the reserved place may be offered to someone else if the reply is a regret. Even if the invitation is refused, it is customary for the person honored by one to send a graduation present or, at the very least, a note of warm congratulation.

A standard form:

The Senior Class

of

Jefferson High School

requests the pleasure of your company

at its

Commencement Exercises

on Tuesday morning

June twenty-fifth

at eleven o'clock

Nineteen hundred and sixty-eight

Portland, Oregon

**GRAPEFRUIT.** *See* FRUITS.

**GRAPES.** *See* FRUITS.

## GRAVY

Gravy usually is served immediately after the dish it accompanies, whether offered by a maid or added by the host, though in a house with a limited staff or none, gravy often is passed from guest to guest after all plates have been served. The standard rule calls for putting gravy over or at the side of the meat only, and then taking a little with each forkful of potatoes or any other food, but today's custom permits ladling a spoonful on rice or potatoes. It is correct to eat the last drop of a delicious gravy, though not by sopping it with a piece of bread held in the fingers. A small piece of bread is broken off, put on the plate, and taken up with the fork.

## GRAVY BOATS AND BOWLS

Gravy may be poured from the lip of a gravy boat or taken with the gravy ladle. The ladle is returned to the gravy with its hollow up and the handle away from the pouring lip, not put on the attached base or the underplate unless the gravy is so hot that the spoon is uncomfortable to pick up. When gravy on a buffet table is kept extremely hot in a lighted chafing dish, the ladle should be put on a plate set adjacent to the serving dish for that purpose. Otherwise the handle becomes far too hot to touch.

## GREETING CARDS

Printed cards carrying good wishes for birthdays and other anniversaries and occasions are widely used and are a pleasant and correct form of communication with only a few exceptions. Such printed messages should never be used to express sympathy after a death or thanks for entertainment, and it is not usual to send cards on religious holidays not observed by both sender and receiver, with one exception. It is the happy custom today for many people of different faiths to celebrate December 25 as a kind of universal holiday for the exchange of gifts and good wishes.

## GUEST BOOKS AND REGISTERS

In a private dwelling, a guest book is never signed with the name preceded by "Miss," "Mrs.," "Mr.," "Dr.," or any other title (contrary to the correct signing of a hotel register). Married people usually sign separately, but one may sign for both, the signer putting his name last: Mary and John Smith, for example, if the husband is writing.

In a public guest register—at a museum, for instance—names are signed as in a hotel register. But unless it is requested, a street address is not given, only the town and state.

In art galleries and other exhibits, a guest register sometimes becomes a mailing list. Add the street address only if announcements are desired.

## GUEST TOWELS

Use them. A surprising number of guests baffle their hostesses by using the corner of a bath towel in order to "save" the pretty little hand towels she has provided. Guest towels should be returned neatly to the rack, though not put on top of the fresh ones or folded so carefully that they appear unused.

## GUESTS

Following are the general rules relating to a guest's behavior.

*Guests are obligated to:*

Accept or refuse all invitations promptly.

Arrive on time, or telephone if unavoidably detained.

Seek out the hostess as soon as possible at a big reception if there is no receiving line, and at some time speak with the guest of honor.

Help make a party successful without being a master of ceremonies, and
assist host and hostess whenever possible, without assuming their duties
or behaving like hired help.

Be moderate in drinking.

Leave at the proper hour.

Say or send thanks or acknowledgments appropriate to the occasion.

Pay for long-distance telephone calls before leaving.

Make good any damage to the possessions of the host or another guest.

Return hospitality in some way, though not necessarily in kind.

And in all other ways observe the admonition often given to children
before a party: "Don't make them glad twice—once when you come
and once when you go."

### Guests do not:

Break an engagement except in a real emergency.

Arrive late for a meal.

Monopolize the guest of honor or any other guest, or the host and hostess.

Act like a host (or hostess) and press drinks on other guests; adjust radio,
television, fire, or windows without being specifically asked; or give
orders or reprimands to servants or children.

Open closets, desk or bureau drawers, or medicine cabinets.

Offer to help the hostess change courses or serve if members of her family
or closer friends are present.

Discuss illness or diets at table.

Feed pets at table.

Remove jackets (men) without invitation.

Circulate with wraps on while saying good-bye if leaving early, or tie up
host or hostess at the door with lingering farewells.

**FOREIGN.** Americans today are playing host to more foreign visitors than
ever before. Cultural and student-exchange programs and the United Nations
are bringing us ever increasing numbers of people from countries all over the
world.

Entertaining a foreign guest requires more perception and tact than does
normal social hospitality. Both host and guest must play the role of a diplomat,
a difficult task even for those who do it on an official level. The following
suggestions make the experience easier and more rewarding:

Remember that American informality is likely to disconcert many foreigners.
It is best to avoid scanty or sloppy dress (which they may consider either indecent or insulting); backslapping and other physical familiarities; first names
at first meeting, and personal questions.

In conversation, stay clear of criticism of the guest's homeland. Asking
questions about his country and customs helps to launch a healthy exchange
of ideas, but host and hostess must be careful to phrase queries so that there
is no implication the guest's country is inferior or backward. Remarks that have
an undertone of bragging about our technical achievements and high standard
of living are scarcely music to a foreign guest's ears. Answer the guest's questions about America as objectively as possible. Do not talk about what things
cost unless specifically asked. We have a reputation of thinking of nothing but
money—don't reinforce it.

In issuing an invitation to a foreign guest, it is best to make sure he has
the telephone number, as well as instructions about how to reach the meeting
place and also an explicit understanding of the hour at which he is expected
and *for what.* In many countries the dinner hour is far later than is common
in the United States, and an invitation for eight-thirty, by which the host means

"after dinner," may be construed by the guest as an invitation to dine. He also should be given clear instructions as to appropriate dress.

Manners and customs vary from country to country. Take it for granted that the foreigner is being courteous by his own standards, even if they differ from ours, and make especially sure that children are briefed before a foreign guest arrives, so that they will make no innocently disconcerting comments.

If the guest has difficulty speaking English and the host does not speak the guest's language, it is tactful to help the stranger find the English word he gropes for, but not to correct his grammar or pronunciation unless asked a direct question about a specific word.

**OF HONOR.** Guests of honor usually are notified of their position by some such invitation as "I'd like to give a dinner [or tea, or whatever] for you." Acceptance means certain duties. Guests of honor are expected to arrive promptly at the time specified by the hostess so that they will be ready to meet all other guests as they arrive. There are a few exceptions to this rule. When the President of the United States, a king, queen, or other high dignitary of a government is attending any gathering, all other guests are assembled before the entrance of the guest of honor. A guest of honor at a public banquet is privileged to arrive just before dinner is served.

The guest of honor usually stands at the right of the hostess in a receiving line (*which see*, for exceptions), or if there is no receiving line, he stays near the door so that it is convenient for the hostess to present each new arrival without having to leave her post near the entrance.

Guests who arrive after a receiving line has broken up must find their way to the guest of honor at some time during a big tea, cocktail party, or reception. If host and hostess are otherwise occupied, latecomers introduce themselves and chat briefly with the honored guest, taking care not to monopolize him.

At a meal, a male guest of honor sits at the right of the hostess, and a female guest of honor at the host's right—except in official circles, where rank takes precedence. (*See* MEALS AND THEIR SERVICE and WASHINGTON.)

A guest of honor at a meal should leave at a reasonable hour since, by formal rules, other guests may not leave first. At an afternoon tea, cocktail party, or formal reception at any hour, other guests leave if it suits them after a stay of about half an hour. The guest of honor is expected to stay through the announced time, such as "from five to eight," and then depart. This rule need not be rigidly observed. When the guest of honor at a cocktail party does not leave promptly at the end of the time specified on the invitation, it may be a signal to other guests that the hostess has planned a small dinner party to follow. In this case, those guests not specifically invited to stay on are wise not to linger.

At a small gathering, guests say good-bye to the guest of honor as well as to host and hostess. At a very large party, a farewell to either host or hostess is sufficient.

It is not obligatory, but it is a customary attention for a guest of honor to send flowers to his hostess either before the party (in time for her to arrange them as part of the decoration of her house) or the day after, with a note of thanks.

**OVERNIGHT.**    *See* HOUSEGUESTS.

**UNINVITED.** In many suburban and rural communities, friends often drop in for a brief call without warning, but it is never a mistake to telephone first and make sure that a call will be convenient. In cities, not even the closest friends arrive without telephoning first.

It is absurd to drop everything for a person who has turned up at his convenience without any consideration for his host's plans. A host or hostess is under no obligation to uninvited guests except to turn them away courteously if their visit is ill-timed. All that is required is an honest explanation: "I wish I could ask you in, but we're just sitting down to dinner," or, "I'm rushing to get ready for a club meeting. Won't you come over tomorrow afternoon?"

The uninvited guest or drop-in neighbor is obligated to accept a courteous excuse readily and gracefully, and take himself off without making any such countersuggestion as, "Go ahead—I'll wait," or, "Let me help you."

See the Index for the list of separate entries relating to behavior on special occasions.

## GUIDES

Government employees in uniform, such as Park Service personnel, who act as lecturers or guides should not be offered tips. In some churches, especially in foreign countries, a regular employee who conducts sightseers around expects a tip. When in doubt, offer one. If it is not appropriate it will be courteously refused. In this case, a donation to the contribution box is obligatory. Hunting, fishing, and camping guides usually expect a tip of 10 to 20 percent. Taxi drivers hired by the hour or half-day as driver-guides are tipped the usual 15 to 20 percent.

Drivers or conductors of sight-seeing buses and boats make it quite evident whether or not they expect tips by where they stand or by a positive hint at the end of a tour. Guides hired individually expect a tip.

When with a group, a sure way to unpopularity is to monopolize the guide's attention or to be aggressive about taking the front row at every stop.

Guides hired by the day usually take lunch with a single patron, a couple, or family group, and at the patron's expense. Guides for a large group pay for their own lunches.

**GUNS.**  See HUNTING AND SHOOTING.

# H

## HAIR

One of the more curious sights in some small towns and in certain city suburbs is teen-agers and young women with their hair skinned up in curlers, not infrequently in full sight of the beaux they intend to dazzle with the resulting curls later in the day. By any rules, this is unhappy taste. Curlers, even under a scarf, belong at home.

Any but the briefest rearranging of one's hair is out of bounds in public, especially at a restaurant table or in an office. It is only sensible to use a pocket comb briefly on windblown hair—immediately after entering a restaurant, for example. Otherwise, fussing with one's hairdo is taboo. And compulsively tugging at or curling a wisp of hair and repeatedly smoothing or touching the hair are at best unattractive mannerisms.

## HANDBAGS

It is equally correct for a visitor to leave her handbag with her coat or take it into a living room, but she does not carry a street bag with her into a dining room. A very small evening purse may be taken to the dining table, but it should be kept on the lap, not put on the cloth.

At a nightclub or a dance, it is customary to lay a small evening bag on the table, but in a restaurant handbags are kept off the table if the rules are followed. A big handbag may be hung on the arm or back of a chair, put on a spare chair, or even on the floor. A small handbag is tucked onto the seat beside the diner or held in her lap.

## THE HANDICAPPED

It is poor judgment to tell a joke or make flippant remarks about the handicapped, since often one has no way of knowing whether or not, among his listeners, there may be someone with a good friend or relative whose disability is a heartbreak.

When dealing with anyone who has a disability of any kind—from stuttering to the infirmity of age—offer any assistance that may be needed, matter-of-factly. Don't make it more conspicuous by oversolicitousness.

The curiosity of children nearly always is aroused by any striking variation in normal gait, appearance, or speech. A child should be trained not to point or stare and not to ask questions within the hearing of anyone with a handicap. Incidentally, children usually need to be reminded that the blind are not necessarily also deaf.

**THE BLIND.** Following are recommendations from The Lighthouse, the New York Association for the Blind, on how to deal considerately with those who cannot see.

In offering to aid a blind person across a street, do not take his arm. Offer yours. The movement of your body will tell him whether he should step up or down. If you need to touch the blind, do so lightly. Don't shove or push them.

In a general conversation, address the blind person by name if he is the one expected to reply. Otherwise, he may not know the remark is addressed to him.

Identify yourself when you join a blind person. Many of the blind conceal their handicap with such resource and grace that sighted people sometimes forget to speak as they approach so that they can be recognized.

Avoid phrasings, descriptions, or gestures that require sight for interpreting them—"about this long" or "the blue of my dress," for instance. Be careful that a shrug or other gesture that modifies your words for the sighted is explained for the blind. Your words by themselves may carry the reverse of the meaning intended.

Don't put a plate or drink in the hand of a blind person as you would serve a small child. Say, "Here is your glass," and wait for the responding gesture. His hand will come out naturally, and then the drink can be put into it without any conspicuous effort.

A blind guest will feel more comfortable and relaxed in new surroundings if he is given a brief description of the room so that he knows the location of doors and the general placement of furniture, particularly of small tables and footstools that could be a hazard to him.

**THE DEAF.** Compromise is required of everyone concerned when challenged by the handicap of deafness. No matter how trying it may be to speak in a raised voice, it is at best thoughtless to maintain part of a conversation at a level that makes a slightly deaf person strain to hear. It is deliberately rude to make remarks below the hearing range of a deaf person sharing a conversation. It also is risky. Not all hearing loss is the same. Sometimes only the higher tones are involved, and the low-pitched aside not meant to be heard may be the one remark that will get through clearly and distinctly. On the other hand, it is inconsiderate of a deaf person to demand abnormally raised voices from everyone in his family—unless his affliction is one that cannot be helped by any mechanical aid.

The deaf deserve every consideration because of the difficulties they meet in the use of hearing aids. Though these devices have been enormously improved in recent years, the best of them are trying to wear in many circumstances. Hearing aids do not select among sounds as the ear does. They may magnify music, wind, the hum of a motor, and other background noises to a steady roar that is nerve-racking to endure for any extended time. Sharp, sudden loud sounds can be extremely painful because they are also greatly magnified, and so it is important to give fair warning to a person wearing a hearing aid if a loud noise is unavoidable.

The fact that a hearing aid is in place does not necessarily mean that it is turned up to effective volume. Therefore, care should be taken not to startle a deaf person by approaching from behind and touching him before he is aware that someone is near.

The first onset of deafness is a particularly trying time. The afflicted person very often refuses to admit his growing disability and covers his own fear of it by irritable complaints that no one speaks distinctly anymore, that he is surrounded by mush-mouthed mumblers; or, rather than ask for raised voices, he withdraws into a seeming inattentiveness. The only way to help the deaf get through the troubling period before a hearing aid is accepted as a necessity is to remember not to speak in a low or indistinct mutter with the head turned away, and, if asked to repeat a remark, to do so without a show of impatience or any implication that the deaf person is too stupid to understand rather then unable to hear.

The important thing to remember is that no one is deaf on purpose. Use imagination in dealing with this disability, which waits for many of us who attain an advanced age.

# HANDIWORK

It is a marked rudeness to knit, crochet, or do any other handiwork at a concert, lecture, or public gathering of similar nature. Even if the work can be done almost automatically, the movement of the hands is distracting to others, and can only be considered an insult to the speaker or performer. On an informal occasion among intimate friends, a hostess may pick up some handiwork—but only if she can proceed with it so casually that it seems in no way to distract her attention from her guests. As for a guest—she does not take out her handiwork unless she is following the example of her hostess. When in doubt, best leave such projects at home in the workbasket.

# HANDKERCHIEFS

Handkerchiefs of linen or cotton are the first choice for both men and women, with linen preferred. Silk and chiffon handkerchiefs are not really useful for mopping the brow or blowing the nose. Often a man wears a silk handerchief as a scarf or ascot or as a decorative accessory in the breast pocket. And a woman finds a big chiffon square an attractive accessory with certain dresses, but carries in addition a practical handkerchief tucked into her purse or pocket.

**CHILDREN.** Even to parties, children do not properly carry extremely expensive or heavily embroidered handkerchiefs that look as if they were borrowed from their parents. Little boys wear white linen ones for dress-up. For everyday, the usual choice is linen or cotton with border stripes in a subdued color—though today a great many parents send small children off to school with a supply of tissues instead of, or in addition to, a handkerchief.

**MEN.** Men commonly wear two handkerchiefs—one mainly for show in the breast pocket, and a supplementary one in a hip pocket. The handkerchief in the breast pocket should be crisp, and folded neatly but casually, rather than with the points lined up too precisely.

**Daytime.** White, white with a colored border or stripes, and a pale shade with perhaps a contrasting border are all appropriate, and initials may be white or colored. For everyday occasions, the color of the handkerchief is usually geared to the color of the tie rather than to the suit; but with formal daytime dress a white handkerchief with a white initial is the correct choice.

**Evening.** With a dark suit and white shirt, a man chooses a white handkerchief. With black tie or tails, he wears a very sheer fine white linen handkerchief either plain or initialed in white, gray, black, or a combination of those colors (never in any other color).

**Initials.** A man uses the initial of his last name if a handkerchief is marked with only one initial.

**WOMEN.** There are only a few rules about handkerchiefs for women. Squares of brilliant solid color or with printed designs are effective with sports and informal clothes, and with many street dresses and suits, but not appropriate with dinner and evening dresses. Extremely handsome handkerchiefs with more embroidery than linen belong in evening bags, and white is the first choice for dressy occasions. However, fine white linen with white or colored initials and a moderate amount of fine handwork is appropriate and widely used for most occasions, day and night.

**Initials.** If only one initial is used, it should be that of the first name—just the reverse of the rule for men.

## HAND-KISSING

The American woman traveling abroad needs to be prepared to accept a kiss of the hand gracefully, but today this pretty formality is encountered increasingly often in the United States as well because of the growing number of foreign visitors. The rules have been drastically changed within the last twenty years. When grandmother made the Grand Tour, it was not correct to kiss the hand of a young unmarried woman, or to kiss a woman's hand before noon or anywhere outdoors except at a social event such as a garden party—and never when she was wearing gloves. Today, Europeans kiss the hands of girls as well as women, uninhibitedly, at any time of day or evening, indoors or out, and plant a gallant smack directly on the back of a hand with far more fervor than once was considered correct. Such salutes are entirely permissible today, though American men generally confine themselves to the formal hand-kiss.

The formal hand-kiss is a gesture rather than an actual kiss. It is used in greeting and farewell when a handshake between a man and woman would be customary in this country. The man takes the woman's hand and bows slightly as he raises it, her palm down, to within a few inches of his lips. If his lips touch her hand at all, it usually is with no more than a brief brushing. The palm of the hand is never kissed in public.

It takes two to make a hand-kiss graceful. An awkward fumbling results if a woman, not alert to the possibility of a hand-kiss, follows through with a handshake while a man is beginning to bow over her fingers. She should extend her hand as she would for a handshake, and then let the man take charge, relaxing her arm so that is not raised like a semaphore. She does not demand a hand-kiss by offering her hand palm down, most especially on the street.

The rule still holds that a man does not kiss a gloved hand. A European sometimes will turn back a short glove or plant a kiss on the wrist above it, however. It is correct to bow over a woman's hand when she is wearing a ball-length glove, but not to raise it fully to the lips.

## HANDS

The way the hands are used reveals—decisively and quickly—good or bad training in the basic rules of social conduct. It is important for youngsters to learn to sit and to stand with their hands easily relaxed in the lap or at the sides, rather than habitually thrust into their pockets, clasped fore or aft, or perched on the hips.

**MANNERISMS.** Controlled gestures add effective emphasis to words, but compulsively repeated mannerisms like stroking the hair, fingering a necklace or other ornaments, jingling coins, tugging at one's clothing, rubbing the hands together, and drumming the fingers are signs of a lack of ease that often communicate nervousness to others.

**NAILS.** Although it is almost a necessity to carry a pocket nail file in any big, dirty city, it is taboo to use one anywhere in the sight of others.

In general, girls do not wear nail polish before high school age, though customs vary in different circles and communities. Many men buff their nails, but conservative taste bans the glassy shine of clear lacquer. Fashions in the color of nail polish for girls and women are constantly changing, but one rule remains the same: It is better to wear no polish at all than polish chipped or in need of renewal. Men wear their nails short and rounded. So do children. Usually, women wear their nails considerably longer and somewhat more pointed, though extravagantly long talons are best left to the birds.

**POINTING.** Pointing is so natural a gesture that it is hard for children to learn the good old rule: Point at an object or to indicate a direction, but try not to point at a person, especially in public.

**SNAPPING.** Snapping the fingers to attract attention (except the attention of a dog) is best avoided because quite a few people take it as an insult. Waiters, bellboys, and porters are not in a position to show resentment at being so summoned, but they are quite likely to feel it.

## HANDSHAKING

A woman makes the first gesture toward a handshake with a man, and a younger woman waits for a much older woman to offer her hand. It is entirely correct for a woman to bow instead of shaking hands, unless she is a hostess, in which case she shakes hands with all guests in greeting and farewell. When stopping to talk with a man on the street, a woman may offer her hand but usually does not, since his right hand is engaged with tipping his hat. In this country women rarely shake hands with other women when introduced, but European women customarily do so.

A man always shakes hands on being introduced to another man unless he must make an awkward effort to reach across others to do so. A very much older man makes the first gesture to a younger one. A host shakes hands with all guests in greeting and farewell.

A firm though light grasp is far more attractive for both men and women than a flipper-like limberness, but men will have the gratitude of women if they remember that a strong grip can be painful, especially to anyone wearing rings.

In general, a woman does not take off her glove when shaking hands, though the rules require it in certain circumstances—when being presented to the President, for example. A woman in a receiving line keeps her gloves on, and so does a woman going through a receiving line (except as noted above). A man removes at least his right glove when going through a receiving line.

If it can be done easily and quickly, a man slips off his right glove before shaking hands, but need not do so if he is burdened with parcels or if it is in any other way inconvenient. In such cases, he correctly leaves his glove on without apology, never saying anything like "Pardon my glove."

An usher wearing white gloves at a wedding does not take one off if a guest proffers his hand in response to the usher's formal bow.

Refusing a proffered hand is an insult unless some sensible reason can be given as explanation, such as having a demonstrably dirty or wet hand.

**HANDWRITING.**  *See* CORRESPONDENCE.

**HANGOVERS.**  *See* INTOXICATION.

# HATS

Today the wearing of a hat is largely a matter of local custom and individual preference—not of etiquette—and men and women need not wear hats on a great many occasions where, not so long ago, it was considered a breach of manners to go hatless. But hat-wearers are still expected to observe the following rules:

**MEN.** Men are required to take off their hats on so very many occasions that some mistakenly remove them when it is entirely unnecessary. Except when greeting an acquaintance, a man properly leaves his hat on in a store, bank, post office, or other public building; in a public vehicle; in the lobbies and corridors of offices, schools, hotels, and apartment buildings; and in the elevators of stores and public buildings (since in these places the elevators are considered extensions of the aisles and corridors).

Following are the occasions when a man is required to take his hat off and leave it off, rather than merely tip it:

On the street or in any other public place when stopping to speak with a woman acquaintance, a much older man, a clergyman, or anyone else who deserves especial respect (though outdoors he does not remain uncovered if the weather is bad).

On entering any place of worship (with the exception of Orthodox and Conservative Jewish synagogues, where a man may be offered a skullcap to wear instead).

During a prayer, burial, dedication, wedding, or any other religious ceremony held outdoors, except Orthodox or Conservative Jewish ceremonies.

During the passing of the hearse in a ceremonial funeral cortege.

During the ceremonies of raising and lowering our national flag, and while the flag is passing in a parade.

During the playing of the national anthem.

During the Pledge of Allegiance.

On entering a private office or residence.

On entering the inner lobby of a theater.

On entering a restaurant.

And, customarily, when sharing the elevator of a hotel or apartment house with a woman, even if she is a stranger, unless his arms are full of bundles or the elevator so jammed as to make the courteous gesture impossibly inconvenient and awkward.

**Tipping the Hat.** A man actually tips his hat by raising it briefly. Touching the brim serves the same purpose; though a bit more casual, it is an entirely correct substitute. A man tips or touches his hat:

When passing a girl or woman of his acquaintance. (Very little girls especially love this courtesy from grown men, though it is not required for them.)

When someone greets a woman he is accompanying, and when she greets anyone.

When a man he is accompanying greets a woman.

When he accidentally blocks a woman's path, bumps into her, or has any other reason to say, "Excuse me."

When asking directions or other information from a passing stranger; under most circumstances, when speaking with a woman receptionist or information clerk.

When he offers his seat to a woman in a public conveyance; when anyone offers a seat to a woman he is accompanying or in any other way shows her a courtesy.

When greeting another man in passing, and always when greeting a clergyman, a much older man, or anyone else who deserves especial respect.

(A man usually does not tip his hat to another man when they stop to talk or when he joins a group of men, especially if they shake hands, since it is awkward to tip his hat and shake hands too. And a woman with her wits about her does not offer her hand to a man with bundles in one hand when he is reaching for his hat with the other.)

**WOMEN.** It is customary for a woman to wear a hat to a formal lunch or an official reception, but by today's relaxed standards not essential.

A hat or other acceptable head covering should be worn when entering churches of certain denominations for a service—notably Catholic and Episcopal churches and Jewish Orthodox and Conservative synagogues. In some parts of the world this rule is rigidly enforced, though in many localities in this country it is not enforced or observed nearly so widely as in the past. When in doubt, it is always safest to wear a hat to a religious ceremony, no matter where it is celebrated.

A woman takes her hat off on arrival for dinner at a private dwelling, but may correctly either leave her hat on or take it off at a lunch, tea, or any other afternoon party. She usually takes her hat off at a reception at which there is to be dancing, but need not unless she prefers to.

Tiny hats need not be taken off in the theater, but it is only considerate to remove a hat that quite obviously will obstruct the view for others—and to do so without waiting to be asked.

## HELLO

"Hello" and variants like "Hi" are the greetings most widely used in the United States among friends and contemporaries. "Hello" is correct on all occasions except after a formal introduction under formal circumstances—in a receiving line, for example—when "How do you do" is the standard response. "How do you do" is also the preferred answer from the very young when they are introduced to their elders, and from anyone introduced to a very dignified or elderly person.

See also TELEPHONE MANNERS.

## HERALDIC DEVICES

Many of the hundreds of thousands of families in the United States who are entitled to use a coat of arms do not realize that they have that privilege. The only requirement is descent in the direct male line (from father to sons) from an ancestor who had the right to use a coat of arms as a distinguishing personal, family, or clan mark. It is not correct to adopt a coat of arms simply because unrelated people of the same surname have a proved right to use it, and American families who wish to establish their right to use a coat of arms must first trace connection to the first ancestor in the direct male line who emigrated to this country. (Public libraries and state historical societies will produce a list of genealogical societies and publications that may be of help.) Then application can be made to the Office of Arms in the country from which the family emigrated, and it will supply corroborating information for a small fee. (A list of such bureaus can be found in *Heraldry and You* by J. A. Reynolds, Thomas Nelson & Sons, New York, 1961.)

Contrary to the belief of many people, the right to use a heraldic device may, but does not necessarily, indicate descent from a titled ancestor, though it is a right to be proud of as evidence of a connection with a long line of known forebears, as a little knowledge of the history of heraldry reveals.

When coats of arms first came into use in Europe in the twelfth century, they were, literally, padded coats or sleeveless jerkins worn over or in place of armor by anyone—titled or not. Since all coats and all armor looked more or less alike, and since a warrior's face was hidden by his helmet, some distinguishing mark was necessary so that people on his side could identify him in battle. Such identification was first painted, later appliquéd or embroidered, on his coat. Later, such devices (known as "charges") were emblazoned on shields. Later yet, as distinguishing family marks, they came into wide use on household articles, letter paper, and so on.

In order to understand the correct use of various heraldic devices by both men and women it is necessary to know what they are and the meanings of certain terms.

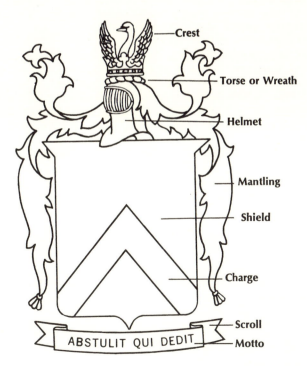

**TERMS AND DEFINITIONS.** The following, selected from the extremely long list of heraldic terms, are the words most frequently used:

*Achievement:* the entire body of the heraldic device, with all its component parts. The main ones are the shield, crest, and motto.

*Argent:* silver.

*Azure:* blue.

*Charge:* any emblem on the shield, such as a fleur-de-lis, griffon, lion, or geometric design.

*Coat of Arms:* the entire body of the device; sometimes loosely used to designate the shield or lozenge alone.

*Crest:* the topmost element of the achievement. Originally, the crest was the identifying device mounted on top of the helmet, attached usually by a wreath or coronet. Some coats of arms do not have a crest, since many countries never employed this device. Also, crests in some cases were not added until later, and then simply as an embellishment. Though the term "family crest" is often used to mean "coat of arms," the word "crest" is not technically correct as a synonym for "coat of arms."

*Dexter:* the right-hand side of the shield, from the viewpoint of the person carrying one.

*Divisions:* traditional configurations or areas into which a shield can be partitioned. They are classified as ordinaries and subordinaries, and are too numerous to give in detail.

*Dominant Symbol:* the main device on the shield.

*Field:* the face of the shield.

*Gules:* red.

*Helmet:* the (often stylized) rendering of a helmet, surmounted by the torse and crest, placed above the shield.

*Impale:* to combine two coats of arms on one shield by dividing the shield in half vertically and showing one full coat of arms on each half.

*Lozenge:* a small, vertically lengthened, diamond-shaped figure on which the main devices from the shield may be displayed. A lozenge is used only by a woman, and in English usage she is permitted only a lozenge, never the full achievement. Long-established American practice permits a woman to use the full arms of the man of her family—her father or her husband.  *See* illustration.

**LOZENGE**

*Mantling:* stylized drapery from the helmet, often shown around the shield.

*Motto:* the family motto—often, originally, a battle cry—set below the shield on a ribbon. The motto is a feature that may or may not be an inheritable part of the coat of arms. By tradition, it was a matter of individual choice, and so, contrary to popular belief, it may be changed or dispensed with if desired.

*Or:* gold.

*Purpure:* purple.

*Quarters:* the fourths of the field, when it is so divided.

*Ribbon:* the same as scroll.

*Sable:* black.

*Scroll:* the ribbon below the shield that carries the motto.

*Shield:* the area or configuration on which the emblems that make up the charge are shown. Usually, it is at least roughly in the shape of a shield, though somewhat stylized.

*Sinister:* the left-hand side of the shield, from the viewpoint of the man carrying one.

*Supporters:* the animals or human figures supporting the shield—a sign of either rank or power. They are not properly used by American families.

*Torse:* the wreath that attaches the crest to the helmet.

*Vert:* green.

*Wreath:* same as the torse.

**USES.** All males inherit the right to use the family coat of arms, and they pass this right along to their sons. A girl uses her father's coat of arms only until she marries. After marriage, she uses her husband's coat of arms, if he has one, or none. (There are certain exceptions, and also differences in rules in European use, but for all practical purposes this rule is the important one to know and follow in this country.)

If, however, the girl has no brothers to inherit her father's arms, she is the heiress to them, which means that she has the right to continue using them and, when she marries, to impale them with those of her husband, if he has a coat of arms. Her children will then quarter the impaled arms (see accompanying illustrations).

### HOW TWO COATS OF ARMS ARE COMBINED

**STAFFORD**

**FITZGERALD**

**IMPALED ARMS**
of the couple when Mr. Stafford
marries Miss Fitzgerald

**QUARTERED ARMS**
used by their children

*Announcements. See* INVITATIONS *below.*

*Bookplates.* The entire heraldic achievement is often reproduced, since the plate is large enough to accommodate it. If full color is used, the name printed underneath should appear in black. A bookplate may also be printed in a single color—some shade of the dominant color in the arms.

*China.* The crest or the full achievement may be used on china, in original colors or in gold or silver.

*Clothing.* The crest or the shield may be embroidered on personal linen or worn on the pocket of a blazer; not common practice for an American, however.

*Decorations.* Painted, embroidered, or tapestry reproductions of family coats of arms are often hung on the wall as a decoration.

*Invitations.* Formal invitations and announcements use a very small coat of arms centered at the top of the page and preferably embossed without color. (Some etiquette authorities sanction the use of the crest alone.) On wedding invitations and announcements from the bride's parents, the device of the bride's family alone appears. If the couple announce their marriage themselves, it is correct either to combine their coats of arms on a single shield or to use the now-shared arms of the husband, but never the wife's coat of arms alone.

*Leather Goods.* The same representation of the coat of arms used on stationery may be stamped in gold on small leather articles such as hand luggage, wallets, key cases, and so on. The same representation used on bookplates may be used on larger luggage.

*Linens.* The crest, shield, or the full achievement may be embroidered on table or bed linen, towels, handkerchiefs, and so on. The rules are the same as for "Silver" below.

*Menu Cards.* The same device, in color, that is employed on stationery may be used.

*Personal Articles.* By American usage, jewelry, cigarette cases, and other such personal articles may, if space permits, carry the full coat of arms. For small objects, however, men often prefer to use only the crest and women a lozenge.

*Place Cards.* Same as "Menu Cards," above.

*Silver.* The proper arms to be engraved on new silver given as a wedding present are those of the bride's family, not those of her husband. This practice stems from the fact that gifts to a bride are considered part of her dowry. If a wedding gift of engraved silver is given by the family of the bridegroom, however, it is always the coat of arms of his family that is used. Once the couple is married, a gift of new silver is engraved with the husband's arms or with combined arms (impaled) if they are used by the couple.

The size of the engraving and the amount of the achievement appearing on each piece are wholly dependent upon its size. Large items such as chafing dishes, coffee servers, trays, or even sugar bowls will accommodate the whole achievement, if this is desired. On small pieces, it is better to use only the crest. In cases where the coat of arms lacks a crest, the dominant symbol on the shield is used.

*Stationery.* The representation of the coat of arms is carried at top-center of the page on family stationery. Since, of necessity, the imprint will be very small, the mantle and helmet may correctly be omitted in order to enlarge the size of the shield. In that case, the crest (if any) would rest on the wreath, directly. above the shield. A woman who follows American practice may use the entire coat of arms on her personal stationery or a lozenge.

For formal invitations color is not used, and the design is embossed in white. On letter and notepaper, the imprint may be shown in the dominant color of the arms.

## HICCUPS

Hiccups are a misfortune, not a social error, however socially embarrassing they may be. Best manners call for making as little of them as possible, since attention often aggravates the attack. The hiccuper ignores a small one and takes the quick bite or swallow that usually stops the attack. If the hiccup is resoundingly loud, he says, "Sorry," once. There is no need to repeat the apology after each succeeding hiccup.

## HIGHBALLS

The highball, a mixed drink of spirits and water or a carbonated beverage, is served with ice in a straight-sided, stemless glass somewhat taller than the standard water glass.

Highballs are served at cocktail parties and, very frequently, an hour or so after dinner. A guest is privileged to ask for one instead of a cocktail before dinner, but a hostess does not automatically serve highballs at that time since such a long drink usually diminishes the appetite rather than fires it.

## HITCHHIKING

In some states, hitchhiking is unlawful. Lawful or not, there is only one rule of safety, sense, and good behavior about hitchhiking for children: DON'T. Hundreds of thousands of youngsters thumb rides safely each day—but never a year passes without its series of tragic abuses of little hitchhikers. It is not easy to forbid hitchhiking where "everyone does it," but responsible parents have no choice, and drivers should help them by refusing to pick up children.

It is equally difficult for a good-hearted driver to skim past a weary, anxious, adult hitchhiker, but the only discreet procedure for women and teen-age drivers is to ignore their appeal, and let grown men or couples be the good Samaritans. All drivers should remember that they have legal responsibilities to any passenger, friend or stranger.

It is only common sense for a driver bound for a distant destination to evade answering the direct question "How far are you going?" Otherwise, he may find it awkward to jettison a tiresome or otherwise undesirable passenger before the end of the run. If a hitchhiker does not give his name and destination when entering a car, the driver should ask for that information. A driver is not obligated to give his own name in return, though he usually gives his last name as a routine courtesy, but does best to volunteer no other personal information.

## HOLIDAYS

In this country we have eight holidays that are observed nationwide by the closing of federal and state offices, schools, stores, and other places of business. But that is just the beginning of the list of holidays observed to almost the same degree in many (though not all) of our states and territories. The anniversary of its admission to the Union is celebrated as a legal holiday in nearly every state, and travelers are often disconcerted to find stores and businesses in a state closed up tight for some other local legal holiday. Far more important as a matter of etiquette, however, are the religious holidays of the various faiths, since these are often celebrated not only as holidays from business but also by other special observances. More than one hostess has been embarrassed to discover, too late, that the date she has chosen for a party is that of a holy day observed by a number of her hoped-for guests.

**NATIONALLY OBSERVED HOLIDAYS.** Technically, we have no national holidays as such, since each state has the right to decide which holidays will be observed within its borders. But for all practical purposes, the following can be considered national holidays because they are always declared legal holidays in all states:

New Year's Day—January 1
Washington's Birthday—February 22
Memorial or Decoration Day—May 30
    (observed in some southern states May 31)
Independence Day—July 4

Labor Day—first Monday in September
Veterans Day—November 11
Thanksgiving Day—fourth Thursday in November
Christmas—December 25

**OTHER HOLIDAYS WIDELY OBSERVED.** In many states, schools and some places of business are closed on certain other days, though federal offices remain open and mail is delivered. Consult a *World Almanac,* available in any library, for the full list of exceptions in various states, territories, and possessions of the United States.

Lincoln's Birthday—February 12
  (all but 17 states)
Columbus Day—October 12
  (all but 16 states)
General Election Day—first Tuesday after the first Monday in November (a half-holiday in all but 17 states; customarily observed only in years of general or presidential elections)

**RELIGIOUS HOLIDAYS.** With the exception of Christmas, religious holidays are not observed by federal declaration, and so mail is delivered and other government offices are open as usual. However, in many communities, offices and stores are closed or staff members of the particular faith are released—on Good Friday and on Yom Kippur, to give just two examples.

Exact dates cannot be given for most religious holidays, since they do not fall on the same date each year. Easter is an example; it falls on the first Sunday after the first full moon occurring on March 21 or any of the twenty-eight days following that date. Therefore, Mardi Gras, the Lenten period, and Assumption fall on different dates each year. The same is true of Jewish holy days because they are also controlled by the lunar calendar.

Among the most important Christian holidays are:

Shrove Tuesday (Mardi Gras)—the day before Ash Wednesday
Ash Wednesday—the first day of Lent
Lent—the forty days preceding Easter
Palm Sunday—the Sunday before Easter
Good Friday—the Friday before Easter
Easter—March or April
Ascension Day—ten days before Pentecost
Pentecost (Whitsunday)—May or June
All Saints' Day—November 1
First Sunday of Advent—November or December
Christmas—December 25
Twelfth Night—the eve of Epiphany
Epiphany—(Three Kings' Day)—January 6

Among the most important Jewish holidays are:

Rosh Hashanah (New Year) ⎫ September
Yom Kippur (Day of Atonement) ⎬ or
Succoth (Feast of Tabernacles) ⎭ October
Hannukah (Feast of Lights)—December
Purim (Feast of Lots)—February or March
Passover (marks exodus from Egypt)—March or April
  (Passover occurs about the same time as Easter, and lasts for eight days.)
Shavuoth (Feast of Weeks)—May or June

**SPECIAL FESTIVE DAYS.** Many people observe the following days with parties or the exchange of gifts or both.

Valentine's Day—February 14
April Fool's Day—April 1
Mother's Day—second Sunday in May
Father's Day—third Sunday in June
Halloween—October 31

**HOME.**   *See* HOUSE AND HOME.

## HOME MANNERS

Good manners are not something to be put on and off like a coat. Manners within the immediate family circle are properly more relaxed than when anyone else is present, but if the basic rules of good manners are consistently broken at home, conspicuous mistakes inevitably will turn up in public.

Children who are required to eat decently, answer properly, and give their mother the common courtesy of notice when they leave the house or return to it will have far fewer problems when "company" manners are needed.

**HOMEMAKER.**   *See* HOUSEWIFE.

**HONEYMOONS.**   *See* WEDDINGS.

## THE HONORABLE

"The Honorable" is a courtesy title. In this country we use it only when addressing or introducing certain high government officials.
   *See* FORMS OF ADDRESS (Government).

## HONOUR

The traditional spelling on formal engraved invitations is "honour." This is the form most often used, though it is entirely correct to instruct the stationer to use "honor" if the standard American spelling of the word is preferred.

## HORS d'OEUVRES

This is the French term for an appetizer served as a first course. In the United States, we usually use "hors d'oeuvre" for an appetizer served at table, and use "canapé" for the small bits of food that may be taken up in the fingers and that are served with drinks away from the table. It is also correct, however, to call cocktail appetizers "hors d'oeuvres."

## HORSE SHOWS

More than 650 horse shows are sponsored by the American Horse Show Association, and there is no telling how many hundreds more gymkhanas, rodeos, and other horseback competitions and exhibits are big yearly events at fairs, clubs, and children's camps.

   The range of formality is enormous. The Tuesday opening night of the eight-day National Horse Show held in Madison Square Garden in New York is a major social event of the autumn, as is "ball night," always the following Friday. On those two evenings many white ties are seen. Black Tie is customary for the spectators in the boxes as well as in other choice seats—though plenty of street clothes are seen elsewhere in the huge house on any evening. Much the same rules of dress are observed on opening nights at the Chicago, Washington, and San Francisco shows, among other major yearly events. But for any outdoor show from the noted Devon Horse Show in Philadelphia to a county rodeo, comfortable town or sports clothes are standard for spectators, with few exceptions.

   Certain rules of behavior are the same everywhere, however. Horse shows are flexible events. Many of them run all day and all evening without intermission, except perhaps for lunch and dinner breaks, and it is customary for spectators to drift away from their seats whenever they like—to get refreshments, look up friends, or circulate as they please—though, just as in the theater, it is not correct to leave one woman alone, especially in a box, if that can be avoided.

The major rules of behavior concern applause, and are based on common-sense consideration for riders and their mounts. It is never correct to applaud during an event—when a competitor takes a spectacularly high barrier halfway around a course, for example—because any sudden noise at such a time can throw a horse off stride. And of course no one should attempt to catch the attention of a competitor or make any sudden move or noise that could startle or distract horse or rider during an event.

When the national anthem of a foreign team or competitor is played, the entire audience rises and stands at attention.

Seating is the same as in a theater. The usual arrangement for two couples, for example, is man, woman, woman, man, but if the view is impeded from one of the seats, a man takes it even if that puts a woman on the outside next to a stranger.

**HOSE, HOSIERY.**    *See* SOCKS AND STOCKINGS for the limited use of these words.

## HOSPITALITY

The dictionary definition of a hospitable person, "one who is disposed to entertain with generous kindness," is packed with more meaning than is apparent at first fast reading. The key word is "disposed." Hospitality is much more than providing fancy food at frequent intervals. That is no more than repeated party-giving. Hospitality as a "disposition" is a pervading mood based on genuine interest in others and on concern for their comfort and pleasure. It has nothing to do with the quality or cost or frequency of entertainment. Hospitality is the ready sharing of the best one has available, with the instinctive generosity that gives a guest the most comfortable chair, the choice portion of food.

## HOSPITALS

A hospital stay can be decidedly more comfortable and pleasant for a patient who knows the rules governing his relations with the staff—and whose friends observe the special rules governing the behavior of visitors.

**DOCTORS.** In addition to visits from his own doctor, the patient can expect visits from one or several staff doctors, including interns. They are there to take care of him during his own doctor's absence, and so their questions should be answered. Interns and male registered nurses wear similar white uniforms—but don't confuse them. If the man in white has a stethoscope, call him "Doctor."

**GIFTS TO PATIENTS.** It is not necessary to take a present along when calling on a friend in a hospital, but most people like to go with something in hand as a tangible token of sympathy and concern. Flowers are nearly everyone's first thought. They are almost always appropriate, but, too often, a patient in for a stay of several weeks finds his room crowded beyond convenience with bouquets at the beginning and barren of flowers toward the end. In many cases, a book or some other item will give more pleasure than another bouquet added to an already big collection. Cut flowers are best sent in their own containers so that busy nurses need not take time to hunt up vases that may be (and almost invariably are) the wrong shape or size. Most hospital rooms are small, and massive bouquets and arrangements are overwhelming in such limited space. A better choice is a bouquet suitable for a very small room at home.

A plant is perhaps the safest choice of all, since it lasts longer and demands less care.

Always suitable are practical presents like cologne, scented rubbing alcohol, pretty book matches, cards for solitaire, lap games, magazines, crossword puzzles, and lightweight books. For small children, simple toys like stuffed animals, dolls, and coloring and picture books are a good choice. If the adult patient is not on a restricted diet, he may enjoy candy, cookies, and other delicacies. They should be packaged in containers with tight tops. Sick people often are hypersensitive to odors—and no hospital room should smell of food. A patient who has many visitors and who enjoys serving drinks to them will welcome a bottle of sherry or liquor, a few glasses more suitable than the bathroom tumblers, easy-to-serve cocktail niblets, and perhaps cocktail napkins.

**NURSES.** To the average patient—or visitor—all members of the hospital staff look like nurses because the uniforms of nurse's aides and the service personnel are similar in some ways to those of nurses, though their training, duties, and the services they can be asked to perform are markedly different. Therefore, it is important to be able to spot those staff members who have professional standing. When in doubt, ask frankly, "What does your uniform mean and what do I call you?" It is the only way to avoid the mistake of offering a tip to a volunteer or asking a registered nurse to change the water in the flower vases.

Among nurses, the registered nurse has had the longest training and has the highest rank. She always wears a white uniform and a white cap, and usually a pin that indicates her R.N. standing. Next comes the licensed practical nurse, who also has completed a specific course of training. She, too, wears a white uniform and white cap. In any one hospital, the caps of nurses in these two categories may all be different in shape because each wears the distinctive cap of the school from which she graduated. A student nurse may be in training for either of the above degrees. All student nurses in a hospital will be dressed alike in uniforms of a distinctive color.

Registered, licensed practical, and student nurses are professionals and must be treated as such. They are under the orders of the doctors and head nurses—not of the patients. They can be asked to perform any reasonable service for the patient's comfort but not to run personal errands. Such requests should be confined to porters and other members of the service staff. A nurse is correctly addressed "Miss" or "Mrs." and her last name, or as "Nurse" if her name is not known. "Sister" is correct to a nursing nun.

A nurse's aide is just what the title indicates. She is a helper who has had some training but who is not a nurse. Her duties and the amount of training given her vary widely from hospital to hospital. All nurse's aides will be dressed alike in uniforms of a color distinctive from that worn by the porters, chambermaids, and so on.

Volunteers never wear caps, and their "uniforms" usually are colored smocks worn over street clothes.

**ROOMS.** Accommodations in a hospital are of three kinds: private rooms; semiprivate, where two or more patients share a room; and wards, where a still greater number share a much larger room.

Patients in a ward or semiprivate room are obligated to treat each other with the greatest consideration they can muster. If stuck with an incessant talker, radio listener, smoker, or a roommate who has an endless stream of disturbing visitors, ask for a transfer. It is just as absurd to suffer in silence as it is to try to mend the ways of a thoughtless companion. Explain the difficulty amiably to the doctor or head nurse. They know that calm and peace of mind are part of a cure, and will do whatever possible to see that these are provided.

Roommates are treated as slight social acquaintances would be. A patient introduces his guests upon their arrival, but roommates do not have to be included in the ensuing conversation. Guests do best not to discuss very personal matters, and to keep speak softly and to limit their stay. Delicacies opened or offered during a visit are passed to everyone in the room, and guests say good-bye to all.

**TIPPING.** The staff professionals—doctors, registered nurses, licensed practical nurses, student nurses—are not tipped. (On occasion, a nurse's aide may prefer a tip to a present. If in doubt, ask the head nurse.) It is customary, however, for a patient in a private or semiprivate room to send a box of candy or cookies out to the desk to be shared by all three nursing shifts, about once a week. It is also customary, though not at all obligatory, to give a private nurse and the floor nurses in regular attendance during any but a brief stay a present on departure. Its cost depends on the length of stay, the price of the patient's room, and his financial status. After a week, a modest gift like a bottle of cologne will do very well. The rare but unpleasant case-hardened nurse need not be rewarded. Other staff members need not be tipped, though it is customary to tip the nonprofessionals. From a dollar a week up to five dollars a month is usual for the maid or attendant who cleans the room. For help with luggage, a porter or doorman is tipped at the same scale as in a hotel. Delivery boys and helpers who handle trays are tipped only if asked for extra service, but after a long stay five dollars is usually left with the head nurse to be divided among these employees. Ward patients are generally not expected to tip or leave presents, but are expected to thank those who have served them, when they leave.

**VISITORS.** The days in a hospital can be very long. Most patients welcome visits eagerly, but a welcome should not be taken for granted. Even the closest friends should telephone and set a definite time for a visit. An unexpected visitor should check at the desk to make sure that the patient is not limited in the number of callers or allowed only the briefest of calls.

Several visitors at the same time can be an exhausting demand on the patient's strength. The unwritten rule is that a visitor is expected to leave very shortly after another caller arrives unless specifically pressed by the patient to stay. A doctor making his rounds in a hospital has a lot to do in a limited time, and so a visitor must leave or withdraw to a waiting room when a doctor enters. The same rule holds when a meal is brought to the patient.

A healthy person often forgets how quickly a sick person tires. Unless specifically urged to stay on, leave after twenty minutes. It is a visitor's duty to watch for signs of fatigue in the patient, and to leave instantly if any appear.

Whenever possible, a visitor avoids discussing his own problems. Generally, nothing is more boring to a patient than to hear about someone else's operation; so let the patient have the floor, but do not press for any details not volunteered. It is lacking in imagination to tell a patient he looks awful—but equally ill-advised to be overhearty and declare, "You don't look a bit sick!" to someone very weak or in pain. Never smoke in the sickroom unless invited to. Even in the corridor, keep the voice low. Do not discuss the patient's condition or affairs in the hearing of others. And, finally, no one with a suggestion of a cold should pay a call on a sick person.

## HOST AND HOSTESS

The details of the duties of host and hostess vary according to circumstances of place, entertainment, and food, but the general rules governing their behavior do not vary. In all cases, host and hostess make every effort:

To arrive before a guest if the appointment is away from home.
To be on hand, at home, and ready to welcome a guest at the appointed time.

To put the comfort and pleasure of guests before their own.
To serve a guest first.
To give a guest the better in all things—the choicest or largest item of food, the
most comfortable seat, the best view.
To avoid all family quarrels before guests, and any quarrel with one.
To be on hand to say good-bye.
To guide conversation but not to monopolize it.

When entering his own house, apartment, or office with a guest, the host
(or hostess) opens the door and stands aside to let the guest enter first unless
the place is so dark that the guest would be at a disadvantage. In that case, the
host sensibly goes first to find the lights. The same rule holds when showing
a guest into any room of the host's house.

*See also* BUSINESS MANNERS; RECEIVING LINES; RESTAURANTS; THEATERS;
and other separate entries.

## HOTELS AND MOTELS

The great popularity of auto travel is bringing about changes in the hotel
industry. Motels now resemble resort hotels in both accommodations and price,
though the traveler can arrive at a motel more informally dressed than at a big
hotel. Otherwise, the rules of behavior are the same for both, with the
following exceptions.

**AMERICAN PLAN.** Under this plan, meals are included in the quoted price.
Tipping varies. If waiters rotate, tip after each meal; if they do not, tip at the end
of a short stay, or weekly during a long one. If in doubt, ask the manager.

**BELLBOYS.** Large hotels have a bell captain stationed at his own desk in
the lobby. Requests to have some one paged or for other service by a bellboy
during a rush period get quickest attention if given to the bell captain. Otherwise, a guest in need of service may summon one of the bellboys stationed
around the lobby. He does this by signaling with raised hand or by calling
"Boy" to one within reasonable distance, rather than by snapping his fingers—
except as a last resort. It is true that bellboys are hardened to that signal, but
anyone in a service position resents being summoned in such fashion. If a finger
snap is used, at least a smile and a courteous gesture should accompany it.

The duty of bellboys is to carry hand luggage to and from rooms, deliver
packages, mail, or ice, and to run other errands. A doorman may unload luggage from a car or taxi, or may summon a bellboy to unload. The usual procedure is for the arriving guest to enter a hotel, once his luggage is unloaded,
and to go directly to the registration desk while the bellboy brings in the bags
and stows them in any convenient place—near the bell captain's desk, the
elevators, or somewhere close to the registration desk.

After the guest has registered, the desk clerk hands a bellboy the room
key. Sometimes one boy takes luggage up on a rear elevator while another
shows the guest to his room. Sometimes the bellboy carries it into the elevator
with the guest. The bellboy follows the guest into the elevator, but leads the
way down the corridor and enters the room first. He turns on lights, adjusts
windows, curtains, and heating or cooling units, and stows luggage on racks
or anywhere the guest directs.

A bellboy is tipped for a service at the time he performs it. The minimum
is a quarter, but more is customary for special service such as a trip outside
the hotel to a store or accompanying a guest to a garage. The standard rate is
a quarter for each bag, though the minimum is at least fifty cents when he
carries one heavy piece of luggage to or from a room. Often, permanent guests
or those staying for a long time find constant tipping a nuisance, and so they

give a tip once a week to the bell captain to be distributed to the boys on his staff.

**CHAMBERMAIDS.** A tip need not be left for the chambermaid after a one-night stay in a modestly priced hotel or motel unless she has been put to extra work to clean up after illness or a party. After a stay of two nights, and always after any stay in a medium-priced or expensive hotel, a tip is usual. It may be handed to the maid, or left on the dresser in an envelope marked "For the maid." The amount varies with the size of the quarters, the number occupying them, and the length of stay. About one dollar a night per bedroom, or somewhat less for a stay of several nights, is the average tip to be divided between day and night maids. Those who spend several weeks at a resort hotel usually give the housekeeper a tip at the end of each week and ask her to divide it properly among the regular and the relief maids.

**CHECKING OUT.** Bags ready to go may be left in the room and the key handed to the bell captain or a bellboy in the lobby with the request to bring the luggage down. More usually, when the guest is ready to leave, he calls the switchboard and asks for someone to pick up the bags. The guest may wait for the bellboy, or go to the lobby, pay the bill, and then claim his luggage at the bell captain's desk. Or, if he is in a hurry, he may carry his own luggage and the key to the lobby.

The desk clerk making out the bill should be told of any last-minute telephone calls and of restaurant charges that may not have had time to reach the accounting department. Otherwise, small charges will follow the guest by mail. A forwarding address is left with the mail desk unless letters are to be forwarded to the address already on the registration card.

**Motels.** A traveler making a one-night stay at a small motel is expected to pay in advance at the time of registration. Unless there are extra charges for telephone calls, the guest may leave without stopping at the motel office, but it is customary to drop the key there on the way out.

**CHECKS.** Usually there is no question about payment by check. However, if a bill is very large or if the hotel has paid out cash for a guest's purchases or for special services, the guest avoids delay at check-out time if he sees the credit manager in advance and gets his formal okay, since many check-out clerks are not authorized to accept personal checks except for routine charges.

**COMPLAINTS.** Make complaints about inadequate supplies or care of the room to the housekeeper. Make complaints about noise in adjacent rooms to the manager or desk clerk rather than to the offenders. If everything about the hotel is displeasing, don't bother—just leave, and pass along a warning to any friends who might be likely to stop there.

**DOORMEN.** It is not necessary to tip a doorman on arrival if all he does is open a car door. A tip is given if the doorman unloads luggage and takes it into the lobby, or parks a car. A doorman gets a quarter when he calls a cab, more if he goes out into bad weather or to any unusual trouble for one. Non-residents who ask the doorman of a hotel to get a cab always give him a tip. Patrons spending several days need not tip a doorman every time he calls a cab, but do give him a substantial tip on departure.

**EUROPEAN PLAN.** This means that meals are not included in the quoted price. Tips are given to all staff members at the time of service with the exception of chambermaids, who are tipped at the end of a short stay, weekly during a long one.

**FORGOTTEN ARTICLES.** Hotel managers suspect that the traveling public has a subconscious urge to be rid of all worldly possessions. The amount of gear left behind each year is staggering. If a valuable item is forgotten, the best procedure is to telephone the hotel as soon as the loss is noticed. If this is not practical, a letter should be sent promptly asking that the item be forwarded.

A tip in keeping with the value of the article should be sent to the manager for the maid who turned in the forgotten item.

**GARAGES.** Boys who pick up and deliver cars to the entrance of a hotel are tipped for each such service.

**INSPECTING ACCOMMODATIONS.** It is usual and sensible to ask a desk clerk to show a room, especially in motels, before registering. If a room proves to be noisy or in any other way unsuitable, the client simply thanks him and leaves without obligation.

**KEYS.** It is not necessary for a guest to deposit the room key at the desk every time he leaves the hotel, but it is customary to do so as a sign to callers that the guest is off the premises. A motel guest who is expecting telephone calls follows this procedure too. Otherwise, he keeps the key to his quarters until ready to check out. A motel guest who departs before the office is open leaves the key inside his room with the door locked by its latch, rather than hanging in the outside lock, or latches the door and drops the key through the mail slot in the office door.

If by accident a key is carried away, drop it in any mailbox. Its attached tag is sufficient identification for the post office to return it.

**LOBBIES.** Customs vary widely. In general, guests dress with some degree of formality when appearing in a hotel lobby. At some resort hotels there is no objection to a guest's crossing the lobby in a bathing suit, but don't take this for granted. If in any doubt, ask at the switchboard.

**PAGING.** A person being paged gives a hand signal to the page boy, waits for him to deliver the message, and tips him if the call is to the telephone. Otherwise, the person requesting the paging tips the boy in advance. Requests for paging are given to the bell captain or, if there is none, to the desk clerk or to a bellboy. A title is used, "Paging Mr. Brown" or "Paging Mr. John Brown," not "Paging John Brown."

**PORTERS.** Hotel porters are tipped according to the services they give, usually fifty cents to a dollar for bringing up a trunk, television set, extra cot or other furniture.

**REGISTERING.** A man alone signs the card without "Mr." preceding his full name or his initials and last name.

A couple is registered as "Mr. and Mrs. Henry York Brown," no matter which one signs. A man never signs his name and adds "and wife."

Neither does a man sign his name and add "and family." He may sign "Mr. and Mrs. H. B. Brown and daughter," or "two children," if the youngsters are very small. For girls over five, and certainly for those of junior-high-school age, he adds "Miss Mary Brown" on a separate line (never omitting "Miss"). A son past kindergarten age is registered on a separate line (without "Master" or "Mr.").

A single woman signs "Miss Mary Ann Brown" (never omitting the "Miss").

A married woman alone signs "Mrs." followed by her husband's name (never "Mrs. Helen Brown" or "Helen Greene Brown").

By today's best practice, a woman traveling with a maid does not follow the old-fashioned form and sign "Mrs. Henry York Brown and Maid." She makes out two cards, or adds the maid's name under hers, but always with "Miss" or "Mrs." preceding the maid's name. If a woman is accompanied by a chauffeur or male secretary, separate cards are used.

Full name and "Miss" or "Mrs." are used when registering a secretary or registered nurse, but "Mr. and Mrs. H. B. Brown, two children and nurse" is correct if the nurse is a "nanny."

A man registering for himself and secretary fills out two separate registration cards (never "H. B. Brown and secretary" on one card, or her name under his on the same card).

A woman who arrives first and registers for herself and her husband or other companions follows the above rules exactly.

Payment is not made at the time of registration in hotels, but usually is made when registering at a small motel for one night.

**RESERVATIONS.** Reservations should be made unless the traveler prefers to gamble on finding suitable accommodations after arrival in a strange city. As a service to travelers moving about without a firm schedule, many hotels and motels will send an inexpensive code message to reserve a room for a departing guest at his next stop. A client should cancel a reservation as readily as possible if his plans change. A reservation usually is not held beyond a specified hour, and so it is important for the client to notify a hotel or motel by telephone or wire if he finds he will arrive much later than expected. Otherwise he may find that his room has been given to someone else.

A deposit is not sent with most reservations. However, if the client wants to be doubly sure of his space during a time when a hotel is crowded, such as during Mardi Gras in New Orleans, it is best to send a deposit.

A reservation should give the hour as well as date of arrival, approximate length of stay, price range desired, and number of people in the party. It is a protection to ask for a confirmation since reservations can go astray.

*A standard letter form:*

[Date]
The Manager
Hotel
[Address]
Dear Sir:
    Please reserve a room with double bed for my husband and myself and an adjoining room with twin beds for our daughters for four nights, September 2 to the afternoon of September 6. We will arrive about 9:00 P.M. Please send me a confirmation.

Very truly yours,
Mary York Brown
(Mrs. Henry York Brown)

[Home Address]

A telegram for reservations is one of the few occasions a married woman signs "Mrs." in a communication.

*A standard form:*

WALDORF-ASTORIA HOTEL
NEW YORK, N. Y.
PLEASE RESERVE ROOM WITH TWIN BEDS FOR FOUR NIGHTS
BEGINNING SEPTEMBER 2, ARRIVING 10:00 P.M. REPLY COLLECT.

MRS. HENRY YORK BROWN
10 MAIN AVENUE,
EASTBROOK, OHIO

A secretary making a reservation for herself and her employer sends a wire in his name:

PLEASE RESERVE TWO SINGLE ROOMS, MYSELF
AND SECRETARY, WEEK BEGINNING SIX P.M.
OCTOBER FIVE. WIRE CONFIRMATION.

HENRY YORK BROWN
[Address]

**ROOM SERVICE.** Hotels usually make an extra charge for meals served in rooms. Even so, the waiter should be tipped rather more than for dining-room service since more of his time is required. He is tipped when he presents the check for payment or signature. The waiter may be told to return for a tray or wagon at a specified time, or room service may be called when the guest is ready to have it removed. If a guest does not want to be disturbed by the waiter, he puts the tray or wagon outside his door.

**SECRETARY TRAVELING WITH EMPLOYER.** When a woman secretary travels with a male employer, the reservation should state the relationship. The hotel automatically reserves rooms on different floors in this case. If by mistake adjoining rooms are reserved, the employer who is registering for himself and his secretary requests a change as a routine protection of his secretary's reputation—and of his own. If the secretary registers for both, she does the same. Separate registration cards are made out. The employer never registers "H. B. Brown and secretary." If employer and secretary need to work together in the hotel, she goes to his room after it has been made up, rather than he to hers. There is no need to keep the door open, and it is sensible and correct to have meals sent up if that is more convenient.

**SIGNING SERVICE CHECKS.** Signing checks in dining rooms and bars is a convenience, especially for a woman entertaining a man, since this avoids any show of money. Also, many people find it practical to have one bill for all the expenses of a stay, as a record for income-tax or expense-account purposes. The amount of the tip is added below the charge with "Tip" or "For waiter" opposite it, and the name of the guest and his room number signed anywhere on the check.

**SOUVENIRS.** Hotel owners have only one word for the "collecting" of such souvenirs as towels, spoons, china, and similar articles. It is "stealing." The few exceptions include items like shoe cloths, which obviously are not washed and reused, and the packets of soap, needles, matches, and other small conveniences that are replaced for each guest.

**TIPPING.** Tips are geared to the quality of the hotel, the size of the accommodations, and the service expected. Many people make their first tips generous as a sign to the staff that they want the best of service and expect to pay for it. The manager, his assistant managers, and the desk clerks are professionals and are not tipped. Neither are social directors, public stenographers, or travel clerks.

Telephone and elevator operators are not tipped by transient guests. Permanent guests usually remember telephone operators and elevator men from time to time or on special holidays. All others who give direct service, such as doormen, bellboys, porters, waiters, and chambermaids, are tipped. A transient guest does not tip a headwaiter unless he goes to some special effort to arrange a big party. Usually a permanent resident gives the headwater a tip about once a month if he patronizes the dining room frequently, but this is not necessary in modestly priced hotels.

**Motels.** A manager is not tipped. A tip is left for the chambermaid after one night in an expensive motel, after a stay of two or more nights in others, and always if she is put to unusual trouble to clean up after a party.

**VALETS.** The standard pronunciation of "valet" in this country is as it is spelled and with accent on the first syllable, not "valay." Hotel valets usually are not tipped, since they run concessions and are in the position of owners or managers, but they are tipped if they do a rush job or one after regular hours. If a bellboy picks up or delivers things for the valet, he is tipped. If the valet makes his own deliveries, his manner will clearly indicate whether or not he expects a tip.

**VISITORS.** A visitor never goes directly to a hotel room unless asked to do so when the appointment is made. Both men and women announce themselves from the lobby through the switchboard, giving the hotel resident a chance to say, "Come up," or, "I'll be down." A man does not ask a girl or very young woman to his room if she is alone. If a man is thoughtless enough to suggest it, she should have no reluctance in answering, "I'll wait for you in the lobby." However, it is common practice to use a hotel bedroom as one would a living room under other circumstances and to ask friends up if that is more convenient for everyone. It is more businesslike to meet strangers and professional acquaintances in the lobby or other public rooms.

## HOUSE AND HOME

"House," "home," "estate," "mansion," and "residence" are high on the list of so-called "problem words" discussed under CONVERSATION because how and when they are used are giveaways of social background.

If in doubt, it is safest to follow the general rule that calls for "house" as first choice when speaking about a dwelling place. "Send it to my house," "Let's meet at your house," "They are buying a new house," are right according to our current customs, but "They're buying a new home" is not—though, trickily enough, "I'm going home" and "She often entertains at home" are correct. The difference lies in the lack of a qualifying word before "home." If "new," "my," or any other adjective or possessive pronoun is added, "home" is seldom correct, and "house" should take its place.

"My childhood home was Louisville" is one of the exceptions to the rule above because the meaning is "Louisville was our home *town* when I was a child." But "The home I grew up in is still standing" is wrong—unless that house was an orphan's home or other institution.

"Home" is also properly used where mood is concerned: "Home is where the heart is," "Keep the home fires burning," and "I feel at home in her house" are good examples.

In any case, "home" is the better choice, even if misused, than such pomposities as "estate," "mansion," and "residence."

**ESTATE.** A real-estate dealer can correctly say, "The Jones estate is coming on the market," when speaking of a handsome big house surrounded by extensive grounds, but anyone who has such a place, and follows the rules, avoids calling it "estate." "I am buying an estate," 'I spent the weekend at their estate," "They have an estate at Pound Ridge," are better forgotten, and "country place" or "big house" used instead.

**MANSION.** By dictionary definition, a mansion is "a large handsome dwelling." Many people live in houses that fit this description, but if it is a private dwelling, "big house" or "huge place" is used—not "mansion." The only exception is in speaking of an official dwelling. "I am going to dinner at the governor's mansion" is correct because that is the official title of the building supplied by the state for his use while he is in office. But "mansion" would not be used to mean the privately owned house of a man who happens to be the governor.

**RESIDENCE.** It is correct to say "my legal residence," but current custom bans as pretentious any such use as, "The party was at my residence," or, "She resides near me." "Residence" is not correctly used instead of "house" or "apartment" except on an engraved invitation or by a domestic employee in answering the telephone.

"The Governor is in residence" is correct with the meaning that he is in town, but "The Governor is at home" is a better choice than "The Governor is at his residence."

# HOUSEGUESTS

*"Visits always give pleasure—if not the coming,*
*then the going."—Portuguese Proverb*

Reduced to simplest terms, the duty of host and hostess is to make the house-guest feel at home, and the duty of the guest is not to act in all ways as if he were at home. Following are the major guidelines for achieving this admittedly delicate balance:

**ARRIVAL.** Under all usual circumstances, the hostess is expected to be at home to welcome houseguests (if she does not meet them at the station). The first order of business is to show a guest his quarters and the bath he will use, and give him a few minutes alone to tidy up after his journey and to unpack. As soon as convenient, a first-time guest is given a tour of the house so that he can orient himself. And, without too much delay, the schedule of meals and the plans for any special entertainment during his stay are explained to him so that he will know what to expect and what is expected of him.

**BEDTIMES.** The rule is explicit: The hostess, not the guest, makes the first move. A houseguest may hint that he is tired and would like to turn in early, but customarily he waits for the hostess to suggest ending the day.

All houseguests are expected to follow the hostess's lead when she suggests bedtime. On occasion, a hostess may excuse herself early and leave her husband and their guests to continue a game or otherwise entertain themselves, but as a general rule a woman does not linger after her hostess retires, and guests of either sex do not stay up after both host and hostess go to bed. In practice, there usually is no problem, since thought waves billow back and forth between the normally aware and considerate hostess and guest, and everyone arrives simultaneously at the idea that it is time to say good night.

On the first night, the hostess usually shows the guest to his room person-ally to see that he knows how to adjust the air conditioner or other equipment, locate the light switches, find extra blankets, and so on, and to make sure that nothing he needs is lacking. She also explains breakfasting hours and customs if she has not done so before.

**BREAD-AND-BUTTER LETTERS.** Thanks at the time of departure, no matter how effusive, are not enough. After any overnight stay, a note (either hand-written or typed) from a guest is obligatory. This so-called "bread-and-butter letter" may be no more than "Thanks for a wonderful weekend" written on a visiting card enclosed with a present, but it is a breach of the rules not to send some message within five days of departure.

A bread-and-butter letter is addressed to the hostess, not to the host or to the host and hostess jointly, and it is written by the wife of a visiting couple. A card accompanying a gift may be signed with both names, but the package is addressed to the hostess.

If a child has been an overnight guest without his parents, he writes his own bread-and-butter note. In most cases, and always if the child is quite young, his mother also writes to thank his hostess.

A houseguest usually sends a message through the hostess to any of her friends who have entertained him during his visit, but is not required to write to them also unless the entertainment was specifically in his honor.

**CHILDREN.** Young houseguests deserve the same considerate treatment that their parents do—and if they get it, life will be far easier for everyone. The experienced hostess does not take for granted that a little child will be content to sit quietly and listen while the grownups talk—a quite common mis-apprehension among childless people that generally results in ruining a visit for all concerned. She lays in some playthings, especially if the child will be confined in a small apartment or house or possibly kept indoors by bad weather, and plans some activities that a child can share.

The duty of other guests is to treat a visiting child as a fellow guest, not as a second-class citizen who should be seen but not heard. Guests are expected to give some attention to the children of the house also, trusting to the parents to see that their offspring do not get carried away and take the spotlight for the entire visit. If a visiting child requires special food, his mother takes the necessary items along and assumes the responsibility for preparing them, especially in the servantless household.

Many parents suffer agonies of doubt and foreboding the first time their children go off to be houseguests on their own. Their gloomy expectation of the worst is usually groundless. Children generally rise magnificently to this social challenge if parents do their part and:

1. Make sure the child clearly understands—and *accepts* the idea—that his host and hostess are, for the duration of his stay, his substitute parents, and therefore are to be *obeyed*.
2. Remind the child that even if meals, bedtime, and the general routine in the house he is visiting differ from those at home, he must not point out these differences and especially must not complain about them ("We don't like broccoli at our house," "My mother says eight is too early for kids my age to go to bed," "Our *maid* does the dishes," and so on.).
3. Explain that he is expected to share the chores and in general follow the lead of the children in the house—short of cooperating in any disobedience or dangerous activities that the hostess's children, made giddy by the presence of a guest, may be inspired to try.

Too many parting admonitions, though, are often worse than none at all; in his state of excited anticipation, the child will either be unable to take them all in or be confused by a flood of instructions. Just be thankful if he remembers to obey his hostess. If he does—and if the hostess is on the job—nothing too disastrous should happen. Being on duty throughout a young visitor's stay is a major responsibility of the hostess. She may have great faith in the trustworthiness, judgment, and resourcefulness of her own youngsters and feel confident about leaving them on their own for short periods (while she does errands, for instance), but she takes a great risk if she blithely assumes that a visiting child has the same qualities. Best practice for the hostess-mother is to invite a child houseguest only if she is prepared to be on duty herself or there is a competent and reliable adult to oversee matters in her absence.

**DEPARTURES.** On some occasions, in a house with a large staff the host and hostess do not get up at the crack of dawn to say good-bye to a guest making an early departure. Instead, farewells are said the night before, and one of the household staff is on hand to provide breakfast and other help. Usually, however, the hostess sees the departing guest off.

A guest's first duty is not to delay beyond the agreed time of departure except in an emergency or unless most urgently pressed to change the original plan. "I wish you didn't have to go!" is no more than a pretty compliment—not an invitation to stay on unless an explicit suggestion of a later departure time or date is made. The departing guest's second duty is to gather up and pack all his possessions so that the hostess is not put to the trouble of wrapping and mailing forgotten items; and to have his bags ready to go in plenty of time so that no one need risk life, limb, and a speeding fine to get him to his train, bus, or plane. (See also "Guest Rooms" and "Tipping" below.)

**ENTERTAINMENT.** The good hostess plans a certain amount of entertainment—a dinner party, sight-seeing, an evening at the theater, and so on—but leaves a reasonable amount of time free for rest or spur-of-the-moment enterprises. She gives her guests a choice of activities for the times when no specific entertainment is scheduled—a walk, tennis, cards, croquet—or asks them to suggest some activity that would particularly appeal to them.

Unless specifically asked for suggestions, however, a guest does not make them or in any other way take charge of entertainment during his visit. He does not, for example, make arrangements to go off with other friends in the neighborhood or involve outside friends in his hostess's plans—except after the most delicate negotiations with her. He may mention the fact that he has friends nearby, but unless the hostess suggests, with unmistakable enthusiasm, getting in touch with them, he discreetly lets the matter slide.

Good guests adapt amiably to all special plans the hostess has made. Of course the guest who would rather rest than take a strenuous hike is privileged to say so and let the more athletic members of the party go off without him, but he joins all the activities that he possibly can if his refusal would cause a dilemma for host and hostess or spoil the pleasure of the whole group.

**EXPENSES.** As a general rule, the host and hostess expect and should be allowed to take care of all food and entertainment expenses—meals in a restaurant or food at home, entrance fees, locker-room charges, and so on. The good guest behaves like a guest, and accepts all such hospitality without fighting for the check at either a supermarket or nightclub. There are plenty of exceptions to this rule, of course, depending on many factors. During an extended stay, a guest who can afford it will occasionally invite his host and hostess to go out for a meal or to the theater at his expense, but under the usual conditions of a weekend visit the guest makes no attempt to be a part-time host and pay for any entertainment. He bides his time and evens the score at some later date.

It is not very logical, but there are certain minor expenses that the guest must take meticulous pains to pay for before his departure. If he makes a toll or long-distance call, he asks the operator for the charges, and pays them before he leaves. It is never correct to ask the hostess to report the amount of his calls when her bill comes in. A houseguest does not offer to pay for the washing of his bed linen and towels, no matter how extended his stay, but he is obligated to pay for all personal laundry, cleaning, and pressing. If the guest's clothes are sent out to a commercial laundry or cleaner, the hostess simply hands over the bill when the things are returned. If she does not do so, the guest makes a point of asking for it, and the hostess accepts payment without argument. If washing is done by an employee, the guest does not pay for that service but does give a tip, usually at the time the clothes are returned if the visit is a long one, otherwise shortly before his departure. Whenever possible, a guest packs with sufficient care so that his clothes do not need pressing. If they do, he tips the employee who performs this service for him.

A guest pays for any taxis he may use by himself—to and from a station or terminal or for a personal trip to town, for example.

**GUEST ROOMS.** A guest deserves fair warning if the house does not have a guest room, or if he is expected to share one with another guest. Many people are delighted to bunk on the living-room sofa or sleep dormitory-fashion in a playroom or attic; but others would rather stay at home than expose themselves to the informality of communal or makeshift quarters, and in simple compassion should be given a chance to refuse an invitation if those are the only arrangements the house has to offer.

Standard equipment for a guest bedroom includes a good reading light over or beside the head of the bed; a well-lighted mirror; a bedside table with a glass and pitcher or Thermos for water; ashtrays, matches, and cigarettes; a selection of reading matter; a clock; a wastebasket; extra blankets; a luggage rack; sufficient drawer and closet space, and hangers for skirts and pants as well as coats; a box of tissues; a pincushion; and perhaps a clothes brush, a small sewing kit, and a radio. A desk supplied with notepaper, pens, pencils, and a calendar is a blessing to a guest making a stay of any length.

**Bathrooms.** Standard equipment in a bathroom for a guest's exclusive use includes aspirin, Band-Aids, and a few other such common items, as well as hand lotion, cologne, bath powder, tissues, hair spray, and similar cosmetic aids that a guest may have forgotten or found too bulky to bring—and always a spare toothbrush in its pristine container.

If the guest finds towels on a rack in his room, it is a clear sign that he is sharing a bathroom through which the traffic is heavy, and that he is expected to keep all his toilet articles in his own quarters. A neatly closed cosmetics or shaving kit may be left in such a bathroom if there is some good place to put it, but the guest does not unpack it and add his toothbrush and other gear to crowded shelves nor leave his towels and washcloth there. It never is amiss for parents to remind youngsters visiting without them to remove that ring in the tub and to leave a used bath mat on the side of the tub rather than on the floor.

**Beds.** In a house with a large staff, beds usually are turned down during the dinner hour and made up while the guest is at breakfast. A guest in charge of his own room removes the coverlet and folds it neatly so that it will not be wrinkled in the morning. He makes up his own bed fairly early in the day, usually right after breakfast, rather than leaving it untidily open.

In a house with few or no servants, a woman guest offers to make up her bed with fresh linen on the day of her departure. If the hostess tells her not to bother with this chore, and if she is leaving early in the morning, she may strip her bed and leave the sheets and blankets neatly folded; or she may spread the bed open to air, which is the standard procedure for a male guest. A guest who is leaving in the afternoon or evening makes up the bed so that the room will look presentable during the day. Any guest who has been bedded down in a living room folds up sheets and blankets before breakfast.

**General Care.** Except in a house with a large staff, guests take care of their own rooms. This means no more than keeping things reasonably neat and attractive—ashtrays wiped out with a tissue, extra used glasses returned to the kitchen, an overflowing wastebasket emptied, and clothes put away in the places provided rather than flung on the chairs. During a stay that extends beyond a long weekend, a woman houseguest runs a dust mop over the floor when necessary, but the hostess usually finds time to do this minor housekeeping chore for a male guest.

**HELPING OUT.** Even the most welcome guests can be a strain unless they help out in two specific ways. (1) In a house with few or no servants, the average able-bodied guest should be fully prepared to contribute a little light labor —at least offer to run errands, help prepare meals, wash dishes, and otherwise share some of the routine chores. (2) If his offer of assistance is countered by the suggestion that he take a walk or a nap, read a good book, or otherwise divert himself alone, there is only one thing to do: Take the suggestion immediately. Every hostess needs a few hours out of each day for routine duties that she can do better and faster alone. The guest who hovers, expecting attention during every waking hour, wears himself out—and his hostess too. On the other hand, a hardworking hostess accepts a certain amount of help from her guests if she wants to make them feel like friends of the family rather than patrons of an understaffed hotel.

**HOUSE PRESENTS.** It is customary, though not obligatory, for a houseguest to arrive with some little gift in hand. If the guest does not take a present, it is usual to send some tangible token of thanks after departure. The value of such presents depends on the circumstances of the guest and the length of the stay, but in no case should a house present be so costly as to suggest payment at hotel rates for private hospitality. Standard house presents are items for general consumption—a bottle of wine or liquor, candy, tinned or homemade delicacies, flowers, a game, a book, scented soap, and so on, or may be something like cologne or perfume for the specific use of the hostess. If there are children in the house, the guest who also takes along some small gadgets for their special use can't go wrong (as long as he avoids noisemakers). If in doubt about the children's ages, cookies or candy are always safe.

**INVITATIONS AND ACCEPTANCES.** Whether an invitation is given in person, by telephone, or by letter, and is for overnight or longer, it should suggest explicit times for arrival and departure and also give the guest an idea of what clothes to bring. For example:

> Dear Betty,
> We miss you! Can you spend the weekend of June 15 with us? I am enclosing a train schedule—the 4:10 on Friday is by far the most comfortable and will get you here in time for a swim before dinner. I'll meet you at the station at this end. Saturday night at the club is fun for dancing (nothing elaborate —short skirts), and for a change we plan a cookout on the shore for Sunday night. Joe takes the 8:15 Monday morning and would love to have you go in with him so he can help with your bags.
>
> > Love,
> > Jane

This tells Betty that she will need a bathing suit, a dinner dress, and flat shoes for the sand, and gives her a chance to suggest any small change in arrival and departure times that may suit her better.

An acceptance should be equally clear about the hours of arrival and departure. If the times suggested by the hostess are not convenient for the guest, it is entirely correct to suggest later arrival and earlier departure—but not the reverse if more than a very slight change is involved. The guest who will arrive at an hour later than was suggested by the hostess should add in the acceptance, "But don't bother to meet me—I'll just pick up a taxi," unless the hostess has made it clear she can adjust her plans to any arrival time that is more convenient for the guest.

**MEALS.** In both a maidless household and a country castle with a full complement of servants, scarcely any virtue is more appreciated in a guest than promptness, particularly promptness for meals. The hostess without hired help who is courageous enough to entertain a houseful of guests certainly deserves that courtesy, and since good servants are hard to find and to keep, so does a hostess who has managed to assemble a competent staff.

If the hostess sets a specific hour for breakfast, the guest is expected to show up on time, dressed and ready for the day. It is not correct to appear at breakfast in a negligee or robe unless the hostess has said that such is the custom of the house. The merciful hostess explains to the very early birds how to find coffee for themselves if they want it long before the family breakfast hour, and when at all feasible she lets slugabed guests sleep as late as they choose. In many houses with a sizable staff, it is the pleasant custom to ask a guest the night before what he would like for breakfast and send it up on a tray to his room at an agreed hour. Very often a hostess with no help also follows this plan, finding it far easier to run up with a tray than to have a guest underfoot while she is getting her house in order.

For all other meals, the basic responsibility of the guest is to be ready to sit down on time.

**SERVANTS.** Unless the hostess or one of her employees has already suggested the availability of some special service (washing a car, for example), the houseguest relays a request for such a service through the hostess. A guest may make any reasonable minor request directly to a member of the house staff, but does not come out with it in the form of an order. No guest, of course, ever properly questions a servant about anything that might be considered a personal family matter. See HOUSEHOLD EMPLOYEES and INTRODUCTIONS for details.

**TIPPING.** Which members of a staff are tipped, and when and how much, are matters that give a great many houseguests more concern than any other point of behavior. The sad fact is that there are no definite answers to these questions. The rules can be spelled out only to a degree because no one set of rules will apply to all circumstances, though there are two basic rules that are always observed:

1. Employees of professional standing (a governess, secretary, companion, and so on) are never tipped.
2. Tips are always accompanied by thanks; they are also given as unobtrusively as possible, every effort being made to avoid giving a tip in the presence of host or hostess.

As a very general rule, a houseguest tips any member of the staff who has given direct service, but does not tip an employee with whom there has been no contact—the chef, for example, in a house with a very large staff. Now for the exceptions—and there are many.

A tip may not be expected or at all proper in some cases in a household with only one regular or part-time employee. For example, if the hostess does some of the cooking herself, it would probably not be in order to tip a part-time maid on hand to help prepare and serve the evening meals during a weekend. Much also depends on the status of such an employee in the community and in the house. When in doubt in such a case, don't tip. If some special recognition seems called for, leave the maid who has the standing of a "mother's helper" a box of candy; or take along some small present for her on a subsequent visit. If sure that a tip will not injure her feelings, slip out to the kitchen when she is alone and give her one or two dollars for a weekend, or a bit more for a longer stay or if she has been put to any undue amount of trouble.

In a house with two or three regular servants—perhaps a cook-waitress and a gardener-chauffeur—everyone is tipped a dollar or so by the weekend guest.

In a really formal house with a large staff, tips can run to a sizable amount. Unless specifically requested not to tip (some hostesses leave a little note in the guest's room to that effect), the houseguest should be prepared to hand out gratuities to all employees who have served him directly. He does not tip the cook unless she has been asked to prepare special dishes because of his dietary limitations, or the gardener unless he has washed the guest's car or otherwise given special service. But the guest should be equipped with bills (not silver) for a butler, houseman, chambermaid, chauffeur, waitress, and so on. And if a guest arrives with a nursemaid or other employee, she too must be supplied with bills to tip the servants who have waited on her; otherwise, the guest is expected to add an extra amount to his own tip to such staff members.

Tips are not given on arrival and seldom at the time of individual service during a visit. They are distributed shortly before the guest departs. If the guest's room is equipped with bells, he rings for the chambermaid and others on call and delivers thanks and his tips. It is also correct to leave a tip on the dresser, though the bills should be in a sealed envelope with the employee's name on the outside. Otherwise, the tip is delivered at any convenient time. The employee usually will be available for a discreet good-bye. If not, the guest makes a detour to the back of the house and tips the waitress, laundress, and so on. A butler or houseman usually will be in the hall when the guest leaves and can be tipped at that time if not before.

A visiting couple tips at about the same rate (or a little less) as would two unrelated guests. If there are no more than three servants, the husband hands out the tips. If there is a very large staff, the wife tips the chambermaid, lady's maid, and perhaps the waitress; the husband tips all male servants.

Following is a rough schedule of what is generally expected in the way of tips for each member of a staff, the exact amounts to be determined according to how much service each has given:

*Woman Guest:* $1 to $2 for overnight; $2 to $5 for a weekend.

*Man Guest:* $1 to $2 for overnight; $3 to $5 for a weekend.

*Guest Couple:* $2 to $3 for overnight; $3 to $5 for a weekend.

*Children:* Very young houseguests visiting without their parents do not leave
   tips. Teen-agers visiting without their parents are not expected to tip in a
   great many households; otherwise, they tip as an adult would but usually at
   the lowest rate suggested above.

## HOUSEHOLD EMPLOYEES

One of the paradoxes of our changing times is that, though fewer families now employ full-time domestic help, more of us deal as temporary employers or as guests with the big staffs once seen only in the most formal households. This change has come about because a fast-growing number of people, whose only regular help in the kitchen is a mechanical dishwasher, turn on special occasions to caterers for the full complement of butler, second men, maids, and drivers. As a result, there is an expanding interest in the rules that apply to household employees of all categories.

**ANSWERING THE DOOR.** In a formal household, an employee who opens the door to a caller smiles in greeting, but if the rule is strictly observed, he waits for the caller to speak first. It is absurd to give this rule a second thought if it is broken, as it often is by the valued maid of all work who properly counts herself a member of the home circle. An air of hospitality at the door is much more important than the stiffly correct observance of this minor detail.

A guest who is expected does not state his name to the employee who opens the door. He says only, "Good morning [afternoon, evening]," adding the employee's name if he knows it; or, less formally to a well-known maid, "Hello, Mary." The employee answers, "Good evening, sir [madam]," or if the guest's name is known, "Good evening, Mr. Smith" (not "Hello").

A caller who is not expected and also is a stranger to the employee announces himself by title and last name, and asks for the specific member of the family he wants to see: "I am Mrs. Smith. Is Mrs. Jones in?"

(For further details, see CALLS.)

**ANSWERING THE TELEPHONE.** "Mrs. Brown's residence" (not "The Browns' residence" or "Mr. Brown's residence") is the standard answer from a staff member employed by a married couple even if the residence is an apartment. "Mr. Brown's residence" is used only if the employer is single. "Apartment" is also correct, and is often first choice if the quarters are very small, and "residence" sounds a bit pretentious.

**BREAKAGE BY SERVANTS.** An employer assumes the responsibility for breakage or other damage to his property caused by his employees. It is not fair to ask a maid to handle valuable fragile china, for example, and then to charge her for the cost of replacement if she breaks it. An employee who breaks anything is obligated to report the damage promptly, but the employer has really only one answer, "I know you didn't mean to do it."

**BUTLERS.** The male member of a couple who are the only employees is sometimes spoken of as a butler, but "houseman" is the technically correct term in this case because "butler" is reserved for the ranking male employee on a large staff.

A butler is called by his last name without "Mr." by children and guests as well as by employers. His first name or a nickname is not used.

**Clothes.** A butler does not wear livery, gloves, a flower, or a moustache. In many houses, he wears some variant of a standard sack suit both day and evening—a black single-breasted jacket with a black double-breasted waistcoat; black or black-and-gray striped trousers; white shirt with a stiff fold-over collar; black four-in-hand tie; black shoes and socks. Or in summer he may wear a soft shirt, black trousers, a single-breasted jacket of gray alpaca or white linen or duck, or a white jacket that has collar and cuffs in black or other solid color or in stripes. This coat is worn with a stiff fold-over collar in the afternoon, and in the evening with a wing collar and black bow tie. Shoes and socks are always black.

Only in a very formal house does a butler need more than the clothes mentioned above. The extremely formal costumes described below are rarely seen today. To serve a formal lunch, a butler wears a tailcoat, but with plain (not silk-faced) lapels; striped gray-and-black trousers; black double-breasted waistcoat; stiff white shirt with white, nonshiny studs or very small gold ones; wing collar with a black bow tie or, less formally, a stiff fold-over collar with a black four-in-hand tie. After six, he wears black trousers (but without a satin stripe) to match his tailcoat; black waistcoat; stiff white shirt with a wing collar and white bow tie.

A butler sometimes supplies his own clothes, but any special jackets are supplied by his employer.

**Duties.** The duties of a butler vary according to the size of the staff. If the staff is very large, his work is mainly directive rather than manual, and he often takes over a large part of the house management—planning meals, ordering food and supplies, and hiring, training, and directing all other members of the service staff. (He does not have jurisdiction over governesses, tutors, companions, social secretaries, and others who have equal social standing with the employer.)

In all but very large households where his work is largely executive, the butler's standard duties include answering the door and telephone, cleaning the silver, serving cocktails, tea, and meals. He serves the main dishes and the wine if he has the assistance of a second man or maid; otherwise he takes entire charge of the service of a meal. If there is no valet, he takes on the valet's duties as well.

**CHAUFFEURS.** Except in very large and busy households, a full-time driver usually takes on extra duties and often doubles as a houseman in serving meals or as a gardener. A chauffeur is called by his last name without "Mr.," or by his complete first name, but in formal practice not by a nickname or diminutive. (See CHAUFFEURS for all other details concerning drivers both in private service and for hired cars.)

**CHILDREN AND SERVANTS.** One of the most important lessons every little child must learn is that rudeness to a household employee or anyone else in a service position is inexcusable and that all requests to any servant must be accompanied by "Please."

Children use the same forms of address to members of the household staff as do other members of the family. A cook called "Mary" by the employers is not "Mrs. Smith" to junior members of the family.

(See "Forms of Address" below for the use of children's names by the staff.)

**COMPANIONS.** A companion occupies much the same position as a relative making an extended stay, and is treated in every way as a social equal, though not as a member of the family on all occasions. For instance, she does not necessarily take all her meals with the family, but may be served in her own room or may eat with a social secretary or other staff member of similar standing. Under no circumstances, however, does she join the members of the service staff at their table.

Members of the family may use a companion's first name or a nickname, depending on her age and other circumstances, but all members of the service staff use "Miss" ["Mrs.," "Mr."] and the last name of a companion.

The duties of a companion are exactly what the word itself implies. They may include shopping, arranging flowers, setting the table for a party, but, as a general rule, not any domestic or personal service beyond that which any member of the family would ordinarily give.

**COOKS.** The word "cook" covers a wide range—from the expert who rates the title "chef" and who does nothing but prepare meals to be served by other staff members, to the jewel beyond price who cooks, serves, washes up, helps with the housecleaning, and pinch-hits as a nursemaid.

A professional male chef is addressed by his last name without title by members of the family, or sometimes by his full first name, whichever he prefers. A female cook is asked at the time of her employment what form of address she prefers, and by her own choice is called either by her first name or by "Mrs." or "Miss" and her last name.

A regularly employed cook usually wears a white or light-colored dress resembling, in its simple cut, a maid's uniform, and a white apron. The combination cook-maid who comes in at the end of the day to prepare and serve dinner may wear such a uniform, but often she wears any simple cotton dress of her own, either printed or in a solid color. Sometimes the employer supplies a cook's uniforms, and sometimes she supplies her own. This is a matter to be decided at the time of employment. A male chef usually wears a white cotton coat or a complete white uniform in the kitchen.

**FOOTMEN.** Only a house with a very large staff that includes a butler would have a regularly employed footman. The man (or men) frequently supplied by an agency to assist a butler at a very formal lunch, dinner, or other party is also known as a "second man," but not as a "waiter." Depending on the occasion, a second man dresses as a houseman does or in formal livery. If he is regularly employed, it is supplied by his employer; otherwise, it is supplied by the agency. Formal livery is a tail suit usually in a dark color other than black—green, maroon, or blue—with silver or brass buttons on the front of the coat and with twelve matching buttons on the tails. With it he wears a stiff white shirt, wing collar, white bow tie, striped waistcoat, and white cotton gloves.

His main duties are to be on hand at the front door to direct guests to places to leave their wraps, to assist the butler in serving a meal, and if there is a regularly employed cook, to assist her in cleaning up after the party.

A full-time second man takes on extra duties, which include acting as valet to male houseguests, cleaning the sidewalks, windows, fireplaces, and silver, and similar chores.

A footman is addressed by his last name without "Mr."

**FORMS OF ADDRESS AND REFERENCE.** Many people avoid the word "servant" completely because of a confusion about when this entirely acceptable word is correctly used and when a substitute is a better choice.

"Servant" and "servants" are explicit and correct in all cases where servants in general are meant. For example, "Her manner to servants is impossible" is the simplest and best way to state that fact. However, in this country, we avoid "servant" when referring to a specific employee and use the job title instead: "That is our cook [or maid or whatever] over there," not "That is our servant."

"The staff" or "our household staff" is always a safe substitute for "our servants." If "our staff" would sound pretentious or absurd when speaking of a combination cook-laundress-nursemaid and her husband who doubles as a gardener-driver-handyman, "the people who work for us at home" or the more informal "the help" is a standard substitute.

Wrong on all counts are the overly elaborate "our cook-lady" and "our cleaning lady," which are as absurd as describing a man as "the odd-jobs gentleman." Every American woman rates the word "lady" on certain occasions (See LADY AND WOMAN), but where her job is concerned, she deserves the dignity of business recognition as a "career woman," "saleswoman," "cleaning woman," and so on.

There is never any excuse for treating an employee like a piece of the furniture and failing to give a routine greeting in the morning, for example. And any order to a servant (or anyone else, for that matter) should be softened by the addition of either a spoken or implied "please," which puts the nonetheless definite command into the courteous form of a request.

**By Servants.** The standard rule is that any remark made by a servant to members of the family or their guests is accompanied by "Sir," "Madam," or a name—and never consists merely of a flat Yes or No.

When speaking of an adult guest, title and last name are used by a servant. If the name is unknown, "the lady [gentleman]" is correct—never "the woman [man]."

When speaking about the employer to an outsider, a servant uses the employer's title and last name. When speaking about the employer to other members of the family, he uses either "Mr.," "Mrs.," or "Miss" with the last name, or "your mother [father]," but not "your wife [husband]" or "the Mrs. [Mr.]"

All employees call very little children by their first names or nicknames. Only in the most formal households are children from about six through their early teens called "Miss Betty" and "Master Billy," for example, and this custom is rarely observed in the United States. Far more usually, girls under about sixteen and boys under eighteen are addressed by first name without any title, especially by employees who have known them since they were small children.

After young people reach their late teens, they are called "Miss Elizabeth" (or "Miss Betty") and "Mr. William" (or "Mr. Bill"), and so on. The employer sets the pattern by using the combination expected: "Has Miss Betty come in yet, Anna?" if that is the way the maid is expected to address and refer to a daughter.

**To Servants.** The employer and his wife, when speaking of each other to a servant, use "Mrs. [Mr.] Brown"—never "my wife [husband]"—and also use the title and last name that the employee is expected to use when they refer to any relatives or friends. If a servant does not use the title and last name in referring to the employer's relatives and friends, he uses "lady" or "gentleman": "the lady next door," for instance. He does not use "woman" or "man" for any social equal of the employer.

**GOVERNESSES.** A governess is treated as a social equal by the family. She takes her meals with them, with her charges, or elsewhere, but never with the service staff. She does not wear a uniform. A French governess is often known as "Mademoiselle" to the entire household, a German governess as "Fräulein," and a Spanish governess as "Señorita." A very young governess sometimes is called by her first name by members of the family, but she is addressed as "Miss" or "Mrs." and her last name by all members of the service staff.

**HEALTH CERTIFICATES.** Some employers ask a prospective employee, especially one who will handle food or be in direct charge of children, for a health certificate. This is by no means a routine request, though a sensible one

If an applicant does not have a health certificate, the usual procedure is for the employer who wants such reassurance to pay his own doctor for taking a chest X ray and a blood test.

**HIRING, FIRING, QUITTING.** Time and trouble are saved for both sides if, when discussing employment, the employer is explicit about working hours, services expected, and especially about any factors that might be considered drawbacks, and if prospective employees are equally definite about services that they are unwilling or unprepared to perform.

In all cases, fair notice is only fair play when employment comes to an end. If for any reason employment is terminated without warning by the employer, payment in lieu of the normal notice of at least two weeks is the standard practice. The courtesy of as much notice as possible is also expected from the employee.

There is no exact rule about severance pay when the association is terminated by the employer, but it is a widespread custom to give a valued and long-term employee a good-bye present in cash. The amount varies according to the circumstances, and may be anything from an extra week's wages for each year of employment to an extra month's pay.

**HOUSEGUESTS.** See HOUSEGUESTS.

**HOUSEKEEPERS.** Big houses that require the services of a professional housekeeper become rarer each year. Today, for all practical purposes, the title "housekeeper" is applied to a deputy housewife—a person who takes charge of things at home for a widower or for a woman who has a job or for some other reason needs a substitute to run the house. If a housekeeper's background is the same as that of the family, she is treated much as a relative would be. If her social background is quite different, she does not (for example) join the family at meals. Such details are agreed upon at the time of employment.

In a very large house with a big staff, the housekeeper is the top executive. She is a professional household manager, prepared by experience to hire and fire the entire staff and supervise every detail of their work, to order supplies and keep the household accounts. She is treated as an executive, though she does not join the family at meals or participate in their social life. Her meals are served by some other staff member. She may take them with a governess, social secretary, or other employee of professional rank, but does not join the service employees at their table. She is addressed by her last name and "Miss" or "Mrs." If a relative or friend is carrying the housekeeper's duties, she usually is known as a "companion" and is treated as a member of the family.

**HOUSEMAN.** "Houseman" or "houseboy" is the correct term for the employee who is the only male on a staff or who perhaps is the only employee. His duties are diverse, depending on the circumstances. Very often a houseboy cooks, serves, cleans the house, acts as a valet, and perhaps as a driver and general handyman. His usual uniform is a white cotton jacket, soft white shirt, black tie, dark trousers, and black shoes. He is usually called by his full first name, or by his last name without "Mr."

**INSURANCE.** It is customary (and only plain common sense) to carry insurance against any injury that might occur to an employee on the premises or elsewhere in the pursuit of his duties.

**INTRODUCTIONS.** See INTRODUCTIONS.

**MAIDS.** The word "maid" is generally used for any female domestic employee who helps out anywhere in the house—from a part-time cleaning woman to a full-time cook-laundress-nursemaid.

**Chambermaids.** Obviously, only a house with a very large staff has a maid assigned to such specialized work. Her duties in the main are to clean the upstairs rooms, halls, and baths; make beds and turn them down in the evening; draw the upstairs curtains, fill bedside carafes, and so on. She may also double as an extra waitress and perform some of the duties of a lady's maid as well. She is called by her first name.

**Clothes.** The standard maid's uniform is a cotton dress with a white collar, usually round. The dress today usually has sleeves ending just above the elbow and may be white, a pale solid color, or striped. It is worn with a white apron, white shoes, and beige stockings. If there is more than one maid, they wear matching uniforms. In a very formal household with several maids, uniforms of darker color and with long sleeves are also provided for use in the afternoon and evening. Black shoes are worn with those. If a maid is expected to wear a uniform, it is supplied by the employer. Maids do not wear caps today except on the musical comedy stage.

**Lady's Maids.** The duties of a lady's maid are defined by her alternate title, "personal maid." She tidies her mistress's bedroom and bathroom but does no heavy cleaning. She washes delicate lingerie, blouses, stockings, and does pressing and mending. She helps her mistress and women guests by packing, unpacking, laying out clothes, and seeing that all accessories are assembled and in good condition. She usually is a trained hairdresser and manicurist.

The daytime uniform of a lady's maid is a dark skirt, white shirtwaist, a small white or black taffeta apron, and black shoes. For late afternoon and evening, her formal uniform is a black silk dress of simple cut ((often of taffeta), a delicate white collar, and a black apron. She supplies her own clothes except for her aprons. She is called by her first name without "Miss" or "Mrs."

**Nursemaids.** In the house, the formal dress for a child's nursemaid is a uniform of simple shirtwaist cut, white shoes, and either beige or white stockings. She does not wear a cap. On the street, she wears any simple suit or dress and coat of her own, and a plain hat, but she often wears her uniform when taking her charge for a walk or to play in the park. Her uniforms are usually supplied by the employer.

A nursemaid is often addressed by the entire family by some special name like "Nanny" or "Jonesy." However, she is asked at the time of employment what she prefers to be called, and by her choice her first name, last name with "Miss" or "Mrs.," or a nickname is used.

**Parlormaid-Waitresses.** The duties of a downstairs maid are dusting and lighter cleaning of the living rooms and helping with the service of meals. In the morning she wears a light-colored uniform. The standard uniform for a maid serving a formal lunch or dinner is black, maroon, gray, or other dark solid color, with collar and cuffs of white organdy; a simply cut white apron of organdy or other material lighter in weight than her morning cotton apron; and black shoes. She is called by her first name.

**Part-Time Maids.** A part-time worker in any category—whether maid, cook, or cleaning woman—who comes once a week or at any other regular interval should be paid when the employer goes away for a short period, unless a clear understanding to the contrary was reached at the beginning of employment. It is not fair to suspend a cleaning woman, for example, without pay for the several weeks of an employer's annual vacation, since it is not likely that she can fill in that time. If her employment is to continue, so should her wages during any such absence.

A part-time worker supplies her own working clothes, though if an employer prefers that a uniform be worn, the employer supplies the uniforms. A part-time worker is asked what she wants to be called, and by her choice her first name or her last name and "Mrs." or "Miss" is used. If the house is more than a short distance from public transportation, the employer is responsible for picking her up and taking her to a bus stop—or for paying taxi fare in addition to her wages. Many employers also pay transportation to and from work.

**MANNERS IN GENERAL.** Meticulous courtesy from the employer is the best way to get correct behavior from the staff. An employer with any consideration for the feelings of others does not discuss servant problems in general or in particular in the hearing of a staff member. An employer may quietly direct a servant to a change of procedure, but properly does not make any sharp complaint or correction in the presence of others.

As a general rule, an employee rises when the employer or a guest stops to talk, and remains standing until asked to sit. During an interview of any length, an employee is asked to sit if the employer is seated.

The employer, any other member of the family, or a guest does not shake hands when an employee on the service staff is introduced or at any routine meeting, but of course a member of the family shakes hands with (or kisses) a valued servant, especially one long involved in family affairs, whenever circumstances call for some special expression of emotion.

An employee who gossips about the private concerns of a current or former employer shows a deplorable lack of discretion (to put it mildly), and should be both discouraged and distrusted. There is little hope that a talebearer will make an exception of anyone.

**MEMOS.** An employer signs a memo to a servant "M. G. Brown" or "M.G.B." —not "Mrs. Brown"—and signs a letter according to the standard rule: Mary Greene Brown.

An employee known in the house by only a first or last name signs a memo "Anna" or "'Jones," as the case may be. An employee known as "Mrs." or "Miss" signs either "A. Jones" or "A.J."—never "Mrs. Jones."

**PART-TIME WORKERS.** See "Part-Time Maids" above and "Social Security Taxes" following.

**REFERENCES.** It is customary to write a letter of reference and give it to a household employee when employment terminates, unless, of course, the employee has been dismissed for such serious misbehavior that no recommendation whatever can honestly be given. It is unfair to withhold a reference under other circumstances, since references in hand are of the greatest importance to anyone seeking a new household job.

A letter of reference must be fair to both the employee and any prospective employers to whom it will be shown. Minor causes of dissatisfaction are not mentioned in such a letter, but neither should fulsome recommendation be written unless it is deserved.

A letter of reference should mention the length of employment and the specific job the employee held, his degree of competence, his character (especially his honestly and sobriety), and the reason the employment terminated. If any of these standard items is left out of a letter of reference, it is a strong hint that the recommendation is given with reservations.

No salutation is needed. "To Whom It May Concern" or "This is to certify" is not necessary as an opening. No closing is required, either, though the letter must be dated and signed—a typed signature is worthless.

A standard form:

December 1, 1966

> Mary Smith has been with us for three years as a combination cook and general houseworker, and I can recommend her highly as a reliable person in every way. She is honest, discreet, sober, prompt, and has been especially valuable to us because of her patience, good nature, and good judgment in helping with our three small children, who love her dearly.
>
> She is leaving us because she wants to devote her mornings to her daughter's family, and we need a full-time maid.

I shall be happy to answer any questions about this exceptionally good, kind, and dependable person.

Mary Greene Brown
(Mrs. Henry York Brown)

10 Main Street
Stamford, Ohio
PLaza 0-0000

(In this letter of reference, Mrs. Brown makes no mention of Mary's cooking—a wide-open hint that good, kind, honest, sober Mary turns out dreadful dinners. Any experienced employer who reads the letter would call Mrs. Brown and get the lowdown about the flaw in this jewel.)

**SOCIAL SECRETARIES.** Men occasionally fill the position of social secretary, but more often it is taken by a woman. She must have a variety of skills. She is an expert typist who can take dictation in shorthand, and is equipped with the other skills of an executive secretary in business. In addition, she has a rounded, legible handwriting and is able to compose both business and social letters for her employers, typing or doing them in longhand as the occasion requires. She is, to some degree, a specialist in entertaining, able to assist in making out guest lists and seating charts, in the planning of menus and in handling other details of parties. Very often she is a confidential secretary in the sense that many financial details may be in her charge—she may keep the household books, pay bills, handle insurance, keep records for income-tax purposes. If there is not an executive butler or housekeeper, she often takes over some of their duties, such as planning meals, ordering supplies, hiring and firing, and in general acting as a deputy of her employer in the management of the household.

A social secretary may live under the roof of her employers all or part of the time, often travels with them, and operates as a companion as well as a specialist in the secretarial field. She supplies her own wardrobe, which must be sizable, since she is called on to join in some of the social activities of the family. She may take some of her meals with the family; otherwise, her meals are served to her alone by another staff member, just as those of a tutor or other professional would be. Though an employee, she is in no way treated as a servant, and is introduced to guests according to the standard rules for social equals.

**SOCIAL SECURITY TAXES.** By law, Social Security taxes must be paid on wages of fifty dollars or more earned in any one calendar quarter. The calendar quarters run from January through March, April through June, and so on. In business and for full-time domestic help, the required deductions and tax payment are a matter of orderly routine, but too often the law is evaded or forgotten for part-time domestic employees. Once a cleaning woman or any other part-time helper is employed on a regular basis, it is the obligation of the employer to take the initiative, ask for the employee's Social Security number, fill out the proper forms (obtained from the nearest Social Security office), and send them in. If an employer does not do this, the part-time worker should request it. Both employee and employer are subject to fine if the law is ignored, forgotten, or evaded. In addition, the employer has a moral obligation to see that part-time workers understand and obey this law. Their status as wage-earners is precarious, their income low. The only income that many of them will have in old age is from Social Security payments. These will be less than rightfully due if each employer does not do his required part.

**TIME OFF.** No self-respecting household employee is going to stay for long if treated like a prisoner. Everyone deserves regular, unsupervised free time, and what an employee does with those hours is not the business of the employer under most circumstances.

At the time of employment there should be a clear understanding about regular off-duty periods. Barring a real emergency, the employer is obligated to honor that agreement. It is entirely reasonable on occasion to ask an employee to switch his time off, if that will be convenient, from one day to another, but it is not fair to ask him to do so frequently or without ample warning. It is never fair to order an employee to make such a concession.

**TIPPING.** The general rule is that only guests who stay overnight or longer tip household employees.  *See* CHAUFFEURS; HOUSEGUESTS.

**TUTORS.** A tutor is treated as a member of the family. Since tutors usually are themselves of college age, they are generally called by their first names, as any other young friend of the family would be, but are given a title and last name by the service staff. A resident tutor commonly serves as a companion to his charges, and is expected to swim, play tennis, and so on during certain hours of the day, in addition to his teaching duties.

**VACATIONS.** Regularly employed staff members are entitled to a standard two-weeks vacation with pay each year. Although the employer decides when such vacations are taken, the actual time is best clearly understood, if possible, at the time of employment so that the employee can make plans.

**VALETS.** Modern custom in this country endorses pronouncing "valet" as it is spelled, with the "t" sounded and the accent on the first syllable; not "valay."

A valet performs duties similar to those of a lady's maid. He sees to pressing, polishing, and otherwise keeping a man's clothes in good order. He packs and unpacks and, unless there is an upstairs maid, turns down beds for male guests, draws curtains, lays out nightclothes, and sometimes assists in serving meals. He is addressed by his last name without "Mr."

A valet's usual dress is a dark blue or black suit, white shirt, black four-in-hand tie, and black shoes and socks. When serving meals he wears a white jacket or, in extremely formal circumstances, a butler's uniform.

## HOUSEMOTHERS

A housemother at school or college is the "head of the household," and has a right to the same considerate and courteous treatment that the young people under her supervision are expected to give at home to a real mother. It is never correct to treat her as a servant, a guard, or a mere figurehead.

When a boarding-school student complains repeatedly to his parents about a housemother's unfairness, unnecessary strictness, or apparent dislike of him, the parent is usually best advised to hear the housemother's side of the story before making an issue of the matter with the school authorities. The child who has not had to conform to many rules at home, or who is slow in adjusting to group living, may rebel against school restrictions and resent correction and discipline at the hands of a housemother who is only carrying out her proper responsibility.

A housemother is not tipped but may correctly be given a present at Christmas or at the end of the school year.

## HOUSEWARMINGS

Housewarming parties are based on an ancient custom—the blessing of a newly finished house by the ceremonial lighting of the first fire on its hearth when the owner moves in. Today's housewarmings celebrate a move to any new quarters, but are held at some time after the furnishing and decoration are complete enough to show off with pride and convenience—usually within weeks of the move but often not for some months.

A housewarming may be a casual party with friends dropping in during an afternoon for refreshments as simple as a nonalcoholic punch and cookies, or an elaborate dance, but an inspection of the premises is an expected part of the event. This does not mean that guests are free to open any closed door or to wander at will from attic to basement, unless asked to explore for themselves. Many people choose to have a series of small housewarming parties rather than one big one so that members of the family will not be so busy greeting and feeding guests that they do not have time to serve as escorts on the tour that is part of the fun for everyone.

An invitation to a housewarming at home calls for an answer. If the party is obviously a big reception, with guests invited to drop by between specified hours, the acceptance can be provisional, but if the invitation is for a definite hour a firm acceptance or refusal is required, just as it would be for any other party. A housewarming of a church, club, or place of business does not require an answer, however, if it is obvious that "come one, come all" is implied in the invitation.

It is customary, though not a requirement, for each guest to bring a small present for the new quarters—a kitchen gadget, or a vase or ashtray, for example.

## HOUSEWIFE

"Housewife" is still the standard title used to mean a married woman who does not carry a job for pay in addition to her work at home. It is the proper word to describe her occupation on such standard forms as applications for insurance, driver's license, and such. "Homemaker" is a coined word widely used in women's magazines. It strikes some people as rather belittling to the hardworking husband who pays the bills and not infrequently mans the washing machine, vacuum, lawn mower, and barbecue grill, and fixes the furnace, plumbing, and car.

## HUNTING AND SHOOTING

The most important rules of behavior for any sport involving the use of firearms concern safety. Anyone who uses a gun must remain constantly aware of its lethal capabilities, not only in the immediate area but also beyond the line of vision. It is more than a breach of etiquette to ignore safety precautions—it is an unpardonable irresponsibility. The other rules concern fair play to the hunted as well as to other hunters.

The most important safety precautions are these:

1. Never point a loaded gun at anyone. This is truly an unforgivable act.
2. Never point an unloaded gun at anyone either. Handle every gun with as much caution as if it were loaded.
3. Never leave a loaded gun unattended. Make it a habit to unload all guns at the close of each day's shooting, and always keep both guns and ammunition well out of the reach of children.
4. Never transport a loaded gun in an automobile.
5. Turn away from companions when loading.
6. Make certain that the safety is on until ready to shoot.
7. Carry a gun with the muzzle pointed toward the ground and away from one's companions, or on the shoulder with the trigger guard upmost so that the muzzle points skyward.
8. Never climb a fence or tree while holding a loaded gun.
9. Be sure of the target, and that the path to the target and beyond it is clear. Never shoot over the horizon (a bullet can carry incredibly far).
10. Don't forget the possibility of a ricochet from water as well as from a rock or tree.

Good sportsmanship does not depend on the sex of the hunter. The woman hunter properly observes the same rules as the man, and expects no special treatment or consideration from the men in the party except where a matter of physical strength may be involved—perhaps in packing a deer out of the woods. Anyone—man or woman—who gripes at discomfort and inconvenience in the field had best take up some other sport.

No true sportsman has respect for the hunter who takes more than the legal limit just because he can get away with it, shoots game out of season, or in any other way breaks the laws, written or unwritten, that ensure conservation by giving wildlife a sporting chance. A standing deer, bear, or other large animal is fair game, but a sitting duck or similar small game at rest is no target for a sportsman.

Giving a fair turn to his companions is also part of the sportsman's credo. If a shooting sequence has been agreed on, he observes it strictly and does not grab a shot out of turn, and he keeps his shots within his own quadrant if zones have been established.

It is the rule that once a hunter has shot at an animal, even if he misses, that animal is his no matter how much easier it might be for someone else to take it. Exceptions are made only if the hunter who missed or merely wounded the game invites a companion to shoot or when it is obviously necessary for someone to shoot in self-defense. Once an animal or bird has been wounded, a hunter is obligated to track it down and finish it off. It is both cruel and unsportsmanlike to condemn a disabled animal to the suffering of a slow death. For this reason, sportsmen resent the hunter who takes a chance shot at an animal that is practically out of range. If he wounds but does not kill it, the whole party must resign itself to what may well prove to be a long and tiresome pursuit (though at some clubs and preserves, staff members will track down crippled game for a guest).

The importance of remaining silent and moving both slowly and quietly will be quickly impressed on the beginner if he does not observe these rudimentary rules, as will the fact that the smell of burning tobacco does as much to betray a hunter's presence as noise.

**CLOTHES.** A guest is expected to bring hunting clothes suitable to the occasion, and if in doubt should make explicit inquiry of his host. Duck hunters, for example, wear clothes of protective coloring—dull browns and greens that blend with the background—and the guest who turns up in a light- or bright-colored jacket is obviously no duck hunter. On the other hand, bright caps and jackets are the standard safeguard for deer hunters who, in wooded areas, might otherwise be mistaken for game.

**DOGS.** A guest is expected to ask his host's permission before bringing his own dog. Each hunter handles and gives orders to his own dog or dogs, but —by the rules—never touches or gives an order to anyone else's dog. When a dog retrieves a bird, no matter who shot it, the bird belongs to the dog's owner—though he is obligated to hand it over if it clearly belongs in the bag of a companion.

**EXPENSES.** Costs to a guest vary considerably according to circumstances. A guest is always expected to bring his own gun, ammunition, and suitable clothes unless, of course, the host specifically states that he will supply them. Technically, what a host is supplying is an opportunity for the *sport* of hunting, and the game bagged by his guests belongs to him. Therefore, on a host's own land or on a preserve where the host is paying all expenses, a guest properly offers his bag to the host. The host generally does not accept it, but it is customary under such circumstances to divide a day's take more or less evenly among the members of a party.

A guest invited to hunt at a club or preserve where there is a fee should be prepared to pay his own expenses unless the host has made it clear that he is assuming all charges for his party, in addition to making the sport available by extending his membership privileges to his guests. These expenses may include a blanket charge for each gun or a set fee for each bird taken. The guest who pays such fees is entitled to keep his bag, but probably will be inclined to make a gift of part of it to his host if the host has been markedly unlucky.

**Tipping.** Guides and handlers are always tipped. Even if a host is paying all other expenses, a guest tips any employee who has accompanied him in the field, cleaned his gun, and so on, just as he would a locker-room attendant at a club. A man who has devoted a full day to a guest as a guide rates about five dollars, but a helper who divides his time among several guests rates about two dollars.

**LEGAL MATTERS.** Many states have strict laws regarding the registration of certain firearms. The gun-owner should inform himself about the local laws when shooting in an unfamiliar locality, since disregarding them can have serious consequences. A hunting license is required almost everywhere today, and the season for each type of game and the bag are regulated by state game laws. Club and commercial preserves, being privately owned and generally privately stocked, may have special rules of their own, but in any case are open only to members and their guests or to clients who pay a fee. Much other privately owned land is posted, and the sportsman who attempts to hunt, shoot, or fish on such land is guilty of trespassing and subject to fine if caught.

**PRIVATE AND POSTED PROPERTY.** Permission must be asked before hunting on private land—even if it is not posted—and thanks are due afterward. Offering the property owner some of the game taken is also a proper gesture. Permission given on one occasion is not blanket approval for years to come. The hunter who fails to close gates, makes breaks in fences, and causes other damage or inconvenience may convince the owner that posting his land is his only recourse.

## HUSBAND AND WIFE

We have some arbitrary customs about the use of "husband" and "wife" that put them into the list of problem words, and here they are:

A woman does not correctly speak of her husband as "Mr. Jones" to any social acquaintance, and a man does not speak of his wife as "Mrs. Jones." In this connection, the only right forms are "my husband [wife]" or, to anyone at all close, "John [Mary]"—even though the listener has not met John or Mary.

When speaking to business friends and associates, "My husband [wife]" is always a safe choice.

When speaking to a domestic employee, the correct form is "Mr. [Mrs.] Jones." "My husband [wife]" is not wrong, though less formal, but a first name is never correct.

A casual acquaintance who has not met a husband (wife) says either, "Does Mr. [Mrs.] Jones like fish?" or, "Does your husband [wife] like fish?" A friend on a first-name basis who does not know the spouse in question says "your husband [wife]" rather than using either the title or first name.

A secretary properly says, "Mr. [Mrs.] Jones is calling"—not, "It's your husband [wife]."

Domestic employees and children say, "Mr. [Mrs.] Jones"—not, "your husband [wife]."

"Bring the husband," "Ask the mister," "Tell your Mrs.," and so on are better avoided, and so is the constant use of "he" or "she," instead of "husband" or "wife" or a first name, as if those pronouns were names in themselves. "The ball and chain," "my better half," "my lord and master," like all clichés, are best used sparingly—if at all.

"Late" wife or husband means one who is dead—not removed by divorce.

"Former wife [husband]" or "ex-wife [husband]" is correct for a divorced spouse—not "Ex" by itself.

# I

## ILLNESS

Serious trouble aside, the victim does best to treat an ache, pain, or illness as a personal secret from anyone who cannot help—never forgetting that "How are you?" is a greeting, not a request for a health report.

When illness is given as an excuse for breaking an engagement, there is only one correct response, no matter how much inconvenience or disappointment the cancellation causes: "I'm so sorry. I hope you will feel better soon," and, if practical, the addition, "Is there anything I can do for you?"

See the Index for illnesses on particular occasions.

**INFORMAL.**  See FORMAL, INFORMAL, SEMIFORMAL.

## INITIALS AND MONOGRAMS

Two or more initials combined in a single design form a monogram. Therefore, strictly speaking, one initial is not a monogram even if it is embellished with elaborate decoration. Neither is a line of three or four initials that do not form an interlocking design. However, the two terms are quite commonly used interchangeably for all such markings, whether one or several letters are involved.

The main purpose of initialing or monogramming is to identify belongings such as handkerchiefs, household linen, or luggage that might become confused with those of others, though initials and monograms are also widely used for their decorative value.

The style of the letters and their size in relation to the size and use of the article to be marked are mainly considerations of taste. Men's handkerchiefs, shirts, and other such personal possessions look best marked with rather small block initials. A woman often uses somewhat larger block initials on sports clothes, but the usual choice for her more delicate and elaborate personal possessions is graceful script initials or an ornamental monogram of intricate detail. Some women like to have completely personal items such as handkerchiefs marked with a full first name.

**CLOTHES.**  If a man indulges himself in such elegant touches as initialed shirts, he chooses two or three discreetly small initials. A woman uses a single decorated initial, several initials, or a monogram on articles of clothing. Handkerchiefs marked to order usually carry more than one initial, though many men and women use the handkerchiefs that come ready-marked with a single initial. If only one initial is used, a man or boy uses the initial of his last name and a woman or girl that of her first name—though this rule is of no great importance and is often broken.

**Trousseaux.**  A prospective bride's wearing apparel is marked with the initial of her first name or with her full maiden initials. She does not have her personal things (except her luggage) marked with the initial of her fiancé's last name before the wedding, though she may add it after the wedding.

**GIFTS.** When in doubt, don't have a present marked. Arrange instead for the store to mark it later at the convenience and by the order of the recipient, who may prefer to exchange an item of clothing for something of a different size or color or, in any case, to choose the style and placement of the initials. All too often, young people are stuck with several identical wedding presents that cannot be exchanged because they are all initialed.

**HOUSEHOLD ITEMS.** There is no problem for the single person when it comes to marking bed, bath, and table linen, silver, matchbooks, or any other piece of household equipment. If one initial is used, it is that of the last name. If Mary Jane Brown (or Mark John Brown) uses three initials of equal size, the sequence is MJB; but the following sequence is used if the initial of the last name is to be emphasized:

$$\text{M}\textbf{B}\text{J}$$

There are a number of correct ways to use initials on all the household possessions of a married couple. Take, for example, the choices and arrangements of initials open to the former Mary Jane Brown who is now Mrs. William Smith:

1. S (last name)

2. M**S**W (her first name, last name, husband's first name. When this combination is used, the family initial is larger and the woman's first-name initial comes first.)

3. MBS   or   M**S**B, her first name, maiden name, family name. She could also choose the initials of her baptismal names (Mary Jane) and her family name (MJS), but this combination, though correct, is considered old-fashioned and not so often used today.

**Bed and Bath Linen.** Any of the preceding combinations is correct, but the first choice for marking "upstairs" linens is the initials of the mistress of the house (the third of the numbered examples).

**Miscellaneous Items.** Cigarette boxes, matchbooks, and other similar articles for general use are marked as shown in the first or second examples.

**Silver.** Any of the markings shown above is correct, but by far the most usual choices are those given in the first two examples. It should be noted that a great many people do not have the jeweler remove or add to the initials on inherited silver. Instead, out of sentiment, they use heirloom pieces "as is"— with the initials of Grandmother or Great-Uncle Hubert unchanged.

**Table Linen, and so on.** Any of the above markings is correct for linen, glassware, ashtrays, and so on, but the most popular arrangements are those shown in 1 and 2.

**Wedding Presents.** It used to be the rigid rule that all linens, silver, and other household presents given before a wedding were never marked with anything but the bride's maiden initials. This rule is completely out of date today. It is entirely correct to have a present marked in any of the three ways above, if the bride's preference is known. See "Gifts" under WEDDINGS.

**LUGGAGE.** It is always best to have luggage marked with two or three initials for quick identification. If an engaged girl's luggage is already marked with her maiden initials, the initial of her new last name is added before the wedding.

**PROBLEM NAMES.** The initials of last names like O'Brian, McGowan, MacChesney, van (or Van) Deurs, von (or Von) Berg, de (or De) Wolfe, duBois,

Du Bois, and DuBois, and all other such combinations present a number of choices. The main consideration is the appearance of the initials in combination with others. O'B is the first choice with the O'Brians, for example, but O alone is equally correct. McG or M, MacC or M, are both correct. When a name is written as two words, with the first one not capitalized (van Deurs, de Wolfe, etc.), the customary method of marking or monogramming is vanD, vonB, deW, and so on. The same is true for such names written as one word: duBois is initialed duB. If, however, the Van, Von, etc., is capitalized and the name written either Van Deurs or VanDeurs, the initial V alone is more often chosen. Under any circumstances, it is correct to use only the initial letter of the name according to the way it is listed in the telephone directory.

**STATIONERY.** *See* CORRESPONDENCE.

*See also* HERALDIC DEVICES for the use of crest, and so on.

## IN-LAWS

There have been so many sour jokes about relatives acquired by marriage that many people, when making an introduction, avoid "in-law" as if it were a dirty word.

*See* INTRODUCTIONS for the substitutes generally accepted today as more cordial.

## INSIGNIA

Insignia are badges, buttons, pins, patches, and other emblems that designate a service and the rank or rating of the wearer. On occasion, a mother or sweetheart is given an airman's wings, for example, to wear as a pin as an evidence of sentimental attachment, but it is poor taste to use the uniform buttons of a police department, fire department, or any of the Armed Services as decorations on civilian clothing.

"Insignia" is the plural (not "insignias").

## INSULTS

"The only gracious way to accept an insult is to ignore it; if you can't ignore it, top it; if you can't top it, laugh at it, it's probably deserved."—*Russell Lynes*

A famous definition of "gentleman" and "lady" is, "One who never insults anyone *unintentionally*." To this can be added, "A lady or gentleman is one who never takes word, deed, or manner as an insult when none was intended."

There is no complete remedy for either the calculated insult or one given under the hot impulse of anger. No matter how regretful or abject the apology, the memory of the insulting words remains. However, when an apology is offered it must be accepted. The acceptance can be stiff if the insult was deliberate. But if the insult was unintentional, the only sensible thing to do, in sympathy for the embarrassment of the left-footed giver, is to laugh and forget it.

**INTERRUPTIONS.** *See* CONVERSATION.

## INTOXICATION

"Wine drunken with moderation is the joy of the soul
and the heart."—*Ecclesiasticus XXXI, 36*

Our language is rich in words that give a fairly accurate idea of how much too much a person has had to drink—high, looping, tight, swacked, stiff, stoned, blotto, to mention only a few. But they all mean "disorderly" to some degree, and that goes for the merrily lit-up victim of just one too many who insists on doing all the talking, to the staggerer who has long since lost the wit to know when—or how—to go home.

So far as etiquette is concerned, it is anyone's privilege to drink as much as he wants in solitary confinement. But displaying the effects of too much to drink in public is an emphatic breach of manners because, in one way or another, a drunk is always a problem.

Dealing with a drunk is a touchy matter. He is detached from reality, in the state that Seneca defined as "voluntary insanity." He is likely to be deaf to logic, and to take any hint that he has had too much as an insult that can be expunged only by one more drink. No one has yet found a good way to deal with the person who has reached that point of irresponsibility, but the rule for the drunk himself is explicit. If he can remember having made a bore, burden, or spectacle of himself—and most especially if he *can't* remember—he is obligated to apologize to his hostess—no argument—since he is sure to have damaged her party in some fashion.

**ALCOHOLICS.** There is a complete difference between the heavy drinker who can avoid being a special problem if he chooses to observe a sensible limit, and the true alcoholic. The heavy drinker can stop after a number of drinks. The alcoholic cannot. One drink is enough to start him on a period of compulsive drinking that ends in stupefaction. There is no way to protect one's self and guests against chronic lushes in either category except to cut them off party lists when possible. However, the alcoholic who faces his malady by refusing all intoxicants deserves both admiration and special consideration.

Some alcoholics make things easier for themselves by explaining the reason frankly when refusing a drink: "No thanks. I had to cut it out—can't handle it." But a great many others choose to keep their susceptibility a secret and to evade drinks by various excuses, from "Not right now" to "I'm dieting." For this reason, it is never kind to urge a drink on someone who refuses, and a host with his wits about him does not make a teetotaling friend conspicuous by such a comment as "Still on the wagon?" He either provides a soft drink, if he knows his guest's preference, or asks, "What will you have?" when offering other guests a choice of hard liquors, and then hands over a nonalcoholic drink without comment.

**HANGOVERS.** The Chinese have a proverb, "The best cure for drunkenness is, sober, to look at a drunken man," and a good solid hangover is a sign that the time has come to remember this wisdom from the Far East. Only the very young think that a hangover is funny or something to boast about. A hangover is tangible evidence that the victim has something to regret besides, at that moment, being alive. Except to someone to whom he owes an apology for his actions while laying the foundation for his suffering, the victim does best to skip references to how he looks and feels, and hope that the pallor, red eyes, and lassitude of the morning-after will be attributed to the beginning of a head cold.

# INTRODUCTIONS

Introductions are governed by three basic rules. There are explicit exceptions to each, explained in the subdivisions following, but no one who keeps in mind the standard shortest form for all introductions and these three rules can go far wrong:

1. Introduce a man *to* a woman.
2. Introduce an adult *to* a much older one of the same sex.
3. Introduce the lower rank *to* the higher rank.

**BASIC FORMS.** Introductions most frequently go wrong (and old Mrs. Smith hears herself being introduced *to* little Johnny) because the person making the introduction tried too hard and used too many words.

When in doubt, forget all such elaborations as "May I present," and fall back on the always safe and correct shortest form, letting the warmth of tone, expression, and manner stand for all extra words: Say (distinctly!) both names, giving first the name of the person to whom another is being introduced—"Mrs. Smith—Mr. Jones" and "General Smith—Captain White," for examples.

Many young people are understandably confused by this so-called "form of safety" because at first thought is seems that Mrs. Smith is being introduced *to* Mr. Jones, since he hears her name before she hears his. Think of it another way, and the logic of this sequence of names comes clear. Saying Mrs. Smith's name first is to catch her attention and prepare her to receive the introduction of Mr. Jones to her. However, what is of paramount importance is the inflection of the words and the manner of the person making the introduction, so that both clearly indicate the meaning: "Mrs. Smith, *this is* Mr. Jones."

Two widely used, correct, but slightly longer forms are "This is Mr. Jones" spoken directly to Mrs. Smith, and then, to him, "Mrs. Smith"; and "Mary [to catch her attention], Mr. Jones," and then to him, "Mrs. Smith."

The most ceremonious form is "Mrs. Smith, I have the honor to present Mr. Jones." It should be forgotten for all ordinary purposes. This form is generally reserved for an introduction to an extremely high dignitary of church or state, to royalty, and of a distinguished speaker to an audience.

"Mrs. Smith, may I present Mr. Jones" is also extremely formal, and is generally used only when making an introduction to an elderly person or a very distinguished one. It is not incorrect, though rather stilted, when making an introduction of a man to a woman under ordinary circumstances. It should not be used when introducing people of the same sex if they are of about equal age and distinction, since the form implies that one person is decidedly older or more important than the other. This form is not used with first names—"Mary Smith, may I present John Jones" is not correct.

Informal but correct and widely used in circles where new acquaintances use first names immediately after meeting are introductions without titles: "Mary Smith—John Jones" (followed by the addition, to him, if it needs to be established that she is married, "Mrs. Smith"). Otherwise, if the title of one person is used, that of the other must also be used (with the exception of certain relatives); "Mary Smith—Mr. Jones" and "Mr. Smith—John Jones" are not correct (unless John is a boy).

**Forms to Avoid.** There are many variants of the correct forms given above, including such statements of fact as "I want you to know," but the best forms are the simplest ones. Better forgotten under all circumstances are "I want to make you acquainted with" and any words that have the overtone of an order like "Make the acquaintance of," "Meet Mrs. Brown," "Shake hands with Mr. Jones," and especially "Meet the wife" or "Meet the Mrs." Also to be avoided is an introduction that by any chance can leave one or both people floundering to recall a last name. "Mary, you remember Joe" can make it difficult if either has drawn a blank and, in turn, needs to make an introduction.

An introduction is a one-way street. The double introduction, "Mrs. Smith—Mrs. Jones. Mrs. Jones—Mrs. Smith," is not used today.

**Identification.** It is often useful to give two strangers some hint of a common interest when making an introduction so that they do not have to fall back on the weather as a subject of conversation—"Mrs. Smith, this is Mrs. Jones, who also collects Sandwich glass," for example—but exact business labels are not given under social circumstances. "This is Mr. Jones, Advertising Manager of City Stores—Mr. Smith, President of Standard Stores" is strictly a business form. But once the basic introduction has been made, it is good social practice to mention their similar business interests in some casual fashion like "Mr. Smith is also in merchandising," and let the two pursue that conversational opening if they like.

Certain family relationships are always mentioned if unknown to the person receiving the introduction: "Mrs. Smith, my daughter Jane," for example. However, some labels of relationship or association are subtly belittling. "Mrs. Smith, this is Bob Hope's cousin! Mr. Jones" sounds as if Mr. Jones's family relationship is his only claim to her interest. It may well be, but unless Mr. Hope is present and there also is some reason for immediately identifying Mr. Jones as his relative, it is better to communicate the exciting fact in some other way than as a label during an introduction.

Avoid the empty label "my friend." "Mrs. Smith, this is my friend, Mrs. Brown" has two unfortunate implications: that Mrs. Brown is the speaker's only friend and that Mrs. Smith is not a friend.

**BASIC RESPONSES.** Any introduction must be acknowledged—no argument about this rule. Not to do so is an affront to the person innocently making an unwelcome introduction, as well as to the person being introduced. A response can be cool—but it must be made.

Technically, the person to whom an introduction is made is the first to say "How do you do" and to extend a hand, but in practice both people usually acknowledge an introduction simultaneously—though a man should, by the rule, wait for a woman to offer her hand unless he is in a receiving line. A smile and bow are actually all the response required, and can serve very well if the manner is properly cordial, but they can be extremely stiff unless the smile and manner are unquestionably warm.

The spoken response correct under all circumstances is an exchange of "How do you do." Nothing more is necessary. The repetition of the name, alone, of someone being introduced—"Mr. Jones"—is also correct, but can easily sound distant. "How do you do, Mr. Jones" is the usual and best form; it implies that the name is important to remember, and also helps fix it in the memory.

A man takes off his hat when being introduced to a woman, but need not do so during an introduction to a man under usual circumstances. If one man tips or touches his hat, the other correctly follows suit.

A man rises when being introduced to a woman even if he is elderly and she no more than eighteen, unless he is incapacitated by illness or some infirmity. Under all usual circumstances, a man rises and shakes hands when another man is introduced. As a general rule, a woman does not rise for any social introduction, though there are some definite exceptions to this rule—notably when she is introduced to a very high dignitary of a church (a bishop and ranks above), the head of a country, royalty, and, as a token of respect for such a man's position, for an introduction to his wife; and a very young woman rises to be introduced to a woman very markedly her senior and for a very old man (provided, in both cases, that she is not seated at a dining table).

A handshake is usual between men, unless the introduction is made across a room or in other circumstances where to rise and shake hands is obviously awkward or impossible. A woman may offer her hand or merely bow, though it should be remembered that in Europe both men and women customarily shake hands during an introduction. As noted before, the person to whom an introduction is made is the first to offer a hand  However, any offered hand must be shaken, even if this rule has been broken. Refusing a proffered hand, except for some good reason such as having a demonstrably dirty or wet hand oneself, is an insult.

**Responses to Avoid.** "How do you do" and "How are you" are the standard responses, but they are empty formulas of greeting, not questions that require an answer other than an echoed "How are you." Certainly they do not call for any detailed report on health or happiness at the moment of introduction.

"Hello" and "Hi" are perfectly good responses under limited circumstances. They are entirely too breezy, though, from a much younger person to an older one who has used the formal "How do you do." And they are not a correct response from anyone under formal circumstances—an introduction in a receiving line, for example.

By today's custom, strictly to be avoided are "Pleased to make your acquaintance," "Delighted," "Charmed," "Honored," and "My pleasure." Some genuine words of pleasure like "I'm so glad to meet you" are correct if followed by an explicit reason ("because my daughter has told me . . ."), but otherwise a standard "How do you do" said with warmth and evident pleasure is better than an effusive or pretentious response.

Especially to be avoided is "You don't remember me, do you?" When this is obviously the fact, it is better to accept an introduction as if a prior one had never been made, or to make any reminder of it definite.

**BUSINESS.** The social rules are very often correctly reversed for business introductions because on some (but by no means all) occasions rank or position (not sex or age) determines which person is properly introduced to another.

Following are the major exceptions to the social rules that men are introduced to women, and younger persons to older ones. It should be remembered that exceptions themselves are also rules *in general*. There are scores of occasions for which exact procedures for business introductions have never been clearly defined as always right or always wrong. When in doubt, follow the standard social rules and don't worry—no one has all these answers. The important thing is to identify each person to the other by business function and affiliation as well as by name—and get on with the business in hand.

Anywhere on business premises, an ordinary caller (man or woman, including an employee's wife or other nonbusiness visitor) is as a very general rule introduced *to* the owner or president of the organization and to the employee's immediate chief.

When a staff member takes a visitor into anyone's private office, the same general rule holds, and a stranger of either sex is introduced *to* the occupant.

When introducing fellow employees on business premises (other than the private office of one of them), the lower in rank is usually introduced to someone in a higher position; a woman secretary, for example, is introduced to a man who has just joined the firm as a top executive. If there is little or no difference in rank, a new employee is introduced to those of longer standing.

When introducing two business acquaintances away from business premises—on the street, for example—the social rules are followed and a man is introduced to a woman.

**Acknowledging.** Staff members and visitors alike usually follow the social rules in responding to an introduction, but some exceptions are correctly made. The occupant of a private office cannot go wrong in rising to receive an introduction in it. A man usually rises for any introduction—but a male caller does not rise when a secretary enters her chief's office and is introduced to him. A woman has to use her own judgment about rising. Common sense has to be the guide, since the rules for all occasions simply are not standardized. A secretary, for instance, does not rise from her desk if a business caller is introduced in passing; but she would rise to be introduced to a person of high rank or special distinction—her chief's wife, for example.

**Business Titles.** Quite the opposite from the social rule, it is both useful and correct to identify business people by rank and affiliation during their introductions: "Mr. Smith, president of City Stores—Mr. Jones, president of Town and Country Products."

The most formal introductions are made by using "Mr.," "Miss," or "Mrs." and the last names of both people. However, both titles are used or both omitted, regardless of age or rank. "Mrs. Smith, this is Mary Brown" is not correct when introducing a saleswoman to an executive or customer.

In business a man properly breaks the social rule and makes a self-introduction under certain circumstances as "Mr. Brown."

Full details about the use of "Mr.," "Miss," and "Mrs." when making a business self-introduction are given under BUSINESS MANNERS.

**CHILDREN.** The rules for adults are (hopefully) followed by children when they make an introduction or are introduced, except that little children do not shake hands with each other, and a girl stands up to be introduced to any adult. Even a small child can learn to observe the following basic rules:

1. Stand when being introduced.
2. Make some response other than a silent stare.
3. Take any proffered hand.
4. Introduce other children to adults, especially to one's parents.

As a child grows older, the refinements can be added, but if a very small child manages to follow these basic rules, no matter how sketchily, he is brilliantly on his way. If a young child says, "This is Billy," without adding his little friend's last name, or responds with no more than a polite smile when he himself is introduced, save until later any corrections beyond an encouraging hint. Painful to child and guest alike at such a time—and therefore not the best of manners from a parent—is criticism of a good try.

Well before the first grade, youngsters should have grasped the fact that any response to an introduction must be accompanied by a smile; and they should long since have learned that a slight bow is also a standard part of a response.

**Adults Introducing.** All children are introduced to all adults (with the exceptions noted under "Servants" below).

A child who is not a relative is introduced by first and last name: "General Smith, this is Betty Jones." The borderline at which a girl graduates positively to the title "Miss" is vague, but it hovers somewhere about sixteen, depending on how well grown for her age she may be. After they reach eighteen, boys and girls are entitled to "Miss" and "Mr." in formal introductions except when introduced by a parent.

(For the rules about introducing one's offspring of any age, see "Relatives" below.)

**COUPLES.** When introducing one married couple to another, the form is "Mr. and Mrs. Smith—Mr. and Mrs. Brown." There is no need to introduce Mrs. Brown first to Mrs. Smith, then Mr. Smith to her, and so on.

**DIGNITARIES AND OFFICIALS.**

See FORMS OF ADDRESS for the correct use of clerical, governmental, military, and other professional titles.

**FORGOTTEN NAMES.** On occasion, everyone draws a blank and cannot recall a well-known name. When, instead of a proper introduction, someone makes some such remark as, "You know Bill Brown, don't you?" it usually is a desperate hint for help. The unidentified person should come promptly to the rescue and state his own name—to the stranger, however; not to the person making the introduction, since that would only emphasize the error.

**GROUPS.** The rule that men are always introduced to women is correctly ignored when introducing a woman or a married couple to a mixed group. If Mr. and Mrs. Smith arrive at a party at which there are already six other guests, first say their names to the group as a whole: "Here are Mr. and Mrs. Smith." (Or "Here are Mary and John Smith" if the first names of the other guests will be used.) Then give the name of each of the other guests, going around the circle from either right or left: "Mr. Jones, Mrs. Green, Miss Brown, Mr. Green, Miss Towne, Mrs. Jones." It is confusing and quite unnecessary in this case to introduce the Smiths to all the women first, or to introduce all the men to Mrs. Smith and then introduce Mr. Smith to all the women, or for handshakes to be exchanged.

If the group is very large—a cocktail party, for instance—a newcomer is introduced to a few of the guests. After that, the roof is considered an introduction for all who are under it, and guests speak with each other as they please without identifying themselves, or make self-introductions *(see below)* if they like.

**GUEST OF HONOR.** When a guest of honor is standing in a receiving line, all other guests, including women, are introduced *to* him. However, no one need bother about this point very much because his very presence in the receiving line is a tacit introduction *of* him to all the people who have been invited to meet him. For all practical purposes in ordinary circumstances, if there is no receiving line, it is safe to follow the standard procedures and introduce a man *to* a woman. Far more important than the form, in this case, is seeing that all guests have a chance to exchange at least "How do you do?" with the guest of honor.

**HOST AND HOSTESS.** A host introduces all guests under their roof *to* his wife. A stranger arriving with strangers, men or women, in tow identifies them *to* his host and hostess. This convention is as old as man—the identifying of the outsider *to* the chief guardian of the cave, the head of the tribe, the king of the castle. By the same token, a hostess logically introduces a stranger under their roof *to* her husband—though often this rule is neither sensible nor graceful to follow. In any case, it need give no one a headache; the hostess can always avoid the stiff formulas of the precedence of names and use some other words that are natural and easy. For example, the natural thing for a hostess to say to ancient, distinguished Mrs. Brown is something like "That's John over there, who has been looking forward to meeting you. John, this is Mrs. Brown."

**LETTERS OF INTRODUCTION.** See CORRESPONDENCE.

**RANK.** When introducing two people who are in the Armed Services, with the younger person having the higher rank, the senior in *rank* receives the introduction. Colonel Smith, fifty years old, is introduced to General Brown, who is only thirty-five. The same rule holds when introducing members of the clergy. *(See* FORMS OF ADDRESS.)

Under all social circumstances, business rank is ignored—men are introduced to women, younger people to older, regardless of their relative business positions.

**RECEIVING LINES.** *See* separate entry.

**RELATIVES.** The relationship is specified (unless it is obvious) when introducing a relative.

A wife never introduces her husband as "Mr.," and a husband never introduces his wife as "Mrs.," except to servants, salespeople, and others in service positions. The standard form is "Mrs. Smith, this is my huband"—never "This is Mr. Jones." If a wife would feel absurd calling an intimate friend "Mrs. Smith" in this circumstance, she says, "Jane—my husband [or John]"; and then, to him, if he does not know Jane's last name, "Mrs. [or Miss] Smith." "Mr. Brown, this is my husband, George Grey," is the correct form if Mr. Brown knows Mrs. Grey under a professional name different from her husband's name—as Miss Mary Ann Green, for example.

A parent does not use "Mr." or "Miss" when introducing offspring of any age. A son and an unmarried daughter are introduced by first name only: "Mrs. Smith, this is my daughter Mary" (if the mother has a different last name through remarriage, "my daughter Mary Tower"). The response to a child is "How do you do, Mary." The formal response to an adult is "How do you do, Miss [Mr.]

Jones." If one's child holds a professional title, it may be given in this fashion: "Mrs. Smith—my son Bill, *Dr.* Jones," or more formally, "my son, Dr. Jones." The form for introducing a married daughter is "Mrs. Smith—my daughter Mary, Mrs. Towne," or more formally, "my daughter, Mrs. Towne."

Brothers and sisters are identified according to the rules given in the preceding paragraph. Half-brothers and half-sisters are identified as "brother" and "sister."

Aunts, uncles, and adult cousins are introduced by title and last name: "Mrs. Smith, this is my aunt, Mrs. Brown"—never "This is my aunt," or "my Auntie Brown."

**Relatives-in-law.** There is nothing incorrect about using "mother-in-law," "sister-in-law," and so on, but the following forms are more cordial and in many cases more explicit, and so they are first choice.

When introducing someone to one's mother-in-law, a good form is "Mama [or whatever she is called], this is Mr. Jones." Then, to him, "Mrs. Smith is John's mother" or "my husband's mother." Either phrase makes the relationship clear. The same form is used for a sister- or brother-in-law: "Mrs. Smith—Mrs. York, my husband's sister."

The relationship and also the last name of a stepparent, stepbrother, or step-sister are mentioned if to omit them would cause confusion. "Mrs. Smith, this is my stepfather, Mr. Jones," is the correct form for someone whose name is White, for example. If the name of both is Jones, "This is my stepmother" is sufficient, but warmer when suitable is "my new mother."

**SELF-INTRODUCTION.** Under all social circumstances, a man of any age does not use "Mr." before his name when introducing himself. He says, "I am John Jones." The same rule applies to an unmarried woman of any age—she does not introduce herself with the title "Miss." Identifying one's self as "Mr." or "Miss" Jones is correct only to servants, tradespeople, or others in service positions, and under certain business circumstances.

It is correct to use a professional title when making a self-introduction, however, since to omit it would lead to confusion about the proper form of address in answering. Therefore a clergyman identifies himself as Father Smith, Rabbi Stern, Canon Jones, and so on. Anyone who expects to be addressed "Dr. Jones" introduces himself by that title.

A married woman making a self-introduction has a choice. Under all usual circumstances, a young married woman says, "I am Mary Smith," and then adds, if it is necessary to establish her title, "Mrs. John Smith." A more formal self-introduction and one often used by an older woman is "I am Mrs. John Smith" (using her husband's first and last names—not just "Mrs. Smith").

**Response.** The use of first and last names in a self-introduction is not necessarily an invitation to use the first name in replying. The formal response to an adult who says, "I am Mary [John] Jones," is, "How do you do, Miss [Mr.] Jones. I am Jane [George] White." Not to state one's own name immediately in response to a social self-introduction (unless one's name is obviously known) is a pointed rudeness.

**SERVANTS.** Following are the standard rules for household employees on the service level—but not for such categories as companions or social secretaries. These procedures also are not strictly applied to the household help that many families of modest means have in some communities—the neighbor whom the employer sees also at school and church, even though she comes in regularly to cook.

If an introduction is made, a domestic employee is always introduced *to* a guest, but generally an employee and guest are identified to each other rather than formally introduced. For example, a hostess might say to a houseguest,

"Anna will take your things," and then to the maid, "I'll show Mrs. Brown her room later." The guest acknowledges this semi-introduction with "Thank you, Anna," and the maid replies with something like "Glad to, Mrs. Brown."

When a servant is introduced, a guest does not offer to shake hands.

As a rule, an employee is not introduced to a guest who is in the house for a meal only. However, on an informal occasion if there is some reason to identify a maid, for instance, the form is "Mr. Brown, this is Anna [or Mrs. Greene, but not Anna Greene] who made the cookies I sent you." Mr. Brown replies: "How do you do, Anna. The cookies were wonderful." And Anna says, "Thank you, Mr. Brown," and nothing more unless the guest asks a question.

To a houseguest, a staff member usually is identified when they first encounter each other if a member of the family is present. Otherwise, when speaking to a houseguest for the first time, staff members identify themselves by whatever name the family uses. For example, a maid who knocks on a bedroom door to offer any service says, "I am Jane, Mrs. Smith. May I do any pressing for you?" If the employee omits the guest's name, the guest does not supply it in this circumstance, but says only, "Thank you, Jane," and adds any request necessary.

A new household employee is introduced *to* all members of the family, little children and grownups alike, by the names each will use to the other. To one's husband, the form is "This is Anna Greene [or Mrs. Greene], who is going to cook for us," and then to Anna, "Mr. Jones." The use of her first and last names without "Miss" or "Mrs." tells him that she will be called "Anna" by the family, and so his reply is "How do you do, Anna." The form for introducing a male employee is "This is Joseph Greene," and then to him, "Joseph [or Greene]—Mr. Jones," thereby telling an adult member of the family which of the two names of the new employee will be used.

When a new employee is introduced to a little child, the form is "Billy, this is Anna" ("Miss" or "Mrs:" Greene only if that is what everyone in the family will call her). If an employee will call an older child or other relative "Miss Jane," "Mr. George," "Miss Jones," or "Mr. Jones," it is also made clear in the introduction: "This is Anna," and then to the new employee, "Miss Jane," or "Mrs. Brown," or whatever.

**TELEPHONE.** *See* TELEPHONE MANNERS.

**TITLES.**

For the use of professional titles, *see* "Self-Introductions" above, and FORMS OF ADDRESS.

**UNNECESSARY INTRODUCTIONS.** There is seldom any point in introducing two people who meet only in passing and who are unlikely to see each other again; therefore, common sense is the best guide about when friends must be introduced.

It is not customary to introduce a companion when stopping briefly for a word with another friend unless there is some special reason to do so. But if the conversation is prolonged, an introduction should be made.

It is quite unnecessary for a host or hostess to introduce a guest who is leaving a party to one who is just arriving unless there is a particular reason to identify them to each other. Let the departing guest speed on his way, without delay at the door.

At a sizable gathering, it is not necessary to introduce all guests individually. Making a determined tour of the room with a newcomer only interrupts conversations to no point, since few people remember names recited en masse.

A repairman identifies rather than introduces himself by name—"I'm the plumber" or "I'm from the gas company"—and a name is not given in return unless there is specific reason to do so.

## INVITATIONS

A formal invitation may be engraved, handwritten, telegraphed, or telephoned, but it always is phrased in the third person. That is the major difference between the formal and informal invitation, so far as wording goes. Informal invitations are all invitations not expressed in the third person. By no means does "informal" in this connection indicate that the event itself will be informal or that dress can be casual. Frequently, one of the many informal invitation forms is used for a small party of stiffest white-tie formality—a small dinner before a big formal dance, for example.

A second difference concerns the appropriate use of formal and informal invitations. It is never correct to issue a formal engraved invitation to an informal party—a barbecue on the beach, for instance.

The rules that govern the wording, spacing, spelling, styles of paper and lettering, addressing, and answering of formal invitations are given in the section following this one. They are quite rigid and should be carefully observed. It is better to extend an invitation in any informal fashion than to ignore the rules for formal invitations in any detail.

There is somewhat more latitude in the forms of everyday or "informal" invitations, spoken or written, but here too certain details are governed by rules that are not correctly ignored. These are explained directly below:

**Rules in General.** There are slight differences in procedure between spoken and written invitations, but the most important matter in all cases is to be explicit about details so that a guest will know what is expected of him and what to wear.

1. When giving a verbal invitation, don't trap a prospective guest by questions like "Are you free Friday night?" or, worse, "What are you doing Friday?" which demands an accounting of another's plans that may be none of the questioner's business. "I hope you can come to dinner next Friday because the Smiths are bringing over their slides of the Grand Canyon" is a good example of an invitation that gives the invitee a chance to refuse gracefully if he wants no part of the Smiths or home movies or travelogues.

2. A man should never put the full burden of choice of entertainment on a woman guest by making a date for a specific time and then saying, "What would you like to do?" A good host takes charge by making some kind of suggestion or suggestions—the movies, dancing, bowling, or whatever—so that his date is not left wondering what to wear. The same rule holds if a guest accepts an invitation to dine in a restaurant. The wide-open "Where would you like to go?" has its built-in financial dangers for the host. It also puts a woman who does not know his preferences in food or the limits of his pocketbook in an extremely awkward position. The only correct procedure is for the host to suggest one special restaurant or a choice of several in his price range.

3. A formal engraved invitation is issued jointly in the names of the host and hostess. An informal invitation, either verbal or written, is correctly issued by the hostess. If a couple is concerned, the hostess telephones or writes to the wife and she replies to the hostess. This rule is properly observed in all written invitations, but in our busy world is very often and sensibly ignored when invitations are given in person. If, for example, it is far more convenient and practical for the host to extend an invitation to a couple through the man, whom he sees daily, he does so—and no one gives the matter a second thought.

4. A last-minute invitation calls for some explanation. If everyone is being invited at the last minute, say so to make sure that no one feels he is being

asked to fill in as a second choice. When a guest is really being asked to fill in at the last moment, a frank account of the emergency is always best because the guest is quite likely to discover the fact for himself anyway.

5. When it is convenient for a guest, he gives his reply in the same form as the invitation. But it is usual and entirely correct to answer an informal invitation in whatever fashion is most convenient—to telephone an answer to a written invitation or telegraphed invitation, perhaps.

6. An invitation to a meal always requires an answer even if it does not carry R.S.V.P. or some other direct request for a reply. The rules say that an invitation to a meal should be answered within about three days—a good procedure to follow with all other invitations whenever possible.

7. A written invitation to tea, cocktails, or a similar party does not technically require an answer if one is not specifically requested. But an acceptance is always correct, and a refusal with explanation is considerate of the hostess's feelings if the guest is not going to put in an appearance.

8. No explanation need be given when refusing a formal invitation, but an explanation must always be given when refusing an informal invitation. There is no necessity for going into great detail. "I'm so sorry, but I'm not free that evening" will serve, but even a vague excuse is better than none.

9. The acceptance or refusal of an invitation should be explicit as well as prompt, though a provisional acceptance is correct, if the rules are observed; it is certainly far better than withholding any answer until the very last moment. For instance, a guest invited to dinner can properly say, "I'd love to come, but I'll have to refuse because I won't know until Monday whether I have to be at a board meeting [or whatever] that night." Such an answer gives the hostess a chance to say, "I'm sorry—I'll ask you another time," if she is planning a small party and must be sure of balancing her list of men and women; or to say: "Monday is plenty of time to let me know. I do hope you'll be able to make it."

10. An acceptance, especially of an invitation for a meal, is a word-of-honor promise to appear, and, like any promise, it should not be broken except for a real emergency. There are occasions, of course, when it is only sensible to postpone a casual date for dinner and the movies, for example, in order to accept an invitation to an unusually festive or important event. But the guest who chronically breaks dates because a better offer comes along does not inspire confidence—or continuing invitations.

11. If a couple is invited to a cocktail party or a similar gathering, one may accept and the other refuse. On the other hand, if the invitation is to a meal, both must refuse if one cannot accept—though there are ways to leave the door open without putting the hostess on the spot. If the refusal is phrased in some such words as, "I'm afraid we can't come because Bob will be out of town," the hostess can say: "I'm so sorry. We'll really miss you," and let it go at that. Or she can go on, "But *you* can come, can't you?" if she can accommodate an extra woman.

12. A husband and wife should never assume that their children are included in an invitation unless "Bring the children" has been a specific part of the invitation. It is permissible to give the hostess a heavy hint—"I'm sorry, but we can't come because our baby-sitter is away"—but never to make an outright suggestion—"We'd love to come if you don't mind our bringing Dolly? She'll be quiet and happy just watching television." (If such a suggestion is made, and

the trapped hostess says anything like, "I'm afraid the poor child would be really bored—we have only one set and it's in the living room . . ." the guest had better make other arrangements for little Dolly—no argument.)

13. The preceding rule applies to a dog also. Never turn up with Fido in tow, no matter how good a dog he may be, unless he has been specifically invited.

14. Asking for an extra invitation for anyone is a touchy matter with few exceptions. Most hostesses welcome an extra man with pleasure. Even so, the request to bring an extra guest is best made indirectly by a tentative refusal: "I'm sorry, but my classmate Mary Brown is visiting us that weekend." This gives the hostess a more graceful choice than does the blunt, "Do you mind if I bring our houseguest?"

**LETTERS.** Handwriting is considered the best form for a note of invitation, but it is not obligatory today when typewriting is acceptable for virtually all correspondence. The address of the writer should appear somewhere on the invitation, and so should the date. The addition of a telephone number indicates a request for a telephoned answer. A signature is always handwritten.

Standard forms *(either typed or handwritten):*

100 Broadview Avenue
July 10

Dear Mrs. Greene,

    Will you and Mr. Greene dine with us on Friday, July 18, at seven o'clock at the Cosmopolitan Club? We are eager to hear about your trip.

Sincerely yours,
May Statten Brown

Plaza 1-2345

April 28

Dear Jane—Do hope that you and Peter can come to us for cocktails at seven, buffet dinner at eight—Friday, May 9— to meet our new next-door neighbors— Robert and Janet Smith.

    Too long since we've seen you!

Love,
Mary Jane

(The address need not be added if the note is to an intimate friend unless it is signed with only a first name that is a common one. When that is the case, adding the address prevents a possible confusion with another Mary, Bob, Bill, or Jane.)

**PRINTED PARTY CARDS.** Commercially printed cards with spaces for time, place, date, and names to be filled in are practical and popular. Their use generally indicates that perhaps twenty or more guests are being asked. If the invitation is to a couple, the envelope is addressed "Mr. and Mrs. George Smith," not to the wife only as is correct for a personal note.

**REMINDER NOTES.** When an invitation is given in person, especially at a party or in surroundings where the invitee does not have his datebook handy, it is practical to send a reminder note to make sure that there is no confusion about time, day, and place. A visiting card or foldover informal can be used with "To remind you—Saturday, June 10, dinner at 7:30" written on it. Or if more details are needed, a little note serves better. It can be handwritten, or typed with only the signature handwritten:

> Dear Jane,
>    Just to remind you that we are looking forward to seeing you and Bob for dinner at 7:30, Saturday, June 10, at the River Club—black tie.
>
>                          Love,
>                          Mary

**REPLIES.** The date and the time are repeated in the acceptance, no matter in what form it is given. So is the place if elsewhere than the host's own dwelling. Only the date is repeated in a refusal.

**TELEGRAMS.** The general form of a brief handwritten note is followed except that "Dear Mary" or any other salutation is omitted:

> MRS. HENRY YORK BROWN
> [Address]
> HOPE YOU AND HENRY CAN COME TO DINNER
> SATURDAY APRIL FOURTEEN AT SEVEN.   LOVE
>                          JANE GRAY

(The answer would be addressed to Mrs. Robert Gray or Miss Jane Gray, as the case may be, and should be wired or telephoned if time is short.)

**VERBAL.** A spoken invitation is never properly given in the presence of an acquaintance who is not included in the plans, and the same holds for a spoken acceptance or refusal. As noted above, a reminder card or note or a telephone call to confirm details is always a good idea if the invitation has been given when the guest has no opportunity to make a record of the time and place.

A spoken invitation from one child to another is always followed up by a call or note from his mother.

**VISITING CARDS.** A visiting card or, far more often used, an engraved foldover informal is practical and correct for an informal invitation or reply if their matching envelopes meet post-office requirements and are at least 2¾ inches by 4 inches in size. The use of either one for an informal invitation generally indicates that about twenty or more guests are being invited, though they can be used for smaller parties. If an invitation in the form below is to a couple, the envelope is addressed to "Mr. and Mrs. George Smith," not to the wife alone, as would be correct for a handwritten note. Because cards and informals are so small, it is both correct and customary to use abbreviations. If the message is in the form of a complete sentence, it may be written on the inside of an informal:

Other examples are under VISITING CARDS.

To meet—
Senator & Mrs John Greene

*Mr. and Mrs. John Brown Smith*

Tuesday. Feb. 14
5<u>30</u>    to    7<u>30</u>

R.S.v.p.                    20 Bank St.

## INVITATIONS, FORMAL

A formal invitation is always expressed in the third person whether it is engraved, printed, handwritten, telegraphed, or telephoned. In addition, there are explicit rules concerning the wording, spacing, spelling, punctuation, paper, lettering, use of names, and addressing. These rules are given immediately below. The reader is then referred—for specific examples—to the subdivision following, under the head "Basic Standard Forms."

**ADDRESSES.** In the body of the invitation and also on the envelope, short house numbers may be spelled or a numeral may be used: "Ten Park Avenue" and "10 Park Avenue" are both correct (though "One" is always spelled out). The same rule holds for numbered streets: "245 East Tenth Street" and "One 179th Boulevard" are both correct. (Note that "th," "rd," "nd," etc., should have a line underneath when handwritten: 179th.) Street, Boulevard, etc., are never abbreviated.

Today, the zip-code number is a standard part of an address, and is correctly used on all envelopes, and also within an invitation when an address follows R.S.V.P.

**ADDRESSING.** *See "Envelopes" below.*

**DATE, HOUR, YEAR.** The date is spelled: "the tenth of May," or "May the tenth" (never "May tenth," "May ten," or "May 10").

The hour is spelled: "at eight o'clock." The standard expression for times other than the hour are: "half after ten o'clock," or "half-past ten o'clock," or "a quarter before eight o'clock" (not "eight fifteen" or "7:45"). "A.M." and "P.M." are not used. When necessary to be explicit about the time of day—in the case of a reception, for example—the words "in the morning" or "in the evening" are added.

The year is not given on an invitation to a strictly social meal or other private party (it is optional on an invitation to a wedding). It is usual and correct to use the year, spelled in full, on formal invitations to business and official events and to fund-raising banquets, balls, and other such functions.

**DECORATIONS.** An invitation bearing the word "Decorations" (usually on the lower right corner) indicates an occasion of white-tie formality. Anyone entitled to wear a decoration or medal is expected to do so.

*See* DECORATIONS, MEDALS, ORDERS.

**Engraving and Printing.** The most formal of invitations are engraved, though process-printing that imitates the raised letters of engraving is also correct today. Ordinary printing is never correct on a formal social invitation, but printing may be used on business invitations that otherwise follow the formal style.

**Lettering.** The most popular engraving styles for invitations are Antique Roman and Script. Other styles widely used for formal invitations of all kinds are reproduced in the WEDDINGS section. It is best to choose from among the traditional styles, and to avoid novelty faces that look like type rather than engraving.

**ENVELOPES.** Title and the first, middle, and last names of the guest are used in addressing a formal invitation. If the invitation is to a couple, the envelope is addressed to "Mr. and Mrs."—not to "Mrs." alone, as would be correct in an informal letter of invitation.

A return address, including the zip-code number, should always be used. Its correct place is on the flap of the envelope. On the most formal invitations, it is embossed in white or sometimes engraved in a pale gray. However, if a colored border is used on the invitation (as it often is today for dances and other parties), the return address can match it.

The stamplike seals and stickers issued by charities during fund-raising campaigns are not correctly used on the flaps of formal invitations.

Double envelopes are used only with wedding invitations and announcements, and invitations to wedding anniversary parties.

**INK.** Black or blue-black ink is correct for formal handwritten invitations and replies, and for addressing engraved invitations. Save the colored inks and the felt-tipped pens for informal notes of invitation.

**NAMES.** A title and the first, middle, and last names of anyone issuing a formal invitation are used: Mr. and Mrs. Henry York Brown ((never John and Mary Brown). The same rule holds if a guest of honor is mentioned in the invitation.

Only the title and last name of the person or persons invited are written on the invitation: Mr. Land, Miss Jones, Mrs. Smith, or Mr. and Mrs. White. The title and full name of the persons invited are used on the envelope, however: Mr. George Ralph Land.

*See* FORMS OF ADDRESS for the correct use of all other titles.

**PUNCTUATION.** Periods are used only after the very few permitted abbreviations: Mr., Mrs., R.s.v.p., and Jr., for example. Commas are used only when necessary to separate words within a line, never at the end of a line.

**R.S.V.P.** These initials stand for the French words *Répondez, s'il vous plaît.* Any invitation that carries them or their translation ("Please Reply") requires an answer. R.S.V.P. and R.s.v.p. are both correct. A period is used after each initial when they are engraved or printed, but the periods are often omitted when the initials are handwritten.

**REGRETS ONLY.** On occasion, these words are used as a compromise between R.S.V.P. and a reply card. This dodge was invented to save both hostess and guests time and trouble though they certainly do not always achieve that purpose. They seem more appropriate for a business party than a social event.

**REPLIES.** All invitations carrying "R.S.V.P." (or the equally correct "R.s.v.p."), "Please Reply," and so on, must be answered as promptly as possible. If the rules are followed, a reply is sent within a day or two after a formal invitation is received.

A formal reply, whether mailed, telephoned, or telegraphed, is worded in the third person. A formal written reply follows the wording and spacing of the invitation almost exactly. A reply to a business invitation may be typed, but all other replies are handwritten.

Unless the invitation requests that the reply be addressed to someone other than the giver of the party (a social secretary, perhaps), the envelope is addressed exactly as the giver's name appears on the invitation: Mr. and Mrs. Henry York

Brown, for example, if the invitation is issued by a couple—never to Mrs. Henry York Brown alone (which is the correct form in answer to an informal invitation).

An acceptance repeats the date and the hour. The place is repeated also if the party is elsewhere than in the home of the giver.

A refusal repeats the date, but not the hour and place. A refusal does not require an explanation, though it always is correct to give one.

One member of a married couple does not properly accept a formal invitation to a meal if the other must refuse. It is correct, however, for only one of a couple to accept an invitation for a cocktail party, reception, or similar event.

**REPLY CARDS.** There is no question that an answer card, with blank spaces to be checked to indicate acceptance or refusal, is the most efficient way to get the prompt replies needed in advance of a big party so that an accurate order can go to the caterer in good time. However, the rule still holds that reply cards are not correctly enclosed in a strictly formal social invitation. This is one of the traditions that is not changing, and so it is best not to break it.

Reply cards are correctly used only with invitations that have some business or charitable or promotional aspect—to banquets, balls, and other festivities for which tickets are sold, for example. An addressed envelope usually accompanies a reply card.

**STATIONERY.** Fine, heavy, white or cream-colored paper is the standard conservative choice for formal engraved invitations, but gaining popularity very quickly are the same fine papers with a narrow border of color. This touch of color is a major breakthrough of long-established rules for formal invitations, but it has won instant approval and is now correct, especially for dances, but is used also for more staid events.

There is a wide range of sizes for engraved invitations. Most often chosen are those that fit an envelope about 6 by 4½ inches. The invitation itself may be on a double sheet that is folded once to fit the envelope, a double sheet that fits without folding, or a single card, depending on the occasion.

Personal letter paper of fine quality and standard size is used for completely handwritten invitations in the third person. Such paper may carry the address or a monogram or heraldic device at the top, but not a printed or engraved name. The invitation is written on the front of a folded sheet, which is preferred to a single sheet.

(See CORRESPONDENCE for further details about letter papers.)

**Business and Fund-Raising.** There is more latitude of choice in the quality, color, and shape of stationery used for formal invitations to such events as the premiere of a movie held for charity, the opening of an art show, or a luncheon, banquet, or ball held for any fund-raising or promotional purposes. Tinted paper and colored ink are often used as eye-catching devices on printed invitations that otherwise conform to regular formal standards.

**For Replies.** Any personal letter paper of fine quality and standard size is used. White or off-white is the most conservative choice. The sheet may be single or double, and may carry the address but not an engraved or printed name at the top. Unmarked paper may also be used. If a double sheet is used, the reply is handwritten on the front, not within the fold.

A reply to a formal business invitation is typed in the standard third person form. A business letterhead can be used if a suitable one is available, or plain paper—though a reply card is usually enclosed with a formal business invitation.

**TELEPHONE NUMBERS.** A telephone number under R.S.V.P. is not correctly used on a formal social invitation. On very rare occasions, a telephone number is engraved in this position if there is an extremely short time between the mailing of the invitation and the party—a real emergency measure more suitable to a business than a social event.

On personal letter paper where a telephone number is so often correctly used, the area code as well as the number is a blessing to distant friends.

**TIME OF MAILING.** A formal invitation is mailed at least two weeks in advance of the event, and very frequently a month in advance.

**TISSUES.** The stationer inserts small pieces of tissue paper to protect the engraving from possible smudging. They are not removed before the invitation is sent.

**WORDING.** The words "request the honour of your presence" are used only in invitations to a religious ceremony such as a wedding. "Request the pleasure of your company" is correct for all other festivities.

The traditional spelling on formal engraved invitations is "honour," though it is entirely correct to use "honor" if the standard American spelling is preferred.

If there is a special guest (or guests) of honor, the standard wording is "to meet Senator John Starr Grey," for example. "In honor of" is used only on engraved (not handwritten) invitations, and is rarely used except for special occasions.

**To Indicate Dress.** It is customary (and a kindness to guests) to indicate in the invitation to any evening event the degree of formality of dress that is expected. If none of the following terms is placed in the lower right-hand corner of an engraved invitation to a party after 6:00 P.M., it can be taken for granted that Black Tie for men and dinner dresses for women are expected, but it is far better to use one of the explicit terms:

"Dancing" (on an "At Home" invitation): White Tie for men; ball dresses for women.

"White Tie" or "Decorations": standard term to indicate full evening dress. ("Formal" is not correct.)

"Black Tie": dinner suits for men; dinner dresses for women. ("Tuxedo" is not correctly used on an invitation as a substitute for "Black Tie.")

"Dress Optional": either dinner suits or dark street suits for men; dinner dresses or dressy cocktail dresses for women.

"Informal": dark street suits for men; dinner or cocktail dresses for women.

## BASIC STANDARD FORMS

A formal invitation may be completely engraved, partly engraved with blank spaces to be filled in by hand, or completely handwritten. Wording and spacing are the same for all three forms.

**Completely Engraved:**

*Mr. and Mrs. Henry York Brown*
*request the pleasure of your company*
*at dinner*
*on Wednesday, May the fifth*
*at eight o'clock*
*100 Broadview Avenue*
*R.s.v.p.*                    *Black Tie*

If the party is elsewhere than at the home of the giver, the form above is changed to read:

*at eight o'clock*
*The Town and Country Club*
*Kindly reply to*
*100 Broadview Avenue*
*Stanton, Connecticut 00000*                              *Black Tie*

If the answer is to go to someone other than the party-giver—a secretary, for example—her name and address are given under the reply request line. The reply envelope is addressed to her, but the reply enclosed follows the standard form above.

*R.s.v.p.*
*Miss Joyce Carol*
*40 Main Street*
*Stanton, Connecticut 00000*

(*Note:* If town and state are used, the zip code must be used also.)

**Partly Engraved:**

(*Note:* This partly engraved form, with spaces to be filled in by hand, is usually on a card about 4 by 5 inches. These cards are useful to those who do a great deal of formal entertaining.)

*Mr. and Mrs. Henry York Brown*

*request the pleasure of the company of*

*at*

*on*

*at*                              *o'clock*

*R.S.V.P.*
*Twenty Exchange Place*
*New York 00000*

**Completely Handwritten:**

*Mr. and Mrs. Henry York Brown*
*request the pleasure of*
*Mr. and Mrs. Barkeley's*
*company at dinner*
*on Wednesday, May the fifth*
*at eight o'clock*

*R.S.V.P.*                    *100 Terrace Avenue*
                              *Miami, Florida 00000*

(*Note:* In a handwritten invitation, the address is moved to the bottom right side, opposite the R.S.V.P.)

**ACCEPTANCES AND REGRETS.**

**Acceptance.** The date and hour are repeated in an acceptance. The place is repeated only if the party is elsewhere than at the home of the giver:

> Mr. and Mrs. Walter Jay Smith
> accept with pleasure
> the kind invitation of
> Mr. and Mrs. Brown
> to dine
> on Wednesday, May the fifth
> at eight o'clock

**By One of a Couple.** It is not correct for one of a couple to accept an invitation for a meal if the other cannot accept, but one of a couple may accept an invitation to a reception or other similar event:

> Mrs. Walter Jay Smith
> accepts with pleasure
> the kind invitation of
> Mr. and Mrs. Brown
> to the wedding reception of their daughter
> on Wednesday, the tenth of June
> at five o'clock
> at The River Club
> but regrets that Mr. Smith
> will be unable to attend

**Canceled Acceptance.** A reason must be given when an acceptance is canceled, and the cancellation must be sent as soon as possible. If time is very short, it is telephoned or telegraphed. Otherwise it is handwritten:

> Miss Mary Locke White
> regrets exceedingly that
> due to the illness of her mother
> she is forced to cancel
> her acceptance for dinner
> on Wednesday, May the twelfth

**Regret.** The time and place are not repeated in a regret. The full name and title are written as they appear on the envelope of the invitation. The simplest form is:

> Mr. John Towne White
> regrets
> that he will be unable to accept
> the kind invitation of
> Mr. and Mrs. Brown
> for Tuesday, the fifth of May

(*Note:* It is not necessary to give an explanation in a formal refusal, except to an invitation from the White House or from royalty, but it is always correct to add on a separate line, after the word "regrets," a phrase such as "because of a prior engagement" or "because of illness."

**CANCELED INVITATIONS.** A formal invitation is canceled only for a serious reason such as illness or a death in the family. If an engraved invitation was used, either an engraved or printed cancellation is correct. If time is extremely short, the cancellations are telephoned or wired. A reason is given in the cancellation whenever possible.

### Engraved, Printed, or Handwritten Cancellation:

*Mr. and Mrs. Henry York Brown*
*regret exceedingly*
*that owing to the illness of Mr. Brown*
*they are obliged to recall their invitations*
*for Wednesday, May the twelfth*

### Telegraphed Cancellation:

MR AND MRS GEORGE STATEN SMITH
[address]
MR AND MRS HENRY YORK BROWN REGRET EXCEEDINGLY THAT
OWING TO THE ILLNESS OF MR BROWN THEY ARE OBLIGED
TO CANCEL THEIR INVITATIONS FOR MAY THE TWELFTH
[no signature]

**Telephoned Cancellation.** In giving a formal cancellation by telephone, no attempt need be made to reach a guest in person; the message is given to a secretary, household employee, or anyone else who answers the telephone. The caller says, "Will you take a message for Miss White?" and then dictates the message in the third-person form of the telegram above. Of course if a host or hostess is making the call and the guest answers, the third-person form is not used.

**POSTPONED INVITATIONS.** No reason need be given for postponing an invitation, though it is not incorrect to include one. The same rules as for a cancellation are followed:

*Mr. and Mrs. Henry York Brown*
*regret that it is necessary to*
*postpone their invitation to*
*dinner from Wednesday, May the fifth*
*to Wednesday, May the twelfth*
*at eight o'clock*
*100 Broadview Avenue*
*R.s.v.p.*

**REMINDER CARDS.** An engraved reminder card with blanks to be filled in by hand is useful to those who issue a great many invitations in person or by telephone. They usually are about 3½ inches by 5 inches. The purpose of a reminder card is to make sure that there is no confusion about day, hour, and place, and perhaps dress. A formal reminder card may also be completely hand-written, and this form is frequently used when the date of a party has been changed by telephone.

A reminder card may be sent following a verbal acceptance, but is never sent if a written acceptance has been received.

Two standard forms:

(approximately half actual size)

This is to remind you that

expect you for

on

at                    o'clock

> *This is to remind you that*
>
> *Mr. and Mrs. John Brown Smith*
>
> *expect you for*
>
> *on*
>
> *at*                    *o'clock*

## VARIATIONS OF THE STANDARD FORMS

**AT HOME.** Somewhat illogically, the words "At Home," "at Home," or "will be at home" on an invitation indicate an extremely formal reception or dance, very often at a club or hotel, and usually a very large guest list, rather than an intimate gathering under the party-giver's own roof—though "At Home" can also indicate a formal reception or dance at a private residence.

An "At Home" invitation is very rarely used today for a tea, cocktail party, or other late-afternoon reception, though it may be used for an event of especial formality such as a debutante reception.

When the word "Dancing" also appears on the invitation, "At Home" indicates a very formal and private dance. An "At Home" invitation may be handwritten on a double fold of plain fine paper, but usually is engraved on a heavy white card about 3½ by 5 inches. It is plain or has only a crest embossed without color.

### "At Home" Invitation for a Very Formal Dance

*Mr. and Mrs. Henry York Brown*
*at Home*                    [or At Home]
*Friday, the third of December*
*at eleven o'clock*
*The Plaza*

R.S.V.P.
100 Broadview Avenue
Stanton, Connecticut 00000                    *Dancing*

### "At Home" Invitation for a Reception

*Mr. and Mrs. Henry York Brown*
*will be at home*
*Friday, the third of December*
*from five until eight o'clock*
*The Plaza*

R.S.V.P.
[as above]

### For a Guest or Guests of Honor:

*In honour of*
*Mr. and Mrs. John Barton Lane*
*Mr. and Mrs. Henry York Brown*
*At Home*
*Tuesday, the seventh of December*
*from nine until eleven o'clock*
*The Assembly Club*

R.S.V.P.
[as above]

### "At Home" Invitation for a Tea or Tea Dance

Though the host is present and fulfills all the duties of a host, and even though equal numbers of men and women are invited, his name usually does not appear on this very formal invitation, unless the party is in honor of a distinguished guest. In that case, the form immediately preceding is used. Otherwise, only the name of the hostess (or hostesses) is used.

**BALLS.** The word "ball" in an invitation indicates a public, semipublic, or official function. It is not correctly used in an invitation to a private dance, no matter how large. The wording and spacing of a formal dance invitation are followed, but the purpose of the ball and the price of admission, and very often the year and the name of the dance orchestra, are added. For a charity ball, it is correct to add a list of sponsors elsewhere on a printed invitation. A reply card and envelope are properly enclosed. The form given under "Banquets," following, is a standard one.

**BANQUETS.** Today, "banquet" is used only for a public, semipublic, or official dinner. The word is never used in the invitation to any strictly social dinner party no matter how large and elaborate it may be. A banquet invitation very often is printed rather than engraved. The wording and spacing follow the social dinner-invitation form, but the purpose of the function, the names of speakers, and the price are added. The dress expected is specified. As on an invitation to a fund-raising ball, a list of patrons or sponsors, speakers, and other pertinent facts may appear elsewhere on the folded sheet. A reply card and envelope are customarily enclosed. There are many correct variations of this standard form:

*The Society of Citizens for Action*

*requests the pleasure of your company*

*at their thirteenth*

*Annual Banquet*

*on Friday, the tenth of February*

*One thousand nine hundred and sixty-six*

*at eight o'clock*

*Grand Ballroom*

*Hotel Pierre*

*R.S.V.P.*
*Mrs. Charles Bernard*
*38 Central Park South*                          *Black Tie*
*New York 10019*                          *Subscription Forty Dollars*

(*Note:* A name and address under R.S.V.P. are omitted if a reply card and envelope are enclosed.)

**BUSINESS INVITATIONS.** Invitations from a firm or organization usually serve a promotional or publicity purpose. They follow the rules for a social invitation, in general, but always make the reason for the party clear. They often are printed rather than engraved, and a return address is printed on the envelope. If printed, a paper other than the formal white or ivory may be used.


Crown Publishers, Inc.

request the pleasure of your company

at a reception

in honor of

Miss Stephanie Sterling

on the publication day of her book

"But Why Can't They Spell?"

Monday, the tenth of October

from five to seven o'clock

Hotel Delmonico


R.S.V.P.
419 Park Avenue South
New York 10016


(*Note:* A telephone number, instead of the address, under R.S.V.P. is also correct on a formal business invitation; it indicates that a telephoned reply is requested.)

**Reply.** The entire form of the business invitation need not be followed. A standard form, typed on business stationery or handwritten on personal stationery:

*Miss Joan Towne*
*accepts with pleasure*
[*or regrets that she will be unable to accept*]
*the kind invitation of*
*Crown Publishers, Inc.*
*to a reception*
*on Monday, the tenth of October*
*at Hotel Delmonico*

(*Note:* Time and place are not repeated in a regret.)

**Dances.** The word "ball" is never correctly used in an invitation to a private dance. *See* "Balls," above.

"At Home" is used only for a most formal reception or dance. *See* above.

"Small Dance" is very often used to indicate a formal party with a sizable but not crushingly large guest list. The word "small" is always omitted in the acceptance.

**Standard Fully Engraved Form.** The fully engraved invitation omits the name of the guest, and so is the least formal:

*Mr. and Mrs. Henry York Brown*
*request the pleasure of your company*
*at a dance*
*on Saturday, the tenth of May*
*at half after ten o'clock*
*The River Club*

*R.s.v.p.*
*25 Maple Terrace*
*Albany, Idaho 00000*

**Standard Partly Engraved Form**

*Mr. and Mrs. Henry York Brown*

*request the pleasure of the company of*

Mr George Thomas Staten

*at a small dance*

*on Saturday, the tenth of May*

*at half after ten o'clock*

*The River Club*

*R.S.V.P.*

[as above]

**DEBUTANTE DANCES.**  *See* DEBUTS.

**GRADUATIONS.**  *See* GRADUATIONS AND COMMENCEMENTS.

**GUEST OF HONOR MENTIONED.** The following is the basic form if a reception, dinner, dance, or any other party is held in honor of a special guest or guests. This invitation probably would be fully engraved for a very large reception, but would be handwritten for a fairly small dinner party. If handwritten, the address would be moved to the lower right in line with R.S.V.P.

*Mr. and Mrs. Henry York Brown*
*request the pleasure of*


*company at a dinner in honour of*
*Mr. John Brian Smith*
*on Wednesday, the fifth of May*
*at eight o'clock*
*The Plaza*

*R.S.V.P.*
*Apt. 6 F*
*38 West 59th Street*
*New York 00000*


(*Note:* "In honour of" is appropriate only on engraved invitations. Anyone who has a supply of the partly engraved invitations shown in this section under "Basic Standard Forms" adapts them to this use by writing "To meet," followed by the title and name of the honor guest, above the engraved name of the host.)

**MULTIPLE HOSTS.** When several individuals or couples issue a joint invitation, their names usually appear in alphabetical order, though in certain cases seniority or marked distinction may dictate the order. For example, if the children of a couple are joint hosts at a party celebrating their parents' Golden Wedding Anniversary, their names might be listed in order of age. The reply envelope is addressed to the one name listed under R.S.V.P., but the enclosed acceptance or regret lists all of the names on the invitation.

> *Mrs. Henry York Brown*
> *Miss Ada Bell Grey*
> *Mrs. Arthur Karl Smith*
> *request the pleasure of your company*
> *at luncheon*
> *on Wednesday, the second of June*
> *at one o'clock*
> *Town and Country Club*
>
> *R.S.V.P.*
> *Mrs. Smith*
> *50 Overlook Drive*
> *[city, state, zip code]*

If this invitation is handwritten, it is changed to read:

> *request the pleasure of*
> *the company of*
> *Mrs. Greene*

(Only title and last name of the guest are used, though the full name is written on the envelope, of course.)

**PATRONS.** For charity balls and other fund-raising events, it is customary to assemble as impressive a list of sponsors as possible, since the use of distinguished names in publicity is of great help in selling tickets. In many states, there are laws prohibiting the use of anyone's name for fund-raising without his explicit permission—and good taste prohibits doing so anywhere. Therefore, some such invitation and reply form as the following is used:

*The Committee of the Charity Ball*
*has the honor to invite*
[title and full name written by hand]
*to be a Patron of the Ball*
*for the benefit of*
*The Emergency Fund*
[etc.]

With this invitation, a reply card is enclosed. It follows the standard form, but with these additions:

Each patron is requested to be responsible for at least four tickets. Tables for ten or more are available.

Name_____

(Please give your name as you wish it to appear on the Patrons' List in newspaper and other releases.)

**REPLY CARDS**

I will / will not    be able to attend the Annual Awards Dinner of
The Society of Citizens on Saturday, April fourteenth.
Please reserve _____ tickets at $12.50 each
a table for eight _____
a table for ten _____
Check enclosed for $_____
(Name)_____
(Address)_____
(The names of my guests are listed on the reverse side of this card.)

**TELEGRAMS.** Telegrams are rarely used for a formal invitation, but are entirely correct if the circumstances call for speed. The form remains in the third person, though abbreviated:

MISS MARY LANE SMITH
[address]
MR AND MRS HENRY YORK BROWN REQUEST THE PLEASURE OF MISS SMITH'S COMPANY AT DINNER WEDNESDAY MAY FIFTH AT EIGHT O'CLOCK AT THE ARMY AND NAVY CLUB. BLACK TIE. R.S.V.P.
[no signature]

(*Note:* No signature is used with the formal third-person form. The words "STOP," "COMMA," and so on, are never used, since standard punctuation is transmitted.

**Formal Telegraphed Reply.** A reply is always telegraphed or telephoned in answer to a telegraphed invitation. It also is correct to telegraph a reply to an invitation issued in any other form, if more practical than a handwritten reply, though the latter is generally preferred otherwise.

MR AND MRS HENRY BROWN
[address]
MISS MARY LANE SMITH ACCEPTS WITH PLEASURE MR AND MRS
BROWN'S KIND INVITATION FOR WEDNESDAY MAY FIFTH.

[no signature]

**TELEPHONE CALLS.** A formal invitation given over the telephone to a household employee or a secretary uses the third person but varies the form somewhat: "Will you take a message for Mr. and Mrs. White? Mr. and Mrs. Henry York Brown hope that they will come to dinner next Wednesday, the sixth, at eight o'clock. Mrs. Brown's telephone number is PLaza 0-0000." The person who receives the call is expected to write the message down and then repeat it to the caller to make sure that place, date, and time have been correctly noted.

**Formal Telephoned Answer.** Much the same form is used: "Will you please tell Mrs. Brown that Mr. and Mrs. Steven White will be happy to dine on Wednesday, the sixth, at eight o'clock" or "regret very much that they will not be able to dine on next Wednesday, the sixth, because of a prior engagement for that evening."

**WEDDINGS AND WEDDING ANNIVERSARIES.** See WEDDINGS.

## INVOCATIONS

An invocation is a prayer offered at the beginning of a meeting or service of worship. When the Pledge of Allegiance is also part of the ceremony, the invocation always precedes it. An invocation is usually given by a priest, minister, or rabbi, but some fraternal organizations and societies have an officer whose duty it is to offer the introductory prayer and in other ways function as a chaplain for the group.

During an invocation everyone stands, eyes lowered, head slightly bowed, showing the respect that is due any prayer. Men remove their hats during an invocation at an outdoor ceremony.

# J

## JAM AND JELLY

Jams, preserves, and marmalades usually are served only at breakfast. If they are to be eaten with toast, they are put on the butter plate, if there is one; if to be eaten with waffles, pancakes, or French toast, they go on the main plate.

Cranberry and the other tart jellies served at lunch and dinner as an accompaniment to meat are put on the main plate, not the butter plate.

See MEALS AND THEIR SERVICE.

**JEWELRY.** See BIRTHSTONES; CLOTHES.

## JEWESS

Say, "She is Jewish" or "She is a Jew." "Jewess" is a displeasing term to Jews.

## JOB

"Job" no longer has the connotation of a minor or subservient state of employment. "Job" and "position" may be used interchangeably—but a really important official is much more likely to refer to "my job" than to "my position."

**JOKES.** See CONVERSATION.

**JUDGES.**  See FORMS OF ADDRESS (The Courts).

**JUNIOR AND SENIOR.**  See NAMES.

# K

## KISSING

The social "kiss"—a touching of the cheeks—is widely used today between people who are no more than affectionate acquaintances. A woman usually does not give a man this greeting in a public place, though there is no firm rule.

In general, an embrace in public between a man and a woman should be brief, no matter how emotionally warm their relationship. That goes for girls and boys, too—in spite of all the evidence to the contrary.

If not already on affectionate terms with a little child, better think twice before demanding a kiss or be prepared for a disconcerting response. Well known to parents is the honest "I don't want to."

**KNIVES.**  See MEALS AND THEIR SERVICE; TABLE MANNERS.

# L

## LADLES

Gravy may be poured from the lip of a gravy boat or taken with the gravy ladle. After use, the ladle is returned to the gravy with its hollow up and the handle away from the pouring lip, not put on the attached base or the underplate unless the gravy is so hot that the spoon would be uncomfortable to touch. The long-handled ladle used in a tureen or a punchbowl should be put back with its hollow up.

## LADY AND WOMAN

Depending on by whom and to whom they are spoken, the words "lady" and "woman" have entirely different overtones, and it is important to have a clear understanding of their rather tricky differences. An innocent misuse of either word can hurt someone's feelings—or reveal the speaker as a bit uncertain of the rules ladies and gentlemen are expected to know.

Every woman rates the title "lady" under certain circumstances. Without exception, under her own roof she is "the lady of the house," for example. She is also "lady" when she is a customer or patron. A salesperson, receptionist, or anyone in a similar position says, "This lady is next"—never "This woman is next." And a customer speaking to a salesperson, waiter, porter, and so on says the same about another patron. Either at home or in an office, an employee says, "A lady to see you," when announcing a caller. A host or hostess says to a waiter, "I am waiting for two ladies"—not "two women."

A woman never correctly uses "lady" when speaking of herself. She does not say, "I am the lady who telephoned yesterday." Instead, she makes the direct statement "I called yesterday," or "This is Mrs. Smith who . . ." Neither does she properly identify herself as "the lady next door"; to both a maid and members of the family, she identifies herself by name or says, "I live next door."

Children use "lady" when referring to an adult unknown by name: "Who is that lady?"—never "Who is that woman?"

Customs vary in different circles, but it is generally best not to lean over too far backward in the use of "lady"—as in "That is the lady who cleans for us." To many people, "cleaning lady" sounds as patronizingly contrived as "handy gentleman" would. "Woman" and "man" are the dignified and correct words to use in connection with job titles—cleaning woman, handyman, for example—just as "career woman" rather than "career lady" is correct. If anyone feels that "woman" in such a connection might hurt an employee's feelings, the problem is best solved by using her name ("This is Mrs. Smith—or Julia—who comes in to clean") or the job title ("our cook," "their maid," and so on).

"Woman" is the correct word to use in speaking about a relative or friend when the emphasis is on the social equality of the listener. A husband speaking about his wife to a social or business acquaintance says, "My wife is that tall woman." Only to a doorman or someone in a similar position would he correctly say "that lady." Women follow the same rule and avoid using "lady" when speaking to acquaintances. "I hear his wife is very pretty" or "such a pretty woman," for example—not "such a pretty lady."

An exception to the above rule is made for a woman of great age. "Such a kind old lady" is correct as an indication of special respect, but the qualifying adjective must be used. "Such a kind lady" has a subservient overtone and is used properly only by someone in a service position. When making a statement of fact, "She is a very old woman" is correct, but so is the more affectionate "a very old lady."

"Mrs. Brown is an aggressive woman, but she *is* a lady" is an example of how tricky the use of the two words can be. In this sense, "lady" is correctly used to mean that a woman can be depended on to observe the best rules of conduct. "She is a great lady" is a great compliment that designates a woman of outstanding character as well as behavior.

And as a closing note on the complications of this subject: "ladies" and "women" are both correct when *writing* about manners.

## "THE LATE"

"The late" is used only in reference to a dead person. It is never used to mean a former wife or husband removed by divorce. "The late" is always used, when applicable, in a release sent to the press. Even though one parent of an engaged girl is dead, both parents are mentioned in the copy: "daughter of Mrs. Henry York Brown and the late Mr. Brown," or, if her mother has remarried, "daughter of Mrs. George Scott Greene and the late Mr. Henry York Brown." "Daughter of Mr. and Mrs. Henry York Brown" is incorrect if either parent is dead.

**LAVATORY.** *See* BATHROOMS AND WASHROOMS.

## LAZY SUSANS

These turntables are suitable at any casual, informal meal. Small ones set in the middle of a table are practical for serving condiments or—at breakfast—jam, marmalade, sugar, cream, and butter. Large ones are useful on a small buffet table, as well as in the center of a small dining table, for the many items that accompany elaborate curries or rijsttafel, or for dishes carrying second helpings.

## LECTURES

There is room for only one lecturer at a time in any auditorium. The obligation of anyone attending a lecture is to listen quietly, no matter what his personal reaction to the speaker and his opinions, and not to attract attention to himself by whispers, groans, or gestures. The time for contradicting a speaker or asking a question is after a lecture, not during it.

A lecturer is applauded after his introduction or, if he is not introduced, when he takes the stage. He is also given the courtesy of at least token applause at the end of his talk. One or two rounds of applause during a lecture are flattering if they are truly spontaneous, but constant interruption by applause is a handicap to a speaker, and is best not promoted by his devoted friends.

Anyone sitting on the platform does not correctly initiate applause, but is required by good manners to join in applause following the speaker's introduction and after his closing words, and also in any general round of applause, unless the applauded statement cannot possibly be endorsed for some individual reason.

A speaker can only feel rebuffed to some degree if a prominently seated member of the audience leaves during his talk. Anyone who must leave early should choose a seat near the rear so that his departure will be inconspicuous.

See BANQUETS; PUBLIC SPEAKING; and for correct seating of a group, THEATERS.

## LEMONS

Lemon wedges are picked up in the fingers, but lemon slices are not. Instead, the juice is extracted by pressing a slice with a spoon. In restaurants, lemon wedges are sometimes served masked with white cheesecloth to prevent squirts, but this is not a correct service at home. The wary diner can, however, prevent a disconcerting squirt from a juicy wedge by piercing it several times with the tines of a fork.

## LENDING.   See BORROWING.

## LENT

Lent is the period of forty days (excluding Sundays) from Ash Wednesday to Easter. Because many Christians observe Lent by fasting and other forms of self-denial, it is not customary to have a big formal ball or wedding during this time, though a small party or informal wedding may be held at any time.

## LETTERS

The person to whom a letter is written is, legally, the owner of the letter itself. Therefore, he can dispose of it as he would of any other personal possession—with one specific legal limitation: he cannot publish it without the writer's permission. For example, an autograph collector may sell the actual letter written to him by a celebrity, but the legal right to *reprint* the letter remains with the writer of it. The writer's permission must be obtained before the letter is used in an advertisement or otherwise in print.

There also are rules and limitations imposed by custom and good taste on both the writer and the recipient.

For these, see separate listings, including CORRESPONDENCE; ENGAGEMENTS TO WED; GIFTS; HOUSEGUESTS; INVITATIONS.

## LETTUCE   See SALADS.

## LIEUTENANTS.   See FORMS OF ADDRESS (Armed Services).

## LIFEGUARDS.   See BEACHES AND POOLS.

## LINEN

"Bed linen," "kitchen linen," "table linen," and "trousseau linen" all are correct terms for towels, sheets, tablecloths, and other such articles for household use even if they are made of cotton or a synthetic fabric. Blankets, however, are not classed as bed linen.

For the marking on linen, see INITIALS AND MONOGRAMS.

**LIPSTICK.**  See MAKEUP.

**LIQUEURS.**  See WHISKIES AND OTHER SPIRITS.

## LOBSTERS

In its shell, this succulent seafood is for informal dining because there is no way to get at the meat except by using the fingers as well as a fork or pick. Nut-crackers are a help, but even if they are provided, the home cook is well advised to crack the big claws of a hot lobster in the kitchen to avoid the risk of spurts of steam and hot juice at the table.

An oyster fork or a nutpick is useful for extracting the meat from the large claws, though quite often only a lunch-size fork and knife are provided. The meat of the small claws can be reached only by breaking them and sucking the meat out.

The roe of the lobster is called the "coral" because of its color when cooked. The name for the soft green liver is "tomalley." Both are special delicacies.

When whole lobsters are served, finger bowls are really needed afterward. The water should be lukewarm, not cool, with a slice of lemon floating in it.

## LOST-AND-FOUND ITEMS

The familiar jingle "Finders keepers, losers weepers" is no more than a statement of what is too often a fact, but by no means does it endorse a finder's keeping every lost item he discovers.

The finder of an article of substantial value is obligated to make an effort to help the owner recover it. "Substantial" value cannot always be gauged in terms of money, and the finder of an article should not judge its worth by its importance to him. Any item that appears to have sentimental associations or other special value—a locket engraved with a personal message, a manuscript, address book, identification cards, letters—may be of great importance to the loser.

If an object carries the owner's name and address, it is generally little trouble to get in touch with him promptly by telephone or mail. Otherwise, the finder can watch the lost-and-found columns in local newspapers. He should also notify (or turn in the article to) the proper authority. Below are special practical procedures for certain items:

**ANIMALS.**  See PETS.

**CLOTHING.**  A single glove or a pair, a handkerchief, or any other small used item found on the street, a park path, or the beach should be picked up and left in some place of greater safety where the owner can see it easily if he retraces his steps in search of it. Coats, fur scarfs, and other articles of substantial value should be turned in, whenever feasible, as a protection to the owner against other passersby who may not be so scrupulously honest. Common sense has to be the guide here, however. Trouble may be spared everyone by leaving a beach robe, for example, right where it is.

**JEWELRY.**  In these days of successful imitations, it is not easy for the ordinary citizen to determine whether a pearl necklace, for instance, is a cheap imitation, a string of good cultured pearls, or the real thing. If in any doubt, it is best to determine its value by showing it to a jeweler, or to take no chances and turn it in to the appropriate agency. Even inexpensive jewelry may have a sentimental value to the owner.

**MONEY, PURSES, AND WALLETS.**  A small bill picked up on the street can reasonably be considered a small windfall and kept by the finder—but a small bill found in a school corridor or within the confines of an office is a different matter. The find should be announced in some fashion. The same rule applies when a purse or wallet is found under any circumstances.

**REPORTING A FIND.** Where and how to report a find depends on the object and the place where it was found.

**On a Public Conveyance.** If the article is found on the seat or floor of a bus, train, plane, or subway, it should be turned over to the driver or conductor, or to the lost-and-found office of the company, or to the nearest police station.

**In a Public Building.** If found in a store, office, museum, hotel, restaurant, theater, or the lobby or entrance of an apartment building, the found article should be turned over to the lost-and-found office, the manager, the cashier, or the superintendent, as the case may be.

**In a Taxi.** Drivers are expected to check their cabs for articles left behind. Usually they immediately turn in valuable lost property such as wallets, jewelry, and furs to a police station. Local regulations govern their procedure about articles of minor value such as gloves. Such items often are reported at the end of a day to the driver's office in the case of fleet-operated cabs. A telephone call to police is the passenger's first move. Name of the cab company, if possible, and details of time and first and last stop will help if the name of the company and the driver have not been noted. The police can then trace the cab through the logs that drivers turn in each day.

The passenger who finds some small article such as a book, gloves, or scarf turns it over to the driver. This is a case where finders most definitely may not be keepers. If a passenger finds what appears to be something of decided value —a purse, wallet, or jewel—the driver's attention should be called to it immediately as mutual protection. After all, the wallet may have been rifled by another passenger who found it first. Examine it with the driver, and if the item is of great value, go with him to the nearest police station to turn it in. If this is inconvenient, ask the driver to find a policeman who can deal with the matter.

**REWARDS.** When a lost article of value is returned by a bus or taxi driver or a stranger, it is customary to offer a reward. If the value of the lost article is nominal or sentimental, the reward should be commensurate with the time and trouble taken by the finder to return it. If the lost article is money or something of substantial value, 10 percent of the value is customarily given as a reward. If the finder has placed an ad, it is only fair to reimburse him for it.

**LUGGAGE.** *See* HOTELS AND MOTELS; INITIALS AND MONOGRAMS; TRAVEL; WEDDINGS.

## LUNCH AND LUNCHEON

"Lunch" and "luncheon" are frequently used interchangeably, but if the rules are followed, "luncheon" is used only for a sizable formal party (though formal invitations to the most elaborate luncheon are worded "request the pleasure of your company at lunch"). Therefore, "Have you a luncheon date?" is not strictly correct. It is most unlikely that anyone will be turned down because of that misuse of "luncheon," but the word is generally avoided as a bit flossy for a routine midday meal.

*See* MEALS AND THEIR SERVICE.

## LUNCH COUNTERS

There is no obligation to leave a tip at a quick-lunch counter, but in many areas it is a growing custom to leave a tip of about 10 percent, especially at an eating bar lined with seats. A tip always is in order for any extra or unusual service.

## LYING

"A liar is far worse, and does greater mischief, than a murderer on the highways."
—MARTIN LUTHER, 1569

Lying is a moral issue—a matter between the liar and his conscience. How to deal with a person caught in a lie, however, is a painful, touchy problem of etiquette.

"You are a liar" is an all-out insult, better not said except by someone prepared to fight, and never if there is the slightest chance that the accused has made an honest mistake rather than a deliberate misstatement of the truth.

A lie certainly should not go unprotested, but the best way to put a liar in his place and still avoid an unpleasant scene is to give him a reasonable chance to reverse himself without too much loss of face. Formula replies such as "I'm sure I misunderstood you when you said . . ." or "Perhaps we're talking about different times," or "I think you've been misinformed because I know that the real fact is . . ." are doubly effective because of their cool politeness.

There is no easy solution for dealing with the chronic liar except to stay as far away from him as possible. The person who will tell a deliberate lie is suspect on every other count, according to J. Edgar Hoover, who put his opinion clearly on the line: "The thousands of criminals I have seen in forty years of law enforcement have had one thing in common: every single one was a liar."

The social fib is, of course, a different matter. Life for all of us would be impossible without certain kindly evasions of the whole hard truth on many occasions—the empty "I'm so sorry," for example, preceding "I've just made other plans for that evening" when refusing an invitation to dinner (even though the "other plans" are to stay at home with a good book).

# M

## MADAM

"Madam" or "Ma'am" is the standard salutation to an adult from a domestic employee, and from a tradesman, waiter, porter, and others who serve the public. Girls who are obviously in their teens are addressed "Miss." Illogically enough, "Mrs." alone is not correct. A courteous manner and no salutation at all is considered better than "Mrs." without a last name, or the empty terms of affection like "dear," "honey," and so on. In some localities and situations where "Madam" would sound hopelessly affected if used to a stranger, "lady" is in common use in such connections as "Lady! You forgot your gloves." Social equals do not use "madam" to each other in social circumstances unless it is combined with a title like "Madam Chairman," "Madam President," and so on.

Teaching small children to use "ma'am" and "sir" to friends of their parents is still the best way to make it easy for them to avoid the rude, flat yes or no when answering.

## MAID OF HONOR. See WEDDINGS.

## MAIDEN DINNER

A maiden dinner is a party at which a bride and her honor attendants and bridesmaids gather while the bridegroom's bachelor dinner is being held elsewhere. A maiden dinner should not be confused with a bridal dinner (also called "rehearsal dinner"), at which all members of a wedding party are entertained following the rehearsal of the ceremony.

See WEDDINGS.

# MAIDEN NAME

A maiden name is the name of the family into which a girl is born. It is not her first (given) name or names combined with her surname. For example, the maiden name of Mrs. John Jones Smith who was Mary Ann Brown is "Brown."

When a woman marries, her husband's name is not substituted for her maiden name, so far as the law is concerned. Legally, her husband's name is added to her given and maiden names, and she becomes Mary Ann Brown Smith.

*See* separate listings such as DIVORCES AND SEPARATIONS; NAMES; SIGNATURES; for details of use.

**MAIDS.**   *See* HOTELS AND MOTELS; HOUSEHOLD EMPLOYEES.

**MAILMEN.**   *See* POSTMEN.

**MAJORS.**   *See* FORMS OF ADDRESS (Armed Services).

# MAKEUP

Fashions in makeup change from year to year, but two basic rules do not: 1. Girls at school, domestic employees on duty, and women at work in an office or other place of business do not wear conspicuously extreme makeup. 2. Extensive repairs to makeup are taboo in public, just as is lengthy fussing with a hairdo.

It is only sensible to make a fast pass with a comb at windblown hair after entering an office building, theater, restaurant, and so on, and it is common good practice for a woman to take out a mirror and use a powder puff or a lipstick, provided she makes such first-aid repairs very quickly and matter-of-factly. With these exceptions, personal grooming of any kind had better be saved for a dressing room.

No doubt about it, lipstick has its problems for everyone, including the men who find themselves the unwitting wearers of it after a kiss. However, it seems to be with us to stay, and so the least a woman can do is to protect other people and their possessions from her brand mark as much as possible. Lipstick properly applied and blotted is less likely to leave the unsightly smears on a cup, glass, or napkin that are one of the least appetizing sights at the table; or to leave towels startlingly encarnadined.

# MALE AND MASCULINE

On an application or any other form with a blank for sex, "male" is the right word to use, rather than "masculine" or "man." "Male" may be used as a noun: "The dog is a male"; or as an adjective, "of the male sex." "Masculine" is always an adjective, but is used only to describe a quality or manner, not a sex: "He is such a masculine little boy." "Male cat" (not "masculine cat") and "male help" (not "masculine help") are correct.

These rules apply to "female" and "feminine" also.

**MAN.**   *See* GENTLEMAN AND MAN.

# MANAGERS

As a general rule, the manager of a hotel, restaurant, beauty shop, or any other business has professional standing, and is not tipped.

**MANGOES.**   *See* FRUITS.

**MANSION.**   *See* HOUSE AND HOME.

## MARMALADE

Marmalade usually is served only at breakfast. When it is to be eaten with toast or other hot breads it is put on the butter plate. If to be eaten with waffles, pancakes, or French toast, it is put on the main plate.

## MASS

Tourists who arrive in a Catholic house of worship when a mass is being read are required to take seats, or come to a complete halt and stand respectfully quiet until the service is completed. It is the worst of manners to move around at this time except to gain the nearest exit. Non-Catholics who attend a mass by invitation (such as a wedding or funeral mass) should rise and sit with the rest of the congregation. They need not cross themselves or speak responses or kneel, but should bow their heads when others do, and lean forward, head bowed, when others kneel.

## MASS CARDS

A person of any faith may send a mass card (sometimes known as "a spiritual bouquet") in token of sympathy to a Catholic friend. Mass cards can be obtained by mail or by calling at any Catholic church and making a donation, in return for which a mass will be said for the repose of a soul.

## MASSEURS, MASSEUSES

Masseurs and masseuses are tipped at the same rate as barbers and beauty-shop operators. A tip of from 15 to 20 percent of the bill is usual at the massager's regular place of business; of 25 percent for a massage given in the client's quarters.

**MATCHES.**    *See* MEALS AND THEIR SERVICE; SMOKING.

**MATRON OF HONOR.**    *See* WEDDINGS.

**MAYORS.**    *See* FORMS OF ADDRESS (Government).

## MEALS AND THEIR SERVICE

This section deals with matters relating directly to the service of all meals at home—from the most formal dinners to the most casual family gatherings. It does not deal, except in passing, with the behavior of diners. That will be found under TABLE MANNERS. Detailed information about other related items and procedures that present special challenges is given under the appropriate separate heads in the usual alphabetical order, but see also the Index for the many references, within other entries, to the service of food.

**RULES IN GENERAL.** Following are the rules that apply to all meals. The additional rules that apply specifically to the service of breakfast, lunch, and dinner are given under those subheads, immediately after this general summary.

**Announcing a Meal.** In a household with servants, the employee who is announcing a meal appears in the doorway of the room where the guests are assembled, catches the hostess's eye, bows slightly, and says in a low voice, "Dinner [lunch] is served." If the room is large and the group is sizable, the employee may need to approach the hostess to catch her attention. Under no circumstances is the announcement made to the gathering at large in the ringing tones of a train announcer.

If the hostess is serving the meal herself without help, she announces that it is ready in any way that suits her, from a breezy "Come and get it!" to "Will you come to the table?"

**Entering the Dining Room.** The hostess leads the way to her dining room, followed by her guests in any convenient order, and the host enters last. The hostess sometimes stands just inside the door of the dining room and directs her guests to their places, but usually she stands behind her own chair and directs her guests to the right and left of the table, and their places, as they enter.

(For the rare occasions when the host correctly enters the dinning room first, *see* "Dinners, Formal," following.)

The guests stand behind their chairs until the hostess makes the first move to be seated; or, if she is to remain on her feet to serve, she tells the guests to take their places. Each man pulls out the chair for the woman on his right.

**Leaving the Dining Room.** At the end of a meal, the hostess catches the eye of one or more of the women, lays her napkin beside her plate, and begins to rise. Everyone rises with her, each man helping the woman on his right with her chair. The hostess leads the way to the living room. The guests follow in any convenient order, with the host last. (*See also* "Leaving the Table" under "Dinners, Formal," below.)

**Seating.** The rules are the same for formal and informal meals: A man and his wife are not seated side by side (except on a special occasion like a wedding breakfast). If there is an unequal number of men and women, the guests are seated so that each has someone of the opposite sex on one side, if possible.

If the hostess directs "Just sit anywhere," a guest should not choose the head or the foot of the table. Those places are always left for the host and hostess. Guests choosing their own places are expected to distribute themselves so that men and women are alternated. Dismaying to any hostess who has taken pains to invite an equal number of men and women is the sight of a covey of women at one part of her table and a lineup of men at another.

The places of honor are to the right of the host and hostess. The next most important places are to the left of the host and hostess. (At formal meals in Washington and in official and diplomatic circles, guests are assigned places at a table according to rank. Thus, the guests of highest rank—an ambassador and his wife, for example—are seated at the right of the hostess and host even if the party is being given in special honor of a couple of lesser rank—a congressman and his wife, perhaps.

(*See* WASHINGTON for further details.)

When there are four, six, ten, fourteen, or eighteen at the table, the host and hostess sit opposite each other either at the ends of the table or in the middle of the longer sides. A woman entertaining alone puts one of her male guests opposite her.

When there are eight, twelve, sixteen, or twenty at a table, the host and hostess cannot sit opposite each other since that would make the alternating of men and women impossible. The host never relinquishes his place. The male guest of honor sits opposite the host in the usual place of the hostess. She takes the first place on the side to the left of the male guest of honor (so that he is still on her right), and the second-ranking male guest occupies the place on her left.

**Service.** The following are the rules that should be observed in even the most casual service because they are based on either the convenience or the protection of the person being served:

All platters and bowls of food are offered from the left of a diner, with the handles of the serving implements pointed toward him and the bowls of spoons and the tines of forks turned down.

Glasses and cups are always filled from the right. The server does not pick up a glass from the table to fill it. However, when filling or refilling a cup at the table, the server picks the cup and saucer up in her left hand and fills it from a pot of hot liquid held in her right hand.

The standard rule is that a used plate is removed from the right and a clean or served plate put on from the left. This rule is rigidly observed in formal service. It is generally observed in informal service also, though it is correct to break the rule whenever some other procedure is obviously simpler and easier, always provided that the server never reaches across any diner.

Stacking dishes at the table for removal is never correct. A butter plate is not put on a dinner plate, for example, if the most elementary rules of good service are observed.

A hostess is never served first—either by the host if he is carving or by a maid. The logic of this rule is open to question, though the rule is not open to change. It can be argued that the food of the hostess is more appetizingly hot when she starts to eat than that of her guests if they are served before she is. However, all the authorities are in agreement that the lady of the house is correctly served first only if she is at the table with her family and no guest is present. This rule does not necessarily mean that a hostess is served last or next to last on all occasions. A maid proceeding counterclockwise around the table with a platter of food properly offers it to the hostess when she reaches her.

(Details of the sequence of service are given fully under "Dinners, Formal" and "Dinners, Informal." Rules applicable only to specific meals are given under the other "meal" subheads.)

Service starts with the woman seated at the right of the host, or if only women are at the table, with the woman in the place of honor at the right of the hostess.

**Table Settings.** These are the basic rules for any table setting, no matter how casual the service:

Candelabra without candles or with the candles unlighted are not correctly part of a centerpiece.

Place cards are used at any meal where they are useful, no matter how informal the setting and service.

With a few exceptions, silver is set in the order of its use, the pieces to be used last being nearest the plate. The tines of a fork point up. The cutting edge of a knife is toward the plate. Knives and spoons are on the right. Forks are on the left. *(Exceptions:* An oyster fork may be either right or left; a butter knife is put on the butter plate, not on the cloth; dessert silver is not lined up with the other implements, but is either on the cloth above the plate or brought in on the dessert plate. A teaspoon is put on the saucer of a teacup or coffee cup, not on the cloth with the other silver.)

Glasses are put on the right above the knives.

A cup is on the right next to the knives and spoons.

A butter plate is on the left, above and slightly to the left of the forks.

If a salad is served with the main course, the plate is on the left. If there is no butter plate, a salad plate occupies its position. Otherwise, it is set to the left of the forks.

A napkin is put on an empty place plate. Otherwise it is on the left beyond the forks.

(Note the illustrations following "Breakfast," "Dinners, Formal," and "Dinners, Informal.")

**BREAKFAST.** A family breakfast, with or without guests, is always an informal meal whether the group sits down together or each member turns up when it suits him.

**Service.** Even in a well-staffed house, a maid does not give as much service at breakfast as does a waiter in a good restaurant or as she herself would in the same house when serving dinner. What service there is, however, follows the "Rules in General" given above.

If a group is being served, with or without a maid, a cold first course like cereal or stewed fruit is generally on the table before the breakfasters sit down —unless they are to help themselves from a buffet. If a maid is then bringing hot foods to the table, she will remove the empty first-course dishes. She may bring in the plates separately if eggs, for example, are being cooked to each person's liking; or put a platter and hot plates in front of the hostess for her to serve. Rather rarely does a maid pass a main dish to each person at the table. Nor does she pass jam, marmalade, syrup, butter, and similar items. They are on the table, to be passed from person to person as needed.

The most popular service of breakfast for a sizable group is from a buffet where eggs, bacon, ham, kippers, and so on, are kept warm in chafing dishes or on hot trays, and such other things as fruits and cereals are lined up for individual choice. Each breakfaster takes his empty first-course bowl to a side table when he returns to the buffet for eggs or whatever he wants next. The hostess supplements this service, if she likes, by serving coffee or making waffles at her place at the table.

In short, any routine that is sensible and causes the least flurry is good procedure, with or without a maid, at this informal meal.

**Table Settings.** Any fairly simple cloth is suitable, as are place mats, but an elaborate lace or embroidered one is not.

A place plate is not a correct part of the breakfast service. If a plate is in front of the breakfaster when he sits down, that is the one he will eat from.

Breakfast plates may be any size needed to accommodate adequately the foods that will be put on them—from dessert to dinner size.

Lunch-size napkins are used.

The correct glass for water is a tumbler, not a footed goblet.

Bread-and-butter plates are optional.

The silver is placed according to the standard rules, with one exception. If a coffee cup is at each place, the spoon is put in the saucer as usual. If, however, the cups are filled at a buffet or elsewhere, the coffee spoon is put on the cloth between the knife and the cereal or fruit spoon.

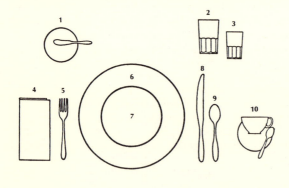

**BREAKFAST PLACE SETTING**
*(with first course in place)*

1. Butter plate and knife
2. Water glass
3. Juice
4. Napkin
5. Breakfast fork
6. Main plate
7. Cereal, grapefruit, etc.
8. Breakfast knife
9. Cereal or fruit spoon
10. Cup, saucer, and teaspoon

**Trays.** A breakfast tray is set as a miniature table would be. By the rule, it is covered with a cloth, though this rule is ignored in many families where informal tray service is regularly used—except for the special trays set for a houseguest or an invalid who needs pampering.

**BRUNCHES.** Brunch is an informal meal for Sundays or other days when people usually sleep late, since it is a combination of breakfast and lunch.

Brunch is served about eleven or shortly after. If an invitation specifies "eleven" or any other definite time, guests are expected to arrive promptly. The mention of a specific hour indicates that the party will be fairly small and that everyone will be served at the same time. An invitation worded "after eleven" implies both a larger gathering and that food will be served continuously for a while during the middle of the day, and so guests are privileged to turn up at their convenience—within about an hour of the stated time. Guests leave about forty-five minutes after the leisurely meal comes to its end, unless specific plans have been made for the afternoon.

Dress is more casual than for a party lunch. Men usually wear sports jackets rather than suits. Women wear simple dresses or, depending on the time of year and the customs of the community, shorts or slacks.

**Food.** The food is a combination of certain breakfast and lunch dishes. Tomato rather than fruit juice is usually offered. In many circles, an eye-opener like a Bloody Mary or a Bull Shot is the standard start. Coffee—lots of it—is always available from the beginning to the end of the meal.

Cereals are not served, and salads are not a typical feature of a brunch.

Scrambled eggs with bacon, ham, sausages, or kippers and one or two light lunch dishes like creamed chicken or seafood on toast usually form the main course.

Waffles, pancakes, sweet rolls, doughnuts, coffee cake, or Danish pastry takes the place of the more elaborate desserts typical of lunch.

**Service.** Brunch is informally served even if there is a maid to clear the used dishes and keep chafing dishes replenished. For any sizable group, the most practical service is from a buffet—following the rules discussed below under "Buffets."

If a group is small enough to be seated at one table, the host and hostess often share the service of foods placed in front of them, and pass filled plates along to the guests.

**Table Settings.** The table is set as for breakfast or an informal lunch.

**BUFFETS.** The word "buffet" originally meant a small room or recess containing a counter and often shelves from which food was served. Then "buffet" came into use as another name for the dining-room sideboard. Today, "buffet" also means any meal at which guests help themselves to part or all of a meal, even if they then carry their plates to a completely set table.

Buffet service is a blessing to the hostess who entertains with little or no help in her kitchen, and an equal boon to the hostess who wants to entertain a group too sizable to be seated comfortably at one table—provided that she plans her food and service carefully.

**Food.** Only two courses, not counting the niblets served with drinks, are usual, and three are the standard limit.

To a very small group, a hostess sometimes hands around a first course like a cold soup or artichokes in the living room before asking her guests to help themselves from the buffet table. And occasionally guests help themselves to salad as a separate course from the buffet. Far more frequently, however, salad goes on the main plate with the other foods, and a dessert is the second course, with or followed by coffee.

Two main considerations govern the menus for buffet meals when the hostess is serving without help in the kitchen. Food that requires any extensive last-minute attention is never a good choice for her. The host is busy enough with drinks, and the hostess with all else she has to do, to take time out for carving both a turkey and a ham, for example, after they have been put on the buffet. It is better to choose a meat that can be carved before the guests arrive (unless the group is very small), or serve a stew, casserole, or something else that guests can easily portion for themselves. And it is essential to choose foods that can be kept at an appetizing temperature until the guests return for a second helping. For example, it is better not to serve a gravy at all unless it and the food it accompanies can be kept reasonably hot for a while.

Coffee is generally not offered with the main course, though of course it may be. Water, wine, beer, cider, iced tea, or any other cold beverage the hostess fancies accompanies the main course.

**Service.** The single most important rule about buffet service for a large group is: Let each guest pick up his own plate. One of the major advantages of this informal meal is that self-service gives people a chance to reassemble themselves in different patterns. The woman who stays planted until the hostess or the man who has been sitting beside her is forced to act like a waiter and bring her a plate has obviously never given a big buffet party herself. Equally defeating to the hostess is the well-meaning volunteer who insists on "helping" by rushing heaped plates to other guests who are still finishing their cocktails.

The hostess starts the service by catching the attention of one or several of her guests and asking them to come to the buffet. A woman guest of honor need not be served first. The other guests do not form a cafeteria line the minute service starts; but neither do they delay too long in going to the table. They finish their drinks and continue conversations as they move toward the buffet.

Sometimes an employee is stationed at the buffet to assist in serving. Sometimes the hostess takes over that duty. More often, the guests simply help themselves to what they want while the hostess serving without a maid takes the opportunity to empty ashtrays, clear away cocktail glasses, and whisk separate little tables into place—unless the guests are to sit at one or more preset tables in the dining room or elsewhere.

If the guests are seated at a number of different tables, host and hostess never sit at the same one. And host and hostess serve themselves last after seeing that all guests are comfortably settled and have everything they need—including salt.

A beverage can be served in any convenient fashion. If the guests sit at a preset table, the host or a maid pours wine after they are seated. If the service is simpler, the guests pick up filled glasses lined up on or near the buffet; or a tray of filled glasses is passed after the guests have found seats.

If there is a maid, she clears the main-course plates and the buffet, and then puts the dessert on it; the guests help themselves. Sometimes, for a relatively small group, a hostess without a maid finds it easier to clear the main-course plates and serve the dessert herself from the buffet with the help of a volunteer. Or she asks guests to serve themselves, and while they are doing so, she can clear away the used plates and glasses.

Either coffee is on the buffet with the dessert, or filled cups, cream, and sugar are passed on a tray after the guests have dessert in front of them.

**Table Settings.** The buffet sideboard or table may be bare, with only tiles or other insulation under the hot dishes, but usually a buffet is covered with a cloth. The food is arranged in any attractive fashion as long as the sequence does not demand backtracking. Rice, for instance, should precede the curry that is to be spooned over it; meat precedes its gravy.

A stack of empty plates at one end of the buffet tells the guests where to start. Unless the guests are to go to preset places, the knives, forks, napkins, and glasses belong at the extreme opposite end of the buffet so that guests need not juggle them while filling their plates. Knives and forks are lined up in an orderly fashion, or can be rolled in separate napkins for easier handling.

Salt and pepper should be made available to guests, no matter where they sit.

**DINNERS, FORMAL.** This division deals with formal private dinners. Public or semipublic dinners are dealt with under BANQUETS. (It is not customary to speak of any purely social dinner, no matter how large or where it is held, as a "banquet.")

A formal dinner, whether for eight or eighty, is governed by strict rules. They are given here in detail, from the arrival of guests to their departure, because all informal service is adapted from them. The correct variations and exceptions are noted in the text under "Dinners, Informal," and other heads, where applicable, in this section.

"Formal" as used here means "ceremonial procedures in *all* aspects." For example, the strictly formal dinner demands the most punctilious service by a completely male staff. This is a finely drawn distinction because many a dinner perfectly formal in all other details is served by a houseman assisted by a waitress, or a waitress alone. But, for all practical purposes, the most important characteristics of the formal dinner are complete and correct service by an adequate staff and all guests seated at one table. If the host carves, if the hostess takes over any part of the service, or the guests pass along plates or serving dishes, the dinner is not formal.

Obviously, completely formal service on any regular basis is largely restricted today to official residences. However, certain of the rules are of moment to the hundreds of thousands of us who are occasionally guests at formally served lunches and dinners, and also to the many families who, on special occasions, turn to caterers for either a complete staff or extra help and equipment for a formal party.

**Before the Meal.** The very first rule is that the hostess must be in her living room ready to welcome her guests at the appointed hour, and guests must never arrive earlier than the time specified in the invitation, but on the dot or a very few minutes after.

A manservant opens the front door, takes wraps, or directs the guests to places to leave them.

The hostess stands just within the entrance of her living room and welcomes the guests as they enter. A man falls behind his woman companion so that she is the first to be greeted.

The host stands near the hostess to welcome their guests in his turn and to make any necessary introductions of guests to each other.

Because the hostess is standing, the male guests must remain on their feet. Women guests may be seated, but since this makes conversation with any of the standing men somewhat awkward, all guests usually stand and chat until the last guest has arrived and the hostess sits down.

If the guests are to be announced, which is usual only at very large formal gatherings, the butler is stationed between the hostess and the living-room entrance. Guests give their names to him according to the rules explained in detail under RECEIVING LINES. He repeats the names to the hostess in a low voice. Otherwise, he serves predinner drinks, which are prepared elsewhere and offered, ready poured, on a tray.

About half an hour is allowed for drinks and talk. In other words, if the invitation is for eight o'clock, the kitchen is geared to serve food at its perfect peak starting at about eight-thirty. Since wine is served during a formal dinner, usually only one round of cocktails is offered. Canapés may be served with cocktails but generally are not.

When the time comes, the butler announces to the hostess that dinner is served. He then goes directly to the dining room and takes his station behind her chair, unless she has instructed him to stand just within the entrance of the dining room and direct guests to their assigned places.

**Beverages.** Only water and wine are served during a formal meal. Coffee and liqueurs are served following it.

**Clothes.** The invitations should specify the degree of formality expected in dress. A formally phrased invitation indicates Black Tie even if it contains no reference as to dress. Women do not wear hats. A woman keeps her small evening purse with her when she goes to the living room. She may leave it there when she goes to the table, but more often holds it on her lap. She never puts it on the table.

**Entering the Dining Room.** At a completely formal lunch or dinner, the rule for entering the dining room is just the reverse of the correct procedure at all other meals: The host enters first, always with the woman who will sit on his right, and the hostess enters last accompanied by the male guest of honor.

An exception to this rule is made if the male guest of honor is a dignitary of extremely high rank (the President of the United States, the head of a foreign government, or a governor in his own state, for example). When the guest of honor is a dignitary oft his rank, the hostess enters first with him; the host enters next with the dignitary's wife, and then the other guests enter paired with their dinner partners.

One of several procedures can be followed to make the pairing of dinner partners in the living room easy and graceful. If the group is relatively small, the hostess takes charge and directs, "Judge Smith, will you take Mrs. Jones in?" and so on. Sometimes, if the party is very large, a seating chart is on display in the entrance hall. The man who opens the door will direct the attention of each male guest to it so that he can find the location of his own place and the name of the woman who will be on his right. Often, little white cards in envelopes— addressed, by title and last name only, to the male guests—are arranged on a silver tray, which is presented to each man on arrival. Each man finds the envelope bearing his name. The card inside bears the name of his dinner partner (Mrs. Brown or Miss Greene). These cards, about the size of a visiting card, are called Name Cards (not Escort Cards). They can be single, but the more useful ones for a very large dinner are the double ones that fold and do not require an envelope. The man's name is written on the front, and his partner's name is inside above a tiny chart with their approximate places marked:

Will you please take:

Mrs. Greene

in to dinner

x

**Food and Wine.** Today, a formal dinner has no more than six courses and frequently no more than four. Very often, only two wines are served, though sometimes sherry is offered with the soup course, in addition to a white wine with the fish and a red wine with the meat, and a dessert wine with the last course. Or champagne only may be served throughout the meal.

A typical elaborate menu:

1. *Appetizer.* Oysters, clams, and seafood cocktails are popular choices. Melon or a fresh fruit cup is a pleasing appetizer to many people, though some do not care for such a first course if cocktails precede the meal.

2. *Soup*—hot or cold. Hot soup is always served in a soup plate at dinner; a cold soup, liquid or jellied, is served in soup cups. At a dinner of many courses, the soup is almost invariably a consommé or bouillon, but a delicate creamed soup like lobster bisque is often chosen if the appetizer or fish course is omitted. Sherry or a white wine accompanies the soup. If olives and celery are served, they are passed at this course.

3. *Fish*—hot or cold. This course is frequently omitted today. The fish should be fairly delicate—filets of sole in a light sauce or a cold mousse, for example.

4. *Meat and vegetables*—always hot. At a formal dinner this course is almost invariably a roast of meat or fowl. Individual steaks are not appropriate because to be truly pleasing they have to be cooked to each diner's taste. Stews, pot roasts, and stout meats like corned beef are reserved for less formal dinners.

   Usually only one vegetable is offered in addition to potatoes. Peas, green beans, braised celery or endive, broiled tomatoes, and mushrooms are among the standard choices. Potatoes are served in tiny balls, *duchesse* or prepared in some other fancy fashion. Whole baked potatoes and large boiled ones do not belong on the formal menu.

5. *Salad or asparagus.* The salad is rarely anything but tossed greens with an oil and vinegar dressing. Asparagus is served hot or cold with an appropriate sauce.

6. *Dessert.* The usual dessert is an elaborate light pudding like a Bavarian Cream, a mousse, ice cream, or sherbet. An assortment of tiny rich cookies is usual with dessert. Pies and layer cakes are not part of the strictly formal menu.

Typical four-course menus:

| | |
|---|---|
| 1. Appetizer or soup | 1. Appetizer |
| 2. Meat and vegetables | 2. Soup |
| 3. Salad or asparagus | 3. Meat and vegetables |
| 4. Dessert | 4. Dessert |

(*Note:* Butter is not usually served at a formal dinner, though dinner rolls, melba toast, and crackers are offered with appropriate foods. However, the ban against butter is breaking down, and it is offered with increasing frequency—which means, of course, that butter plates and knives must be provided.)

**Leaving the Table.** The hostess leads the way. Unless the men are to remain at the table for their coffee and liqueurs, they accompany the women out of the dining room, paired if they have entered in that fashion. The host then leads the men to another part of the house for coffee and liqueurs (or perhaps the hostess retires with her group). In strictly formal procedure, coffee is served to the two groups separately—anywhere convenient, depending on the size of the house—and they reassemble after about half an hour.

**Service.** The major distinguishing procedures of formal service are as follows:

Place plates are on the table when the guests enter. From then on, no guest is left without a plate in front of him until the table is cleared and crumbed just before dessert is brought in.

The first course is brought on, glasses are filled, and bread is passed after the diners are seated.

A used plate is removed from the right and its replacement is put on immediately from the left.

Second helpings are not offered.

No serving dish (except those carrying bonbons, salted nuts, and tiny cookies) is put on the table at any time. Olives, celery, gravy, sauces, and bread are offered to each diner individually.

The server does not put anything from a platter onto a diner's plate himself. Any food brought in on a platter or serving dish is offered to each diner, who must help himself.

The server does not hold a platter or serving dish by its rim. He presents it on the flat of his left hand, with a napkin underneath to protect his hand against the heat. If necessary, he steadies a large heavy platter with his right fingers on the rim.

There are correct variants to the following order of service, but these are the procedures most generally followed:

Ideally, there is one server for each six or seven diners.

At a dinner small enough to be handled by one server (eight guests at the very most), the service starts with the woman seated at the right of the host and proceeds counterclockwise around the table, with the host served last.

At a dinner for twelve or fourteen, service is started simultaneously from both ends of the table, beginning with the woman on the host's right and the man on the left of the hostess.

At a very large dinner, service for each six people starts simultaneously with the women on the host's right, the woman six places to her right, the woman six places beyond her, and so on around the table.

At a very large dinner, the butler directs the service by the footmen, and serves only the wine himself. At a small dinner, he serves food as well, assisted by a footman.

### Service, Details by Courses.

1. The first course, whether appetizer or soup, is brought in ready-served and put on the place plate.
2. Bread or crackers are offered to each diner.
3. The water glasses are then filled from the right. (The server never picks up any glass to fill it.)
4. If the first course is soup, and a wine is to accompany it, the wine is then poured.
5. If the second course is soup, the appetizer plate is removed from the right and the filled soup plate is immediately put on the place plate from the left.
6. The place plate is picked up with its empty dish and immediately replaced by an empty plate before the fish course is served. The fish is then offered on a platter to each diner, who helps himself. Wine for that course is then poured.
7. Clean plates are put on in the same fashion before the main course. The platter of meat is offered first. The server then returns and offers vegetables to each diner. A sauce is offered immediately after the dish it complements. Bread is passed, and then the wine is poured.
8. The same procedure is followed for the salad course. (However, wine is not served with salad.)

9. Before dessert is served, each place is cleared. Salt and pepper containers and place cards are also removed. The table is then crumbed from the left of each diner—a matter of using a folded napkin to brush any bits of bread into a tray or plate held just below the rim of the table.

10. The dessert plates—often with finger bowls on them, flanked by the dessert silver—are brought in. (See FINGER BOWLS for details.)

11. Dessert is served. If bonbons have been on the table during the meal, the guests help themselves. Otherwise, bonbon dishes may be put on the table at this time or offered individually, and then put on the table. The same rules of service apply to plates of small cookies.

12. If finger bowls were not brought in on the dessert plates, after dessert has been eaten each dessert plate is removed and immediately replaced by a finger bowl.

**Table Setting.** A formal dinner (or lunch) requires one table large enough to accommodate all the diners comfortably. Chairs should be placed about a foot apart to allow room for service.

A formal dinner table is covered by a cloth with an overhang of a foot or more. A silence pad of felt is used under a damask cloth. The wood is allowed to show through a lace or embroidered cloth.

Dinner-size napkins are used. They are put on the empty place plate, which is always on the table before the meal is announced.

Place cards are a standard part of a formal meal if more than eight are at the table. A place card is laid on the napkin, or on the cloth above the place plate.

The silver is placed as described under "Rules in General," in the order in which it will be used, except that dessert silver is brought with that course.

The correct water glass is a stemmed goblet. It is set above the knives. The glasses for wine are set to the right in a row or irregularly grouped—the glass to be used first set farthest to the right.

Butter plates were never provided in the past at the strictly formal dinner, since breads were offered without butter, but the ban is now lifted and they are not considered incorrect and so are sometimes provided.

Individual salt and pepper containers are set at each place, or larger ones are set between each two diners. Individual containers are set above the place plate and slightly to the left of its center.

An individual ashtray is set directly above the place plate with two or three cigarettes on it and matches in tiny boxes or narrow folders nearby. Or cigarettes may be in open silver, crystal, or china containers set near the centerpiece within easy reach of each three diners. Ashtrays to be shared are set between each two diners.

The hostess does not use a bell to signal for service.

### FORMAL PLACE SETTING

1. Salt and pepper
2. Ashtray, cigarettes, and matches
3. Water glass
4. Wineglasses
5. Fish fork
6. Main-course fork
7. Place plate
8. Napkin
9. Place card
10. Main-course knife
11. Fish knife
12. Soup spoon
13. Oyster fork (an alternate position is on the left of the other forks)

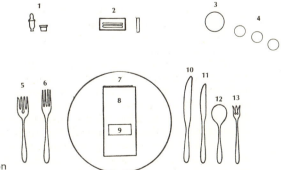

**Time of Arrival and Departure.** In this country, eight or eight-thirty is the formal dinner hour. Guests stay a minimum of about an hour after coffee is served, and generally leave not much after eleven. By the rules, the guest of honor makes the first move toward departure and, except in emergencies, the other guests do not leave before he does.

**DINNERS, INFORMAL.** This division covers all dinners that vary in any degree from the ceremonial procedures discussed above—from the party so elaborate in number of courses, service, and appointments that it is more accurately described as "semiformal" than "informal," to the simplest dinner cooked and served by the hostess.

**Beverages.** Water is served if no other beverage is offered, but at many tables water is not served if wine accompanies the meal. Iced tea, iced coffee, cider, or any other drink may be served instead of water, but of course not with wine. At a casual dinner, hot coffee or tea accompany the main course if that suits the taste of the family. By today's custom, however, coffee is served with or following dessert at a party dinner.

**Courses.** There are no limits except those of practicality. Very often, and especially if a hostess is serving with little or no help, even a party dinner consists of only two courses—meat and vegetables and perhaps a salad, followed by dessert.

Salad is popular as a first course in the West. Many people prefer it after the meat course, and others like it with the main course.

**Food.** There are no restrictions except the taste and pocketbook of the family. Main-course foods that call for finger bowls (steamed lobsters in their shells, for instance) are best not served at dinners with any pretension to formality.

**Service with a Maid.** If the hostess has a maid as well as a cook, the service can be very close to formal in most aspects. For example, the maid may open the front door, and the hostess can welcome her guests as they enter the living room; and the maid may pass hot canapés or offer the first round of cold ones before setting the platter down for guests or hostess to hand around. A host generally takes charge of mixing and serving drinks, however.

One maid should certainly not attempt completely formal service for more than six people. And if she is both cook and waitress, other short cuts are not only correct but in far better taste than any struggle for more pretentious service. Relishes, jelly, and a cold first course may be put in place, and water glasses filled, before dinner is announced.

Iced-tea and iced-coffee glasses may also be filled before the meal, or filled with ice only, before the guests sit down, and then the beverage is poured from a pitcher. Sugar (and cream for iced coffee) is then passed by the diners themselves.

Wine is poured after the diners are seated.

Butter is on the butter plates, or passed by the diners.

The standard rules for announcing and seating given under "Rules in General" are followed.

If there is no first course, and the maid is to offer main-course foods to each diner individually, the main-course plates are on the table at each place. The maid brings in the meat platter and offers it, always from the left of each diner, starting with the woman on the host's right, and proceeding counterclockwise straight around the table. (Some hostesses instruct a maid to bypass them and return after all others are served. But such backtracking can be awkward and delaying, and so whichever procedure calls least attention to the service is correct.) The maid then makes return rounds with the vegetables, gravy, hot breads, and the salad bowl if salad is served with the main course. If the group is small, the maid offers most of these items individually. There is great latitude in the details of good informal service, however. A maid generally will bring in two bowls of vegetables, one in each hand, and offer first one and then the other to each diner. And if the group is sizable and the maid is also the cook, the sensible and correct routine is to put the gravy, bread, and perhaps the salad bowl on the table after the meat and vegetables have been offered individually, and let the diners pass along such dishes at their convenience.

A maid may offer the wine, but the host usually takes over that duty.

It is customary to offer a second helping of all main-course foods. The hostess uses a hand or floor bell to signal the maid when anything is needed.

It is never correct for a maid to start clearing used plates until everyone at the table has finished with a course.

In all usual circumstances, a maid follows the standard rule: Take off from the right; put on from the left. However, in informal service it is entirely correct to reverse that order when another procedure is obviously more convenient. And it is in no way necessary or usual for one maid serving alone to replace a used plate immediately with a clean one, as required in formal service. Instead, the usual and correct routine is for the maid to pick up two used plates, going around the table as before, and carry them to the kitchen (or set them on a tray or sideboard for later removal) and return with two clean or served plates, which she puts in place before removing the used plates of the next two diners. In other words, she does not trot back and forth empty-handed, but follows any routine that gets food on and off most inconspicuously.

If the host is to carve, the maid brings in the roast and a stack of hot plates If he is to serve the vegetables also, she puts those dishes to his right. If she is to assist him in serving, she stands at his left and takes each filled plate to the guest for whom it is intended—or first to the hostess if she is adding the vegetables. A usual sequence of service in this case is women first, starting with those on the right and left of the host; then men, starting with those beside the hostess, with the hostess receiving the next to last plate while the host is helping his own.

Before dessert, a maid clears the table of everything but glasses and dessert silver (if that was part of the place settings instead of being brought on with dessert). Dessert is brought in ready-served, two plates at a time, or if finger bowls are brought in on the dessert plates, the maid offers a platter of dessert from which each diner helps himself individually. Or the maid may bring in a stack of dessert plates and put them in front of the hostess if she is to serve. If the maid is to assist the hostess in this kind of dessert service, she follows the same routine as when taking served plates from the host. Most often, however, the maid disappears at this point to straighten the living room and prepare the coffee service, and the hostess sends the filled dessert plates down alternate sides of the table—without making a big deal of women-first. The host gets the next to last plate, of course.

Coffee may be served at the table with dessert, but if coffee in demitasses is on the program, it is far better served in the living room so that the maid can get on with clearing and washing up the dinner dishes without delay. The usual procedure is for the maid to take a tray with cups, cream and sugar, and a pot of coffee to the living room, set it before the hostess, and then retire to other duties.

**Service Without a Maid.** The combination hostess-cook-waitress has a fourth duty, which is to fulfill her other three without apparent pressure. She can meet this not inconsiderable challenge if she plans her menu and service with some cunning. Her chief aim should be to spend as little time away from her guests as possible—both before dinner and during the meal. The hostess who acts like a hired cook and isolates herself in the kitchen for half an hour before she announces dinner, or who is forever jumping up and down during a meal, is no hostess at all.

If the group is at all sizable, buffet or semibuffet service is her best solution. Nearly always, she does best to serve a first course in the living room or to skip this course so that she need clear the table only once—of the main plates as she serves the dessert.

While her guests are finishing cocktails, she gets everything needed to the table. She fills the water glasses; puts the wine at the host's place, ready for him to pour; brings in the meat, vegetables, hot bread, and so on. She puts the meat and vegetables at the host's place if he is to serve, or in front of her place if she is to help plates from there. Sometimes the host carves and asks the woman at his right to serve the vegetables; the plates are then passed along by the diners. Sometimes the diners pass separate bowls of vegetables around the table after the meat has been put on each plate. If the table is very small a hostess often will ask her guests to be seated, and she will stand to serve the main course from a buffet or side table, putting each plate in front of a guest as she fills it. At this time the host may walk around the table filling the wineglasses, or he may sit in his place and pour the wine as the guests pass their glasses up to him.

The sequence of service is not a matter of status-shaking importance at such casual family-style dinner parties, though at a small table the woman guest of honor gets the first plate, as usual, and the other women (with the exception of the hostess) are then served, then the men.

If the host is carving a bird, he will ask each guest about preference for light or dark meat and so there will be no confusion about where a plate is to go. In this case, the host sends the first plates to the women on his right and left, and then follows the procedure above. However, when there is no need for consultation about a guest's preference, the host (or hostess, if she is serving) simply dispatches the plates down alternate sides of the table as they are filled, and if the guests are not told to do otherwise, they pass them right along, the host and hostess getting the last two as usual.

Although the hostess may have to go out for more hot bread, she does not leave the table if she can avoid doing so until she brings in dessert. If, however, it is more convenient for her to offer a second helping to each person individually, she presents a platter or bowl from the diner's left; but it is never correct for her to attempt to give as much service as expected of a maid because her place is at the table, rather than bobbing up and down. When she changes plates, she observes the rule of "off from the right and on from the left" if this is convenient, but always does what is simplest for her—short of reaching across a diner or stacking plates at the table for removal.

When clearing the table before dessert, she removes meat and vegetable dishes, but need not follow a maid's procedure and remove salt and pepper containers, though if it is convenient she sets them on a sideboard. She never crumbs a table as a maid might do.

By using a tea cart as a service table, some hostesses manage never to leave the table at all during a meal. The cart is stationed at the right of the hostess within easy reach. On its top the dessert, dessert plates, and silver are waiting. When the time comes to clear the table, the guests pass their used plates (without stacking them) to the hostess. She does not scrape and stack them when they reach her; she merely takes the silver off (if she wishes to) and puts it in an empty dish provided for that purpose on the lower shelf of the cart. The plates are then stacked on the lower shelf. Next, the hostess transfers the dessert and its plates to a place in front of her, and puts the main-course food platters and bowls on the top shelf of the cart if there is no room for them below.

A hostess can also manage not to leave the dining room by following a somewhat similar plan—removing the used plates to any kind of serving or side table, and then portioning the dessert from her place or a buffet.

**Table Settings.** The setting for an informal dinner sometimes conforms very closely to a formal setting, but the following variations are also correct:

Either mats or a tablecloth is correct.

Dessert implements may be on the table, as shown in the accompanying chart.

A butter plate is a convenience, but it is not an essential as it is at a formal lunch, for instance.

Salad may be served with the main course, either on the main plate or on a separate salad plate.

A teaspoon is not properly put on the cloth with other eating implements. If coffee or tea is to be served with the main course, the teaspoon is on the saucer. An iced-tea spoon, however, is correctly set on the cloth at the right of the knife.

An iced-tea or iced-coffee glass may be on its own small plate on a coaster or set directly on the cloth or mat.

Condiments, relishes, jelly, and all such complementary foods may be on the table from the start of the meal.

Small side dishes for soupy foods like creamed corn are not correct except in the most casual of "family style" settings.

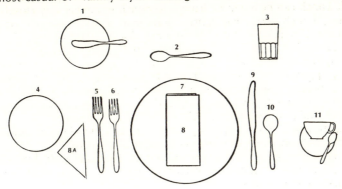

**INFORMAL PLACE SETTING**
*(Lunch or Dinner)*

1. Butter plate and knife
2. Dessert spoon (see also below)
3. Glass
4. Salad plate (if served with the main course)
5. Main course fork
6. Salad fork
7. Main plate*
8. Napkin (if no first course is on the table)
8A. Napkin (may be on the empty main plate or on the cloth)
9. Main course knife
10. Soup spoon
11. Cup, saucer, and teaspoon (if a hot beverage is served throughout the meal)

---

*The first course may be on the main plate with or without an underplate. If salad is the first course, the positions of the salad and main-course forks are reversed.

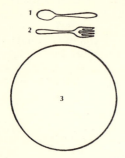

If two dessert implements are needed: 1. Dessert spoon or knife, handle pointing right. 2. Dessert fork, handle pointing left. 3. Main-course plate. (Or dessert silver can be brought in on the dessert plates.)

**LUNCHES.** "Lunch" and "luncheon" are often used interchangeably, but whenever in doubt choose "lunch," which is always correct. If the rules are followed, "luncheon" is used only in speaking of a sizable social, official, or business event, and so "Have you a luncheon date?" is not strictly correct. It is most unlikely that anyone ever turns down an invitation because of this misuse of "luncheon," but for the everyday gathering the word is generally avoided as sounding a bit pretentious—and formal invitations to even the most elaborate midday meal are worded "request the pleasure of your company at lunch."

**Food.** Lunch can be anything from a sandwich to a meal very closely resembling dinner, though somewhat lighter foods than usual at the end of the day are the standard choice. The list of good lunch dishes is almost endless. Soufflés, sweetbreads on toast, and chicken à la king in patty shells are examples of main dishes often served at a party lunch. Chops and cutlets, broiled chicken and fish are also appropriate, but—except in restaurants—roasts and extremely heavy stews are generally reserved for dinner. Soups and desserts tend to be more delicate also, though there is no hard-and-fast rule. Hearty salads, spaghetti, tamales, and similar dishes are suitable for informal lunches.

**Formal Lunches.** The completely formal lunch is closely akin to the formal dinner in most details, with the following major differences:

A formal lunch cannot be given without an adequate staff, but it may be served by a waitress or waitresses instead of the male serving staff required at a ceremonially served dinner.

The usual hour for a formal lunch is one o'clock. Guests leave about half an hour after the end of the meal, rather than stay for the longer period usual after dinner.

Women are relieved of their wraps and gloves on arrival, but may keep their hats on. The hostess, of course, wears no hat unless she is entertaining away from home.

Three courses are customary today: soup or appetizer, main course, and dessert. Sometimes at a very elaborate lunch there will be a fourth course—perhaps a seafood or fruit cocktail before the soup; or a salad served as a separate course after the main dish.

Water or both water and wine are the beverages served during the meal. Wine is not a requirement. If it is served, only one wine is customary, though on occasion sherry is served with the soup and another wine with the main course. A cocktail or sherry is usually offered before the meal.

Hot coffee is always served, but never until after dessert, and then in demitasses. Liqueurs are not usual with the coffee, but are correct.

A full damask cloth with a deep overhang is not correct on the formally set lunch table. Any handsome cloth without much or any overhang is appropriate; or mats may be used. Lunch-size napkins are correct.

Hot breads are a standard part of the formal lunch. Butter, butter plates, and butter knives are always provided.

Soup is served in soup cups, not soup plates.

Salt and pepper containers are not removed when the table is cleared for dessert.

Otherwise, the rules for service and table settings are the same as for a formal dinner party.

**Informal Lunches.** Any of the procedures for service and table settings given under "Buffets" and "Dinners, Informal" are followed, depending on the size and character of the party.

In the summertime, iced tea or iced coffee is often served instead of water. By today's custom, hot coffee (or tea) is generally served with dessert, in which case standard-size cups are used. But serving hot coffee, tea, chocolate, milk, buttermilk, beer, or any other beverage throughout an informal lunch is entirely a matter of the hostess's choice.

Soup is served in soup cups unless lunch consists only of a thick hearty soup and a dessert. In this case, soup is more appropriately served in a soup plate or bowl.

**OUTDOOR MEALS.** The range of formality for alfresco meals is enormous—from a dinner on a terrace at a fully set and formally served table, to the most casual of paper-bag lunches carried to a park. Therefore, no special rules of service bind the host and hostess—except to have an alternate plan in case of inclement weather—and they are free to make any sensible adaptation of the procedures given at the beginning of this section under "Rules in General" on all informal occasions like barbecues and picnics.

**SUPPERS.** Supper is always an informal meal to some degree. It is served either at the end of the day in place of dinner, or about midnight at a dance, or after the theater or other evening entertainment.

Any of the procedures for service and table settings given under "Buffets" and "Dinners, Informal" above are correct.

A supper in the early evening is a casual light meal appropriate if dinner has been served at midday or in the afternoon, as it is in some families on Sundays, Christmas, and other holidays. A supper of this kind closely resembles a substantial breakfast or a simple lunch—or may be just a reappearance in some fashion of the turkey, ham, or roast left over from the preceding dinner.

A late supper for guests can be anything from a selection of cheeses, cake, and coffee, to a generously varied buffet, or even a quite fancy three-course meal such as is served at many dances.

See the Index: FOODS for the complete listing of edibles that present special problems in serving and eating; see also special events like clambakes, dealt with separately, for other matters relating to eating discussed within separate entries.

**MEATS.** See CARVING.

**MEDALS.** See DECORATIONS, MEDALS, ORDERS.

# MEDICINE CABINETS

Other people's medicine cabinets are as irresistible to some visitors as the forbidden box was to Pandora—even though they know that taking a secret peek at a host's pharmacopoeia is as out of line as snooping in his checkbook. Let them ponder Pandora's fate.

A guest in emergency need of first-aid items like bandages is certainly privileged to open a medicine cabinet. But the guest who rummages through a cabinet, reading labels out of curiosity, is abusing the hospitality of the house. And anyone who passes along such information as "I know she takes pep pills.

There's a huge bottle of them in her medicine cabinet," exposes himself as a Peeping Tom.

Needless to say, medicines dangerous to children should never be left within their reach.

## MEDICINES

If medicine must be taken in public it is best done matter-of-factly, as inconspicuously as possible, and with no comment. No excuse is necessary, and an explanation of any kind is better skipped, especially at table.

It is not good sense to offer anyone a medicine that can be obtained only by a doctor's prescription. The fact that a medicine cannot be dispensed by a druggist without a doctor's order means that some safeguard is needed against its unrestricted use.

## MEETINGS

When someone is officially presiding at a meeting, it is not correct for anyone else to speak without first gaining recognition from the chair. Interruptions or comments without such permission are out of order.

See CLUBS.

**MELONS.**  See FRUITS.

**MEMORIAL SERVICES.**  See FUNERALS.

## MEMOS

A memo to a domestic employee, the milkman, and so on is not properly signed "Miss Smith," "Mrs. Brown," "Mr. Jones." It is a minor matter, but if the rules are followed both men and women sign such messages with initials and last name: "M. J. Brown," or with initials only "M. J. B."

## MEN'S FURNISHINGS

"Men's furnishings" is sometimes used to mean the many small items of clothing such as ties, socks, handkerchiefs, scarves, and belts, but all authorities agree that "men's accessories" is the correct term.

**MENUS.**  See BANQUETS; MEALS AND THEIR SERVICE; RESTAURANTS.

**MESDAMES, MESSRS.**  See CORRESPONDENCE.

## MESSENGERS

Messenger boys who deliver packages, flowers, or telegrams need not be tipped, though it is customary to tip them just before Christmas, and at other times if they have taken any unusual pains or come an unusually long way, especially in stormy weather. A messenger making a pickup is usually asked to wait outside until the item is brought to him, but if he has to wait for more than a few moments, it is only common courtesy to offer him a place to sit.

See also "Delivery Men and Boys" under TIPPING.

**MIDDLE NAMES.**  See INVITATIONS; NAMES; VISITING CARDS.

**MINISTERS.**  See FORMS OF ADDRESS (Clergy).

## MONEY

No one is well dressed without plenty of small change in a pocket or purse. We live in a vending-machine age. The person who is forever cadging dimes and quarters for everything from fares to telephones, tolls, turnstiles, and toilets

—or wasting time by running off to break a bill—is out of step with the times. We also live in a tipping age. Unless one has small change readily available for taxi drivers, delivery boys, waiters, doormen, barbers, beauty-shop operators, bellboys, and so on, the handing over of obligatory tips becomes a big, boring, delaying production for everyone concerned.

It is pretty hard to agree with the familiar saying "The love of money is the root of *all* evil," though putting undue emphasis on money by asking price-tag questions about income and other personal matters is certainly the root of social poison ivy.

See CONVERSATION for the explicit taboos in talking about money. The handling of money and other aspects of the subject are mentioned in countless separate entries from ALLOWANCES to TIPPING. Also see the Index.

**MONOGRAMS.** *See* INITIALS AND MONOGRAMS.

**MONSIGNOR.** *See* FORMS OF ADDRESS (Clergy).

**MORMONS.** *See* FORMS OF ADDRESS (Clergy).

**MOTELS.** *See* HOTELS AND MOTELS.

## MOTHER'S DAY

Mother's Day is the second Sunday in May, but there is no need to fix the date in memory—merchants will fill the papers with reminders, as they also will for Father's Day, the third Sunday in June. Many people deplore the whole idea of these special days because they feel that the commandment "Honor thy father and thy mother" is better observed in other ways—and daily.

## MOURNING

A few women still wear the unrelieved black of deep mourning for a season following a bereavement, and half-mourning during additional months, but today many families do not believe in this outward show of their grief, and make no radical changes in their wardrobes.

**CLOTHES.** One of the reasons we seldom see full mourning dress today is that a woman does not correctly wear the complete black of formal mourning to her place of employment, though a man may wear a mourning band to work if he chooses.

For the record, here are the standard rules for the wearing of full or half-mourning:

*For a husband, wife, child, or parent:* six months to a year.

*For a sister, brother, grandparent, aunt, or uncle* three to six months.

*For other relatives:* one to two months.

*For a friend:* only in very exceptional cases does anyone except a relative go into mourning.

*Children.* It is no longer the custom for little children or boys and girls under sixteen to wear mourning. Instead, they wear clothes of subdued colors to the funeral of a close relative.

**Men.** In this country, formal mourning for men is seldom more than a black mourning band attached to the left sleeve of any standard street suit or overcoat. A mourning band can vary in width from about two inches to four-inches. It is made of felt or other nonshiny material, and circles the sleeve half-way between shoulder and elbow. A mourning band is not attached to sports jackets or other casual clothes. If a man wears a mourning band, he wears black shoes, black socks, and a black tie, a white shirt and handkerchief, and a hat with a black band.

**Women.** The traditional full mourning costume calls for unrelieved black clothes, including stockings, of nonshiny materials. Women of the immediate family may find long, concealing black veils a comfort during a funeral, but today long veils are not worn with full mourning thereafter. Gold jewelry (except a wedding ring) is not worn with full mourning dress. Neither are other jewels, except for an engagement ring and pearls, jet, or black onyx. Only colorless nail lacquer is correct.

Half-mourning, which is far more frequently seen, is either all white relieved with touches of black, or all black relieved with touches of white or sometimes lavender; beige stockings; plain gold or silver jewelry, but no colored stones. Nail lacquer is colorless or of a very pale shade.

**FLAGS.** The flag of the United States is flown at half-mast only by official decree, never by a family or firm as a symbol of individual loss.

For other details, *see* FLAG OF THE UNITED STATES.

**FLOWERS.** Anyone in mourning or half-mourning does not correctly wear a flower.

**FUNERALS.** *See* separate entry.

**PUBLIC APPEARANCES.** Nearly always, anyone who has suffered a great loss feels like avoiding big public gatherings for a while; on the other hand, some bereaved people find it easier to try to let life go on much as usual— another reason why few people today go into deepest mourning dress. A woman in deep mourning does not stay in complete seclusion, but by the rules she does not go to the theater or other public place associated with festivity. She confines herself to very small private gatherings. She goes to church, of course, and may go to a wedding, though she usually refuses an invitation to a large wedding reception rather than have her full mourning dress add an inappropriate note of sadness.

*See also* WEDDINGS.

**STATIONERY AND VISITING CARDS.** Black-bordered writing paper and visiting cards are virtually never seen today.

## MOVIES

The rules are the same as those given in detail under THEATERS, with the following additions and exceptions:

**ENTERING AND SEATING.** It is routine to consult all members of a party about where to sit if there is any latitude of choice, since many people can see best from the rear of the house, but others are at a disadvantage unless close to the front. A couple follows an usher down the aisle side by side. If there is no usher and the theater is dark, a man takes his companion's arm to steady and guide her, or goes first to find seats if that is more practical.

**NECKING.** Don't.

## MOVING

A cardinal rule for anyone moving to a new home or office is to inform everyone, well in advance, of any part of the change affecting them. The terms of a lease usually specify that a landlord must be notified a month or more in advance of a move (or be paid in lieu of notice), but it is only considerate to tell him the news earlier than the specified date when possible, and also allow him to show his property to prospective new tenants at reasonable times. If moving out of a community means resigning from office or committees in local organizations, earliest notification possible should be given so that replacements can be chosen and trained in orderly fashion.

**CHANGE OF ADDRESS.** Notice should be sent in advance of an actual move to friends, magazine publishers, shops where charge accounts are maintained, and to all others in regular touch by mail. The local post office can supply printed change-of-address postcards without charge. These are useful but not especially attractive, and many people prefer to use some other style for the announcement. *See* ADDRESSES for a standard form.

**THE MOVERS.** Moving is such hot and heavy work that it is only kind to have cold soft drinks on hand to offer the men; if the process of packing is a long one, sandwiches and coffee will be welcome. It is also a good idea to keep simple first-aid remedies within easy reach until everything else is out of the house.

Someone—a member of the family, relative, or friend—should be on hand during both the loading and the unloading. For insurance purposes, the householder or his representative should also assist the driver in making an inventory that indicates the condition of furniture and other possessions at the time they are picked up and also when delivered.

**TIPPING.** Tips are not obligatory, but it is the general custom to tip moving men. The rate varies widely. A householder in average circumstances making a short move that is completed by two or three men in one day or less usually tips each man two or three dollars. If the men are asked to handle many small items with special care (and do so), or if a move is complicated by wrangling big heavy piece of furniture up and down narrow stairs, or if extra pains are taken to safeguard things moved in a pouring rain, the rate may be a bit higher. The amount of the tip is not geared to a percentage of the bill as a waiter's tip is. This is a case where a tip is given as a token of appreciation for care and for cheerfulness in giving the little extra services that make moving less chaotic and exhausting.

*See also* FAREWELL PARTIES; HOUSEWARMINGS.

## MUSEUMS, ART GALLERIES, EXHIBITS

The conventional route through a room in a museum or any other exhibit is to the visitor's right as he enters. It is simpler for everyone to move in this fashion if the gallery is crowded, rather than to buck the stream of traffic, though it is entirely sensible to go back through a crowd for another look at a particular item. Experienced museum-goers usually move to the right even if a gallery is empty because quite frequently items are arranged to be viewed in sequence, starting from the right of the entrance. Care should be taken not to pass in front of anyone who is examining a painting or sculpture from a few steps back, or to pass as quickly as possible, and comments should be kept low and discreet.

When moving with a group and a guide, a sure way to unpopularity is to monopolize the guide's attention or to be aggressive about taking a choice place near him at every stop.

In this country, the guides connected with a museum who take groups on regularly scheduled lecture tours have professional status and are not usually tipped. There are exceptions. When in doubt about tipping, inquire at the booking desk. Abroad, museum guides are much more likely to expect a tip in addition to the standard fee charged by the museum.

## MUSIC AND MUSICIANS. *See* CONCERTS; ENTERTAINERS; NIGHTCLUBS; OPERA; and also the Index.

## MUSSELS          •

Mussels are seldom served raw since they are extremely hard to open except by steaming, but are served in any of the other ways suitable for clams and oysters.

Atlantic Coast mussels are safe to eat at any time of the year when gathered from unpolluted waters, though they are at their best between October and April. Pacific Coast mussels must never be eaten during summer and autumn months (May through October). During this time they extract from the plankton on which they feed a substance that can reach a concentration in their flesh that is poisonous to man.

**SMOKED.** Canned smoked mussels, served with cocktails, are eaten from toothpicks.

**STEAMED.** Mussels are thoroughly scrubbed and the tough beards cut off before steaming. Only tightly closed ones are used. The shells are heaped in a kettle with a tight top and steamed in no more than an inch of seasoned water or white wine until the shells open. One or two minutes is enough. The mussels may be removed from their shells and added whole to a spaghetti sauce or to a chowder. They frequently are served cold in a ravigote sauce as a first course, or hot after being chopped and stuffed into half shells. Often they are served straight from the steamer, heaped in their shells on a soup plate, with a white wine or a marinara sauce. Mussels served in their shells are eaten with an oyster fork. Bits of bread are dropped into the sauce and eaten with the little fork or with the soup spoon, which usually is also provided. Finger bowls are customary after mussels served in this fashion.

**MUSTARD.**  *See* CONDIMENTS AND RELISHES.

## MY DEAR (Use of)

Logic indicates that the reverse should be true, but a letter that begins "My dear Mrs. Smith" is more formal than one beginning "Dear Mrs. Smith." Therefore, "My dear Mrs. Smith" should be used only in formal letters to strangers and to people with whom the acquaintanceship is slight. In all other cases, "Dear Mrs. Smith" is used. "My dear Jane" is not used, since the formal, distant "my" combined with a first name is a contradiction in terms. But "My dearest Jane" is entirely correct.

When spoken, "My dear Mrs. Smith," "My dear Jane," "My dear John," and so on, can easily sound superior and patronizing. The same is true of "My dear girl" (or "boy," "chap," "fellow," or "child"), unless said with such unmistakable tenderness and love that it is clear no reproach or protest is intended.

# N

## NAIL FILES

Although it is sound practice to carry a pocket nail file, it is poor taste to use it anywhere in public, or in the presence of others in an office or place of business.

## NAIL POLISH.  *See* HANDS.

## NAMES

Explicit rules govern the use of names and titles in speaking and in writing.

Details relating to special occasions and circumstances are given under many separate headings. The rules for signing one's name, for example, are found under CORRESPONDENCE; CHRISTMAS; GUEST BOOKS AND REGISTERS; HOTELS AND MOTELS, among many other entries. (See also Signatures in the Index.) Following are the rules that do not belong exclusively to any one category, and certain other rules about which questions are most frequently asked:

**ASKING FOR A NAME.** Among the several ways to ask for a person's name, any is better than "What was the name?" That question implies that the name was once known but was not worth remembering and, grammatically, carries the macabre implication that the owner is dead.

**In Person.** In business, a direct "Your name, please?" or "What is your name?" from a receptionist or someone else who needs to know for a good reason is better than the overelaborate "Whom shall I say is calling?" which is more often used by a butler than a business employee.

Under any social circumstance, the best way to ask for a name is by a self-introduction ("I am John Brown") rather than the direct question "What's your name?" since such a self-introduction calls for the other person to give his name in return.

**On the Telephone.** "Your name, please?" "May I take a message?" "Will you leave your name?" and "Who is calling?" are good business and social forms to the person who does not volunteer his name. Never correct is the caller who demands, "Who's this?" before announcing his own name.

**CHANGING ONE'S NAME.** Anyone is free to change both his first and last names, so far as the law is concerned. A few of our states require a court order before a person may use a name other than that on his birth certificate, but in most states a person can take a new name without going to court, provided that there is no intent to defraud. However, in all cases, anyone who wants to use a self-chosen name on a document that requires a birth certificate must have the new name legalized in court. Otherwise, the document will carry the name on his birth certificate no matter how widely known he may have become by the name he has adopted. The court proceedings are simple. A petition is filed, and in due course a hearing that takes only a few minutes is held. A judge usually grants a change of name readily if the petitioner gives any good reason. In general, a legal change of name is refused only if there is intent to evade responsibility or if the new name infringes on the rights of another person.

Each year thousands of people seek legal relief from names that for one reason or another make life difficult. Garbič (pronounced Garbitch) is a completely dignified name in Yugoslavia, but being identified as "Garbage" in this country made one family miserable. They changed their name to Gage. When Mr. Wytwytsky changed the spelling of his name and shortened it to White, he had centuries of American custom behind him. We would be reading about the battle of Boncoeur Hill had not the pre-Revolutionary French émigrés, as part of their pursuit of happiness, changed the spelling of that family name to Bunker. And children would be reciting "The Midnight Ride of Apollos Rivoire" if Paul Revere's father had not anglicized his Huguenot name when he arrived from the Isle of Guernsey.

**Announcements.** A legal change of name need not be announced in any formal fashion (except the required publication of the court order in some periodical of record), but it is practical to mail an announcement if one's circle of business and social acquaintance is large.

The standard form is a white card, about 4 inches by 6 inches, engraved or printed in black, mailed in an envelope to match:

*Mr. Athanasios Tschernych*

*announces that by permission of the court*

*he has changed his name to*

*Ethan Cherne*

If only the last name of a family is changed, a standard form is:

*Mr. and Mrs. Richard Worms*
*announce that by permission of the court*
*they and their children*
*have taken the surname*
*West*

If first names as well as the surnames are changed, a standard form is:

*Mr. and Mrs. Roberto Fulano*
*Miss Luz Fulano*
*Mr. Guillermo Fulano*
*wish to inform you that*
*by permission of the court they have taken the names*
*Mr. and Mrs. Robert Fuller*
*Lucy Fuller*
*William Fuller*

**Divorcées.**  A divorce is not in effect when an interlocutory decree is granted. A woman remains Mrs. Henry York Brown, for example, until final divorce papers are issued by the court after the required waiting period. After that, she ceases to use her former husband's given names. She either takes back her maiden name (by court permission) and becomes Miss Mary Greene, or she drops her ex-husband's given names, substitutes her maiden name, and becomes Mrs. Greene Brown. Or she may substitute another family surname. For example, she might use her mother's maiden name and become Mrs. Maitland Brown, to avoid such absurdities as Mrs. Brown Brown, Mrs. Little Child, Mrs. Short Knight. Or, if her maiden name is one like Frank, Alexander, or John, she may prefer to use some other family name to avoid the impression that she has married a second Mr. Brown.

A woman divorced several times may take back a former husband's last name. This is often done if there are children by that name, but usually not otherwise.

Letters to a divorcée are never correctly addressed Mrs. Mary Brown except as noted below under "Women in Business."

**FIRST NAMES.**  In many circles, it is the custom to use first names immediately after an introduction. Some people do not care for this extreme informality, but, by today's standards, it is stuffy to make a point of the matter in most cases. However, if the point does need to be made, an older person need only address a breezy young first-name user casually by title and last name within the next few sentences, and so make clear that he or she prefers to follow the rules. In social life, a woman makes the first move to use given names when a man of about equal age is introduced, and so does any decidedly older person of either sex; in business life, the employer or ranking executive, regardless of age or sex, has this privilege. In all cases, a very young person who is addressed by his given name by a much older person waits for an explicit invitation to use a first name in return.

Little children often innocently call an adult by the first name they hear their parents use. If this in inappropriate, it is the duty of the parents, not the friend, to correct the child. In speaking to servants, however, children follow the lead of parents. They are not expected to say "Mrs. Smith" to a cook called "Jane" by their elders.

**Junior, Senior, and Numerals.** Though "junior" means "younger," a man uses it as part of his name only if his name is exactly the same as his father's. He does not use "junior" if his name is the same as that of any other older relative, and does not use the numeral "2nd" to distinguish him from his father, for the reasons explained below.

The rule that a man does not continue to use "Jr." after the death of his father is correctly disregarded if the older man was extremely prominent and continues to be mentioned frequently in the press and elsewhere after his death. In such case, the son properly continues to use "Jr." to avoid confusion. An outstanding example of good sense correctly taking precedence over any such general rule as this one is found in the Rockefeller family. The first John D. Rockefeller is now consistently referred to as "John D. Rockefeller, Sr.," to make it crystal clear that the founder of the fortune is being mentioned, not his son of the same name who also became world-famous in his turn (though "Sr." after a man's name is not ordinarily correct). And John D. Rockefeller, Jr., retained the "Jr." after his father's death, and is so referred to today, after his own death. This is a case, like that of Franklin D. Roosevelt, Jr., where "Jr." actually becomes a permanent part of a name to distinguish one man from another—and is not an appendage to be dropped when a father of the same name dies.

In social correspondence and on social calling cards, either "Jr." or "junior" (no capital) is correct. The abbreviation "Jr." is preferred in business use. A son who acquires a title ("Dr.," "Colonel," "Rabbi," for example) drops "Jr." unless his father also has the same title as well as the same name.

A man never uses "Sr.," though on occasion it is correct for others to add "senior" to the name of the older man when referring to him (though not when addressing a letter to him) if confusion with his son would otherwise result. "Senior" or "Sr." is used only by a widow, in circumstances explained below.

**Numerals.** The use of a number after a man's name means that he has the identical name of an older living relative other than his father. There is only one exception to this rule. If a living grandfather, father, and son have the same name, the father uses "Jr." and the son uses "3rd."

In social uses, "second" (no capital), "2nd," and the Roman numeral "II" are correct. The simple numeral "2" is not used. For business cards and correspondence, "2nd" is preferred to "second."

**Women.** A widow correctly adds "Sr." to her husband's name if it is the same as that of her son, to avoid confusion with her daughter-in-law, who of course drops "Jr." when her husband does—after the death of his father. Both "senior" and "Sr." are correct.

A girl never uses "Jr." after her name even though it is the same as that of her mother. For example, if her mother, Mrs. John Jones in private life, is widely known professionally as Miss Marianne Jones, a daughter of the same name does not use "Miss Marianne Jones, Jr." To avoid confusion with her famous mother, her cards and letters to her may read: "Miss Marianne Jones, 2nd" (or "second"). "Younger" is also correct, but this word is less often used because of the implication that the famous mother is old. The best way to avoid the confusion is for the girl to use her middle name on her cards and in formal correspondence—"Miss Marianne Lee Jones," for example.

**LEGAL NAME.** "Mr.," "Mrs.," or "Miss" is not signed to a legal document. A married woman's legal signature is her given name, her maiden name, and her husband's last name: "Mary Greene Brown." A man's legal name is the one that appears on his birth certificate, but the man with a very long name—perhaps with several middle names—may use a shortened version if that is the way he is generally known in business: "John Paul Hutchinson," rather than "John Paul Cornelius Henderson Hutchinson." A woman with a very long name is also privileged to shorten it somewhat.

**MAIDEN NAME.** A maiden name is the name of the family into which a girl is born, not her given name or names combined with her surname. For example, the maiden name of Mrs. John Jones Smith who was Mary Brown is "Brown."

When a woman marries, her husband's name is not substituted for her maiden name, so far as the law is concerned. Legally, her husband's name is added to her given and maiden names.

**MIDDLE NAMES.** As a general rule, middle names are spelled out for any formal social use. For example, on wedding invitations or social calling cards, the names Mr. [or Mrs.] Henry York Brown and Miss Jane Towne Grey are better form than using one or two initials with the surname. If someone dislikes his middle name, if to use it causes confusion, or if it makes a name hopelessly long on a calling card, it is better to drop it entirely than to use an initial, unless to do so would cause confusion. But if John Darling Smith is fed up with jibes about his middle name, he is privileged to use John D. Smith to avoid confusion with the many other John Smiths.

**NICKNAMES.** The use of nicknames and diminutives is a sign of affection and usually of fairly close acquaintanceship. Nicknames are best not used when speaking to or of adults known very slightly or not at all, though there are many exceptions. When a celebrity is commonly known in the press by a diminutive or nickname, it is entirely correct for a stranger to use it in speaking about him, if he likes, though it would be deplorable taste for a stranger to so address the celebrity under social or official circumstances—for example, to address General Eisenhower as "Ike."

The use of a nickname to make a false show of intimacy in order to impress others is almost sure to backfire eventually. For example, Mary and Ralph Jones, prominent in local society, may be known to their families and very close friends as Buzzie and Rafe, but anyone not in this inner circle risks exposure as an absurd show-off if he says, with an implication of familiarity, "Buzzie and Rafe Jones will be there." There is far too good a chance that the boaster may find himself, in due course, being introduced to Buzzie for the first time in front of the very person he tried to impress.

It also is not a good idea to assume that a nickname or diminutive not already in common use will be welcomed. Many a "Henry" regards with loathing the breezy acquaintance who decides to call him "Hank." It is entirely correct to take a firm stand and to scotch the use of a disliked diminutive by saying amiably, "No one calls me that because I really don't like it."

Nicknames and diminutives are not properly used on social calling cards, but are sometimes used on business cards. In the latter case, such usage is entirely a matter of individual choice.

**WIDOWS.** After her husband's death, a woman does not drop his first names and become Mrs. Mary Brown. She continues to use Mrs. Henry York Brown on her cards, and mail should be addressed to her under that name.

**WOMEN IN BUSINESS.** All rules of etiquette are based on what is most practical and considerate for all concerned. Therefore they are changed or modified by changing times. The rule that "Mrs." must never be used with a woman's first name, as in "Mrs. Mary Smith Greene," is one that is being widely ignored today to adapt to the need of married women in business.

Some professional women solve the problem by continuing to use their maiden surnames in business after marriage. Miss Mary Smith, for example, will use "Mrs. John Greene" only in her social life. Others use "Miss" as a business title with the husband's surname, and are addressed Miss Mary Greene at the office, Mrs. John Greene in social life. Others prefer to make their status as married women clear, and so the form Mrs. Mary Smith Greene is being widely used today in business by married women and divorcées, especially if they have children. Since business and social activities so often overlap, more and more we find divorcées, especially, using "Mrs. Mary Greene" both socially and in business. This form is not correct according to strict rules, but wide use is giving it increasing status, especially for divorcées who achieve any degree of distinction in business on their own.

## NAPKINS

Napkins folded in rosettes, cocked hats, and other complicated shapes are out of style today, and a rectangle, triangle, or other simple fold is the standard choice.

If there is an empty place plate on the table at the beginning of a meal, the correct place for the napkin is on it. In all other cases, the napkin belongs on the left, next to the forks. There is no need to bother about where to put a napkin enclosed in a ring. Thanks to the paper napkin, the unattractive custom of making one napkin serve for several meals is now an unregretted thing of the past.

**SIZE AND STYLE.** A handsome table covering calls for napkins that more or less match it in design, color, and material. Damask napkins are generally used with a damask cloth, though they can be of a different color. An ecru cloth decorated with embroidery looks most attractive with the napkins made to go with it, or with others very similar in character. A lace cloth calls for fine linen napkins with hemstitched or otherwise decorated borders. Very popular today are table coverings of patterned cotton and other simple materials, and so are plastic and straw mats for casual meals. Napkins of bright cotton, coarse linen, or colored paper are good choices with them.

**Cocktail.** Formal occasions call for cocktail napkins of fine linen—either five to six inches square, or rectangles of about five by six inches. On other occasions, any material from heavy linen to fringed gingham is suitable. Today, however, most people use the pretty little paper cocktail napkins that are available in an endless variety of colors and decorations.

**Dinner.** Extremely large napkins from twenty to twenty-two inches square are properly used only at dinner, and are generally characteristic of a quite formal table setting. On all ordinary occasions, napkins about eighteen inches square are the most popular size for both lunch and dinner, and are suitable at any meal.

**Lunch.** Napkins about fourteen to sixteen inches square are termed "lunch size." They can be used at informal dinners, but generally are reserved for breakfast, informal lunches, and supper.

**Paper.** Paper napkins are now widely used on casual occasions. They are not appropriate at a meal with any pretensions to formality, and they look absurd with fine china and crystal. But they are such a blessing to anyone running a house with no help in the kitchen that they are standard equipment in many families for everything but real party meals. Paper napkins are treated exactly as are napkins of cloth. At the end of a meal, a paper napkin is laid on the table beside the plate, never wadded into a ball and left in a cup or glass.

**Tea.** Tea napkins are about the size of a woman's handkerchief. They are generally of fine linen.

**USAGE RULES.** A large dinner napkin is laid across the lap in a double fold. Smaller napkins can be used in the same way or completely unfolded. It is not correct to tuck a napkin in at the belt or neck—except that of a very young child.

A guest waits for the hostess to pick up her napkin before touching his own. At the end of a meal, the napkin is not refolded. It is laid casually on the table at the right of the place setting after the hostess gives the signal that the meal is ended by putting her own napkin on the table.

## NATIONAL ANTHEMS

Our national anthem, "The Star-Spangled Banner," is often played before the opening of concerts, plays, sports events, and other large public gatherings such as dedication and graduation ceremonies. During wartime, playing the national anthem is obligatory at any public gathering, but otherwise it is a matter of choice.

Men, women, and children (except the disabled or infirm) rise promptly and stand quietly, weight evenly distributed on both feet, until the playing is finished. A man removes his hat and holds it in his right hand over his heart. Boys do the same. A hatless man may place his right hand over his heart or stand with both arms relaxed, but never with hands in pockets or clasped. A woman or girl may place her right hand over her heart, left arm relaxed, or may stand with both arms relaxed; she should never clasp her hands or put them on her hips or into her pockets.

No one should smoke, eat, drink, chew gum, whisper, or move about during the playing of any national anthem. People walking in the street or down an aisle stop and remain at attention until the anthem is finished.

It is not proper to clap after the playing or singing of the national anthem, and under no circumstances is any arrangement of, or improvisation on, the music of the national anthem used for dancing, though parts of it are sometimes incorporated in an opera or other musical work.

**FOREIGN NATIONAL ANTHEMS.** In this country, our own anthem always is played before that of a foreign country. Foreign national anthems are usually played in honor of a head of state, ambassador, or other distinguished official guest at some public ceremony. Americans are obligated to rise and stand quietly. It is the gravest discourtesy not to do so, no matter how bitterly opposed one may be to the policies of the government concerned or the personal behavior or record of its representative.

**When Abroad.** Americans and all other nationals rise and stand at quiet attention, just as they would for their own anthem, when the national anthem of the country they are visiting is played. This participation is not an endorsement of the policies of, or a pledge of allegiance to, a foreign country. It is a courtesy expected of visitors.

**OTHER PATRIOTIC SONGS.** None of the above rules apply to other patriotic songs such as "America the Beautiful," "Columbia the Gem of the Ocean," or "God Bless America," but when such songs are being sung by a soloist or choral group, respectful silent attention is expected. "Hail to the Chief" is played as a signal that the President of the United States is about to enter and that all present must stand.

**SINGING.** All of us are expected to know at least the first and last stanzas of "The Star-Spangled Banner." It is not obligatory to sing them, but it is customary to do so or at least to murmur the words.

THE STAR-SPANGLED BANNER
Francis Scott Key, 1814

O say, can you see, by the dawn's early light
What so proudly we hailed at the twilight's last gleaming?
Whose broad stripes and bright stars, through the perilous fight,
O'er the ramparts we watched, were so gallantly streaming?
And the rockets' red glare, the bombs bursting in air,
Gave proof through the night that our flag was still there:
O say, does that star-spangled banner yet wave
O'er the land of the free and the home of the brave?

On the shore dimly seen through the mists of the deep,
Where the foe's haughty host in dread silence reposes,
What is that which the breeze, o'er the towering steep,
As it fitfully blows, now conceals, now discloses?
Now it catches the gleam of the morning's first beam,
In full glory reflected, now shines on the stream:
'Tis the star-spangled banner! O long may it wave
O'er the land of the free and the home of the brave!

And where is that band who so vauntingly swore
That the havoc of war and the battle's confusion,
A home and a country should leave us no more?
Their blood has washed out their foul footsteps' pollution.
No refuge could save the hireling and slave
From the terror of flight or the gloom of the grave:
And the star-spangled banner in triumph doth wave
O'er the land of the free and the home of the brave.

Oh! thus be it ever when freemen shall stand
Between their loved homes and the war's desolation!
Blest with victory and peace, may the heaven-rescued land
Praise the power that hath made and preserved us a nation.
Then conquer we must, when our cause it is just,
And this be our motto: "In God is our trust."
And the star-spangled banner in triumph shall wave
O'er the land of the free and the home of the brave!

**NECTARINES.**  *See* FRUITS.

**NEGRESS**

This word is not acceptable to Negroes. Use "Negro" for both sexes.

**NEIGHBORS.**  *See* APARTMENTS; CALLS; HOSPITALITY.

**NEWSPAPER ANNOUNCEMENTS.**  *See* ANNOUNCEMENTS in the Index.

**NICKNAMES.**  *See* NAMES.

**NIGHTCLUBS**

In nightclubs and similar places where a floor show, dancing, or other entertainment is offered, the rules given under RESTAURANTS hold, with the following additions and variants:

DANCING. If the host dances at all, he invites each woman at his table to dance, starting with the woman on his right, before taking a turn with his wife. The male guest at the hostess's right asks her for the first dance. Other men usually dance first with the women seated immediately to their right and left. Any man who dances at all must invite his hostess to take a turn with him. Anyone is privileged to beg off from dancing, but under all usual circumstances a woman is not left alone at a table.

**PHOTOGRAPHS.** The host rather than a guest usually orders and pays for pictures from a staff photographer. If a picture is taken, a copy is ordered for each single person and for each married couple.

**SEATING.** The best seats face the dance floor or stage, and these are ceded to guests when such allocation of seats is practical. This is not always easy, of course, if the party is sizable and conventionally seated, with host and hostess opposite each other and guests of honor to the right of each; and so no great point need be made of it except in a small group.

**TIPPING.** Expect to tip everyone who gives even minor service, and at the high rate customary in an expensive restaurant. This includes the cigarette girl, washroom attendants, the house photographer, and the doorman on departure —even if all he does is open the door of a waiting cab.

Entertainers are not generally tipped, though there are exceptions. Wandering musicians who stop to serenade a table expect a tip in cash. If a solo entertainer like a piano player is asked for special numbers, it is customary to slip him a dollar or so "for a drink." An entertainer who joins a party for a while is not tipped, but always is offered a drink.

**NOBILITY.**   *See* FORMS OF ADDRESS (Foreign).

**NURSEMAIDS.**   *See* HOUSEHOLD EMPLOYEES.

**NURSES.**   *See* HOSPITALS.

## NUTS

If salted nuts are passed at the table, the diners put them on their butter plates or, if there are none, on the tablecloth. A big bowl of nuts in their shells is a traditional and delightful part of festive family feasts, and many people feel that Thanksgiving, Christmas, and New Year's dinners are not complete without them as the last course. Often, nuts and fruit form the centerpiece on such occasions. Walnuts, pecans, Brazil nuts, and hazelnuts are the usual choice.

# O

**OBITUARIES.**   *See* FUNERALS.

**OFFICE PARTIES.**   *See* BUSINESS MANNERS.

## OLIVES

Very small olives may be put in the mouth whole and the pit taken out with the fingers after the meat is eaten, but the customary procedure is to eat an olive in several nibbles and keep the pit out of the mouth. Olives passed at the table are put on the butter plate, if there is one, and the pits are returned there.

**ONIONS.**   *See* GARLIC AND ONIONS.

## OPEN HOUSE

An open house is a practical way to entertain a sizable number of friends without too much effort because refreshments can be anything from coffee and doughnuts to an elaborate buffet spread.

An invitation to an open house at home calls for an answer. A guest who cannot accept should say so definitely, but this is one of the few occasions when a provisional answer is correct if there is a real chance that the guest will be able to make it. "We always spend New Year's Day at Mother's but we'd love to come if we can get back from the country in time," for example.

An invitation to an open house at an office, club, church, and so on does not require an answer.

An open house may span four or five hours, but guests usually stay for an hour or less. An invitation to an open house at home does not mean that each person invited is free to turn up with half a dozen friends in tow. It is generally understood that a guest may bring along a companion without checking with the hostess—though it is always safest to do so. A community open house means "come one, come all."

An open house differs from a housewarming (*which see*) in that the whole house is not necessarily open for inspection.

## OPERA

The rules are the same as those given in detail under THEATERS, with the following additions and exceptions:

**APPLAUSE.** The conductor is applauded when he first appears, and usually on his subsequent returns to the pit. It is customary to applaud the set at the beginning of each scene if applause will not interfere with the mood of the music or interrupt a singer. Many operas were written and staged to give leading members of the cast an entrance, and applause may be given for the first appearance of anyone in a major role if it will not interfere with the performance. Applause at the end of an opera should be reserved for the real end of the work—that is, when the orchestra, as well as the singers, has finished.

Programs at the Metropolitan Opera in New York carry the message "The audience is respectfully but urgently requested to refrain from applauding after arias," but it is common practice there, as well as elsewhere, to applaud at the end of certain arias that were written as show-stopping pieces—though it is never appropriate to applaud an aria, no matter how brilliantly rendered, if applause interferes with the mood and music, as it would in Wagnerian music dramas, for example. Applause in the middle of an aria is the worst of musical manners, sure to draw outraged scowls and hisses of "Quiet!" When in doubt, save applause for the end of a scene or act—with the exception of *Parsifal*, which is the only "sacred" music drama. Applause is never correct during or after a presentation of *Parsifal*.

Shouts of "Bravo" are not incorrect, but it can be noted that at the major opera houses in this country such shouts come mainly from the younger enthusiasts among the standees and in the upper galleries. "Bravo" is always correct to compliment a man, woman, or ensemble. Some opera buffs demonstrate their knowledge of Italian with "Brava" for a woman and "Bravi" for more than one person.

**CLOTHES.** Street clothes may be worn to any performance. However, it is customary for men in boxes and for many in the orchestra to wear either White Tie or dinner jackets for the opening performance of the season and on other gala evenings. In New York, Monday is traditionally a dressy night at the opera, for example.

**ENCORES.** It is not correct to call for encores at the opera in this country; at the Metropolitan in New York, for instance, encores are strictly prohibited no matter how insistent the applause. In Europe, singers will respond to a demand for repetition.

**ENTERING AND SEATING.** Opera lovers take the entertainment very seriously, so it is even more important to be seated before the performance begins than it is in the theater.

The procedures for entering, checking wraps, and seating are the same as given in detail under THEATERS, though certain differences are observed in boxes at the opera.

Boxes are usually built to accommodate six or eight people. Those facing the stage customarily have three places in the front row. Side boxes may have three or four places along the rail. The rule is "No men in the front row"—if there are enough women in the party to fill the front or railside seats. Therefore, if three or four couples who are strangers to one another occupy the same box, each man sits behind his woman companion in a box facing the stage; in a side box, the women sit next to the rail and the men sit beside them.

If a hostess has a party of six and a box facing the stage, she takes the right-hand front seat, placing her ranking woman guest in the left front seat (the host behind her) and the third woman in the front center seat. In a box for eight, three women take the front seats as above; the fourth woman sits in the second row flanked by two men, and the host and the fourth man take chairs in the third row.

In a side box the hostess takes the railside seat farthest from the stage, and the men occupy the inner row.

If there is an anteroom behind the box, patrons leave their wraps there. The host or a male guest makes sure that the door or curtain between the anteroom and the box is completely closed so that a crack of light does not shine into the eyes of the singers or of people in opposite boxes.

**LEAVING.** Anyone who must leave before the end of a performance is expected to depart between acts, not during one. At the end of an act he may move to an empty aisle seat at the back of the house (if there are any) so that he can slip out later without disturbing others, or join the standees for the part of the act he has time to see before leaving.

**LEAVING A BOX.** A major rule is that, under all ordinary circumstances, a woman is not left alone in a box during an intermission; some male member of the party is expected to stay and keep her company. It is not usual for a woman to leave a box unless a man in the party accompanies her.

Anyone who must leave a box before the end of the performance explains to the hostess and takes a rear seat before an act begins so that he can slip out without further word to her when the time comes.

**ORANGES.**   *See* FRUITS.

**ORCHESTRAS.**   *See* APPLAUSE; CONCERTS; ENTERTAINERS.

**ORDERS (of Merit).**   *See* DECORATIONS, MEDALS, ORDERS.

**ORGANIZATIONS.**   *See* CLUBS; FRATERNITIES AND SORORITIES.

**OVERCOATS.** *See* COATS.

## OYSTERS

At a formal meal, raw oysters served as a first course are brought in after the guests are seated, but in a house with little or no help in the kitchen they are put on the table just before the guests enter the dining room.

Oyster forks are a necessity with raw oysters. Lacking them, better choose another first course. A raw oyster is taken in one bite, never cut. A wedge of lemon is the usual accompaniment. Oyster crackers are put on the butter plate, or if there is none, on the tablecloth.

**COCKTAILS.** Oyster cocktails are served in their sauce in stemmed first-course cocktail glasses or in bowls set in cracked ice.

**FRIED.** A standard fork is used for large fried oysters. They may be cut with the fork. Tartar sauce is the classic dressing—or a wedge of lemon.

**HALF SHELL.** The shells are embedded in cracked ice or put directly on the plate. A small cup of cocktail sauce may be in the center of the plate, or only a wedge of lemon may be served. The shell is steadied with the fingers of the left hand while the oyster is detached and picked up with the oyster fork. The shell is not lifted and the oyster slurped from it except at a clambake or other very casual meal. Cooked oysters served on the half shell are eaten with an oyster fork.

**OYSTER CRABS.** These minute baby crabs are found also in mussels, and often turn up in a serving of whitebait. They are a great delicacy.

# P

## P.C., ETC.

For the correct use of the abbreviations *p.c., p.f., p.p.c.,* and *p.r., see* ABBREVIATIONS.

## PACKAGES

Today, because nearly everyone stretches the budget by patronizing cash-and-carry stores, more people are toting their own packages. But the change in buying habits has not made all the old rules entirely outmoded. It is still not strictly correct for anyone attending a religious service to carry a package into a house of worship. An exception can be made for a small, discreetly wrapped parcel, though certainly not for an armful of bundles or for a single enormous one. And as a matter of common sense, it is better not to look like a delivery boy or a shopping housewife on a business occasion of any importance.

A man is expected to help a woman with heavy or bulky loads whenever his strength is needed, but when he joins a woman who is carrying a small parcel he is not obligated to carry it for her. When a man and a woman are shopping together, he usually picks up her first purchase and carries it. After that, they divide their packages, since both look absurd if one is empty-handed and the other is clutching an armful of parcels.

**PAGE BOYS.**   *See* HOTELS AND MOTELS; WEDDINGS.

## PAGING

A person being paged in a hotel usually gives a hand signal to the page boy, waits for him to come over and deliver the message, and tips him if the call is to the telephone. Otherwise, the person who requested the paging tips the boy in advance. Requests for paging are given to the bell captain or, if there is none, to the desk clerk when a bellboy is not immediately available. The boy should always be given a title to use and asked to page "Mr. [Miss] Brown" or "Mr. John Brown."

Only in an extreme emergency should paging be requested at any such public gathering as a concert, theatrical performance, lecture, or banquet. A delay in reaching a member of the audience by this means is inevitable because a chairman, house manager, or other person in charge cannot be expected to make such an announcement until there is an intermission of some kind. Anyone who has reason to think he might be paged should leave his name and table or seat number with the telephone desk as well as with the headwaiter or head usher to that he can be reached quickly and also inconspicuously.

## PARADES

The place of honor in a car moving in a parade is the right-hand place on the back seat.

See FLAG OF THE UNITED STATES.

## PARLIAMENTARY PROCEDURES

The standard work on the rules governing procedures at all kinds of meetings is *Robert's Rules of Order,* available at any public library and at most bookstores.

## PARSLEY

Parsley is delicious, and the sprig on a plate is not for decoration only. A diner eats it if he wants to. He generally does not help himself to parsley garnishing a serving platter, but there is no reason for someone who enjoys its pungent taste not to do so if he pleases.

## PARTIES

Business parties have their special rules and so do the different kinds of private parties, but two basic rules apply to all parties from the most formal of balls to the backyard barbecue:

1. It is the duty of the host and hostess to see that all guests feel at home.

2. It is the duty of all guests not to take advantage of this courtesy by behaving as if actually at home.

See the Index.

## PART-TIME WORKERS.  *See* HOUSEHOLD EMPLOYEES.

## PARTY CALLS

The formal call, or visit, and the leaving of calling cards at the house of a hostess within a few days after any entertainment is a thing of the past. After most small parties the thanks of the guest on departure are all that is required, though a telephone call or a note of appreciation for a good time is welcomed by any hostess, and in some parts of the country a little note of appreciation for the entertainment is customary. When in doubt, send one.

## PARTY-CRASHERS

Small boys have always felt that slipping under a turnstile or over a fence at a circus or carnival is a prerogative of their particular low-income group—more a challenge to match wits with the ticket taker than conduct unbecoming to an honest citizen. Adults are inclined to be indulgent with small fry who play this game, but there is no reason whatever to be indulgent with anyone who applies gate-crashing techniques to any kind of party.

The problem of adult crashers is not too hard to handle at a party given at a club or hotel. Admission cards and someone to collect them at the entrance will winnow out those people who are thick-skinned enough to risk the embarrassment of being turned away at the door. Some few may bluff their way in, but they run an even greater risk. Almost inevitably they will be spotted as freeloaders by the host or hostess, and snubbed—if not actually expelled.

What has become a real problem and one far more difficult to handle is the growing fashion among teen-agers to take for granted that any party for people their own age is to be regarded as a come-one, come-all open house, and that anyone who hears about the event—even at third or fourth hand—is privileged to turn up. This kind of party crashing is usually done in gangs of four, six, or more acquaintances who, quite naturally, feel that there is safety if not propriety in numbers. Things are now so out of hand in some areas that gangs will crash a party even if they do not know the boy or girl giving it. This custom is largely confined to suburban communities, but it is dismaying if not frightening parents all over the country, not in just a few scattered localities. Party-crashing is not one of those silly but harmless teen-age fads that are best endured until they have run their course. Crashing a party under any circumstances is an inexcusable breach of the most elementary decent manners, and parents who condone it are doing a far-reaching disservice to the community. Even if the custom is well established in a neighborhood, parents are not helpless. All it takes is a few families concerned enough to get together and agree to turn crashers away at the door, and also to forbid their children to attend any party unless the guests are sternly restricted to those who received an invitation.

Police departments are already concerned about party-crashing as a source of trouble, in that it is a mild (and sometimes not so mild) form of "breaking and entering." They are ready to help control it as a behavior problem.

**PASSOVER.** *See* HOLIDAYS.

**PASSPORTS.** *See* TRAVEL.

**PEACHES, PEARS.** *See* FRUITS.

**PEDESTRIANS.** *See* STREET MANNERS.

**PEERAGE.** *See* FORMS OF ADDRESS (British).

## PEOPLE, PERSON, PERSONS

"People" is properly used to mean large numbers of human beings who have something in common: the people of France, the peoples of Africa, thoughtful people.

"My people" is also widely used to mean "my family" or ' my relatives." However, a businessman who refers to his employees as "my people" runs the risk of sounding patronizing, and a bit like Ole Massa befoh de wah. "My staff," "my employees," and "the people who work here" are safer choices.

"Nice people" is widely used in the South with a special meaning most closely approximated by "gentlefolk," and is an excellent substitute for that old-fashioned word.

"Person" means an individual. It is grammatically correct to say, "Look at that person," but actually a bad choice because, in common usage, "person" in this context has an overtone of superiority or criticism.

By the rules, "I met six persons" is correct, but it sounds absurd. This is another case where being correct is stuffy and pretentious. It is better taste to go along with everybody else and say, "I met six people."

**PEPPER.** *See* SALT AND PEPPER.

## PERFUME

It would be hard to find a man, woman, or child today who does not use some kind of perfume daily. Virtually all soaps, after-shave lotions, shaving creams, bath powders, and so on, come with more or less emphatic scents built in. And, by the millions, well-groomed men use a splash of toilet water or cologne as a regular after-bath routine.

As a rule, only women wear actual perfume, which is the strongest and longest lasting of the bottled fragrances. (Toilet water is next in strength, and cologne is still lighter.)

Little girls love to experiment with their mothers' bottles of sophisticated scents, but (when they can be outguessed) are appropriately restricted to the light, flowery colognes. Girls in their teens, if they obey the rules of current taste, have to content themselves with toilet waters and colognes of flowery rather than musky character, much as they long for the *femme fatale* elixirs that, according to the advertisements, drive men mad. Today's custom limits men to the bracing scents of spice, pine, lemon, lime, and so on, though in many households everyone uses and enjoys the same garden-scented toilet soap.

The choice of a fragrance is so very largely a matter of individual taste that only general rules are established. The time of day, the occasion, and the weather, as well as a woman's personality, all should be taken into consideration when she is deciding which perfume—and how much of it—to wear. A woman dressing for a party can use perfume with a far more lavish hand than a woman dressing for a day at work.

Heat and humidity intensify perfumes, and so the heavy musky ones are more appropriate—and appealing—in cool weather than in midsummer. Such exotic scents are also best reserved for social occasions or used very sparingly indeed by businesswomen during working hours. It is never sound practice to turn up in the morning smelling as seductive as an Oriental dancer.

Toilet water and cologne may be splashed on the skin with a reasonably free hand, since their fragrance is not overpowering and dissipates more quickly than does perfume. Perfume is applied in light touches or sprays, also on the skin, since its alcohol if not its other ingredients can drastically affect the color of cloth if applied directly to it.

Both "perfume" and "perfumes" are correct plurals for "perfume." A "perfumery" is a factory where perfumes are manufactured. The word is not used in any such way as "She has so much perfumery," or "the perfumery department."

## PERSIMMONS    *See* FRUITS.

## PERSONAL REMARKS.    *See* COMPLIMENTS; CONVERSATION.

## PERSPIRATION

"Ladies glow, gentlemen perspire, and horses sweat" was the rule about the use of these words in polite circles in Grandmother's time. Today we are less delicate about such matters, and a modern girl coming off a tennis court in the blazing sun is likely to describe herself forthrightly as "sweating," if she really is dripping, and use "perspiring" for a lesser "glow."

As the multimillion-dollar sale of deodorants and antiperspirants shows, we also face the fact that a "glow" can make itself disastrously evident in other ways besides bedewing the brow. A standard part of personal hygiene for both men and women is the regular use of underarm deodorants. An antiperspirant is equally necessary—to keep blouses, shirts, and dresses free of underarm stains.

Both a deodorant and an antiperspirant (usually combined in one dispenser today) should be used without fail before trying on clothes in a shop.

## PETS

It is estimated that 33 percent of the families in this country have a dog, a cat, or both. And there is no telling what the population of pet rabbits, guinea pigs, hamsters, white mice, turtles, chameleons, goldfish, and birds may be. Therefore, it would be hard to find anyone who is not involved at some time in some way with the problem of behavior around pets.

**ALLERGIES AND FEARS.** Some people are allergic to animal fur and cannot be in the same room very long with a cat or dog without suffering the distress of swelling eyes and running nose. Other people have a panic fear of some or all animals that has nothing to do with logic. A newborn kitten can fill one person with the same terror that a harmless garter snake or mouse causes in another. Reassurances that a pet is in no way dangerous are meaningless. In simple compassion for guests afflicted with either of these difficulties, banish pets from the room during their visits.

**CATS.** No one has yet found a way to control the love duets of cats allowed free range of the outdoors. Otherwise, cats present few special problems as pets except as shedders of hair—no minor matter to the guest who arrives in immaculate dark clothes and departs looking more than a little tweedy.

**CHILDREN AND PETS.** Nowhere does a person reveal basic good or bad manners more decisively than in dealing with pets. The child who handles all pets gently, never teases or frightens his own or any other animal, and keeps his caged animals clean, well fed, and otherwise comfortable has learned a basic rule of decent conduct to human beings as well: Give special consideration to the helpless, the handicapped, or the otherwise disadvantaged. Too often, well-meaning friends set a bad example by giving a pet to a child who has no suitable place to keep it or who is too young to handle it properly. Prime examples of thoughtless gifts are the baby chicks and rabbits, given by the thousands on Easter, that are doomed to short, painful lives because of loving mishandling and inadequate living conditions.

**DOGS.** The familiar saying "There's no such thing as a bad dog—only bad dog-owners," may not be strictly true, but for all practical social purposes it is. Any dog can be taught good manners. It is the owner who needs a lesson in manners if his dog begs at the table, jumps up in welcome and rakes the guest with his paws, or barks excessively.

A dog properly barks when a stranger sets foot on his territory. That is his job as guardian. A dog barks when he is in trouble. No one can blame him for that. But it is unfair to both the pet and the neighbors to leave a dog shut up alone if he is not trained to wait in silence for his owner's return. Anyone harassed by the frequent and prolonged outcry of a lonesome shut-in dog usually gets results with a mildly stated complaint: "I'm sure you don't know it, but your dog barks the entire time you are away." If the owner does not take action, a formal complaint to the building superintendent, the A.S.P.C.A. (American Society for the Prevention of Cruelty to Animals), or the police is the logical next step. It may start a feud—but who wants to make a chum of anyone who is indifferent to the comfort of both his pet and his neighbors anyway?

Few things are more disconcerting to a guest than the dog who scratches a pleading paw against him during a meal. An owner who encourages his dog to beg by slipping him handouts at the table puts a guest in an impossible situation. It is hardly a compliment to the cook if the guest shares what is on his plate, but shoving Fido away is direct reproof to the owner for allowing the dog to be a nuisance.

On city streets where local law requires walking a dog on a leash, the obligation to take him to the edge of the street when he needs to relieve himself is so obvious that it would not seem to need comment—but a surprising number of owners act as if public sidewalks are any dog's privy.

A dog-owner also needs to remember that, fascinating as his pet's accomplishments are to him, most visitors will get restive if they are required to listen to an extended conversation about the animal and its remarkable ways.

Visitors also have strict obligations. Too many make trouble by thoughtlessly inviting dogs to jump up beside them on a forbidden couch or otherwise encouraging a pet to banned behavior. The dog cannot be blamed if he responds. But it is the dog that will be reproved—not, unfortunately, the visitor.

It is never by the rules for a visitor to arrive with his dog in tow unless he has been specifically invited to do so, or to assume that his hosts will donate the remains of the roast or provide other food even for an invited animal. A responsible guest takes his pet's food with him, and asks for a plate or pan of the host's choosing, rather than allowing the pet to polish off the leftovers on a dinner plate.

**LOST OR ABANDONED ANIMALS.** It is never anything but cruel to abandon a house pet in the mistaken belief that its instincts will enable it to forage for itself. Abandoned dogs have been known to die of heartbreak even if strangers saved them from starvation; cats can suffer the same emotional trauma. Because cats are less demonstrative than dogs, they have the reputation of being more attached to places than to people. But anyone whose cat is a house pet knows that this is not the fact. A cat feels more comfortable in familiar surroundings, just as any living thing does, but it also forms deep attachments to people. An abandoned cat will cling to the place where it has always found food and shelter, not for the place alone but in the frightened hope that the people it misses will return there.

A city pet accustomed to life with a family can very rarely feed itself efficiently if abandoned in the country, and it is generally doomed to starvation if abandoned in the city. A pet rabbit can feed itself if it is turned loose in fields or a park, but it is very likely to fall prey to other animals. The same is true of any wild animal that has grown up as a pet.

If a pet cannot be taken along when a family moves, and a new home cannot be found for it, the only responsible thing to do is to turn it over to the local Humane Society, the A.S.P.C.A., or a similar organization. If they cannot find a new owner for it, the pet will be painlessly destroyed. It is hard for an owner to face this possibility, but it is far kinder to give the pet this alternative than to abandon it to the almost certain anguish of slow starvation.

When a stray pet, obviously hungry and thirsty, turns up at one's door, it deserves first aid—water, food, and perhaps shelter in bitter weather. However, it is fair neither to a lost pet nor to its owner to confine and keep the animal without making some effort to return it to its home. An animal wearing a license or other identification tag is clearly a valued pet, and the duty of the finder is unmistakable. He should get in touch with the agency that issued the tag—all it takes is a telephone call—and the agency will then check its records and get in touch with the owner. If the animal wears a tag issued by an agency located some distance away, the likelihood is that the pet was lost while on a trip with its owner. In such case, calls to the local police and pound are practical measures because, if the owner is in the neighborhood, his first sensible move is to notify these local agencies and give them a description of the lost pet and the approximate time and place when the animal was last seen.

If such an apparently lost and distressed animal wears no license or tag, the police and all nearby animal shelters should be notified by the finder, who can then decide what he wants to do—keep the animal or turn it in to a shelter.

Although there is no law saying that a person who finds an animal must advertise for the owner, anyone who understands the attachment people have for their pets, and vice versa, will put an ad in the local paper. If he does not place an ad himself, he is at least obligated to watch the lost-and-found columns of the newspapers for a notice inserted by the owner.

If in doubt about the correct procedure or the correct interim care of an animal, the finder can get help and guidance by calling his local zoo, A.S.P.C.A., or Humane Society.

It is customary to offer a tangible token of thanks to a finder who has sheltered one's pet. In some cases, a tip is welcome; but if money is inappropriate, a box of candy, some flowers, or a similarly impersonal small gift shows the owner's gratitude graciously.

**TRAVELING PETS.** *See* TRAVEL.

## PEW CARDS

The purpose of pew cards is to ensure a preferred place in a house of worship on any occasion when a great many guests are invited to a ceremony, though they are mainly used for extremely large weddings (*which see*).

**PEWS.** *See* CHURCHES. For details about pews traditionally reserved on certain special occasions, *see* FUNERALS; WEDDINGS.

## PICKET LINES

Crossing a picket line is a matter of principle, not of etiquette. Each of us is privileged to make his own choice.

## PICKLES

Pickles served on a plate with a sandwich may be picked up in the fingers and eaten a bite at a time, or carved with knife and fork.

When offered as a relish with a main course, chopped or mixed pickles are put on the dinner plate, not on the butter plate, and are eaten with a fork. Only tiny whole gherkins are put on the butter plate and picked up, as are olives, in the fingers.

## PICNICS

To some people the word "picnic" means the simplest of snack foods—sandwiches, cookies, fruit, and pop. To some it means a hamper packed with silver, a cloth, and a complete meal from cold cocktails to hot coffee. To others it means a cookout featuring anything from wieners to steak. Whether the occasion is simple or elaborate, of major importance to its success is packing to keep hot things hot and cold things cold in transit—and to make sure that nothing essential is forgotten. Many a corn roast has been ruined because the salt—or the corn—was left at home. The best insurance against such a disaster is making a complete checklist and ticking off each item as it is packed. The experienced picnic-giver also expects the unexpected and has an alternate plan in case of a sudden storm. And, depending on the picnic site and the time of year, he carries a judicious selection of the nonedibles that can make the difference between comfort and discomfort: insect repellents, suntan lotion, soap, sponge, and paper towels, and a simple kit of first-aid needs for cuts, burns, and skinned knees.

No specific rules govern manners at the picnic table, but it is an absolute "must" for picnickers to leave the site uncluttered and clean and to douse a fire thoroughly.

*See* the instructions given in detail under BEACHES AND POOLS; and CAMPING.

## PIES

Pie, hot or cold, plain or *à la mode,* open or under pastry, meringue, or another topping, is probably America's favorite dessert.

A broad-bladed pie or cake server is almost an essential, when pie is portioned at the table, to get each piece intact to the dessert plate. Many people feel that pie, especially apple pie, is not complete without a piece of sharp cheddar cheese on the side. The cheese is sometimes served with the pie, or it can be passed separately.

Not too long ago, to eat the filling and leave the crust was considered an insult to the hostess's pie-making skill. Polite guests had to resist the often strong temptation to leave the limp or leathery undercrust that is characteristic of some pies. Today, though it is still a compliment to the pie-maker to eat the undercrust, the widespread emphasis on reducing diets has made it less reprehensible to leave it. However, when in doubt, don't.

## PILLOWS

The houseguest who goes to sleep with her lipstick on will be remembered by her hostess.
    *See* INITIALS AND MONOGRAMS for rules for marking bed linen.

## PINEAPPLES.  *See* FRUITS.

## PIPES.  *See* SMOKING.

## PITCHERS

At informal meals, a pitcher of water, milk, iced tea, or a similar drink is sometimes set on the table if second helpings are likely to be needed. An iced wine mixture like *sangría* is served from a pitcher. Otherwise, wine is served from a carafe if not from its original bottle.

## PITS, SEEDS, AND STONES

The general rule is that what goes into the mouth on a fork or spoon is taken out on it, and what goes in with the fingers is taken out with them. The pit of a stewed cherry, for instance, is taken out of the mouth with the spoon, but fingertips take out the pit of a fresh one. There are exceptions. For example, watermelon seeds are much more efficiently handled with fingers than a fork, but efficiency stops short of using the cupped palm. When practical, avoid the whole problem—cut out the pit or stone of cooked fruit with the spoon, and eat olives and small fruits in several bites without putting the pit in the mouth.

## PLACE CARDS

Place cards are standard at sizable, extremely formal lunches and dinners, but they can be used at any meal, no matter how informal.

The basic, always correct, place card is of plain white cardboard, about two inches long and one and a half inches high, or slightly larger, either single or a foldover. Such a card may carry a narrow border, initials, a monogram, or an heraldic design.

At informal parties, place cards can be as fancy and colorful as the hostess likes. Sometimes, little cutout figures are used at special celebrations, or a place card is in some way fastened to a favor.

A double card stands on the cloth just above the place plate. A single card is laid on top of the napkin if that is on the place plate, or in the center of the place setting; or, if a first course is in place when the guests sit down, on the cloth above the place plate.

At a formally served table, the place cards are removed when the table is cleared and crumbed just before dessert is served. If the cards are attached to favors they are left on the table, since the guests may want them as souvenirs.

**NAMES.** Names on a place card are always handwritten. On informal occasions, anything goes—first names, diminutives, nicknames. But for a party of any formality, only a title and last name are correct: Mrs. Brown, Miss Green, Dr. Jones—unless there would be confusion between two guests with the same title and last name, in which case the first name is added (Mrs. John Smith and Mrs. Henry Smith).

Place cards serve two equally important purposes. They tell guests where the hostess wants them to sit, and give guests a hint as to how to address their neighbors—particularly helpful in government and other special circles.

Where most professional and governmental titles are concerned, the title and last name on a place card are correctly the same as a hostess would use in speaking formally to the guest—Senator Smith, Canon Jones, Colonel Brown, and so on. However, certain specific exceptions are always made at official or public functions. In the case of dignitaries of exceedingly high rank, the title only is used. For example, "The President" is the only correct form on a card marking the place of the President of the United States. This rule applies to all federal officials through cabinet rank, and so at public or official meals the place cards would correctly read "The Vice President," "The Chief Justice," "The Speaker," "The Secretary of State," "The Attorney General," and so on. (This tells a neighbor that the correct formal address is "Mr. President," and so on. Details about this use of the title alone, in direct address, are found under FORMS OF ADDRESS.) The same rule applies to diplomats of ambassadorial and ministerial rank: "The Ambassador of France." It also applies to clergy of the rank of archbishop and higher: "The Archbishop of Boston"; and to governors and mayors: "The Governor of New York."

It should be emphasized that these rules concerning the use of title alone do not apply at small private dinner parties (except in the case of "The President" and "The Vice President," which are the only correct forms under all circumstances). If using only the full title would seem stilted or pretentious within a small group, the hostess can properly write "Archbishop Brown," "Ambassador Blanco," "Secretary Smith," "Governor Jones," and so on.

## PLACE PLATES

At the most formal dinners and lunches, a plate always is before the guest from the moment he sits at the table, with one exception. Just before dessert the table is cleared of all dishes and is crumbed; then the final course is served. Therefore, at elaborately served meals, place plates (sometimes called service plates) are on the table when guests enter the dining room. If a place plate is empty, a folded napkin is on it. If a cold first course is in place, the napkin is in its usual position at the left.

Place plates usually are about the size of a standard dinner plate. They may be part of a matched dinner service, but need not be, though they always should be chosen to complement any smaller plate that will be put on them. In strictly formal service, the place plate is removed when the first course is served and immediately replaced by another, but often today a cold first course is in place on it, or is brought in and placed on it. If there is no first course, the place plate is exchanged by the server for a hot main plate.

If a first course is followed by soup, the place plate remains until the soup course is finished. It is then removed with the soup bowl and its underplate, from the right, and immediately replaced from the left with a warm dinner plate.

At elaborate lunches, the procedure is exactly the same as for dinner if place plates are used. They often are omitted.

Place plates are not used at breakfast with the exception of wedding breakfasts.

## PLACES OF HONOR

At a dining table on social occasions, the place of highest honor for a man is to the right of the hostess; for a woman, to the right of the host. The places of second highest honor are to the left of host and hostess.

At the speakers' table at a public lunch or dinner, the places of honor are (1) to the right of the presiding officer and (2) to the left, regardless of the sex of the guests, even though this seating may put two men or two women side by side. The same rule holds for the seating of honored guests on a platform and in the lineup of officials in a reviewing stand.

In a car on an ordinary social occasion, there no longer is any place of honor. Passengers enter, arrange themselves, and get out in any order that is most practical, comfortable, and safe. On official occasions—in a parade, for example—the place of honor in a car is on the right in the back seat.

*See* AUTOMOBILES; *also* RECEIVING LINES; THEATERS; and other separate listings for special details.

## PLANES    *See* TRAVEL.

## PLATTERS

The only important rule about serving platters is that they are always offered from a diner's left.

## PLEDGE OF ALLEGIANCE

The text of the Pledge of Allegiance is: "I pledge allegiance to the flag of the United States of America and to the Republic for which it stands, one Nation under God, indivisible, with liberty and justice for all."

It is customary for parents and other visitors to a schoolroom to stand, place the right hand over the heart, and join in the ceremony with the children, though it is also proper procedure for them merely to stand at attention. Citizens of other countries rise in token of respect to the ceremony but do not join otherwise.

## PLUMS.    *See* FRUITS.

## POCKETBOOKS.    *See* HANDBAGS.

## POINTING

Pointing is so natural a gesture that it is hard for children to learn—and follow—the rule: It is correct to point at an object or to indicate a direction, but it is generally not the best of manners to point at a person.

## POKER.    *See* GAMES.

## POLICE

"Officer" is the proper form of address to a policeman on duty, though anyone who can read police insignia will naturally use "Sergeant," "Captain," or whatever title is appropriate.

On social occasions, members of the police force are introduced as "Mr."

## POLITICS.    *See* CONVERSATION.

## POMEGRANATES.    *See* FRUITS.

## POOL.    *See* BILLIARDS; *also* BEACHES AND POOLS.

## PORTERS

Hotel porters are tipped according to the services they give—usually 50 cents to a dollar for bringing up a trunk, television set, or other furniture.

Porters in the uniform of an airline, such as the men who handle luggage from plane to claiming area, are not tipped, but porters who carry luggage elsewhere in an airport are tipped, just as are the porters who carry luggage in train or bus stations. The standard minimum tip in most places is 25 cents for each piece of luggage, but in some big cities the rate is higher. It is usual to tip slightly more for extremely heavy pieces, or if the porter carries luggage an unusually long distance or stands by to find and help load a cab.

## POSTCARDS.   See CORRESPONDENCE.

## POSTMEN

A postman is not tipped for the regular performance of his duties, even though he may go to some extra trouble and make several return trips—with registered mail, for example. However, in many big cities, it is customary to give the regular postman a present at Christmastime—usually money tucked into a Christmas card rather than handed out as a tip would be to a delivery boy.

## POSTPONEMENTS.   See INVITATIONS; WEDDINGS.

## POSTURE

The importance of good posture cannot be overemphasized because posture has a direct result on both manner and manners. Proper posture can make a short person look taller and a fat one seem thinner. It can lend an inexpensive costume an air of elegance, and can endow the person of simplest background with the look of royalty.

Poor posture can cause physical discomfort as well as physical unattractiveness. The person who walks with shoulders bent and pelvis forward encourages an unflattering bulge of the stomach and also invites backache. Poor posture leads directly to poor manners at table. The person who does not sit erect is tempted to support his slouching shoulders by putting one or both elbows on the table, or to bend over his plate, bringing his mouth to his food instead of his food to his mouth.

## POTATOES

Potato chips are picked up and eaten from the fingers, and so are any deep-fried potatoes that are served crisp and brittle. The standard-size French fried potatoes are cut into bite-size pieces with a fork and eaten from it.

According to the rules, a boiled potato is not mashed on the plate and then mixed with butter or gravy, but there seems to be no valid reason why an adult should not do so if he fancies this preparation standard for little children.

If potatoes are baked in foil, the foil is removed before they are brought to the table in any but the most casual service. A potato baked in its skin is usually broken (not cut) open in the kitchen just before it is brought to the table. If it is served unbroken, the diner breaks it with his fingers or slits it first with his fork, and then spreads it open, adds seasonings, and eats the mealy interior from the shell, cutting the shell with his knife and fork and eating it also, if he likes.

Butter is not put directly on a potato with a serving knife or pick. It is first put on the butter plate or, if there is none, on the side of the dinner plate. It is transferred to a potato (or anything else on a dinner plate) with the dinner knife, not the butter spreader. However, sour cream or gravy is ladled directly onto a baked potato with the serving spoon.

In formal service, the waiter ladles gravy on or beside the meat, but a guest helping himself to gravy ladles some over mashed potatoes if he wants to.

**PRECEDENCE.**   See WASHINGTON for details of seating dignitaries by the rules of protocol governing rank. See the Index for rules of precedence in entering a room, leaving a party, and so on.

**PRESENTS.**   See GIFTS, and the Index.

## PRESERVES

Jam, preserves, and marmalade usually are served only at breakfast or at informal home-style meals. When they are to be eaten with toast or other hot breads, they are put on the butter plate. If they are to be eaten with waffles, pancakes, or French toast, they may be put on the main plate. Jelly served as an accompaniment to meat is put on the main plate.

**PRESIDENT OF THE UNITED STATES.** See FORMS OF ADDRESS (Government); WASHINGTON.

## PRESSING

A staff member who presses clothes for a houseguest is tipped. The tip may be given at the time the clothes are returned, but more usually is given on the day of departure. When a cleaner is called and garments are sent out to be pressed, the guest pays the charges. It is the guest's duty to ask the hostess what the charges are, and the hostess should be matter-of-fact about stating the amount and accepting the payment. Hospitality does not properly include paying for such personal expenses.

In a hotel, the bellboys who pick up and deliver things for the valet are tipped. If the valet himself makes the delivery, his manner will clearly indicate whether or not he expects a tip. Hotel valets usually do not, since they operate concessions, though it is only fair to tip one who does a rush job.

**PRIESTS.**   See FORMS OF ADDRESS (Clergy).

**PROFESSORS.**   See FORMS OF ADDRESS (Academic).

## PROMOTIONS

The announcement of a promotion is sent to the press, or made in any other fashion, by an officer of the firm or organization, not by the person receiving the promotion.
*See* BUSINESS MANNERS.

**PRUNES.**  See FRUITS.

**PUBLIC OPINION POLLS.**   See SURVEYS.

## PUBLIC SPEAKING

Sooner or later, virtually everyone has to say a few words in public—introducing a speaker at a meeting, presenting or accepting a prize, making a committee report, responding to a toast. The first and most important virtue in any speaker is brevity. If asked to speak for five minutes, don't take fifteen. Have a watch handy and keep an eye on it.

Covering all the necessary points in an allotted time demands preparation. Organize a speech so that the main points follow in a logical progression; then time the speech. The best speakers try to give the impression that they are talking extemporaneously or from rough notes because no speech, however brilliantly written, is as interesting and effective when read. If a speech must be completely written in advance, rehearsal is doubly important so that the speaker will have the appearance of speaking casually rather than of reading a lecture. On such occasions, oversize type is essential unless the speaker can clearly see ordinary type at fingertip distance, since the script is best left lying inconspicuously on the stand or table in front of him. In any case, a speaker should be sufficiently familiar with his written speech to glance up frequently from it or from his notes and so make the audience feel he is addressing them directly, not the microphone only.

Even if speaking without notes, it is vital to avoid an unfocused, blind stare over the heads of the audience, whether they number six or six hundred. Don't talk to the wall, the ceiling, or an imaginary vanishing point. Address the entire audience by glancing occasionally right, left, and center, not forgetting the balcony if there is one.

A good start and an effective closing are the biggest hurdles. An experienced speaker often protects himself by memorizing his opening and closing remarks, and then—in between—depending on no more than a series of index cards on which salient points, statistics, exact quotes, and other such matters are noted. Thus, if he draws a blank or forgets the sequence of ideas, a steady reminder is at hand to put him back on the track.

If humor does not come naturally, forget it. There is no law that says a speech must start with a joke or wisecrack, though there is considerable evidence that many people are not aware of this consoling fact. As another general rule, don't begin any speech with a self-belittling statement. "Unaccustomed as I am . . ." is one of the most threadbare of clichés. Apologizing for lack of preparation or for not being qualified as an authority seldom wins a speaker admiration for his frankness and humility. Instead, the audience wonders why the program committee was so inept as to choose him and why he was so ill-advised as to accept. Even when the speaker is a last-minute replacement and really is not prepared or qualified, the explanation can be far more gracefully made by the person introducing him.

Of no little importance are a speaker's appearance and mannerisms. A woman speaking from a platform of any appreciable elevation should remember that, since she is somewhat above the eye level of the audience, an inch or so of a slip that barely clears her hemline will be noticeably in view to the audience, and her pants may also be clearly visible if she sits with her knees apart. What to do with the hands is a problem best thought out in advance because ramming them deep into pockets, draping them on the hips, or clutching the speaker's stand as if it were a life preserver lends an air of tension and unease, as does any nervously repeated gesture.

Also of special importance is a speaker's use of the microphone. Under usual circumstances, a microphone has been adjusted and tested for correct volume before it is needed, and the speaker merely needs to speak more or less directly into it, in a natural tone; of course, if he wanders away from it, or turns his head aside, it will not amplify his voice. There is no need to lean into the mike, and it is best not to pick one up or touch it because even the slight sound of the fingers or of a ring clinking against the mike will also be magnified. By the same token, a speaker must turn away from the mike if he has to cough or sneeze, since any such sudden noise can sound like a bomb blast.

Unless other arrangements have been specifically made, a speaker is required to be on hand a few minutes before the announced time of a meeting. If there are several speakers, all stay to the end of the program as a routine courtesy to the others. If a speaker must leave early, he mentions the fact to the presiding officer in advance so that a formal explanation can be made to the audience during the chairman's introductory remarks.

**AUDIENCE.** The duty of the audience is simple and definite: It should hear the speaker out in silence. Occasional applause is welcome, but constant bursts of applause can ruin the timing and effectiveness of the best speaker. Interruptions from the floor, boos, and catcalls are taboo—no argument. So is table-hopping during the speeches at a lunch or dinner meeting. Couples or groups who fall into conversation during a speech are being inexcusably rude to the speaker, the chairman, and the program committee, as well as to their neighbors. No matter how inept or boring a speaker has been, he deserves at least a token round of applause—if only in thanksgiving that he has at last ceased.

**INTRODUCTIONS.** The shorter the introduction of a speaker, the better it usually is. Identify him adequately, give any special reasons for his appearance, acknowledge any special effort he has made to accept the invitation, and then let him have the floor.

The speaker remains seated while he is being introduced. At the end of the introduction, he rises and (if necessary) moves into place. His first words are an acknowledgment to the person who made the introduction—by name, not by title alone ("Thank you, Mr. Smith"; not "Mr. Chairman," for example). The speaker's salutation to the audience then follows, varying according to circumstances. In a small group, a smile and slight bow can serve if "Ladies and gentlemen," "Fellow committee members," or a similar greeting would be absurdly stilted. A formal salutation to a large gathering, however, follows an exact pattern. The speaker first addresses himself to the presiding officer by title only, "Madam President"; he then says, "Honored guests" (if there are other speakers or guests of honor present), and finally, to the audience, "Ladies and gentlemen" or "Members of the Society," or whatever else is suitable.

**PRESIDING OFFICER.** Whoever is conducting a meeting or otherwise officiating as chairman of the event always says a few words of thanks to a speaker immediately after the conclusion of his remarks. After a meeting, the presiding officer makes a point of seeing that a distinguished speaker, particularly a woman, is accompanied to an exit and put into a cab or seen comfortably on the way. On some occasions, it is appropriate for several of the officers or committee members to arrange to take the guest speaker out for drinks or other refreshment after the meeting breaks up. Under any circumstances, thanks at the conclusion of the event are not enough. A formal note of thanks from an officer of the sponsoring group or the individual in charge should always be dispatched the next day, or as soon thereafter as possible.

**RADIO AND TELEVISION.** For a formal appearance on television, a guest is generally advised in advance about what shade of color will televise best according to the background, and also about any special makeup if it is necessary. As a general rule, it is best not to wear brilliantly faceted necklaces or pins or other flashing jewelry that will cast a blazing reflection into the camera. Because the microphone picks up all noises in the studio indiscriminately, clanking bracelets can be a problem.

Broadcasts are timed to the split second, and so it is essential to follow the lead of the moderator, especially when appearing with other speakers, so that everyone on a program will have a fair share of the time, and particularly not to interrupt—nothing but a jumble of meaningless sound results when two people talk through a mike at once.

A disaster can be the result if everyone in the studio does not watch the "On the Air" light. When it is red, everything said in the studio is going over the air. Even if the program seems to have been brought to a formal close, wait in silence until that red light changes to green.

# PUNCH

Though punch can be made of a wide variety of ingredients, it usually is based on liquor or wine (or a combination of them) and citrus juices, sugar, plain or carbonated water, and perhaps also liqueurs, tea, and spices. Occasionally, small fruits and berries are added. Certain punches are served either cold or hot. Non-alcoholic punch is usually served cold, and punches containing carbonated water and sparkling wines are invariably served cold. (The same drink served from a pitcher instead of a bowl is called a "cup," or "wine cup.")

**DRINKING.** Any punch is best taken in small, cautious sips, even if it does taste like fancy lemonade. A great many punches honestly earn their name from the wallop they carry. The delicious (and not infrequently disastrous) Fish House Punch is a notable example of a mixture that slides down so easily and then hits so hard.

**SERVING.** At receptions, punch very frequently and practically takes the place of cocktails, highballs, and other drinks that have to be mixed more or less to order, or of champagne, because punch is less expensive and also easier to serve.

Traditionally, punch is ladled from a bowl and served in a glass cup with one handle, though small Old-Fashioned glasses or cocktail glasses without a foot are very frequently used. A punch cup or glass is filled about two-thirds full. The punch bowl and its cups are commonly placed on a table by themselves, rather than on the one containing food.

**Cold.** A cold punch is a favorite refreshment at dances, and is frequently the first choice at a large, casual reception like an open house or housewarming. Continuous chilling is achieved by floating a big block of ice in the bowl. (Ice cubes dilute the punch too rapidly.) Milk punches, however, should not be cooled in this manner.

**Hot.** Hot punch, wonderful in cold brisk weather, was the original punch. It dates from Anglo-Saxon times (the word "wassail" derived from "Waes Haeil," which meant "Be healthy!"). Today, eggnog and hot punch are the traditional drinks to serve at Christmas, on Twelfth Night, and at New Year's. A hot punch is served in a cup with a handle, and if metal cups are used, they should have insulated handles or they will become uncomfortably hot to hold.

## PUNCTUALITY

"Punctuality is the politeness of kings."—(attributed to) *Louis XVIII* of France
On a less exhalted level: "Punctuality is the art of arriving for an appointment
just in time to be indignant at the tardiness of the other party."
—*The Left-Handed Dictionary*
"Punctuality is the ability to guess to the minute exactly how late a girl
will be for an appointment."—*Vittorio de Sica* (ibid.)

Chronic lateness is one of the most irritating breaches of the basic rules of good manners because it shows a deliberate indifference to the value of other people's time. Anyone who will be as much as fifteen minutes late for an engagement at an exact hour should, if possible, telephone and give the approximate time of his arrival, rather than leave the other person wondering if the date has been forgotten or if there is confusion about the time and place.

It is just as important to be punctual about leaving. If invitations to a cocktail party, for example, state "five to seven," guests are privileged to turn up as late as six-thirty, but are not expected to linger on and on past the specified ending time.

Exactly the same rules hold for both business and social engagements. The people who break them regularly deserve to be paid back in their own coin— but that way lies only double trouble. The whole code of manners would break down if everyone were treated as he deserved to be, instead of by the rules.
See TARDINESS in the Index.

## PUNISHMENT

It is often necessary to correct small children for some breach of manners, but actual punishment—from a scolding to a spanking—in the presence of a guest usually is a greater punishment for the guest than for the child. It is far better to divert the child or banish him, and deal with actual punishment after guests have gone. The purpose of punishment is to drive home a lesson. Too often, parents who punish a child for showing off are themselves showing off—demonstrating what firm disciplinarians they are.

**PURSES.** *See* HANDBAGS.

# Q

## QUARRELS

> "I recommend to you this moral!
> In real life it takes only one to make a quarrel."—*Ogden Nash*

Everyone involved in a quarrel shares responsibility, no matter who started it, because it takes two to *continue* a controversy. Quarreling in public can only bore if not embarrass bystanders, and families who bicker, squabble, wrangle, or fight in front of guests break the laws of hospitality. A guest is obligated never to start a quarrel with anyone while under another's roof. If neighbors must quarrel, they do better to have it out strictly between themselves, rather than in the presence of other adults or of their own children.

**QUESTIONS AND ANSWERS.** *See* CONVERSATION.

**QUITTING.** *See* RESIGNATIONS.

# R

## R.S.V.P.

These letters stand for the French *Répondez, s'il vous plaît*. They are in very wide use in this country. Their translation, "Please reply," is equally correct, though never abbreviated to P.R. Both R.S.V.P. and R.s.v.p. are correct. When these initials appear on an invitation, an answer is obligatory.

**RABBIS.** *See* FORMS OF ADDRESS (Clergy).

**RADIOS.** *See* TELEVISION AND RADIO.

## RADISHES

Unless radishes are served as part of a mixed salad, they are taken from their serving bowl with the fingers and put on the butter plate or, if there is none, on the side of the salad or dinner plate. Radishes are sometimes buttered and dipped into salt that has been spooned or sprinkled onto the side of the plate, but are never dipped directly into an individual open saltcellar.

## REACHING

The rule says: Never reach across another person to pick up an article, to point, to ring a bell, to help oneself to food, or for any other reason—but this is much too sweeping a dictum to follow invariably. If it is impossible or unreasonably awkward to avoid reaching across someone, reach (except at table)—but say a quick word of apology.

## REAL ESTATE

Not infrequently, trouble develops between buyer and seller, landlord and tenant, because one or both are vague about the points of business etiquette covering their relationship. And even more frequently, the real estate agent is caught in the middle because of a client's ignorance about his function and profession.

**AGENTS.** The real-estate agent offers an extraordinary bargain in services. He invests his time, training, and special knowledge with no charge to either party unless he is successful in bringing the right people together and making a deal for them. If the rules of fair play to him are understood and observed, buyer and seller both profit from his services—and so does he.

A real-estate agent's income is a percentage of a sale or rental price. In some parts of the country, the agent's percentage for negotiating a *rental* is paid by the tenant. The commission for a sale is almost invariably paid by the seller, but a prospective buyer also has a positive financial obligation to the agent.

In the first place, the agent does not make appointments to show properties because he is lonesome. Time is money to him, just as it is to every other professional. Therefore, the person who consults a real-estate agent should be frank about his circumstances—the overall price he can afford, what down payment he can make, and whether he wants to close a deal immediately, next month, next year, or is merely looking over the neighborhood to see if it suits him.

If an appointment to look at a property must be canceled, inform the agent as promptly as possible. The time of an owner as well as of the agent may be totally wasted if the client simply fails to appear.

Properties frequently are put on what is known as "multiple listing." This means that several different agencies are working on the sale and that the agent who makes the sale gets the lion's share of the commission. Therefore, if one agent offers to show a property to a prospective buyer that another agent has already shown to him, the buyer is obligated to mention that fact. If he finally decides to buy that property, he is expected to conclude the deal through the agent who first showed it to him—it being obviously unfair to let one man invest time, gasoline, and telephone calls in his behalf and then allow another agent to collect the cream of the profit.

"Exclusive listing" means that one agency only has the right to conclude the deal. Obviously, it is sharp practice on the part of both buyer and seller if they attempt to conclude a deal directly, once an agent has been delegated to handle the property.

**BUYERS AND RENTERS.** The person looking at a house for sale or lease cannot go wrong if he behaves like a guest in the place when the owner or current occupant is present. He asks permission before opening a closet or entering a closed room. And he takes particular pains not to make derogatory comments in front of owner or tenant, remembering that the house and the furnishings represent the taste of the occupant—or at least what the occupant has been willing to endure. In other words, a buyer can easily put himself on the right road if he remembers, when negotiating for a property, that he is making an impression as a new member of the community and that later, under different circumstances, he is almost certain to meet both the agents he has dealt with and the owners of the houses he has considered: at church, school meetings, while shopping, or socially.

A renter can fulfill his obligations to an owner if he behaves as responsibly about damage as a houseguest or a borrower of personal property should. An owner has every right to expect his property to be returned to him, at the end of a rental period, clean and otherwise in as good condition as the renter found it, barring damage caused by a leaking roof or other matter that is not his responsibility, and expecting what is described in leases as "reasonable wear and tear." For example, at the end of six months, the renter is not expected to pay for the cleaning of upholstered furniture that has had normal use. But if a large hole has been burned in a couch, he is by all rules of fair play obligated to repair the damage.

**LANDLORDS.** Any standard lease usually provides that the owner may inspect his property "at any reasonable time"—a fair-enough stipulation if it is not abused. On the other hand, any man's dwelling—rented for a day or leased for ten years—is his castle, and the owner should expect to enter only with the tenant's permission and by appointment.

## RECEIVING LINES

The whole purpose of a receiving line is to make it easy for each guest at a large gathering to be greeted by the host and hostess and introduced to the guest of honor without delay or confusion. A receiving line is a standard part of a formal or official event of considerable size, but also is appropriate on an otherwise quite informal occasion—if it is the most practical way to accomplish the same purpose.

**ANNOUNCERS.** An announcer officiates only at large and formal events, never at small or informal ones. He serves an extremely useful function if many of the guests are unknown or only slightly known to the first person in the receiving line.

An announcer usually is the hostess's butler or a butler supplied by a caterer. At a wedding reception, the announcer sometimes is a relative or close friend of the bride's family, usually a man, though occasionally a woman is asked to serve in this capacity. At business, official, and diplomatic events, the announcer usually is an aide or other member of the host's professional staff.

An announcer stands just ahead of a receiving line, and in no sense participates as part of it—beyond his special duty, which is to relay the name of each guest separately to the person heading the line. The announcer does not shake hands with an arriving guest, even if he himself is a personal friend of the party giver. He keeps his hand pointedly at his sides so that guests will not offer to shake hands, gives only a cordial and inquiring look and a slight bow as a guest approaches, and says, "What name, please?" if the guest does not state it. He does not identify himself in return. Of course, if he is good old George, childhood friend of a guest, he gives and gets a special smile, but other social exchanges are saved until later.

(Additional details are under "Going Through a Line" below.)

**FORMATION AND PLACEMENT.** A receiving line usually stands just inside the main room in which the gathering is held, but may be placed anywhere that is most comfortable and convenient—at the far end of a garden or along one side of a ballroom at some distance from the entrance, for example.

A receiving line takes its place as the first guests arrive (with the exception noted under RECEPTIONS), and remains in place for widely varying lengths of time, depending on the occasion. Usually, the line breaks up after about three-quarters of an hour. At a very large reception for a noted guest of honor, the line may stay intact much longer. The general rule is that the receiving line stays in place until the majority of the guests have arrived. It generally does not re-form at the end of a party, but if it does, that is a clear sign it is time for guests to leave.

A receiving line may be no more than host and hostess, or hostess and guest of honor; it is always best to keep the line as short as circumstances allow. Receiving lines at wedding receptions have to be long, but on all other occasions the line customarily includes no more than six at the most. Except for the occasions noted below, the hostess stands first in line, nearest the entrance. The host stands second unless there is a guest or guests of honor, in which case he stands last. If the host is not standing in the line, he stays near it to introduce guests coming off the line to others nearby.

If there is more than one guest of honor, the hostess has some latitude of choice and can set up her line in any way that seems to her most tactful. Following are the rules most widely observed unless very high dignitaries of state or church are involved.

If a man and woman who have no personal connection but who are of nearly equal distinction are being jointly honored, the woman usually stands next to the hostess; and if a married couple are being honored jointly—on a wedding anniversary, for example—the wife usually precedes her husband in the line. This arrangement, logically, is based on the rule that women are introduced before men. However, some hostesses prefer to alternate men and women in a receiving line, and it is not unusual to see this equally correct order: hostess, male guest of honor, his wife, host.

If two married couples are being honored, the elder couple stands next to the hostess, then the younger couple. If the honored couples are of about the same age and distinction, the hostess has what is, at best, an awkward choice. She can place the couple she has known longer beside her, let alphabetical order of names decide position, toss a coin—or abandon the whole idea of a receiving line.

**Business and Official.** The social rule calling for a hostess to stand first in line is reversed at business and official events. If a business reception is held at the host's dwelling, his wife always receives with him—but he stands first in line. At a business reception held elsewhere, the wife (or husband) of anyone in the receiving line does not join it unless there is some business reason to do so. Instead, the wife of the host (or, if she is not present, someone on his staff) is detailed to see that the wife of a guest is not left alone. If wives stand in line, the rules below under "Dignitaries" are followed.

**Clubs, Schools, and so on.** The officers of an organization or class stand in the order of their rank: president, vice-president, and so on. Wives, husbands, and dates do not stand in such a receiving line.

**Debuts.** *See* separate entry.

**Dignitaries.** The United States Department Bureau of Protocol approves the following in receiving lines of an *official* nature:

Official Host
Guest of Honor
Wife (or Husband) of Guest of Honor
Official Hostess
*or*
Official Host
Guest of Honor
Official Hostess
Wife (or Husband) of Guest of Honor

**Weddings.**  *See* "Receptions" under WEDDINGS.

**GLOVES.** The first rule about gloves and receiving lines is: Take both gloves off or, when appropriate, leave both on. A man never wears gloves when standing in a receiving line or going through one. A woman standing in a receiving line can keep her gloves on or leave them off, as she likes. In the evening, if she is wearing long gloves, it is customary to keep them on. A woman going through a receiving line has the same choices with some few exceptions. She may choose to leave short gloves with her wraps, for example, but if long gloves are part of her costume, she keeps them on. If she is being presented to the President of the United States, the head of another country, the Pope or other dignitary of very high rank, she will be instructed if protocol calls for removal of her gloves. If in doubt, she should take them off.

**GOING THROUGH A LINE.** Guests must go through a receiving line immediately after checking their wraps under all usual circumstances. At an enormous reception, if the line of guests waiting to be received is extremely long and also if the receiving line is not stationed in such a position that to bypass it would be conspicuous, a guest may postpone the duty briefly and take some refreshment, chat with friends, or dance first; but all guests who arrive before a receiving line breaks up must go through it. Not to do so is a marked mistake. Guests who arrive after a receiving line has dispersed must find the host and hostess as readily as possible, and also say a few words to the guest of honor. It is an outstanding rudeness to go to any reception, eat, drink, and leave without meeting the guest of honor.

A woman precedes a male companion through a receiving line, with the exceptions noted below under "Washington."

The hostess always mentions a guest's name as she offers her hand—"Good afternoon, Mrs. Jones," and so on. However, a hostess challenged to remember the names of scores of acquaintances within a brief time can draw a sudden blank, and if she does not welcome a guest by name, the guest promptly helps her by stating it so that she can make the introduction to the next person in line without the embarrassment of admitting her failure.

Anyone who does not know the hostess makes a self-introduction—"I am John Jones [Mary Jones], a classmate of your daughter Jane," for example, or: "I am Mrs. George White. My husband serves with Mr. Brown on the board at the club."

A married woman identifies herself as "Mrs. Harold Jones." An unmarried woman gives her first and last name without "Miss" (except to an announcer). A man never uses "Mr." with his name (except to an announcer), though if he has a professional title he uses it so that his hostess can identify him properly to the next person in line.

The hostess says, "How do you do, Mrs. [Miss, Mr.] Jones," and makes the introduction to the guest of honor if one is necessary. All guests generally are introduced to both men and women guests of honor when they are standing in a receiving line, though there are exceptions at debuts and weddings (which see).

**Announcer.** The routine is quite different if there is an announcer. All guests give both title and name to him. A man alone says, "Mr. Jones." An unmarried woman says, "Miss Jones." A married woman alone says, "Mrs. Jones." (She adds her husband's first name only if it is needed to avoid confusion with others of the same last name). If her husband is with her, he says, "Mr. and Mrs. Jones." The announcer gives the name separately to the hostess, however—"Mrs. Jones," and after the hostess has greeted her, "Mr. Jones."

A man arriving with his daughter or any other woman not his wife gives her name first to the announcer ("Miss Jones"), and after the announcer has repeated her name to the hostess, he states his own to the announcer, "Mr. Jones."

A man arriving with his family gives his wife's name first to the announcer, then those of his daughters, then those of his sons. Girls over twelve are identified to the announcer as "Miss Jones." Girls under twelve are identified to him by first and last name without "Miss," but the announcer then gives a little girl a thrill by adding the title and announcing her as "Miss Mary Jones." The same rule holds for identifying boys under twelve to the announcer, who adds "Master" or makes it a really memorable event by adding "Mr."

**Colleges.** At a faculty reception at a man's college, the student goes first through the receiving line. He gives his name ("John Jones") to the hostess and then introduces his companion by her title and last name. If many hundreds of students are going through a long receiving line, he does not hold up the procession of guests by repeating her name all along the line. Instead, his date follows him and gives her own name (without "Miss") after she has been presented to the first in line. The student observes the same procedure if his parents are with him, but after stating his own name, he adds, "My mother," and then, "My father." He does not repeat his parents' last name unless it is different from his.

At a woman's college, the student goes first, introducing herself without title, "Mary Jones," but a girl introduces her escort by title, "Mr. White." However, if he needs to give his own name, he omits the title and uses his first name, "William White."

**Washington.** At official or diplomatic receptions in Washington, a man takes precedence over his wife and is announced and goes through a line first. The reason behind this rule of protocol is that guests are present in their official capacities. A few years ago, before we had any woman ambassadors, cabinet officers, senators, and so on, this presented no problem because it was always the husband who held the office. Today, this rule is not logical, but it is still observed, since it makes things more orderly; at an official White House reception, for example, the husband of a woman senator is directed by the aides to precede his wife through the receiving line.

At any kind of private and entirely social gathering, the standard rules are observed, of course.

**WEDDING.** *See* "Receptions" under WEDDINGS.

# RECEPTIONS

We use the word "reception" today to mean a formal gathering, other than a meal, in honor of some person or occasion. The major differences between a reception and a tea or cocktail party are that a reception can be held at any time of the day or evening; that a receiving line is formed; and that there is far wider latitude of choice in refreshments. There may be no refreshments at all, as in the case of a huge civic reception held in honor of a visiting dignitary, or there may be an elaborate supper such as sometimes is served at an evening reception.

**DURATION.** A reception usually lasts about two hours, but circumstances govern the duration. When hundreds of people are invited to pass along a receiving line to be presented to a celebrity, a reception may span the better part of an afternoon. A very small reception—for instance, one held before a public banquet to give committee members and a limited number of other important guests a chance to speak with the guest or guests of honor—may last only half an hour.

**GUEST OF HONOR.** The guest of honor arrives promptly, shortly before the designated time, and stays to the end of the time announced in the invitation. Only the president of a country, a reigning monarch, or a very high dignitary of church or state makes an entrance after all the guests are assembled. At such ceremonial events, the general rule is that all guests remain until the guest of honor departs.

An experienced guest of honor learns to avoid an aching hand by giving a quick grip and releasing a guest's hand before the grasp can be returned with well-meant but thoughtless force. A woman who must shake hands with a great many guests saves herself anguish by transferring a ring to her left hand until the receiving line breaks up.

A guest of honor usually sends flowers to the hostess either in advance or on the day after the reception, and always writes a note of thanks to her.

**GUESTS.** The main obligation of a guest who arrives before a receiving line breaks up is to go through it. (*See* RECEIVING LINES.) The guest who arrives later must find the host and hostess as soon as possible, and must make a point of saying a word or so to the guest of honor. It is a marked discourtesy to arrive at a big party, eat, drink, make merry with friends, and leave without completing these duties.

At a private reception the roof is an introduction, and guests speak with strangers without being formally introduced. This rule holds only in general at large public receptions. Strangers may introduce themselves, but a guest does not break into a group of complete strangers deep in conversation without some signal that he is welcome.

At a small reception, a guest says good-bye to host or hostess and the guest of honor before departure. At a very large reception, going through the receiving line is enough—guests may leave without further word to host, hostess, and guest of honor unless an easy opportunity to speak to them presents itself.

**Length of Stay.** The time of arrival and length of stay vary widely according to the character of the reception. For a small reception preceding a meal such as a wedding breakfast or a public dinner, guests should arrive promptly at the hour specified. At an evening reception at which there will be dancing, the invitation often gives only the opening hour—10:00 P.M., for example. In this circumstance, a guest is privileged to arrive as much as an hour later, or about half an hour before supper, if the time for it is specified, and may stay as long as the music continues. If an invitation specifies a period such as "three to six," a guest may arrive at any time before five-thirty. It is never correct to arrive only a few minutes before the closing hour or to stay much past it.

Usually a guest stays somewhat longer at a small gathering than at a very large one. A guest may stay for the full duration of the party, but forty-five minutes to an hour is the usual length of stay, and half an hour is sufficient. Even if a guest of honor does not leave at the specified closing hour, other guests are required to do so. (When the guest of honor stays on, his remaining indicates that the hostess has made special plans for a small segment of her party for the rest of the evening; only those specifically invited are expected to remain also.)

**INVITATIONS.** Here, again, the range is wide. Invitations may be printed, engraved, or given by telephone. No matter how formal or informal the form of an invitation, it should give the duration of the reception and the name of the guest of honor, if there is one.

An engraved or printed invitation to attend a public or semipublic reception does not require an answer unless "R.S.V.P." appears on the invitation. An invitation in handwriting indicates a small gathering, and an answer is required even if "R.S.V.P." is omitted. The reply follows the form of the invitation.

*See* INVITATIONS for details.

**RECEIVING LINES.**   *See* separate entry.

**THANK-YOU NOTES.** A note of thanks is not required or customary after a large reception, except, of course, from the guest of honor. Close friends frequently send a note of thanks after a small reception.

**REFERENCES.**   For letters of reference or recommendation, *see* BUSINESS MANNERS and HOUSEHOLD EMPLOYEES.

## REGRETS

"R.S.V.P." on any invitation means that an answer is required, and it is just as important to send regrets promptly as it is to send an acceptance. "Regrets Only" on an invitation also requires a prompt answer if the invitation cannot be accepted.
   *See* INVITATIONS.

**RELATIVES.**   *See* INTRODUCTIONS.

**RELIGIONS.**   *See* CONVERSATION; FORMS OF ADDRESS (Clergy).

**RELISHES.**   *See* CONDIMENTS AND RELISHES.

## REMINDER CARDS

Sending a reminder of the time and place of a party is often a practical gesture —particularly if an invitation has been given verbally under circumstances where the guest had no means of making a record of the details. A note or telephone call to the guest will serve the purpose.
   For the use (and the standard form) of a formal engraved reminder card, *see* INVITATIONS.

**RENTING.**   *See* REAL ESTATE.

## REPLY CARDS

A response card is useful and correct with an invitation to a business event and also to fund-raising balls, banquets, and theater parties no matter how "social" some of their aspects may be.
   For standard forms and other details, *see* BANQUETS and INVITATIONS, FORMAL.

## RESERVATIONS

It is remarkable how many hotels, restaurants, and countless other places will make firm reservations for space or services with no other guarantee than the word of a client given over the telephone. So much time is saved and so much peace of mind provided by this system of mutual trust that, from selfish reasons alone, it is important to cancel a reservation as soon as possible if plans change. It is a real abuse of good faith to make a reservation and neither show up nor cancel.
   *See* HOTELS AND MOTELS for correct written and telegraphed forms.

**RESIDENCE.**   *See* HOUSE AND HOME.

## RESIGNATIONS

. For nearly everyone, there comes a time when quitting in a blaze of verbal fireworks is almost irresistibly tempting. Better think twice. There may be two sides to the matter. Just as an employer is best advised not to fire in fury, the employee is best advised to quit in cool good order. A blistering outburst gives a momentary satisfaction, but no one can know what the future holds or be sure that, later on, dealings of some sort with the previous employer may not be necessary.
   On the other hand, there are times when a real injustice calls on the outraged spirit to protest, no matter what the consequences. In such a case, let the

false fellow have it—but in full awareness that a door is being slammed on that relationship forever.

The rule about giving notice works both ways. Just as an employer is obligated to give an employee fair notice that his employment is terminating, an employee is obligated to give an employer the same chance to adapt to a change.

*See also* BUSINESS MANNERS; CLUBS; HOUSEHOLD EMPLOYEES.

**RESPECTFULLY.** See CORRESPONDENCE and FORMS OF ADDRESS for the very limited use of this word as the complimentary close of a letter.

## RESTAURANTS

The rules for business and social entertaining in a restaurant are the same.

**ACCIDENTS.** If a diner accidentally breaks a glass or plate he does not offer to pay for it, since it can be taken for granted that such losses are covered by insurance. However, a bill for damages can be expected for deliberate breakage (of glasses smashed at a bachelor dinner after the toast to the bride, for example).

If a patron causes any spectacular spilling of food or drink, he apologizes briefly for the trouble he has caused the waiter and leaves a larger tip than usual.

If an employee is responsible for an accident that damages a patron's clothes, all that the management is expected to do, beyond apologizing profusely, is ask to have the bill for cleaning sent to them in due course; and all that the patron can do is accept the apology with the best grace possible.

If a fellow diner causes a spill that seriously damages clothes, he makes the same offer. The victim generally refuses to accept it under the philosophic reasoning that in every life some rain (and other substances) must fall.

**CAFETERIAS.** If all the tables are occupied, a patron may take his tray to any empty place, but "Are you saving this place?" is the standard courtesy before taking a seat at a partially occupied table It is the growing custom to leave ten cents per person for the busboy who cleans away the tray and dishes.

**CHECKING.** A man checks his hat and coat. A woman checks bulky parcels, but usually does not check her coat unless it is wet. (Some restaurants will not check fur coats because their insurance does not cover them, and some will not check women's coats because they have no room.) A man takes any items a woman wants to check, hands them to the attendant, and keeps both checks himself. When leaving, he asks for the woman's wrap first, and helps her into it before putting on his own. He pays the tip for both, even if the woman is his hostess. If there is a line waiting at the checkroom, a woman stands to one side, out of the way, rather than in the line beside him.

**CHOOSING.** It is the host's obligation to offer a choice of restaurants if he does not want to make a definite selection of one himself. "Where would you like to go?" puts a guest in an embarrassing spot if he is in any way uncertain about his host's finances and tastes, since it makes him responsible for determining the price of the meal—and the character of the food and service.

**CLOTHES.** In many restaurants, a shirt-sleeved diner would be as conspicuous as one in a bikini. Since a restaurateur  is within his rights to set up standards for his own establishment, as long as he does not violate the laws, a prospective patron who is politely turned away because of too casual dress has no reason to feel insulted. A tie and jacket are routine at any but the most informal eating places.

**COMPLAINTS.** As a general rule, if food and service are both impossible, the best thing to do is endure them in silence—and never go back. Point out an honest mistake, of course, and send back an overdone steak if a rare one was ordered. But it is not fair to blame the waiter if the quality of the cuisine in general is poor—that is the chef's responsibility. If the service is so bad that a complaint is called for, send for the headwaiter and complain to him, and so avoid any further dealings with a waiter who has already proved himself incompetent.

**DRINKS.** A cocktail is part of a meal for many people. Unless he is certain of a guest's wishes, a host says, "What will you have to drink?" rather than, "Do you want a drink?"—which implies that he himself does not. If a guest asks for a cocktail, the host orders tomato juice or something similar if he does not want anything stronger, but does not let his guest drink alone. The routine for the guest who does not want alcohol is the same if his host orders a drink. The important thing for both is to be specific about what they really want. Too often, both host and guest politely order unwanted cocktails because each thinks the other wants one.

(For service at a bar, see "Meeting In" below.)

**DRIVE-INS.** Flicking the car light is the standard signal to a waitress that attention is wanted. If this does not produce results, the lightest touch of the horn is all that good manners permit. Since drive-in restaurants are completely informal, only one other rule need be observed: Don't drive off leaving an unappetizing kitchen midden of paper cups, napkins, straws, wrappers, and half-eaten food on the pavement to greet the next customer—or for the hardworking little waitresses to pick up.

Waitresses who bring trays to a car expect a tip. Ten percent is adequate. Tips are not expected from patrons who get out of the car and pick up their own orders.

**ENTERING AND SEATING.** The main rule to remember is: Let the host and hostess take charge. When several people are dining together and dividing the check, the women stand back and let one of the men deal with the preliminaries with the headwaiter.

After checking wraps, the host steps forward and tells the headwaiter the number in his party or asks for the table reserved in his name. The women follow the headwaiter or a waiter he summons. If the group is sizable, the hostess goes first so that she can most efficiently direct the guests to their places. In a group of two couples, the hostess follows a woman guest of honor. The host brings up the rear, though a man entertaining a sizable group without a hostess often goes first, again because this makes it simpler to seat guests as he wants them. When a couple is entertaining, the wife tells the guests where to sit, and a guest waits for a sign from her (or the host, if he is entertaining without his wife) before choosing a place. The only exception occurs when two people are being seated: The waiter pulls out the chair with the best view—quite literally, if there is anything to see out of a window; otherwise, the one facing the room —and the woman (or the guest if two women or two men are concerned) takes it.

If there is no captain or waiter to lead the way to a table, a couple does whatever is practical. If the place is crowded, the man goes first. Otherwise, he usually suggests a table and follows his companion to it. She usually takes the seat farther from the entrance.

If a waiter does not pull out a chair and seat a woman, her escort does so, and helps her off with her coat before taking his place. (A woman captain or waitress does not pull out a chair except for someone who obviously needs assistance.)

A man with two women seats the decidedly older, or if one is his wife he helps their guest, though if the waiter is helping one he helps the other. If no waiter is on hand, the second woman seats herself rather than wait for the man to rush around to seat her also. If she needs help with her coat, he offers it after the first woman is comfortably settled.

At a free-standing table for four, six, or ten, host and hostess sit opposite each other, just as they would at home; at a table for eight or twelve, the male guest of honor sits opposite the host, with the hostess on his left. If two couples are dining together and splitting the check, the two men sit opposite each other.

In a booth, two people sit opposite each other. If there are two couples, the women take the seats against the wall. If the couples are married (or otherwise related) each man sits beside the other's wife. If the couples are not married, the men follow the rule above, or sit beside their dates, as they choose.

In a semicircular booth, the two outside seats are taken by men. The arrangement for two married couples is: host, guest wife on his right, hostess, guest husband. Otherwise, couples assort themselves as they like, with the men on the outside. The same rules are followed for larger groups.

At a banquette, two people sit side by side with a woman (or guest) on a man's right. In a party of four, the women sit against the wall and the men opposite, on the chairs, each man across from the other's wife or date.

**HANDBAGS AND GLOVES.** Nothing belongs on the table except the food, the necessary equipment for eating it, and the restaurant's decorations. Handbags and packages belong on the lap, hung on the arm of a chair, set on the seat of a banquette, or put on the floor out of the waiter's path. Gloves are not put on the table either.

**LEAVING THE TABLE.** Under all ordinary circumstances, the hostess makes the first move to leave, though if the host (or a hostess entertaining without a host) delays unduly in sending for the check, a guest is entirely correct in saying frankly, "I have an appointment . . ." or giving any other excuse for making the first move.

**For a Washroom.** When a couple enter a restaurant—after a long drive, for example—and the man says, "Do you want to wash your hands?" the answer should not be No because the question may mean that he wants to be excused. If a group enters under the same circumstances, it is usual to find a table first and then for the hostess to say, "Do you want to come with me?" to the other women. They all follow her, leaving the men free to find their own washroom. If a group is going on after a meal to a theater or elsewhere, the hostess makes the same suggestion when the host sends for the check. If time is pressing, she adds—for the benefit of her husband—"We'll meet you at the checkroom." Otherwise, all return to the table.

Staff members are alert to a patron's needs. Anyone in search of a washroom usually is given directions in response to no more than an inquiring glance. Otherwise, ask for "the ladies' room," "the men's room," or "the washroom." "The rest room" and "the bathroom" sound faintly absurd in a restaurant, and "the little girls' room" and other delicate evasions are a bit cute when used to a staff member.

As a general rule, her companions do not all go away from a table and leave one woman there alone. If it is necessary for a member of the party to leave the table during the meal, no more than "Excuse me—I'll be right back" is necessary. Of course, if anyone is absent for an undue time, the hostess goes to see if a woman guest is all right and the host checks up on a male guest; or a waitress or waiter can be sent to investigate.

**LUNCH COUNTERS.** This is such casual eat-and-run feeding that common sense sets the rules. Patrons do not dally for a cigarette or a chat if others are waiting for seats, and at a crowded stand-up counter they move back as soon as served.

Technically, a tip is not necessary at a lunch counter, but it is increasingly the custom to leave a dime or about 10 percent of a tab over a dollar. A tip always is in order for extra or unusual service.

**MEETING AT.** A man usually does not ask a woman with whom he is dining alone to meet him at a restaurant—he calls for her and takes her there. This general rule can, of course, be broken for practical reasons, but they should be good ones, and call for an excuse from him, as well.

A host (hostess) is expected to arrive a few minutes before the appointed time, and a guest should arrive promptly or no more than a few minutes late. (*See* "Tardiness," below.) If a table has been reserved, the first person to arrive may wait near the entrance or ask to be seated.

Usually a guest who arrives before his host does not order a drink while waiting, but there is no absolute rule. In crowded restaurants, there often is no comfortable place to wait except at the bar. Unless the bar is also crowded, the early guest can take a seat there without ordering a drink. Otherwise, he orders a drink to justify his place at the bar, or stands in any place he can find outside the main stream of traffic.

In many hotels, a cocktail lounge adjoins a restaurant. This is a good place for a sizable group to meet, and here the host orders a drink for his first guests as soon as they arrive, and for others as they join the party. In general, it is more thoughtful to ask a woman or elderly people to meet in a cocktail lounge than a bar, especially if there is a chance that they may arrive before the host does. Some women do not feel comfortable alone at a bar, and chairs are more easily managed by the elderly than bar stools.

If the table is ready before drinks are finished at the bar or in a lounge, the patron does not carry his glass with him. He leaves it for the waiter to transfer.

**NIGHTCLUBS.**    *See* separate entry for the special rules observed in places that feature floor shows, dancing, and other entertainment.

**ORDERING.** À *la carte* means that each dish is priced individually. *Table d'hôte* is less expensive than the same number of courses chosen à *la carte*, but the choice of dishes is likely to be more restricted and the portions smaller.

In general, dining out is a more pleasant occasion and there is less confusion in the serving if all at the table follow the host's lead and take the complete dinner or the same number of courses that he suggests à *la carte*. If the host says, "Do you see anything you like on the dinner?" it is a clear hint that he would rather not order the more expensive specialties in the à *la carte* section, and the guest chooses from the dinner menu or suggests skipping the appetizers and soups before one main dish à *la carte*.

Since a guest properly hesitates to order too expensive a meal, or too many courses, the host who is not counting the cost may suggest, "What would you like first? The oysters are good here," and so on. In some very expensive restaurants, a woman is handed a special menu without prices. The only prudent course for her is to wait for the host to suggest Steak Châteaubriand or Golden Pheasant, or to ask him to order, saying, if necessary, "I don't eat seafood [or whatever], but otherwise I'll have what you do."

If the group is small, the host asks each guest what he would like and transmits all orders to the waiter, giving his own last, always. When there are six or more at table, this procedure places an almost impossible demand on the host's memory, and so it is correct with larger parties for the waiter to take each order separately, starting with the person on the host's right.

**PAYING.** When the meal is finished, the host (or if there is none, one of the diners) asks the waiter for the check. It is quite correct—and only sensible— to look the check over (rapidly!) to make sure it is right. If an error has been made, take for granted that it was an honest mistake, and point it out pleasantly to the waiter or headwaiter, whichever is available. Sufficient bills are put on the tray and then covered by the check, facedown.

If diners are to share costs, the mathematics of dividing up the bill should be kept as brief as possible. The most efficient way to avoid delay and discussion is to ask for separate checks when ordering. Otherwise, let one person serve as accountant and collect from the rest at the table; or serve as banker, and the others settle accounts with him afterward.

If a host intends to pay by bank check where his credit is not established, he does best to see the headwaiter before his guests arrive so that there will be no conversation about the bill at the table.

Some men are old-fashioned enough to feel uncomfortable if a hostess displays cash in public. Women who entertain frequently in restaurants, as many businesswomen do, solve the problem by carrying a credit card and adding the tip to the bill when they sign it. If a woman does not have a charge account or a credit card, she can estimate the approximate cost of the meal in advance and give the headwaiter more than enough cash to cover it; he simply brings her the change at the end of the meal. Or she can slip some bills to one of her male guests and ask him to pay the check for her, but today's sensible procedure is to let her pay the check in any way she likes, with as little fuss as possible.

**Check Grabbers.** A major rule for guests is: Let the host be a host, and don't take the edge off his hospitality by attempting to grab the check. Let him take care of the tab and tips, thank him, and return the favor at some other time. Even more out of line, however, is the chronic check dodger who is always looking the other way when the check is presented to a group that has agreed to share expenses.

**RISING.** A man rises from a restaurant table when a woman stops to speak to him or his companion, and all men rise when a woman arrives to take her place in the group—unless, of course, they are pinned down in a booth or banquette. The hostess does not rise except for a very old or distinguished woman guest. A woman guest does not rise for anyone joining a group already seated in a restaurant.

**SEATING.**   *See* "Entering and Seating" above.

**SERVICE.** In moderate-priced restaurants, the waiter brings each individual portion already served and sets it in front of the diner. In more expensive restaurants, if all at the table are having the same main dish, the waiter presents the serving platter to the host first for his approval. The host does not serve himself. All he does is nod, or murmur "Fine." The waiter then puts the platter on a serving table and transfers portions to plates, or serves the diners if plates are at their places, serving the host last. The same procedure is followed when an individual order is presented to a diner. He nods approval, and the waiter then transfers the food from the serving platter for him, boning a fish or giving other attention to any item that needs it.

In too many restaurants, a waiter will snatch a diner's empty plate before others at the table have finished eating. It is the host's duty to signal him to leave the clearing until everyone has finished the course.

**SMORGASBORD.**   *See* separate entry.

**STAFF.** Any special request to a staff member is accompanied by "Please" or a manner that says the same thing, and a special service requires "Thank you" or a nod of acknowledgment. An order for food need not be accompanied by "please," but it certainly should not be flung at a waiter like a command. A nod or other recognition of a waiter's presence is routine when he comes with a menu.

The standard way to attract a waiter is to gesture to him with a hand raised at about eye level or to call "Waiter," or, if necessary, to tap a glass lightly with a spoon or knife. Waiters resent being summoned by a snap of the fingers, a hiss, or a whistle. It is as illogical to call a waitress by saying "Miss!" as to summon a waiter by calling "Mr." Her title is "Waitress," and that is what she should be called.

**TARDINESS.** If anyone is decidedly late for a meal in a public place, common sense controls the behavior of those who arrived on time. On social occasions, the host orders drinks, if he likes, but does not place an order for food until all his guests are assembled. At a business lunch, a host does not delay others for one unpunctual guest. When business friends are meeting during the normally brief lunch hour, the first to arrive orders after a reasonable wait, especially if each member of the group is paying his own check. In either business or social circumstances, if a host has one guest only, he does not order his own meal until his tardy guest shows up, unless an inexcusable delay of twenty minutes indicates that the appointment probably has been forgotten. The guest who reaches the same conclusion after a reasonable wait for a tardy host either orders or leaves. In the latter case, he leaves a message in case his host does eventually show up.

**TIPPING.** The basic rate for a restaurant tip is 15 percent. Twenty percent is standard if extra service has been given, if a very long time was spent at the table, or if a check is very small, and also for service in an expensive restaurant.

If wine is ordered through a wine steward, figure 15 percent for the food and cocktail bill and an additional 10 percent for the wine steward, given directly to him—he will make himself available to receive it when the bill is presented. (He is not tipped at the time of service.) A busboy is not tipped, since he gets his share from the waiter. The headwaiter is not tipped unless he has been consulted in advance about the plans for a sizable party or has rendered some other special service. His tip is always in bills, and varies from one dollar to five, depending on what he has done and the expensiveness of the restaurant.

The checkroom girl gets twenty-five cents or, in an expensive restaurant, fifty cents. The coins that a washroom attendant displays in a saucer indicate the tip expected. A doorman is not tipped when a patron enters, but is tipped when the patron leaves if he calls a cab or has parked or watched the patron's car.

## RETURN ADDRESSES

A return address is correct on any letter, business or social, formal or informal.
    *See* CORRESPONDENCE for correct forms and placement on an envelope.

## REVEREND

> "Call me Mister, call me friend,
> A loving ear to all I lend,
> But do not my soul with anguish rend,
> PLEASE stop calling me Reverend."
>     —HENRY LEWIS, Episcopal Chaplain

"Reverend" is an adjective. It is never correctly used as a noun or title, as in "I'll ask the Reverend." And to say "Yes, Reverend" is as much a breach of the rules as to say "Yes, Honorable" to an official who has the right to use that title.
    *See* FORMS OF ADDRESS (Clergy) for further details.

## REWARDS.    *See* LOST-AND-FOUND ARTICLES.

# RIDING

Riding, like boating, has had a tremendous surge of popularity in recent years. There are now more than three and a half million horses maintained for pleasure riding in this country, and every year the number of private and rental stables, dude ranches, pony clubs, and hunt clubs increases. Thousands of new riders each season are learning that there is more to the sport than climbing into a saddle and staying there.

**Rules in General.** Each form of riding—farm style to fox hunting—has its special traditions, but all share certain rules of etiquette that fall into two main divisions: good manners to other riders, and good manners to one's mount.

Each horse is an individual with its own quirks of character, but as a species horses are notable among animals as extremely mannerly. Don't insult (and possibly startle) a horse by mounting without ceremony. Give him a chance to see his rider, before swinging into the saddle. Never forget his comfort. If he is to stand for any protracted time, loosen his girth.

A horse is just as capable of surprise, discomfort, and weariness as the rider. Only in the movies is it dashing for a rider to take off or race back at a hell-for-leather gallop. The experienced pleasure rider takes off at an easy pace, and never brings his horse back to the stable in a lather. He never "steers" by sawing or jerking the bit against a horse's sensitive mouth, or holds him on an uncomfortably tight rein. He never puts a horse to a fast gait on a paved surface, down a steep hill, or over terrain pocked with holes.

Horses will instinctively avoid stepping on or hurting any person or animal, but they also are easily startled. A sudden move that will cause one's own mount or another horse to shy is taboo. It is also the rider's responsibility to keep a safe distance from others. Allow the full length of a horse when following another rider, and generous clearance for stirrups if riding beside a companion or passing someone.

Horses are inclined to follow the leader. In all usual circumstances, do not pass another rider at full gallop. If leading other riders—especially, inexperienced ones—call out or give a hand signal before suddenly changing gait. And never put a horse to a jump unless entirely sure that the riders following can also take it, since their mounts are likely to go after the leader.

As a most important safety precaution, be extremely careful about smoking in and around a stable. Hay is highly inflammable. If smoking while riding in the woods or dry open country, stub the cigarette out on a bootheel and make sure it is completely out before tossing it away.

**CLOTHES.** There are two especially important rules about correct riding clothes, formal or informal. They must be comfortable—and that means meticulously well cut and fitted; and they should not be frilly, flimsy, or fancy.

There are strikingly different fashions in the various kinds of riding clothes, but within each classification there is very little latitude for individual choice. Riding clothes are either right and in good taste, or conspicuously incorrect. The best protection a beginner can have is the advice of a really knowledgeable friend or a really good, conservative outfitter.

Members of a hunt club wear what amounts to a uniform: a formally cut riding coat in a solid dark color (or the bright red known as "pink") with the club's distinctive collar and buttons; breeches in white, buff, or whatever other shade is chosen by the club; a waistcoat; standard high black riding boots; collarless shirt with a stock; gloves of buckskin, pigskin, heavy capeskin, or knitted string; a hunting derby or silk—all as prescribed by the club. With formal riding clothes women wear their hair severely confined—no curls, floating strands, or pony tails. Anyone invited to ride with a hunt as a guest should consult with his host before accepting if he does not have formal hunting clothes, since some hunts take a dim view of anyone who turns up in clothes suitable for other kinds of riding.

Regulation formal riding clothes for the country or a park allow a little more latitude. Standard is a jacket of characteristic cut: slightly longer than a sports jacket, more fitted through the waist, with a center split in back. This coat may be made of tweed, melton, gabardine, or whipcord; patterned in small checks, herringbones, or very muted plaids; but loud colors are never correct. Also standard are riding breeches in a plain color worn with high brown riding boots with rounded toes and flat heels; or jodhpurs with their regulation shorter boots; a plain shirt with attached collar and a four-in-hand tie, or a collarless shirt with a stock; a soft felt hat, a derby, or no hat. A waistcoat is always worn with a stock, but otherwise is optional.

For more casual riding in the country or a park, an ordinary sports jacket serves very well or, in summer, no jacket and a shirt with attached collar, perhaps open at the neck and with sleeves rolled up. Well-cut breeches and well-fitting brown boots are the main requirements. A soft hat, a cap, or no headgear is correct.

At many resorts and children's camps, completely informal riding clothes are the rule. The most popular combination is blue jeans and a sports shirt with a pullover sweater. Moccasins or other sports shoes with a small heel can be worn. Boots afford a protection to the ankle and leg that is a real comfort, but they are not an essential investment for the holiday rider who is going out a few times for relatively short periods.

Clothes for riding in a Western saddle at dude ranches and elsewhere have their own special style. Pendleton pants, levis, and blue jeans are correct, as are high-heel, pointed-toe cowboy boots, though the ones with fancy appliqués of colored leather at the top are generally left for the drugstore cowboy. Shirts of any cut and color, plain or plaid, are correct. So are short leather jackets, sweaters and bright neckerchiefs, and any kind of comfortable headgear from a cap to a sombrero.

Thousands of vacationers who have never been on a horse go each year to dude ranches and have a splendid time under the watchful eyes of the "dude wranglers," who are fully prepared to teach them all they need to know. A beginner is likely to make mistakes if he outfits himself before he arrives at a dude ranch. If he has any doubt about the correct clothes to buy, by far the best procedure is to wait and buy his outfit after arrival—from a good local outfitter. But, under any circumstances, it is not advisable to go out in brand-new jeans. The stiff seams can abrade the knees severely in an afternoon. New jeans should be thoroughly washed to soften them before they are right for riding.

**TIPPING.** Tipping is a somewhat touchy matter, and the best thing to do is make discreet inquiry before offering tips to certain specific people. Some riding instructors can be tipped. Others, like golf pros, will be offended if offered money but can be given a present.

If a host has his own stable, a guest for a weekend tips the groom who has served him from $2 to $5, depending on the amount of service. Such a tip is given toward the end of his stay, not after each ride. If several grooms have served him, the guest may leave a sum with the head groom to be divided among the stable staff. The same rule applies to dude ranches.

Tipping customs at rental stables vary. An owner or manager is not tipped but in some localities it is customary to give a stableboy fifty cents or a dollar. In other places no tip is expected, though one is generally welcome.

**RINGS.** *See* BIRTHSTONES; DIVORCES AND SEPARATIONS; ENGAGEMENTS TO WED; JEWELRY; WEDDINGS.

**RISING.**   For the many occasions when men, women, and children are expected to rise to their feet, *see* SITTING AND STANDING.

**ROLLS.**   *See* BREAD.

**ROYALTY.**   *See* FORMS OF ADDRESS (Foreign).

# S

**SAILING.**   *See* BOATING.

## SALAD

At formal meals, salad is served as a separate course following the main course. Otherwise it is served at any time that suits a family's fancy—as a first course, with the main course, or after it.

When salad is offered with a main course, separate salad plates or individual bowls are generally used because cold greens and hot meat, salad dressing, and gravy are not the most appetizing combination on one plate. In this service, the salad plate is put to the left of the main plate. There is no sense or logic in this placement (except for the left-handed), since the diner must reach across his main plate, endangering his cuff, for each forkful of salad. But that is the iron-clad rule. Those who rebel against it at home risk trouble when dining out.

Salad is cut with a fork when possible, but there is nothing wrong about using a knife when one is needed, as it is with a thick wedge of iceberg lettuce or stout ribs of escarole.

Any bowl that complements the rest of the service in general style makes a good salad container. Glass, pottery, china, and wood are the leading favorites.

## SALARY AND WAGES

Everyone who holds a paid job, from janitor to president, is a wage-earner. But by today's custom, "wages" is used only for the earnings of unskilled workers and domestic employees. An executive is not likely to care what his pay is called, but many people do. And so "salary" is always a safer word for the income of anyone on a regular job—from office cleaning staff to manager, and including domestic employees.

**SALESMEN.**   *See* SHOPPING; TELEPHONE MANNERS.

## SALT AND PEPPER

Salt and pepper should be within easy reach of each person at a table. Repeated requests for the salt are, at best, a tiresome interruption to the conversation, and many guests will suffer what is, to them, underseasoned food rather than ask repeatedly for salt that has been passed out of reach.

Glass-lined or china saltshakers are by far the best choice, since salt corrodes and blackens silver very quickly. Ground pepper should not be left for any length of time in a shaker; once peppercorns are broken and exposed to air their flavor deteriorates rapidly. Light-colored foods should not be seasoned in the kitchen with cracked black pepper because it shows up in suspicious-looking specks. Use white pepper, cayenne, or Tabasco.

One of the more curious habits of some diners is to sprinkle salt all over a serving before taking even one exploratory taste. It is of course entirely correct to season any dish to one's own liking, but it is no less than an insult to the cook and the hostess to scatter salt on untasted food.

See also MEALS AND THEIR SERVICE and TABLE MANNERS.

## SANDWICHES

Sandwiches have come a long way since the fourth Earl of Sandwich, hungry and unwilling to leave the gaming table, asked for some meat between two slices of bread to sustain him—and gave the world a name for the combination of foods that, itself, must have been invented immediately after bread.

Today, with sandwiches ranging from hamburgers heaped with onion, tomato, lettuce, catsup, and relish, through the towering "hero" concoctions, to the fried, grilled, and open-face ones drenched with gravy, "sandwich" no longer necessarily means "finger food." It is now customary to serve any sandwich at the table—even those as easily handled with the fingers as a Swiss cheese on rye —with a knife and fork. The diner can take it from there. If he likes, he can carve bites and eat them with his fork. Or deal with the sandwich in his fingers. It is a minor matter, but in the latter case it is usual to cut or break a standard-size sandwich into fourths.

## SAUCES

A good sauce is one of the joys of the table. By all means, eat the last delicious drop by breaking off a piece of bread to mop it up—but use a fork, not the fingers. A ladle is returned to the sauce, not to the underplate of a sauceboat.

## SCULPTRESS

A sure way to draw a pained look from a woman sculptor is to call her a "sculptress," which she considers just as absurd as calling a woman painter "paintress."

**SEAFOOD.**   See CLAMS; CRABS; etc., and FISH.

## SEALING WAX

There is nothing wrong with using sealing wax on an envelope, but it is out of fashion today because most people are hard-pressed enough for time to answer letters—let alone for fancying them up in this fashion.

## SEALS AND STICKERS

Stamplike seals and stickers distributed during fund-raising campaigns are not used on the front of an envelope, but may be used to seal the flap. They are not correctly used on formal announcements or engraved invitations.

**SECOND, 2ND.**   See NAMES.

## SECOND HELPINGS

A second helping of any course is not offered at a formal meal, but "seconds" usually are offered at a lunch or dinner party at home.

See TABLE MANNERS.

**SECRETARIES.**   See BUSINESS MANNERS; SOCIAL SECRETARIES.

## SECRETS

> "If you would wish another to keep your secret, first keep it
> yourself."—Seneca, circa A.D. 60

There are times in every life when one needs to confide to a trusted friend a personal matter that is not, and should not be, generally known. Sometimes sharing a piece of secret good news makes it better. Sometimes sharing a sorrow or setback makes it easier to bear. Sometimes recounting the details of a personal problem almost magically opens the way to a solution. Sometimes it is only sensible to give restricted information in confidence to someone who otherwise might make a disastrous blunder. In general, though, one of the surest signs of social maturity is the ability to keep confidential matters to one's self, remembering Jean Paul Richter's warning, "Whoever lets go the smallest part of a secret has lost the power to keep the rest." For that reason, "Can you keep a secret?" is a double-edged question if the speaker is passing along anything that was told to him in confidence—it clearly shows that he, for one, cannot.

## SECURITY CLEARANCE

A "security clearance" is required by the United States Government of people being considered for certain federal positions. This means that an investigation of an applicant's loyalty as well as suitability on other counts is made usually by the Federal Bureau of Investigation but sometimes by the Central Intelligence Agency. Their checking is largely a matter of questioning the candidate's friends and business associates.

Very nearly always, an F.B.I. agent telephones for an appointment, but on occasion one will just ring the bell. If he arrives unannounced at an extremely inconvenient time, it is not necessary to drop everything, but arrangements should be made to see him promptly because, in the performance of his duties he is being of service to every citizen.

Any such agent always shows his identification on arrival without being asked. Sometimes an agent will telephone for additional information after he has made a personal call, but no one is obligated to answer telephoned questions concerning a security clearance unless the credentials of the agent have been established beyond all doubt.

It is quite all right to report to the person being investigated what questions the agent asked and what answers were given to them, but it is not very discreet to mention the investigation to others without permission of the candidate. In some cases, the applicant for a federal post may not want his current employer, his friends or family, to know that he is applying for a government job until he is cleared and the appointment made.

**SEEDS.**   *See* PITS, SEEDS, AND STONES.

**SEMIFORMAL.**   *See* FORMAL, INFORMAL, SEMIFORMAL.

**SENATORS.**   *See* FORMS OF ADDRESS (Government).

**SENIOR.**   *See* NAMES.

**SEPARATIONS.**   *See* DIVORCES AND SEPARATIONS.

**SERVANTS.**   *See* HOUSEHOLD EMPLOYEES.

## SERVICE PLATES

These are usually called place plates (*which see*), to avoid confusion with the serving plates, platters, and other dishes on which food is offered.

**SHERRY.**   *See* WINES.

**SHIPS.**   *See* BOATS AND SHIPS; TRAVEL.

## SHIRT SLEEVES

It is to be hoped that the convention requiring men to wear jackets on certain occasions, no matter how hot the weather, will soon join the rack and thumb-screw as a bygone form of torture. Until that day, common sense and common compassion should temper the rule that a man must never dine in his shirt sleeves. It is the clear obligation of a hostess whose house is not air-conditioned and who is entertaining in blistering weather to tell her male guests to shed their jackets as soon as they arrive. Needless to say, men who hope for this consideration will wear belts instead of suspenders.

**SHOOTING.** *See* HUNTING AND SHOOTING.

## SHOWERS

A shower is a popular way for a group to provide a "dowry" of equipment for a new house or part of a trousseau or a layette for an expected baby.

There are only two major rules that need to be remembered about this fes-tivity. It is not correct for a very close relative to give a shower—the request for presents should not come from so close to home. And only those who know the honored guest well enough to want to contribute a present should be asked.

Invitations are issued in any informal fashion, but they usually specify the general category of presents—"pots and pans," "kitchen gadgets," "linen," "lin-gerie," and so on. It is also a good idea to specify favorite colors and such de-tails. Very frequently a low price limit is set, and guests are instructed to find some present "under two dollars," for example.

A shower can be any kind of party, but generally is a lunch or an afternoon gathering if only women are invited, a cocktail or after-diner gathering if both men and women will attend.

Anyone who accepts an invitation takes a present, and very often those who cannot show up send one. The hostess gives a present in addition to providing the refreshments. The usual procedure is for the guests to hand their presents to the hostess as they arrive, or to put them in some place she has designated. Then, after everyone has had a first round of refreshments, the guest of honor opens the packages, reads out the messages, and displays the gifts around the circle. Sometimes, each guest in turn hands over a present in person, when the time comes to open them. In either case, a card should be enclosed to avoid eventual confusion as to who gave what.

## SHOPPING

Salespeople are subject to several occupational hazards, not the least of which is the dictum, obviously not based on fact, "The customer is always right." Because a salesperson seldom can show justified resentment of unmannerly treatment without risking his livelihood, customers are doubly obligated to cor-rect and considerate behavior.

The first requirement in dealing with anyone who serves the public is a manner that implies a request for assistance—not a flat order for it—and, at the end of the transaction, spoken or implied thanks instead of walking away as unceremoniously as from a vending machine.

The second main requirement for customers is to mind their manners to each other. The word does not seem to have reached a great many shoppers that "First come, first served" is a basic rule. The aggressive (or, to be charitable, absentminded) customer who barges up to a counter and demands attention ahead of everyone else deserves smiting down. In a busy store, a salesperson cannot be expected to keep track of waiting customers, so it is up to the buyers themselves to thwart the people who play the little shopping game of "Me first, no matter what." In this case, as in most others where a protest is necessary, an amiable statement of fact will do the trick. "I am next, and this lady and that gentleman are also waiting" is all it takes to establish precedence—and to help the harassed salesperson out of an awkward spot.

If salespeople themselves ignore or break the rules of service, that is the misfortune of the shop-owner. The best way to deal with flippant, unduly breezy or familiar, bored, curt, or otherwise incompetent salespeople is to refuse to meet them on their own level, continue to behave according to the standard formulas of politeness—and take one's patronage elsewhere.

**FORMS OF ADDRESS.** The standard form of address to any adult customer is "sir" or "madam." Most salespeople use these words comfortably, since they are only giving what they expect to receive when they, in their turn, are customers. However, if "sir" or "madam" would sound stilted, a cordial manner will serve just as well—"This way, please," for example, instead of "This way, sir." "Can I help you, Mrs.?" is not correct, and "Miss" is not properly used except to girls obviously in their teens or younger, though these conventions are of minor importance.

Experienced salespeople always refer to customers as "ladies" and "gentlemen": "This lady is next"—never "This woman [man] is next." Customers use the same formula when referring to each other. On the other hand, "saleslady" is generally considered an old-fashioned term today, and we give the ladies their proper recognition as career women by speaking of them as "saleswomen."

## SHRIMPS

Shrimps served as a first course in a cocktail sauce should be small enough to eat in one bite. Shrimp cocktails need an oyster fork. Shrimps served as a main course are eaten with a dinner fork. The boiled or smoked shrimps served before dinner with cocktails are speared with a toothpick, dipped into sauce, eaten in one bite, and the toothpick discarded in an ashtray—not returned to the platter.

## SIDE DISHES

The small, separate side dishes, sometimes used by family-style restaurants for individual helpings of vegetables, are also used for family meals at home when creamed corn, stewed tomatoes, or any other vegetables with runny sauces are served. They are not used at formally served meals.

## SIGNATURES

A title is never correctly part of a signature on a letter of any kind, an application blank, or a legal document. And a very good general rule about signing one's name elsewhere is: When in doubt, don't add "Mr.," "Mrs.," "Miss," or any other title. There are some specific exceptions, though, and also times and places where a woman properly adds her title but a man does not.

For a list of exceptions *see* SIGNATURES in the Index.

## SILVER

"The silver" is used to mean table knives, forks, and spoons even if they are made of tin, but inconsistently, "the sterling" is not properly used in this sense even if the knives, forks, and spoons are solid silver.

## SIR

"Sir" is the standard American form of address to a male customer from tradesmen, salespeople, waiters, waitresses, information clerks, and all others in service positions—who, of course, are entitled to be addressed as "sir" in their turn when they are off duty and the roles are reversed. Contrary to what some people think, there is nothing subservient about this use of "sir," since all male citizens rate it equally when they are patrons or customers. In other words, we give with dignity what we expect to receive under the same circumstances.

Adults do not use "sir" in social circumstances except when speaking to someone who rates special respect because of extreme age or very high rank. In the latter case, "sir" is used to avoid undue repetition of titles like "Mr. President," "Your Highness," and so on, when the use of "Mr." and a last name is not suitable.

Teaching small children to use "sir" is the best way to make it easy for them to avoid a flat "yes" or "no" when speaking to an adult whose name is unknown or forgotten.

After girls reach high-school age, they generally drop the use of "sir" that is appropriate to childhood—except when speaking to men of great age and distinction or to teachers in those schools and colleges where "sir" is standard from all students. Young men continue the use of "sir" much longer and use it more widely than do girls, though they are well advised to find a substitute in many circumstances. A man in his thirties, for example, often does not take kindly to this mark of respect for his years from a strapping college boy.

## SIRENS

Behavior when a siren sounds is not a matter of etiquette. It is a matter of law, but it is so important that it is included here anyway. All cars must pull over to the extreme right. They may proceed with caution within a block, but must never cross an intersection until there is complete certainty that the vehicle sounding the siren will not be blocked or slowed. Pedestrians must also stay out of crossings.

## SITTING AND STANDING

Our rules about taking or keeping a seat when others are on their feet, and about when rising is required, are well standardized. They are among the most important for children to learn quite early so that the conventional procedures will become automatic behavior rather than "company" manners.

**RISING.** Everyone, young and old, rises when the national anthem is played in public. The other basic rules that follow apply in general under all circumstances, but there are exceptions. The ill, the infirm, or otherwise incapacitated are always privileged to do what is comfortable and practical rather than to follow any general rule blindly.

There are also many times when these rules are modified, and full details of such correct changes are given under separate headings, including BUSES; BUSINESS MANNERS; FLAG OF THE UNITED STATES; INTRODUCTIONS; RESTAURANTS; TABLE MANNERS; and TOASTS, among many others.

### A Child Stands:

When being introduced to anyone.

When greeting and saying good-bye to a guest.

When a markedly older person (stranger or acquaintance) stops, in passing, to chat or ask a detailed question.

When his elders do during a religious or civil ceremony.

When in doubt as to the proper procedure.

### A Man Stands:

When being introduced to a woman, teen-age girl, or a man.

When a woman first joins a group or for the exchange of greetings with her anywhere.

When his host or hostess first appears to greet him.

When a markedly older person (particularly a woman, whether she is a stranger or acquaintance) stops to chat or ask a detailed question.

When the regular congregation stands during any religious service.

When others stand in court or during other ceremonial civil procedures.

*A Woman Stands:*

When being introduced to a woman very decidedly her senior, to a very high dignitary of the church or government, and—as a mark of respect for his rank —to the wife of such a dignitary. She does not rise for the introduction of a woman of about her own age or younger unless she is the hostess.

When greeting and saying good-bye to any of her guests.

When either her host or hostess enters to greet her if she has been admitted and asked to take a seat by someone else.

When the regular congregation stands during any religious service.

When others stand in court or during other ceremonial civil procedures.

**SITTING.** After entering a dwelling or private office, a guest normally waits for a host or hostess to indicate a seat before planking himself in a place of his own choice. Any guest, especially a man, waits for his hostess to sit before he does so unless she has obvious duties that will keep her on her feet.

Under even remotely formal circumstances, people who follow the rules sit reasonably erect with one or both feet on the floor—not propped against a low table, hooked around the legs of a chair, or tucked up in a position that puts the shoes in contact with upholstery. Tilting a chair back on its rear legs is all right on a porch if the chair is very sturdy, but it is too casual behavior anywhere inside a dwelling or office, and is correct at table.

For women, the ban against sitting with legs crossed at the knee is as outmoded as the bustle. However, women's legs look far more attractive crossed at the ankles or above the knee—one knee propped directly over the other results in an ugly bulge of the calf. Anyone making a formal call, sitting on a speaker's platform, or applying for a job looks a bit too free and easy with her knees crossed. Lining the feet up side by side gives a babyish look. The most graceful position is with knees together and both feet on the floor, but with the toe of one shoe at about the instep of the other shoe—at one side or the other.

## SKATING

When skaters of widely different degrees of proficiency share a rink—or a country pond—faster skaters usually keep to the outside and leave the center ice to figure skaters. The following rules are standard almost everywhere:

1. Don't smoke while skating, or discard cigarette butts, matches, candy wrappers, or any other debris on the ice.
2. Don't carry unnecessary impediments such as a camera, spare jacket, radio, or equipment bag while skating. Such gear can cause a dangerous spill if dropped in the path of another skater.
3. Always skate with the traffic. The nonconformist who tries to buck it is a menace to himself and everyone else.
4. Obey the posted regulations or the orders of the official guards as to restricted areas, skating in groups, jumping, speed skating, Conga lines, etc.
5. Don't come to a halt in a busy part of a rink or pond to greet a friend or hold a reunion. Pull out of the mainstream for any stop.
6. When taking a rest break, don't sit on the rails or lean against them. Leave the ice or sit in a designated rest area on it.

**CLOTHES.** A skating costume of satin or other fancy material looks splendiferous in an ice show but out of place on a pond or public rink. Women usually wear slacks or fairly full skirts, with sports shirts or pullovers, and, at an outdoor rink, a warm cap and jacket or heavy sweater. Men wear slacks, shirt, pullover, and a heavy jacket or extra sweater when needed. Skaters usually have less trouble with the cold than with becoming overheated, and so an extra sweater for use during rest periods is practical.

**SPECTATORS.** Spectators at a competition properly withhold cheers and applause while a figure is being performed. Even at racing events, grandstand enthusiasm is out of place if it drowns out the starter's signals or interferes with the concentration of the participants.

**TIPPING.** At most rinks no more than a quarter tip is usual for checking, and a dime may be acceptable where the majority of the patrons are teen-agers, particularly at small rinks or in the less populous areas. Skating instructors are tipped according to the charge for a lesson—a dollar tip for instruction costing five dollars or more, and proportionately less for cheaper lessons. In the case of group instruction of beginners, a tip is rarely given or expected.

# SKIING

One of the most popular sports today, skiing is also probably one of the world's oldest forms of transportation. A ski museum in Oslo has a pair of skis thought to date back 2,500 years.

Safety is no small factor in this exhilarating sport. The prohibitions and tips in the list below are observed automatically by experienced skiers; skiing would be safer and more fun for everyone if beginners observed them too.

1. Don't push ahead of others in a lift line. (Only a class group with an instructor or a ski patrolman is privileged to do so.)
2. Sit or stand still on the lift (no swaying, swinging, or bouncing), having first made sure that no scarf or other item of apparel is dangling loosely where it can get caught.
3. Keep ski tips up and skis pointed straight ahead while on a lift, and hold poles by the shaft (not with the straps around the hand).
4. Get off a lift as smoothly as possible, without attention-seeking gymnastics.
5. On the slopes, match hill and skill. Beginners do not belong on intermediate and expert slopes. A novice who refuses to admit his limitations is courting disaster.
6. Before taking off, look up the hill to make sure no other skier is already in motion, descending on the same path. A *moving* skier ahead, lower down on the slope, also has the right of way.
7. When it is necessary to pass close to another skier, warn him by calling out "To your right" or "To your left."
8. Move over to the side when stopping for a breather or a chat with someone.
9. Never ski alone—particularly cross-country or outside a supervised area. Notify *someone* (the area manager, ski patrol, or Forest Service) of destination and time of planned return, and check in when safely back. Otherwise, a rescue party will be sent out.
10. Always ski under control—even at the bottom of the run. Many accidents occur at the foot of a slope because skiers bent on making a flashy finish fail to slow down soon enough.

**CHAPERONAGE.** Thousands of young people today take off for a skiing weekend in couples or groups without chaperonage and without causing a flicker of an eyebrow. One of the lodges that house men and women in separate wings or in dormitories is considered sufficient chaperonage in itself for young people who can be trusted by their parents to behave themselves anywhere.

**CLOTHES.** Skiing outfits for men and women differ little, except that women's ski clothes usually are brighter in color and have more decoration. Experienced skiers of both sexes find the layer system of clothing comfortable and practical: underwear in a lightweight, absorbent, knitted fabric (often consisting of two layers) that will not become clammy; stretch pants, which should fit well but allow freedom of movement, as should all skiing clothes; shirt of wool or cotton, woven or knit, turtleneck or tailored; sweater, which may provide enough warmth on mild days; and also a quilted or down-filled parka; double-layered socks or two pairs, the inner pair lightweight, the outer pair heavier—of wool, if preferred—and ski boots, which must be particularly well fitted, since they are equal in importance to the skis themselves.

Avoid waterproof clothing. It causes perspiration because it traps the body heat, and when the skier is not active (as in the lift lines and on the lift) he is likely to get chilled. Water-repellent fabric makes for greater comfort, since it is a protection against the moisture of air and snow and woven closely enough to be an efficient windbreaker.

The spectator who stays out for more than a brief period needs more protection than the skiers themselves—warm boots and a warm parka or a hooded coat in three-quarter length, perhaps also an extra sweater or scarf. A long, heavy fur coat, however, can be tiring and awkward to climb about in.

Sweaters or sports shirts and skirts or slacks are standard both day and evening in the lodge—even at the dressier ski lodges. The young man who takes along a white shirt, tie, sports jacket, and well-pressed slacks is prepared for almost any occasion; a woman may need a dress to wear for a certain special evening, but will be conspicuous in a fussy or low-cut dress even then.

**Accessories.** The smaller accessories permit more variation. For instance, head-covering may be the helmet type, a ski cap with or without earflaps, a wool mask, or a simple headband that covers the ears and keeps the hair from blowing. Whatever headgear is chosen, it should fit snugly.

There is an equally wide variation in gloves. Many skiers prefer mittens, sometimes two pairs. Some prefer gloves with a thin liner, and others the combination style—a mitten with finger space for the index finger. Whatever the choice, a long wristband is practical.

Ventilated sun goggles are practically a must. So is sunburn lotion. All items for personal grooming should also be taken along, since a chronic borrower is a nuisance anywhere.

**EQUIPMENT.** Having the right equipment and keeping it in good condition are important to both the safety and the fun of skiing. The beginner should ask —and heed—the advice of his instructor about skis, bindings, and poles before investing in equipment that may be unnecessary, inappropriate, or even dangerous for an amateur—unless, of course, he knows a reliable dealer and is willing to be frank and realistic about his own capabilities. (Automatic release bindings are a help in falls, and a leather Arlberg strap or some substitute will avoid the danger and inconvenience of a runaway ski.) Don't forget ski wax.

**EXPENSES.** The group-project ski weekend is usually a Dutch-treat affair. Each skier, regardless of sex, pays his own way entirely—travel, lodging, meals, lift tickets, and so on—though there is no rule that forbids a young man from taking one of the girls in the party to dinner as his guest. Popular with young people on a limited budget is the all-expense ski-weekend excursion, which covers all charges and often the tips as well. Here, each person pays his whole tab when he buys his ticket.

If a man invites a woman to be his guest at a ski resort, he pays all expenses, including transportation.

**FALLS.** The beginner who learns, right at the start, *how* to fall is taking out insurance against serious injury. The best skiers know that it is often better to fall deliberately and safely than to risk life and limb in an attempt to avoid a tumble. After a spill, look around for dropped items that may be a hazard for others on the slope—cigarette package, matches or lighter, gloves, coins, candy bar, compact, and so on. And always fill in sitzmarks.

If a companion is hurt in a fall, or if a skier finds someone on an isolated slope who has been injured, no attempt should be made to move him if there is a possibility of a broken bone. Stay with him, keep him warm and awake, and set a pair of skis upright in the snow, crossed to form an X, as a signal to the ski patrol.

**TIPPING.** A ski instructor or pro is not tipped. Employees at a ski lodge are tipped as at any hotel. The ski tow is paid for by a fixed fee, and attendants are not tipped.

**SLANG.** *See* CONVERSATION.

# SMOKING

"Tobacco is a dirty weed: I like it.
It satisfies no normal need: I like it.
It makes you thin, it makes you lean,
It takes the hair right off your bean;
It's the worst darn stuff I've ever seen:
I like it."
—*G. Hemminger*

"A custom loathsome to the eye, hateful to the nose, harmful to the brain, dangerous to the lungs, and in the stinking fume thereof resembling the horrible Stygian smoke of the pit that is bottomless."—*James I of England, Counterblaste to Tobacco, 1604*

Of all the ways that people differ, few are more apparent in day-to-day life than those that separate the smoker from the nonsmoker. A smoker feels that any unusual restriction of his use of tobacco is an arbitrary violation of his liberty. The nonsmoker feels exactly the same way about being forced to breathe smoke-filled air. It takes imagination and constant compromise to preserve their uneasy truce.

**Rules in General.** The sad fact all smokers must face is that most of the rules of manners concerning their habit begin with "Don't."

Don't smoke—because it indicates a lack of respect—in any place of worship, during any religious ceremony out of doors, during any formal civil ceremony indoors or out, in a court of law, during the playing of the national anthem and the ceremonial raising and lowering of the national flag. For the same reason, take a cigarette (cigar, pipe) out of the mouth when being introduced to or when greeting anyone.

Don't break the laws that prohibit smoking in city buses, subways, certain stores, and certain parts of theaters.

Don't smoke in any crowded or confined public place like an elevator because it exposes others to discomfort, if not the risk of burns, and because there is no provision for the disposal of ashes and stubs.

Out of common consideration, don't smoke in a sickroom unless the patient suggests it, or in a nursery. Don't smoke in a doctor's waiting room or similar places if ashtrays are pointedly lacking.

Don't permit a cloud of smoke to blow directly into or across the face of anyone. A nonsmoker who takes a seat (if he has another choice) beside a smoker and then asks him to extinguish his cigarette, cigar, or pipe is out of line; but so is the smoker who joins a nonsmoking group in any confined place and lights up without first asking permission.

Don't ignore any of the written or unwritten laws of safety. Never smoke near open containers of gasoline or other highly flammable substances. Never throw a lighted stub out of a car even if there is no danger of starting a roadside fire—the wind can fling it back or into a passing or following vehicle or against a pedestrian or animal.

Don't put down a lighted cigarette even momentarily on a shelf, mantel, table, or other piece of furniture, or anywhere else except securely within an ashtray—not propped against the edge from the outside. Never abandon a stub to burn out by itself anywhere. Don't risk getting into that dangerous habit by letting stubs burn out on a lawn, for example.

Don't treat porches, patios, public corridors, the floors of taxis, and other such places as ashtrays.

Why don't all of us swear off? As Mark Twain made clear: "It's easy! I've done it a thousand times."

**ASHTRAYS.** As an almost unbreakable rule, don't use a wastebasket, unlighted fire, or empty fireplace, potted plant, and especially any dish that has been used for food as an ashtray. If there are no ashtrays in a waiting room, private office, living room, or on a dining table, it is clear evidence that smoking is not welcome, and a visitor does not properly ask permission to smoke—and certainly does not light up without permission and then ask for an ashtray.

Except as part of a table setting, tiny pin-tray-size ashtrays are a poor choice, since they quickly overflow and need frequent emptying. Few sights and smells are unlovelier than an ashtray heaped with stubs, but the nervous hostess who leaps to empty every ashtray after a couple of stubs accumulate is as disconcerting to her smoking guests as the hostess who leaves a heavily loaded ashtray immediately under the sensitive nose of a nonsmoker.

**CALLERS.** It is never correct for a visitor to enter a dwelling or a private office carrying a lighted cigarette, cigar, or pipe, and it is customary to ask permission before lighting up if others are not smoking.

**CIGARETTES.** A hostess is expected to have a reasonable supply of cigarettes (and matches) in conveniently placed boxes or open containers for her guests, but it is also the convention for a guest, especially a heavy smoker, to take along an ample supply of his own. A woman who is the guest of a man in a public place also starts out with at least some cigarettes of her own, but if she needs more he gets them for her as a routine part of his expenses as her host.

**Lighting.** It would be hard to imagine any "help" that a woman needs less than aid in lighting her cigarette. Nonetheless, a man is expected to light a woman companion's cigarette under most social circumstances. Women should remember that this little attention is a grace note, not an ironclad requirement, and not demand it by waiting pointedly with an unlighted cigarette until a man produces a match. Equally tiresome is the man so assiduous as a fire-bringer that he leaps across a room to spare any woman the effort of lifting a lighter. If a man does not have matches handy when a woman takes out her own, it is in no way necessary for him to take the packet from her and light her cigarette. This elaborate byplay can be a bore to her if she is a heavy smoker—especially if he absentmindedly pockets her matches.

When a man offers a cigarette to a woman or to another man, he always lights the other's cigarette before lighting her own. A woman lights a cigarette for a woman, but does not do so for a man even though he may have accepted a cigarette from her. Lighting a cigarette in one's own mouth for someone else is done only by request—for a driver, for example, who cannot easily light his own.

A sizable number of people are made uneasy if three cigarettes are lighted on one match. The superstition that this brings bad luck had an honest beginning during World War I. A lighted match held that long gave a sniper ample time to take accurate aim. The taboo is senseless away from a battlefront, but the superstition persists, and so the usual procedure when in doubt about a stranger's feelings is to light two cigarettes and casually strike a new match for the third, without comment.

**Offering.** A hostess always offers a cigarette to any nearby guest before lighting one for herself. Otherwise, a woman generally does not offer her cigarettes to a man unless he is momentarily without any. A man offers a cigarette to either a man or woman companion when he takes out a packet or case to help himself. If a woman companion accepts a cigarette on the first offer, he offers her another each time he takes one, but need not do so if she has refused or has taken one from her own supply. The whole pack of cigarettes is offered. The donor may pop one up to make it easier to extract, but does not take it out in his fingers for another person. Nor does he put a cigarette in a woman's mouth in public, unless she is driving or there is some other practical reason to do so.

**CIGARS.** Many people who find cigarette smoke not unpleasant are distressed by the heavier aroma of cigars. Therefore, it is customary to ask permission of the hostess before lighting a cigar in her house or closed car. If she counters with an invitation to try her special brand of cigarettes, better accept. Her objection to the cigar—though only implied—is clear.

If the rule is followed, a cigar is not worn clamped in the mouth, but is held in the hand between puffs. Every effort should be made to keep the end as dry as possible—not chewed or frayed. As for the dead stubs, someone had better see to clearing them away without delay.

**EMPLOYEES.** Most firms have their own specific rules about the times and places when the staff is permitted to smoke. Under all conditions, an employee properly takes a cigarette out of his mouth when addressing a client or customer. Domestic employees are certainly privileged to smoke when alone, but a well-trained house servant does not smoke when on duty in sight of guests.

**MEALS.** A lighted cigarette should not be carried to the table. If ashtrays are provided, it is a signal that smoking is expected—but only in a restaurant is it correct to light a cigarette while waiting for the first course to be served. At home, smoking is confined to times between courses. It is always a mistake to stub out a cigarette on a used plate or douse it in the dregs of a cup, to light a cigarette from candles at table; and at a formally served meal a guest does not correctly put a pack of cigarettes on the table.

**PIPES.** Pipes are taboo at the table, and a pipe should never be lighted in an enclosed space, especially in mixed company, without first asking permission. Pipe-smokers often develop marked mannerisms like punctuating every few words with puffs, a habit that has driven more than one listener wild. Sucking on a gurgling pipe rates along with blowing on soup to cool it. Rubbing a meerschaum on the face to color it is a ritual best performed in privacy. So is pipe cleaning because of its inevitable by-product: an ashtray littered with strong-smelling residue and stained cleaners.

# SMORGASBORD

Traffic generally moves clockwise around a smorgasbord table, or any other buffet table not set against a wall, because this route puts the right hand in a comfortable position for serving a plate held in the left. This minor point is certainly to be ignored, however, if traffic happens to be moving the other way.

In a restaurant, a party first settles itself at a table for drinks and perhaps a soup course brought by a waiter. When the time comes, the hostess leads the way to the smorgasbord spread, and she correctly goes first or among the first around the table. Men and women guests follow in any easy order, more or less paired. The host is always the last to serve himself on the first round. After that, guests return in any order they please, and as many times as they like, for additional helpings. The practicality of a smorgasbord is the chance afforded each diner to choose helpings of a size and variety to suit himself, and so the rule is that each person goes back for his own refills. A hostess does not help herself first, of course, at a smorgasbord table under her own roof.

## SNAILS

Snails are served on metal plates with small round depressions that hold the filled shells upright. The shell is held steady with the metal snail-clamp in the left hand. The meat is pulled out with a pick or oyster fork and eaten in one bite. Shells may then be picked up in the fingers and the buttery, garlic-flavored liquid tipped into the mouth, or small pieces of bread may be speared with the fork and used to sop it from the shell.

## SNEEZING

The custom of saying "God bless you" or "Gesundheit" to a sneezer stems from the superstition of primitive peoples that some part of the soul escapes momentarily with a sneeze, giving an evil spirit a chance to enter unless the way is magically blocked by such words. If this "magic" exorcism is spoken at all, once is enough. Forcing the already breathless sneezer to repetitions of "Thank you" is no help to him.

## SNOBS

Webster's Dictionary defines a snob as: "**1.** One who blatantly imitates, fawningly admires, or vulgarly seeks association with those he regards as his superiors; **2a.** one who tends to rebuff the advances of those he regards as inferior; **b.** one who has an offensive air of superiority in matters of knowledge or taste."

In his *Book of Snobs,* William Makepeace Thackery said the same thing in another way: "You, who despise your neighbour, are a Snob; you, who forget your own friends, meanly to follow after those of a higher degree, are a Snob; you, who are ashamed of your poverty, and blush for your calling, are a Snob; as are you who boast of your pedigree, or are proud of your wealth."

Herbert Agar notes that snobs appear to be confused about the laws of nature: "Snobs talk as if they had begotten their own ancestors."

And Eleanor Roosevelt disposed of snobs gently but finally: "No one can make you feel inferior without your consent."

## SOCIAL SECRETARIES

Social secretaries fall into two categories—the private social secretary who devotes time to one employer, and the public social secretary who is retained when needed to help with one major social event such as a debut, wedding, or ball.

**PRIVATE SOCIAL SECRETARY.** Men occasionally fill this position, but more often it is held by a woman. The private social secretary must have a variety of skills similar to those of an executive secretary in business. She needs to be an expert typist, capable of taking dictation in shorthand. In addition, she should have a rounded legible handwriting and be able to compose both business and social letters for her employers, typing or doing them in longhand as the occasion requires. She must, to some degree, be a specialist in entertaining, able to assist in the preparation of guest lists and seating charts, in the planning of menus and other details of parties. If there is no executive butler or housekeeper, she often takes over some of the duties of these employees, such as planning meals, ordering supplies, hiring and firing, and acting in general as a deputy of her employer in the management of the household.

The private social secretary sometimes lives under the roof of her employers and functions as a companion as well as a specialist in the secretarial field. She supplies her own wardrobe, which must be sizable since she is included in some of the social activities of the family. She does not take her meals with the domestic staff. When she does not eat with the family, a meal is served to her by another staff member.

**PUBLIC SOCIAL SECRETARY.** An experienced social secretary is of great value in helping with any sort of large social event because she can give sound counsel about the services of caterers, florists, and musicians, as well as other matters. She is prepared to order and address invitations, deal with replies, aid with the guest list and seating for a charity ball or banquet, and take over as many of the complicated details of a big private party as an employer wishes. Since the public social secretary may be needed for as long as several months, though not for full time, she usually charges a flat fee rather than a weekly salary.

## SOCKS AND STOCKINGS

"Hose" and "hosiery" are commercial words, used by shops and manufacturers to describe merchandise. A customer may ask for "the hosiery department," since that is what the merchant calls a section of his store, but she asks to be shown stockings, not hose or hosiery. Men follow the same rule. They ask to be shown socks, not hose. "My hose" and "my hosiery" are in the same slightly too pretentious category as "my wearing apparel" instead of "my clothes," and "my residence" for "my house."

No one appears in stocking feet except under completely informal circumstances. Women often slip their heels out of their shoes in the dark of a theater and under a concealing table. It is never correct (or practical) to take one's shoes off entirely in such places—the risk is far too great that they may be kicked beyond easy recovery.

## SORORITIES.    *See* FRATERNITIES AND SORORITIES.

## SOUP

A diner correctly fills a soup spoon by moving it toward the far rim of his soup bowl, and also tips the bowl away, not toward, himself to make the last spoonfuls available. In general, soup is sipped from the side of the spoon, but this convention is ignored for soups containing sizable pieces of solid food, which are easier to take from the point of a large soup spoon. If an exploratory sip shows that the soup is scalding, the rest of the spoonful is held above the plate for the few seconds needed to cool it, since blowing on soup or spooning it into the air to reduce its temperature is incorrect.

**BOWLS, CUPS, AND PLATES.** In extremely formal service, soup plates are used only at dinner, and soup cups and bowls are reserved for use at lunch, but these fine distinctions are ignored in everyday life.

The smallest of these containers is the bouillon cup, used for clear soups only. It has two handles and a matching saucer. It is customary to lift this cup by one of its handles and drink the soup in a series of sips, using the spoon only for the first few tastes and for any bits of barley, rice, or vegetables that may be floating in it.

A cream-soup cup also has two handles and a matching underplate, but it is somewhat larger than the bouillon cup. Any soup served in it is eaten with the spoon.

Informal soup bowls, usually made of pottery, come in a variety of sizes and may have one handle, two, or none. They also are served on an underplate —either salad or dinner-plate size.

The standard soup plate that is almost as big as a dinner plate is served on an underplate only slightly larger than itself. Any liquid soup, clear or thick, is correctly served in a soup plate, but jellied soups are served only in a cup or bowl.

**CRACKERS AND CROUTONS.** If crackers (including oyster crackers) are passed, the diner puts them on his butter plate; or if one is lacking, on the underplate of a cup or bowl; otherwise on the tablecloth—but never directly into the soup. Oyster crackers may then be put into the soup a few at a time, but crackers of any kind are not correctly crumbled and dropped into soup. However, croutons or other tiny garnishings that are offered with a serving spoon are dropped directly into the soup.

**LEMON.** Lemon slices usually are served floating in a soup. If lemon wedges are passed, the diner puts one on his underplate, if there is room; otherwise, on his butter plate.

**THE "MEAL IN ITSELF" SOUP.** Bouillabaisse, cioppino, gumbo, and other soups that are actually stews are often served as a main course accompanied by French bread or bowls of dry rice. Standard wide soup plates are used for them, and a fork as well as a spoon usually is provided. The classic service of such main-dish soups is from a tureen on the table in front of host or hostess.

**SPOONS.** A bouillon spoon has a round bowl and is served with the standard clear-soup cup. A cross-soup spoon is the same shape but slightly larger; it is used with the standard cream-soup cup or with a bowl, though a dessert spoon can serve as a substitute. A standard soup spoon for use with a soup plate is almost the size of a serving spoon and of the same shape. Again, a dessert spoon is a correct substitute.

A spoon should not be left in a soup cup at any time. Between sips it is put on the underplate. The spoon is left in the standard wide soup plate between sips, since there is not room to put it on the underplate.

**TUREENS.** A soup tureen is used only for the service of a thick hearty soup. It is a pretty piece of table equipment, and is useful when either host or hostess is serving, especially if second helpings are to be offered. A covered earthen casserole makes a good substitute for a tureen, but since a casserole lid has no opening for the ladle handle, an extra plate is needed for the ladle, thus making it possible for the cover to sit down firmly and keep the soup appetizingly hot.

# SPAGHETTI

Authorities disagree flatly about the correct way to eat spaghetti. Some say that the proper method is to wind a few strands around the tines of a fork without the aid of a spoon, until a mouthful has been neatly bundled. Others endorse winding with the aid of both spoon and fork, which seems by far easier and neater, and they provide a dessert spoon for the purpose. The spoon is held in the left hand, the fork in the right. The fork is twirled with its tines against the bowl of the spoon until one mouthful is rolled up with no ends dangling.

All authorities agree that dangling ends should not be bitten off and allowed to fall back into the plate—not an easy rule to follow. In an emergency, however, bite them off instead of sucking them into the mouth.

If the winding method is too much of a challenge, it is entirely correct to cut a mouthful of spaghetti with the side of the fork. The entire plateful should not be cut at one time, however, except for a small child—in which case both knife and fork are used for the cutting.

Sauces and cheese may be distributed through the spaghetti by lifting and turning the strands, but the real spaghetti expert combines the pasta and sauce with each mouthful. Any sauce remaining is eaten with the spoon, or bits of bread are dropped into it, one at a time, and eaten with the fork.

## SPARERIBS

This delicious cut of pork is best served only at a barbecue or an informal family dinner, since it is hard to eat with knife and fork. Pick up a rib in one hand rather than two. Nibble at it as neatly as can be managed—and give thanks to the hostess who has plenty of extra paper napkins at hand.

**SPATS.** *See* CLOTHES.

## SPITTING

The dreadful spittoon is happily now no more than an item of interest to antique collectors, and with it has disappeared the word "expectorate" from common use. Today, we use the the forthright "spit" as consistently as we avoid that action at the table, on the street, or anywhere else except in solitude.

**SPOONS.** *See* MEALS AND THEIR SERVICE; and "FORKS, KNIVES, AND SPOONS" under TABLE MANNERS.

**SPORTS MANNERS.** *See* GAMES, and also the individual sports for the rules governing the behavior of spectators, players, and participants.

**STACKING DISHES.** *See* MEALS AND THEIR SERVICE; TABLE MANNERS.

## STAG PARTIES

The rules say that when a man gives a stag party, the women in his family stay out of sight. But like so many other established customs, this one can be ignored whenever it is obviously absurd to follow it to the letter. The important thing is to know the standard procedure and to observe it to all practical limits.

For example, it is not the correct hospitable gesture for a man's wife to help him receive his guests, even if she withdraws afterward. In all ordinary circumstances, she stays out of sight from the beginning. The festivity may be fun, but it is no longer a stag party if a wife, mother, sister, or daughter flits in and out bearing drinks and food. If there is a maid, she may properly appear to serve refreshments, but the usual procedure in a servantless household is to set up a bar and buffet so that the men can serve themselves without assistance. If the house is sizable and so arranged that the host's wife or other female relative can unobtrusively set out food when the time comes for it, that is all to the good, but she does not help to serve it or appear to remove empty plates and glasses. And, by the rules, unless the men have retreated to some other part of the house quite separate from the dining area, the cleaning up is left for the morning after.

## STAIRS

As a general rule, a man lets a woman precede him when going up a flight of stairs too narrow for two to use comfortably side by side. Also as a general rule, a man leads the way when descending a narrow staircase. He always does so if the stairs are dark or dimly lighted or extremely steep, because this puts him in the best position to offer a steadying hand or to be of aid if his companion stumbles. Otherwise, there are no explicit rules about the matter—so long as the man does not race ahead and leave a woman to trail, squawlike, behind him.

On a wide moving stairway, a man and woman together step on side by side. On a narrow one, a man lets his companion step on first, and a younger person stands aside for an elder. Otherwise, all comers take their turn as they do in any queue in a public place. "'Escalator' is a trade name denoting the product of one manufacturer, though it is often used to mean any moving stairs.

**STANDING.**   *See* SITTING and STANDING.

**STARING**
Don't.

**"THE STAR-SPANGLED BANNER."**   *See* NATIONAL ANTHEMS.

**STATIONERY.**   *See* CORRESPONDENCE.

**STEPCHILDREN, STEPPARENTS.**   *See* INTRODUCTIONS; also "Announcements" and "Invitations" under WEDDINGS.

**STEWARDS, STEWARDESSES.**   *See* TRAVEL.

**STICKPINS.**   *See* CLOTHES.

**STONES.**   *See* PITS, SEEDS, AND STONES.

**STRAWBERRIES.**   *See* FRUITS.

**STRAWS**
Drinking straws are fine for soft drinks served in their bottles and for thick milk-shakes whipped up at home, but in general they belong at the soda fountain rather than the dining table. They are not provided with iced tea or coffee, for example. A long-handled spoon or a metal sipper is the usual choice for these and other long iced drinks.

**STREET MANNERS**
A man or boy walks on the curbside whether he is in the company of one or more women or girls—not between two women, for example, unless both are in need of his actual support. The reason is obvious: he gallantly takes the position more exposed to splashes or other hazards from traffic in the road. How-ever, when a man is accompanying a woman for only a few steps, or they change directions frequently when window-shopping, it is absurd for him to make a big point of dodging around to the curbside if it is awkward to do so.

On a path so narrow that a man and woman must walk in single file, the woman does not trail him squaw-fashion. She goes first. The man leads only if the way is dark or there is some other practical reason—to test a spongy or slip-pery surface or break trail for her through a heavy crowd, for example. By the same token, when a man and women are walking side by side, he falls behind her when it is necessary to make room for another person to pass. And when the paths of a man and woman cross, a man cedes the right of way to her.

As a general rule, a man does not hold on to the arm of a woman, and she does not take his arm when they are walking along a street. He properly offers his arm or takes the elbow of a companion if she needs steadying while crossing a rough stretch or assistance at a curb or on stairs. But he does not automatically grip her elbow at a crossing or other place that she can perfectly well manage without his help. For her part, a woman with her feminine wits about her lets a man take charge by following his lead when crossing a street. There are few things that make a man feel more inept than the little lady who darts masterfully ahead of him or who hangs back mistrustfully, when he starts across an inter-section. Let him be the one to stop, look, and listen—the common-sense pro-cedure for any pedestrian, even if he has the right of way. Being in the right does not lessen the pain of a broken leg.

On a relatively empty sidewalk, pedestrians stroll on the right or left side, as they please. On a crowded sidewalk, "keep to the right" is the rule, though it is curious how many people break this elementary traffic law and assert their independence by bucking the oncoming stream. On a country road or any other thoroughfare without sidewalks, pedestrians walk facing the oncoming motor traffic as a safety measure.

"Sorry," or some other brief apology, is required from anyone who jostles against another on the street, who finds it necessary to push through a group or pass between people in conversation. In turn, people who stop to talk on a crowded sidewalk should pull out of the mainstream. One of the insoluble mysteries of human behavior is why so many people, especially those coming out of revolving doors, stop dead in front of an exit for a chat.

Anyone who wants to be popular with a neighbor does not use his lawn habitually as a public thoroughfare, no matter how convenient a shortcut it may provide, but this rule does not generally hold for children and dogs for the excellent reason that it is all but impossible to enforce.

A man tips or touches his hat when greeting any woman on the street. If he stops to talk he takes a cigarette, cigar, or pipe out of his mouth. Many men make a point of remaining uncovered when stopping to exchange a few words with a woman—but not, of course, in cold or inclement weather. (*See also* HATS.)

If it is easy to do so, a man slips off his right glove before shaking hands. If it is awkward to do so, he correctly leaves it on, and skips any such words as "Pardon my glove."

A man walking with a woman for any distance carries bulky packages for her, but does not relieve her of a magazine, a small parcel, or a closed umbrella, though he takes an open umbrella from her and holds it over her unless, of course, he is carrying his own.

*See also* AUTOMOBILES; BABY CARRIAGES.

## SUBWAYS

In spite of a good deal of evidence to the contrary, there *is* a code of etiquette for subway riders. A woman with a male companion steps in first, and when they reach their stop he steps out first *when practical*. This means that as often as not a man correctly dodges into a car first if he needs to grab a door that is about to slam against his companion. And at a stop, if a woman is nearer the door, she steps out first because what is fastest and least uncomfortable for all concerned takes precedence over usual pedestrian rules during a subway's brief stops. At rush hours, jostling is inescapable as the train buckets along its tube, but an occasional "Sorry" makes the shared misery easier to bear, just as a certain amount of resigned good nature does.

## SUGAR

For use on berries or waffles, granulated sugar may be served in a shaker, but powdered sugar is a better choice for berries. Granulated sugar is served with cold drinks such as iced tea because it dissolves more quickly than lump sugar.

Tongs are the proper implement for serving lump sugar. If they are not available, better not serve it. The rule that only lump sugar is correct with after-dinner coffee is absurd and may be ignored. A whole lump of sugar in a tiny cup is far too much sweetening for many people, and so granulated sugar is correct by today's custom. Some stores now stock lump sugar in a miniature size that is ideal for after-dinner coffee, but this is not available everywhere. For the formal service of hot tea, lump sugar is still the correct choice.

Either a sugar bowl and spoon or a shaker is correct for serving powdered sugar.

For other rules of service, *see* COFFEE; TEAS.

## SUPERSTITIONS

Superstitions are as old as man. Few people today have any real belief that bad luck follows the breaking of a mirror, eating with thirteen at the table, and so on through the long list. However, quite a number of people have at least a passing feeling of uneasiness, which in itself can lead to trouble, if circumstances force them to defy certain of the ancient taboos. There are, for example, those who know that the belief is absurd but who can't forget the association of Friday the thirteenth with disaster. If they are forced to start a journey under this cloud, the nagging thought that the auspices are all wrong can build up enough tension to precipitate a mishap. Therefore, when someone shows reluctance to accept a third light from one match, or after certain words is impelled to knock on wood or cross two fingers, best not argue or take any notice. Put it this way—it's bad luck.

## SUPPER

"Supper" is used occasionally instead of "dinner" for the meal at the end of the day to indicate that the food will be simple and the service informal—Sunday supper, for example. Otherwise, as generally used today, "supper" means a light meal served at about eleven or later in the evening.
See MEALS AND THEIR SERVICE.

## SURVEYS

A national census is taken every ten years by our Federal Government. It is, of course, important to see the people employed for this task and to cooperate with them because the information they gather is of benefit, in one way or another, to all of us.

As for other so-called "census takers" who are really survey makers, everyone can use his own judgment. But no survey taker should be admitted or given any information before he shows his credentials, and if there is a degree of doubt about the genuineness of a surveyor who calls on the telephone, ask for his name and the office number of his sponsor, and offer to call back.

Today, an enormous number of subjects is surveyed by private industry, ranging all the way from the popularity of public figures to what soap a family prefers. Some surveys serve useful purposes in the upgrading of products, improvement of packaging, and so on. Therefore, if the surveyor rings the bell or telephones at a convenient time, it is sensible enough to answer any impersonal questions he asks. However, it is risky to answer certain other queries. Be wary about seemingly innocuous questions like how many times a week the whole family goes out regularly or what vacation dates are the family's preference. Canny burglars have been known to make things easy for themselves by dropping such queries into a "survey" on the use of leisure time, for example.

**SUSPENDERS.**   See CLOTHES.

**SWIMMING.**   See BEACHES AND POOLS.

## SYMPATHY

A gift, letter, or telegram sent as a token of sympathy calls for an acknowledgment of some kind. A telephone call or personal thanks during a conversation will serve in some cases, but a brief note is usually best if much time will elapse before seeing or speaking to the donor.
See CALLS; CONDOLENCES; FUNERALS.

**SYNAGOGUES.**   See TEMPLES AND SYNAGOGUES.

# T

**TABLE D'HOTE.**   *See* A LA CARTE.

## TABLE MANNERS

Probably the single most important rule about table manners is: Don't have two sets of them. All of us dress and act more casually in the family circle than in public, but it is a mistake to extend this latitude to table manners.

There is nothing complicated or restrictive about good table manners. They are based on simple common sense about what is most practical, comfortable, considerate, and attractive when eating in company, and if standard behavior is observed at family meals, there will be no need to worry about children's "company" manners elsewhere.

**ACCIDENTS.** The spilling of food or drink is the most common of accidents at table, and usually is the source of far keener embarrassment to the person who caused the mishap than to anyone else. Nearly always, spillage at the table is the work of two people, one of whom makes a move unexpected by the other. Even if an accident is clearly the fault of a waiter, waitress, or fellow diner, nothing is gained by a show of annoyance from the victim, who is bound by custom to accept an apology and any needed assistance with as little flurry as possible. The hostess who delivers a sharp reproach to a maid at such a time only adds to the embarrassment of everyone. The best a hostess can do is take the responsibility (which actually is hers, for providing inept service), say, "I'm so sorry," and then concern herself with the necessary repairs.

When a drink is spilled on the table, a guest uses his napkin to mop up a flood that is an immediate threat to himself or his companions. Otherwise, he waits for a maid or his hostess to take action.

A guest who drops a spot of gravy, jelly, or other food on the cloth picks it up with any clean implement and puts it on the side of his plate. Common sense is the guide to dealing with food dropped on the floor. A dropped cracker or other dry food that will not damage the floor covering is often better ignored than retrieved, but if a beet, strawberry, or other stain-producing food skitters off the plate, it is only sensible to bend down and recover it. If an implement is dropped, the rule says it must not be polished off and used, but that another must be provided by maid or hostess.

**ANNOUNCING AND SEATING.**   *See* "Entering a Dining Room, and Seating," below.

**ASKING FOR SOMETHING.** Asking for something not on the table is permissible under very few circumstances. Certainly, if a standard item such as a napkin or a knife is missing, a guest asks the hostess for it, or indicates the lack to a maid, but a guest should not ask for anything not supplied to all others at the table. For example, even though a guest heartily dislikes adding salad to a plate of hot meat and vegetables, he is not privileged to request a separate salad plate; and even though a meal is ruined for him unless coffee is served with the main course, he must do without it then unless the hostess offers it. A guest also must wait for the offer of a second helping of anything served from the kitchen. If the hostess does not suggest a second helping, she has a reason, and her embarrassment is only increased if she has to explain a delay in her service or the lack of sufficient quantity to go around a second time.

In restaurants, the above rules are relaxed to some degree. It is entirely correct to ask a host or hostess to send for mustard, catsup, or other condiments. As a general rule, a guest relays all orders through his host, rather than signaling a waiter himself. But if he wants more water, for example, and can indicate his wish while a waiter is serving him, he does so, since that is simpler than to interrupt conversation by relaying such a routine request through his host.

**BEGINNING TO EAT.** All guests wait until the hostess gives the signal to begin any course by picking up her own fork or spoon. In small groups, this means that everyone waits until all are served, since the hostess never is served first if the rule on which all authorities agree is observed.

(*See* MEALS AND THEIR SERVICE for service details.)

At a very large party, however, guests are expected to start eating when their plates are put in front of them so that the food will not grow cold, though the first few guests to be served wait for the hostess to say, "Please start," rather than fall to as if starved. When the hostess issues that instruction, it should be obeyed. Delaying until she is served is an uncalled-for reproof to others who obeyed her request.

At a big public dinner, it is not necessary to wait until all at one table, or those seated opposite at a long table, are served. As soon as two are served, they start to eat.

**BELCHING.** This unhappy surprise can be dealt with only by saying "Excuse me" and trying to suppress the next one.

**BEVERAGES.** No liquid of any sort should be taken when there is food in the mouth—with one exception. An extremely hot mouthful of food, taken by mischance, is properly cooled by a quick sip of cold liquid. The napkin should be used lightly before taking a drink, to avoid leaving an unsightly smear of food or lipstick on the edge of glass or cup.

**BLOWING ON FOOD.** There are no exceptions to the rule that bans blowing on a bite of food before it is put into the mouth, or blowing with the mouth open to cool a blazing-hot bite inside it.

**BONES.** Picking up bones in the fingers is for only the most informal meals. The only exceptions are the smaller joints of frog's legs and very small game birds. These may be picked up in thumb and fingertips and held while the meat is bitten or pulled off. Paper frills, sometimes used to cover the charred bone-tips of chops and crown roasts, are decorations only, not an invitation to pick up the piece in the fingers.

There are very few exceptions to the general rule that anything put into the mouth with fork or spoon is taken out on the same implement. However, the little splinters of bone sometimes left by a butcher's cleaver, bits of gristle, small fishbones, shot, tiny or slippery seeds, or anything else that is awkward if not impossible to extract on a fork is taken out in the fingertips.

**BREAD.** A whole slice is never buttered at one time. A bite-size piece is broken off and buttered just before it is eaten. Biscuits, hot rolls, and hot toast may be buttered whole, but small pieces are broken off for eating if the hot bread is bigger than two bites. A piece of bread held in the fingers is not used as a pusher, but it is entirely correct to drop a bite-size piece of bread into a sauce and then eat it with a fork. If there is no butter plate, put bread on the cloth (with the exception of sticky rolls, which are put on the main plate).

If hard rolls are on the butter plates when guests take their places at a public dinner, or are brought to the table before a first course is served in a restaurant, they may be eaten before the first course appears. At home, guests wait for the hostess to start, before eating anything.

**BUTTER.** Butter taken from its own serving dish is put on the main plate if butter plates are not provided, not on bread or a roll laid on the cloth, because a serving knife must not be used to put butter directly on top of any food. Butter for a baked potato, for example, is put first on the butter plate or, lacking one, on the side of the main plate, and then transferred with the fork or dinner handle on the table.

**BUTTER KNIFE.** This tool is used only for foods that go on the butter plate.

It is not used to transfer butter to food on the dinner plate. The dinner fork or knife is used for this purpose. The butter knife stays fully on the butter plate when it is not in use, never propped with its tip on the edge of the plate and its handle on the table.

**BUTTER PLATE.** Only butter, bread, olives, radishes, and celery are put on the butter plate at lunch and dinner. Honey and marmalades are put on the butter plate at breakfast. At all other meals, jellies, preserves, pickles, cranberry sauce, mustard, catsup, chutney, and other condiments that complement meats are put on the dinner plate. Olive stones are returned to the butter plate. Bits of bone, the seeds of spiced fruit, corncobs, and the residue of anything else from the dinner plate are returned to it, not put on the butter plate.

**CHILDREN.** Any child old enough to take a place at the table is ready to master the simple rules that make eating a pleasant sight. He will have far fewer problems in later years if taught from the beginning that company manners for children are no more than everyday manners for grown-ups.

**CHOKING AND COUGHING.** One of the most embarrassing mishaps at table is a paroxysm of choking. If a bit of food goes down the wrong way and cannot be dealt with readily by one good cough, the best procedure is to signal to the host or hostess the need to recover in private, and leave the table. Only the man at her left half-rises to help a woman with her chair when she leaves the table in such an emergency, and when she returns. Choking usually is damaging only to the makeup and emotions, and so the less notice taken of it, the better. Thumps on the back often complicate matters. Choking can sometimes be extremely dangerous, however, and unless a guest returns promptly either the host or hostess should investigate.

**CONVERSATION.** By the rules, some few subjects are not mentioned at the table.

Save all discussion of the cost of food for another time—most especially if a guest is present.

If there is a maid, do not start to talk about a matter not meant for her ears, during one of her absences from the dining room—a pointed silence when she returns can only make her and everyone else self-conscious.

Don't mention the details of illnesses. Even an oblique reference, like "I won't go into detail at the table," is unfortunate, since it puts active imaginations to work on unpleasant possibilities.

A lively difference of opinion, if kept on the amiable level, makes conversation spirited, but the table is not the place for quarrels, sulks, lectures—or monologues.

At a small table, keep conversation general. At a long table, conversation can break into two or more groups, though no guest should pointedly ignore, throughout the entire meal, anyone seated next to him. At large and formal dinners, the hostess usually starts chatting with the man on her right unless conversation is kept general. A bit later she turns to the man on her left. This is known as "turning the table." Guests need not end their conversations abruptly and whip around like weathervanes, but they are expected to follow her lead without too much delay so that no one person will be left stranded.

At a business lunch or dinner, the guest waits for the host to start discussion of business.

**CRACKERS.** *See "Soup," below.*

**CUPS.** Only the smallest children are permitted the babyish gesture of picking up a cup in both hands. A cup is put down between sips, not held at mouth level, with the elbow propped on the table. When a cup is passed for more coffee or tea, the spoon stays in the saucer, not propped against the side of a plate.

**CUTTING.** Whenever practical, food is cut with the side of the fork. A large piece of food is not cut up into bite-size pieces all at once, except of course for very little children. When food already in portions is offered, such as individual molds of aspic, the portion should not be cut and part left on the serving platter.

**DUNKING.** The sopping of toast, doughnuts, cookies, rolls, or any other breads in beverages or soups is taboo, except at a meal eaten out of sight of others, because dunking leaves an unappetizing residue of crumbs or grease in the cup, and the dripping piece of food is, itself, not an appetizing sight.

**EATING TABOOS.** A mouthful of food means a small bite, not a mouth really full of food. Good manners demand small-enough bites to make possible an answer or comment at any time.

Little children naturally eat with the mouth more or less open and an innocent smacking of lips. They need to be trained to overcome this unsophisticated habit, since a mouthful of half-chewed food is one of the world's least alluring sights. All food must be chewed with closed lips, no exceptions, and any such marked mannerisms as chasing bits of food around the cheeks and teeth with the tongue should be avoided. The Germans have different verbs for the eating of foods by humans (*essen*) and the gulping and gobbling of food by animals (*fressen*). Enough said.

Good posture leads naturally to bringing food to the mouth, not the mouth to the food. The eater who sits with his feet on the floor, not hooked around the legs of his chair, and with elbows off the table finds it difficult to slump over food and shovel it in.

**ELBOWS.** There is nothing wrong with putting one or both elbows on the table between courses when leaning forward in conversation. Otherwise, the rules about elbows are as easy to remember as they are rigid: Keep them off the table at all times when an implement, cup, glass, or a piece of food is in hand; keep them close to the sides when cutting food; apologize if an elbow touches a neighbor at a table.

**ENTERING A DINING ROOM, AND SEATING.** At a strictly formal dinner, the host and the woman who will be seated at his right lead the way to the dining room.

(*See* MEALS AND THEIR SERVICE for this and other details of ceremonial procedures.)

Under all other circumstances, the hostess leads the way, followed by her guests in any convenient order, and the host enters last. The hostess may stand near the door to direct her guests to the places she has chosen for them, but usually she stands behind her chair. As they enter, each guest waits to catch her eye. One of the commonest mistakes young people make is to move impetuously along one side of the table, risking an awkward backtracking to a place assigned on the opposite side. Guests never choose places for themselves unless the hostess directs them to sit where they please. If she does do so, her woman guests take care not to choose places next to other women, unless, of course, women outnumber the men.

All guests remain standing behind their chairs until the hostess gives the signal to sit. Then each man pulls out the chair for the woman on his right. As she sits he pushes it smoothly under her, being careful not to throw her off balance by touching her bending knees with it.

No one touches a napkin until the hostess puts hers in her lap. If she leaves it on the table after all are seated, it is a sign that she is waiting for quiet before grace is said.

**EXCUSES.** Apologies for service, equipment, or the quality of the food only call attention to a lack that might otherwise go quite unnoticed. If a dog runs away with the turkey, and the startled guests are served baked beans as a substitute, of course the whole sorry tale should be told. But if the stuffing is soggy or the gravy lumpy, the hostess does best to make no comment. Apologies will not improve the taste of a disaster, and they leave guests with nothing much to say except some hollow contradiction.

**FINGERS.** Food should be touched with the fingers as little as possible. Pieces of chicken or sticks of French-fried potatoes are not eaten from the fingers on occasions with any pretension to formality. Brittle bacon may be picked up in the fingers if cutting would splinter it to crumbs, but the best way to handle greasy or sticky foods is with a fork.

(*See* separate listings for such foods as artichokes, lobsters, and so on.)

Licking the fingers to clean them is taboo. If they cannot be satisfactorily wiped off with the dry napkin, dampen a corner of it by tilting the water glass —not by dipping the napkin into the glass.

A sure way to infuriate a waiter is to summon him with a snap of the fingers.

**FOREIGN MATTER.** Unintended additions to food can turn up in the best-run households and restaurants. They should be coped with as inconspicuously as possible out of consideration for the feelings of others at the table. In a restaurant, if a hair, cooked fly, or bug is a startling added entry in a serving, a gesture to the waiter is enough—he will whisk in a new serving. In such case, the least comment, the better, either from the concerned hostess or the unfortunate guest.

Things are a little more difficult at a private party. Even the most perfect-looking apple can harbor a juicy worm, for example. The best procedure is to say nothing, conceal him under a peeling, and hope that he does not start traveling. Deal with a little green lettuce crawler in the same way, and ignore the rest of the salad if the sight of this clean little vegetarian has made the entire helping unappetizing.

**FORKS, KNIVES, AND SPOONS.** Once used, an implement is never returned to the cloth. When not in use, it is left fully on the plate, not propped against the side of a plate with its handle on the cloth.

**Knives and Forks.** The fork may be lifted to the mouth with either hand.

The American style is to cut a piece of food with the fork in the left hand, lay down the knife, transfer the fork to the right hand, and lift the food with the tines up. When this method is used, the fork is held with the thumb on top and the palm up, not with the thumb under and the fingers in a fist, palm down. Food is not speared with the tines down and lifted in this position when the fork is in the right hand.

The European style, in which the fork is held in the left hand both to cut and to eat food, is correct and certainly more efficient, though less often seen in this country. The fork is held lightly, forefinger advanced (not grasped in a fist), and tines down during the cutting. It is then lifted to the mouth with the tines still down. The knife is not used to heap extra food on the back of the fork.

The knife is not held in either hand while the fork is being raised with food on it. Food that does not need cutting or that is cut by the fork is eaten with the fork held in the right hand (except by the left-handed) on both sides of the Atlantic.

When not actually in use, the knife and fork are left at any convenient angle to each other until the diner has finished a course. To signal that he has finished, he places the knife and fork diagonally across his plate parallel to each other, handles to the right. The fork, tines up, is put nearer to the diner, and the blade of the knife is turned toward the fork. The knife and fork stay on the plate when it is passed for a second serving. The tines are left up, since this position is the best safeguard against dropping the fork. Serving forks, however, are returned to the platter with the tines down.

**Serving Implements.** When presented on a platter of food, the tines of forks and bowls of serving spoons are turned down and are returned to that position. A gravy ladle is returned to the gravy boat or bowl with the bowl up, not to the base or underplate unless the handle is becoming too hot for comfort. Long-handled ladles used for serving punch or soup are returned with the hollow up.

**Spoons.** The rules say that a spoon must not be left in a cup, that it is not correct to hold a spoon aside with a finger when drinking, and that a used spoon should be put on the saucer or the underplate of a glass—not returned to the tablecloth or propped against the side of the main plate. Therefore, the diner confronted with coffee served in a mug or iced tea served in a glass without an underplate obviously faces an insoluble problem. Whatever he does, he breaks one of the rules. Let him take cheer. Nobody cares what he does. Coffee served in a mug is so informal that anything goes. He can hold the spoon aside if he likes, or do what is more sensible and safe—prop it against his main plate. A straw or metal sipper is usually left in a glass, and a long iced-tea spoon may be, but no one has ever been cut off a list because he laid it on his butter plate rather than risk a stab in the eye from it.

When not in use, a bouillon or a round soup spoon is put on the underplate, but a standard-sized soup spoon is left in a wide soup plate both between sips and when the diner has finished. The bowl of the spoon is not turned down as a signal that the diner is finished. The spoon is left with the hollow up, since in that position it is least likely to be dropped when the plate is removed.

When dessert is served in a small bowl on a wide underplate, the spoon is left in the bowl until the diner has finished, then put on the underplate. If the underplate is quite small, the spoon is left in the bowl.

A spoon is held with the thumb on top of the handle, never grasped in the fist with the back of the hand up. A soup spoon is always filled by moving it away from the diner. The soup bowl or plate is tipped away from the diner also, not toward him, to make it easy to spoon up the last of a liquid.

Liquids are taken from the side of a spoon, not the tip. Solid food is taken from the tip, but the whole bowl of the spoon should never be put inside the mouth.

**GLOVES.** Long gloves worn with an evening gown are taken off completely after a woman is seated at table. They should not be left on the arms with the fingers tucked back at the wrist. This is correct only if she is taking some refreshment while standing or seated away from a table—at a reception, for example. Gloves are put anywhere but on a table.

**GRACE.** In many households, food is blessed only at family meals. In others, the family custom is observed when guests are present. Not infrequently, a first-time guest is embarrassed by hearing himself chattering along in an increasingly pointed silence and then noticing that he is the only one who has placed his napkin in his lap. This experience is the best possible proof of the wisdom of keeping an eye on the hostess and following her lead. If grace is to be said, the hostess leaves her napkin untouched until after the "Amen," and so one glance in her direction after all are seated gives the answer to the stranger in the house.

**GRAVY AND SAUCES.** A gravy or sauce may be added by the host if he is carving, or may be passed by a maid or from guest to guest after plates have been served. Gravy properly is ladled mainly on the meat rather than poured over everything on the plate, though it is entirely correct to put a spoonful on rice or mashed potatoes. Gravy may be poured from a gravy boat or the ladle may be used. The ladle is returned to the bowl, not put on an underplate after use, unless the gravy is so hot that the ladle handle is growing uncomfortable to touch.

**HANDBAGS.** A handbag is not taken to a dining-room table at home. A small evening purse may be carried to the table and held in the lap, never put on the cloth.

Neither a handbag nor an evening purse is put on the table in a restaurant or at a banquet or other public meal. A big pocketbook may be hung on the arm or back of a chair or even put on the floor. A little one is tucked beside the diner on the chair seat or held in her lap. Exceptions are made only at small tables where a full meal is not being served, such as those at a nightclub or dance. There, a small evening bag is customarily put on the tabletop.

**HANDS.** The left hand properly remains in the lap during most of the eating time, not propped against the table edge. It is inviting trouble to make gestures with a loaded fork, and not the best of manners to gesture with any implement in hand. All gestures at table should be restrained to some degree. A sweeping gesture can connect disastrously with a dish being passed.

One hand is put on the table if assistance is needed to rise, but both hands are not used to shove the chair back from table when leaving.

**HATS.** Women guests may keep their hats on at a lunch party at someone's house, but always take them off at dinner in a private dwelling.

**HELPING THE HOSTESS.** A guest should not offer to help the hostess if able-bodied members of her family are making no move to do so. However well meant, such an offer implies criticism of her family for not lending a hand. The same is the rule for a guest being entertained for the first time when others obviously intimate in the house are present. A male guest never volunteers to help clear a table and serve the next course if the host remains seated, which he does, rather than leave the table abandoned by both host and hostess.

In a maidless household, the hostess serving a sizable group usually needs help in changing courses, but an experienced guest asks if help will be welcome, before springing up to volunteer. If one woman guest rises to help the hostess, the other women do best to remain seated. If every woman at the table jumps up to help, a hostess can only be dismayed by the interruption of conversation and by the confusion that comes from too much help, no matter how well meant.

At a big buffet dinner, both men and women earn the appreciation of the hostess if they volunteer a certain amount of help in clearing, but always without assuming the duties of a professional maid or waiter. A thoughtful man (or woman) guest will take his empty plate and that of another guest to a sideboard, for example, but unless a specific offer of help is accepted, guests do best not to start a parade to the kitchen.

**KNIVES.** *See "Forks, Knives, and Spoons," above.*

**LATE ARRIVAL.** A hostess usually delays a meal no more than fifteen to twenty minutes for a tardy guest. Then, rather than condemn her other guests to overdone food, she goes ahead.

What to do about rising from a table to greet a tardy guest is always a problem—except for women guests, who never rise from a table to greet a newcomer, no matter how old and distinguished. The rule that both host and hostess rise to greet an arriving guest and that male guests rise for a woman newcomer is sometimes extremely awkward to follow at the dining table, especially if there are many guests.

At a large dinner party, if a staff member opens the door, the hostess does not rise when the late guest is shown into the dining room, since all men would then be required to rise. The late guest always goes to the hostess for the briefest of greetings and then proceeds to the empty chair without explanation at that time. If the guest is a woman and she has her wits about her, she signals to her host and any other men who are politely preparing to get to their feet not to do so, and slips into her seat before introductions can be made. Only the man at her left half-rises to help her with her chair. A late-arriving male guest gives the same signal to the host, and takes his place without other delay than his brief greeting to his hostess.

At a very small party in a private dwelling, the men do not rise if it is the hostess who leaves the table to answer the doorbell, but very likely will rise when she returns to the table with a tardy woman guest, though the guest (never the hostess) can follow the same procedure as at a large party, say, "Please don't get up," and slip into her place.

At a restaurant, it is often virtually impossible for men seated on a banquette or in a booth to rise to greet a tardy guest, and no more than a token half-rise is expected of anyone pinned down in such a seat. This is a situation where common-sense behavior from all concerned is the best guide to the best manners. Of course, if the hostess herself is late and her guests have been seated at a restaurant table, her male guests rise when she finally shows up, no matter how awkward it may be for them to extricate themselves from chairs in a crowded space.

If the reason for a guest's tardy arrival is absurd or amusing or newsworthy, the details make an enlivening anecdote for the table at large. If the delay is due to sad or bad news, illness, or an unpleasant accident, all explanation is best skipped until it can be given to the hostess alone.

If the first course has been cleared and the main course already served, the best procedure is to provide the late guest with what others are eating, though a first course may be brought in if that does not cause delay in serving others or prolong the absence of a hostess operating without a maid.

**LEAVING FOOD UNFINISHED.** An empty plate is a compliment to the cook, but there is no rule that calls for a guest to clean a plate that was heaped beyond his appetite. He does make an attempt to eat at least a little of everything set before him, however, unless he has an allergy to a specific food. In that case, he leaves the troublemaking item on his plate, without comment.

**LEAVING THE TABLE.** If a guest leaves the table briefly during a meal, only the man on a woman's left rises, or half-rises, to help her with her chair. All others remain seated when she leaves and when she returns.

If a woman guest must say good-bye before a meal is finished, all men rise unless she has the good sense to insist that they not do so, and she makes her getaway with the least commotion possible. If there is no staff member on hand to show the guest out, the host goes to the door, or the hostess may go instead with a woman guest if that is more convenient for everyone.

**At the End of a Meal.** It is never correct to push one's plate back or aside as a signal that a course is finished, and the diner who finishes first does not push his chair back out of line with the others, hook one arm over the back, tilt his chair back on two legs, sit sideways with one elbow on the table, or put his napkin on it. His napkin stays in his lap until the hostess gives the signal that the meal is ended by laying her napkin on the table and beginning to get up. Guests follow her lead, each man helping the woman to his right with her chair. Chairs are pushed back in any way convenient except by shoving with the hands against the table. A man does not leave his chair and that of the woman to his right lined up under the table precisely as they were found, but he does push them back toward the table to clear the way for others and to leave the dining room looking reasonably orderly. In a restaurant, chairs are left for a waiter to adjust, though a diner should not walk away leaving his chair blocking an aisle or otherwise in a position of inconvenience to other patrons.

If women are to withdraw alone, all men rise, but the host gives the signal to the other men by staying at his place. A woman never stays at the table with the men when the hostess withdraws with other women at the end of a meal. Otherwise, all guests follow the hostess in any convenient order. After leaving the dining room, dinner partners usually separate to speak with others, though there is nothing wrong with their staying together to finish a conversation.

**MASHING FOOD.** A bite at a time may be mashed, but a whole boiled potato, for example, is not mashed at one time and combined with butter or gravy. Small portions of a baked potato may be lightly mashed to amalgamate butter, but today's rules say that potato is best not taken out of its skin and completely mashed in preparation for eating.

**NAPKINS.** A guest leaves his napkin on the table until his hostess picks hers up. (See "Grace," above.) Lunch-size napkins usually are opened completely. Dinner-size napkins usually are left folded once. A napkin should not be tucked in at the neck or the belt except by small children. Usually there is no danger of its slipping to the floor if the elbows are kept off the table and the left hand stays in the lap, where it properly belongs when not in actual use, rather than propped on the table edge. The napkin should be used lightly before taking a sip from a cup or glass (to avoid leaving a greasy smear on the rim)—but be careful not to leave the napkin encarnadined with lipstick or otherwise unappetizingly stained. Food that must be taken out of the mouth is never removed by or into the napkin, and the napkin should not be raised as a screen during the removal of food in the fingers.

At the end of a meal—if the fingers are sticky from handling fresh fruit, for example—tip the water glass to dampen a corner of the napkin rather than dip a corner of it into the glass. A napkin should not be used as a handkerchief to mop brow or neck in hot weather, and it is inexcusable to use a paper napkin for nose-blowing. No one correctly puts his napkin on the table until the hostess puts hers beside her plate, which she does as a signal that she is about to rise and leave the table. A napkin should be laid neatly, but never precisely refolded, to either the right or the left of the plate. A paper napkin should not be crushed into a wad and dropped into glass, cup, plate, or ashtray.

**ORDERING.**   *See* RESTAURANTS.

**PASSING DISHES.** A diner leaves his knife and fork on his plate when he passes it back to the host or hostess for a second helping. Serving dishes are presented from a diner's left whether offered by a maid or passed from guest to guest. For example, a hostess who is starting a serving platter or bowl around the table picks it up and holds it for the guest on her right while he helps himself. He then takes the dish and holds it for the person on his right, and so on around the table. The hostess is the last to serve herself, when the dish completes the circle.

In a maidless household, the hostess often takes pains to plan a meal that does not require constant running back and forth to the kitchen. She may, for instance, have a tea cart beside her place with dessert on the top, and the bottom shelves empty for the stowage of used dinner plates. The guests pass used plates to her—but not even a butter plate is properly piled on a dinner plate. The hostess does not scrape and stack dishes at her place before putting them on the service cart, though she usually concentrates silver in some one place on it. Condiments, relishes, jellies, salt and pepper servers, and others items usually cleared before dessert are left on the table unless the hostess asks that they be passed to her.

In a restaurant, a plate should be passed to a waiter if it is obvious that he will have to lean across the table to the discomfort of another diner to reach it. Otherwise, it is left in place until he can remove it properly.

When a hostess asks some such question as "Will you have some cranberries?" the answer should never be "No, thank you," if the dish is within easy reach. In a circumstance of this sort, the question is an implied request to pass a dish to others.

**PETS.** Don't feed them at the table—no argument.

**PROBLEM FOODS.** See separate listings for ARTICHOKES; CORN; LOBSTERS, etc.

**PUSHERS.** Using a piece of bread to push food onto a fork is taboo.

**REACHING.** When conversation is lively and a guest's needs are not noticed, he has no choice but to wait until he can ask for something to be passed. It is all wrong to reach across another diner or to the other side of the table in any circumstances.

**READING.** Except when eating alone, it is permissible to read at table only at breakfast, and even then a member of the family does not read unless a houseguest is supplied with at least a portion of the morning paper. But at breakfast there is no reason why the head of the house may not glance over mail or a paper while the rest of the family does the same or talks.

**REFUSING FOOD.** As a general rule, a guest is expected to take at least a token helping of any main dish offered him. If for any reason he does not want a certain food, all that is called for is "No, thank you" when the dish is offered. A slightly lifted hand or any small, courteous sign to maid or waitress will also suffice. Emphatic gestures of refusal are neither correct nor graceful. If the host is serving, a guest may properly make such a request as "No dressing and gravy, thank you," but it is not necessary to add an explanation—"I'm on a diet," for instance. All references to allergies are best skipped too, especially such clichés as "I love onions but they don't love me." So is any such direct question as "Are there cucumbers in the salad?" It is better to take a very small helping and leave it, if one taste betrays the presence of a troublemaking ingredient, or to refuse a helping without comment.

**RISING.** When a hostess is serving a meal without help from a maid, the men at her table do not rise when she gets up to clear plates or get more food.
See also "Leaving the Table" and "Late Arrival" in this section)

**SALT AND PEPPER.** It is an insult to a cook worthy of the name to sprinkle salt all over one's food before taking a taste. Celery, radishes, or any other food is never dipped into an open salt cellar, even an individual one meant for the use of one person. Nor should a small heap of salt for dipping be put on the cloth. For this purpose, salt is put on the edge of the butter plate or, if none is served, on the dinner plate. If a little salt spoon does not accompany an open salt cellar, take a pinch of salt with the fingers or on the tip of a clean knife or spoon.

**SAUCES.** See "Gravy and Sauces," above.

**SEATING.** See "Entering a Dining Room, and Seating," above.

**SECOND HELPINGS.** Second helpings are not offered at formal meals, but usually are offered at most dinner parties at home.
(See "Asking for Something," above.)

The knife and fork are left on the plate when it is passed at table to host or hostess for a second helping.

Even if a hostess does not want a second helping, she takes a token second portion if a guest does so, unless she has other food on her plate and can make a pretense of eating as long as any guest is doing so.

**SEEDS AND STONES.** When possible, seeds and stones are not put into the mouth. Instead, fruit is cut away from them and they are left in the bowl or on the plate. Olives and small fresh fruits are eaten from the stones in several bites. In the case of a small stewed fruit, the stone is cleaned well in the mouth and returned to the underplate with the spoon. Tiny seeds, like grape seeds, and slippery watermelon seeds are removed in the fingertips. Olive stones are returned to the butter plate, or to the dinner plate if no butter plate is provided. Only away from table are they put in an ashtray. Stones of stewed fruit are put on the underplate if they have been in the mouth. Otherwise they are left in the bowl.

**SERVANTS.** By strictly formal procedure, a guest accepts services without paying any attention to the waiter or waitress beyond a courteous signaled or murmured "No, thank you" in refusing a dish. A guest does not say "Thank you" after being served or offered any dish. He does express thanks for special attention such as the replacement of a dropped napkin, but a nod and smile do equally well. Incidentally, in Europe, a thank-you when a dish is offered indicates that the guest does *not* care for any.

A guest smiles or murmurs a greeting to a maid who has served him frequently before, when she reaches his place for the first time during the service of a meal, but does not start a conversation, even with someone who may have been an employee of his own at one time. There are exceptions to all rules. It is absurd to behave stuffily and cut short a happy outburst of greeting from a familiar but not very well-trained maid when her intention is nothing but kindness. In general, any conversation with the staff serving a meal is left to the host or hostess. The same rules hold in restaurants.

Without making a point of it, the hostess keeps an eye on the service. If it is in any way inept, she should not give conspicuous reproof and most certainly never make any disparaging comment that can be overhead by the one serving. She may give instructions in a very low aside when the maid is near, but does best not to show any evidence of dismay until later. She never gives any order without adding "please," or implying it in her manner and tone.

**SERVING.**    See "Forks, Knives, and Spoons," above.

**SMOKING.**    Lighted cigarettes should not be carried to the table. If ashtrays are in place on the table, a guest is privileged to smoke between courses, but if there are no ashtrays, the hint should be respected. A guest who, under these circumstances, asks, "Do you mind if I smoke?" is taking unfair advantage, since a hostess cannot very well say, "Yes, I do."

In a restaurant, it is entirely correct to take a cigarette while waiting for the first course to be served—but not at home, not even if cigarettes and matches are on the table.

It is never correct to light a cigarette from a candle, and it is the worst of manners to use a sauce, dessert plate, or any other dish meant for food as an ashtray, most particularly if it has the smallest bit of food left on it.

**SOUP.**    The soup spoon is filled by moving it away from the diner, never toward him. It is correct to tip the soup plate to make the last spoonfuls available—always away from the eater, never toward him. It is customary to lift a cup of clear soup by one handle and sip it, after any garnishes or solids have been eaten with the spoon, but all thick and creamed soups are eaten only with the spoon even when served in a bowl with handles. Blowing on a spoonful of hot soup is taboo. So is spooning soup into the air to reduce its temperature.

If no butter plates are on the table, oyster crackers are put on the tablecloth. They may be eaten from the fingers or dropped whole in the soup. Bigger crackers are eaten from the fingers, not crushed to bits and dropped into the soup. If croutons are passed with a serving spoon, they are put directly into the soup. Lemon wedges are put on the underplate of a cup or bowl, on the butter plate if the soup is served in a big soup plate.

When finished, the diner leaves the soup spoon resting on its bowl in a wide soup plate because in this position the spoon is less likely to drop when the plate is removed. A spoon never is left in a soup cup—it should be put on the underplate when not in use.

**SPILLED FOOD.**   *See "Accidents," above.*

**SPITTING OUT.**   It is inexcusable to spit out food into the napkin or hand. In the very unlikely case that an actually spoiled piece of food is served—one tainted clam on the half-shell, for example—forcing it down would be foolhardy. There is only one sensible procedure: Remove the suspect mouthful as inconspicuously as possible with a spoon or fork and—unpleasant as the sight of a lump of half-eaten food is—return it to the plate.

A burning-hot piece of food should be cooled by taking a sip of water, never by removing it from the mouth. The same goes for the fiery taste of hot pepper relish—wash it down; don't take it out.

**SPOONS.**   *See "Forks, Knives, and Spoons," above.*

**STACKING DISHES.**   Clean plates are brought in stacked if host or hostess is to serve a course at table, but there is never any occasion when it is good manners to stack used dishes at the table. A properly trained maid never sets a butter plate in a dinner plate before removing it, for example, or stacks other used dishes. If guests pass used plates to the hostess to stow on the lower shelf of a tea wagon or other service arrangement, the plates are passed separately. When they reach the hostess, she does not scrape and stack them on the table for removal in one load. Correctly, she sets them one by one in the place she has provided off the table, stacking them there if she wishes.

**STIRRING FOODS.**   Only little children are permitted to make a whirlpool of mashed potatoes and gravy or to reduce ice cream to a mush before eating it. Others combine each bite of potatoes with a little gravy on the fork.

**TABLE-HOPPING.**   *See BANQUETS; RESTAURANTS.*

**TOOTHPICKS.**   A toothpick is never used in public, and it is startlingly bad manners to use the tines of a fork, the tip of a knife, or a fingernail as a toothpick at the table. If a bit of bone or other sharp piece of food cannot be dislodged by an inconspicuous leverage of the tongue, there is nothing to do but endure the discomfort until the matter can be dealt with in private.

**TURNING THE TABLE.**   *See "Conversation," above.*

**WAITERS.**   *See "Servants" above.*

**WINE.**   A guest refuses wine by saying, "No, thank you," or by making a slight, restrained gesture of refusal to the server, never by turning down the glass or covering it with the palm of the hand. A sip of wine may be taken as soon as a glass is filled, but it is always best at the beginning of a meal and also toward the end to follow the lead of hostess or host, since, if a toast is to be proposed, all are expected to take the first sip together, with the exception, of course, of the person toasted.

A small portion of wine is poured into the host's glass first, whether he is serving or a waiter is doing so. The host takes a sip to make sure of the quality. Then the service proceeds, the host's glass being the last one filled to the proper level.

*See WINE, for other details of service.*

**WIPING TABLEWARE.**   Don't polish silver with the napkin. There are no exceptions to this rule, either at home or in a restaurant.

## TABLE SERVICE, SETTINGS.   *See MEALS AND THEIR SERVICE.*

## TACT

The dictionary definition of tact is "a quick or intuitive appreciation of what is fit, proper, or right; fine or ready mental discernment shown in saying or doing the proper thing, especially in avoiding what would offend or disturb; skill or facility in dealing with men or emergencies." Eddie Cantor went to the heart of it: "What a fellow has when he won't change his mind but can change the subject."

Tact is also just another name for the kindness on which all rules of etiquette are based. It is automatic with anyone not so completely absorbed in himself as to be unaware of the needs and feelings of others.

## TANGERINES. See FRUITS.

## TARDINESS

No one can help being late once in a while, and so we have developed special conventions for the behavior of both the latecomer and others involved. These are somewhat different on different occasions. Because there are so many of them, they are listed under Tardiness in the Index.

## TAXIS

"Cab" is less often used in this country than "taxi," perhaps because it is easier to shout the latter, but either word is correct. However, a screamed "Taxi!" or a piercing whistle by a woman is certainly not attractive—and even a man appears a bit ridiculous if he resorts to great semaphore sweeps of the arm and frantic leaps out into the traffic. Such public gymnastics to attract the attention of a cabdriver are strictly for emergency use.

Competition for taxis at rush hours is one of the unhappier challenges of big-city living. Courteous people do not race up the street and grab a taxi just a few yards before it reaches someone who obviously has been waiting longer —but a lot of otherwise nice people do not seem to have gotten the message. When strangers queue up for taxis at a station, hotel, or on a street corner, a man takes the first one if he has been waiting longer than a woman. If he is kind enough to let a woman much his senior, or one heavily burdened with packages, have the first cab, he should be warmly thanked for a gracious and somewhat unusual courtesy.

A woman with her feminine wits about her makes no move to hail a cab when she is with a man. Ask any man what he thinks. Eager-beaver cab-hailing by his date comes high on a man's list of feminine social sins.

**ENTERING AND LEAVING.** If there is no doorman, the man opens the cab door—and the woman lets him do it. She takes the far seat. The old rule that a woman must sit at a man's right in the rear seat of a car is utter nonsense today. It had its origin in horse-and-buggy days when a man took the place nearer the street to protect his companion from being splashed by passing vehicles. In this day of one-way traffic and compact cars, it is both purposeless and impossibly awkward for a woman to take the seat nearer the curb and force a man to scramble past her. In extremely bad weather, when a man leaves a woman in a sheltered place while he gets a cab and rides back in it, he does the sensible thing and swings the door open for her without getting out. This is a case where good sense amends the rules of normal polite behavior, since it is far more considerate to get her sheltered quickly than to leave her exposed while he climbs out to help her in. If two men and one woman are sharing a cab, one man gets in first so that she sits between her two escorts. If one man and two women share a small cab, the man enters last and sits on the right, where he can get out most easily to help them alight. If the cab is roomy, he sits in the middle if he wants to.

A man gets out first, with few exceptions. If one-way traffic has put him on the far side from the curb and a doorman is on duty, he follows a woman out. He follows her out if they are in a cab so compact that it means awkward effort to climb over her.

In bad weather, the man pays the driver before getting out. Otherwise, he helps the woman out before paying. Unless she needs to take shelter, she waits nearby while he pays the driver through the front window. If a man is dropping a woman and keeping the cab, he asks the driver to hold his flag, takes his companion to her door or to the entrance of her apartment or hotel, before continuing.

**INSTRUCTIONS TO THE DRIVER.** Instructions are given to the driver by the man, or by the hostess if two women are sharing a cab. If more than one stop is to be made, the driver is told so when given the first address. In general, it is best not to be a back-seat driver and tell the cabbie what turns to take unless he obviously is not well acquainted with a neighborhood. Taxi drivers are licensed, subject to police inspection, and governed by strict regulations. The vast majority are honest and can be trusted to choose the best and fastest route through one-way streets and around traffic jams.

**LITTER IN CABS.** Cabs are not mobile ashtrays. Don't fling cigarette stubs on the floor or leave a cab in any other way untidy for the next passenger.

**LOST-AND-FOUND ARTICLES.** Drivers are expected to check their cabs for articles left behind. Usually, they take any valuable lost property such as wallets, jewelry, and furs to a police station without much delay, but turn in articles of minor value to the cab headquarters at the end of the day. If a cabdriver goes to particular pains to find a passenger in order to return a lost article, he should be given a tip that will rather more than compensate him for his time. If he returns a sizable sum of lost money, 10 percent is the expected reward.

The passenger who finds a small article in a cab—a book, gloves, or a scarf —turns it over to the driver. This is a case where finders most definitely may not be keepers. If a passenger finds something that appears to be of decided value, such as a handbag, wallet, or piece of jewelry, the driver's attention should be called to it immediately, and they should examine it together for mutual protection. After all, the wallet may have been rifled by some other passenger who found it first. In case of an item of great value, the passenger should go with the driver to the nearest police station to turn it in. Lost articles are kept by the police for varying lengths of time depending on their value. If not claimed, they become the property of the finder.

**MANNERS TO DRIVERS.** In big cities, drivers do not usually help passengers in and out of their cabs, even if traffic conditions permit it. The exceptional ones who volunteer to aid with luggage expect and deserve an extra tip. Passengers say "thank you" when they tip under any circumstances.

Rules in some cities forbid cabdrivers to refuse a fare to any point within the city limits, but the driver about to go off duty frequently—and understandably—will ask a passenger bound for a distant suburb to excuse him. Out of simple consideration for a hardworking man, the passenger should let him go and find another driver.

The garrulous cabdriver will sometimes take the hint implicit in monosyllabic replies from his passenger—and shut up. The truly incorrigible "gabby cabby," on the other hand, responds only to more outspoken treatment. The passenger who wants to refer to some notes, plan for his next business appointment, or think out a problem is best advised to say so unmistakably: "I have to go over some notes. Would you mind if we didn't talk?"

There is, of course, the other side of the coin. Many people chatter away in a cab as if the driver had neither ears, sense, feelings, sex, race, religion, or color.

**PAYING.** Cabdrivers are not expected to change very large bills. If the passenger's lack of small bills necessitates a stop for change, the driver deserves an extra tip. Having change ready before the destination is reached helps prevent traffic jams. If the fare is to be shared by passengers, they should settle up after leaving the cab unless they can do so expeditiously and not keep the driver and the cars behind him waiting while they solve their monetary problems.

When a man for some reason sends a woman home alone but feels obligated to pay her cab fare, he helps her in, asks the driver the approximate fare, and pays him, adding an appropriate tip. He does not hand the money to the woman. On arrival, she thanks the driver but does not tip him anything extra unless by miscalculation he has not been sufficiently well paid or tipped. When a woman asks a man to call a cab for her, she pays her own fare.

**SHARED CABS.**  Some cities have regulations against strangers' sharing cabs loaded at transportation terminals. In other cities, starters fill cabs with strangers who are going in the same direction. In cities where cabs have a flat rate within certain zones, this presents no payment problem. Each passenger pays the full amount shown on the meter and gives a tip. The driver does not clear his meter until he drops the last passenger.

When acquaintances share a cab, the first one out hands over approximately half of the fare and tip to the passenger who is continuing, if the two stops are within reasonable distance of each other. If the first stop is only a brief run and the second is much longer, the first passenger to get out gives full fare and tip to that point to the passenger who is going on.

When strangers share a cab, each pays the driver.

**TIPPING.**  The usual minimum tip in big cities is fifteen cents when the fare is under fifty cents; twenty or twenty-five cents under a dollar, and about 20 percent above it. It is not fair to skip or skimp a tip, since tips are a recognized part of a cabby's income. In many small towns, drivers do not expect any tip—but it is worth giving one for the novel experience of hearing genuine thanks. When several stops are made to pick up and drop passengers sharing a cab, the driver should be tipped rather more than a single passenger would give for the same distance.

Doormen who find cabs are tipped according to the circumstances. A hotel doorman who helps with luggage is tipped. A doorman who does no more than open the cab door for a hotel resident need not be tipped, but if there is heavy competition for cabs along that street and he uses his influence with drivers known to him, or if he must make any special effort, especially in bad weather, he gets anything from twenty-five cents up. A nonresident who asks a hotel doorman to summon a cab always is expected to tip. Doormen at department stores are not tipped for summoning cabs, but doormen at nightclubs expect a tip from departing patrons if they do no more than raise a languid hand to summon one.

**TEA DANCES.**  *See* BALLS AND DANCES.

## TEAS

Somewhat different procedures are followed at small and large tea parties, but one rule about tea itself is always observed. Tea cools quickly, and so a trayful of filled cups is never offered. Each cup is filled and served individually.

**CLOTHES.**  A hostess wears any suitable afternoon dress for a tea at home. She does not wear a hat unless she is receiving at a club, hotel, or other such place. Traditionally, guests arrive hatted and gloved in honor of the festivity, but today this is entirely a matter of personal preference and local custom. A guest does not take her hat off, but removes her gloves before accepting tea.

**INVITATIONS.**  One of the major differences between large and small teas is the length of time a guest is obligated to stay—nearly always clearly indicated by the way the invitation is expressed.

If only the beginning hour is mentioned, a very small party is indicated, and a guest is expected to arrive at the mentioned time, or very shortly thereafter, and stay for about an hour. For example, "Can you come to tea next Tuesday at four-thirty to meet my house guest?" means that a guest who accepts should turn up no later than quarter to five and stay until about six.

A guest who can stay for only a short time should make that clear when accepting: "I'd love to come, but I can't make it until [or will have to leave] a little after five because I have to pick up the children."

An invitation to a large tea, telephoned or mailed, always specifies the hour of departure. An invitation that reads "four to six" indicates that a guest is welcome to arrive at any time between four and five-thirty and should leave by six-fifteen, unless specifically invited to stay longer. A guest generally stays a half-hour to forty-five minutes at a big tea, though it is correct to stay for the entire time.

A printed invitation to a tea sponsored by a church, club, or other organization does not require an answer unless it carries "R.S.V.P."

A handwritten invitation requires an answer even if it does not carry a request for one.

Under most circumstances, it is correct for a guest to ask her hostess if she may bring a friend with her, but the formality of asking permission should be observed, except for a community or other semipublic tea.

**LARGE TEAS.** The hostess does not pour at a large tea, since her first duty is to welcome her guests as they arrive and to make introductions. Instead, she honors two of her friends by asking them to preside at the table for her. Their main obligations are to arrive shortly before the stated hour and to keep their places at the table until the crowd thins out and late-comers have been supplied with refreshments. A pourer is an assistant hostess as well as a guest, but she keeps her hat on and does not rise to greet other guests.

Both tea and coffee are served at a large tea. Traditionally, the dining room curtains are drawn; the table is covered with a cloth and has a pretty centerpiece. Candles are not used unless they are lighted. At one end of the table is the coffee service—pot, cream pitcher, and sugar bowl or bowls (either granulated or lump sugar, or both, may be served). The matching silver tray is not covered with a cloth. At the other end of the table on its tray is the tea service, which includes a pot of strong tea suitable for serving with milk, a pot of hot water for diluting the brew for those who like a more delicate tea, the milk pitcher, thin slices of lemon and a pick, a sugar bowl (with tongs if the customary lump sugar is served), a silver strainer if one is not built into the pot, and a container for the dregs remaining in cups brought back for refill.

Cups, saucers, and spoons are to the left of each pourer, stacked so that they are within easy reach. All the cups and silver need not match and, indeed, seldom do. Few households are equipped with enough china serve fifty or more guests, and so borrowing extra equipment is a routine part of a big tea.

Platters of food are arranged on one or both sides of the table, along with dessert plates, and forks if they will be needed for an iced cake. Napkins are put on the cloth or stacked between the plates. Paper napkins sometimes are used, but elegant little linen tea napkins are still the first choice.

Two kinds of food are offered at a formal tea—small delicate sandwiches and a variety of sweet pastries suitable for eating from the fingers, though sometimes slices of cake are offered.

At a large tea, help is needed in the kitchen to keep the platters of sandwiches and cakes replenished, the pots of coffee and tea filled, and to provide extra cups as needed. Very often, these duties are entrusted to a young relative and several of her friends too junior to be guests but happy to join the party in this fashion. The youngsters take their share of goodies in the kitchen as they go about their duties as substitute maids, but are otherwise treated as guests and are not expected to do any major dishwashing or tidying at the end of the party. The mother of any little girl asked to help is always invited to the tea, of course.

Unless it is summer and the door can be left open in welcome, a member of the family or a friend of the hostess is assigned to answer the bell. She introduces herself, directs guests to places to leave their wraps, or to the room where the hostess is.

The hostess makes it easy for each guest to find her immediately after arrival by staying near the entrance of her living room. At the beginning of the party when few people are present, a guest is introduced around the circle. Once the room is well filled, the newcomer is introduced only to guests in an adjacent group or so. After that, self-introductions are in order.

When she is ready, after greeting her hostess, the guest makes her way to the tea table. Unless there is a rush at the moment for refreshments, she introduces herself to the pourer and chats for a minute or so if she likes. If the pourer is hard-pressed, the guest says only, "Thank you" when she receives the cup filled to her specifications, helps herself to food, and moves away to find a place to sit—if there is one.

No attempt is made to provide chairs for all guests at a large tea, since a guest is expected to drift around and speak with as many other guests as reasonable. The concentration of the refreshments in the dining room makes this easy. Anyone pinned down in a corner or stuck with a stranger too long can always say, "Let's get some more tea," and move purposefully back into the mainstream, where she can introduce her companion to another group and then be free to circulate.

A guest does not leave without having had a few words with the guest of honor, if there is one, introducing herself if that is the simplest thing to do. She need not say good-bye to the guest of honor or the pourers, but does thank her hostess before getting her wraps. She sets an empty cup down in any convenient place—in or near the dining room if she can without too much effort. If the party has thinned out, the hostess goes with her to the door. Otherwise, the hostess says good-bye to departing guests in her living room and they let themselves out.

**SMALL TEAS.** The tea service is set up in advance in the living room whether the hostess is serving with or without the help of a maid, so that only the pots of tea and hot water need be brought in after the guests arrive. The tea table may be a small one of standard height covered with a cloth, or the hostess may prefer to set the tea tray directly on a bare coffee table. The tray itself is not covered with a cloth. If it is big enough, it carries the cups and plates stacked for easy access, as well as the tea service. Otherwise, they are set to the server's left, with plates of small sandwiches and cakes also at hand.

The hostess may serve her first guests as soon as they arrive, or wait until most of the guests are present. As noted under "Invitations," guests are expected to arrive promptly when invited to a small afternoon tea. The hostess asks each guest how she likes her tea, and then adds milk or lemon and sugar to order. If a maid is on duty, she delivers each cup as it is filled. Otherwise, the guests pass cups and plates along if convenient, or each guest rises to get her cup and plate, though a young guest will aid the hostess by serving any markedly older guest. If men are present, women guests remain seated and the men serve them. As a general rule, the hostess remains seated and a guest offers such assistance as passing second helpings. Men do not get up when the hostess goes out for more tea.

The hostess rises to greet each guest, and also to say good-bye. If a host is present, he sees each guest to the door. Otherwise, the hostess does so.

# TEEN-AGERS

"When I was a child, I spake as a child, I understood as a child; but when I became a man I put away childish things."—*New Testament, I Corinthians 13:11*

Teen-agers have many extremely tough problems, but the rules governing their manners are not among them. As far as manners go, teen-agers are grown-ups and are expected to observe the basic rules that govern the conduct of men and women. The very few procedures that are different for boys and girls are explained in detail where any sensible young person would expect to find them —under specific topical headings along with the standard rules for the adults they soon will be.

See INTRODUCTIONS, for example, for the explicit exceptions of the regular rules that are made when boys and girls are being introduced and are themselves making introductions; and VISITING CARDS and CORRESPONDENCE for the correct use of their titles; also Teen-agers in the Index for the many other special references to this age group.

**TELEGRAMS.**   See CORRESPONDENCE; INVITATIONS; TIPPING.

## TELEPHONE MANNERS

> "In heaven when the blessed use the telephone they will say what they have to say and not one word besides."—*W. SOMERSET MAUGHAM*

There is nothing confusing about good telephone manners—except why so very many people ignore them. Alexander Graham Bell gave the first public demonstration of his marvelous invention in 1876. Since then, the device has been developed to a range of performance close to magical, but the basic rules for using it have remained the same for many years:

1. Speak directly into the transmitter to avoid a muffled or indistinct transmission of speech. When talking in a noisy place, don't shout. It is much more effective to pitch one's voice under surrounding noise than over it. Don't shout anyway. A controlled low tone goes through the instrument much more clearly and pleasantly than a voice raised above normal volume.
2. During an interrupted telephone conversation, don't press the transmitter against the chest or rib cage to block out a comment not meant for the person on the other end of the wire—it does not always work. Cover the transmitter with the hand.
3. Don't lay the instrument down noisily on a hard surface. The resulting clatter is magnified and can be unpleasant, if not actually painful, especially to a listener wearing headphones. For the same reason, don't drop the instrument roughly into its cradle, jiggle violently to attract the attention of the operator, or cough directly into the transmitter.
4. When calling, let the bell ring at least five times before hanging up. Most people are not all alone by the telephone waiting to grab it at the first ring, and are understandably annoyed to hear only a dial tone after dropping a demanding task and rushing to answer. Give the callee a reasonable chance to reach the telephone from any part of his house—or perhaps garden.
5. If an unfamiliar voice answers, don't ask either, "What number is this?" or, "Who is this?" The correct procedure for the caller is to ask, "Is this Plaza 0-1234?" or to state his own name and ask to speak with the person he is calling. A number dialed by mistake is none of his business—and the identity of a stranger answering a correctly dialed number may not be, either. (*See also* "Wrong Numbers," below.)
6. The caller who goes by the rules remembers that telephones are not yet equipped with TV screens. He identifies himself immediately by name or in some other fashion, and does not take for granted that his voice will identify him as soon as he begins to speak.
7. Without fail (unless the house is on fire), a caller should ask if it's a conven-

ient time for the callee to talk unless the conversation can be completed in about the same time it takes to ask that question. It is always possible that the callee's own house is on fire or that he is in no mood (for other pressing reasons) to settle down to chat at length at the caller's convenience.

**ANSWERING—OR NOT.** The telephone is a glorious convenience, but each subscriber is its master—not its slave. There is no rule, law, or reason that obligates a subscriber to answer the bell. And there are scores of occasions when it is more considerate of everyone concerned to let it ring unanswered. Gian-Carlo Menotti's one-act opera *The Telephone* deals with one of them. The hero, thwarted in making a proposal of marriage because his beloved cannot resist interrupting his declaration to answer her telephone, rushes away in desperation in order to get her full attention—by calling her up.

If a conversation must be interrupted to answer the telephone, it should be done without indecent haste. Nothing is more disconcerting to a visitor than to be cut off in midsentence because his host or hostess leaps to answer the telephone like a fireman responding to an alarm. The implication is that almost anything is more important than the visitor and what he is attempting to say.

Certainly there are many times in both business and private life when it is necessary to interrupt a conversation to deal with an incoming call. When the telephone rings, the least a visitor should do is come quickly to the end of a sentence. But the very least the subscriber should do is to give the visitor this chance, and then make some apology like "Sorry, but I have to take this," as he prepares to answer.

**BOOTHS.** Don't smoke in a telephone booth. One cigarette can make the little closed room smell like an old ashtray to the next user.

**BUSINESS CALLS.** The major difference between business and social calls (*see below*) is in the use of "Mr.," "Mrs.," and "Miss," which are correct for more frequently in business than in social telephoning. The basic rule in business is that a title and last name are the standard correct form on occasions where the first name is of no importance to the business in hand or to the person relaying the name.

A man who needs to identify himself in relation to his function in the firm may answer either, "Complaint Department—Mr. Brown," or "Complaint Department—Brown speaking." He does not correctly use "John Brown" unless there is another Mr. Brown in his department and there also is some reason to make clear to the caller which one is speaking.

First and last names are generally reserved for the use of executives. A secretary says, "Mr. York's office. Miss Greene [not Mary Greene] speaking." The caller may say to her, "Mr. Brown calling Mr. York," or Brown of Consolidated," or if he is a frequent caller and especially if he is on the executive level, he says, "John Brown" (adding the name of his firm if further identification would be helpful). Under no circumstances does a man identify himself respectfully as "Mr. John Brown." If he gives his first name, he omits "Mr."

A woman is always correct in identifiying herself by title, since this saves time by making it unnecessary to ask, "Miss or Mrs.?" However, it should be noted that the more important the position that either a man or woman holds, the more likely such executives are to avoid the more stilted title and last name and use "John Brown" or "Mary Smith" when identifying themselves. When in doubt, follow the standard social rules.

**Secretaries and Switchboard Operators.** Somewhat special rules govern the responses of the people on the front line of defense, and valuable beyond estimate to any firm are the go-betweens who observe these rules. If a caller does not give his name, the operator or secretary says something like, "Who is calling, please?" (not the unceremonious demand "Who's this?" and certainly not the slightly macabre "What was the name?" which sounds as if the caller is speaking from the spirit world). If her chief is not in or is busy, she says something like: "Mr. York is not available [or here] right now. May I help you?" or: "He is on another line. Do you wish to wait?" (but never "He's not here," or "You'll have to call back"). That flat "have to" is a phrase infuriating to most people—second only to the words "Hold it, please, Mr. Brown calling you," if Mr. Brown does not come on the line immediately.

**CRANK AND NUISANCE CALLS.**   For reasons that the authorities cannot explain, anonymous nuisance calls that are either annoying or frightening are on the increase. Many of the most distressing come from foolish or actually unbalanced people who select a name at random from the telephone book and either hold on to the telephone without speaking or make obscene or threatening remarks. There is only one way to deal with such calls. Hang up immediately. Don't ask questions. Don't answer them. Don't reply to offensive comments or abuse. A response only encourages such a caller. In all cases, hang up on anyone who refuses to identify himself.

If the calls persist, call the telephone company and ask for instructions. In communities all over the country, the telephone company is working with the police and other authorities to curb abusive, obscene, and harassing misuses of the telephone. They have ways to trace the caller, including a device that (unknown to the caller) can activate an alarm and alert an operator assigned to tracing duty.

The seriousness of this problem cannot be overemphasized, especially to those youngsters who think that telephoning to strangers is a harmless indoor sport. New York State, among others, now has a law that provides for a year's imprisonment, a fine up to $500, or both, for a caller who makes obscene remarks to a woman or a child under sixteen or who threatens to commit a crime against any person. And what might be even a worse blow to a teen-ager— anyone caught making harassing calls faces the loss of his telephone service.

**DIRECTORY LISTINGS.**   It is correct to list a name in the telephone book in any way that suits the subscriber best. Usually, a home number is listed under the name of the male head of the house, but there is no rule that says this is the only correct listing. Not infrequently, a professional man who wants to avoid business calls at home lists that number under his wife's name. It is also quite usual for a man to differentiate between his business and home listings in this fashion, which has the advantage of making clear how he should be formally addressed in invitations, and so on:

Brown, Henry Y. lwyr 20 West Av..........................RE 0-2345
Brown Henry York res 100 Chestnut St.......................PL 0-1234

"Mr." is not used, but "Dr." or "M.D." is. "Miss" and "Mrs." may or may not be used with a woman's name. A single woman often lists her initials rather than her first name to avoid crank calls from strange men.

**DISCONNECTIONS.**   If a connection is broken, the person who placed the call is the one who calls back.

**ENDING A CALL.**   The established rule is: The person who makes the call ends it, and the person called is expected to allow the caller this courtesy. If this rule were observed strictly, some of us would never be off the telephone, and so everyone is privileged to ignore it in one of the several possible polite ways. A busy executive may say, "Thank you for calling," as a hint that he is ready to hang up, and the caller who does not respond to this tacit request has missed his cue. "I'm so glad you called. We must get in touch more often" is one of the many gentler variants constantly used in social life. And of course it is always correct to shut off a long-winded speaker with any acceptable explanation—"I wish we could talk longer, but I'm due at a meeting."

A call should be ended with an unmistakable good-bye of some sort, so that the other person is not left wondering if the connection was broken and therefore in doubt about whether to call back.

Deliberately hanging up in the middle of a conversation is a deliberate insult.

**EXTENSIONS.** Listening on an extension, unless both speakers know they are being overheard, is eavesdropping—taboo by all standards.

**GUESTS.** A guest does not use the telephone under usual circumstances without first asking permission. If a guest has arranged to be called at his host's number, he so informs his host upon arrival. A strict rule is that a guest is obligated to find out the charges and pay for any long-distance calls before his visit ends. It is never correct to ask a host or hostess to relay the amount of such charges when the bill comes in.

**OPERATORS.** Telephone operators are among the most carefully trained of all public servants. They meet a demandingly high standard of efficiency and helpfulness. Ordinary politeness to them pays the highest dividends. It also is only a simple necessity to keep on good terms with the company because, as one supervisor, tried beyond endurance by a subscriber's abusive language, suggested, "Perhaps you would care to make other arrangements?"

**PARTY LINES.** When a conversation on a party line is frequently interrupted by another subscriber who obviously wants to use the line, it is only common courtesy to end the conversation as quickly as possible and give the other subscriber a chance at the shared facility. Anyone sharing a party line is privileged, in a real emergency, to interrupt a conversation, explain his urgent need, and ask that the line be freed at once. It is a legal offense not to clear the line immediately in such instances.

**PHONE.** The abbreviation "phone," like "bus," has made its way completely into common use, and is now considered just as good usage as "telephone."

**REQUESTS TO RETURN CALLS.** By the rules, a person calling to thank someone does not ask to be called back if he cannot reach the person he wants to thank. He either leaves a message of thanks with a third party or keeps on trying to reach the person who has done him a favor.

When the person called says, "May I call you back?"—especially when he offers no explanation—it is clearly evident that the callee is caught in an emergency or some inconvenient situation. The only correct reply in all but exceptional circumstances is the briefest possible answer: "I'll be here for an hour," or, "I'm at Plaza 0-1234," for example.

**SALESMEN, SOLICITORS, AND SURVEY MAKERS.** All telephone calls are to some degree an invasion of privacy in that they are interruptions made at the caller's convenience. Calls from salesmen, particularly those who launch into a lengthy preamble before announcing that the subscriber has "won" that free dancing lesson or whatever, come under the general classification of nuisance calls. They can be infuriating interruptions. On the other hand, many telephone salesmen are shut-ins trying to make a living in perhaps the only way open to them, and they deserve a measure of consideration. There is no need to let a telephone salesman waste one's time, but it is just as easy to say, "Thank you, but I am not interested," as to slam down the receiver without an answer.

Solicitors for charities and political causes usually are volunteers who are doing their duty as good citizens, as they see it. There is no need to listen to them, either, but these hardworking, unselfish people deserve to be cut off with courtesy.

The making of public opinion surveys by telephone is a big business that serves many useful functions. When convenient it is sensible to answer impersonal questions such as inquiries about which TV programs the family likes best. Cooperation with the surveyor might just possibly raise the standard of programs. But make sure that questions from a stranger really serve an honest purpose. It is extremely unwise to answer questions about vacation plans or other absences. A favorite dodge of burglars is to represent themselves as "making a survey," and with a few seemingly innocent questions like "How many nights a week does your whole family eat in a restaurant (go to the movies, and so on)?" the so-called "survey taker" gets all the information he needs for selecting a safe time for breaking and entering.

Under all circumstances, if in doubt about a stranger's credentials, ask him for his office address and number and offer to call him back.

**SOCIAL CALLS.**   The standard answer from the subscriber or a member of his family or one of his friends who answers a home telephone is "Hello." (Under most circumstances, a visitor—especially a man visiting a woman—does not answer the telephone unless asked to.)

The standard answer from a domestic employed by a married couple is "Mrs. Brown's residence." "Mr. Brown's residence" is correctly used only if the employer is single. "Apartment" is also correct, and is sometimes preferred by a single man or woman living in a small one. A well-trained domestic never answers "Hello."

If a servant answers the telephone, the caller identifies himself by title and last name. "This is Mr. [Miss, Mrs.] Brown. Is Mrs. York there?" It is also correct when identifying one's self or leaving a message with a child or an unknown person to follow this rule. For example, "Please ask your mother to call Mrs. Greene," or, "Please tell Miss White that Mr. Jones will be fifteen minutes late." First and last name without title are not generally used in such cases unless there might possibly be confusion about which Mrs. Greene was speaking.

A first name only should not be left with someone who does not know the caller. For example, "Please ask her to call Ann" may give someone a hard half-hour of telephoning to a series of Anns before the right one is reached.

If the person calling breaks the rules and does not state his name immediately, a member of the family says, "Who is this, please?" A servant says, "May I tell Mrs. Brown who is calling?" A visitor does not ask; it is none of his business.

If the person called is not at home, a member of the family says, "Mother [or she] is not at home. May I give her a message?" A servant does not use "she." The correct answer is "Mrs. Brown is not at home. May I take a message?"

When making a social call, even to a stranger, the caller correctly identifies himself without title: "John Brown." A single woman also gives her name without title: "Mary Green." A married woman does not identify herself as "Mrs. Jones." She may say, "This is Mrs. Ralph Jones," but first choice is "Mrs. York, this is Mary Jones," and then the establishment of her marital status by some other means—for example, "My husband serves with Mr. York on the school board." Such use of one's name is never an invitation to the other party to use it in return. Mrs. York correctly answers, "Hello, Mrs. Jones."

The social caller can be forgiven all other sins if he makes it a strict habit to ask, "Have you time to talk?" before launching into any but the briefest conversation. Anyone who telephones near a mealtime is especially obligated to ask, "Are you in the middle of dinner?" and to end the talk readily if the reply is anything like "We were just about to sit down." When a caller neglects to find out if his interruption is inconveniently timed, the callee is privileged in any case and obligated in some to make an excuse and offer to talk later. During either a family meal or a party, protracted absence on the telephone is a rudeness to all present.

**Children.**   A little child who cannot take a message should not be answering the telephone—but, of course, that doesn't mean he won't do it. So it is only the better part of sense not to depend on little Johnny to get a message straight, remember it, or even to go get Mommy. He may well feel that he has discharged an interesting task with complete social aplomb if he says, "Hello," and then goes back to his blocks.

A child old enough to use the telephone is old enough to begin to establish the base for good telephone manners in the future. He should be taught to give his name when he calls: "This is Johnny. May I speak to Harry?" (instead of "Is Harry there?").

**Teen-agers.** What can be done about teen-agers and the telephone except ponder Guy Lombardo's words: "Many a man wishes he were strong enough to tear a telephone book in half—especially if he has a teen-age daughter."

**WRONG NUMBERS.** Everyone makes a mistake in dialing once in a while. The rules for both caller and callee are clearly established. Too often the caller demands accusingly, "Who is this?" or, "What number is this?" instead of, "Is this Plaza 0-1234?" If he impulsively makes either of these mistakes, his question should not be answered. The correct reply to these incorrect questions is "What number do you want?" as a preliminary to helping him correct his mistake. (In the event of getting a wrong number on a toll call, the caller may say, "Will you please tell me what number I have reached so that I can ask the operator to remove the charge from my bill?" Under these circumstances, the callee is correct in giving the caller the requested information—at least the area code, if he prefers not to give his full number. But the telephone company will still remove the charge from the caller's bill if he notifies the operator, whether he is able to identify the wrong number he reached or not.)

Completely out of line is the wrong-number caller who hangs up without so much as an "I'm sorry." The routine reply to a wrong-number apology is "All right" or "No trouble"—though no one can be blamed for gritting out the words a bit stiffly if the careless dialer has chosen the middle of the night to make his mistake.

## TELEVISION AND RADIO

No doubt about it: For good or ill, television and to a lesser degree radio are home courses for everyone in manners, speech, and behavior, and they continue to modify many local differences in accent and etiquette. The variety of behavior examples afforded by the complete run of broadcast programs can be confusing to young children; but that very variety is as much of an opportunity as a problem for parents because for every tasteless, vulgar, and ungrammatical commercial and program, there can be found—with perhaps a little effort—an example of standard good procedure in situations of every kind. Among these are *some* of the panel and discussion shows, where interruptions are politely but positively suppressed by the moderator if the panelists fail to apologize for interrupting or to give a good excuse or an explanation for doing so.

As for the interruptions that these marvelous "boxes" themselves can be, the rules are clear:

1. Both the owner wired for sound by a pocket radio or portable television set and the owner of a home set are required by ordinary consideration for all within earshot to keep the volume at a level that does not become an invasion of privacy. Broadcast sound carries farther than many people realize. Late at night, especially, a set located near an open window can, quite unintentionally on the part of the owner, be an active nuisance to a neighbor. Don't give anyone, within the house or elsewhere, the unhappy necessity of complaining about the volume of the sound.

2. As a general rule, turn off a program when a guest arrives. Some people

enjoy background music during a conversation. Others find even low music disturbing and the mutter of broadcast words particularly so. This rule certainly does not apply when an unexpected guest arrives in the middle of a program of special interest to a listening group. The standard procedure then is for the hostess to explain the special reason for continuing the program, and for the guest to respond immediately by joining the company in silence. If, on the other hand, the program is only a minor diversion for the adults present, the host should click it off unless he is certain that the unexpected visitor will also find it of interest. However, it is only fair in most such cases to allow a child to see a favorite program to the end, though with the sound turned down to its lowest effective level.

3.  If watching a television program is planned as part of an evening's entertainment, that fact should be made clear when the invitation is given. Anyone who accepts is obligated to watch with a minimum of distracting talk. The program may prove boring to some members of the party, but they are required to endure it in comparative silence, except during commercials, until the host takes merciful action and turns the sound down or off.

4.  Let the host be the engineer. A guest who adjusts a set is always out of line unless he is specifically asked to do it. He can ask for the sound to be turned up or down, but "Hands off" is the rule for him.

## TEMPLES AND SYNAGOGUES

"Temple" or "synagogue," not "church," is the name given to a Jewish house of worship. "Synagogue" is used by Orthodox congregations. Conservative congregations use either "temple" or "synagogue." Reform congregations use "temple." The proper form is Temple Emmanu-El, for example, not Emmanu-El Temple. "Synagogue" generally follows the name.

When anyone of another faith enters a temple or synagogue, he is expected to follow the customs of the congregation about head covering. If the men present are wearing hats, a male visitor keeps his on. If an usher or other attendant at the entrance hands a head covering to a hatless man, he is required to accept and wear it, no matter what his own religion may be.

See CHURCHES for the rules of respectful behavior that are the same in all houses of worship.

## TENNIS

Tennis is still a game where the observation of traditional customs is of supreme importance in spite of two fairly recent and controversial innovations—the "lace panties revolution" in the clothes for women players, and the Van Alen Simplified Scoring System (VASSS), in which points are figured on a straight 1-to-31 basis as opposed to the standard series of six-game sets.

**CLOTHES.** The long-standing rule for tennis clothes for both men and women, "White is right," still holds, and correct getups for men remain unchanged. Men wear white trousers or shorts (but nothing so short or tight as basketball or swimming trunks), a short-sleeved white sports shirt or T-shirt (but not a cotton undershirt).

The standard dress for women is still the white one-piece, short-skirted tennis dress, or not too short shorts and a sports shirt, though brief shifts are increasingly seen in some circles. It is always safer to find out in advance the degree of formality and conformity in dress that is expected when going to play at a new club or in the company of new companions. Clanking jewelry still remains taboo.

Both men and women wear short white socks and white tennis shoes with the rubber soles necessary to provide a safe grip on a cement court and also needed on a grass or other soft-surface court to protect the court itself.

**COURTESIES.** A booklet issued by the United States Lawn Tennis Association giving the official rules that govern every aspect of championship play is available free at sporting-goods stores. It is a good thing to have on hand, since many of the rules are also customarily observed in less formal play. Under any circumstances, meticulous courtesy is the basis of all the rules. If, for example, one player offers the other his choice of the side of the court on which to begin play, the one choosing the more advantageous court automatically cedes to the other the right to serve first. The same rule holds if first choice is decided by the traditional spin of the racket—the winner may choose either the court of his preference or first serve, but does not have first chance at both choices.

In the absence of an umpire, it is the responsibility of the server to call the score after each point (his own score first) and also the score in games at the end of each game or whenever the players change courts. The receiver, however, always calls any close serves, either good or out, since the server may not be able to tell if his ball hit inside or just past the line. If the rules are observed strictly, the receiver does not touch any serve that is out, but in most informal play it is customary to stop bad serves when convenient, in order to keep balls off the adjoining courts or to save time in chasing them. When this results in confusing the server, the *receiver* is expected to offer to replay the point. In other words, good sportsmanship is the main obligation of both players, rather than any niggling controversy about who is "right."

It is traditional tennis courtesy to praise a good shot made by either an opponent or one's doubles partner, or to commiserate for a bad one, but a running stream of comment can be tiresome. Relative quiet is expected, and, of course, any really disgusted comment on a partner's play takes the fun out of the game for everyone. The loser, no matter how dismayed, is expected to congratulate the winner without alibis; and the gracious winner will take care of any excuses that can rightly be made for the loser.

Common sense is the basis of the rule that stray balls must not be retrieved from an adjoining court while play is in progress there. Wait for a break in the play, since anyone wandering around the edges of the court will distract the players even if a ball is being retrieved from well behind the base line. It is also common sense to initial tennis balls in order to avoid misunderstandings about their ownership.

When others are waiting for either a public or private court where reservations are not made, players are expected to cede a court on the completion of a set (not hang on to it the whole afternoon), or suggest a doubles match, so that the waiting time for others is reduced. But it is never good practice for inexpert players to accept such an invitation from obviously skilled players who have been playing a fast game. Players waiting to take possession of a court reserved for a specific hour usually suggest that the set in progress be completed, but accepting their offer is not good practice if it means cutting deeply into their allotted time.

Women players should not expect preferential treatment, but men are expected to give them a certain amount of it. In mixed doubles, a male player usually takes the more active court and does the major share of retrieving, but he does not concentrate his shots toward the woman player on the other side of the net if she is the weaker of the opposing twosome.

**HOST AND GUEST.** The guest at a club supplies his own racquet and takes along at least three new balls, which he should make no point of salvaging for his own use on another day. They usually represent his only expense, since the host is expected to pay for everything else. However, if a locker-room attendant gives a guest some special service, he rates a tip—a dollar in a private club, fifty cents or less at a public court.

Any tennis court needs some care. The guest invited to play at a private court is certainly more likely to get a repeat invitation if he lends a hand with its upkeep—whether this be sweeping or the more arduous rolling, raking, or weeding—unless there is a regular caretaker for such chores.

**SPECTATORS.** People waiting for a court, as well as the spectators at any tennis match, are expected to keep their voices down and make no move that will distract or unnerve the players. Loud conversation, attention-getting cheers, boos, groans, catcalls, and kibitzing are out of line. Applause is saved for the intervals between points, not given during play. And only good points are applauded—never a miss or other error even though it means a much-desired advantage for a favorite player.

# THEATERS

The following rules of audience behavior apply at all theatrical and musical entertainments.

For additional rules governing behavior at events other than dramas and musical comedies, *see* CONCERTS; LECTURES; MOVIES; OPERA.

**APPLAUSE.** It is customary to applaud a distinguished set when the curtain rises. The first entrance of a star or extremely popular supporting player often is greeted with applause. Very occasionally, an unusually effective scene within an act of a drama draws spontaneous burst of clapping, but, though flattering, it is seldom welcome since it breaks into the mood and action. Applause at a musical comedy is a different matter; the prolonged applause that calls for an encore is welcome after any number. Even after a disappointing show, patrons in the front rows are obligated by ordinary politeness and sympathy to clap at least a little when the company takes a curtain call.

For further details, *see* APPLAUSE.

**BOXES.** The places in boxes are not separately numbered, and so the first comers have the first choice of locations. If several couples occupy a box, the women sit next to the rail and the men take the inner row. A hostess takes the seat against the rail farthest from the stage. If only women are in her party, she gives the railside seat to one of her guests and, if necessary, sits in the second row herself.

**CHANGING SEATS.** As a general rule, patrons stay in the seats that they have bought. If there are empty seats after the first intermission, they may move to seats that suit them better, but most people choose to move within the same section rather than from the top balcony to the orchestra, for example.

**CHECKING.** A woman does not usually check her coat unless it is wet. A man is much more comfortable if he checks his, since—for reasons unknown —it is against custom for a man to spread his coat over the back of the seat and sit on it. If a man prefers not to spend the brief time required to check and retrieve his wraps, he holds his coat and hat in his lap or puts them under his seat.

A woman stands aside, rather than in line, while a man is checking and retrieving his belongings.

**CLOTHES.** Patrons in the choice seats in the orchestra often wear Black Tie and evening dresses on an opening night and at a gala or benefit performance, but there will also be a comfortable number of people in less formal dress, since it is correct to wear street clothes to a theater at any time. A woman's hat, unless it is no more than a skullcap, is bound to interfere with the view of those behind her. It is not enough for her to ask the person immediately behind if her hat is in the way—a hat can block the line of view for people in several other rows. Therefore, it is routine procedure for a woman to take off any hat except the very smallest without being asked. If she does not, "Do you mind taking off your hat?" is a correct and sensible request.

**CONVERSATION.** Too many people chatter along throughout a show as if they were at home watching television. Once a performance has started, conversation rightly ceases; and during a performance, good manners call for the suppression of sighs, groans, and all other attention-distracting sounds and gestures.

**ENTERING AND SEATING.** Tardiness is distracting and therefore discourteous to performers and audience alike, and so patrons should make every effort to be in their seats before the curtain goes up.

A host or hostess lets guests go first past the ticket taker. Once inside, guests stand aside while the stubs are handed to the usher stationed just inside the entrance, who points out the correct aisle. If an usher is at the head of the aisle, the host hands over the stubs and steps aside to let his guests go first. If the usher is far down the aisle, the host leads the way or he may walk down beside one of the women in his party, depending on how crowded the aisle is. He then directs his guests to enter the row in the order of seating he has planned, unless his wife is present, in which case she tells the guests where to sit.

When a man and a woman (or a hostess and a woman guest) are at the theater, the man (or hostess) takes the aisle seat or the one closest to it. When two couples are being seated, the men occupy the seats next to strangers, and the women sit side by side between the men. In this situation, if a woman leads the way into the row, she takes the third seat and stands until the man following has passed in front of her to reach the fourth seat. Since this is at best awkward and delaying, usually the man who will occupy the far seat is directed to go in first. If the couples are married, the wife of one usually sits beside the husband of the other. Much the same procedure is followed in larger parties, with the members switching seats, if they like, between acts.

Once a patron is seated, if others need to pass by to get to their seats, he either turns his knees aside or rises to make room. The newcomers say, "Thank you" or, if late, "Sorry," but in any case do not push past without some recognition of the cooperation given them.

In this country we face the stage when entering a row, but in England patrons face the people they are passing. Either way, particular care should be taken not to let sleeves or handbags drag against the heads of patrons already seated in the row ahead.

**INTERMISSIONS.** A man should ask a woman if she wants to go to the lobby during an intermission. If she does not want to, it is correct, though not usual, for him to excuse himself and leave her. In a group, however, it is not customary to leave one woman alone while the rest of the party goes out. Someone is expected to stay and keep her company. An elderly woman who prefers to remain seated should certainly do so, but a younger one who merely does not want to make the effort should nonetheless join the group rather than oblige someone to stay with her. "Excuse me" is the usual way of requesting passage past patrons who are keeping their seats.

The man on the aisle steps out and aside for the woman beside him and then follows her up the aisle; the rest of the party follow two by two. In returning, a woman precedes a man down the aisle. The main obligation of those who go to the lobby at intermission is to get back to their seats before the curtain rises.

**LEAVING.** Aisles are crowded when a show breaks, and a group joins the stream as best it can. Many people find that no time is lost by remaining seated until the first rush is over and then walking out without being pushed and jostled. In any case, each man in a group follows a woman in the party to try to give her what protection he can from the press of the crowd.

Unless it is really necessary to leave before the final curtain, patrons are expected to keep their seats until the cast has taken its curtain calls because it is disconcerting to performers as they bow their thanks for applause to see half the audience making for the exits.

A guest is not privileged to suggest leaving because the show is a bore. If the performance is truly a great disappointment, the host or hostess may broach the idea of leaving, but properly cannot insist if the guest wants to stay.

**MEETING AT.** In pleasant weather a host or hostess waits outside the theater for a guest; otherwise, in the outer lobby. If there is any chance that a guest may be late (especially if several guests are being entertained), it is best to have an understanding in advance that a ticket for the tardy guest will be left in his name at the box office.

**OPENING NIGHT.** Flowers for a member of the cast are best sent in a vase or basket, and should be timed to reach the theater before seven o'clock on an opening night. The sheaf of cut flowers sometimes presented to a woman star when she takes a curtain call usually is a tribute from the management, and all other flowers are sent to the dressing rooms. Opening-night telegrams are one of the theater's happy conventions, and the more a player receives, the better. Incidentally, it is best not to send a message specifically predicting a long run before an opening. Theater people consider it bad luck.

On an opening night, personal friends (and their guests) may make their way backstage after the final curtain without being announced. They use the doors leading to the stage from the auditorium, not the exterior stage door. Such calls are generally very brief and limited to a few words of congratulation and praise.

**REFRESHMENTS.** Candy or drinks bought in the lobby at intermission are consumed there or may be taken to someone who has remained seated. In the latter instance, empty drink containers are set on the floor under a seat before the performance resumes. If candy is to be eaten during the performance, crackling wrappings are best removed before the curtain goes up.

It is customary, though not at all obligatory, for a host to suggest a drink or other refreshment after a performance, especially if dinner has not preceded a theater party. If the host does not make this suggestion, one of the other men in the party may make it, in which case that guest picks up the tab, of course. Anyone who for good reason does not want to extend the evening is privileged to refuse with thanks.

**SEATING.** *See* "Entering and Seating," above.

**STANDEES.** It is an unwritten law that a standee has a continuing right throughout the performance to the place against the rail that he has taken on entering. Standees habitually seek a seat in a lounge to rest during intermissions, in full confidence that other standees will not grab their places during this absence. (If there are empty seats after the first act, a standee can usually secure one or two of them for himself and a companion by giving a dollar to one of the ushers.)

**TIPPING.** The coins displayed in the saucer of the washroom attendant indicate the tip expected—usually twenty-five cents for an attendant who provides a towel or gives any special service. Twenty-five cents is the standard tip to the checkroom attendant for each claim stub. The doorman gets twenty-five to fifty cents if he secures a cab or gives other extra service. Ushers are tipped in Europe (10 to 15 percent of the cost of a seat), but not in this country— except as noted under "Standees" above, or for taking a note backstage.

**VISITS BACKSTAGE.** An intermission is not the time to pay a visit backstage, but performers usually welcome a brief call from a friend at the end of a performance. Under all usual circumstances, a stranger who attempts to meet an actor or actress in this fashion is out of bounds, of course. And, except on opening nights, even a friend does not go backstage unannounced. The standard procedure is to hand a note (with a fifty-cent tip) to an usher at the first intermission. Any short message like "Enjoying your performance—hope to see you backstage after the show," written on a calling card or a leaf from a memo book, will serve. The usher brings back the player's answer during the next intermission.

WASHROOMS. If a man says, on entering a theater, "Do you want to go to the lounge?" the answer should be Yes, since his question may mean that he himself wants to be excused. A woman who wants to use the washroom need only say, when reaching the lobby, something like "I'll join you here shortly." A man tries not to leave a woman alone in a lobby, but if he finds it necessary to excuse himself during an intermission, he steers her close to a ladies' room and then says something like "I'll meet you here."

## THIRD, 3RD.  *See* NAMES.

## THIRD PERSON

Use of the third person when speaking directly to anyone is a formal form of address used mainly by servants. "Does Madam care to wait?" and "Will the Admiral leave a message?" are examples.

## TIES.  *See* CLOTHES.

## TIPPING

Tipping is a tiresome custom, but it is with us to stay. It is absurd to fight it. The only sensible thing to do is learn the rules about who, when, where, and how much—and then follow them.

**Manners in General.** Easy good manners in tipping call, first of all, for readily available small change. The woman who makes a doorman, porter, or cabdriver wait while she churns through her purse for a tip makes an awkward spectacle of herself and everyone else involved, and there is little excuse for a man—with all those pockets—who fumbles for change or must overtip unless he makes everyone wait while he sends a bill to be changed. A tip found readily and handed over casually is the mark of a person accustomed to service. So is giving the correct amount. The overly lavish tip is second only to the niggardly one as a mark of inexperience.

Certain tips are obligatory. Tips are a standard part of the income of bellboys, porters, waiters, and beauty-shop employees. It is cheating to skip or skimp tips to them and to many others who serve the public—though by no means to all who do so. Tips to people in certain public-service positions are an insult. A good general rule is: Don't tip government employees or anyone with professional or managerial standing (with the exceptions noted below).

The manner in which a tip is given is also important. Even if the tip is an obligatory one, the fiction is maintained that it is a reward for exceptional service. Either a casual word, gesture, or smile indicating thanks is a correct part of a tip handed directly to anyone.

ABROAD. Americans abroad frequently neglect to give certain obligatory tips, or tip far too much because unaware of local customs quite different from ours. It is a widespread custom in many foreign countries to add 10 to 20 percent to the total of certain bills "for service." This charge is entered as a separate item on a hotel bill, but not on a restaurant bill if *service compris* or other words meaning "tip included" are printed on the menu. When in doubt, ask, "Service complete?" In a restaurant, if the answer is Yes, it means that an acceptable tip, which will be divided among the staff, is a built-in charge. In practice, however, any small coins brought as change are left for a waiter, and exceptional service always is rewarded by an extra amount, usually no more than 5 percent. If the answer is No, tip the standard 15 to 25 percent, depending on the character of the restaurant, length of time the table is occupied, and amount of extra service requested. Washroom attendants are always tipped, and except in a few countries theater ushers must be tipped. Even if a stout service charge is added to a hotel bill, additional tips are required. Porters, bellboys, and room-service waiters are given small change at the time of service, and tips in addition to the standard service charge on the bill are given at check-out time, or earlier on the day of departure, to everyone else on the staff who has given direct service. This includes the chambermaid, valet, elevator boys, concierge, doormen, and the man who shines shoes left outside a room. Don't worry about finding all these people. They will make themselves available. As a general rule, it is better to give these tips separately, not in a lump sum to the concierge to be divided at his discretion.

See also "Guides" below.

**AIRLINES.** No one connected with an airline is tipped, including the men who bring luggage from plane to claiming station, unless they also act as porters and carry bags to or from the entrance of the terminal.

**APARTMENT HOUSE STAFF.** The services of the staff are supplied as part of the rent, but many residents of higher-priced apartment houses give staff members who serve them directly a monthly tip. A building employee asked to give any extra service, such as moving heavy items to and from a storage room, helping load a car, walking dogs, or anything else not strictly a routine duty, should be tipped. In addition, all staff members, including the superintendent, usually are tipped at Christmastime, though a superintendent with managerial status generally gets a bottle or other gift rather than money. Amounts vary according to the size and character of the apartment house and the income of the resident. Guests of an apartment-house resident should tip members of the staff if they carry luggage, park a car, or give any other special service.

**ATTENDANTS.** Rest-room, checkroom, and locker-room attendants are almost always tipped.

See separate entries like CLUBS and individual sports for details.

**BABY-SITTERS.** They are considered professionals, and are not tipped as a routine practice.

**BARBERSHOPS.** Tips in barbershops depend on how many employees are involved in the service. In most shops, 15 to 20 percent is customary. If a manicurist, shoeshine boy, or other specialist is used, each is tipped separately, and the overall tip runs from 20 to 25 percent. An owner or manager who works only at the appointment desk has professional standing, and is not tipped. The owner who works along with his employees is offered a tip, and is given a chance to accept or refuse.

**BEAUTY SHOPS.** In most shops, 15 to 20 percent is customary if one operator does a shampoo, set, and manicure, with an additional fifteen cents or twenty-five cents to the dressing-room attendant. If several operators are involved, each is tipped separately and the overall tip runs from 20 to 25 percent.

Tips may be left at the desk when the bill is paid. More often they are handed to each operator or dropped into an apron or shirt pocket, always with spoken thanks. As in a barbershop, an owner or manager who works only at the appointment desk has professional standing and is not tipped. The owner or manager who works along with the staff should be offered a tip and given the chance to accept or refuse.

**BELLBOYS.** A bellboy usually is tipped for each service at the time he does it. The minimum is a quarter, more for any special service such as a trip outside the hotel for some item at a store, or for going with a guest to a garage. When he handles luggage, the rate in all but luxury hotels is a quarter for each bag, though the minimum is fifty cents when he carries one or two pieces of luggage to or from a room, and usually more for large or extremely heavy bags.

**BOAT CREWS.** The captain and mate of a privately chartered fishing boat are professionals and are treated as such with one exception. They usually expect and will accept tips, just as do most professional guides. Captain and crew are not tipped on a large, privately owned boat. But a waiter and the steward or stewardess of a privately owned pleasure boat are tipped at the end of a cruise of several days, just as the household staff of a large country place would be after a weekend. If a guest is taken out to a boat in a club launch, the launchman is not tipped. If the guest finds his own water taxi, the operator is tipped just as a taxi driver would be.

**BUS DRIVERS.** These are professionals, and are not tipped unless they also serve as guides on a sight-seeing tour. If they expect a tip they will make it crystal clear.

**BUSBOYS.** Because waiters share their tips with the busboys assisting them, a separate tip is not necessary.

**CADDIES.** *See* "Golf," below.

**CAFETERIA STAFF.** Customs vary widely. In many localities it is now quite usual to leave the busboy who clears a table in a cafeteria about ten cents per person.

**CATERER'S STAFF.** The host tips the caterer's staff at about the same rate customary in a good restaurant. The tip is most conveniently handled by adding 15 percent to the caterer's bill and letting him make the distribution to the staff, though in the case of a small staff the tipping may be done individually, or a sum to be divided among them may be handed to the individual who presents the bill. Guests do not tip the caterer's staff.

**CHAUFFEURS.** The usual tip for the driver of a hired car is about 20 percent. It may be given to him in cash, or added to the bill he presents to a charge customer to sign. The general rule that servants are not tipped unless a guest makes an overnight stay is followed for the drivers of privately owned cars. A guest who is run across town after lunch, for example, says "Thank you," and is not expected to tip, and never tips if the owner is in the car under this circumstance. However, if the chauffeur makes a long run into town from the country after a dinner party, a tip is in order. This can be anywhere from one to five dollars, depending on the hour, distance, size of party, and weather. The driver who takes a guest of a few hours to and from a station is not tipped. He is tipped one or two dollars by an overnight guest, depending on the length of the stay and the amount of service given during it. An extra tip is expected if a chauffeur washes a guest's car or runs any special errands.

**CHECKROOM STAFF.** It is never a mistake to offer a tip to a checkroom attendant in a public place. The usual amount is a quarter. If tips have been prepaid, as at some banquets and dances, or if forbidden, as in some clubs and museums, it will be courteously refused.

**CHEFS.** These professionals are not tipped.
*See* "Cooks" below, for exceptions.

**CHILDREN.** A guest may make a present of money to a child, but children should not be tipped for running an errand or doing any other routine service to make a guest comfortable, since they are expected to share the duties of hospitality. If a neighbor's child is hired to mow the lawn or feed the cat, he should be paid the sum agreed and may be given a present (or an extra sum for extra time and service), but is not tipped since he is a social equal.

**CIGARETTE GIRLS** *See* "Nightclubs," below.

**CLUB STAFF.** Each club has its own rules. Some prohibit tipping. Some add a service charge to meal checks so that small change is never needed. In others, tips are given on a pay-as-you-go basis to locker-room and checkroom attendants, waiters, and doormen, with a quarter the usual minimum. The guest of a member leaves the tipping to his host under usual circumstances. The non-member who has been given a guest-member card takes care to tip for all services, however, if tips are permitted by club rules.

**COOKS.** The general rule is that staff members not seen by a patron or a guest are not tipped. A cook who ranks as a chef is a professional and is not tipped. However, if a cook or chef in a hotel is asked to prepare fish or game brought in by a sportsman, payment for that special service is in order. It is the custom, especially in the South and West, for a regular guest in the house of friends to seek out a cook and slip her a tip occasionally. Any cook who has the status of "mother's helper" or companion is not tipped.

**DANCES.** Tipping at a party at anyone's house is not correct. Parking attendants, checkroom and washroom attendants may be offered tips at a private party at club or hotel. If the host has already taken care of them, the tips will be refused. At public or subscription dances guests tip for all services as they would in a nightclub.

**DELIVERY MEN AND BOYS.** Railway Express drivers and delivery men from department stores and furniture shops are not tipped, though it is only fair to offer payment for extra services—the opening of heavy crates, for example, if such work is not part of their regular duties. The boy who makes deliveries for a market is tipped if he has made the trip in driving rain or snow, even if it is not the local custom to tip for grocery deliveries. Liquor-store delivery boys are tipped. All delivery boys who bring ice and other supplies for parties are tipped. In higher-income neighborhoods it is the custom to give Christmas tips to laundrymen and others who make regular deliveries. Boys who deliver flowers and telegrams usually are tipped during the Christmas season. At other times a tip is not obligatory unless the weather is dreadful and trip unusually long and troublesome. Boys employed by special messenger firms are tipped, when necessary, by the person who pays for the trip, and so the receiver need not do so.

**DOORMEN.** The patron of a theater, restaurant, or shop and a resident of an apartment house or hotel need not tip the doorman for opening the door of a car when it pulls up or of a cab already waiting. He should be tipped a quarter if he makes some special effort to get a cab, helps with luggage, or parks a car. A nightclub doorman is tipped for opening a car door for a departing patron, however, and any passerby who joins regular patrons of an establishment who are waiting for cabs is expected to hand over a tip, and must always do so if he asks the doorman to signal a cab for him. A resident at an hotel or apartment house usually tips his doorman on a fairly regular basis.

**ELEVATOR OPERATORS.** In hotels, elevator boys are not tipped unless they have given some unusual service. In apartment houses the regular staff usually is tipped at Christmastime, and it is customary to tip for special services such as parking a car or bringing in heavy luggage.

**ENTERTAINERS.** An entertainer of professional standing is never tipped. A host is expected to "buy a drink" by handing over a bill to a piano player in a modest café if he has asked for special songs. The strolling minstrel regularly employed in a restaurant is not tipped if he moves on after one selection. If asked for another, he expects a tip—and if he sticks around a tip probably is needed to get him on his way.

**FIREMEN.** A present for some extraordinary service may be given, never a tip.

**GARAGE ATTENDANTS.** Men who deliver cars from hotel garages are tipped. Men who handle cars in a transient parking garage or lot are generally not tipped. Employees in a garage where a car is kept on a monthly basis are tipped when they go to some special effort to dust a car or load it. Garage mechanics are seldom tipped. However, if one works overtime in an emergency he deserves and usually will accept a dollar or so if accompanied by some such words as "I owe you a drink."

**GAS-STATION ATTENDANTS.** In spite of all of that good, cheerful, free service—no tip.

**GOLF.** A golf pro is a professional. He can be given a drink or a present, but not a tip. A caddie master is not tipped. Fifty cents a round is the average minimum tip for a caddie, though the amount varies regionally and in different clubs. If two players share one caddie, he should be given a double tip.

**GOOD SAMARITANS.** Tipping a stranger who volunteers help in an emergency is a delicate matter and can be decided only by guess and instinct. The motorist who is so extremely kind as to stop to help change a tire, for example, may be insulted if a tip is offered. In most circumstances, the Good Samaritan is giving a service that he could not possibly be hired to do. On the other hand, if the Good Samaritan is someone who apparently could use the money, a tip may be offered on the basis of appreciation for the time that he otherwise would have devoted to his own interests. Appearances are deceiving, though. Millionaires as well as migrant workers wear blue jeans, so it is essential to feel one's way carefully in this matter.

**GUESTS.** The general rule is that only a guest who stays overnight in a private residence tips a domestic employee. In a restaurant or club, the tip is part of the host's obligation. Let him pay it.

**GUIDES.** Government employees in uniform who act as lecturers or guides, such as Park Service personnel, should not be offered tips. In some churches, especially in foreign countries, a regular employee who conducts sightseers around expects a tip. It is perfectly proper to offer one. If not appropriate it will be courteously refused. In this case, some donation to the contribution box is obligatory. Hunting, fishing, and camping guides usually expect a tip of 10 to 20 percent. Taxi drivers hired by the hour as driver-guides are tipped the usual 15 to 20 percent. Drivers or conductors of sight-seeing buses and boats make it quite evident whether or not they expect a tip by where they stand or by a positive hint at the end of a tour. Guides hired individually expect a tip.

**HEADWAITERS.** A tip is not given unless a headwaiter is asked for a ringside table or other special consideration, or unless he has made some special effort in planning an elaborate party or has been of direct help otherwise. Even so, he is not tipped if he is the owner.

**HOSPITALS.** See HOSPITALS.

**HOTELS.** Tips are geared to the quality of the hotel, the size of accommodations, and the service expected. Many people make their first tips generous as a sign to the staff that they want the best of prompt service and expect to pay for it. The manager, his assistant managers, and the desk clerks are professionals and are not tipped. Neither are social directors, public stenographers, and travel clerks. Telephone and elevator operators are not tipped by transient guests. Permanent guests usually remember telephone operators and elevator men from time to time or on special holidays. All others who give direct service such as doormen, bellboys, porters, and waiters are tipped at the time of service. A tip is left for the chambermaid on departure. A transient guest does not tip a headwaiter unless he goes to some special effort to arrange a big party. A permanent resident usually gives the headwaiter a tip about once a month if he is a frequent patron of the dining room. Valets are not tipped consistently.

*See* HOTELS AND MOTELS for full details.

**HOUSEGUESTS.** The general rule is that a houseguest does not tip any staff member whom he does not see, but there are exceptions depending on the length of stay, the size of the staff, and the relation of the guest to the host. A chef is not tipped but a cook of less pretensions may be, and should be if she has been put to any special effort to prepare dishes for someone on a diet, for example. In a house with a large staff, the maid who takes care of a room, the person who does any pressing, the waitress, houseman, and chauffeur are tipped at time of departure.

See HOUSEGUESTS, for details.

**LAUNDRYMEN.** Delivery men are not tipped, though it is the custom in high-income neighborhoods to remember at Christmastime all who give such regular services.

**LIFEGUARDS.** They are professionals and therefore not tipped.

**LOST-AND-FOUND ARTICLES.** When a package, umbrella, scarf, or similar article is found by an employee of a store, restaurant, or other such establishment and turned in to the Lost and Found Department, a tip is not customary. However, when a wallet, purse, or valuable piece of jewelry is found by a janitor, cleaning woman, hotel chambermaid, taxi driver, porter, or waiter, a reward should be given. The amount varies so considerably with the circumstances of the loser and the finder that it is impossible to arrive at rules, except that if a sizable sum is involved about 10 percent is customary. In the case of a lost pet, the finder should be reimbursed for any expenses he has incurred in advertising his find or taking care of the pet, and on occasion, a tip may be given.

**LUNCH COUNTERS.** Customs vary widely. Increasingly, it is the practice to leave a minimum of ten cents for the server at a quick-lunch counter and about 10 percent of a check at the lunch bars serving complete meals.

**MAIDS.**   See "Houseguests," "Hotels," and "Motels" in this section.

**MANAGERS.** As a general rule, a person with the title of manager (in a hotel, restaurant, beauty shop, or any other business) has professional standing and is not tipped. If a manager performs the same services as do his employees, a tip should be offered, however.

**MARKETS.** Clerks and butchers who serve in small shops are sometimes tipped at Christmastime by regular customers. Owners and managers are not. Employees in big supermarkets are rarely tipped even at Christmas. Delivery boys usually expect a quarter for bringing a heavy load to the house, though in some localities it is not the custom to tip for delivery of groceries. Boys who carry merchandise from check-out counter to car as a standard service provided by a supermarket usually do not expect a tip, but will take one when it is offered for a special service.

**MASSEURS AND MASSEUSES.** About 20 percent is the standard tip for services at the operator's regular place of business, about 25 percent if the operator goes to the client.

**MESSENGERS.** Boys employed by bonded messenger service firms usually are not tipped by the sender from whom they pick up a package or by the person to whom they deliver it, but they will accept a tip and should be given one if asked to wait or go to any other special trouble. Messenger boys delivering flowers and telegrams count on receiving tips at about half their stops; though a tip is not obligatory, it is always welcome. A tip is customary when a delivery is made just before Christmas, and at other seasons also if the messenger has taken any unusual pains or come an unusually long way, especially in bad weather.

**MOTELS.** The man behind the desk is not tipped, even if he helps with luggage or brings ice. No tips are expected in modestly priced motels. Where rates are the same as in a good hotel, a tip is left for the chambermaid, especially after a stay of several days, and always if she has been put to any extra trouble to restore order.

**MOVERS.** *See* MOVING.

**NEWSBOYS.** There is no need to tip boys who sell papers on the street or at stands, except for special service. In some localities, boys with regular paper routes are not tipped when they collect the monthly bill, but usually are at Christmas. In others, the regular paper boy expects a tip more frequently.

**NIGHTCLUBS.** A headwaiter is not tipped unless asked for a special table or other consideration. An entertainer is not tipped, though one invited to join a table for a while should be offered a drink as any other guest would be. In modest clubs, a piano player can be offered a dollar or more "for a drink," if asked to play special selections. Everyone else is tipped. A quarter is minimum to a dressing-room attendant, even if the only service is saying "Good evening"; for the cigarette girl who brings her tray to a table; for the checkroom girl and the doorman, even if he does no more than open a door of a waiting car. A waiter is paid as in an expensive restaurant—a minimum of 20 percent of the tab.

**NURSES.** *See* HOSPITALS.

**PAGE BOYS.** They share the delicate talents of bellboys when it comes to letting a client know that a tip is expected. A quarter is the usual tip if one is indicated.

**PARKING LOTS.** The average parking-lot attendant is not tipped unless he is asked to go to special effort to keep a car in front, ready to pull out. Boys who take a car at a nightclub, hotel, or café and park and deliver it are tipped. Even if the client parks his own car in the "free" space at a nightclub, when an attendant is on duty he expects a tip for watching it.

**POLICEMEN.** A present for some extraordinary service may be given, never a tip.

**PORTERS.** All porters and redcaps are tipped. In many stations the rate is fixed at twenty-five or thirty-five cents for each piece of luggage. It is customary to add a tip above any such set rate, the extra amount depending on time and service given.

*See also* "Trains," below.

**POSTMEN.** A mailman is not tipped for the regular performance of his duties. However, in many big cities and other areas it is customary to give the regular delivery man a present at Christmastime—usually money tucked into a Christmas card rather than handed over directly as a tip would be to a delivery boy. The amount depends on the number of regular postmen on a route and the circumstances of the householder. Christmas tips are not obligatory, but are in the nature of presents given freely.

**PRIVATE DINNERS.** An employee of the host is not tipped except by an overnight guest.

For exceptions, *see* "Chauffeurs" and "Cooks," above.

**PUBLIC DINNERS.** Often the waiter's tip is included in the price of admission to public or club functions, but an extra tip is called for if a waiter is asked to give any special service. If tip is not included, a salver will be passed by a waiter, usually just before the dessert course. Men tip for themselves and their guests. The waiter does not ask women to tip when men are at the table, but a woman unaccompanied at a public dinner should pay her own tip and not allow the man who happens to be seated beside her to pay, or skimp the waiter by ignoring him. The usual tip for a public, semipublic, club, conference, or convention meal is less than the tip an individual would leave at a restaurant in the same hotel. A dollar per person is usual for meals between eight and ten dollars. If a host has filled a whole table, it is his duty to get the eye of the waiter with the silver tray and tip for his whole party. Coatroom attendants may or may not have been tipped in advance by the dinner committee. The best plan is to offer a tip. It will be refused if other arrangements have been made.

**REST ROOMS.**    *See "Washrooms," below.*

**RESTAURANTS.**    The maître d'hôtel or headwaiter is not tipped unless special attention has been given to advance planning of a party. In such case about 10 percent of the total bill is customary. Waiters are tipped about 15 percent, but 20 percent is usual today in big cities, and 25 percent is not unusual for exceptional service. If two or more waiters serve a table, one tip is left with whichever presents the bill. The busboy need not be tipped since the waiter shares his tips with him.

If a wine steward serves the wine, he is tipped about 10 percent of its cost, but usually no sum under a dollar. If drinks are taken at the bar, a tip of 15 to 20 percent is left for the barman even if charges are put on the table check. A quarter is standard for the hatcheck girl. A washroom attendant gets ten cents to a quarter. A doorman is tipped a quarter or more if he goes to some effort to call a taxi or if he parks a car, but usually not for opening the door only, except at nightclubs.

**ROOM SERVICE.**    Even if a hotel makes an extra charge for meals served in a room, the waiter gets the standard tip of about 15 percent of a tab, and 20 percent if the charge is quite low, with fifty cents the minimum.

**SALESPEOPLE.**    Clerks in stores and markets are not tipped.

**SERVICE CHARGES.**    Even in hotels and restaurants where a percentage is added to the bill, supposedly to cover tips, it is customary to add a small additional tip for waiters and to tip others for extra services at the time they are performed.

**SHIPS.**    Officers are not tipped. This includes the purser. Tips are given at the bar and elsewhere for any bills paid at the time of service. Otherwise, tips are handed out at the end of a voyage. About 10 percent or slightly more of a fare is the usual amount devoted to tips. Of this, about 40 percent goes to the room steward or stewardess, 40 percent to the dining-room steward; the remaining 20 percent is divided among the others who have given direct service.

*See* TRAVEL, for details.

**SHOESHINE BOYS.**    Who could face himself after walking away without tipping a small sidewalk entrepreneur a dime or so? It is also an understood part of the deal that a customer tips the shoeshine man who makes the rounds of an office, operates a regular stand, or is available in a barbershop. The rate depends on the place and the client.

**SIGHT-SEEING TOURS.**    The guide for a sight-seeing tour usually makes it quite clear whether he will welcome tips. The courier who acts as social director as well as guide or lecturer for a group on a travel tour is not tipped, but often is given a collective present by the members of the party at the end of a successful holiday.

**SPORTS EVENTS.**    *See* separate listings.

**STARTERS.**    It is not necessary to tip a cab starter at a station. He is there to see that passengers are loaded in their proper turn.

**TAXIS.**    In all big cities cabdrivers expect tips and should get them, since tips are part of their livelihood. In some small towns, the drivers do not take tips for granted—but accept them with a gratitude heartwarming to anyone accustomed to the offhand manners of cab jockeys in big cities. The usual tip is fifteen cents for a fare under fifty cents, twenty or twenty-five cents under a dollar, and about 20 percent over a dollar.

**TELEPHONE GIRLS.**    They are not tipped except very occasionally by a hotel guest who makes special demands on the switchboard, such as a series of conference or long-distance calls, or incessant local ones if he asks an operator to act as a secretary and place them for him.

**THEATERS.** Ushers are not tipped in this country. An exception is made if an usher is asked to take a message backstage, and a standee sometimes slips an usher a dollar for an unoccupied seat. Checkroom and rest-room attendants are tipped. So is a doorman in the unlikely event that he can secure a cab.

**TRADESMEN.** Owners in selling positions are not tipped. Only their delivery boys are.

**TRAINS.** Conductors are not tipped. A Pullman porter expects a dollar a night from a passenger occupying a berth or roomette, and a bit more from one in a compartment. On a daytime trip, a porter expects from twenty-five cents to a dollar, depending on the service he has given. Waiters and bar-car attendants are tipped as in any good restaurant. *See also* "Porters," above.

**VALETS.** *See* HOTELS AND MOTELS; HOUSEGUESTS.

**WASHROOMS.** There is seldom any doubt about the expectation of the attendant for a tip. If that little saucer with its display of coins is in evidence, a tip should be left even if the attendant does no more than hand a towel, since tips are a standard part of the income on that job. In department stores, rest-room attendants are on regular salary and expect no tip, except for some exceptional service.

**WINE STEWARDS.** A separate tip of 10 to 15 percent, but usually no sum under a dollar is given to a wine steward.

**YACHTS.** *See* "Boat Crews," above.

## TOAST

A whole slice of toast may be buttered at one time, but pieces are then broken or cut off— the whole slice is not lifted to the mouth. When a platter of food on toast is offered, an entire portion, including the toast, is taken even if the toast is not wanted. It need not be eaten, but should not be left on the platter.

## TOASTS

Drinking to the health and happiness of a person or the success of an enterprise is a custom that goes far back in ancient times. We get the word "toasting" for this ceremony through another old custom—the serving of a piece of toast in the goblet with mead or other alcoholic brews. The bread, when saturated, sank to the bottom, and so when someone proposed a health and challenged "Toast!" the cup had to be drained in order to slide the toast down after the drink.

Today, in all but a very few cases, it is not necessary or customary to drain a glass when drinking a toast. A sip is enough. Indeed, teetotalers need only go through the motion of drinking, merely raising a glass to the lips without taking even a token sip. However, it is the greatest rudeness not to join a toast in at least this ritual gesture. When glasses are not drained, a series of toasts may be drunk from the same glass of wine.

A toast usually is drunk with wine, but may also be drunk with beer, punch, or whiskey. It is not strictly correct to *propose* a formal toast with water, cocktails, or liqueurs, but of course individuals can "toast" one another by lifting glasses of any liquid, including milk.

A toast may be proposed and drunk without rising. On formal occasions, the person proposing the toast stands to make it and all others stand to drink it except the person being toasted. Under any circumstances, the subject of a toast does not raise his glass until the others have drunk, since that would be drinking to himself. After the others are seated, a man (except the President of the United States or other very high dignitaries) rises and bows his acknowledgment or says a brief "Thank you," and then may lift his glass to them or may propose a toast to the host and hostess or some other member of the party, depending on the circumstances. A woman does not rise to acknowledge a toast unless she is making a speech in answer.

**BACHELOR DINNER.** The first toast is always to the bride, and is always proposed by the bridegroom. Glasses are drained and, in the past, were broken (*see below*). The best man then proposes a toast to the groom, but the glasses are not drained or broken after any toast but the one to the bride.

**BANQUETS.** Toasts at a public or semipublic dinner are proposed with the dessert or at the end of the meal, since very frequently both the giving and accepting of toasts on these occasions involve speeches. The presiding officer or a toastmaster proposes the first toast. Other toasts may follow, but they are proposed only by those seated at the speakers' table, not by a member of the general audience, and anyone at the speakers' table must first gain the toastmaster's attention and permission before proposing a toast.

**BREAKING GLASSES.** At one time it was the custom to snap the stem of a wineglass with the fingers or to fling the glass into a fireplace after drinking a toast on certain very special occasions, especially after the toast to the bride at the groom's bachelor dinner. This custom is rarely observed today, and certainly not unless the person proposing the toast sets the example.

**CASUAL TOASTS.** Often, when several people are drinking or dining together, they raise their glasses—and sometimes clink them—without words as a symbolic toast, or use traditional sayings that mean "to your health," such as "Skål" (Scandinavian), "Salut" and "A votre santé" (French), "Prosit" (German), "Salud" (Spanish), and so on. They do not rise, and since the toast is a mutual exchange of good wishes, all drink together. Likewise, at a party, sometimes one person raises his glass to another across a table or a room, and they drink a silent toast to each other.

**CHRISTENINGS.** The first toast at a christening party is proposed to the child's health and happiness by a godfather at the end of the christening lunch or dinner, or when drinks are first served at a reception.

**ENGAGEMENTS.** The girl's father proposes the first toast to his daughter and her fiancé at an announcement party. In the absence of her father, the closest of her male relatives who is present performs this duty.

**FIRST TOASTS.** At a private party, the first toast usually is proposed as soon as the first glass of wine is poured (with the exceptions noted). The host (again with the exceptions noted) proposes it to the person or the couple being honored—the new graduate, the couple celebrating a wedding anniversary, the person whose birthday it is, the special guest of honor, and so on. Under certain circumstances, the first toast is properly made to someone absent. For example, the first toast would be to the President of the United States at a public dinner sponsored by his political party, even if he is not there.

**WEDDING BREAKFASTS, RECEPTIONS, ETC.** The best man proposes the first toast, always to the bride and groom jointly. Both bride and groom rise in acknowledgment, and he says a few words of thanks.

## TOILET WATER

Toilet water is second in strength to perfume, *which see*.

**TOILETS.**   See BATHROOMS AND WASHROOMS.

## TOOTHPICKS

Toothpicks are not properly made available at the table, and it is startlingly bad manners to use the tines of a fork or the tip of a knife as a substitute. If a bit of bone or other sharp piece of food cannot be dislodged by an inconspicuous leverage of the tongue, there is nothing to do but endure the discomfort until it can be dealt with in private.

Toothpicks used with cocktail food are put in an ashtray, never under any circumstances returned to the serving platter.

## TOWELS

For some curious reason, a surprising number of guests who would be shocked at the idea of using another person's napkin will ignore the lineup of fresh guest towels and dry their hands on someone's used bath towel—to the bafflement of the hostess. Guest towels are not an ornament. No matter how fancy, they are meant for use. A used towel should be put back on the rack neatly—but not refolded so that it seems untouched. The hostess who provides paper towels is sure to provide a wastebasket for them, and that is where used ones belong.

It is inconsiderate to scrub off makeup, especially lipstick, on a towel. Any hostess who has pretty bath linen is almost certain to have tissues available. Otherwise, use toilet paper. These rules should be observed in hotels also. Hotel towels should not be used as shoe-polishing cloths, either.

*See also* HOUSEGUESTS; INITIALS AND MONOGRAMS.

## TRAVEL

Today, more of us are traveling more frequently and to more distant places than ever before. Wherever we go, around the world or to the next city, and for whatever purpose, business or pleasure, each of us is an ambassador from his own community. An open mind (specifically, a resistance to boasting that "our ways are best," and a receptivity to what other people have, in their turn, found best) will make any trip more rewarding for the visited as well as the visitor— as will observance of these six rules that form the credo of every experienced traveler:

1. Don't try to see the world in two weeks. It is far better to make fewer stops and really see what each place has to offer than to race so far and fast that the main results of a trip are memories of porters, taxis, hotel rooms, packing and unpacking—and a crying need for a vacation to recover from the holiday.

2. Make firm reservations when traveling in peak holiday seasons, but don't plan an activity for every hour of every day in advance. Travel is both stimulating and exhausting. Leave some open time for rest as well as for the unexpected opportunities for fun.

3. Travel light. No one has more than two hands, and every bag over two per person is a hazard because almost inevitably there will be occasions when all porters and cab drivers seem to have vanished for lunch.

4. Take only noncrushable clothes. Avoid taffetas, organdies, and other fabrics that need pressing after each packing. Concentrate on the dependable knits, soft silks, and drip-dry materials.

5. Carry sizable sums in traveler's checks.

6. Take more money than seems necessary.

**BON VOYAGE PARTIES.** Many people love to have a group of friends see them off. Others much prefer a welcome home party to the big send-off that frequently only adds to the flurry and confusion of departure. Under any circumstances, a surprise party just before departure or any scheme to "pour" someone aboard is neither sensible nor kind. Nearly always, a bon voyage party several days in advance of departure is the most practical.

*See also* "Gifts for the Traveler" and "Ships," following.

**BUSES.** Touring by bus is enormously popular because it is economical. It is also an excellent way to see many parts of the country not reached by other public transportation, and is comfortable and not too confining if enough stopovers for sight-seeing and sleeping are scheduled.

**Clothes.** All but short-run buses are air-conditioned, and so the same clothes suitable for train and plane travel are appropriate. Women are most comfortable in lightweight dresses that will not wrinkle badly or bind during long hours of sitting. A jacket or topcoat for use at stops should be kept at hand. Passengers heroic enough to take overnight bus trips often slip their feet out of their shoes and loosen belts and collars, but otherwise they do not make any change from usual daytime dress.

**Drivers.** On the bus the driver is the government. What he says, goes. His primary responsibility is to keep his bus on schedule—safely. That takes all his attention on the road. Talk with him at stops, but while he is at the wheel do not engage him in conversation or in any other way distract his attention, except in a real emergency such as an illness that calls for an unscheduled stop.

**Food.** Ask about scheduled stops when buying a ticket. Some few deluxe nonstop buses on special runs carry a stewardess who serves sandwich meals, though most buses on long runs make stops for meals at the regular hours and often make shorter "coffee break" stops between, especially if there is no toilet aboard. Some passengers prefer to take picnic lunches and eat them in their seats. Nothing wrong with that so long as peelings and wrappings are disposed of neatly and children are kept from leaving the upholstery sticky or stained.

**Luggage.** The space in the overhead racks is limited at best, and is needed for wraps and light hand luggage. Heavy or bulky luggage is stowed in the baggage boot, and only smaller bags containing essentials needed during the trip should be carried aboard. Generally, it is entirely safe to leave possessions of minor value in one's seat during a stop, but just as on any train or plane, it is not wise to leave valuable objects like fur coats and cameras unguarded.

**Seats.** It is possible to reserve a seat on some buses at the time the ticket is bought. On others, the first passengers in line have the first choice. Many people consider the front pair of seats on the right the best because they give an unobstructed view of the road. Others choose seats toward the center, since this location is subject to somewhat less motion than seats in the extreme rear. Except for the sight-seeing advantages of window seats, there is not a great deal of difference in comfort because modern buses are equipped with shock absorbers that control undue motion anywhere, front or rear, and antiglare glass and air conditioning make the shady and sunny sides equally pleasant. Even if seats are not reserved, each passenger has the right throughout the trip to the seat he selected on boarding. He does not lose it after a meal stop, for example. The customary way to avoid confusion is to leave a magazine or some other minor possession on the seat as a sign to new passengers that the place is already claimed.

**Tipping.** A bus driver is not tipped even though he has assisted a passenger with luggage. Porters in bus stations are tipped at the regular rate—at least twenty-five cents per bag; fifty cents for each if he has carried luggage for any distance or has been kept waiting for it—and usually a quarter more in addition.

**CHILDREN.** Long trips are no fun for little children, and they in their turn can be trying to other passengers. But parents who take some standard precautions will not come back agreeing with Robert Benchley: "There are two classes of travel—first class, and with children."

1. Take along toys (small, non-noisy ones) to keep them amused, and also expect to be a fairly assiduous social director. Looking out of the window is not enough to keep children quiet and in their seats. In short order, scenery all begins to look alike to them unless a game gives it meaning—counting spotted cows, red barns, out-of-state license plates, and so on.

2. Avoid the disasters of motion sickness to whatever extent possible. Don't "entertain" a child by letting him fill up on candy and carbonated drinks at stops or in transit. Take plain crackers along for snacking. Keep a sharp eye

out for that telltale pallor around the mouth, and be prepared at all times to protect clothes, upholstery, and other passengers from an upheaval.

3.  Take along a small pillow (except on planes, where they are always available) so that a child can nap comfortably—and trust to luck that he will feel like doing so.

**CUSTOMS.** The possessions of travelers are subject to customs inspection at any national border, and a stiff import tax may be due on items exceeding a specified cost or quantity (notably cigars, cigarettes, and liquor). It is, therefore, a sound precaution to register any foreign-made possessions with the United States Customs before taking them out of this country—a German or Japanese camera, for example. Otherwise, an import tax may be levied when they are brought back to the United States.

**GIFTS FOR THE TRAVELER.** A bulky box of candy or any other sizable or heavy gift presented just before departure is nearly always a mixed blessing to a traveler. Either he has to jam it into a carefully packed bag (and perhaps pay an overweight charge on a plane); or, if his heavy luggage is already checked through, he is forced to carry it aboard himself and find room for it in his seat. For a woman, a small flower to wear is often a welcome little last-minute present, but many women feel that an orchid or a large corsage makes them look too much like Madam Chairman of the Club leaving for a convention.

*See also* "Ships," following.

In general, bon voyage presents are best delivered well in advance of departure so that the traveler need not go off laden with duplicates. Passport cases, film, stick cologne, clear plastic envelopes of various sizes, and other lightweight, nonbreakable, and leakproof articles are good choices. A thoughtful present for the traveler headed abroad is a packet of bills and coins in the currency of the country of his first stop so that he has money in hand on arrival for tips and cab fares.

**GUIDES.** The person in charge of a group on a trip of any length is variously known as a courier, tour guide, or tour director. He or she operates as a social equal and, indeed, is usually considered the star of the party. Guides of this status are never tipped, though very often a group shows appreciation at the conclusion of a happy trip by taking up a collection and giving the courier a present of some kind. On sight-seeing buses and other shorter trips, a guide will make it quite clear if a tip is welcome. A quarter from each client is sufficient for a guide who has moved around with a party of thirty or more people for several hours to half a day. If the group is between ten and fifteen people, tips usually run from fifty cents to a dollar, depending on the length of the tour and the services rendered. Individual guides hired by the hour or the day generally receive from 10 to 20 percent of the basic fee.

The difference between a good guide and a poor one can mean the difference between a delightful and profitable excursion and a tiresome and somewhat profitless one. The hotel desk is usually the best source of information about reliable guides and guided tours. Taking a guide who offers his services in the street is risking time with a person who may be ill-equipped for the duty or whose main interest may be in steering the traveler to shops and restaurants where the guide gets a rake-off.

The guide hired for a short time will indicate whether he expects to eat with his client—and at the client's expense. If the guide says something like, "I'll come back for you in an hour," then he expects to pay for his own meal and eat it alone. If he makes no such statement, the patron usually suggests, "You'll lunch with us, of course," and if the offer is accepted, pays for the guide's meal. Sometimes, however, if the price set for a tour specifies the inclusion of all expenses, the guide will pay for his patron's lunch and his own as well.

**HOTELS AND MOTELS.**   *See* separate entry.

**INSURANCE.** A short-term floater covering personal possessions against loss and damage is a sensible precaution, easily available at quite low cost. Ask any travel agent where and how to get one.

**LUGGAGE.** The day of trunks for travel is virtually past. Today, most travelers use lightweight hand luggage of various sizes and do not worry if the pieces are mismatched so long as they are attractive and in good condition. The most generally useful pieces are:

*Overnight bags:* pieces small enough to fit under a plane seat or overhead in the rack on a train or bus, and just big enough to carry cosmetics, night clothes, slippers, and other items needed in transit.

*Weekenders:* pieces approximately twice the size of an overnight bag; roomy enough to accommodate several changes of clothes and shoes. These need to be somewhat sturdier than an overnight bag, since they are likely to be tossed about in luggage compartments.

*Hanger-bags:* fold-over pieces that, to some degree, take the place of a wardrobe trunk, though they are much more compact, lighter, and far easier to handle. They carry an almost unbelievable number of dresses, suits, and coats, and are particularly useful because they are in effect a traveling closet. They also cut down drastically on crushing, as well as on the time needed for unpacking and repacking.

Even if luggage is initialed, it should be tagged with the owner's name and home address. If for any reason a traveler does not want to have this information on the outside of a bag, his name and address should be on the inside. Luggage seldom goes astray, but when it does there can be a disastrous delay in recovering it if it carries insufficient identification.

**PASSPORTS.** A passport is a requirement for travel by a United States citizen nearly everywhere outside our own country. Canada, Mexico, Bermuda, and some of the West Indies are the main exceptions (though other documents proving citizenship are required when entering those countries and also when returning to the United States).

Even if a passport is not required, any traveler entering the United States must have a valid International Certificate of Smallpox, signed by a doctor and also stamped by his Department of Health, indicating that he has been vaccinated within the preceding three years. This evidence of vaccination is also required by many foreign countries before a traveler may cross their borders, and in a number of areas other inoculations may be required by foreign quarantine regulations or, in any case, are no more than basically prudent safeguards. Typhoid, paratyphoid, and smallpox inoculations are all the protection needed in most places, though yellow fever shots are a requirement for travel in parts of South America, and other shots are considered wise for certain parts of Africa and India.

Any travel agent can supply information about passports and inoculations, or a request to the Passport Office, Department of State, Washington, D.C. 20524, will produce printed rules and regulations.

Many people have no marked reaction to inoculations, but since some may experience a day or so of discomfort, it is sensible to have them several weeks before departure. The application for a passport should not be left until the last minute, either, since applications must be sent to Washington, D.C., for processing.

An applicant for a passport needs proof of citizenship by some such documentary evidence as naturalization papers, a birth certificate, or a previous passport. In addition, the applicant must establish his identity to the satisfaction of the Clerk of Court or Passport Agent who processes the application. Among the documents acceptable as identification, provided that they contain the signature and either a photograph or physical description of the applicant, are a previous passport, a driver's license, or a business, industrial, or government identification card or pass. If such documents are not available, the applicant will need to have an identifying witness who has known him for at least two years. Also needed at the time of application are two duplicate full-face photographs (not larger than 3 by 3 inches or smaller than $2^{1}/_{2}$ by $2^{1}/_{2}$ inches) taken within the previous two years. A group photograph is preferred when a wife and/or children are included in the passport. Photographs may be in color or in black and white.

**Names.** Usually a person's legal name is the one correctly used on a passport. However, if an entertainer, writer, or business person uses another name consistently in all his relationships and activities, both professional and social, he can make arrangements at the time of application to use that name on his passport even if his name has not been legally changed. When a person uses one name (perhaps his actual legal name) socially and another name in his professional life or career, both names can be put on the passport. Make inquiry at a passport bureau about the affidavits that are required.

**Visas.** A visa is usually a stamped notation on a passport indicating that the passport-holder has permission to enter a specific country, defining the purpose of the visit, and stating the length of stay allowed. Few countries require American citizens to secure visas for brief visits. Among those that do, many require a fee and some a photograph. Consult a travel agent or write to the nearest consular office of the particular country for an explanation of the requirements. When these have been met, the passport (with fee, photograph, and any other necessary material) is then sent to that consular office for stamping. A circular may be obtained from the Passport Office of the Department of State, Washington, D.C., 20524, which gives further information, including the address of the embassy or consulate in cases where a country has only one or two offices in the United States through which a visa can be obtained.

**PETS.** The regulations about traveling pets vary considerably, and so it is important to investigate them thoroughly before deciding to take or send a pet on a journey even within the boundaries of the United States. In some states, dogs are not permitted in certain public camping grounds. A pet may enter any state in a car without formality, but in some states pets arriving by train or other common carrier will need a health certificate or a rabies inoculation or both.

Some foreign countries readily admit pets accompanied by a health and a rabies inoculation certificate. Others quarantine all incoming pets (at the expense of the owner) for from three to six months. The Tourist Information Bureau or the consulate of a foreign country can supply the needed information, and travel agents can easily check the regulations. Check the regulations also before buying a pet abroad to bring back to the United States. In general, this is no problem. All that is usually required for a dog entering the United States is a health certificate and evidence of recent rabies inoculation, but there can be exceptions, and at certain times some kinds of animals and birds have been refused entry entirely or have been subject to lengthy quarantine.

As a general rule, buses do not accept pets, even small ones in carriers, as passengers. It is risky to attempt to take a pet aboard in a carrier without getting formal permission in advance.

Some railroad systems will allow a pet in a carrier to accompany a passenger. Other lines will carry animals only in crates in a baggage car, and may require animals to wear a muzzle.

Some airlines will allow a small pet to ride in the cabin with its owner if it can be carried in a case no bigger than 18 x 18 by 12 inches, but usually these lenient airlines have a quota and will permit only one or two pets in the cabin on any one flight. So a reservation for pet as well as passenger is a necessity. Other airlines will carry pets only in a special pressurized and air-conditioned baggage compartment. For such a journey, a strong shipping crate that meets their exact specifications is required. This is supplied at the owner's expense. (Ready-made crates usually are available at airports.) Charges for the flight are made on the basis of both weight and displacement.

Pets are not allowed to share the owner's cabin aboard ship, but most ships (not all) have roomy kennels with an attendant in charge who feeds and waters the traveling animals. Owners can visit these kennels and walk their dogs, though usually in restricted areas.

All of this may sound more formidable than it really is. Pets can travel comfortably if the owner does his part in advance, investigates the regulations thoroughly, and also consults a veterinarian about medications that will aid the pet during transit. Dogs can suffer from motion sickness on a trip in a car or train, and seasickness is a common problem with animals. It is customary to get a prescription for a sedative for a highstrung pet, and give this to him about an hour before departure. Some travel experts think that the devoted owner usually needs one too.

**PLANES.** There are two main classes of accommodations on planes: first class, and what is variously known as coach, economy, tourist, or thrift class.

Many planes are all one class. In others, a small first-class section forward is divided from the rest of the cabin. In it the seats are roomier, there is more leg room between them, meals are more elaborate, and free luggage allowance is usually somewhat more generous on international flights. Those are about the only differences, except that the cost is markedly higher. In this day of fast jet flight, many people who can well afford first class choose the regular coach space.

**Bargains in Airports.** In certain airports, limited amounts of liquors, cigarettes, perfume, and other items may be bought, free of both import and export taxes, by passengers in transit. Inquire at the tourist bureau of the country to be visited about their airport shops, and also check United States rules and regulations regarding imported items before stocking up on "bargains" that may be refused entry or subject to stiff taxes.

**Checking In.** Plane companies provide regularly scheduled bus service from a central terminal or other midtown point to an airport. This service is not included in the price of the ticket. Passengers leaving from a midtown terminal can have their luggage weighed and—with the exception of the pieces they will take into the cabin—checked through right at this terminal, and their tickets validated. Thereafter, all they need do at the airport is show ticket or loading pass at the proper gate when their flight is announced as ready for loading.

Plane companies ask passengers who are not checking in at a midtown terminal to arrive at the airport for checking in at least half an hour before departure time of a domestic flight, and an hour before an international flight. It is sensible to comply with this request. The choice of seats is made when the ticket is validated, or, if seats are not assigned at that time, the passengers first in line have the first choice.

Anyone on crutches or in a wheelchair or accompanied by an infant will usually be taken to the plane in advance of other passengers if this special attention is requested. Airports have wheelchairs for the use of passengers who need them.

Seats just in front of the wings or well behind them are considered the best because they provide an unobstructed view of the ground.

**Clothes.** Clothing suitable on the street is appropriate, though it should be chosen with consideration for any expected difference of temperature at the destination. For transcontinental and overseas flights, a woman finds a dress with an easy belt and skirt most comfortable. On overnight flights, some people replace their street shoes with soft folding slippers, but no other undressing is usual.

**Delays.** If the departure of a flight is very much delayed, on some occasions an airline will issue tickets for free meals at the airport, or supply overnight accommodations if a night flight is canceled or delayed until the next day. Therefore it is wise to inquire what provisions will be made in such emergencies before making arrangements on one's own.

**Drinks.** Liquors are available on most (though not all) flights after 11:00 A.M. Alcoholic drinks are complimentary in first class, but passengers in economy classes pay for them by the drink, though wines frequently are served free in all classes on overseas flights. A passenger is privileged to carry his own flask, but the pilot has authority to put an intoxicated passenger off the plane at any stop. It should be remembered that planes are pressurized to the point of comfort but not necessarily to the same pressure as ground level, and for this reason drinks can have a quicker effect in the air. On nearly every flight, coffee, tea, chocolate, and fruit juices are available without charge.

**Food.** Meals are served without charge on most flights spanning normal mealtimes except on a few short shuttle jumps. On some economy flights a charge may be made for each meal, but it is not enough to worry about in view of the overall saving in the price of excursion or special-season tickets. On many morning flights, coffee and a sweet roll are offered as a sort of second breakfast after takeoff.

**Forms of Address.** The names of the plane's personnel usually are posted somewhere in plain view. Titles and last names are used. The young women on duty in the cabin are addressed as "Stewardess" or "Miss Jones." The chief pilot is addressed as "Captain."

**Illness.** Airsickness is rare in today's jets, which ride smoothly above or through most turbulent weather. The paper "burp bags" that once were standard equipment at every seat are seldom seen now, though a stewardess will produce one rapidly in response to a ring. Stewardesses are trained to give first aid, but passengers with chronic afflictions should carry with them any special medications they are likely to need, not pack them in luggage to be stowed in the baggage compartment.

**Luggage.** On international flights all luggage, whether carried aboard or checked through, is weighed—with the exception of a purse, briefcase, camera, an extra coat, and perhaps a small net or bag of books or packages. If the luggage weight exceeds the specified free limit, overweight charges are collected at the time of check-in.

On domestic flights, there is no weight limit for a specified number of bags of limited size. Ask for details when buying a ticket because regulations change and overweight charges on a long flight can be an ugly blow to a limited budget.

On short flights, passengers are sometimes allowed to save time in reclaiming their baggage by carrying all gear aboard themselves and stowing big pieces in a luggage dock just inside the entrance to the plane. On most flights, however, passengers are required to send bulky luggage to the baggage compartment Exceptions are made for delicate gear like portable typewriters, tape recorders, and big camera cases. Usually, the owners are asked to carry these aboard to avoid any possibility of damage to them in loading or transit.

It is dangerous to stow heavy items on the overhead shelf. They must be put under the seat, elsewhere on the floor, or in an empty seat.

**Packing.** The experienced plane traveler thinks twice before packing liquids, especially in breakable containers, in luggage that is checked through. Not all luggage compartments are pressurized, and very frequently liquids will be forced out of bottles with seemingly tight stoppers or screw tops. One broken bottle of perfume, lotion, or liquor can ruin the contents of an entire bag.

**Radios.** Transistor radios must not be played on planes because they can interfere with the pilot's transmission of signals.

**Reservations.** Plane companies make it very easy to secure reservations. Tickets can be ordered by telephone, and will be held for pickup until a couple of days before departure. If a passenger's plans change, he should cancel his reservations promptly even if the ticket has not been paid for. A last-minute cancellation may deprive another traveler on the standby list of the space because he cannot get to the airport in time. Failure to cancel space for which a ticket has been issued may cause the loss of a percentage of the price when a refund or another flight is requested.

If a ticket has been bought some time in advance of a trip, the passenger should confirm by telephone the reservation (day, hour, and flight number) a few days before departure. It is essential to reconfirm space reserved on another flight when a passenger makes a stopover during a trip. This can be done at the air terminal when debarking or later by telephone. But not to do so well before flight time risks loss of the space.

**Special Services.** Stewardesses are prepared to refrigerate formulas and other special items of diet, and to heat them when needed. Magazines are standard equipment on most planes, and many planes carry free postcards and writing paper. Flight bags are usually supplied free to first-class passengers, or may be bought for a moderate price. Blankets and pillows are available on all overnight flights, and some airlines supply soft slippers on request. Radiograms may be sent in transit. Other conveniences may be available. When in need, ask the stewardess.

**Tipping.** The only people connected with air travel who are tipped are the porters who help with luggage. Twenty-five to fifty cents per bag is the expected rate. Bus drivers, stewardesses, and all other employees of an airline are thanked for good service but never tipped.

**Toilets.** Washrooms on planes are not usually marked separately for men and women. They are plainly labeled and usually have a sign that flashes "Occupied" when they are in use. The experienced traveler waits until this sign flashes off and then makes his way along the aisle. Since leaving one's seat is forbidden when the "Fasten Seat Belts" sign is on, the passenger who wants to tidy up before deplaning should get to the washroom well before the plane starts its approach to the airport.

**SHIPS.** Travel by ship is so enormously popular that it is advisable to book passage months rather than weeks in advance, whether on a luxury liner or a freighter.

**Accommodations.** Big passenger liners usually offer three classes of accommodations: first class, cabin (second) class, and tourist (third) class. Many smaller passenger ships offer only two classes. Cruise ships and freighters are all one class. On any ship, the cost of passage varies quite widely, according to the size of the cabin and the number of people occupying it. The first-class section on any ship is relatively small; the cabin and tourist classes are by far the most popular on a big liner. Many young people who can afford first-class space prefer the tourist section because it is less formal and more lively, and they are likely to meet more people of their own age in it.

First-class passengers have the run of the ship, but cabin and tourist passengers can visit the first class and use its facilities only by the invitation of an officer or as the guest of a first-class passenger.

Private baths can be taken for granted in first-class space, and in virtually all cabin classes. Private baths are available with some tourist cabins, but most passengers in this class will find themselves sharing a bathroom with quite a number of other people.

The passenger occupying a cabin without private bath does well to see his cabin or bath steward as soon as possible after the ship pulls out (just ask any steward where to find him) and reserve the bath time of his choice. Once a bath time is assigned, it is necessary to observe it promptly. The passenger who is late or overstays his allotted time throws everyone who comes after him off schedule. Passengers go to and from their cabins in robe and slippers.

**Boarding.** It is best to arrive at the ship at least an hour before sailing time, and to board two hours before sailing time if friends are turning up to say good-bye, since they will be required to leave the ship at least half an hour before sailing time.

**Bon Voyage Gifts and Parties.** The time is past when big baskets of fruits and tinned delicacies were welcome presents. In this day of rapid crossings and elaborate shipboard meals, perishable edibles are likely to be a waste and tinned ones useless—except to be passed along as presents after the passenger leaves the ship. Candy, wine or liquors, books, games, and (for certain passengers) flowers are now first choice for bon voyage presents given at the moment of departure. Bouquets are suitable if the passenger has a large stateroom, but even a single large bunch of flowers can be a problem for anyone in an inexpensive shared cabin, where space is usually extremely limited.

With as many as 2,000 passengers streaming aboard a big liner, there is a lot of orderly flurry and confusion before sailing time. Be sure to give potential visitors the cabin number, or arrange to be in some specific place to meet them. Countless people turn up to say "Bon voyage" and never do find their friends on a big ship.

Bars do not open until after sailing, and all the ship's service personnel will be on the run getting passengers settled. Don't depend on getting last-minute service of glasses and ice. The passenger who wants to offer drinks to his friends needs to place an order for setups and canapés in advance, and provide his own liquors, though his travel agent can take of these details for him.

**Cabins.** The choicest accommodations in any class are the outside cabins, since they have portholes, but all modern passenger liners are air-conditioned and so inside cabins are also comfortable, though they lack a view. Passenger ships have stabilizers so that there is no marked advantage to a cabin amidships, except on a freighter or other vessel without stabilizers. Staterooms have beds. The least expensive cabins often have upper and lower bunks, usually assigned at the time the ticket is purchased. However, it is customary for anyone sharing a cabin with a stranger to relinquish a lower bunk to someone very much older or incapacitated if the ship is crowded and no other accommodation is available after sailing.

**Clothes.** In the first class, any clothes appropriate at a dressy resort hotel are suitable. It is usual, but not mandatory, for passengers in the first class on most ships to dress for dinner (Black Tie) except on the first and last nights of a voyage and on Sunday nights. It is customary to dress when dining at the captain's table, on the night of the ship's concert, and on other special occasions.

In the cabin and tourist classes and on freighters, passengers do not wear formal clothes. Women change from shorts or sports slacks, if that has been their daytime costume, to afternoon or simple dinner dresses. Men put on shirts and ties and, in the cabin class, usually change to dark suits. On cruise ships, passengers wear formal dinner clothes for dinner or not, as they choose. For any meal aboard, some degree of formality in dress is expected in a dining salon.

Passengers who want to lunch in bathing suits or other extremely casual clothes order a tray brought to the deck.

**Cruises.** Cruises are simply extended sea vacations with land stopovers for sight-seeing and shopping. The ship is used as a hotel while it is in port. Life aboard is much the same as on any other passenger ship. The major difference is that tips are not given all at once at the end of the voyage except on very short cruises. If a cruise lasts two or three weeks, half of the amount is given in the middle of the voyage and the remainder at the end. On longer cruises, tips are given at regular intervals, usually when the ship puts in at a major port, so that the staff has money to spend ashore.

**Deck Chairs.** Deck chairs are free on some ships, but don't take it for granted. The experienced traveler sees the deck steward as soon as possible after sailing, pays a fee from two to four dollars, and chooses the location he prefers for the chair that will be for his exclusive use during the voyage. (On some ships, a reservation can be made when the ticket is bought.) On big liners, chairs cannot be moved. If in doubt about a desirable location, ask the steward to recommend the best spot—the shady or sunny side, the protected or windy areas. A name card is attached to the rented chair. Other passengers may occupy a reserved chair briefly, but do not move it and always relinquish it immediately when its owner shows up. Steamer rugs can be rented. It is not correct to take blankets and pillows from one's cabin for use on deck.

**Drinks.** Drinks may be charged on some ships, but on others are paid for when served. The barman is usually tipped at the time of service.

**Fellow Passengers.** It is correct to speak to fellow passengers when a reasonably easy opportunity affords the chance; or a ship's officer or social director may be asked to make an introduction. As a general rule, it is a good idea to go slowly because it is easy to get stuck with a group that may not wear well. The passenger list usually is published the first day out. Get it from the purser. It is not at all unlikely that a longtime friend—or enemy—may be aboard.

**Fire Drill.** On the first day out, fire drill will be called. It is of paramount importance that all passengers turn out for this practice and listen carefully to the instructions.

**Food.** Meals are a major diversion aboard ship. In addition to breakfast, lunch, and dinner, bouillon is usually served on deck and in the lounges at midmorning. Tea is offered in the afternoon. Many ships also provide a midnight buffet.

On a sizable ship, the dining salons will not accommodate all the passengers at one sitting, and so the three major meals are available at two different hours. Passengers choosing the earlier hour are obligated to finish promptly so that the table can be cleared and relaid for the next sitting. Anyone with a decided preference for the earlier or the later mealtime sees the dining-room steward or purser, as the case may be, as soon as possible after sailing. Otherwise, a sitting will be assigned arbitrarily. (On some ships, a table reservation can be booked when the ticket is bought.)

The passenger who finds himself seated with uncongenial tablemates can ask to be moved to a different table, and his request is generally complied with. A passenger does not ask to be seated at the captain's table. Dining with the captain is by his invitation only. Customarily he rotates the guests at his table if he shows himself in the dining room at all. An invitation to join the captain at a meal is a social compliment and is treated as any other social invitation would be. It must be accepted or regretted promptly. The invitation can be refused, of course, for any good reason, but the excuse should be stated when regrets are sent. On many large liners there is no captain's table because the passenger list is too long and he is too busy to be a social figure; he solves the problem by dining in his own quarters.

Passengers sharing a table introduce themselves. Conversation is kept general, much as it would be at a private dinner party, with no one ignored.

**Freighters.** Freighters quite frequently have fairly luxurious accommodations and excellent meals, but whether they carry four or forty passengers, the cargo sets the schedule of departure, arrival, and stopovers. Freighters often are directed by radio to detour for unscheduled stops to pick up cargo, and so passengers on tight schedules may sometimes be inconvenienced. But for travelers with sufficient time, freighter travel has special attractions, including somewhat lower fares (considering the extra time and meals) than passenger liners offering the same quality of food and cabins on a shorter run.

**Illness.** Today, no one need worry about seasickness. There are plenty of safe-and-sane pills on the market to control it. Experienced travelers subject to motion sickness take their own pills with them, but the cabin stewards and stewardesses, the ship's pharmacy or doctor, can also supply these remedies. Freighters seldom carry a doctor, but regular passenger vessels will have one aboard. Patients with chronic or sporadically recurring ailments should see the doctor early in the trip and explain the nature of their troubles so that he will be prepared in case he is needed.

**Luggage.** It is important to check well in advance about the rules for getting luggage aboard. On some lines, luggage can be sent to a ship a day or so before departure. On others, luggage is accepted only on the sailing date. Each piece of luggage should be tagged with the name of the owner and also the port of debarkation, especially if it is to be sent to the hold. If a cabin is shared, storage space will be very limited, and so only the pieces of luggage carrying things actually needed during the voyage should be sent there.

**Personnel.** The ship's personnel is divided into two main categories: the captain and all the people concerned with the operation of the ship, and the people who are engaged chiefly in catering to the personal needs of the passengers. Requests for services can be given to the people in the latter category, but it is an outstanding breach of etiquette to ask members of the operating crew, either officers or men, to run errands or give any other personal service.

Use the captain's title when speaking to him, either "Captain" or "Captain Smith." Address all other officers (and these include the purser and chief steward) as "Mr." with the last name, or just skip any form of address if the last name is not known, and let a courteous manner serve instead. Passengers seldom come in contact with the crewmen except on freighters. There the usual form of address is "Sailor" or the last name only. "Steward" or "Stewardess" is the correct form of address for the people who give direct service in cabins, dining rooms, and elsewhere.

**Problems.** Do not take personal problems to the captain. The ship is his job. Instead, see the purser (or someone in his office). He is an executive officer, and also a highly trained specialist in direct charge of all passenger relations in addition to his other duties, and all problems can be cleared through him.

**Tipping.** Barmen usually are tipped at the time of service, and waiters always are when they give special cabin or deck service, just as a room-service waiter in a hotel would be. Otherwise, happily, it is not necessary to dip constantly into pocket or purse for change. Tips are distributed on the morning of the last day if the ship is docking in the afternoon. They are given the night before if the ship is docking in the morning.

Do not tip any officer or sailor, but do tip all stewards, stewardesses, and others who have given direct personal service (except, of course, the ship's doctor). When in doubt, ask the purser.

The total of the tips depends on the length of the trip, the price of accommodations, and the number of people in a party. A single passenger tips about 10 percent of the price of his ticket—somewhat more in first class, and as little as 5 percent in tourist class. When there are two or more in a party occupying the same quarters, about one-fourth of the one-person rate is added for each extra person.

The rough rule is that about 80 percent of the total amount set aside for tips is evenly divided among the people who have given cabin and table service. The rest is divided among deck stewards, the bath steward, pool attendant, and others who have devoted a smaller amount of time to the passenger. The head dining-salon steward occupies the same position as a maître d'hôtel in a good restaurant and is tipped if he has given any special service. The wine steward is tipped if his services have been used.

On a freighter, tips are divided equally between the cabin and the table stewards.

**TRAINS.** Planes get there fast. Buses are less expensive. But trains are first choice with many pleasure travelers because they combine a chance to look at the countryside, comfortable sleeping accommodations, and some freedom to move around while under way.

**Accommodations.** There are two classes available to rail travelers: first class (generally called "Pullman") and coach.

Coach travel is decidedly less expensive, has limited or no porter service, but can be very comfortable on good trains. Some coaches have reclining seats and footrests and, at each end of a car, a sizable dressing room as well as the standard toilets. On some trains, coach seats can be reserved when tickets are bought, and this assures adjacent places for people traveling together. On other trains, passengers take coach seats on a first-come, first-choice basis. It is quite common practice for economy-minded passengers on a train that carries both coach and Pullman cars to use the inexpensive coach space during the day and move to a sleeping car at night, and so enjoy the advantages of both classes at less than the top rate. Coach passengers are welcome in all dining cars and, if the train carries them, in the special high-level sight-seeing cars with picture windows, skylights, or clear domes that afford spectacular views. First-class lounges, however, are not available to them.

A Pullman ticket is more expensive to start with. An extra charge is added if the passenger reserves any of the special spaces—from an overstuffed swivel chair in a parlor car for a daytime run, to a drawing room. The old-fashioned sleeping cars that made up into curtained berths at night have almost disappeared in favor of cars composed entirely of separate rooms, each containing its own toilet, washbasin, and one or more sleeping places. The smallest of such rooms is provided in what is called a slumber or siesta coach. It is suitable for one person, as is a roomette, which is slightly bigger. A bedroom has two berths —a lower, and an upper that folds out of sight in the daytime. A compartment has two lower berths and more floor space than a bedroom. A drawing room has two lower berths and one upper, and the toilet is concealed behind a door instead of disguised as an extra seat. A bedroom suite is two bedrooms that can be made one by a wall that folds up. All the above accommodations have a space where clothes can hang wrinkle-free.

**Clothes.** Any street clothes from spectator sports clothes to suits are appropriate. Some women change to slacks at night for comfort in coaches, but it is not customary for sit-up travelers to change to dressing gowns or other very informal clothing for sleeping. It is not wise to leave fur coats or other valuable items unguarded in lounge cars or other open spaces.

**Drinks.** Both alcoholic and nonalcoholic beverages are sold in lounge and dining cars, and for an additional service charge passengers in private rooms can order either drinks or setups, though state liquor laws are observed. Drinks are not served while a train is passing through a dry state, or on Sunday if local law prohibits.

**Food.** Most long-distance trains provide dining cars. Some have counters for snack service in addition. Sandwiches, nonalcoholic drinks, fruit, and candy are offered from baskets or carts in some coaches. And, of course, anyone who wants to can take along a picnic lunch.

In a dining car, there is always a captain in charge of seating. Passengers wait for his signal and do not choose tables for themselves. Only a courteous nod is required when a stranger joins one's table. There is no need to engage in conversation, though it is entirely correct to do so anywhere on a train if a fellow passenger responds encouragingly to casual remarks.

**Luggage.** In coaches, luggage is stored in racks over the seats, or sometimes in a luggage dock near the exit. It is a violation of the safety rules to leave luggage in the aisles. In first-class sections, the train porter will help the passenger stow luggage and get it to the platform when his destination is reached.

**Special Services.** When buying a ticket, ask what special services may be available. Premier trains offer various special features, including "ship to shore" telephones, and some have a space set aside for shower facilities and barber and valet services, among other extra comforts.

**Tipping.** Waiters and barmen are tipped just as they would be in a good hotel—15 to 20 percent of the tab. Porters who give room service of meals are tipped a bit more. The porter in a coach or parlor car gets fifty cents to a dollar, depending on how much service he has given. Porters taking care of passengers in Pullman space usually rate a dollar a night, and somewhat more if extra service has been given. Conductors are not tipped.

**TRAVEL AGENTS.** The biggest bargain in the travel field is the services given free to his patrons by the travel agent in booking transportation and, in some cases, making other reservations. Contrary to widespread belief, however, all the services of the travel agent are not free, and many people go wrong in dealing with travel agents because of confusion on this point. Time is money to a travel agent, just as it is to anyone else in business. He makes no charge when providing the following services to a sizable group, but if he is asked to give lengthy consultation about an independent trip, make complicated arrangements for many one- or two-day stops, book the services of guides, provide tickets for theaters, music festivals, and so on, and deliver a detailed typed itinerary, he will make a charge. The relatively modest fee he asks for such extensive services is also a big bargain because he can do in days what it would take the individual weeks of research, letter-writing, or cabling to do for himself.

Any travel agent will welcome and make no charge for reasonably brief preliminary consultation about a trip. He will supply free brochures and will gladly answer questions about passports, the best seasons for travel in different localities, costs in general, and scores of other matters that he can quickly clear up because of his professional know-how and his ready access to timetables and other reference materials. The client is under no obligation to this point. He is privileged to walk out and take his business elsewhere with no more than a "Thank you" if he does not like or have confidence in the agent.

Otherwise, these are the rules that a client is expected to observe:

1. If a travel agent has devoted much time to consultation, give him at the very least the chance to book the major amount of the transportation. It is totally

unfair to use a travel agent as a free information bureau and then bypass him completely.

2. Don't try to impress the travel agent. Be frank about a small budget, and give him a chance to stay within its limitations. His job is to please—not to trick the client into extra expenditures.

3. Expect to pay any previously agreed fee for his work if the trip is canceled after he has completed the arrangements.

4. If the agent has made hotel and other reservations without charge, the client is obligated to reimburse him for any long-distance calls and cables he may have made if the trip is canceled.

**TRAVELERS AID.** The National Travelers Aid Association is a nonprofit organization dedicated to helping the person traveling by any means (including a car) who needs assistance. Anyone—young or old, rich or poor, citizen or alien, sick or well—is eligible for help. There is a unified network of local Travelers Aid Societies and cooperating agencies with bureaus in about 3,000 cities and towns in the United States and Canada. In big cities, a Travelers Aid booth or desk is usually to be found in any depot or terminal. Elsewhere, its location will be listed in the telephone directory. The bureaus are staffed by both paid and volunteer workers. The help they give may be comparatively simple—aiding the incapacitated, the confused, and children to make connections; straightening out matters for travelers who have lost their tickets or money; sheltering the lost or strayed. In other instances, help may extend to casework by trained social workers.

There is no charge for these services if the traveler cannot afford to pay. Those who can pay are expected to make a voluntary contribution (tax-deductible). In some cases a fee for extensive services will be suggested, but charges are always adapted to the traveler's circumstances.

## TRAYS

All trays are used without a covering, with three exceptions. Breakfast, lunch, and dinner trays are regarded as miniature dining tables and usually are covered with a little mat or cloth, though one is not essential. Trays used in any other kind of service, from one carrying a single glass of water to one carrying a complete tea or coffee set, are used without covering.

## TROUSSEAUX

Traditionally, a bride's trousseau included her clothes and all the bed, table, bath, and kitchen linen needed for her new house, and often china and silver as well. In today's use, "trousseau" means a bride's wardrobe only, though many brides collect or are given a sizable amount of household linen.

The bride or her family supplies all her personal wearing apparel. Women friends properly give lingerie, negligees, and other such items as engagement or shower presents, but clothing is not suitable as a wedding present. Household linens, however, are often given to young couples if they·let it be known that such "trousseau" items will be welcome.

## TRUTH

"A truth that's told with bad intent
Beats all the lies you can invent."
—*William Blake, Auguries of Innocence*

Good manners being what they are in this sorry world, *see* LYING for the proper time and place to tell the truth, the whole truth, and nothing but the truth.

## TURNING THE TABLE

At large and formal meals, the hostess usually starts chatting with the man seated on her right unless conversation is kept general. A bit later she turns to the man on her left and talks with him. This is known as "turning the table." Guests are expected to follow her lead without too much delay, since otherwise some guests would be stranded between companions whose attention was directed away to right and left.

## TUTORS

A tutor is a professional, and may be given a present in appreciation of special service but is never tipped.

See HOUSEHOLD EMPLOYEES for rules concerning tutors in residence.

## TUXEDO

Though "tux" and "tuxedo" are very widely used, some people make a point of using "dinner jacket," "dinner suit," or "black tie" instead. This is not a matter of any great importance, but it should be noted that Black Tie (not Tuxedo) is the correct term on a formal invitation to indicate that a man is expected to wear a dinner suit, rather than a street suit or full evening dress.

# U

## UMBRELLAS

A man's umbrella is always black. The whole rainbow range of color is open to women. A man does not carry a woman's furled umbrella for her, but he does take her opened one and holds it over her—unless, of course, he is carrying his own.

The superstition that opening an umbrella indoors is bad luck is now all but forgotten—and a good thing this is because an umbrella becomes an unsightly mass of wrinkles unless allowed to dry open.

**UNCLE.**  See AUNT AND UNCLE.

**UNIFORMS.**  See HOUSEHOLD EMPLOYEES.

**UNITED NATIONS.**  See FORMS OF ADDRESS (United Nations).

**USHERS.**  See BALLS AND DANCES; FUNERALS; THEATERS; WEDDINGS.

# V

**VALETS.**  See HOTELS AND MOTELS; HOUSEHOLD EMPLOYEES.

## VEGETABLE JUICES

Fruit or vegetable juice is not served as a first course at a strictly formal lunch or dinner.

## VEGETABLES

When one vegetable is served as a separate course, a salad-size plate is used. A large artichoke is the exception. It needs a larger plate to accommodate the leaves as they are discarded. All cooked vegetables, including corn on the cob, served with the main course are put on the dinner plate. Only radishes, fresh celery, spring onions, and raw carrot sticks are put on the butter plate. At a formal meal, vegetables are not served in little side dishes clustered around each dinner plate, but some families find this so-called home-style service practical for creamed corn, stewed tomatoes, and other soupy vegetables.

SERVING. Vegetables may be brought to the table in separate platters or bowls, or in a compartmented dish. The serving spoon and fork are offered with the bowl, tines down, and left in that position after use. All service of food is from the diner's left, and so when serving dishes are to be passed by guests, they should be started around the table counterclockwise. This makes it easy for each diner to hold the dish while the person on his right helps himself, and so on around the table. When any vegetable is offered on toast, a guest helps himself to a complete unit. He need not eat the toast, but should not leave it on the serving platter.

For details about special eating and serving problems, see ARTICHOKES; ASPARAGUS; AVOCADOS; CORN; POTATOES.

## VENERABLE

"Venerable" is used under certain circumstances when writing to or making a public presentation of an archdeacon of the Anglican or Protestant Episcopal churches. It is not correct to use "Venerable" alone in conversation (such as, "Yes, Venerable") or in writing ("Dear Venerable").

See FORMS OF ADDRESS (Clergy).

## VESTS AND WAISTCOATS

A vest is the garment that matches a street suit in fabric. "Waistcoat" is the correct word for the single- or double-breasted garment worn with formal day or evening clothes whether it matches the coat in color or not, and also for the garment that is different in color or material from a suit of any kind.

See CLOTHES.

## VETERINARIANS

"Veterinarian" is such an awkward, long tongue-twister that most doctors of veterinary medicine are resigned as well as accustomed to being called "Vet" in all but formal circumstances. "Veterinarian," however, is the correct word to use when introducing this kind of doctor to an audience at a banquet or on other such occasions; and under no circumstances is "Mr." substituted for "Dr." The rules given under DOCTORS apply also to veterinarians, most particularly the rule banning any request for specific medical advice under social circumstances. For reasons unknown, a great many people who would not dream of asking any other doctor for personal advice at a party feel free to ask a veterinarian, immediately after being introduced, exactly what should be done about Rover's diet.

## VISITING CARDS

Business cards differ from social cards in several marked ways. In a pinch, a social card may be used as a business card, with business address and telephone number written in, but a business card is never properly used for social purposes. A major difference between a man's business and social cards is that "Mr." is never used on a business card, always used on a social card.

## BUSINESS CARDS

**ADDRESSES.** A business card usually carries the full address (always including the zip code number) and the telephone number, though the card of a top executive often carries only his name and that of the firm. There is a good deal of latitude allowable in spacing and spelling, but following are the specifications most generally observed:

The number of a building is not spelled out (with the exception of "One"), but spelling is used for streets with numerical names through "Tenth." "One Tenth Avenue" and "2 Tenth (not 10th) Avenue" are correct.

Above "Tenth," the name of a street is abbreviated (72nd Street).

The name of a city is never abbreviated. The name of a state may be abbreviated, though it is spelled in full if space permits. (Correct and incorrect abbreviations of state names are listed under CORRESPONDENCE, Business.)

The words "Street," "Avenue," "Boulevard," and so on, are spelled in full as first choice. Ungainly length of the lines of the address is better controlled by using a smaller type size than by resorting to abbreviations.

**COLORS.** The most conservative business cards are white with black lettering. Tinted paper and colored inks are often chosen by beauty shops, flower dealers, specialty stores, restaurants, and the like for the cards used by their salespeople and for other promotional purposes, but as a general rule cards printed in bright inks on either white or tinted papers are not used by their executives.

**DESIGN.** There is enormous latitude in the design of a business card and the placement of the lettering, but these two rules are universally followed:

The name of a high-ranking executive is placed above the firm name:

JOSEPH H. REINER
VICE-PRESIDENT

| CROWN PUBLISHERS | 419 PARK AVE. SOUTH |
| BONANZA BOOKS | NEW YORK, N. Y. 10016 |
| OUTLET BOOK CO. | (212) 685-8550 |

The name of a junior executive or a salesman is placed below the name of the firm:

MU 5-8550

CROWN PUBLISHERS
BONANZA BOOKS   •   OUTLET BOOK CO.
CLARKSON POTTER INC. • HARLAN PRESS

| ROBERT J. FASNACHT | 419 PARK AVENUE SOUTH |
| SALES REPRESENTATIVE | NEW YORK, N. Y. 10016 |

**NAMES AND TITLES.** Correct use of names and titles is markedly different for business and social visiting cards.

**Names.** Both first and middle name are usually spelled in full on a social card, but initials may be used on a business card, and a middle name or initial may be dropped. John Brian Jones, J. Brian Jones, John B. Jones, J. B. Jones, and John Jones all are correct in business usage.

The use of a nickname on a business card is not the conservative practice, but it is entirely a matter for the individual to decide. The same is true of diminutives like Billy or Betty, and shortened names like Will. Such abbreviations as Jos., Wm., Chas., are not correct.

"Junior" is not spelled in full on a business card. "Jr." is correct. So are "2nd" and the Roman numeral II (not "2" or "second").

**Titles.** A man never uses "Mr." on a business card, but women use "Miss" or "Mrs."

(See CORRESPONDENCE, BUSINESS, for the rules governing the use of these titles with the first name of a married woman and a divorcée.) If a woman's name appears without a title, it is taken for granted that she is addressed "Miss."

"Dr." is not used on a business card to indicate either a medical or academic title. "John B. Jones, M.D." and "Mary Greene Jones, Ph.D." are the correct forms.

**SIZE AND STYLE.** Business cards are larger than social cards, and men and women use the same size. The standard dimensions are about $3\frac{1}{2}$ inches by 2 inches or slightly larger.

The most formal business cards are engraved, but process printing that imitates the raised lettering of engraving is far more widely used. It is entirely correct, and so is ordinary printing.

Plain white cardboard without a raised or colored border is the conservative choice, though white parchment is often used because it has the advantage of being thinner and therefore more practical for anyone who distributes a great number of cards in any one day.

The standard lettering is one of the variants of Roman or block letters. Script is not correct on business cards, though occasionally a woman connected with a firm dealing in cosmetics or a similar specialty may use it.

**TELEPHONE NUMBERS.** A telephone number is a standard part of a business card. It is sometimes omitted on the cards of the loftiest of executives, but usually is carried on all others. The prefix is spelled in full: PLaza (not PL).

**USES OF BUSINESS CARDS.** A business card is used for any *business* purpose exactly as a social card is used for a social purpose. However, it cannot substitute for a social card. For example, a business card is not properly enclosed when sending a nonbusiness present to a friend. In this circumstance, it is better to use a blank card than a business card because enclosing a business card indicates that the donor is acting in his business capacity for his firm.

## SOCIAL CARDS

Strict rules govern the size, style, and use of social visiting cards.

**ADDRESSES.** An address on a social card is entirely a matter of individual choice. If one is forever scribbling his address on a card with only the name, it is obviously simpler to have it engraved. Only a home address is used, however. A business address is never correct on a social card. A club address may be used by a nonresident member who wishes to be reached there by mail as a regular proceeding.

An address is always placed in the lower right-hand corner. If an address is used at all, today's first choice is to use the city, state, and zip code as well as the street address. Abbreviations are not correct. Street, Boulevard, and so on are spelled in full. So are state names. The number of a building is not spelled out with the exception of "One." Spelling is used for streets with numerical names through "Tenth." Above "Tenth," the name of the street is abbreviated (82nd Street).

**BLANK CARDS.** For complete details, *see* CARDS.

**CALLS.** The formal call has virtually disappeared except in diplomatic, military, and certain governmental circles, and visiting cards today are used almost entirely for other purposes.

For all details of the formal call, *see* CALLS.

**CHILDREN'S CARDS.** Some people feel that it is a bit affected to supply children with cards. Others feel that the sooner a child learns the proper use of visiting cards, the better. Cards for children are correct, but certainly far from customary even for teen-agers. Cards for little children are slightly smaller than standard for grown-ups. Teen-agers use standard sizes.

Many young people get their first cards as a high-school graduation present so that the card can be enclosed in the graduation announcement or invitation. (It should be emphasized that an engraved card is in no way necessary for this use; a blank card with a handwritten name is entirely correct.)

A boy does not rate "Mr." before his name on a card before he is eighteen and also has finished high school. "Mr." may be added after he is eighteen, but usually is omitted until he is on his own after graduation from college.

It is correct to use "Miss" on the card of a girl of any age, but the first choice for a girl under twelve is without that title. After she is sixteen, and always after her graduation from high school, a girl's card carries "Miss."

**ENVELOPES.** Visiting cards usually are ordered with matching envelopes. When a card is enclosed with a present, especially one sent by a shop, it customarily is slipped into its matching envelope. The envelope may or may not be sealed; it may be left blank, or the addressee's first or full name may be written on it if there is any chance of confusion.

A card left during a formal call is never enclosed in its envelope.

In the past, visiting cards could be mailed in their tiny matching envelopes, but in 1959 the Post Office Department ruled: "Envelopes which are less than $2^3/_4$ by 4 inches are non-mailable." Today, therefore, the larger fold-over "Informal" is much more widely used for mailed messages, though a visiting card can be slipped into the envelope for an Informal, for mailing. Stationers carry these envelopes in open stock. A recommended size is $3^5/_{16}$ inches by $4^3/_8$ inches.

**FOLD-OVERS.** A man does not use fold-over cards, but they are correctly used by a couple or a woman. A fold-over card, widely known as an "Informal," is not strictly a visiting card and cannot properly be substituted for one in certain specific uses—in making a formal call or for enclosure in a graduation invitation or announcement, for example. However, fold-overs are discussed here because they can be substituted for a standard visiting card in virtually all other situations —for enclosure with presents and for invitations and other short messages. Many people order a small number of standard cards and a larger number of fold-overs at the same time.

A fold-over closely resembles a visiting card except that the name is on the front of a double fold of heavy paper somewhat lighter in weight than visiting card stock. It is larger than a visiting card—about 3 by 4 inches—and therefore meets the Post Office mailing regulations. Fold-overs always come with matching envelopes. In style, placement of the name or names, and placement of an address if one is used, the engraving on the fold-over is the same as for a visiting card.

A message may be written on the front or within the fold. No salutation is used if a message is put on the front, and "Miss" (and, on occasion, the last name too) is usually struck through in ink, following the rule for visiting cards when an added message is completed on the front. "Miss" is not struck through if the message is written within the fold.

The following examples show standard forms and uses of the fold-over.

*Message on the outside:*

BaRBECUE ———

Sunday, June 15 — AT 6 —

*Mrs. Stuart Wendell Danforth*

R.S.V.P.          50 Valley Road —

CongratulatioNS —

Miss Llewellyn Hill

*Message on the inside* (salutation and signature may be used, or not):

Happy to join
you on Sunday
June 15 at six —

**INTRODUCTIONS ON CARDS.** On occasion, a visiting card with a hand-written line added is given to the friend who is to be introduced, instead of an actual note of introduction. Handing over either a card or note of introduction is not enough, however. It is also necessary to telephone or write, explaining that a card of introduction has been given, so that the call from the person being introduced does not come as a complete surprise. If this follow-up is skipped, the person presenting the card is put in an extremely awkward position, and the recipient is in doubt about what is expected of him.

Both of the following forms are correct:

**INVITATIONS ON CARDS.** Either a visiting card in one of the larger sizes or, more often, a fold-over with a few handwritten lines added is often used for an informal invitation, though this use implies that there will be twenty or more guests, as does the little printed fill-in invitation card. A prompt reply is called for, but if the party giver wants to make doubly sure of answers, "RSVP" is correctly added. The answer may be sent by note or on a visiting card or fold-over; if a telephone number has been written in on the invitation, it is a sign that a telephoned answer is preferred.

**JOINT-NAME CARDS.** Many married couples have more use for a joint-name card (Mr. and Mrs. Henry York Brown) than for separate ones. It is not correct to strike out the "Mr." or "Mrs." on such a card to indicate that a present or message is from one of the couple only.

**MAILING.** For the regulations, see "Envelopes," above.

**NAMES AND TITLES.** The rules are exact regarding names and titles—there is little latitude of choice here.

**Names.** The first and middle name are generally spelled in full—"Miss Mary Matilda Brown" (not "Miss Mary M. Brown") and "Mr. Henry York Brown" (not "Mr. Henry Y. Brown") are standard choices. There are exceptions, of course. In the case of very long names, either a first or middle initial can be used—or the first and last names only can be used.

"Jr." and "Sr.," rather than full spelling, are today's choice. The Roman numerals "II" and "III" are preferred to full spelling and also to "2nd" and "3rd."

**Titles.** A man always uses "Mr." on his social card. "Esquire" or "Esq." and "The Honorable" or "Hon." are never used on a card, social or business.

A woman always uses "Miss" or "Mrs." on her social card. A married woman or a widow never uses "Mrs." with her first name on her social card, and if the rule is strictly observed, a divorcée does not, either. Today, custom is rapidly modifying this rule for divorcées.

See NAMES for full details.

The name of a married woman matches the name her husband uses on his social card. If he chooses to drop his middle name and use "Mr. Henry Brown," she does not have her cards engraved "Mrs. Henry York Brown."

A widow continues to use her husband's name without change, except that she adds "Sr." if her married son has the same name as his father. This is done to avoid confusion with her daughter-in-law, since the son drops "Jr." after his father's death. A man never uses "Sr."

"Dr." is a correct abbreviation on a social card. An unmarried woman doctor uses her title on her social card: Dr. Mary Ann Smith. A married woman doctor, however, does not; she uses the standard social form: Mrs. Henry York Brown. When "Dr." precedes a name, initials denoting an academic degree are not used following it. "M.D.," "Ph.D.," and other such initials are correct only on a business card, and when they are used "Dr." is omitted.

**SIZE AND STYLE.** The engraving on social cards is always black. For women, script or one of the variants of Roman lettering is the most popular. A joint "Mr. and Mrs." card is often engraved in script. Ordinarily, a man does not use script unless he is in the diplomatic corps. In that service, script is the standard style for men and their wives also. Always to be avoided is any style of lettering that looks like a printer's type rather than engraving.

---

### VISITING CARD PLATES

| | |
|---|---|
| SCRIPT | *Mrs. William Wilson Carver* |
| LONDON SCRIPT | *Mrs. Cornelius Grant Arlington* |
| WINDSOR | Mrs. Frederick Arthur Hewitt |
| MAYFAIR | Mrs. Jay Barclay Woods |
| ST. JAMES | *Mrs. Stuart Wendell Danforth* |
| ANTIQUE ROMAN | Mrs. Thomas Gordon Belknap |
| NORMAN | Mrs. Robert Wellington Cameron |
| HAMILTON | *Mrs. Oren Jacques Chandler* |
| SHADED ROMAN | MRS. EDWIN DANIEL MEADE |

---

The samples of engraving above are reproduced through the kindness of Tiffany & Co. Among their clients, Script and Antique Roman are the most popular with women, followed by St. James and Norman as second and third choices. Antique Roman is the leading choice among their male customers.

**Paper.** Fine white cardboard is the usual choice, though light cream-colored cardboard is sometimes used. The card is plain, never with a plate-marked border.

**Size.** Cards vary slightly in size depending on the length of the name, which should not look crowded. A man's card is somewhat narrower than a woman's, usually about $2^{13}/_{16}$ inches long by $1^{1}/_{2}$ inches wide. A woman's card may vary from $2^{13}/_{16}$ inches by 2 inches, through $3^{1}/_{2}$ inches by $2^{1}/_{4}$. "Mr. and Mrs." cards have the same proportions as a woman's card, but may be as large as $3^{1}/_{2}$ by $2^{1}/_{2}$ inches.

**STRIKING OUT TITLE AND LAST NAME.** There is no hard-and-fast rule about this matter. It is correct to enclose a card with a gift without striking out "Mr." or "Miss." However, by far the most usual custom today is to strike a light line through the title if a message is added, and to strike through both the title and the last name on a card sent with a gift or message to a friend who is on a first-name basis. The whole engraved line is struck through if a nickname or a diminutive is signed to a message.

Customary forms (for both men and women):

**TELEPHONE NUMBERS.** A telephone number is not correct on a social card, though it may be used on a fold-over informal card.

## VISITORS' REGISTERS

A visitors' register in a museum, exhibit, or other public place is signed as a hotel register would be. So is a visitors' register in any place of business. A guest book in a private dwelling, or at a private party held away from home, is signed informally with "Mr.," "Miss," and "Mrs." omitted.

See also FUNERALS; WEDDINGS.

**VISITS.**   See CALLS; HOSPITALS; HOUSEGUESTS.

**VITAL STATISTICS COLUMNS.**   See Newspapers in Index.

## VOLUNTEERS

Without the help of unpaid volunteers, the work of virtually all clubs, charities, political organizations, and nonprofit community groups would grind to a standstill. But all too often the efforts of a reliable group of volunteers is defeated to some extent by those people who willingly volunteer but consider a promise to do a job in no way binding if the task proves boring, hard, or inconvenient.

An employee can be fined, fired, or called on the carpet if he neglects an assigned task, but there is no really effective way to control or discipline an irresponsible volunteer, as most committee chairmen know to their sorrow. For this reason, a volunteer is doubly obligated to fulfill his promises to the letter.

# W

## W.C.

The most commonly used term for "toilet" in Europe is "the W.C." (water closet). Since the toilet often is in a separate room from the bathtub and washstand, anyone asking for a chance to wash his hands may get exactly that. Ask forthrightly for the toilet or the W.C.—pronounced *doobleh-vay-say* on the Continent.

**WAGES.**  *See* SALARY AND WAGES.

**WAISTCOATS.**  *See* CLOTHES; VESTS AND WAISTCOATS.

**WAITERS AND WAITRESSES.**  *See* in the Index.

**WALKING STICKS.**  *See* CLOTHES.

**WARRANT OFFICERS.**  *See* FORMS OF ADDRESS (Armed Services).

## WASHINGTON

Certain special procedures, quite different in a number of aspects from those correct in other parts of the country, are observed in official circles in Washington. Members of our government are well briefed on these conventions, or, when in doubt about any point of precedence, they can turn to the office of the Chief of Protocol in the U.S. State Department—as indeed can anyone else, though the services of that department should not be requested in matters that can easily be cleared through other sources—through reference to the information following in this section and in the FORMS OF ADDRESS section, for example.

Discussed here are the major points that will be helpful to the visitor in Washington who is invited to attend an official function, and to anyone who has occasion to entertain in the capital or elsewhere by the rules of Washington protocol.

1. All guests stay until the guest of honor leaves at any formal official function at which guests are required to arrive promptly—a dinner, for example. All guests at the White House stay until the President and First Lady withdraw.

2. A newcomer with official standing makes the first calls on his official connections. He does not expect to see the person on whom he calls. He merely leaves the correct number of cards (*see* VISITING CARDS) as a formality—a method of announcing his presence in his new post. A newcomer, however,

does not make the first entirely social call on someone he would like to know, but observes the regular social rules and waits for a resident of longer standing to call first.

3. The rules of precedence are extremely important in official circles, and should be observed on official occasions.

A man precedes his wife through an official receiving line in Washington— just the opposite from the custom in entirely social circumstances (see RECEIV- ING LINES for details).

Guests at a meal are seated according to rank. This means that a guest of honor and his wife possibly are not given their usual places at the right of the hostess and host if someone of higher rank is present. For example, if the guest of honor is a Senator, and a member of the Cabinet is present, the Senator is seated at the left of the hostess and the Cabinet member has the place at her right. If two Cabinet members or other officials who outrank the guest of honor are present, they usually are seated at the right and left of the hostess, and the guest of honor is assigned a place farther down the table. However, it should be noted that precedence is sometimes waived by request for certain officially arranged functions.

Incidentally, in government and diplomatic circles, the word is pronounced "preeceedence," with the accent on the second syllable and the e in the first and second syllables pronounced to rhyme with "free."

The State Department does not release an official order of precedence, but the following unofficial list is the one generally observed in diplomatic circles, and can be safely used as a guide:

## ORDER OF PRECEDENCE

The President of the United States
The Vice President of the United States
The Speaker of the House of Representatives
The Chief Justice of the United States
Former Presidents of the United States
The Secretary of State
The Secretary-General of the United Nations
The President of the United Nations Security Council
The President of the United Nations General Assembly
Ambassadors of Foreign Powers
Widows of former Presidents of the United States
The United States Representatives to the United Nations
Ministers of Foreign Powers (Chiefs of Diplomatic Missions)
Associate Justices of the Supreme Court and Retired Associate Justices
The Cabinet
   The Secretary of the Treasury
   The Secretary of Defense
   The Attorney General
   The Postmaster General
   The Secretary of the Interior
   The Secretary of Agriculture
   The Secretary of Commerce
   The Secretary of Labor
   The Secretary of Health, Education, and Welfare
   The Secretary of Housing and Urban Development
   The Secretary of Transportation
The Senate
Governors of States

Acting Heads of Executive Departments (in the absence of the Cabinet member)
Former Vice Presidents of the United States
The House of Representatives
Under Secretaries of State
Administrator, Agency for International Development
Director, United States Arms Control and Disarmament Agency
Chargés d'Affaires of Foreign Powers
Secretaries of the Army, the Navy, and the Air Force (ranked according to date of appointment)
Director, Bureau of the Budget
Chairman, Council of Economic Advisers
Chairman, Board of Governors, Federal Reserve
Under Secretaries of the Executive Department and Deputy Secretaries
Chairman, Joint Chiefs of Staff
Chiefs of Staff of the Army, the Navy, and the Air Force (ranked according to date of appointment)
Commandant of the Marine Corps
The Secretary-General, Organization of American States
Representatives to the Organization of American States
Director, Central Intelligence Agency
Administrator, General Services Administration
Director, United States Information Agency
Administrator, National Aeronautics and Space Administration
Chairman, The Atomic Energy Commission
Director, Defense Research and Engineering
Director, Office of Emergency Planning
Administrator, Federal Aviation Agency
Chairman, Civil Service Commission
Director, the Peace Corps
Special Assistants to the President
Deputy Under Secretaries of the Executive Departments
Assistant Secretaries of the Executive Departments
United States Chief of Protocol
Members of the Council of Economic Advisers
Active or Designate United States Ambassadors and Ministers (career rank, when in the United States)
Under Secretaries of the Army, the Navy, and the Air Force (ranked according to date of appointment)
Four-Star Generals and Vice Admirals
Assistant Secretaries of the Army, the Navy, and the Air Force (ranked according to date of appointment)
Lieutenant Generals and Vice Admirals
Ministers of Foreign Powers (serving in Embassies, not accredited)
Deputy Assistant Secretaries of the Executive Departments
Counselors of Embassies or Legations of Foreign Powers
Major Generals and Rear Admirals
Brigadier Generals and Commodores
Assistant Chiefs of Protocol
The Secretary of the Senate

**Seniority.** Precedence between two officials of equal rank is determined by their length of service in all but a few cases.

The precedence of diplomats of equal rank is determined by the dates on which their credentials were presented at the White House, not by the relative size and importance of their countries. It should be noted that a foreign official of equal rank with an American official is given preference, though no one ever outranks our President under an American roof or anywhere else in this country.

The Speaker of the House of Representatives outranks all members of Congress. Otherwise, a Senator outranks a Representative, regardless of length of service.

The President pro tem of the Senate outranks all other Senators. Other Senators are ranked according to their length of service. The precedence of Senators sworn in on the same day is determined, by State Department practice, alphabetically by their own last names. The same rules apply to Representatives.

The Chairman of the Joint Chiefs of Staff outranks all officers of any branch of the Armed Services. Otherwise, the precedence of officers of the same or a comparable rank in all services is determined by the date of their appointment to the current rank.

A wife is seated according to the rank of her husband.

**NAMES.** When speaking to the President, the Vice President, the Speaker of the House, the Chief Justice, and Ambassadors, their titles alone are used—"Mr. Speaker," for example; not "Mr. Smith." A member of the Cabinet is addressed as "Mr. Secretary" with two exceptions: "Mr. Attorney General" and "Mr. Postmaster General" are the correct forms of spoken address to those two members of the Cabinet.

Further details relative to introductions and correspondence are to be found under FORMS OF ADDRESS (Government).

**PLACE CARDS.** In general, the rules above are observed, and titles alone are used for persons of Cabinet rank and higher, though there are exceptions for certain other ranks.

*See* PLACE CARDS for examples and further details.

**THE WHITE HOUSE.** The degree of formality observed in White House entertaining varies with each administration, but no first-time guest at the White House need worry about what will be expected if the following simple rules are kept firmly in mind:

1. A guest must arrive several minutes before the hour specified. It is an unforgivable error not to be on hand when the President makes his entrance.
2. Our chief executive is addressed "Mr. President" or "Sir," not "Mr. [Last Name]." The First Lady is addressed "Mrs. [Last Name]."
3. A guest never leaves before the President and the First Lady withdraw.

For the rest, guests will be guided so efficiently by a staff that has the most beautiful of simple, easily formal American manners that they will never be at a loss as to where to go and in what order.

The visitor's welcome starts with the greeting of the alert but steadily courteous guards at whichever gate he enters. If an admission card was enclosed in the invitation, it is given to the guard, who, under any circumstances, has a list of the expected visitors that he checks before passing anyone in.

There is parking space for guests driving themselves, but the usual and most comfortable procedure is to arrive by cab or chauffeur-driven car. Guests are relieved of their wraps as they enter, and there will be plenty of aides of all degrees to show the way.

**Clothes.** For lunch, tea, or an afternoon reception at the White House, a woman wears any suitable street-length costume and gloves. A hat is optional during the daytime, but a woman does not wear a hat after six o'clock to a White House function. A man wears a conservative business suit for daytime appearances at the White House.

As noted above, the degree of formality in dress can vary quite widely between administrations. Under one President, there will be many White Tie dinners and receptions; under another, Black Tie rather than White Tie will be the general rule, and there also may be many evenings when dark street suits are the President's preference.

In any case, there will be no confusion about what to wear in the evening to the White House because the invitation will make this matter clear, in one way or another. An engraved invitation, for example, will include a separate card with "White Tie" or "Black Tie" engraved on it. If such a card is not enclosed, a dark suit for men and a short cocktail dress for women are indicated. When White Tie is specified, women wear long formal dresses. Long gloves are customary, though not obligatory, with dresses that have brief or no sleeves. If in doubt about what to wear, call the White House and ask for the office of the Social Secretary.

**Gifts.** It is never correct to take a gift to the White House unless the gift has been cleared through an aide.

**Invitations.** An invitation to the White House is a command and must be accepted even if it means canceling a prior social engagement. There are, of course, some few acceptable reasons for refusing. Among these are illness, absence from Washington, the recent death of a close relative, and a family wedding. If a refusal is necessary, the reason must always be stated.

Very often, a state dinner or other formal gathering at the White House must be arranged on short notice, and invitations—especially those to out-of-town guests—will be wired or telephoned. In such cases, a prompt answer by wire or telephone is called for. In any case, the answer to a White House invitation should be given within twenty-four hours if the rules of protocol are observed. It may be mailed or delivered by messenger, or, if the guest is out of town, wired.

An engraved invitation calls for a handwritten answer in the standard formal third-person style, though the wording is slightly different from the regular form in that "have the honour to accept" (instead of "accept with pleasure") is correct, and "regret exceedingly" (instead of "regret") is used. However, if the time is short, a telephoned answer to the office of the Social Secretary at the White House is very much preferred to a delayed answer in writing (though such a telephoned answers should then be confirmed in writing in one of the following standard third-person forms).

If other instructions about addressing the reply are not included in the invitation, the only correct forms are:

If the invitation is from the President:

> *The President*
> *The White House*
> *Washington, D.C. 20500*

If the invitation is from the President and his wife:

> *The President*
> *and Mrs. Smith*
> *The White House*

If the invitation is from the President's wife, there is a choice of forms. The first below is the most formal and is endorsed by the State Department. However, also correct, and very widely used outside diplomatic circles, is the second example below:

> *Mrs. Smith*         or         *Mrs. John Jones Smith*
> *The White House*                 *The White House*

Standard formal answers:

*Mr. and Mrs. Henry York Brown
have the honour to accept
the kind invitation of
The President and Mrs. [Last Name]
for dinner on
Wednesday, the tenth of June
at eight o'clock*

or

*Mr. and Mrs. Henry York Brown
regret exceedingly
that owing to Mr. Brown's
absence in Rome
they will be unable to accept
the very kind invitation of
The President and Mrs. [Last Name]
to dine
on Wednesday, the tenth of June*

**Tours.** Nearly 2,000,000 people take the regularly scheduled tours through certain portions of the White House each year. The smallest group is admitted at 8:30 in the morning on what is known as the V.I.P. tour. Tickets for it can be obtained through one's congressman. Other tours do not require a reservation, though it is wise to make special arrangements for very large groups.

**WASHINGTON'S RULES OF CIVILITY.**  For George Washington's 110 "Rules of Civility and Decent Behavior in Company and Conversation," *see* CHILDREN AND MANNERS.

**WASHROOMS.**  *See* BATHROOMS AND WASHROOMS.

**WATCHES.**  *See* CLOTHES.

**WATER**
Water is always provided at a formal meal, even if several wines are also served. In very formal service, water glasses are filled after the diners are seated at the table. On less formal occasions, it is usual and correct to fill the glasses with ice water just before the meal is announced. And, it should be noted that water is often not served on everyday occasions if iced tea, beer, or wine is provided.

A water glass is filled or refilled from the right so that the server need not reach across the diner.

Stemmed goblets are the standard formal choice for lunch and dinner, though this rule is blithely ignored on many everyday occasions. Tumblers are correct for water at breakfast and always are used when water is served away from the table.

**WATERMELONS.**  *See* FRUITS.

**WATER-SKIING**
All too often, water-skiing is more fun for the skier than for everyone else within striking distance. Out of consideration for nearby swimmers, fishermen, and others on or in the water, the water-skier and his boatman need to obey the following rules:

1.  Avoid skiing through congested areas, and also be alert at all times for swim-

mers farther from shore who might be startled by a heavy wake or endangered by the boat, towline, or skis.

2. Observe all the standard "rules of the road" when meeting, overtaking, or crossing the course of another boat.
3. Run parallel to the shore except when making necessary turns.
4. Come in slowly when landing, to avoid collisions with swimmers or a dangerous spill in shallow water.
5. Don't clown after a spill. The skier who falls must let his driver know at once that he is all right; otherwise, nearby boats are obligated to stand by to see if his driver needs help in assisting him. The fallen skier should also give the standard position signal (holding up one ski) so that his driver can locate him quickly, and other boatmen can keep out of the path of his returning towboat. His driver, of course, returns with all safe dispatch, never leaving the fallen skier floundering alone as a gag.
6. Use a towboat with a rearview mirror unless there is an extra person aboard to keep an eye constantly on the skier.

## WEDDING ANNIVERSARIES

Some husbands and wives exchange gifts on each anniversary of their wedding, and close relatives remember the date with a card or a gift. But, as a general rule, special attention is paid only to the anniversaries that are considered major milestones: the first, tenth, fifteenth, twenty-fifth, fiftieth, and seventy-fifth.

By custom, specific materials have come to be associated with each anniversary year, as follows:

|       |                                          |
|-------|------------------------------------------|
| 1st   | paper, plastics                          |
| 2nd   | cotton                                   |
| 3rd   | leather                                  |
| 4th   | linen, silk, rayon, nylon                |
| 5th   | wood                                     |
| 6th   | iron                                     |
| 7th   | wool, copper, brass                      |
| 8th   | bronze, electrical equipment             |
| 9th   | pottery                                  |
| 10th  | tin, aluminum                            |
| 11th  | steel                                    |
| 12th  | silk, linen                              |
| 13th  | lace                                     |
| 14th  | ivory                                    |
| 15th  | crystal, glass                           |
| 16th, 17th, 18th, 19th not traditional categories | |
| 20th  | china                                    |
| 25th  | silver                                   |
| 30th  | pearl                                    |
| 35th  | coral, jade                              |
| 40th  | ruby, garnet                             |
| 45th  | sapphire, tourmaline                     |
| 50th  | gold (the Golden Wedding anniversary)    |
| 55th  | emerald, turquoise                       |
| 60th  | diamond, gold                            |
| 75th  | diamond, gold                            |

**INVITATIONS.** Invitations to a wedding-anniversary celebration can range from formal engraved ones to telephone calls.

A standard form:

Mr. and Mrs. John Jones Smith

request the pleasure of the company of

[name of guest, handwritten]

at a dinner to celebrate

the fiftieth wedding anniversary of

Mr. and Mrs. Henry York Brown

on Wednesday, the tenth of March

at eight o'clock

The West Country Club

R.S.V.P.
[home address]
[city, state, and zip code]

If the couple's children are giving the party jointly, their names may be listed on the invitation:

Mr. and Mrs. Arthur Arnold White

Miss Judith Jane Brown

Mr. Walter Raleigh Brown

request the pleasure of

[etc.]

R.S.V.P.
Miss Brown
1040 Park Terrace
Elmhurst, Oregon 00000

If there are so many children that their names would crowd the invitation, the form can be:

In honor of

the fiftieth wedding anniversary of

Mr. and Mrs. Henry York Brown

their sons and daughters

[etc.]

# WEDDINGS

All weddings are formal ceremonies in that they must conform to certain civil procedures even if they are not solemnized by religious ritual. For the sake of clarity in discussing the many possible degrees of formality, weddings are dealt with here in three main categories:

1. *Ceremonial*: applied, in this book, to the most elaborate as to dress and other details.

2. *Formal*: applied to weddings somewhat less elaborate than the Ceremonial.

3. *Informal*: applied to all weddings of simpler character.

The major differences are given in the accompanying chart; additional details will be found in this section under separate heads in their alphabetical order.

There are countless variations, all correct, that can be made in many of the standard procedures given here. However, it cannot be too emphatically emphasized that it is essential to discuss all details relating to a religious wedding ceremony, in a house of worship or elsewhere, with the clergyman or a member of his staff, because what is entirely suitable in one faith may not be according to the rules of another faith.

| | Ceremonial Wedding | Formal Wedding | Informal Wedding |
|---|---|---|---|
| **Announcements and Invitations** | Engraved | Engraved | Engraved Announcements: optional Invitations: informal |
| **Attendants** | Best Man Bridesmaids: four to twelve Honor Attendants: two (usually a maid and a matron of honor; both may be married or single) Optional: flower girls, pages, ring bearer | Best Man Bridesmaids: two to twelve Honor Attendants: one or two Optional: Same as ceremonial | Best Man Bridesmaids: none Honor Attendants: one |
| **Decorations** | Elaborate flowers at the reception and (if permitted) in the church. Ribbons the full length of the aisle. Optional: awning and carpet outside; canvas on the main aisle | Same as Ceremonial, though aisle ribbons may enclose only the reserved section | Simple, if any No aisle ribbons |
| **Dress** (*see* separate heads in this section for further details) | Bride, daytime or evening: Elaborate wedding gown, usually floor length, but may be waltz length Headdress with a short, medium, or long veil Train: optional Groom, before six: cutaway or black sack coat and striped trousers After six: White Tie | Bride, daytime or evening: Same as Ceremonial Groom, before six: same as Ceremonial, or dark suit or, in summer, white linen suit After six: White Tie or dinner jacket | Bride, daytime or evening: Wedding gown (no train), an afternoon dress or her going-away dress or suit—depending on time and place Groom: Dark suit or his going-away suit |
| **Guests** | Usually 100 or more | Any number; usually 75 or more | Any number; usually under 50 at the ceremony—often only close relatives and friends |
| **Location** | Usually in a house of worship, but may be elsewhere (faith permitting) | Same as Ceremonial | Same as Ceremonial, or in a church parlor, judge's chambers, town clerk's office, etc. |

| | Ceremonial Wedding | Formal Wedding | Informal Wedding |
|---|---|---|---|
| Marriage | Usually performed by a clergyman but (faith permitting) by a judge or other civil authority | Same as Ceremonial | Same as Ceremonial |
| Reception | Music: dance orchestra of five or more pieces<br>Receiving line: with announcer<br>Refreshments: champagne, bride's cake, and elaborate food—usually a three-course meal (buffet or semi-buffet) but with the bridal party seated at one table, and usually a seated parents' table also. (Optional: individually boxed pieces of groom's cake) | Dancing optional but usual; orchestra of three or more pieces<br>Receiving line: announcer optional and not usual in an intimate circle of friends<br>Refreshments: champagne or punch, bride's cake. Food and service may be as elaborate as for Ceremonial reception or somewhat simpler, depending on time of day. (Optional: individually boxed pieces of groom's cake) | Optional, though a large reception follows a small and simple ceremony<br>Music: optional<br>Receiving line: optional, depending on number of guests<br>Refreshments: may be only champagne or punch and a cake; or small seated meal; or buffet meal for a larger number |
| Ushers | At least one for each 50 guests, but usually the same number as bridesmaids | Same as Ceremonial | Two or none |

**AGE OF CONSENT:** The age of consent is the age at which young people can marry without parental permission. It is established by law in each state, and varies widely. Details are given under "License," following.

**ALTAR BOYS.** Altar boys are also known as "candle lighters," since their main duty is to light the tapers used during a candlelight ceremony. There usually are two altar boys, though there may be more. Boys over ten years and under fourteen who are relatives of either the bride or groom are most often chosen to serve in this capacity. They wear regular suits even if the groom is in formal day or evening clothes.

Customs vary widely from church to church in different parts of the country. Sometimes the candles are lighted about half an hour before the ceremony; sometimes just before the bride's mother is seated, and the altar boys then take places determined during the rehearsal. If there are no specially appointed altar boys, a member of the church staff lights the candles.

**ANNIVERSARIES.** For details about the celebration of wedding anniversaries, *see* WEDDING ANNIVERSARIES.

**ANNOUNCEMENTS.** *See also* the introductory text under "Invitations," following.

**Formal.** Formal announcements are governed by explicit rules. Unless these are followed, it is better to announce a marriage in an informal fashion.

1. A formal announcement is never sent to anyone who has received an invitation to the wedding or reception.
2. *Addressing:*   The rules are the same as for "Invitations," following in this section.
3. *Answering:* No answer is required to a formal announcement, though it is correct and certainly kind to send a little note of good wishes in answer. Depending on circumstances, this note may be addressed to the bride, the groom, or the parents of either.

4. *By whom sent*: The groom or his family does not issue a formal announcement. The announcement is made by the bride's family, whether or not they have attended the ceremony.
5. *Enclosures*: An "At Home" card giving the bridal couple's new address is usually enclosed to personal friends (but not to strictly business friends). Or the new address may be engraved in the lower left-hand corner of the announcement:

> After the first of August
> 38 Elm Drive
> Waco, Texas 00000

6. *Format*: Size, paper, and all other physical details of the formal announcement are the same as for a formal invitation. Double envelopes are used.

---

Mr. and Mrs. Lewis Alexander Wilkins

have the honour of

announcing*the marriage of their daughter

Marjorie Ellsworth

to

Mr. Robert Emmons Peterson

Thursday, the twenty-fifth of October

One thousand, nine hundred and sixty-two

Saint Bartholomew's Church

New York

---

* Or "have the honor to announce"; or "announce."

7. *Gifts:* The person who receives an announcement is not obligated to send a wedding present. If a present is sent, it is addressed "Mr. and Mrs. John Jones Smith."
8. *Mailing date:* Announcements are never mailed before the ceremony, but it is customary to post them on the same day or a day or so following.
9. *Standard forms:* With a few changes, the wording is like that of an invitation. The actual place of the ceremony is not mentioned unless it was in a house of worship, which may be given, or not. But the date, year, and city (state also, if needed, to identify a small community) are always given.

*A mature bride or one with no close relatives.*

In these and similar cases, the bride and groom issue the announcement jointly:

> *Miss Mary Ann Brown*
> *and*
> *Mr. John Jones Smith*
> *announce their marriage*
> [etc.]

*Divorcées:*
The parents (or other relatives if the parents are not living) of a young divorcée may make the announcement, in which case her given name and former husband's last name are used (no "Mrs."): Mary Brown West.

If a divorcée and her groom announce the marriage jointly, she uses her maiden name and her former husband's last name: Mrs. Greene Barkeley.

*Widows:*
The marriage of a young widow may be announced by her parents, and her name used without "Mrs."—Mary Brown West.

A widow of mature years usually makes her own announcement jointly with the groom, and uses the same name she has been using on her social calling cards: Mrs. Henry York Brown.

*See* "Invitations" for all other details.

**Informal.** The bride, groom, and their parents write or tell the news to their various friends in any way that suits them.

**Press.** Announcements to be printed in the society columns are addressed to the Society Editor, and should arrive several days before the date of the ceremony so that copy can be prepared to appear the day following or perhaps on the following Sunday.

A picture of the bride in her wedding dress can be sent with the announcement if the bride cares to have a photograph made in advance. (The newspaper will send its own photographer if it wants a news shot of both bride and groom —usually taken as they leave the church.)

Information can be telephoned to a newspaper, but it is far better to type a release, double-spaced and on one side of the paper only.

Some newspapers have standard announcement forms, which are mailed out in response to a telephoned request. The following form is an example. It is a good guide to the various details that can be included in a press announcement. (*Note:* In all cases, give the names of both parents, living or dead, of the bride and the groom.)

Society Department
WEDDING FORM
(Please Type or Print)

Bride's Name_____

Bride's Parents_____

Address_____ Telephone_____

Bride's Schools_____ When?_____

Bride's Affiliations_____

Bridegroom's Name_____

Bridegroom's Parents_____

Address_____ Telephone_____

Bridegroom's Schools_____ When?_____

Bridegroom's Affiliations_____

Wedding Date and Time_____

Wedding Place_____

Reception Place_____

Honeymoon _____

Future Home_____

Bride's Honor Attendants_____ | Best Man_____

_____ | Ushers_____

Her Other Attendants_____ | _____

_____ | _____

_____ | _____

_____ | Clergyman_____

Giving Bride in Marriage_____

Bride's Gown_____

_____

Veil_____ Bouquet_____

Attendants' Costumes_____

_____

_____Flowers_____

Decorations at Church_____

Decorations at Reception_____

Bride's Mother's Costume_____

Bridegroom's Mother's Costume_____

Going Away Costume_____

_____

Notes: _____
(Please return several days PRIOR to wedding)

If a newspaper wedding form similar to this one is not available, a typed release should follow the pattern of the one given below. The name of the person issuing the release can be that of a social secretary or anyone else to whom the newspaper can direct inquiries for additional information. The names of the bridesmaids, the schools and club affiliations of the bride and groom, the place where the reception is to be held, and other such information may also be included.

From:

MRS. HENRY YORK BROWN
10 West Boulevard
City, State 00000

PLaza 0-0000

Mr. and Mrs. Henry York Brown of 10 West Boulevard announce the marriage of their daughter, Mary Ann, to Mr. John Jones Smith, son of Mr. and Mrs. William Gregg Smith of Chicago. The wedding will be held on June 10 at St. George's Church in Boston. The couple will be attended by [names of the maid of honor and best man, and their places of residence, but no street address if they are from out of town]. After a two weeks' motor trip, the couple will return to New York City, where Mr. Smith is completing postgraduate work at Columbia University.

If the bride and groom make the announcement jointly, the so-called impersonal form is used in the release. It is the same as the form above except that it begins "Announcement is made of the marriage of Miss Mary Ann Brown and Mr. John Jones Smith," and so on.

**Press, Paid Announcements.** A paid wedding announcement in the Vital Statistics columns is not strictly correct by the standard rules of etiquette, but this is one of the rules that is being changed by changing times. In large cities there is not room in the society pages for individual news stories about every marriage that takes place in the community. Therefore, it is a growing custom in some localities to use this way to publish an announcement that has not found a place in the news columns.

**"AT HOME" CARDS.** These cards are practical but by no means obligatory. They may be included with invitations and announcements to personal friends, but are not enclosed with announcements to business acquaintances, since their purpose—to announce the couple's new address and the date when they will be in residence there—is a social one.

Names are omitted on At Home cards sent with an invitation to a wedding because the invitation is mailed before the bride has a right to use her new name.

Street names are used as they would be on a formally addressed envelope, without abbreviations such as "Ave." or "St." The state and the month are spelled in full, and a zip code is always used.

An At Home card is about 3 by 4 inches.

Good form both before and after the marriage:

*At home*

*after the fifteenth of November*

*296 East 72nd Street*

*New York 10021*

Good form after the marriage:

*Mr. and Mrs. John Jones Smith*

*After the fifteenth of November*

*296 East 72nd Street*

*New York 10021*

**ATTENDANTS.** The term "bridal party" means the bride, the groom, and their attendants, including ushers. In very simple weddings there may be no attendants, but at least two are usual: a best man and a maid or matron of honor. At a ceremonial or formal wedding, attendants may include all the following:

Altar boys (also known as "candle lighters")
Best man
Bridesmaids
Flower girls
Maid of honor
Matron of honor
Page boys (also known as "trainbearers")
Ring bearer
Ushers

(Details of the selection and invitation of the attendants, their duties, dress, and expenses, are given under separate headings, following.)

**Relatives.** Any relative may serve as an attendant, and it is customary to ask certain relatives to serve in particular capacities. For example, a sister of the bride (if she is of appropriate age) is the usual first choice as maid or matron of honor. A brother of the groom is usually chosen as best man, if he is old enough to carry the best man's very heavy duties. It is also customary to ask all other sisters and brothers of the bride and groom to serve as bridesmaids and ushers—if, of course, they are of suitable age. The best man is usually about the age of the groom, but need not be, and the father of the groom sometimes serves as best man. The mother of the bride seldom serves as matron of honor because she has too many other duties. When a mature widow remarries, a daughter of appropriate age may serve as honor attendant; and a grown son may serve as best man for his father.

**BACHELOR DINNER.** A stag dinner before a big wedding is traditional, though today many grooms prefer to skip it. The event is the groom's last fling with his friends in farewell to bachelor freedom, and so women are never invited. The best man and the ushers are always invited, and other male friends may be. The party may be given by the groom, the best man, or any male relative or friend; or a group may chip in as joint hosts to the groom. The best man makes the arrangements or helps with them if the groom is the host. Invitations are informal and are generally given by telephone or in person.

A bachelor dinner usually is held in a private dining room of a club or restaurant or at a bachelor's own quarters. Experience proves that it is wiser to choose a date several days in advance of the wedding rather than the evening preceding it. The groom may give his presents to the best man and ushers at this party or at some other time, as he prefers.

A distinctive feature of the bachelor dinner is the toast to the bride. It is proposed by the groom. He rises, and all others rise also. He lifts his glass and says, "To the bride." All glasses are drained and—today—usually returned to the table intact rather than snapped at the stem or flung into a fireplace. If the groom does break his glass (so that it can never be used for a less honorable purpose), all the guests also break theirs—and the restaurant or club adds a charge to the bill.

Champagne is the traditional wine for this toast, but cocktails, whiskey, beer, or grape juice can serve as substitutes.

The bride sometimes gives what is called a "maiden dinner" for her attendants and other women friends on the same evening as the bachelor dinner, though this is not a traditional custom.

**BANNS.** Banns are proclamations in a house of worship of a couple's intention to marry. They are made on three successive Sundays or holy days before a wedding in the churches of both bride and groom if they attend different ones. Their purpose is to inform the community, and also to give anyone who has reason to do so a chance to protest the marriage. Many faiths do not practice this custom. In those that do, the testimony of reliable witnesses can sometimes be substituted for the publication of banns. Guidance in this matter is best supplied by one's own clergyman.

**BEST MAN.** Next to the bride's mother, the busiest person at a big wedding is the best man. He is chosen and invited to serve by the groom. He may be a relative of either the bride or groom, but usually is a close friend of the groom. Generally the best man and the groom are about the same age, though the best man may be decidedly younger or older. On rare occasions, the groom's father serves as best man or, in the case of a remarriage fairly late in life, the groom's grown son.

At Protestant weddings, the best man need not be of the same faith as the groom. Catholics and Jews are governed by special rules. Inquiry should be made before asking a man of one of those faiths to serve at a wedding in another faith.

The best man may be married or single. If he is married, his wife is asked to attend prewedding parties (except the bachelor dinner) with him.

It is a great compliment to be asked to serve as best man, and the invitation cannot be refused except for very good reason. Considerable thought should be given to the selection before a man is actually invited. The best man's duties are extensive, and he also may be put to quite a bit of expense in time and money. Therefore, it is important to ask someone who can afford to accept and who is a reliable administrator as well.

**Clothes.** If the groom is in street clothes, the best man wears a similar suit, and his accessories match those of the groom—except, perhaps, for his tie. If the groom is in formal day or evening dress, the best man dresses to match with the exception of his boutonniere—a white flower usually different also from the boutonnieres of the ushers.

**Duties.** The best man holds himself ready to help the groom in any way that he can, but specifically his duties include:

Accepting, whenever possible, invitations to any prewedding parties.

Attending the rehearsal.

Calling for the groom on the wedding day in plenty of time to help him pack and dress; making sure the groom has the marriage license and any other documents needed for the ceremony; and taking charge of the bride's wedding ring until it is needed during the service.

Making sure that the couple's tickets, passports, luggage checks, and any other such items needed for the wedding trip are with the groom's going-away clothes.

Seeing that the groom's going-away clothes are complete, and having them delivered to the place of the reception if the groom is changing there before leaving on the honeymoon.

Making arrangements in advance to stow the luggage of both the bride and groom in a car or taxi during the reception so that there is no delay at the time of departure. (If their first stop is a local hotel, the best man registers for them in advance, perhaps delivers a major part of their luggage in advance, orders champagne and flowers if the groom wants them waiting, and gives the groom the room key so that he need not stop at the desk for it.)

Giving the fee to the clergyman (unless the groom has mailed it) either before or after the ceremony, but always in the vestry or other appropriate place—never in the church itself.

Signing as a witness, if required.

Retrieving his own and the groom's hat and gloves from the vestry after the ceremony, and taking them to the reception.

Helping to get special guests to the reception if other arrangements have not been made for them.

Acting as announcer at the reception if asked to take over this duty.

Proposing the first toast (to the bride and groom).

Reading congratulatory telegrams aloud (if this is done) at some time during the reception.

Dancing with the bride after she has taken a turn with the groom, her father-in-law, and her father.

Helping the groom change to his going-away clothes, and taking charge of his wedding clothes.

Checking to make sure that the luggage of both bride and groom is properly stowed in their car or taxi.

Summoning the parents of the groom for a private farewell before the young couple make their traditional dash from the reception.

**Expenses.** The best man pays for his own clothes except for his tie, gloves, and spats (if worn), which are a present from the groom, as is his boutonniere.

If he lives out of town, the best man pays his own travel expenses. The groom, however, pays his hotel expenses or makes other arrangements to put him up.

The best man is obligated to give a wedding present.

**BIBLE AND PRAYER BOOK.** A bride may prefer to carry a prayer book or a Bible instead of a bridal bouquet. She hands it to her honor attendant after reaching her place at the altar, just as she would a bouquet. Even if she is in simple street dress, the book may be marked with white ribbons decorated with flowers. If the bride wants the clergyman to use her prayer book for the ceremony, the markers are not decorated with flowers or in any other way. In this case, she hands the book to the clergyman instead of to her honor attendant. He hands it back to her before she leaves the altar if there is a formal recessional. Before the receiving line forms, the bride gives the Bible or prayer book to the honor attendant or a member of the family to be set aside in a safe place.

**BLOOD TESTS.** A blood test made within thirty days of the wedding date is required by virtually all states before a marriage license is issued.

See "License" for details.

**BREAKFAST.** "Wedding breakfast" is the standard name for a meal served after the ceremony at any hour until about one thirty in the afternoon, even though both time and menu are typical of lunch.

For seating and other details, see "Reception."

**BRIDAL DINNER, BRIDE'S DINNER, AND SO ON.** It is easy to confuse the following terms, and for that reason their alternate names are generally used:

The bridal dinner is also called the rehearsal dinner. It is a party given after the rehearsal of the ceremony.

The bride's dinner is also called the maiden dinner. It is a parallel to the groom's bachelor dinner.

The bride's lunch is also called the bridesmaids' lunch. A special party the bride gives for her attendants during the week before the wedding, it can also be either a tea or a breakfast instead of a lunch. Sometimes it replaces the maiden dinner if the bride does not choose to give a party on the night of bachelor dinner, and many brides skip both such parties. There are no special rules for the bridesmaids' party except that men are not asked.

**BRIDE.** Hairsplitters refer to her as "the bride-to-be" until the day of her wedding, but generally an engaged girl is referred to as "the bride" during the weeks of parties and preparations before the wedding as well as on her wedding day and during her honeymoon. After the honeymoon, she becomes "a recent bride."

**Bouquet.** *See "Flowers."*

**Clothes.** What the bride will wear is determined by the degree of formality of the wedding, where it is held, and the hour, but there are some general rules that apply to all wedding dresses:

The dress is never cut very low and is never off-the-shoulder.

The arms are usually covered—by long sleeves or by long gloves if the sleeves are extremely short. Gloves are not correct if the dress has long sleeves, and need not be worn if the sleeves are just above the elbow or longer.

Jewelry is generally restrained and simple, though the bride may wear a handsome heirloom necklace with an appropriate dress, or the groom's wedding gift of jewelry if it is suitable to her costume.

White or off-white is worn only at a bride's first wedding, though a first-time bride may wear a delicate pastel shade if she prefers. A bride never wears black.

A formal wedding gown may be floor-length, with or without a train; or it may be "waltz length"—thirteen inches from the floor. It is worn with a headdress—a circlet of pearls, a wreath of flowers, and so on—with or without a veil. The veil may be long or short, of tulle or lace. The shoes are pumps, without decoration, to match the dress.

Full bridal array is not usually worn at an informal wedding, though it may be if the wedding is not held in a judge's chambers or other business background. The bride's costume can be as elaborate or as simple as she wishes—from a long or short dress to a suit—according to the time and the place of the ceremony and reception. It may be white or any color except black.

**Duties.** Since the bride's family is responsible for virtually all preparations (and expenses) of the wedding and reception, her duties are extensive. They include:

Collating her invitation and announcement lists with those of the groom, and seeing that both sets are addressed and mailed.

Going with the groom to apply for the marriage license, to choose the wedding ring or rings, and to call on the clergyman who will officiate.

Choosing her bridesmaids and other attendants, issuing them invitations to serve, and deciding the style, color, and fabric of their costumes.

Attending the rehearsal.

After the wedding, writing special notes of thanks to the clergyman, her attendants, and all other friends who took some special part in the ceremony—a soloist, for example. (These notes can be combined with her thanks for wedding presents.)

Sending handwritten notes of thanks for all wedding presents.

**Expenses.**   The long list of expenses paid by the bride or her family are given under "Bride's Father."

**BRIDEGROOM.**   "Groom" and "bridegroom" are used interchangeably, during the same period shortly before and after the wedding, as "bride" is used.

**Clothes.**   It should be noted that the groom need not be dressed to the same degree of formality as the bride except for a ceremonial wedding. (See the chart at the beginning of this section.) For example, at a formal daytime wedding the bride may correctly wear a lovely long wedding gown and the groom may correctly wear a dark suit, white shirt, solid or striped tie, black shoes and socks (or in summer a white suit), rather than rent a formal daytime costume of cutaway or black sack coat and striped trousers. If formal clothes are rented, sufficient time should be allowed to have them fitted—they are a sorry sight unless they do fit well.

After six, the groom may wear a dinner jacket or a dark suit (as above).

At an informal wedding, day or evening, the groom may wear his going-away suit; or, if a large reception will follow a quiet ceremony, dress appropriately for it.

**Duties.**   Compared to the bride, the groom has fairly light duties. They include:

Getting his invitation and announcement lists and those of his family to the bride in plenty of time.

Going with the bride to choose the wedding ring or rings, to apply for the license, and to call on the clergyman who will officiate.

Making certain that all legal, health, and other certificates are in order.

Choosing and inviting the best man.

Choosing the ushers (almost always in consultation with the bride), issuing them an invitation to serve, and briefing them about their costumes.

Making all arrangements for the honeymoon.

Attending the rehearsal.

Remembering to thank the bride's parents for the wedding and reception—as well as for their daughter.

Writing a note of special thanks to his best man.

**Expenses.**   The groom pays for:

1. The bachelor dinner.
2. The clergyman's fee (if a relative or friend performs the ceremony, a gift instead).
3. Flowers: A corsage for the bride to wear on the wedding trip. (The bride's parents usually provide her bouquet, but in some communities it is customary for the groom to pay for it.)
   Corsages for both mothers and grandmothers. (Sometimes the bride's father supplies the flowers for her mother and grandmother.)
   Boutonnieres for his best man, ushers, his father, and himself.
4. The honeymoon.
5. Lodging for his best man and ushers if they live out of town.
6. The marriage license.
7. Presents: A wedding present for the bride, usually jewelry; a present as well as gloves and ties for his best man and the ushers.
8. The wedding ring.

**BRIDEGROOM'S PARENTS.**   It should never be forgotten that the wedding is an important event in the lives of the groom's parents also. Though they have few responsibilities, they are of course drawn into all the prewedding festivities. They attend the rehearsal and are especially honored guests at the wedding and reception. The groom's mother stands in the receiving line. His father often does also.

**Clothes.** The costume of the groom's mother more or less matches that of the bride's mother in style and formality. The groom's father dresses to match his son.

**Duties.** The groom's mother helps her son with the lists of relatives and friends who are to receive invitations and announcements, and sees that they reach the bride's mother in plenty of time for checking against her lists, and addressing and mailing.

**Expenses.** In addition to a wedding present, the groom's parents usually give the bride a special present for herself, traditionally a piece of jewelry.

**BRIDE'S FATHER.** The bride's father shares with his wife as many of the arrangements for ordering decorations, transportation, and other such things as he chooses, but usually his main obligation is to pay the bills.

**Clothes.** His costume matches the groom's in degree of formality.

**Duties.** Beyond lending moral support, his duties include attending the rehearsal, escorting his daughter to the church and down the aisle, and acting as the host at the reception.

**Expenses.** The bride or her family pay for the following:

1. Announcements, invitations, and postage.
2. Clothes: The bride's wedding dress and trousseau. Sometimes, though not usually, costumes for the bride's attendants.
3. Decorations for the church.
4. Fees: All fees connected with the ceremony except for the clergyman's fee. *See* details under "Church Expenses."
5. Flowers: Bouquets for the bridesmaids and usually the bride's bouquet, though sometimes the groom supplies that. Corsages for the bride's mother and grandmother (sometimes the groom also supplies these).
6. Lodging for the bride's attendants who live out of town.
7. Presents: A gift to each of the bride's attendants; also the bride's wedding present to the groom.
8. Photographs at the wedding and the reception.
9. Reception: All expenses, including decorations, food, music, tips.
10. Rehearsal party, though the groom's parents may give it.
11. Ring for the groom if there is a double-ring ceremony.
12. Transportation for the bridal party to the ceremony and then to the reception.

**BRIDE'S MOTHER.** The bride's parents are the official host and hostess at the wedding and reception, and as such bear the responsibility for practically all arrangements and expenses.

**Clothes.** For a morning wedding, the bride's mother wears a pretty daytime dress (usually light in color, though it need not be), hat, and gloves. She does not wear a long dress even if her daughter is in a full-length wedding gown. For a formal afternoon wedding, she wears a dressy cocktail dress, hat, and gloves. For a formal evening wedding, she wears a dinner dress or full-length gown, usually not extremely low-cut, however. Depending on the requirements of her church and local custom, she wears no head covering with an evening dress, or merely a small arrangement of flowers or of flowers and veiling in her hair.

**Duties.** In addition to helping her daughter plan all the details of the wedding, the bride's mother usually supervises their execution. Her heavy responsibilities include:

Consulting with the groom's mother about the lists for invitations and announcements, ordering the required number, and seeing that they are sent at the proper times.

Choosing her own dress and informing the groom's mother of its style and color so that she in turn has plenty of time to plan her costume.

Making arrangements for decorations and music at the wedding and reception, and for the flowers for the bride's attendants.

Ordering the refreshments and making all other plans for the reception.

Making arrangements to house out-of-town bridesmaids and other special guests.

Seeing that transportation to the church is provided for the wedding party, and making arrangements for the parking of guests' cars, and so on.

Helping to open and keep orderly lists of the wedding presents.

Receiving at the reception.

And in all other ways seeing that things go smoothly in spite of the natural flurry and excitement.

**BRIDESMAIDS.** The bride chooses her bridesmaids from among her friends, and customarily includes her sisters and those of the groom if they are of suitable age.

*See also* "Maid and Matron of Honor."

There may be any number of bridesmaids, though more than twelve is unusual since a great parade of bridesmaids makes a wedding look more like a theatrical production than a religious ceremony.

Bridesmaids may be married or single. They usually are about the age of the bride, but need not be. On some occasions all the bridesmaids are children or teen-agers. By Protestant rules, bridesmaids need not be of the same faith as the bride, but inquiry should be made before asking a Catholic or Jewish girl to serve, since she may be governed by special restrictions against active participation in religious services outside her faith.

The bride issues the invitations to serve. They should not be given by her mother or anyone else except in unusual circumstances. The invitation to be a bridesmaid is an honor that can be refused only for a very compelling reason. Therefore careful thought should be given to the choice, since a bridesmaid is usually put to a certain amount of expense.

**Clothes.** The bridesmaids' dresses, shoes, and headdresses are always alike in fabric and cut, but may be different in color. The dresses may be long or short, but usually are a style suitable for later use. Bridesmaids wear simple jewelry or none at all—usually no more than a strand of pearls.

**Duties.** A bridesmaid holds herself ready to help with addressing invitations, arranging decorations, and similar tasks, but specifically her duties include:

Accepting, whenever possible, all invitations to prewedding parties.

Attending the rehearsal.

Arriving promptly at the bride's home at the specified time on the day of the ceremony.

Standing in the receiving line at the reception.

**Expenses.** The bride chooses the style, fabric, and color of the clothes of all her attendants, but they pay for their own. (The bride's parents, if they wish, may correctly pay for the costumes of their daughter's attendants, but this is not the usual custom.)

Each bridesmaid gives a wedding present, or all the bridesmaids may join in buying one substantial gift.

An out-of-town bridesmaid pays her own traveling expenses, though the bride's parents may make her a present of the trip, if they choose. The bride's parents make arrangements for her to stay in their house or with friends, or otherwise take care of her living expenses.

**Junior Bridesmaids.** A girl too old to be a flower girl but much younger than the bridesmaids is often included in the bridal party as a junior bridesmaid. This honor is usually given to girls between ten and fifteen—very often to little sisters of the bride and groom who long to be "members of the wedding." There may be one junior bridesmaid or many.

Her expenses are the same as those of the other bridesmaids. Her clothes may match theirs or be different in cut and color—and it is just as well not to challenge a very junior bridesmaid with unaccustomed high heels.

A junior bridesmaid goes to the rehearsal party and the reception, but need not be invited to all prewedding parties if she is very young.

**CAKES.** The ceremonial sharing of a wedding cake by the bride and groom is ancient and worldwide "magic" to ensure happiness, good luck, and abundance in their life together. It was part of the marriage ritual of Roman tribes before recorded history. And the white man found both the American Indians and the Fiji Islanders practicing the custom when he first set foot in their lands.

**Bride's Cake.** This is another name for the standard wedding cake that is the most important item of refreshment following the ceremony. It is unthinkable to omit it, though the Groom's Cake (see below) may be.

The cake for the first-time bride, by tradition, has white icing and decorations—except for the little groom, if a bridal couple is used on top. The little figures of bride and groom are not used as decorations if the bride has been married before; and the cake is iced in a pastel shade or in white with pastel decorations. A wedding cake may be made in any shape—rectangular, round, heart, or ring. Nothing is written in icing on a wedding cake—with one exception: A cake baked and iced to resemble a wedding ring usually has the initial of the bride's first name on the left and of the groom's first name on the right. Large wedding cakes are made in several tiers to facilitate cutting and serving them in attractive segments.

The traditional wedding cake is a dark fruit cake, but also popular today are white fruit cake and white or pale-gold pound cake. Sometimes the small top layer of a tiered white cake is made of dark fruit cake and sealed in a tin under the icing. It and its decorations are removed by a waiter or the person in charge of serving (after the bride has cut the first slice from a lower layer), and are saved for the bride and groom to enjoy on their first or any subsequent anniversary.

Little gold or silver trinkets wrapped in waxed paper sometimes are inserted after the cake is baked. They are put in the layer that will be served to the attendants—those for the women on the left and those for the men on the right. Some distinctive flower or leaf in the icing or narrow white satin ribbons mark their location so that the person who serves the cake can make sure each attendant gets one and learns what fortune has in store. A button or dog for a man and a cat for a woman foretells single life for another year. Dice signal exceptional luck coming to a man. A thimble tells a woman that her industry will be richly rewarded. For both a man and a woman, a heart means a happy romance—new or continuing; a ring means "next of your sex in the bridal party to wed"; a little wishbone promises fulfillment within a year of any wish made on it; and a coin foretells riches to come.

**Cutting.** At a seated meal, the wedding cake usually is part of the table decoration—placed so that the bride can reach it conveniently when the time comes for cutting it. If there is no bridal table, the cake stands with the other refreshments on a buffet or on a separate table at a more convenient location.

The cake is cut at the end of a meal or after refreshments such as cocktail sandwiches have been served. If only cake and champagne are offered, the cake is cut after everyone has been served a round or two of wine.

The bride stands to cut the cake. If the bridal party is seated at a table, all men rise with her unless this would make it difficult for other guests to see, in which case she asks them to keep their seats. Women at the bridal table remain seated. If there is no separate table for the bridal party, the attendants gather around the bride and groom, and other guests stand near, to watch the cake-cutting.

The groom stands beside the bride, his hand over hers to help her guide the knife. Sometimes the knife is a special one engraved with the initials of the bride and groom and the wedding date—a wedding present that makes a charming keepsake. The knife handle is usually decorated with white ribbons in which flowers are knotted. If the groom is in dress uniform, his dress sword (not decorated with ribbons and flowers, of course) is traditionally used for the first cut.

The bride cuts only the first slice. She and the groom then simultaneously feed each other a small piece. After this ceremony, a waiter or someone else finishes the cutting and serving.

**Groom's Cake.** This term is confusing to many people because it is not often used today. It is just another name for little pieces of wedding cake that are boxed in advance and distributed as souvenirs to the guests. The groom's cake is traditionally dark fruit cake with white icing.

**Souvenir Pieces.** If there is no groom's cake packaged for easy transport, every wedding guest cannot expect to take a piece of cake home. It is customary to supply each bridesmaid and other unmarried woman with a little extra slice, since everyone knows that a girl who sleeps with a piece of wedding cake under her pillow will see her future husband in her dreams. It is usual also to send a piece of wedding cake to any especially dear relative or friend who is not able to attend the reception. (A supply of cellophane bags to protect the unpackaged pieces will be useful.)

The tiny white boxes used to package wedding cake may be square, rectangular, triangular, or heart-shaped, and either plain or monogrammed with the initials of the bride and groom. A box is put at each place at the bridal table, and at all other places if the entire party is seated. Otherwise, the boxes are passed on trays by ushers, bridesmaids, or waiters. Or heaps of the little boxes may be left near the exit so that guests can help themselves when leaving. A guest is expected to take only one—not to load up with several as souvenirs, unless invited to take an extra box as a memento for an invalid, a small child, or someone who could not be present. The bride usually saves several boxes to share with her husband on major anniversaries of the wedding, such as the first, tenth, twentieth, twenty-fifth, and fiftieth.

**CANCELED.** If all plans to marry are canceled before the wedding invitations are mailed, the procedures given under ENGAGEMENTS are followed.

If invitations to the wedding have already been mailed, the procedures are different. In both cases, all wedding presents are returned.

First of all, the close relatives of the bride and groom and all members of the bridal party must be notified by telegram, telephone, or in person before the formal cancellation notices are sent. Speculation inevitably follows the cancellation of a wedding at so late a date. The best way to keep gossip to a minimum is to give the fewest personal details possible. "They changed their minds," though obvious, serves far better than lengthy explanations or recriminations. No one should press for details.

If time allows, the cancellation notice is sent in much the same form as the original invitation. If time is very short, everyone who received a formal invitation must be notified by telegram or in any other informal and rapid fashion.

A formal notice of cancellation is printed on a single card, not a double fold, and a single envelope is used. Paper is similar to that of an invitation. See "Invitations," following, for examples of standard forms.

If a release has been sent to newspapers, they also must be notified as quickly as possible—by telephone, if time is extremely short; otherwise, by a typed release headed by the name and address of the person issuing the release so that the editor can check for details or make sure that the news is not the work of a very misguided practical joker.

A standard form:

> *Mr. and Mrs. Henry York Brown of 10 West Avenue*
> *announce that the marriage of their daughter, Mary Ann,*
> *to John Jones Smith, which was scheduled for June 10,*
> *will not take place.*

See "Invitations to the Ceremony" for the procedures if invitations are recalled but the wedding will take place on the date scheduled, and for postponements.

**CANDLE LIGHTERS.** See "Altar Boys."

**CATHOLIC SERVICES.** See "Ceremony, Differences from Basic Protestant."

**CEREMONY, BASIC PROTESTANT.** What follows here is a summary of the most ceremonious and usual Protestant procedure in church, which is correct (with certain alterations) in all denominations; needs only simplification for smaller and simpler weddings; and can also be adapted to a wedding performed by a judge or other civil authority elsewhere than in church. The details are to be taken as a general guide only, since they are subject to almost endless variations depending on the place, size, and degree of formality of a wedding.

The important special differences observed in Orthodox and Roman Catholic ceremonies, and in Episcopal and civil ceremonies, follow immediately after this summary. See also "Ceremony, Jewish."

The rules for wedding guests are found under "Guests" and "Receptions."

**Assembling at the Church.** The ushers arrive about an hour before the time of the ceremony, put on their boutonnieres, which have been sent to the church, and wait in the vestibule, ready to seat the guests.

For details, see "Seating."

Guests begin to arrive about half an hour before the ceremony, and should make a point of coming early enough to be seated at least ten minutes before the service is to begin.

The groom and best man arrive together about half an hour before the ceremony and wait in the vestry.

The bride's attendants assemble at the home of the bride (or the place where she is dressing). They may dress there or arrive already costumed except for their bouquets, which are given to them before they leave for the church.

The bride, her parents, and the attendants leave the house at about the same time, in this order: the bride's mother in the first car, alone (or she may take one or two of the attendants with her); next, the bride's attendants in other cars; last, the bride, accompanied only by her father or whoever will give her away. She sits on his right.

The bride's mother and the attendants arrive at the church about ten minutes before the ceremony. They assemble in a secluded part of the vestibule or a room near it. The bride and her father arrive shortly thereafter and join them.

The groom's parents should arrive before the bride. They wait in the vestibule, but not with the bride's attendants.

An usher notifies the groom as soon as the bride arrives.

Just before the hour of the ceremony, the main church doors are closed and no one is seated by an usher thereafter except the groom's parents and the mother of the bride. (Guests arriving late must slip into seats in the rear or in the gallery.)

An usher escorts the parents of the groom to their pew.

Then the mother of the bride is escorted to her pew.

Two ushers march side by side to the head of the aisle, turn, and loop the pew ribbons into place from front to back.

Two other ushers (or men from the sexton's staff) unroll the aisle canvas from front to back.

The ushers join the bride's party, now lined up in the order determined at the rehearsal. If there is an uneven number of attendants in any category, the shortest walks first, alone. The rest follow, paired according to height, with the shorter ones in the lead. (The ushers are never paired with the bridesmaids in the processional.)

**Going to the Altar (the Processional).** It should be noted that there are many correct variations of the following procedure. The positions taken by the ushers and bridesmaids after they reach the chancel are also subject to many different arrangements according to the size and shape of the church.

The organist, who has been playing appropriate selections, lets the music fade and then begins the wedding march.

At the first strains of the wedding march, the congregation rises and the clergyman enters, followed by the groom, who in turn is followed by the best man.

The clergyman takes his place in the chancel and faces the congregation.

The groom stands on the right of the aisle (on the clergyman's left) and faces the procession. The best man stands on the groom's left, also facing toward the procession, a step farther from center and a step nearer the pews.

(A rehearsal is essential if a formal procession is to move with the proper grace and dignity. The "hesitation" gait is not used today, but the correct slow pace needs to be practiced. A space of four pews between each pair of attendants and a space of six or seven pews between groups of attendants are usual.)

The customary order of the procession is:

1. The choir (if any) in pairs, singing.
2. The junior ushers, paired. When they reach the head of the aisle, they divide, take positions determined at the rehearsal, and turn to face the bride as she comes down the aisle.
3. The ushers, paired. They divide and take positions as above.
4. The junior bridesmaids, paired. They take positions as determined at the rehearsal.
5. The bridesmaids, paired or singly, depending on the number. They divide and stand in front of the ushers.
6. The bride's honor attendant (if there are two, they may walk side by side; or walk singly, with the chief attendant following the other). The chief honor attendant takes a position on the left, opposite the best man. If there are two honor attendants, the other stands a step farther from the center and a step nearer the pews.
7. The ring bearer. He stands beside the best man.

8. The flower girls. They stand with or in front of the bridesmaids. (If a little page boy is acting in an honorary capacity, he may precede the flower girl or walk beside her.)
9. The bride on her father's right arm.
10. The page boys (if any) holding the train.

(*Note:* If the ring bearer is acting in an honorary capacity only, and is very young, he takes a seat—determined at the rehearsal—in one of the front pews. Very young flower girls and honorary page boys are also withdrawn from the procession near the head of the aisle.)

**The Processional:**

(1) Clergyman. (2) Bridegroom. (3) Best man.
(4) Ushers. (5) Bridesmaids. (6) Maid of honor.
(7) Flower girl. (8) Father of the bride. (9) Bride.
The positions of other members of the bridal procession and further details, are given in the text.

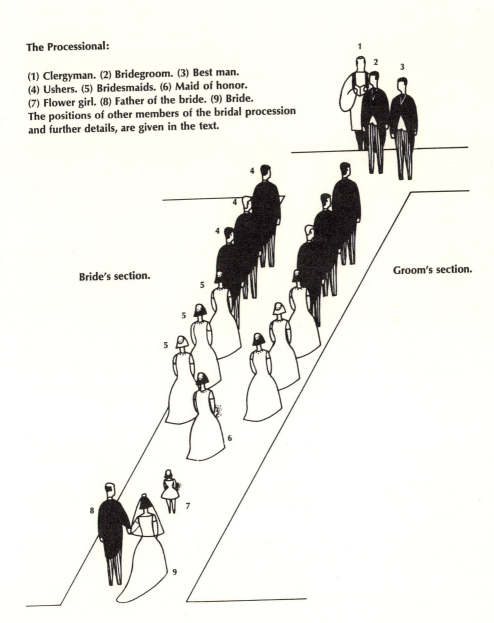

Bride's section.

Groom's section.

As the bride and her father reach the chancel steps, the groom steps forward and takes his place beside her in front of the clergyman. The bride relinquishes her father's arm and shifts her bouquet to her left hand. Many minor details from here on are determined in the rehearsal—with, of course, the advice and consent of the clergyman. For example, at this point in some ceremonies the bride gives her right hand to the groom, who may hold it in his right hand, or he may be instructed to put her hand in the crook of his left arm; or the bride and groom may stand side by side without touching until later in the service.

The music ceases and the marriage service begins.

**Marriage Service.** The marriage ceremony is in two main parts: the betrothal, and then the exchange of vows and the blessing. (Sometimes the bride and groom partake of communion in the second part.)

Depending on the size and shape of the church, the betrothal may be held at the foot of the chancel steps, and then the clergyman, bride, groom, the bride's honor attendants, the best man, and the ring bearer move up to the altar for the exchange of vows and the blessing. Or the entire service may be conducted in one place. Since all such matters are decided during rehearsal, there is no need to list the numerous possible variants here.

When, during the betrothal, the clergyman asks, "Who giveth this woman?" the bride's father may take her right hand and give it to the clergyman without verbal response. Or, in other ceremonies, her father says only, "I do," and then takes his place in the front pew.

When he reaches his place beside his wife, the congregation sits down.

If the bride is wearing a veil over her face, it may be turned back at the end of the betrothal, or it may not be lifted back until the second part of the marriage is completed. If the service is to be completed at the altar, the choir or organist provides soft music while the clergyman leads the way, followed by the bride and groom, then the bride's honor attendants, the best man, and the ring bearer. The rest of the bridal party remain in place, facing the altar.

The bride hands her bouquet (or prayer book or Bible) to her chief honor attendant, who has already handed her own bouquet to the second honor attendant or to a bridesmaid. (If the bride's own prayer book or Bible is to be used, she hands it to the clergyman.)

When the time comes, the best man hands the ring to the groom. He hands it to the clergyman, who blesses it, and returns it to the groom, who puts it on the bride's finger. (In some ceremonies, the best man hands the ring directly to the clergyman.) In a double-ring ceremony, the bride's honor attendant gives her the groom's ring at the same time the best man hands over the bride's ring. The rings are blessed together, and the bride puts the groom's in place immediately after she receives hers.

When the ceremony is complete, the clergyman congratulates the couple, and then they exchange a kiss if the rules of the church permit. (If the bride has been wearing a face veil to this point, she first turns to her honor attendant for help in raising it.)

**Recessional.** After the kiss is exchanged, the bride retrieves her bouquet from the maid of honor. The maid of honor then lifts the bride's train out of her way as the couple turn and face the aisle. The bride takes the groom's right arm.

The congregation rises, and the bride and groom start the exit march. They do not move swiftly, but at a faster pace than for the entrance march. (They may stop briefly to receive the congratulations of her parents and then his.)

If the ring bearer and the flower girl have been standing during the ceremony, they follow the bride and groom. Otherwise, the bride's honor attendant

On this page are two customary arrangements for the wedding party at the altar:
(1) Clergyman. (2) Bride. (3) Groom. (4) Father of the bride. (5) Best man.
(6) Maid or matron of honor. (7) Bridesmaids. (8) Ushers.

retrieves her own bouquet and is next in line—alone, if the best man has at this point made an exit through the vestry to pick up the groom's hat and gloves; or on the best man's right arm. If there is a second honor attendant, she goes out on the arm of the chief usher. Or the bride's two honor attendants may join the recessional side by side—again, a matter to be planned during the rehearsal.

The bridesmaids, paired, follow, and then the ushers, paired; or if there is an equal number, each bridesmaid may go out on the right arm of an usher.

When the bride and groom reach the end of the aisle near the church entrance, her parents sit down and the entire congregation does also. Unless there is to be a receiving line at the church, the bride and groom and her attendants get immediately into the waiting cars and go to the place of the reception, leaving only those ushers who have special duties.

One usher comes back up the aisle. He escorts the bride's mother out on his right arm. Her father follows a pace behind. Another usher comes to escort the groom's mother out, with the groom's father following. Grandmothers are then escorted out in the same fashion if they are to share a car with the parents to the place of the reception. Then two ushers release the ribbons, and the congregation is free to leave.

When leaving for the reception, the bride and groom take the first car, which is the one the bride used when coming to the church; the bridesmaids are in the next cars, and then the bride's parents followed by the groom's parents. The parents may take anyone they like with them, of course. The guests follow in their own cars or in cars provided by the bride's family.

**CEREMONY, DIFFERENCES FROM BASIC PROTESTANT.** Wedding ceremonies in all faiths are much more alike than different. Lady Bird Johnson emphasized this fact when speaking of the elaborate formal wedding of her younger daughter: "This is a wedding just like any other wedding—one boy, one girl, one church, one reception."

However, there are some special differences in the rituals and requirements among Christian faiths and between the Christian ceremony and the Jewish ceremony (which is discussed under "Ceremony, Jewish," below.)

**Church Ceremonies in General.** Traditionally, a wedding is held in the bride's regular church, but it may be held in the groom's—or in any other church if appropriate arrangements are made.

Usually the bride's clergyman officiates if the wedding is in his church, though with his permission someone else may do so. For example, if a relative of the bride or groom is a clergyman, they may want him to serve or to share the service with the resident clergyman. In any case, the resident clergyman is first consulted and then adds his formal invitation to that of the bride and groom.

Most churches have specified hours and days when weddings may be held. It is essential to confer with the clergyman before making any positive plans concerning him or his church.

A chapel is often the first choice if the guest list is small and the congregation would fill only the first few rows in the main body of the church. In a chapel there still may be bridesmaids, ushers, formal wedding dress, and other components of a formal wedding; or, of course, the wedding can be very simple as to dress, attendants, and decorations.

In some faiths, weddings may be performed only in a house of worship unless special official permission is granted for a wedding to be held elsewhere. In others, it is quite usual for a clergyman to perform a marriage in a private residence, garden, club, or hotel. He *must*, however, be consulted to make sure that decorations, music, and all other details have his approval.

Usually no fee is charged for the use of a church itself for the wedding of a member or members of the congregation, though certain other fees are charged. Nonmembers pay a standard fee for the use of the church.

*See "Church Expenses."*

**Civil Ceremonies in General.** Civil ceremonies fall into two main divisions: very simple marriages held in the office of a city, town, or county clerk, or in a judge's chambers; and quite elaborate weddings performed by a judge, governor, mayor, or other nonreligious official at a private residence, hotel, or other place appropriate for a formal gathering.

Rings are not exchanged during a civil ceremony, and the father of the bride does not give her away. At an elaborate civil wedding, he may escort her to the place where the groom, best man, and the official who will perform the ceremony are waiting, much as he would in a church.

If the marriage takes place in a clerk's office or judge's chambers, the bride's costume is not more elaborate than a pretty cocktail suit or dress. A wedding dress and veil are not appropriate in such business backgrounds. The bride does not carry a bouquet, though she may wear as elaborate a corsage as the groom chooses. She may or may not wear a hat. She lays her gloves and purse aside during the ceremony. Often, there are no official attendants or, at most, a best man and maid or matron of honor. Usually only a few relatives and friends witness the ceremony. A large reception may follow even the simplest civil ceremony, or there may be a festive lunch or dinner for only the small wedding party.

A civil wedding at home or in a garden, club, or hotel can be simple, charming, and quiet, or there can be the full run of attendants as elaborately dressed as for the most formal of church weddings. In either case, the bride correctly wears a wedding gown with veil and train if she wishes.

A town clerk or similar official charges a small fee for performing a wedding ceremony. The amount varies from place to place, but is usually under five dollars. The groom ascertains the amount in advance and hands it over in an envelope either before or after the ceremony.

A high-ranking official like a judge, governor, or mayor is generally not asked to perform a marriage ceremony unless he is a friend or relative of one of the families. A fee is not offered to such an official. Instead, after the ceremony, the groom sends him a gift ranging from a box of fine cigars to a case of wine or something else appropriate, and the bride writes a note of appreciation.

**Double Weddings.** A double wedding is a pretty and practical way to avoid double expenses when two relatives or extremely close friends are to be married at about the same time. (Some faiths permit double weddings only if the brides are related.) Here are the most important variations from the standard ceremony:

1. The brides may share one set of bridesmaids and other attendants; or each bride may serve as the honor attendant for the other; or each bride may have her own complete set of attendants. Each groom may have a best man; or each may serve as the other's best man; or one best man can serve both grooms.
2. The brides and the bridesmaids (if there are two sets) need not be dressed alike, though of course they should be dressed in an equal degree of formality and the styles and colors of the dresses should harmonize. The grooms and ushers, however, all dress alike.
3. If the brides share one set of attendants, the procession to the chancel is the same as outlined under "Ceremony, Basic Protestant," except that the older bride on her father's arm precedes the younger bride on her father's arm.

If the brides are sisters, the younger is escorted by a brother, uncle, or other relative, who leaves her at the head of the aisle, since the father will give both of his daughters away. Or a father may escort both daughters, one on each arm, if the aisle is wide enough.

If each bride has her own set of attendants, the order is: all the ushers first, then the older bride's bridesmaids, her maid or matron of honor, the older bride on her father's arm; the younger bride's bridesmaids, her honor attendant, and finally the younger bride on her father's arm. Or both sets of bridesmaids may follow the ushers; then the older bride's honor attendant, the older bride and her father, the younger bride's honor attendant, and last the younger bride and her father.

4. The bridegroom of the older bride and his best man stand nearer the congregation. When both couples take their places in front of the clergyman, the older bride and her bridegroom stand on the left as they face the altar.

5. The ceremony may be read once with the vows repeated separately; or the whole ceremony may be read twice, one immediately after the other. In the latter case, the first couple remain in place during the second ceremony but do not exchange a kiss until the second ceremony is completed.

6. If there are two complete sets of attendants, each bridal party may leave the altar as a separate unit, the older bride's leading; or the order may be the older bride and her husband, the younger bride and her husband, followed by the attendants in any order determined at the rehearsal.

7. The seating of the families in church follows the order of the bridal procession—the mother and father of the older bride sit in the first pew, with the closest relatives with them; the parents of the younger bride take the second pew; or the parents of both brides may sit together in the front pew. The same arrangements are followed by the parents of the grooms.

8. At the reception, the usual order of the receiving line is as follows:

    Mother of the older bride (if the reception is at the home of the younger bride, her mother stands first in line)
    Mother of the older bride's groom
    Mother of the younger bride
    Mother of the younger bride's groom
    Older bride
    Her husband
    Her honor attendant
    Younger bride
    Her husband
    Her honor attendant
    Bridesmaids

9. See also "Invitations to the Ceremony," following.

**Episcopal.** Weddings in the Episcopal faith differ from the general procedures described under "Ceremony, Basic Protestant," in the following particulars:

Special permission is needed for an Episcopal marriage service to be held outside a church, and is granted only in an emergency.

The ceremony follows a prescribed ritual, and no variation is permitted.

Music must be liturgical. Soloists may be permitted but are not usual.

One of the couple must have been baptized in the Episcopal faith.

The clergyman must be consulted at least three days before the marriage, by church law.

A divorced person cannot be married in the Episcopal church without special permission.

Many Episcopal churches do not permit a wedding during Lent or on Sundays.

A ceremony in the morning or at high noon usually includes Holy Communion for the bride and groom.

A Nuptial Mass may or may not follow the marriage. The ritual of this Mass is virtually the same as that in the Roman Catholic faith.

The bride takes part in the rehearsal; a substitute is frowned on.

The bride goes up the aisle on her father's left arm, not his right.

The father of the bride does not say "I do" when the clergyman asks, "Who giveth . . . etc." He puts the hand of his daughter in that of the clergyman without oral response.

### Locations Other than a House of Worship.

1. Civil weddings performed in a city, town, or county clerk's office, a judge's chambers, or other similar places are extremely simple in all details. Usually no more than two witnesses and a very few close relatives and friends attend. The bride wears a pretty dress suitable to the time of day and a corsage, but she does not appropriately wear a formal white wedding dress and veil. A large reception, a small one, or none may follow.

2. Marriages in a church parlor, rectory, parish house, or clergyman's study are usually attended by only the closest of relatives and a friend or two. The bride may correctly wear a white wedding gown and a veil and carry a bridal bouquet, but she seldom dresses so formally unless there is to be a large and rather formal reception.

3. A wedding at home or in a club or hotel may be as elaborate and formal or as simple as the bride and her family choose. Faith permitting, it may be performed by a clergyman or a civil official. There is no rule that it must be held in the bride's home if a relative or friend offers a bigger or more conveniently located house (though a wedding or reception is held in the home of the groom's parents only under usual circumstances).

Wherever a home wedding is held, the bride's mother acts as hostess in that she stands first in the receiving line, if one is formed after the ceremony. The bride's family pays all expenses, including tips for the regular staff (unless a generous relative or friend has given the decorations and refreshments as a wedding present).

If a clergyman officiates, the rules for a wedding in a house of worship are followed in general, but he should always be consulted about all arrangements, and a special room should be provided where he can change to his vestments. The altar, set up to the clergyman's specifications, is usually a small table covered with a white cloth. It may be backed by an elaborate bank of flowers, but need not be.

For a big wedding, a caterer will bring in enough of his standard chairs to seat all guests, or just enough seats for the immediate family and a few older guests may be provided. If the room is large and seats are provided for everyone, the ushers can be posted near the entrance to escort guests to their places.

There may be a wedding procession just as in church, with the bride entering on her father's arm, or the bride and groom may take their places alone, depending entirely on their wishes and, of course, the size of the quarters.

The receiving line often forms in front of the altar, with relatives going up first to give the bride and groom their best wishes. If the reception is to be held in another room, the garden, or somewhat later at a club or hotel, any variation in procedure that is suitable to the space may be followed immediately after the ceremony.

4. A garden wedding can also be elaborate or very simple. It can be held in any suitable outdoor spot—from the lawn of a country estate to the roof garden of a hotel. The procedures are the same as for a home wedding. At a large wedding, a tent or covered dance floor is frequently used for the reception.

5.  Shipboard: There is a widely held—but mistaken—belief that a marriage conducted by the captain of any ship at sea is legal. Such a marriage is legal only if the laws of the state in which the ship is registered give a ship captain the authority to perform a marriage; or if the country of registration or the state where the company owning the ship is incorporated recognizes the legality of a common-law marriage. Otherwise, such a marriage is worthless.

However, it is sometimes possible to arrange for a wedding to take place on board shortly before a ship sails if the honeymoon couple is booked for the voyage. The service may be performed by the ship's chaplain or, with his permission, by a clergyman who comes aboard for that purpose. Arrangements also can be made on some ships for a reception in one of the lounges, with refreshments served by the ship's barmen and waiters.

**Military.**  A military wedding differs only slightly from any other wedding. Customarily, the best man and ushers are members of the Armed Services, though civilians may serve. Those who are entitled to (including guests) wear dress uniforms for a formal wedding, regular uniforms for an informal wedding. Civilians, both male attendants and the fathers of the bride and groom, match the groom in formality of dress. For example, the civilian father of the bride or groom and any civilian ushers wear either White or Black Tie at a formal evening wedding if the groom is wearing full-dress uniform.

A charming part of some military weddings is the arch of sabers through which the bride and groom pass after the ceremony. This arch is traditionally formed by the ushers on the steps just outside the church. Civilian ushers join the line but stand at salute while the others hold their sabers high, points touching. It is not customary for the bridesmaids and other attendants to pass under the arch of sabers.

If a service chaplain performs the ceremony, he does not receive a fee.

At the reception, the wedding cake is cut with the groom's dress sword, if he is wearing one.

**Orthodox Catholic.**  The wedding rituals in the various branches of the Catholic Church other than the Roman Catholic are similar, though there are differences between the Eastern, Greek, Russian, and Rumanian Orthodox services. All, however, have a beautiful pageant-like quality. The bride and groom hold lighted candles during part of the ceremony. The priest places gold crowns or wreaths of flowers and ribbons on their heads. Their rings are switched three times, and there are other impressive rituals.

An Orthodox Catholic wedding service may last from one to nearly two hours. Since it is customary for the congregation to stand during the entire service in some Orthodox churches, it is important for wedding guests of other faiths to be prepared for that eventuality.

**Roman Catholic.**  A Roman Catholic wedding can be celebrated with or without a Nuptial Mass, but is always held in a church unless in some extreme emergency special permission is granted for it to be solemnized elsewhere. Special permission is also required if the church is outside the bride's parish.

The ceremony follows a prescribed ritual, and no variation is permitted.

Music is liturgical, though the *Lohengrin* and Mendelssohn wedding marches are allowed, and soloists are permitted.

Catholics may be married at any time of the year. However, special permission is required for a Nuptial Mass to be read during Lent or Advent.

If a Nuptial Mass is to follow the ceremony, the wedding must be held in the morning because a Mass may not be celebrated after noon (or one o'clock Daylight Saving Time). If there is no Nuptial Mass, the wedding may be held at any time except after six o'clock in the evening on Sunday.

Holy Communion is usually received during the Mass by bride and groom (unless they have partaken earlier in the day) and by the Catholic members of the bridal party and sometimes by the parents.

At a large Catholic wedding, small Mass books containing the marriage service and the Nuptial Mass frequently are provided so that guests unfamiliar with the rituals can observe the proper procedures. In any case, it is helpful for non-Catholic guests to know that a Nuptial Mass may be a Low Mass, lasting a half-hour (organ and soloist); a High Mass, lasting forty minutes (choir); or a Solemn High Mass, lasting one hour (choir, three priests officiating).

The maid of honor and the best man must be Catholic if a Mass is part of the ceremony; otherwise, special permission is required if a non-Catholic serves in either of these positions. Bridesmaids need not be of the Catholic faith.

The bride's father does not give her away. He takes his place in his pew as soon as she is in place beside the groom.

The bride may carry a white rosary with her bouquet or in place of it.

All women in the church wear some kind of head covering.

Civil marriages are not recognized by the Catholic Church, but it is possible for a non-Catholic and a Catholic to be married by a priest—in church or elsewhere. This, however, is a matter about which the priest must be consulted.

**Jewish.** Judaism in America has three main divisions: Orthodox, Conservative, and Reform. The wedding ceremony in all three has some similarities, but the differences in viewpoint result in certain dramatically visible differences in ritual procedure at the ceremony. It is always necessary to discuss in advance all details of the wedding with the rabbi who will perform the ceremony.

Most rabbis prefer a wedding to be held in the synagogue or at home, though some will officiate elsewhere. Jewish weddings are not permitted on the Sabbath (from sunset Friday to sunset Saturday), nor on various holy days and major festivals or during certain specific periods in the Jewish calendar. An Orthodox or Conservative ceremony should not begin until at least an hour and a half after sunset on a Saturday or on the evening after a festival—to allow time to travel to the wedding and to give florist and caterer time to carry out their advance work.

All males, guests as well as men of the wedding party, wear head covering during an Orthodox or Conservative ceremony (and sometimes at a Reform wedding)—usually black or white skullcaps (yarmulkes). Male guests who arrive at the wedding without headgear will be given these, and men of other faiths should accept and wear them, conforming with the customs of the congregation.

In all types of Jewish wedding ceremonies, it is proper for the bride to wear a head covering. At an Orthodox wedding, the bride wears a veil that covers her face; at a Conservative ceremony, too, the bride generally wears a face veil. Reform practice is less insistent on this point. Women attendants also wear a head covering if the wedding is ultra-Orthodox. At Reform weddings, women attendants may be bareheaded. (Again, it is best to consult the rabbi to make sure of his preference.)

At an Orthodox ceremony, the bride wears either a long-sleeved dress or a short-sleeved one and gloves. As at any religious ceremony held in a synagogue, women attendants, members of the family, and guests are sometimes requested to avoid décolleté or sleeveless dresses unless a coat, jacket, or stole is part of the costume. (These "cover-ups" can be removed for the reception.)

The processional at a Jewish ceremony admits of several variations. Traditionally, the rabbi and cantor lead the procession. They may be followed by first the bride's grandparents, then the groom's grandparents. The ushers, paired or singly, are next in line, followed by the best man. Then comes the groom, with his father at his left, his mother at his right. He is followed by the bridesmaids, singly or paired; then the maid of honor. Last in line is the bride, her father at her left, her mother at her right. (If a flower girl and ring bearer are used, the ring bearer follows the maid of honor; the flower girl immediately precedes the bride and her parents.)

Whether the traditional processional is carried out in every detail depends on several factors, among them the size of the synagogue or room where the ceremony is to be held, the preference of the rabbi, and the width of the aisle. For example, some rabbis enter from a side door rather than walk in the procession. Sometimes the grandparents do not take part in the processional. And, in cases where the aisle is not wide, parents may walk directly ahead of their child —the groom's parents in front of him, the bride's in front of her. Or both fathers

**Jewish processional: This is a standard arrangement of the entering wedding party, but see the text for a number of admissible variations.**
This is a standard arrangement of the entering wedding party,
**(1) Cantor. (2) Rabbi. (3) Ushers. (4) Best man. (5) Groom between his parents. (6) Bridesmaids. (7) Maid of honor. (8) Bride between her parents. (9) Canopy (huppah).**

may walk with the groom and both mothers with the bride, though this is not a very common practice. Still other variations in the traditional Jewish processional are possible, and at some Jewish weddings the standard processional illustrated earlier is used. (Whatever procedure is followed, particularly if there will be many participants, it is as advisable to hold a rehearsal as for a wedding in any other faith.) If the parents are not part of the processional, the bride's parents are seated at the right of the aisle and the groom's at the left. Reform congregations reverse this seating arrangement.

An Orthodox or Conservative wedding ceremony takes place under a canopy known as a "huppah," which may be either fixed in position or held over the bridal couple by four men. (Reform Judaism does not insist on the use of a huppah.) It is usually made of velvet or silk and may be richly embroidered or decorated with fresh flowers and greens.

The bridal couple stand under the huppah, the bride at the groom's right. (At ultra-Orthodox and some Orthodox weddings, when the bride reaches the canopy, her parents lead her seven times around the groom before she takes her place beside him.) The groom's parents stand at his left, and the bride's parents at her right. Bride and groom face the rabbi and cantor, who stand beside or behind a small cloth-covered table on which are placed wine (sometimes two goblets or glasses are used) and a fragile glass wrapped in cloth. Although the order of the service varies from rabbi to rabbi and from tradition to tradition, it usually includes a betrothal benediction recited over a cup of wine from which bride and groom sip, a ring ceremony, the reading of all or part of the Ketubah (written marriage document or "contract"), the chanting of the Seven Benedictions (over the second cup of wine), and the breaking of the cloth-wrapped glass by the groom—a reminder to the assembled congregation of the destruction of the Temple in Jerusalem, which they must remember even in times of greatest joy. (In Reform practice, the breaking of the glass is optional; and the reading of the Ketubah is not usual, though some rabbis may use a modified wedding agreement.) The ceremony is generally concluded with a benediction pronounced by the rabbi.

**Standard arrangement of the wedding party during an Orthodox or Conservative Jewish wedding ceremony:**
**(1) Cantor. (2) Rabbi. (3) Groom. (4) Bride. (5) Groom's parents. (6) Bride's parents. (7) Best man.**
**(8) Maid of Honor. (9) Ushers. (10) Bridesmaids. (11) Canopy (huppah).**

A guest of another faith attending a Jewish wedding should conform with the customs of the congregation. At ultra-Orthodox weddings, women sit separated from the men, but this will be indicated to guests as they arrive. Otherwise, guests sit wherever they choose or according to the plan of the person who is supervising the wedding arrangements.

The reception following a Jewish wedding is like any other wedding reception except that a meal opens with the recitation of the blessing over the bread, and closes, in traditional practice, with the recitation of Grace After Eating and the repetition of the Seven Benedictions.

**CHURCH CARDS.** A church card serves as an admittance ticket. Enclosing such a card with a wedding invitation indicates that the church will be closed to the general public shortly before and during the ceremony, and that only those holding cards will be admitted.

Church cards are needed only for houses of worship at which many sightseers wander in and out, or at weddings where the prominence of bride, groom, and guests might inspire great numbers of the idly curious to attend uninvited.

A church card is engraved on plain stock in the same style as the invitation. A standard form:

*Please present this card*

*at St. George's Church*

*Wednesday, the tenth of June*

(*Note:* "Saint" may be abbreviated on the card but is correctly spelled out on the invitation.)

**CHURCH EXPENSES.** Usually no charge is made for the use of a house of worship by a member of the congregation. In this case, the father of the bride often makes a special contribution. Otherwise, an established rental fee ranging from $25 to $100 or more can be expected. In addition, members of the regular staff—the choir, organist, and soloist—are paid for their services (if used), and the sexton is always paid for his services in opening the church if they are not included in the rental fee. If a friend performs as organist or soloist, a present instead of a fee is sent. The bride's family assumes all these expenses.

**CLERGYMAN.** It should never be taken for granted that any clergyman asked to perform a wedding ceremony will be able to do so. Each is governed by the regulations of his faith. Therefore, as a proper formality and also for purely practical reasons, the bride and groom are obligated to pay a formal call on the clergyman.

If a clergyman from outside the specific church is to perform or share in the ceremony, an invitation must be sent to him by the resident clergyman.

The clergyman and his wife are always asked to the rehearsal party and the wedding reception.

**Fees.** The clergyman's fee is in the nature of a donation, and therefore there is no customary or fixed amount. For a small, intimate wedding, it may be as little as $10; for a large, ceremonial wedding, it may be $200 or more. It is always paid by the groom, and can be presented in different ways—mailed before the wedding; or handed (always in an envelope) to him, usually by the best man, in the vestry before the ceremony or after the ceremony in any appropriate place, but never in the church itself.

If the fee is paid by check, the check is made out to the clergyman, not to the church.

### CLOTHES.

*See* the chart at the beginning of this section; also separate headings—"Bride," "Best Man," and so on.

### CLUBS.

For weddings held in clubs, hotels, and elsewhere, *see* "Ceremony, Differences from Basic Protestant."

**CONGRATULATIONS.** It is never correct to say "Congratulations!" to the bride, since the word implies that by skill, luck, or consistent effort some goal has been achieved. Though all these may have entered the picture, the fiction is maintained that the groom is the one who has wooed and at last won. Say "Congratulations!" to him. But give the bride "Best wishes for happiness."

**CONSULTANTS.** A wedding consultant is a specialist who is equipped by experience to advise about most procedures and to take over all details, from addressing invitations to making arrangements for the reception. For a very large wedding, the services of a wedding consultant are well worth the fee. They are especially useful to a mother and bride who hold jobs or have other heavy demands on their time, or to a bride whose mother is ill or dead.

Consulting services in special categories are supplied without charge by most of the following:

**Caterers.** Any large catering establishment can give sound advice about receptions. If supplying a large staff, some caterers will also supply a superbutler who can act as adviser on many details and can also serve as the announcer at the receiving line.

**Churches.** The clergyman or, more often, the sexton or some other member of the church staff can give guidance about decorations, choice of music, seating arrangements, and other procedures, even if there is not a rehearsal.

**Department Stores and Shops.** When the wedding dress and bridesmaids costumes are bought at one shop, a good deal of service is often given without extra charge. A shopping consultant who is an expert on wedding clothes will help plan the color and style of dresses for the bridesmaids, as well as for the bride and the mothers. She will also suggest where men's formal clothes can be rented. A shop often can make arrangements for a fitter to stand by and help bride and bridesmaids with any last-minute adjustments that may be needed.

Gift counselors at department, jewelry, and other stores will set up a registry for patterns of china, crystal, and silver so that friends can readily check what pieces are lacking.

**Hotels.** Usually a hotel's banquet manager is prepared to help plan and supervise all details of the reception as part of the hotel's service. He can also advise on proper formation of the receiving line and other such matters.

**Jewelers.** The counsel of a fine jeweler carries authority because of his constant experience with local customs. He gives advice without charge about the marking of engagement and wedding rings; the proper wording and lettering for invitations, announcements, and enclosure cards; the proper engraving on presents for attendants. And, of course, he will also register silver, china, and crystal patterns so that duplication can be avoided.

**Musicians.** The leader of a dance band generally is well informed about standard reception procedures—choice of music, the right time for the first dance, the cutting of the cake, and the toast to the bride.

**Photographers.** If candid pictures are to be made, a professional photographer is another experienced adviser who is likely to have special knowledge of procedures at receptions.

**Police.** Consult the office of the chief of police if special traffic problems are anticipated at a very large wedding or if ropes may be needed to limit crowds of the curious who otherwise might block the entrance of the church. There is no charge for such police assistance.

**Social Secretaries.** The services of a paid social secretary are invaluable if a large number of invitations and announcements are to be sent. Experts are available on a part- or full-time basis through special bureaus and employment agencies in all big cities.

**Transportation Companies.** The company that supplies the limousines can assign extra men to see to the parking of guests' cars.

**Travel Agents.** Unless a travel agent is asked to make very complicated plans for a long trip, he will make no charge for securing most hotel reservations and buying and delivering tickets.

**DATE AND HOUR.** The date selected for a wedding is a matter of personal choice—within the limitations, of course, of the rules of each faith. A very quiet marriage ceremony may be conducted on virtually any day, though a big formal church wedding is not appropriate in some faiths during Lent or on Christmas and other special days. Weddings are generally not held on Sunday and, in the Jewish faith, are not permitted on the Sabbath and, in general, not on certain holy days or festivals.

The most popular hours for weddings are at about noon, followed by a wedding breakfast; in the late afternoon, followed by a reception; after six, followed by a dinner and dance; and after eight, followed by a dance and supper.

**DECORATIONS.** Before giving an order to a florist or making other plans to decorate a church, it is essential to consult with the sexton or a similar church official. Some houses of worship have restrictions about where flowers may be placed and how many may be used. Under any circumstances, it is necessary to reserve a convenient time for the installation of decorations.

**Awning, Canvas, and Carpet.** Is is a sensible precaution to arrange for an awning and carpet outside the church if there is a likelihood of bad weather.

A carpet or white canvas is often used on the main aisle at a big wedding, especially if the bride is wearing a train. Its purpose is to protect the train and, if the church is not carpeted, to muffle the sound of the steps of the bridal party. A strip of carpet is laid when the church is decorated, but a canvas is not put down until just before the wedding march starts. It is unrolled from a spool with two handles, from the foot of the chancel to the rear of the main aisle, by two ushers or men from the sexton's staff.

**Flowers.** Floral decorations may range from none at all to an altar massed with blooms, great sprays in windows, and smaller bunches tied with white ribbons to the pews along the main aisles. White flowers are traditional, but flowers of any color are correct.

**Ribbons.** Very often white ribbons are used only to mark the reserved sections. These ribbons, generally available from the florist in charge of decorations, are arranged in short lengths so that the ushers can easily unhook and replace them. At large weddings, white ribbons sometimes are strung the entire length of the center aisle after the mother of the bride has been seated. Just before the wedding march begins, two ushers start from the front of the church and walk back toward the entrance, looping the ribbons over the ends of the pews as they go; or they may start from the rear of the church and enclose the congregation in the same fashion. If ribbons are used, guests do not leave their places until the ushers have removed the ribbons after the recessional.

**DIVORCE PROBLEMS.** Certain special procedures established by custom are usually followed if the bride, groom, or their parents are divorced.

**Bride.** A divorcée does not wear white or a veil, and the giving-away part of the ceremony is omitted. Usually a divorcée has a simple, quiet wedding, either religious or civil, and contents herself with as large and festive a reception as she pleases. Her children, if their father is living, sometimes attend the reception but not the ceremony; sometimes they go to both—the decision depends on their ages and what their mother feels is best for them.

**Bride's Parents.** If the bride's parents are divorced, several choices of procedure are open, according to how amiable their relations are. Whenever possible, divorced parents put aside their differences at least long enough to give a daughter as happy a send-off as possible. Following are the rules if both parents attend, but of course it is not obligatory that both do so.

The bride's mother usually gives the wedding and reception. She sits in the first pew, and if she has remarried, her husband sits beside her. Her former husband sits in the second or third pew, with his wife (if any) beside him. The bride's father calls for her at her mother's house to escort her to the church. If relations are extremely stiff, he does not go to the reception. If he does go, he acts as a guest, not as the host. If the bride's mother has married again, her husband acts as the host. The bride's father usually does not stand in the receiving line, though if the divorce has been a friendly one, he may do so.

If the bride has made her home with her father for many years, he probably will give the wedding and the reception. If he has remarried, his wife accompanies him to the ceremony and acts as hostess at the reception. If the bride's mother attends the ceremony, she sits in the first pew. If she has remarried, her husband may or may not accompany her. The bride's father sits in the second or third pew with his wife (if any) beside him. Whether or not the bride's mother, with or without her husband, will attend the ceremony and also the reception is entirely a matter of the cordiality of the relationships and the wishes of all concerned, but mainly of the bride.

**Groom.** The status of the groom does not affect the character of the wedding itself, religious restrictions aside. If it is a first marriage for the bride, the wedding may be as ceremonial in dress and procedure as she pleases. Unless the children of the groom have made their home with him, they usually do not attend the ceremony. They may or may not attend the reception, depending on the circumstances.

**Groom's Parents.** The groom's mother sits in the first pew. The groom's father sits in the second or third pew. If they are remarried, their spouses may or may not attend. Both of the groom's parents are invited to the ceremony and reception under all usual circumstances, and the matter of refusal or acceptance is left to their discretion.

**Invitations and Announcements.**

Examples of the wording of invitations and announcements are given under those heads in this section.

**Remarriage.** If two people decide to remarry each other again after being divorced, the whole matter usually is kept as quiet as possible so that the past difficulty will be quickly forgotten. Usually no formal announcements are sent, no notice is sent to the press, and their children do not attend the ceremony, since that would only emphasize the prior trouble.

**DOCUMENTS.** A marriage license is always necessary (see "License"), and other documents in addition may be needed. Depending on the faith and other circumstances, these may include a baptismal certificate, a confirmation certificate, and a letter from the church where either the bride or groom is a regular communicant if the marriage is to be performed elsewhere.

**DOUBLE.**

For procedures at a double wedding, *see* "Ceremony, Differences from Basic Protestant."

**ELOPEMENTS.** An elopement does not necessarily mean that a young couple are defying the wishes of their parents or marrying without their parents' consent. Often, an elopement is arranged with the full knowledge and blessing of both families, for a number of reasons. When the bride and groom are of different faiths, an "elopement" and a civil ceremony sometimes avoid family dissension about the service on religious grounds. Sometimes, when parents are divorced, an elopement resolves what would be an awkward situation at the church and reception. And sometimes elopements are planned because the bride and groom want to avoid the problems and expense of a large wedding and reception.

Plans for such technical "elopements" are not kept secret from the families. The usual procedure is for the engagement to be announced to at least the closest relatives and friends and perhaps the press, and then the couple "elope" on a planned date and telephone to their parents immediately after the ceremony.

**Announcements.** Formal announcements may be, and usually are, sent after an elopement even if the marriage has been kept a secret for several months or more. The announcements follow the standard forms given under "Announcements," and "At Home" cards usually are enclosed.

If the engagement was announced in the press, notice of the marriage may be sent but usually is not if the marriage has been kept secret for some time. No mention is made of the elopement in a formal announcement or in a press release.

**Gifts.** The rules say that a wedding anniversary need not be sent following the announcement when there has been an elopement, but loving relatives and close friends usually send gifts anyhow.

**EPISCOPAL.** *See "Ceremony, Differences from Basic Protestant."*

**EXPENSES.** Under certain conditions a young couple may decide to share the expenses of a wedding reception, but this is a personal matter. According to tradition, the bride or her family assumes virtually all the expenses of the wedding and reception.

Details are given under "Bride's Father" and "Bridegroom." The expenses of the attendants are given in detail under "Best Man," "Bridemaids," and other separate heads.

**FLOWER GIRLS.** There usually is only one little flower girl, if any, and seldom more than two. A flower girl may be as young as three years, though the duty is a real challenge to such a small child, and the risks are obvious. Usually, she is not older than seven unless tiny for her age. The very young flower girl is withdrawn from the processional as she passes one of the front pews, since standing quietly without innocently taking the spotlight away from the bride is too much to expect of her. If she does remain with the bridesmaids, she walks in the recessional but does not stand in the receiving line as a general rule. Very young flower girls often do not go to the reception, especially if it is an evening one, but the bride makes a point of thanking all such small attendants after the ceremony. The flower girl's parents are invited to the rehearsal and also to pre-wedding parties, though the flower girl herself may not be.

**Clothes.** A flower girl usually wears clothes appropriate to her age, but sometimes she is dressed in a period costume or a miniature version of the bridesmaids' dresses.

**Duties.** She attends the rehearsal. During the processional, she either scatters rose petals in the bride's path or merely carries a basket of flowers or a tiny bouquet.

**Expenses.** The parents of a flower girl pay for her costume, but its style and color are chosen by the bride. The little girl and her parents may send a joint wedding present, or she may send one of her very own.

**FLOWERS.** The season of the year, the time, place, and the degree of formality of the wedding will be the controlling factors in choosing correct flowers for decoration and for the bridal party, but in all cases there are certain traditional customs that should be observed.

**Best Man.** The best man's boutonniere is always white but is slightly different from the groom's and also from the ushers'—a white camellia, perhaps, if the groom is wearing a sprig from the bridal bouquet and the ushers are wearing white carnations. The groom supplies the best man's boutonniere.

**Bride.** The bridal bouquet is traditionally white, but a touch of color is also correct, and if the bride is wearing a pastel-colored dress her bouquet may match or complement it in color. The bride's going-away corsage sometimes is part of her bouquet. It is removed, of course, before she tosses her bouquet at the reception. For a formal wedding the bride's family usually provides her bouquet as part of her costume, and the groom then sends her a separate going-away corsage. However, in some circles, it is customary for the groom to pay for the bride's bouquet.

**Bride's Attendants.** The bridesmaids carry identical bouquets, which may be of any color that suits their dresses.

The bouquet of the maid or matron of honor is usually slightly larger and may differ otherwise. If the wedding is informal and there is only one attendant, she may simply wear a corsage.

A flower girl may carry a basket of flowers, or of petals if she is to strew them, or a small nosegay.

The ring bearer and pages wear white carnations or other small white flowers.

The bride's family provides the flowers for all her attendants.

**Groom.** The groom's boutonniere traditionally is a sprig from the bride's bouquet. It may be a small cluster of lilies of the valley or a single white gardenia or camellia. The florist sends it along with the boutonnieres for the best man and ushers. The groom pays for it.

**Guests.** Generally only members of the bridal party and parents and grandparents of the bride and groom wear flowers at the ceremony, but there is no reason why a guest may not wear a flower with a suitable costume.

**Parents.** The mothers and grandmothers of the bride and groom wear corsages. Customarily, the bride's father supplies the corsages for her mother and grandmother and his own white boutonniere, usually a carnation. The groom (or his father) supplies corsages for his mother and grandmother and a white boutonniere for his father. However, it is correct—and usual in some circles—for the groom to provide the corsages for the bride's mother and grandmother as well as for his own relatives.

**Place of Ceremony.** Since rules and customs about decorations vary considerably in different houses of worship, it is important to consult the clergyman about the flowers to be used and their placement, as well as about when they may be installed.

**Reception.** The flowers at a reception may be of any kind or color, though flowers on the tables are traditionally white.

**Soloist and Organist.** If a personal friend is singing or playing at the ceremony, the bride's family provides a corsage for a woman, a white carnation for a man.

**Ushers.** A white carnation is the traditional "badge" for the ushers at a wedding. The groom provides them.

**GARDEN.** *See "Ceremony, Differences from Basic Protestant."*

**GIFTS.** A formal invitation to a wedding does not obligate the recipient to send a wedding present, but it is customary for anyone invited to the reception to send a present. An informal invitation to a wedding is more personal, and so a guest usually feels under more obligation to send a present.

Whenever possible, presents are sent about two weeks before a wedding. It is entirely correct to send one after the ceremony. It is never the best idea to take a present to the ceremony or reception, though not incorrect.

A wedding present should be something of use to both bride and groom rather than something personal for the bride. All items for their house, car, and garden fall into this category. If in doubt, send something that can be exchanged.

**Addressing.** Any present sent before the wedding is addressed to the bride, not to the bride and groom, though the card may carry some such message as "Best wishes to Betty and Joe," or "Love to you both." A present should not be sent to the bride's office except under special circumstances—if she lives in a walk-up apartment where there is no one to receive packages, and her parents live in a distant city, it is only sensible to use her office address.

After the wedding, a present is addressed to the couple jointly (Mr. and Mrs. John Smith). It is sent to their new address or may be sent in care of either family, to be forwarded.

**Damaged.** If a present sent from a local shop arrives broken or damaged, the bride usually calls the shop and arranges for a replacement herself, without mentioning the matter to the donor. If the shop is not identified by the box, or the present is something unique that cannot be duplicated (like a piece of heirloom china), the bride reports the damage to the donor. Only a very thoughtless donor mails a package uninsured, and so replacement of a damaged present usually represents no additional expense.

**Display.** Wedding presents are not put on display at a wedding reception held in a club or hotel or in the social rooms of a church. They sometimes are displayed at a wedding reception in a private residence, or at a tea or cocktail party held a day or so before the wedding. Displaying gifts is not usually today's custom, though it is entirely correct. The presents, along with the cards of the donors, are generally put on tables covered with white or pastel-colored cloths. Checks are customarily displayed so that the signatures, but not the amounts, show; or a little card with "Check from Aunt Mary" is placed with the other presents.

**Exchanging.** It is entirely correct to exchange almost any wedding gift, and it is absurd to keep one that is a duplicate or otherwise useless or inappropriate. The bride makes the exchange herself, if possible. At some later date she may inform the giver that she has done so, explaining why and emphasizing the great pleasure she takes in its replacement. Needless to say, a family heirloom may not be taken to an antique shop and traded for something else. And discretion also has to govern exchanging certain other gifts, no matter how foreign to the taste of the bride and groom they may be. But no couple need give a second thought to exchanging eight silver cocktail shakers, for example, for one dishwasher, if that is their pleasure.

**Initials and Monograms.** Wedding presents are best not initialed or monogrammed, with few exceptions. Usually, even if the bride has registered her silver pattern with a shop, the pieces are sent plain so that she can have them all marked alike. If a present is to be initialed, it is important to query a member of the bride's family to see if she prefers the initials of her new name or her maiden initials.

**Money.** Stocks, bonds, and gift certificates, as well as checks, should be made out to the bride if given before the ceremony. Often, a letter is sent to the bride to say that a gift of stock will follow, but the actual certificate is not delivered until after the marriage. In this way, it can be made out in both names.

The proper form is Mary Ann Smith (or Mary Brown Smith) and John Jones Smith (not Mr. and Mrs. John Jones Smith).

**Obligatory.** The bride and groom usually exchange other wedding presents in addition to their rings. Since these, as well as the following obligatory presents, are mementos of a sentimental occasion, they should be something of lasting value and for personal use.

The bride always gives each of her attendants a present, usually a compact or piece of jewelry. The bridesmaids' presents customarily are identical, with a somewhat more valuable one for the maid of honor.

The groom gives his best man a cigarette case, cuff links, or something similar, and presents of slightly less value to the ushers.

The parents of the groom give the bride a special present for herself, usually jewelry, in addition to the present or presents that they give the couple jointly.

The bride's parents usually do not give the groom a personal present since he is receiving from them the bride herself, as well as the wedding and reception.

**Returning.** Even if a wedding is postponed for a long time, the wedding gifts are not returned. If, however, all plans to marry are canceled, then all gifts must be returned with a note of thanks. The same is true if one of the couple dies before the wedding.

When a couple is divorced, the wife is technically the owner of all wedding gifts, though if something of special value was given by a relative or friend of the groom, that item usually—and fairly—remains with him. And if a wedding present from the groom's family was heirloom jewelry, silver, china, or furniture, a divorced wife of any sensitivity leaves such a family treasure with her former husband, unless there are children to inherit it.

**Second Marriage, etc.** According to the rules, there is no obligation to send another present when a woman marries again if one was sent to her on her first marriage. Most relatives and close friends ignore that chilly regulation and send another gift in token of their continuing hope for their happiness.

**Thanks.** The bride must write a note of thanks for each present—no argument. The groom may add a postscript if he wishes, and he may also send a letter of his own, after the bride has written, to someone who sent a particularly touching or lavish present. But the bride must first go right down the list and send their dual thanks even to his relatives and friends unknown to her.

Notes of thanks are best sent in small batches as the gifts arrive. In any circumstances, they should be sent within about three weeks after the wedding. Otherwise, the donors are left to wonder if their presents arrived safely. Notes can be brief—even written on hotel stationery during the honeymoon—but they should be handwritten. If many presents are expected, it is practical to get a Wedding Gift Register (a good shower present) so that an orderly record of the gifts and the names and addresses of the donors can be kept by anyone who opens the presents for the bride.

The bride addresses her note of thanks to the wife if the present came from a couple. The letter may start "Dear Mr. and Mrs. Brown," or simply "Dear Mrs. Brown" with a reference made to Mr. Brown in the body of the message. After the wedding, the bride begins her letters to the groom's relatives just as he would ("Dear Aunt Mary and Uncle Bill"), even though they may be unknown to her. If several friends join in giving one present, separate notes of thanks may be sent, or only one note that expresses thanks to all if they live or work at the same place. If dozens of fellow workers signed one card, it is palpably absurd to write individual notes; one letter suitable for posting on a bulletin board is addressed to some one individual on the list, usually the ranking executive.

Any kind of printed card of thanks is incorrect, but printed cards acknowledging the arrival of a gift are sometimes used when hundreds of gifts are received. Such cards are never a substitute for the bride's own note. All they do is notify a donor that his gift has arrived and indicate that there may be some delay before a note is received from the bride herself.

A standard form, before the wedding:

*Miss Mary Ann Brown*
*wishes to acknowledge the receipt*
*of your wedding gift*
*and will write a personal note of*
*appreciation at an early date*

For cards mailed after the wedding, the bride's new name is used:

*Mrs. John Jones Smith*
*wishes to acknowledge the receipt*
*of your wedding gift*
*and will write a personal note of*
*appreciation at an early date*

**GIVING THE BRIDE AWAY.** In some faiths, no one gives the bride away. In others, it is a usual part of the ceremony but is not obligatory, and therefore may be omitted.

The bride's father traditionally escorts her up the aisle and gives her away. If he cannot be present, a close male relative, a legal guardian, her stepfather, or a friend of her parents may serve as his deputy. A brother under twenty-one may escort her up the aisle but does not give her away.

The mother of the bride may give her away, though such is not the usual procedure. In this case, a male relative escorts the bride to the altar and then withdraws to his pew, and at the proper time the bride's mother says "I do" from her place in the front pew.

The ceremony of giving away the bride is generally omitted if the bride is a mature widow or a divorcée, but need not be.

**GLOVES.** The wearing of gloves by members of the wedding party is a matter of the time of year and the formality of the clothes.

**Bride.** At an informal wedding, if the bride is in street clothes she lays aside her gloves with her purse before the ceremony begins. She may or may not wear gloves with a formal wedding gown, though if her sleeves are extremely short she usually wears full-length ones. She does not wear gloves if her sleeves are long. If the bride wears gloves of any length during the ceremony, the seam on the underside of the ring finger is opened so that when the time comes, she can free her finger easily to receive the wedding band.

**Bride's Attendants.** Even if the bride wears gloves, the bridesmaids and other attendants do not necessarily have to wear them—though they may.

**Groom, Best Man, Father of the Bride.** The groom wears white kid gloves for a ceremonial evening wedding; white or gray buckskin gloves for a formal daytime wedding; no gloves or, in winter, his usual street gloves to an informal wedding. He usually leaves his gloves in the vestry, but if he is in formal dress he sometimes wears them into the chancel and removes and hands them to the best man as the bride comes up the aisle.

The best man's gloves match the groom's. If the groom wears gloves into the chancel, the best man does also, but he removes his right glove before handing over the ring.

The father of the bride wears clothes and gloves to match those of the groom in formality.

**Others.** The mothers of the bride and groom and the guests wear gloves suitable to their costumes and keep them on during the ceremony.

**Receiving Lines and Receptions.** All women standing in a receiving line keep their gloves on. Fathers in the receiving line take their gloves off. Women going through a receiving line keep their gloves on, but a man removes his or takes off the right one if the receiving line is at church. Men leave their gloves with their hats and wraps if the receiving line is elsewhere.

At a wedding breakfast or other seated meal, all women wearing gloves, long or short, take them off. For less formally served refreshments, a woman wearing long gloves may tuck them in at the wrists, but a woman wearing short gloves takes them off.

**Ushers.** Ushers wear white kid gloves at a formal evening wedding; white or gray buckskin gloves at a formal daytime wedding; none at an informal wedding. They do not take them off while officiating, and also keep them on during the ceremony.

**GRANDPARENTS.** Grandparents are treated as specially honored guests in all ways. They are asked to the rehearsal dinner. During the ceremony they sit in the row immediately behind the parents of the bride and groom. They sit at the parents' table, if there is one, at the wedding reception, though they do not stand in the receiving line with the parents.

**GUESTS.** The main responsibility of a wedding guest is to arrive in time to be seated at least ten minutes before the hour of the ceremony. If there are ushers, guests wait to be escorted down the aisle (see "Seating" for details). And guests do not leave their pews, even if the side aisles are open, until the ushers have escorted the parents of the bride and groom from the front rows and have removed the center aisle ribbons.

Guests of other faiths follow the custom of the congregation as to head coverings and also in matters of ritual, as far as possible. For example, a Protestant is not expected to cross himself during a Catholic ceremony, and need not kneel. However, he should lean forward with head bowed when others kneel, and should stand and sit when the congregation does.

**Clothes.** Guests are not obligated to match the wedding party in the degree of formality of their dress, though most guests usually approximate it if they are also going to an evening reception.

Men wear dark suits to an informal wedding. Dark suits are also appropriate at the most elaborate daytime wedding even if the men in the wedding party are wearing cutaways and striped trousers. At an evening wedding and reception, if the groom is in White Tie, male guests may wear either White Tie or dinner jackets. If the groom is in Black Tie, most of the guests will be also, but there probably will be a showing of dark suits at the reception as well.

At a morning wedding, women make a point of wearing pretty hats and gloves and, if going to the reception also, festive-looking dresses appropriate to the time and place. At an informal evening wedding or a formal afternoon wedding, they wear dressy afternoon clothes, hats, and gloves. Evening dresses are worn to a ceremonial or formal evening wedding and reception, though if the ceremony is in church the shoulders are usually covered in some fashion. In many parts of the country it is no longer customary for women guests to wear head coverings in church at evening weddings, but inquiry should always be made of a member of the bridal party because in certain faiths a head covering of some sort is obligatory during a religious service and a guest with a bare head would be uncomfortably conspicuous.

Corsages and boutonnieres are generally worn to the ceremony only by members of the wedding party—including, of course, the parents and grandparents—but there is no reason why a guest should not wear a flower or flowers also.

### HOME WEDDINGS.

*See* "Ceremony, Differences from Basic Protestant" for weddings elsewhere than in a house of worship.

**HONEYMOONS.** At one time, the word "honeymoon" meant the first month after marriage. Today, the word is generally used to mean the wedding trip specifically, and so we hear "They are taking their honeymoon later," "They are off on a three months' honeymoon," as well as "They aren't having a honeymoon."

The honeymoon starts at the moment the bride and groom leave the reception and go off by themselves. Some newlyweds are amused by practical jokes and feel a bit disappointed if handfuls of rice are not planted in their luggage or if a "Just Married" sign is not surreptitiously attached to their car. But many other couples, especially dignified and older ones, are embarrassed by such pranks. Better give the matter a second thought, and abandon any plans for practical jokes if there is the slightest suspicion they will be unwelcome.

**HONOR ATTENDANTS.** The maid and matron of honor and the best man are known as "honor attendants."

**INVITATIONS TO THE CEREMONY.** The form in which invitations are issued depends largely on the number of guests. For about fifty guests, invitations are usually informal (given by letter or orally), and then perhaps engraved announcements are sent to many other friends.

If a sizable number of friends and acquaintances are asked to the ceremony but only some of them are asked to the reception, engraved invitations to the wedding are sent to all and separate reception cards are enclosed to the selected smaller list.

If a very few relatives and close friends will attend the ceremony, and a large reception is to follow, invitations to the wedding may be given informally and engraved invitations issued to the reception.

Or an invitation to both the ceremony and reception may be combined on one engraved sheet.

Informal invitations are given in any convenient way—by telephone, in person, or by handwritten note. The bride's mother may make a point of herself writing or telephoning to guests on the list of the groom and his family; but, depending on circumstances, the groom and his family often share in extending invitations in any way most convenient and efficient for all concerned.

Formal invitations are governed by explicit rules, given below. Unless these are followed exactly, it is better to send the invitations in an informal fashion.

**Addressing.** For a large wedding and reception, it is important for the bride, groom, and their families to start compiling their lists almost as soon as the engagement is announced and the size of the wedding has been decided. Working out lists for those who will receive invitations to the wedding, the wedding and the reception, the reception only, or announcements only, and checking to avoid duplication, is a demanding task. Disastrous oversights are almost certain if plenty of time is not allowed. The lists also must be carefully checked because an announcement is not correctly sent to anyone who receives a formal invitation.

The groom and his family send their lists for invitations and announcements to the bride, and then she, her mother, and friends address the entire list unless this task has been turned over to a social secretary.

The rules for addressing are the same as for other formal invitations (*which see*), with emphasis on the following:

1. It is not correct to send a wedding invitation to a business address unless the home address is unknown and also in some way difficult to ascertain.
2. Typing is not correct. Handwriting is obligatory.
3. Only black or blue-black ink is correct.
4. A formal wedding invitation or announcement is always enclosed in two envelopes. The flap of the inner one is not gummed and is never sealed. The addressee's title, first, middle, and last name appear on the outer envelope, but only title and last name are put on the inner envelope, with some few exceptions. If the bride is addressing the envelopes herself, it is correct and charming to write on the inner one "Grandfather," "Aunt Mary and Uncle Bill," and so on, for her close relatives, if she likes, but she follows the standard rules for her friends.
5. It is both correct and important to use a return address. Thousands of invitations go astray each year, and hurt feelings result, because return addresses were omitted.

   The return address is embossed on the flap. White embossing is standard, though the return address in pale gray is also correct. Some authorities consider printed address stickers permissible, but stickers are not in keeping with the formality of the rest of the invitation, and many people regard them as inappropriate as well as unattractive.
6. The words "and Family" are not correctly used following a name or names on the envelope.
7. Standard forms for both envelopes are given below.

   *To one person:*
   Outer: Mr. John Barr White
   　　　　(*address*)
   Inner: Mr. White

   *To a married couple:*
   Outer: Mr. and Mrs. George Moore Bell
   　　　　(*address*)
   Inner: Mr. and Mrs. Bell

   *To a couple with children under 18:*
   Outer: Mr. and Mrs. George Moore Bell
   　　　　(*address*)
   Inner: Mr. and Mrs. Bell
   　　　　Joan, Jean, and Michael

   *To a couple with grown children:*
   (One invitation may go jointly to the father and mother with the name of one son or daughter on a separate line, or a separate invitation may be sent to each grown child.
   Outer: Mr. and Mrs. John Joseph White
   　　　　Miss Mary Birch White
   　　　　(*address*)

Inner: Mr. and Mrs. White
     Miss White

*To relatives under the same roof,* such as an aunt and nephew (separate invitations are usually sent, but one may be addressed to both):
Outer: Miss Amelia Towne White
     Mr. John Charles White
          (*address*)
Inner: Miss White
     Mr. White

*To sisters over 18:*
     Outer: Misses (*or* The Misses) Mary and Margaret White
          (*address*)
     Inner: Misses White (*or* The Misses White).

*To brothers over 18:*
     Outer: Messrs. (*or* The Messrs.) Luke and John White
          (*address*)
     Inner: Messrs. White (*or* The Messrs. White)

**By Whom Sent:** The groom never issues formal engraved invitations, and only in extremely exceptional circumstances (explained in "Standard Forms," following) would a member of his family do so. A formal invitation is sent in the name of the bride or someone close to her.

**Costs.** The bride or her family pays for invitations, announcements, and stamps.

**Enclosures.** The separate cards most often enclosed with an invitation are an "At Home" card and a reception card. A church (admittance) card and a pew (reserved seat) card can be added. Details are given under separate heads in this section.

By the traditional rules, a response card with blanks to be filled in is not correctly enclosed with an invitation to a wedding or wedding reception. However, this is the one rule about formal invitations that is beginning to change—reply cards are seen more and more frequently when the guest list is extremely large. Their advantages are obvious: they produce answers more promptly, and they are far easier to file than are the formal folded handwritten answers.

**Format.** A formal invitation, whether engraved, handwritten, or telegraphed, is always phrased in the third person. The spacing, spelling, and words are completely standardized, and variations should not be made.

1. Abbreviations: All abbreviations except "Mr.," "Mrs.," "Dr.," "Jr.," and "Sr." are avoided. ("Junior" and "senior" are correct but are not the modern first choice.) Roman numerals are used after a name, not "2nd" or "3rd."
2. Lettering: The most formal invitations are engraved, but the fine process printing that produces raised letters closely resembling engraving, at somewhat less cost, is also correct. Ink is always black. Script or one of the shaded Roman type styles is traditional and the best choice. Novelty lettering or any that resembles type used by printers should be avoided. Any good stationer can show samples of the standard styles.
3. Names: "Miss" or "Mrs." does not precede the bride's name, with the exceptions shown under "Standard Forms," following.
4. Paper: The correct paper for invitations and announcements is white or off-white of a fine, heavy quality, with double envelopes to match. It is most often plain, but may have a raised (plate-marked) border. A double sheet

### Engraved Copper Wedding Plates

| | |
|---|---|
| SCRIPT | *Mrs. George Fenwick Faulkner* |
| LONDON SCRIPT | *Mrs John Low Venable* |
| WINDSOR | Mr. and Mrs. David Wetherell Joyce |
| MAYFAIR | Mrs. Percival Harold Clayton |
| ST. JAMES | *Mrs. Richard Evans Brooks* |
| ANTIQUE ROMAN | Mr. and Mrs. Lewis Alexander Wilkins |
| NORMAN | Mr. and Mrs. Richard Murray Barton |
| HAMILTON | *Mr. and Mrs. Oren Chandler* |

The samples of lettering above are reproduced by the courtesy of Tiffany & Co. The two most popular styles with their clients are Script and Antique Roman, followed by St. James and Norman.

with the engraving on the outside is traditional. When folded once again, it fits an inner envelope about 5 by 6 inches, which is enclosed in a slightly larger matching envelope. If tissues are in place to protect the engraving, they are not removed. Invitations on a double sheet of paper that does not need a second fold to fit the same size envelope are less usual, but they are also correct.

A folded invitation is put into the envelope with the fold down and the enclosure cards within the fold. Unfolded invitations are put in the inner envelope with the engraving facing the back of the envelope, and with enclosure cards in front of the engraving. The inner envelope is put in the outer envelope, flap first, with its flap facing away from the flap of the outer envelope. Inner envelopes are not gummed and are not sealed in any way.

5. Punctuation: Punctuation marks are used only when necessary within a line, as in "Wednesday, the tenth of June" (no comma at the end of the line), or after abbreviations like "Mr."

6. "R.S.V.P." is not used on an invitation to attend a church wedding (unless an invitation to the reception is combined in the main body of the invitation), but is used on an enclosed reception card. An invitation to attend a wedding in a private residence, a club, or hotel implies that refreshments will be served, and so "R.S.V.P." is added even though the reception is not specifically mentioned. The city, state, and zip code should be added to the street address when a reply is requested. (The one exception is for New York City addresses—in this case, the state name is dropped, and the correct form is New York 00000).

7. Spacing: See the samples, following, for the traditional sequence of words and spacing of lines.

8. Spelling: Whenever possible without crowding a line, numbers are spelled out rather than expressed in figures. Numbered streets are spelled, but house numbers are not unless they can be spelled in one word. "Fifteen Fifth Avenue" is correct. So is "545 Fifty-seventh Street."

   Time and date are also spelled out. "Wednesday, the tenth of June" is correct, not "Wednesday, June 10 (or 10th)." The hour is spelled. If the ceremony is to be held on the half- or quarter-hour, the form is: "at half after four" or "at half past four," "at a quarter before four" or "at a quarter past four."

   The year may or may not be used on an invitation (but always is used on an announcement). If the year is used, it is spelled out: "One thousand nine hundred and sixty-eight" or "Nineteen hundred and sixty-eight."

   "Honour" is the traditional spelling, though "honor" is also correct.

9. Wording: "The pleasure of your company" is never used on an invitation to a religious ceremony. "The honour of your presence" is the only proper wording, and it is also best used when a judge or other secular official is performing the marriage. "The pleasure of your company," however, is the only correct form on a separate reception invitation.

10. Zip Code: *See* "R.S.V.P." above.

**Mailing Date.** Formal invitations may be mailed as much as a month, but never less than two weeks, before the date of the wedding.

Announcements are usually mailed the day of the wedding or the day following—except, of course, in the case of an elopement.

**To Whom Sent.** Invitations are sent to all close relatives of the bride and groom, even if it is quite certain that they will not be able to attend.

Invitations are also sent to all who are sure to attend—the groom's parents, the bridesmaids and ushers, and the clergyman, for example—since they may want to keep the invitation as a souvenir.

An invitation is not properly sent to one member of a married couple. If one is asked, the other must be also.

It is only romantically sympathetic of the bride and groom to see that the fiancée of a bridesmaid and the fiancée of the best man or an usher get an invitation. There is no need, though, to invite just any current best girl or beau of an attendant.

It should be emphasized that invitations rather than announcements are sent to relatives and close friends who live in distant places and cannot possibly accept. This is a charming custom because it indicates that the couple wish the recipient could be present. It also puts these special people on the list of those who will be the first to receive a formal communication about the event, since an announcement would not be mailed until after the wedding.

A formal engraved announcement may be sent to a much wider circle of acquaintances than is the invitation to the wedding and the wedding reception. An invitation to a wedding reception more or less obligates the guest to send a present, and many people feel that an invitation to a wedding does also; therefore, announcements are often sent to business friends and less intimate friends, to avoid seeming to make a tacit request for a wedding gift. Or, if the wedding and reception are small, invitations are given informally and formal announcements are sent to all those not invited to the ceremony and the reception.

## STANDARD FORMS

*Basic Standard Form.* The following wording is the standard form on which all formal wedding invitations are based.

Mr. and Mrs. Richard Evans Brooks
request the honour of your presence
at the marriage of their daughter
Frances Pearson
to
Mr. Stuart Wendell Danforth
Thursday, the twenty-second of October
at four o'clock
Church of the Heavenly Rest
New York

*Optional additions*: It is correct to add the year, spelled in full, after the line giving the hour of the wedding. The name of the state is added if the town is not well known. If the church is not well known, or if there is any chance that guests might confuse it with another of a similar name, its address is added. Such an invitation would read:

at four o'clock
One thousand nine hundred and sixty-eight
Saint George's Church
100 Revere Avenue
Eastbrook, Maine

## At a Private Residence, Club, or Hotel

It is understood that refreshments will be served following a ceremony at home or in a club or hotel, and so "R.S.V.P." is added. The state is not added if the city is well known, but is included if there might be a chance of confusion, or if R.S.V.P. is used, as in the examples following:

*House of the bride or her parents*:

at half after four
Ten Fifth Avenue
Eastbrook, Maine 00000
R.S.V.P.

*House of a relative or friend*:

(The bride's parents issue the invitation, as above, but added is "at the residence of, etc." and under "R.S.V.P." the residence of the bride's parents, since replies are sent to them.)

at four o'clock
at the residence of Mr. and Mrs. John Hall Ball
1042 Sunset Avenue
Baycrest, New Jersey

R.S.V.P.
247 West Avenue
Wilton, New York 00000

*At a club or hotel*:

at seven o'clock
The River Club
New York

R.S.V.P.
940 Fifth Avenue
New York 00000

## If the Bride's Parents Are Divorced

The bride's mother usually issues the invitations, but if the bride has made her home with her father, an aunt, grandparents, etc., the person with whom she has lived for many years usually issues the invitations.

*A divorced mother's invitation reads*:

Mrs. Greene Brown
[her maiden name and her former husband's last name]
requests the honour of your presence
[etc.]

*A divorced and remarried mother:*

Invitations may be issued in her name alone, or jointly with her husband. The first form below is often used if the bride's father is living, though the second may be used if the bride is devoted to her stepfather. The second is always used if her father is dead.

*Mrs. John Charles Ball*
*requests the honour of your presence*
[etc.]

or

*Mr. and Mrs. John Charles Ball*
*request the honour of your presence*
*at the marriage of her daughter*
*Mary Ellen Brown*
[etc.]

("Her daughter" is used to make the relationships clear.)

*A divorced and remarried father:*

In this case, the invitations always read "Mr. and Mrs. Henry York Brown," but "his daughter" is used to indicate that the mother is either dead or divorced.

*If divorced parents have both remarried:*

With the divorce rate being what it is, things are getting complicated, and so we are creating a number of new rules. Today, it is a growing and very pleasant custom for divorced parents who have maintained a friendly relationship to join formally in giving their daughter a happy send-off, even if one or both have remarried. If it seems a comfortable and graceful arrangement for all concerned, they can certainly ignore the traditional regulations and issue the announcements jointly. It is less usual for them to issue the wedding invitations jointly, but who is to say that it is not "correct" if that seems to them the natural way to launch their daughter in her new life? In this case, the invitation or announcement would read:

*Mrs. William Graham Tower*
*and*
*Mr. Henry York Brown*
*request the honour of your presence*
*at the marriage of their daughter*
[etc.]

### If the Bride's Parents Are Legally Separated

When their relationship is at all amicable, and especially if their circles of friends overlap, the fact of their separation is ignored and invitations read:

*Mr. and Mrs. Henry York Brown*
[etc.]

Otherwise, the parent with whom the bride lives issues the invitation alone:

*Mrs. Henry York Brown*
[etc.]

### If a Parent Is Widowed and Remarried

*A widowed and remarried mother:*

The invitation is issued by the bride's mother and stepfather, but "her daughter" is used. The bride's last name is given to make the relationship clear.

> *Admiral and Mrs. William Graham Tower*
> *request the honour of your presence*
> *at the marriage of her daughter*
> *Mary Ann Brown*
> [etc.]

*A widowed and remarried father:*

The invitation is issued as above by the bride's father and stepmother with "his daughter," but only the bride's given name or names are used, since her last name is the same as her father's.

### If the Bride Is an Orphan

The invitations are issued by a close relative—a grandparent, an aunt or uncle, an older brother or sister, depending on the circumstances. If a relative issues the invitation, the relationship is mentioned. If the relative is married, "Mr. and Mrs." is always used. Or if the bride has no close relatives, she may issue the invitation herself.

*A relative's invitation:*

> *Mr. and Mrs. John Charles Evans*
> *request the honour of your presence*
> *at the marriage of their sister*
> *Alice Jane Greene*
> [etc.]

(The bride's last name is given if she is Mrs. Evans' sister to make the relationship clear.)

*A godparent's or close friend's invitation:*

The relationship is not mentioned, and this is one of the very few cases when "Miss" correctly precedes the bride's name.

*If the bride issues the invitation:*

An older bride often issues her own invitation rather than draft a distant relative to do so. The same form is used by the young bride who does not have close relatives. The following forms are among the very few in which "Miss" and "Mrs." are correct.

> *The honour of your presence is requested*
> *at the marriage of*
> *Miss Mary Ann Brown*
> *to*
> [etc.]

### If the Bride Is a Divorcée

The parents of a very young divorcée usually issue the invitations when she remarries. A mature divorcée usually issues her own invitations.

*A young divorcée:*

> Mr. and Mrs. Henry York Brown
> request the honour of your presence
> at the marriage of their daughter
> Mary Brown Smith
> [etc.]

(Note that "Mrs." is not used with the divorcée's name.)

*A mature divorcée:*

> The honour of your presence is requested
> at the marriage of
> Mrs. Brown Smith
> [etc.]

### If the Bride Is a Widow

If her parents or a relative issues the invitation, as is usual if she is quite young, her name is given as "Mary Brown Smith" (no "Mrs.").

If she issues the invitations herself, as is usual with mature widows, her name is given as used on her calling cards, not "Mrs. Mary Brown Smith."

> The honour of your presence
> is requested at the marriage of
> Mrs. John Jones Smith
> [etc.]

### If the Bride Is Widely Known Under a Professional Name

In this case her legal name is used and her professional name is given below it, in smaller letters and in parentheses.

> Mary Ann Brown
> (Dolores Darcy)

### If the Invitations Are Issued by the Groom's Parents

Under most unusual circumstances—for example, if the bride is a foreigner without close friends in this country—the groom's parents may give the wedding.

> Mr. and Mrs. George Nelson Smith
> request the honour of your presence
> at the marriage of
> Miss Maria Delorme
> to their son
> [etc.]

### If the Bride or Groom Is in the Armed Services

The only differences in form are in the use and placement of military titles.

*If the bride is in the service:*

Her rank follows her name.

> Mary Ann
> Lieutenant, Women's Army Corps

*If the groom is in the service:*

A commissioned officer's rank precedes his name if his rank is Captain or higher in the Army, or Lieutenant (senior grade) in the Navy. Otherwise, his rank is given below his name.

*Colonel John Dewey Anderson*
*United States Army*

*John Dewey Anderson*
*Ensign, United States Navy*

If the groom is a noncommissioned officer, petty officer, enlisted man, cadet, or midshipman, his rank or rating does not precede his name (and neither does "Mr."). It may be used as in the first example below, but the recommended form is the second example below.

*John Dewey Anderson*
*Corporal, United States Army*

or

*John Dewey Anderson*
*Signal Corps, United States Army*

### Double Weddings

*If the brides are sisters:*

The name of the older sister is given first.

*at the marriage of their daughters*
*Mary Ann*
*to*
*Mr. John Jones Smith*
*and*
*Elizabeth Jane*
*to*
*Mr. George Arthur White*
*[etc.]*

*If the brides are cousins or friends:*

If the brides are about the same age, the order is alphabetical, and each bride's last name is used. If one bride is somewhat senior to the other, her name comes first. However, if one girl's parents are much senior, or if her grandparents are issuing the invitation with the other bride's parents, the older couple or individual takes precedence. Or separate invitations may be sent, of course. Or two standard invitations may be engraved facing each other on the inside of the usual folded sheet.

*Mr. and Mrs. Henry York Brown*
*and*
*Mr. and Mrs. Peter Bell White*
*request the honour of your presence*
*at the marriage of their daughters*
*Mary Ann Brown*
*to*
*Mr. John Jones Smith*
*and*
*Rosemary Jane White*
*to*
*Mr. William Hart Black*
*[etc.]*

**Double Invitation or Announcement.** Some families like to follow a custom seen more often in Europe than the United States, and to join in issuing the invitations and announcements. Following is a popular form, though there are a number of correct variants. The engraving appears on the inside of a double fold. The bride's parents' message is always on the left. R.S.V.P. can appear at the usual place at the lower left, if the ceremony is at home or at a club or hotel, but appears on the reception card if the ceremony is in a house of worship:

<table>
<tr><td>Mr. and Mrs. John Vance Vincent<br>request the honour of your presence<br>at the marriage of their daughter<br>Amelia Ann<br>to<br>Mr. Jean Paul Smith</td><td>Mr. and Mrs. George Fenwick Smith<br>request the honour of your presence<br>at the marriage of their son<br>Jean Paul<br>to<br>Miss Amelia Ann Vincent</td></tr>
</table>

*Saturday, the first of October*
*at four o'clock*
*Saint George's Church*
*Chicago*

### If a Wedding Is Postponed

If time is very short, all who received invitations must be notified by telegram or other fast means. If there is time to order invitations giving the new date, they follow the style of the original invitation, except that they are printed, again to save time. Block lettering or any other type face that appeals can be used. New reception cards are enclosed, of course, and they require answers just as the original ones did.

*Mr. and Mrs. Henry York Brown*
*announce that the marriage of their daughter*
*Mary Ann*
*to*
*Mr. John Jones Smith*
*has been postponed from*
*Wednesday, the tenth of June*
*until*
*Saturday, the eighteenth of August*
*at six o'clock*
*The Country Club*

*R.S.V.P.*
*204 Highland Avenue*
*Ross, California 00000*

### If Invitations Must Be Recalled

Invitations to a wedding are recalled for two reasons: because all plans to marry are canceled; or because, since there has been some such emergency as a serious illness or death in the family, only an extremely small and quiet wedding will be held on or near the announced date. In both cases a single card (instead of a double fold of paper) and a single envelope are used, and the notice is printed instead of engraved in order to save time.

*If the marriage is canceled after invitations are sent:*

Mr. and Mrs. Henry York Brown
announce that the marriage of their daughter
Mary Ann
to
Mr. John Jones Smith
will not take place

(*See "Canceled" in this section for details.*)

*If the invitations are recalled for other reason:*

An explanation is often given if plans for a big wedding are canceled, but the wedding will take place as scheduled. However, no explanation need be given.

Mr. and Mrs. Henry York Brown
regret that they are obliged to recall
the invitations to the marriage of their daughter
Mary Ann to Mr. John Jones Smith
owing to the death of Mr. Smith's father
Mr. George Fenwick Smith

To the above can be added the following lines:

The ceremony will be held privately
in the presence of the immediate family

*If invitations to a reception must be recalled:*

Mr. and Mrs. Henry York Brown
regret that owing to a death in the family
they are obliged to recall the invitations
to the marriage reception of their daughter
on Saturday, the sixteenth of June

The marriage ceremony will take place
as originally planned

**INVITATIONS TO RECEPTIONS.** When a wedding is held in a house of worship, the reception invitation usually is enclosed with the wedding invitation, but in some circumstances one of the forms below may be more practical. Note that "The pleasure of your company" (never "The honour of your presence") is used on any separate invitation to the reception only.

**Reception Card Enclosed with a Wedding Invitation**

This is the most practical form when fewer guests are invited to the reception than to the wedding. The card is about 3 by 4 inches and matches the invitation in style of engraving.

Reception
immediately following the ceremony
The Cosmopolitan Club

R.S.V.P.
845 Fifth Avenue
New York 00000

or

*The pleasure of your company*
*is requested at the reception*
*after the ceremony*
*25 Eastlake Drive*

*R.S.V.P.*

## Invitation to the Reception Only

The form follows that of an invitation. Double envelopes are used.

*Mr. and Mrs. Henry York Brown*
*request the pleasure of your company*
*at the wedding reception of their daughter*
*Mary Ann*
*and*
*Mr. John Jones Smith*
*on Wednesday, the tenth of June*
*at five o'clock*
*Mark Hopkins Hotel*
*San Francisco*

*R.S.V.P.*
*312 Golden Gate Avenue*
*Belvedere, California 00000*

If the reception is at the residence of a friend, the invitation reads as above, except for the following change:

*at five o'clock*
*at the residence of*
*Mr. and Mrs. John Towne White*
*1043 Grace Circle*
*Ross, California*

## Combined with the Wedding Invitation

If all invited to a ceremony in church are also invited to the reception, the invitations may be combined. "R.S.V.P." is added.

*Mr. and Mrs. Henry York Brown*
*request the honour of your presence*
*at the marriage of their daughter*
*Mary Ann*
*to*
*Mr. John Jones Smith*
*on Wednesday, the tenth of June*
*at four o'clock*
*Saint John's Church*
*and afterwards at the reception*
*The Garden Club*
*Denver*

*R.S.V.P.*
*[address]*
*[City, State, Zip Code]*

### A Delayed Reception

On occasion, a reception may be given several days or more following a wedding. For example, the parents of the groom might give a reception some weeks after the ceremony, if it took place in another city, to introduce their new daughter-in-law to their friends. Or the parents of the bride, or the parents of the bride and groom jointly, might give the reception when the couple return from their wedding trip.

*In honour of*
*Mr. and Mrs. John Jones Smith*

*Mr. and Mrs. Henry York Brown*
*Mr. and Mrs. George Fenwick Smith*
*request the pleasure of your company*
*Sunday, the thirtieth of June*
*four to seven o'clock*
*The Garden Club*

*R.S.V.P.*
*Mrs. Brown*
*10 West Avenue*
*Atlanta, Georgia 00000*

An answer to the above invitation, always handwritten, would read:

*Miss Marian Millbrook*
*accepts with pleasure*
*the kind invitation of*
*Mr. and Mrs. Brown*
*and Mr. and Mrs. Smith*
*[etc.]*

**INVITATIONS, REPLIES TO.** Replies to wedding and wedding reception invitations are also governed by exact rules:

1. A formal invitation to a wedding in a house of worship does not require an answer unless a reception invitation is also enclosed.
2. A formal invitation to a wedding at home or in a club or hotel does require a formal answer because, even if no mention is made of a reception, it is understood that refreshments will be offered after the ceremony.
3. An informal invitation to a wedding anywhere always requires a reply. A handwritten note of invitation implies that very few guests are expected. It must be answered promptly, just as any other personal letter of invitation must be.
4. Replies should match the invitation in degree of formality. A formal reply is always in the third person.
5. The envelope is addressed exactly as the name of the sender or senders appears on the invitation: to "Mr. and Mrs. Henry York Brown," for example, not to "Mr. and Mrs. H. Y. Brown" or to only one of a couple.
6. Standard Forms: A formal reply is handwritten in black or blue-black ink on conservative social letter paper that does not have a printed name at the top. The standard-size double sheet is the usual choice, but a single sheet or note-size paper is also correct. There is no need whatever to go shopping for heavy white paper to match that of the invitation. The spacing follows that of the invitation closely.

## A Formal Acceptance

The date and time are always repeated in a formal acceptance, and it is usual to repeat the place also. When the wedding and reception are at the same place, the shorter form below may be used, as it may be for an invitation to the reception only. Or it is correct to repeat the entire invitation as shown in the longer forms.

*Mr. and Mrs. William Bond Grant*
*accept with pleasure*
*the kind invitation of*
*Mr. and Mrs. Brown*
*for Wednesday, the tenth of June*
*at four o'clock*
*The Plaza Hotel*

or

*Mr. and Mrs. William Bond Grant*
*accept with pleasure*
*the kind invitation of*
*Mr. and Mrs. Brown*
*to the wedding reception of their daughter*
*Mary Ann*
*and*
*Mr. John Jones Smith*
*on Wednesday, the tenth of June*
*at five o'clock*
*The River Club*

or

*Mr. and Mrs. William Bond Grant*
*accept with pleasure*
*the kind invitation of*
*Mr. and Mrs. Brown*
*to the marriage of their daughter*
*Mary Ann*
*to*
*Mr. John Jones Smith*
*on Wednesday, the tenth of June*
*at four o'clock*
*Fifth Avenue Presbyterian Church*
*and afterward at*
*The River Club*

## A Formal Regret

The day and date are given in a formal regret, but the hour and place are not. The shorter form is always correct, though an explanation of the refusal is more cordial, even if not necessary.

*Mr. and Mrs. William Bond Grant*
*regret that they are unable to accept*
*Mr. and Mrs. Brown's*
*kind invitation for*
*Wednesday, the tenth of June*

**or**

> *Mr. and Mrs. William Bond Grant*
> *regret exceedingly that*
> *their absence from the city\**
> *prevents their accepting*
> *Mr. and Mrs. Brown's*
> *kind invitation for*
> *Wednesday, the tenth of June*

## A Combined Acceptance and Regret

Invitations to a wedding breakfast or other reception differ from invitations to other meals in that both husband and wife need not refuse if only one is able to attend. It is entirely proper for both to go to the ceremony and only one to the reception; or for both to miss the ceremony and only one to attend the reception. In such cases, the standard reply is:

> *Mrs. William Bond Grant*
> *accepts with pleasure*
> *the kind invitation of*
> *Mr. and Mrs. Brown*
> *to the wedding reception of their daughter*
> *on Wednesday, the tenth of June*
> *at five o'clock*
> *The Plaza Hotel*
> *but regrets that Mr. Grant*
> *will be unable to attend*

**JEWISH.**  *See "Ceremony, Jewish."*

**KISSING THE BRIDE AND GROOM.** The groom is always the first to kiss the bride. After most ceremonies he kisses her before they leave the altar, though some faiths do not approve a kiss at the altar. This matter will be made clear during consultation with the clergyman or at the rehearsal. Where a kiss at the altar is customary, it is given after the clergyman offers his congratulations and before the couple turn to face the congregation.

When going through the receiving line, only guests on close terms with the bride kiss her. Others shake her hand. Relatives of the groom who are strangers to her properly kiss her on the cheek in token of warm welcome to the family, but his male friends are most certainly not privileged to do so. The bride's female relatives usually kiss the groom, and there are those who think it is a standard part of the fun for the bridesmaids and other young single women to leave him well besmeared with lipstick, but care should be taken not to put the bride to this disadvantage.

**LICENSE.** A marriage license must be obtained before a wedding can be performed in any state, and the bride and groom must apply together, in person, for it. The license must be issued by a marriage license bureau in the state in which the wedding will be held. A license issued by one state is not valid in another.

It is best not to delay making application for the license until the last few days before a wedding. In some states, a license will not be issued until at least five days after the filing of the application. In others, a license is not valid until several days after the date of issue. And if the special requirements discussed below are not met at the time the application is made, there may be a considerable additional delay.

---

\*Or "illness in the family," "a previous engagement," etc.

(Note: Consult a current *World Almanac,* available in any library, for each state's requirements for age, with and without parental consent; blood tests; and the waiting time for a license.)

**Age.** All states have laws controlling the age of marriage either with or without parental consent. In quite a number of states, a girl as young as fourteen and a boy of fifteen can be married if they have the consent of parents or guardians. In other states, parental consent is required for both men and women under the age of twenty-one. However, according to the *World Almanac:* "In most states, the court has authority, in an emergency, to marry young couples below the ordinary age of consent, where due regard for their morals and welfare so requires."

**Birth Certificates.** Applicants for a marriage license who look young for their years may be asked to produce their birth certificates. They can avoid having to make a return trip to the license bureau by taking proof of their age with them when making application.

**Blood Tests.** Virtually all states require a blood test made no more than thirty days prior to the wedding date, before a marriage license will be issued. A written and signed medical report must be submitted when the license is applied for. It usually takes several days for a report on a blood test to be returned to the doctor, and so sufficient time should be allowed.

**Divorced Persons.** In some states, a divorced person is required to show a certified copy of a final decree of divorce when applying for a marriage license. The license may be refused if the divorce is not valid in that state.

**Expenses.** The charge for a marriage license is fixed by local law, and usually ranges from two to five dollars. The groom pays for the license. As a general rule, each of the couple pays individually for blood-test reports or other documents concerning health that may be required.

**Foreign-born Persons.** Naturalized citizens will need to submit proof of citizenship when applying for a license. Citizens of another country will be asked for proof of identity and age as well as citizenship. A passport serves well for this purpose.

**Health Requirements.** In some states persons suffering from certain maladies may not marry, and a doctor's report in addition to the usual blood test may be required. Check local laws.

**Proxies.** The principals are required to appear together at a marriage license bureau to make application for a license. Consult a judge, other official, or a lawyer if the circumstances are such that one or both of the principals cannot appear.

**Term.** A marriage license is usually good for sixty days, but it is advisable to check local law to make sure that a license dated more than a month before the marriage is valid.

**LUGGAGE.** The bride does not take luggage marked with the initials of her maiden name on her honeymoon. If she is not getting new luggage, the initial of her husband's last name should be added before the wedding. For example, if Mary Jane Brown has been using luggage marked MJB and her new name will be Smith, she instructs the luggage shop to remark her bags either MJBS or MJB . If she is using new luggage, the usual marking is MBS.
S

**MAID AND MATRON OF HONOR.** Traditionally, a bride has at least one honor attendant no matter how simple the wedding may be. The honor attendant may be married or single. She usually is a sister of the bride or her closest friend, and is of about the age of the bride, though she need not be. On very rare occasions, the bride's mother serves as the matron of honor, but this arrangement is likely to be awkward because the mother of the bride has so many other duties to perform.

In a large wedding party there often are two honor attendants, usually a maid and a matron of honor. Both may be married or single, and either one may be designated the chief honor attendant.

The bride herself chooses and invites all her attendants. Invitations to be a member of the wedding party are not issued by her mother or anyone else except in some unusual circumstances. In some religious denominations, the honor attendant must be of the same faith as the bride unless special permission is given for someone outside that faith to serve. Sometimes an invited honor attendant (or bridesmaid) is obliged to decline the invitation to serve because her own faith prohibits her participation in a religious service of another faith or because she would feel seriously ill at ease doing so. Therefore, inquiry about such religious restrictions and feelings is best made before inviting anyone to serve.

It is a great compliment to be asked to serve as maid or matron of honor. The invitation is not refused except for a valid reason. Because of this fact, and also because the duties of an honor attendant are numerous and she may be put to some expense, due thought should be given to the choice.

If the honor attendant is married, her husband is invited to attend prewedding parties and, of course, the ceremony and reception.

**Clothes.** The costume of the maid or matron of honor matches the dresses of the bridesmaids in general style, but may be somewhat different in cut and usually is a different color or a different shade of the same color, though it need not be. If the bride has only one attendant, she dresses in any costume that goes well with that of the bride.

**Duties.** The maid and matron of honor are expected to help in all possible ways with plans for the wedding, but specifically their duties include:

Accepting, whenever possible, invitations to any prewedding parties.

Helping to address invitations and announcements and to open and list wedding presents, as well as arrange decorations—if asked to.

Attending the rehearsal.

Arriving at the bride's house in time to help her dress for the ceremony.

Making sure that the ring finger of the bride's left glove is slit and seeing that she has the traditional "something old, something new, something borrowed, something blue" to wear.

Seeing that the bride has a handkerchief, and carrying it for her if she does not have an appropriate place to conceal it in a long sleeve or glove.

Seeing that the bridesmaids' costumes are in order and that they have their bouquets before they leave for the church.

Helping the bride to pack, and making sure that the bride's going-away costume is complete and delivered to the proper room if she is changing to travel clothes at a reception away from home.

Standing near the bride during the ceremony, holding her bouquet during the service, and helping to raise her veil.

Taking charge of the groom's ring and handing it over at the proper time during the service.

Adjusting the bride's train before the recessional.

Signing as a witness, when required.

Standing in the receiving line.

Helping the bride change to her travel clothes.

Seeing that the bride's luggage is delivered to the best man in good time to be stowed with the groom's in the car or taxi.

Taking charge of the bride's wedding dress if the bride changes into her going-away costume away from home.

**Expenses.** On rare occasions, the bride may make a present of their costumes to any or all of her attendants, but usually they provide their own according to the bride's choice of color and style. The bride's family provides the bouquets. Other expenses of an honor attendant include sending a wedding present and paying for her own transportation (with a few exceptions) if she lives out of town. The bride's family pays for her hotel or otherwise takes care of housing her.

**Maiden of Honor.** This is the title given to a junior bridesmaid if only one serves. Little girls from about ten through their early teens are often made members of the wedding by being asked to serve in this capacity.

**MAIDEN DINNER.** A maiden dinner is a party at which a bride and her honor attendants and bridesmaids gather while the bridegroom's bachelor dinner is being held elsewhere. A maiden dinner should not be confused with a bridal dinner (also called "rehearsal dinner") at which all members of a wedding party are entertained following the rehearsal of the ceremony.

**MILITARY.** *See "Ceremony, Differences from Basic Protestant."*

**MOURNING.** If a death occurs in either family just before the wedding, the feelings of the bride and groom govern any changes of plan. The wedding may be held as scheduled, it may be postponed, or invitations to a very large wedding and reception may be recalled (*see* "Invitations" for the procedure) and only a quiet wedding without bridesmaids and ushers be held on the announced date. In this case, the bride may wear her wedding gown or a simpler costume, whichever is most appropriate if time and place are changed.

Under any circumstances, neither the bride nor any of her attendants wears black. The groom, best man, ushers, the father of the bride or of the groom, do not wear black sleeve bands.

It is correct for someone recently bereaved to remain as a member of a wedding party. All depends on the feelings of the individual. If the loss is recent and of someone very close, an attendant may feel it best to withdraw rather than risk marring the otherwise joyous mood of the day because of his or her personal sorrow. If a woman in mourning remains as a member of the wedding party, she lays black clothes aside for the occasion and wears a costume to match those of the other attendants.

It is proper for someone recently bereaved to attend a wedding or any other religious service. Anyone who is in deep mourning usually attends the wedding ceremony but declines the invitation to the reception unless it is to be a small, quiet family gathering. There is, however, no reason why the recently bereaved should not attend the reception as well if they can conceal their sorrow temporarily in what should be a time of rejoicing in the happiness of bride and groom.

A woman wedding guest in deep mourning adds a touch of white or lavender to her dress and does not wear black stockings. A male guest in mourning need not remove the black band from his sleeve.

**MUSIC.** The regulations concerning the music that may be played at a wedding in a house of worship vary. In some faiths only sacred music is permitted. In others, secular songs like "Oh, Promise Me" and "I Love You Truly" may be sung by a soloist. In all cases, however, it is essential to consult the clergyman or the organist before making a definite selection of music.

In those churches that permit secular music, the "Bridal Chorus" from Wagner's *Lohengrin* ("Here Comes the Bride") for the processional and the wedding march from Mendelssohn's *A Midsummer Night's Dream* for the recessional are traditional.

More latitude is possible in the selection of music to be played during a ceremony performed outside a house of worship, but if a clergyman is to officiate he most certainly must be consulted in this circumstance also. If a judge or other nonreligious official performs the marriage, there are no restrictions as to the choice of music except the personal taste of the bride and groom.

**Organist.** If the regular professional organist of the church plays for the wedding, he receives his regular fee. If an outside organist is to play, it is the standard courtesy to gain the permission of the clergyman or the regular organist first. If the visiting organist is a personal friend, it is customary to give him a present rather than a fee.

**Reception.** Any music is appropriate, but the first dance in which the bride and groom circle the floor once alone is by tradition a waltz.

**Soloist.** A professional soloist engaged to sing at the ceremony is paid his regular fee. If a friend is asked to sing, a present instead of a check is usual.

**PAGE BOYS AND TRAINBEARERS.** Page boys used to have a real function when brides wore immensely long trains too heavy to be managed without support. Since these are almost unheard of today, page boys are rarely part of a wedding party. On occasion, a boy too young to serve as an usher and too old to be a ring bearer is included as an honorary page boy. He walks in front of a flower girl or beside her, or if there is no flower girl, directly in front of the bride and her father in the processional, and after her in the recessional.

During the ceremony he stands in a place determined at the rehearsal. He may go to the reception or not, depending on his years.

**Clothes.** He dresses according to the choice of the bride—usually in a dark-blue suit or, especially in summer, a white one or, on occasion, a special costume—ruffled shirt, shorts, and a colored sash, for example. It is not the customary or formal procedure to dress him in miniature evening clothes.

**Duties and Expenses.** He attends the rehearsal. His parents pay for his clothes. He joins his parents in sending a wedding present, or can send one of his own separate from theirs.

**PARENTAL CONSENT.** *See* "Elopements"; also "License."

**PEW CARDS.** The purpose of a pew card is to ensure a preferred place in a house of worship on any occasion when a great many guests are invited to a ceremony, though these cards are mainly used for extremely large weddings. A pew card may be sent with the invitation, but more often is sent after an acceptance is received.

Engraved visiting cards are usually used when specific pews are assigned. "Pew 6" (or whatever the number) is handwritten in black ink on the upper left-hand corner of a visiting card. The bride's mother works out the seating chart and marks the cards, using her own for the guests on her list and the cards of the groom's mother for the guests on the list from the groom and his parents.

The above procedure is obviously so complicated—and the possibility of hurt feelings so great—that today's custom is not to assign pews but only to ensure places in a reserved section for special guests. If a church (admittance) card is used, a handwritten line "Within the ribbons," or "Bride's reserved section," or "Groom's reserved section" can be added for special guests. Otherwise, visiting cards, marked as above, or little fill-in cards available through many stationers are used.

**PHOTOGRAPHS.** The formal studio portrait of the bride in her wedding dress and veil, either full length or head and shoulders only, is usually made two or three weeks before the wedding so that proofs can be considered without haste and prints can be sent to the press in sufficient time to be prepared for publication close to the wedding date. (Glossy prints 10 by 14 inches should be ordered for newspaper use.) A picture of the bride and groom together is not sent to a newspaper. If the editor wants one, he sends a cameraman to make a shot of the couple as they leave the church.

**Candid.** Pictures of any religious service should not be taken within a house of worship without the permission of the clergyman, and few clergymen will grant it; but candid shots outside the church and at the reception are customary, and they make a charming record to be treasured. It is generally better to hire a professional to take such pictures than to depend on the services of an amateur. Customarily, a full set of candids is ordered for the bride's parents and also the groom's, in addition of course to the set for the bride and groom. And generally one or two special shots in which they appear to particular advantage are sent to the attendants and special guests.

**Wedding Party.** When to take a picture of the whole wedding party is a problem. It is awkward, at best, to have it taken before the ceremony. It is also extremely awkward to have a studio picture made of the bride, groom, attendants, and both sets of parents if a reception follows the ceremony immediately, since that leaves no one to welcome the guests as they arrive at the reception. Very often the best solution is a candid group picture made just before the receiving line forms. In any case, thought should be given to the feelings of the guests, who should not be left too long alone at the place of the reception while the wedding party poses for a studio portrait, or made to wait around unduly before the receiving line forms.

**POSTPONED.**   *See* "Invitations."

**PRAYER BOOKS.**   *See* "Bible or Prayer Book."

**PRESS RELEASES.**   *See* "Announcements."

**PROCESSIONAL.**   *See* "Ceremony."

**RECEIVING LINES.** A receiving line, whether at the church or at the reception, may be set up in several ways, but certain basic rules govern all of them:

1. A wedding receiving line is composed of two parts that may be at some distance from each other or in one continuous line: first, the parents' line; then the bride, groom, maid of honor, bridesmaids, and junior bridesmaids.
2. The best man, ushers, and little children never stand in the receiving line.
3. Guests always reach the parents' line first. The bride's mother stands nearest the entrance (except in "Special Circumstances," given below). If the groom's mother is present, she always stands second or third in line. Frequently, just the two mothers receive, and the fathers stand nearby but not in line, so that they are free to move about, speak with guests, make introductions, and so on. Or, if the groom's father knows only a few of the guests, he stands in the line between the two mothers while the bride's father circulates. Or both fathers may be in the line.

> **A standard receiving line:**
> **(1) Announcer. (2) Mother of the bride.**
> **(3) Mother of the groom. (4) Father of the groom.**
> **(5) Bride. (6) Groom. (7) Matron of honor.**
> **(8) Maid of honor. (9) All the bridesmaids.**
> **(10) Father of the bride. He stands near the end of the line,**
> **but is free to move about to chat with guests, and make introductions.**

1       2       3       4               5       6       7           8           9           9

10

An alternate standard receiving line:
(1) Mother of the bride. (2) Mother of the groom.
(3) Bride. (4) Groom. (5) Matron of honor.
(6) Maid of honor. (7) All the bridesmaids.
(8) Father of the bride. (9) Father of the groom.
The two fathers are standing near the end of the line,
but are free to move about to make introductions.

If all four parents are in the line, two arrangements are correct:

| | |
|---|---|
| Mother of the bride | Mother of the bride |
| Father of the groom | Father of the bride |
| Mother of the groom | Mother of the groom |
| Father of the bride | Father of the groom |

4. The bride always stands on the groom's right, with one exception—if he is in uniform, her correct place is on his left. The standard place for the bride is first in her part of the line. Only if the available space makes it impossibly awkward for her to stand first and also on the groom's right does she stand second in line—an arrangement that should be avoided unless there is no other solution.

The traditional order is:

Bride
Groom
Matron of honor
Maid of honor
Bridesmaids (according to height)

**Bouquets.** Flowers look lovely in the receiving line, but unless the bride can hold her bouquet comfortably in her left hand or over her left arm, she sets it aside. The bridesmaids usually hold their bouquets, but may set them aside.

**Gloves.** All women in a formal receiving line keep their gloves on. If the receiving line is at the church, women guests do also. If the receiving line is elsewhere, a woman guest may leave her gloves with her wrap before going through the line, though if long gloves are part of her costume, she keeps them on. A man always takes his gloves off.

**Going Through the Line.** An announcer is not used for a small reception, but it is practical to have an announcer at a large reception if many of the guests are unknown or only slightly known to the mother of the bride. The announcer may be a butler, the best man, or another guest.

Full details are given under RECEIVING LINES.

If there is no announcer, guests unknown to the mother of the bride identify themselves so that she can make the introduction to the next person in her line. Acquaintances also do well to state their names. At a time of such festive excitement, the mother of the bride cannot be expected to recall the names of scores of her daughter's friends—not to mention those of her new son-in-law—whom she may have met previously only in passing. A receiving line is no place for guests to stop for more than a few words. They should move along with reasonable dispatch. It usually happens that the chain of introductions breaks down somewhere along the line. A guest unknown to the bride should identify himself when he reaches her part of the line so that she can repeat his name to the groom, but he merely shakes hands with the bridesmaids without giving his name, unless there is some special reason to do so.

The bride and groom take care of introducing each other to their own relatives and friends, if need be, and such introductions are made with some brief hint as to the guest's identity. "John, this is Mrs. Greene who sent us the lovely ladle," is always tactful—if the bride has a reliable memory about the donors of the various wedding presents. The groom tries, as far as possible, to keep an eye on the oncoming line so that he can say, "Mary, this is Mr. Greene, my father's partner"—and make self-identification by the guest unnecessary.

Only her relatives and close friends kiss the bride—and care should be taken not to leave anyone in the receiving line marked with lipstick—as too often happens.

**Special Circumstances.** If the bride's mother is not present, her father stands first in line unless he has remarried, in which case the bride's stepmother takes the usual first place of the hostess. If the bride's father is not remarried, he sometimes asks a relative—grandmother, aunt, older daughter, and so on—to receive with him. If the relative lives with the father, she stands first in line; otherwise, he usually stands first with his honorary hostess beside him, and then the groom's mother.

If the reception is in the residence of someone other than the bride's parents, the line is formed in the standard fashion; the lenders of their house do not join it.

If the mother of the bride is divorced but her relations with the bride's father are cordial, he attends the reception but does not receive with her. She receives alone or with the mother of the groom (if she is present); or, if the bride's mother is remarried, the bride's stepfather acts as the host and the bride's father has the status of a guest.

**RECEPTIONS.** A receiving line is not formed at a small, informal reception, but the usual components of a large reception are a receiving line, music, dancing, and refreshments suitable to the hour.

**Arriving.** Guests provide their own transportation to the reception, though in suburban communities the ushers are often delegated to ferry guests without cars from the wedding to the reception. Guests should proceed to the reception without great delay—but also without haste, in order to give the wedding party sufficient time to reassemble and to form the receiving line. In all usual circumstances, guests go through the line in the order of their arrival, and do not correctly bypass a long line waiting to be received, or take refreshments first and go through later.

**Cutting the Cake.** The cake may be cut as soon as the receiving line breaks up if the refreshments are no more than the cake and champagne or punch. If a wedding breakfast or other meal is served, the cake is cut after the main course is finished.

*See "Cake" for details.*

**Dancing.** At a small reception, records usually serve for background and dance music. At a large reception, three to five musicians are usual—or there may be a full dance orchestra. They play any suitable selections, but do not play dance music until the receiving line breaks up, since no one dances until the bride and groom have made one turn around the floor alone to the traditional opening waltz. The bride's father with the groom's mother, and the bride's mother with the father of the groom, then join them for the second turn around the floor. Then the best man and maid of honor, the bridesmaids and ushers, join in, and other guests follow them.

The bride's second dance is with her father-in-law while the groom dances with her mother. The third dance sees the bride with her father and the groom with his mother. There is no strict rule, however, since some parents may not care to dance. The bride then takes a turn with the best man and each usher while the groom dances with the honor attendants and each bridesmaid. Bride and groom then dance with other guests if time and strength hold out.

**Decorations and Accessories.** Flower decorations for a first-time bride are traditionally white, but may be of any color. White book matches with the first names or the initials of the bride and groom in silver or a pastel color, as well as paper cocktail napkins printed in the same fashion, are often used.

**Expenses.** All the expenses of the reception are assumed by the bride or her family, though a relative or godparent sometimes pays for the reception as a wedding present. Usually this happens only if the bride is an orphan, or is so far from home that her parents cannot be present, or in other exceptional circumstances.

**Guests.** At a wedding reception the roof is an introduction, and guests need not wait to be formally introduced before speaking to each other. Except in unusual circumstances, guests are expected to stay until the bride and groom depart.

A guest is not obligated to write a note of thanks to the hostess, but close friends frequently telephone or send a little note complimenting the mother of the bride on the success of the party.

**Leaving, Bride and Groom.** After refreshments and as many dances as time permits, the musicians give a fanfare or some other musical cue to the guests that the bride is about to toss her bouquet before changing for her wedding trip. As everyone knows, the girl who catches the bridal bouquet will be the next to marry. Traditionally, the bridesmaids are given preference, and so they gather nearest the bride, who usually turns her back to let chance play its part in the outcome. If the bride has only one attendant and she is not married, other girls gather near but allow the attendant to catch the bouquet if she possibly can. If the bride wants to have her bouquet preserved by the florist, the girl who catches it returns it to the bride's mother. Otherwise, she keeps it.

The bride's mother, the honor attendant, and the bridesmaids often all go with the bride to help her change. The best man assists the groom to change, and sees that the luggage of both bride and groom is delivered to their car or taxi.

The parents of the bride and groom usually go for a private word of good-bye to the young couple before their departure. The wedding party may come back together—parents first, then the bridesmaids, and last of all the bride and groom together. Or all but the bride and groom may come back a few minutes before the couple make their traditional dash for the door.

In the meantime, the ushers have been putting a "Just Married" sign on the back of the car or tying racket-making tin cans and old shoes to its rear bumper —or preventing others from playing such pranks if they suspect the bridal couple would be dismayed rather than amused by them.

Tossing rice over the bride and groom as they leave the church or the reception for their honeymoon is an ancient custom. It symbolizes good wishes for happiness, luck, and fertility. Sometimes only the attendants are supplied with rice just before the couple dashes from the reception. Sometimes bowls of rice are placed at convenient places near the exit so that other guests can join in the ceremony. Rice should be tossed, not thrown with any force, since the grains can sting if hurled at close range. It is also slippery underfoot, and for this reason many people now skip the rice-throwing ritual or substitute confetti.

**Refreshments.** As guests come off the receiving line, champagne or some other drink usually is made available to them. Waiters may be circulating with trays, or there may be a bar and buffet, depending on the size of the party, what food is to be offered, and when substantial food is to be served.

If the refreshments are to be no more than cocktail sandwiches, the wedding cake, and champagne or a punch, the reception resembles a tea or cocktail party. Several seating arrangements are possible if more substantial food is offered. Here are the general rules:

1. Buffet: The formality and size of the party govern the seating. Quite often at a sizable party there will be a bride's table and a parents' table (described below), and all others present find places at smaller tables accommodating four to ten. Or there may be no special tables, and the bride and groom sit together wherever they please.

2. One table: If the wedding meal includes so few guests that all can be seated at one table, the bride's mother and father sit at the ends, opposite each other, in the usual position of host and hostess, with the bridegroom's mother on the host's right, the wife of the clergyman on his left; the father of the groom at the right of the bride's mother and the clergyman on her left. The bride sits at the groom's right on one of the longer sides of the table. They are flanked by the best man and the matron or maid of honor. Other attendants and guests fill in the rest of the places. Or if the bride's parents are not present, the bride and groom sit side by side at the head of the table, the bride on the groom's right.

3. Bride's table: Usually, only the bride, groom, and their attendants sit at this table. Sometimes the wife of an usher or the husband of a bridesmaid is included, but usually not. The bride sits on the groom's right at the head. The maid of honor is on his left and the best man on the bride's right, with bridesmaids and ushers alternating in the other places. When possible, this group sits at only one side and the ends of a long table (or around the outside of a horseshoe table) so that other guests will have an unobstructed view of the cake-cutting.

4. Parents' table: There is no parents' table unless there is a bride's table, and need not be one at all. The bride's father and mother sit opposite each other, with the groom's parents in the places of honor to their respective rights. The clergyman sits on the left of the bride's mother and his wife to the left of the bride's father. Grandparents and any extremely distinguished guests sit with them.

5. Place cards: Place cards are generally not used on the smaller tables for the guests, but they are a convenience and are usual at the tables for the bridal party and the parents, and also if everyone is seated at one large table.

**Toasts.** The first toast is traditionally proposed by the best man to the bride and groom. All (except the bride and groom) rise and drink to their health and happiness. The groom then rises and says a few words of thanks from himself and the bride, and usually proposes a toast to the bride's parents or to both sets of parents jointly. Other toasts may follow. Glasses are not drained after each toast—and, indeed, better not be if it appears that there will be many. The bride's father often keeps this ceremony from extending too long by proposing a collective toast to the bridesmaids and then to the best man and ushers, thereby guaranteeing that no one in the bridal party is overlooked.

The toast may be given at any time convenient during the reception—as soon as all guests are supplied with a first glass of wine, or before or after the cake is cut.

**RECESSIONAL.** *See "Ceremony."*

**REHEARSAL.** A rehearsal is not held if the bride has only one or two attendants. Instead, just before the ceremony, the clergyman explains the procedures—sometimes to the bride and her attendant and, separately, to the groom and best man; sometimes to all the principals together.

A ceremonial or formal wedding, however, is a complicated performance, and a rehearsal is a true necessity.

A rehearsal may be held at any time. The usual hour is in the late afternoon or early evening (depending on the availability of the church and the convenience of the clergyman) two or three days before the wedding.

There is no point in holding a rehearsal unless everyone who will participate is present. Usually no one else attends, though if a rehearsal party is to follow, the wife or husband of an attendant may watch if it is inconvenient to meet at the end of the rehearsal—and of course the groom's parents are invited.

The clergyman or one of his assistants is in charge. The entire procedure is practiced—how the ushers escort single guests, couples, and family groups to their seats; the formation of the processional and the pace at which it moves up the aisle; the ceremony; and the recessional. The marriage service is not spoken, but it is discussed in detail so that there is no uncertainty about when the bride's veil is lifted, when the bouquet is handed to the honor attendant, and so on.

In some faiths, it is traditional for the bride not to take an active part in the rehearsal but to watch while a stand-in rehearses for her. This custom is not widely observed today, since it leaves the bride at an obvious disadvantage. The Episcopal Church, for one, frowns on the use of a substitute.

Wedding costumes are not worn at the rehearsal, of course.

**REHEARSAL PARTY.** Some kind of party is usual after a rehearsal: a lunch, dinner, tea, or cocktail party, depending on the time of day. The bride's mother usually gives the party, but the groom's mother or anyone else may do so.

The parents of the bride and groom, the clergyman, and his wife are always invited. So is the husband or wife of a married attendant or usher, and the parents of children who are members of the bridal party. Some few special friends who have come from out of town for the wedding are sometimes asked also, but usually the party is confined mainly to those who have participated in the rehearsal.

Invitations are issued in any informal way and accepted or regretted in the same fashion. Sometimes the bride and groom give their presents to the attendants and ushers at this party.

**REPLY CARDS.** Enclosing a response card with blanks in which to indicate acceptance or regret for a wedding or reception invitation is not a correct procedure if the traditional rules are followed. However, this rule is beginning to change because reply cards have definite practical advantages, especially when the guest list is extremely large. They elicit faster responses, for one thing, and are far easier to file than the formal folded written responses.

**RESERVED SEATS.** *See* "Pew Cards."

**RICE.** *See* "Reception."

**RING BEARER.** A ring bearer may be as young as about four and usually is no older than seven unless he is small for his years. He walks in the processional just before the flower girl, or may be paired with her if this gives both of them the steadying companionship likely to be needed by very young ones. If he walks with the flower girl, he is on her right so that he can take his position next to the best man at the head of the aisle, which he must do if entrusted with the actual wedding ring. More often he carries a prop ring. In either case, the ring is attached to a white satin cushion by an easily broken thread.

If he is very small, he and the prop ring on its cushion are taken out of play by someone in a front pew as he passes. He does not join the recessional unless he has taken part in the ceremony itself, and he does not stand in the receiving line.

A ring bearer goes to the rehearsal. He often does not go to the reception, especially if it is an evening one and there is a chance that the excitement will inspire him to clowning or noisy showing off.

**Clothes.** A ring bearer usually wears a regular little-boy suit of navy blue or white with knee-length shorts, or he may have a special costume of white shirt, short pants, and a tailored sash. It is not customary or formal procedure to dress him in miniature evening clothes to match the groom's costume.

**Expenses.** His parents provide his clothes according to the choice of the bride. He joins his parents in sending a wedding present, or may send one of his very own separate from theirs.

**RINGS.** The groom pays for the bride's wedding ring. She or her family pays for his if there is a double-ring ceremony.

The bride and groom usually choose the rings together. If because of illness or any other reason the bride does not assist in the choice, the groom borrows a ring of hers that fits perfectly so that the jeweler can determine the right size, since—traditionally—she never removes the wedding ring after it is put on her finger during the marriage ceremony. (The bride removes her engagement ring before her wedding or wears it on her right hand until after the ceremony.) Once the ring is chosen, the bride does not see it again until the wedding day. The jeweler sends it to the groom or to the best man as directed, and sends the groom's ring to the bride or her honor attendant.

Any words may be inscribed inside a wedding ring, of course, but the usual inscription is the date of the wedding and the initials of the groom and of the bride's maiden name.

A man's wedding ring is usually plain gold without decoration. He wears it on the ring finger of the left hand, just as a woman does. A woman's wedding ring should match her engagement ring in metal and style. A heavy gold band does not go well with a diamond set in platinum, for example. A woman's wedding ring may be engraved, chased, or set with stones. A ring with stones is not practical for the bride who intends to follow the custom of never removing it, since most of them require regular cleaning and sometimes repair if tiny stones drop out.

If rings are not part of the wedding ceremony, the groom may put a wedding ring on his wife's finger at any time that seems to him appropriate after the ceremony.

**SEATING AT THE CEREMONY.** At Christian weddings, the bride's side of the church is to the left of the center aisle as the guests enter. The groom's side is to the right.

At Reform Jewish ceremonies, the above rule is followed. At ultra-Orthodox Jewish weddings, women sit on one side, men on the other; otherwise, in Orthodox and Conservative congregations, guests sit where they choose or according to the plan of whoever supervises the wedding.

These traditional divisions of families and friends are also followed at weddings held elsewhere than in a house of worship, but friends do not divide into two arbitrary clans under all circumstances. If the groom is from another city and comparatively few of his friends can attend, tactful friends of the bride will take places on his side rather than leave it markedly empty.

If there is no center aisle in the church, the left main aisle is used for the procession to the altar and the right main aisle for the recessional. In this case, the bride's side is the left half of the center section; the groom's is the right half. Their families divide the first rows of the center section, but friends may be seated in the side sections as well as behind the relatives in the center section.

The parents of bride and groom sit in the first row, with the fathers in the aisle seats.

See "Divorce Problems" for exceptions.

At a large wedding, a number of front rows are roped off by white ribbons to indicate that they are reserved for relatives and perhaps a few close friends. Ribbons sometimes are strung down the main aisle along the remaining pews after the bride's mother has been seated just before the wedding march starts. Ribbons are not used unless there are ushers. If there are no ushers, those guests who are not relatives and who arrive early take care not to occupy the first few rows even if there are no ribbons.

Ushers should be at the church for final instructions about an hour before a large wedding, since guests will begin to arrive half an hour before the ceremony. Ushers stand inside and to the left of the entrance so that they are in a position to offer the right arm to guests. If there are ushers, both men and women wait to be properly escorted to seats even though this may mean a small delay.

Ushers greet guests with a smile and the small bow usual with any greeting, but do not offer to shake hands. Ushers and guests do not exchange names, though they may do so if there is some special reason to identify themselves. If the guest does not say, "The bride's side," or "The groom's side," the usher asks, "Where would you like to sit?" The guest then gives his relationship in some such fashion as "I'm the groom's nephew," or "I'm a friend of the bride's mother," to explain in which part of a section he belongs.

To a woman, an usher offers his right arm, bent with the forearm horizontal and his hand at about the middle of his waistcoat. She puts her left hand inside the crook, not on top of his forearm.

Couples are taken down the aisle together by one usher, the woman on the usher's arm and the man following, not beside, his companion.

A man alone walks on an usher's right but does not take his arm. If two men are being seated, the elder walks on the usher's right and the younger follows or, if the aisle is wide, walks beside the elder.

If several members of a family arrive together, the usher gives his arm to the eldest lady and the rest follow, first women and then men.

If there is a head usher, he escorts the groom's parents to their places just before he goes to see if the wedding party is ready. Other guests may be seated by other ushers during this brief period, but no one is seated by an usher after the mother of the bride enters, and latecomers must slip into seats in the rear or in the gallery.

When the church doors are closed, the ushers join the bridal party if they are to walk in the processional. Otherwise they take seats.

**SECOND MARRIAGES.** The status of the groom does not affect the character of the wedding. If it is a first marriage for the bride, the wedding gown, bridal party, ceremony, and reception may be as elaborate as she and her parents choose.

If the bride has been married before, she does not wear white and does not correctly wear a formal wedding gown and veil, but she may carry a bouquet, and may invite a large number of guests to both the ceremony and reception. Usually, however, if the bride is remarrying, only a few guests are invited to the ceremony, though the reception is often a large one.

**SHIPBOARD WEDDINGS.** *See* under "Ceremonies, Differences from Basic Protestant."

**SHOWERS.** Wedding showers generally are held six weeks to a month before the marriage. If only women are invited, a shower may feature lingerie for the bride, or some category of household items. If both men and women are invited, gifts are usually confined to some type of household item.

**Gifts.** If the invitation specifies "Linen," "Kitchen," "Garden," or any other category, guests are expected to choose gifts within that classification so that, when several showers are scheduled, the couple will not find themselves with twenty chopping boards and no bath towels. Often a hostess keeps a list of needed items so that guests can check with her for suggestions and thereby avoid choosing duplicate gifts or items of the wrong color.

The shower guest usually takes the gift along to the party, but may correctly send it in advance to the house of the hostess. Whether the gift is taken or sent, a card should be enclosed to avoid the otherwise inevitable confusion about which donor gave which gift.

**Guests.** The guest list should be most carefully considered because anyone invited to a shower is expected to supply a present whether attending or not, and this obligation can be a real burden to a friend invited to attend a series of showers for the same couple—and obligated to send a wedding gift as well. If there are to be several showers, the guest lists are usually worked out with the mother of the bride and often—unofficially—with the bride herself, unless the shower is to be a surprise party.

**Hostess.** The mother or sister of the bride does not give a shower, since that would be a request for presents from too close to home. An aunt, cousin, or friend of the family often sponsors such a party, however, and of course supplies the refreshments as well as a present.

**Invitations.** Guests are invited in any informal way—by telephone, note, or the little printed fill-in invitations found in greeting card shops.

**Refreshments.** A shower may be any kind of party from a breakfast to a midnight supper.

**Thanks.** Only verbal thanks need be given to the donors present, but notes of thanks are sent to absent donors. The guest of honor usually sends flowers to the hostess in advance of the party and always telephones thanks the day following it.

**SUPERSTITIONS.** Even brides who place no faith in superstitions generally observe certain long-established customs that are supposed to bring good luck.

With her wedding costume, the bride wears "something old, something new, something borrowed, something blue, and a sixpence [dime] in her shoe" to ensure health, happiness, and good fortune.

The superstition that it is bad luck for a bride to look in a mirror between the time she is fully dressed for the ceremony and the completion of the marriage service is ignored today. So, quite generally, is the taboo against the groom seeing his bride on the day of the wedding until she meets him at the altar, though one vestige of that ancient custom persists: If the bride is wearing a formal wedding gown, the groom is supposedly defying the gods of good luck if he sees her in it before she approaches him for the wedding ceremony.

The bride tosses her bouquet as a symbol of farewell to her maiden state. And, as everyone knows, the girl who catches it will be the next to marry.

If a girl sleeps with a piece of wedding cake under her pillow, she will see her future husband in her dreams.

Rice tossed over the couple after the ceremony ensures an ever-full pantry and an abundance of all other good things, including children.

Old shoes and tin cans are attached to the back of the couple's car to attract the attention of strangers, who are expected to add their good wishes to those of friends.

The groom carries the bride over the threshold of their first home, even if it is a hotel room, as a symbol that he has captured her at last.

**TELEGRAMS.** Relatives and close friends who are unable to attend a wedding often send congratulatory telegrams. Such messages are addressed to the new couple (Mr. and Mrs. John Jones Smith), or to a member of either family with the instruction to relay the message to the newly married pair.

Congratulatory telegrams are sometimes read aloud by the best man during the reception. Some person other than the busy best man should be delegated to open and assort them before they are handed to him to read aloud. If they are not read at the reception, they are tucked into the luggage of the bride and groom.

A congratulatory telegram calls for a little note of thanks from either the bride or groom within a reasonable time.

**TIME OF DAY.** *See* "Date and Hour" and "Ceremony, Differences from Basic Protestant."

**TROUSSEAU.** In the past, a bride's trousseau included her clothes, all the bed, bath, table, and kitchen linen needed for her new house, and often china and silver as well. In today's use, "trousseau" means the bride's personal wardrobe, though many girls do collect a sizable amount of trousseau linen. The bride or her family supplies all her clothes, but of course friends may give her lingerie and other items for personal use, such as perfume, handbags, and so on, as engagement presents. Such things are not suitable as a wedding present. By today's sensible custom, blankets, household linen, and similar items are correctly given to practical young couples as wedding presents if they let it be known that such things would please them.

Except for the bride's luggage, the personal items in the trousseau are marked with only the initial of her first name or her maiden initials, and she adds the initial of her husband's last name after the wedding if she wants to. Silver, household linen, and other such presents may be marked before the wedding in any way the young couple chooses.

*See* INITIALS AND MONOGRAMS for the customary choices.

**USHERS.** When there are only about fifty guests, there may be no ushers, or two may be asked to serve. Otherwise, one usher is usually required for each fifty guests if the seating of a large number is to be handled efficiently. However, if there are six or more bridesmaids, an equal number of ushers is usual even if not actually needed, since an even pairing of men and women makes prewedding parties gayer. When there are several ushers, one is chosen as the head usher—to be more or less in charge of the others.

Technically, the ushers are attendants of the groom, and so he is privileged to select them. But it is customary for him to consult with the bride, and choose some of her relatives and friends too. Under any circumstances, he includes those of her brothers (as well as his own) who are of suitable age. It is the groom's duty to issue the invitations to the ushers, though in some circumstances the bride's parents may do so—if the groom is from out of town, for example, and does not know the young men who are available for this duty.

Ushers are usually of about the age of the groom, but need not be. Also, they need not be of the same faith as the bride and groom, and may be married or single. An usher's wife is invited to the prewedding parties with him (except the bachelor dinner) and to the wedding and reception.

Since an invitation to serve as an usher is an honor, it is never refused except for explainable good reason.

**Clothes.** The ushers dress to the same degree of formality as the groom and best man. Their ties, gloves, and boutonnieres are identical, since they are a gift from the groom, but their suits may differ in some details—the cut of the collar on a dinner jacket, for example. For an informal daytime wedding they need not wear identical suits, of course, but the groom should specify— after the invitation to serve has been accepted—what he expects his ushers to wear so that all will be in dark suits, summer linens, or whatever.

**Duties.** Besides the duties given in detail under "Seating," the ushers' responsibilities include:

Accepting invitations to prewedding parties, when possible.
Attending the rehearsal.
Putting the pew ribbons in place just before the ceremony.
Joining the processional and recessional, on occasion.
Removing pew ribbons and escorting special guests from the front pews after the ceremony.
Going with the bridesmaids to the reception, if special cars are provided; or helping to drive the wedding party and special guests there.
Helping to make the reception a success.
Dancing with the attendants, both mothers, and the bride before devoting themselves to friends not in the wedding party.
Helping the best man with the luggage of the bride and groom.
Distributing rice or confetti, if it is to be thrown.
Clearing the way for the bride and groom when they are ready to make their dash for the door.
And thwarting such horseplay as "Just Married" signs if the bride and groom might be embarrassed by it.

**Expenses.** An usher is responsible for the cost of any clothes he needs in order to be dressed like the other ushers. He also pays for his own transportation if he lives out of town and, of course, sends a wedding present.

**Junior Ushers.** A boy of junior-high-school age may feel especially honored by an invitation to serve as a junior usher, but usually is asked to serve only if the ushers are to wear informal dress because a young man under college age does not correctly wear a formal daytime cutaway or White Tie. However, a boy of fifteen is just about ready for his first Black Tie, and so he can correctly dress to match ushers in dinner jackets.

**WIDOWS.**   *See* "Invitations" and "Second Marriages."

**WEEKENDS.**   *See* COLLEGE WEEKENDS; HOUSEGUESTS.

## WHISKEY AND OTHER SPIRITS

The enormous family of alcoholic drinks is divided into two main categories: those made by fermentation followed by distillation (the whole run of strongest drinks from aquavit to whiskey); and those like beer and wine (*which see, separately*) made by fermentation only.

Unsweet alcoholic drinks made by distillation are known as "spirits" and "liquors." The markedly sweet are called "liqueurs" or "cordials." (Though there is a technical difference, the words "liqueur" and "cordial" are commonly used interchangeably. *See* "Liqueurs" below.) "Liqueur" is also applied to an aged but not sweet liquor so very fine and smooth that it can be served straight after dinner, as liqueurs are—"liqueur brandy," for example.

The most widely used spirits in this country are brandy, gin, rum, vodka, and whiskies. The person who drinks hard liquors usually has a decided preference for a particular one of these tipples, and a whiskey drinker generally has an equally decided preference for one of the three most popular types, blended, bourbon, and Scotch. It is neither necessary nor customary for a home bar to be stocked with a saloon-like variety, but it is considerate and customary to offer guests a choice of whiskey and gin; and if Scotch is offered also, to have on hand some other whiskey that does not have its distinctive smoky taste.

The following terms confuse a good many people:

1. *Aging.* All liquors do not need aging or improve by it, but some are not suitable for drinking until aged for a specified number of years. Longer aging improves the quality of others. Aging is done before bottling, since liquors do not continue to mellow and mature to any appreciable extent in the bottle as some wines do.

2. *Neat and Straight.* These words are used interchangeably to designate any liquid exactly as it comes from the bottle—with nothing added, not even ice. "Straight" also has a technical meaning that does not concern the ultimate consumer; to distillers it indicates a liquor that has not been blended (*see* under "Whiskies" below).

3. *Proof.* This word is the technical term used to give the alcoholic content of spirits. For all practical purposes, in the United States a proof number is *double* the percentage of alcohol in the product. For example, a bottle of 90 proof gin is 45 percent alcohol. Pure alcohol is 200 proof, and far too powerful to take straight. Therefore, distilled water is always added to all distilled liquors during the manufacturing process.

**BRANDY.** "Brandy" is a broad term applied to liquors distilled from a wide variety of substances, including beets, grains, sugarcane, fruits, and berries. Brandies made from fruits and berries are generally so labeled: Peach Brandy, Cherry Brandy, Blackberry Brandy, for example.

The word "brandy" used alone means that the liquor was distilled from grapes. "Brandy" comes from the Dutch *brandewijn,* or "burnt wine," and refers to the process of distillation from wine or from the residue of the wine press called "marc." Brandy made from marc is inferior but very strong. Brandy is aged before bottling.

Among other places, parts of France, Spain, Portugal, Australia, Italy, and the United States produce brandy. The most celebrated brandies are cognac, made from white grapes in the Département of Charente, and armagnac, made in the Département of Gers, both in France. Bottles labeled "Fine Champagne" contain the choicest cognac. Stars on a label do not indicate age; they designate the quality of the cognac—the more stars, the finer the quality. However, the number of stars and their relation to quality vary from vintner to vintner. Initials are also used to indicate quality: C—Cognac, E—Especial, F—Fine, O—Old, P—Pale, S—Superior, X—Extra. V in advance of an initial stands for "Very."

**SERVING.** Fruit brandies, especially, are used in certain cocktails. Brandy is also served with soda or water as a highball, and on the rocks. But the classic occasion for brandy is after dinner with or immediately following coffee, neat or combined about half and half in the glass with a liqueur.

After a formal dinner, coffee, brandy, and liqueurs are sometimes offered to men at the table after the women have withdrawn elsewhere to take coffee and a choice of drinks. Usually, however, a tray with brandy and several liqueurs in either decanters or their original bottles is brought to the living room, and the hostess offers the guests a choice with or immediately after coffee.

Brandy combined with a liqueur is served in a liqueur glass. Straight brandy may also be served in a liqueur glass or in the traditional snifter or inhaler, which is a short-stemmed glass with bulging sides and a rather small opening. When served in a snifter, the brandy is warmed by cupping one or both hands around the bowl—the heat of the hands brings out the aroma, which of course is held in by the small opening. When a liqueur glass is used, the warming process is of course omitted. Brandy snifters range in size from the small ones with a total capacity of about six ounces, to the very large, holding as much as twenty or so ounces (though no more than about two ounces at a time are poured into any snifter). Most popular are the middle-size snifters holding eight to ten ounces.

**GIN.** Since gin is almost entirely pure neutral spirits, it can be made from many substances, but usually it is produced from grain. Various botanical flavorings are added after the liquor comes from the still, but it is juniper berries that give gins their distinctive taste. The one exception is sloe gin, which is really a pink liqueur colored and flavored with sloe berries. Gin gets its name from the French *genièvre*, which means "juniper." Gin does not need aging.

**Serving.** Dry gins are best for cocktails. Some people prefer the slightly sweeter gins served on the rocks. Any gin can be used in long drinks like a Tom Collins or Gin and Tonic (quinine water), since the mixers conceal the basic flavor of the gin.

**LIQUEURS AND CORDIALS.** A liqueur is a potent spirit to which sweetening, flavoring, and sometimes coloring are added before it is bottled. Some liqueurs like Benedictine, Cointreau, Chartreuse, and Grand Marnier are made by complicated and closely guarded formulas. Others may have the flavor of only one fruit, berry, or herb or other aromatic added.

Liqueurs are made in one of three ways. Fine liqueurs are made by what is called the distillation method. In this process one (or perhaps fifteen or more) flavoring ingredients are added to a spirit that, after a waiting period, is then redistilled and sweetened. Excellent liqueurs are also made by the infusion method. In this process crushed fruits, herbs, or other flavorings, and a sweetening are added to a spirit and steeped in it until their flavor is absorbed. The solids are strained out before the resulting liqueur is bottled. (The words "liqueur" and "cordial" are widely used as synonyms, but—technically—a cordial is a liqueur made by the infusion process, a method that is quite easy to follow at home.) The third method of manufacture is known as the essence process. It produces liqueurs of the least fine quality. Essential oils, either natural or artificial, and a sweetening are added to a spirit, which is then bottled.

Liqueurs are used in cooking—a Grand Marnier soufflé is a noted dessert—and are widely used to flavor cut-up fresh fruits and as a sauce over ice cream and puddings. They are used in cocktails too, and also make a good long drink combined with soda and ice in a highball glass. But mainly they are served straight with or immediately following after-dinner coffee.

**Serving.** In addition to being powerful in taste, liqueurs are extremely strong. Few are less than 30 percent pure alcohol (60 proof), and some range as high as 160 proof. Therefore, they are served in small amounts and are sipped slowly, never tossed down. The standard tiny liqueur glass has a stem and has a total capacity of about an ounce—never more than two ounces. It is filled no more than two-thirds full.

If liqueurs are decanted, clear glass or crystal bottles are appropriate to display those that have spectacular colors. But a liqueur may correctly be left in its original bottle. Usually a choice of several liqueurs and a brandy is brought in on a tray, and the hostess offers her guests their preference. Many men prefer straight brandy to the extremely sweet liqueurs, or a mixture of about half-and-half brandy and liqueur. If only one liqueur is offered, the little glasses already filled may be passed on a tray.

**RUM.** Rum is distilled from fermented molasses or other sugarcane products. This liquor was developed by early British settlers in the West Indies from a native drink called "Kill Devil." The name "rum" is believed to derive from a Devonshire word "rumbullion," meaning "a great tumult"—probably because of the effect of the liquor on sailors, to whom grog (rum and water) became a standard drink. Rum drinkers usually have a preference for one of the three major types: the very pale rum, lightest in color and taste; golden rum, which is somewhat heavier and darker; and dark rum, which is the heaviest and strongest in taste. Rum needs to be aged. Colorless when it comes from the still, it gets its color from the casks or by the addition of caramel.

**Serving.** Rum is a favorite ingredient in punches and cocktails. It often is served on the rocks or in a highball glass diluted with soda, water, or soft drinks.

**VODKA.** The best vodka is made from fermented grain. It is white, crystal clear, and somewhat fiery in taste. Since it has no distinctive flavor, it leaves less of a "breath" than other hard liquors. In Europe it is often served cold in shot glasses and downed neat. In this country it is served in any of the ways that gin is. Vodka does not require aging.

**WHISKIES.** The word "whiskey" derives from the Gaelic *usquebaugh*, which means "water of life." The taste of whiskies varies enormously, depending on the kind of mash, the water, and the methods of processing, aging, and blending.

All whiskies are distilled from a fermented mash. Bourbon is made principally from corn, with very small amounts of grains to regulate the fermentation and aging processes. Other standard American whiskies (including Canadian) are made from rye, wheat, and other grains. Straight Scotch is made from pure barley malt. (Incidentally, Scotch whiskies are spelled "whisky." All other whiskies are spelled "whiskey.") Almost all Scotch whisky sold outside of Scotland is a blend of about 25 percent straight (barley malt) Scotch and 75 percent Scotch grain whisky or aged neutral spirits. Irish whiskey is made from both malted and unmalted grains, including barley.

Malt is made by allowing moistened grains to sprout and then stopping the growth by rapid drying. Scotch gets its characteristic smoky flavor from malt dried over fragrant peat fires.

Inferior whiskies can be made from many things besides cereals. Moonshiners have been known to distill fermented potatoes, and a bootlegger's "whiskey" may be no more than straight alcohol with water, coloring, and flavoring shaken up with it.

**Aging and Coloring.** All whiskey is colorless when it comes from the still. Color is acquired during the aging and finishing processes. Whiskies need to be aged (from four to eight or more years) before they are bottled. The length of the aging affects the quality. Scotch and Canadian whiskies are aged in used bourbon barrels and occasionally in wine casks, which contribute flavor as well as color, and—as do all casks—absorb fusel oil and other substances that mar the flavor and quality. Bourbon distillers are charred white oak casks to give that whiskey its distinctive bouquet, color, and mellowness. Very small amounts of caramel and other substances are often added to heighten the color.

**Blended Whiskies.** What goes into a blended whiskey is a closely guarded manufacturing secret because blending is one of the ways a brand is given its special characteristics. Blending is done by combining several different whiskies (often as many as a dozen different kinds) and perhaps neutral spirits. The object is to produce a smooth, mellow, light-bodied product of distinctive taste. There can be inferior blends, of course, made with poor whiskies. Bourbon is never a blend. It is the product of one distillation only.

**Bottled in Bond.** The label "Bottled in Bond" is not a guarantee of superiority as some people mistakenly believe. It means only that a whiskey has been inspected by the government, is four years old, and is 100 proof. Less than 10 percent of the whiskey sold in this country is bottled in bond.

The strip stamp that seals the top of a bottle means only that the required revenue tax has been paid. A green strip stamp signifies that the whiskey was bottled in bond. All other whiskies carry a red revenue strip stamp.

**Serving.** If whiskey is served "neat" or "straight" in a shot glass, it is accompanied with a chaser of water on the side. An Old-Fashioned glass is used for whiskey on the rocks, or whiskey, ice, and the very small amount of water that many people prefer to a cocktail as a predinner drink. A straight-sided water glass or a highball glass is used for whiskey and soda or whiskey diluted with a soft drink—ginger ale, for example (though even the thought of combining a good whiskey with any soft drink turns the knowledgeable devotees of firewater pale).

As noted above, but deserving of double emphasis, most whiskey drinkers have a marked preference for Scotch or a whiskey devoid of its smoky taste, and so it is standard practice to offer guests a choice. But the choice is offered by category, not brand name—for example, "Will you have Scotch or bourbon?" (not "Will you have Dewar's White Label or Old Taylor?").

For other details about this pleasant subject, *see also* BEER AND ALE; COCKTAILS, GLASSES; MEALS AND THEIR SERVICE; WINES.

## WHISTLING

Constant low whistling has been known to drive one's fellow workers mad, and so it is best to forget the Seven Dwarfs' advice, "Whistle While You Work," when anyone is within hearing. It is a superstition in the theater that whistling, particularly backstage, will bring bad luck, though the reason for this long-established belief has been forgotten. The taboo against any kind of whistle aboard a naval vessel is equally strong. It probably originated in the possibility of confusion with the boatswain's pipe commonly used to whistle orders.

Waiters, waitresses, porters, and bellboys strongly resent being summoned by a whistle, and rightly. Such a signal is better saved for calling a dog or used in an emergency by a man desperately trying to get a taxi.

**WHITE HOUSE.** *See* WASHINGTON.

**WHITE TIE.** *See* BLACK TIE, WHITE TIE; and CLOTHES.

## WIDOWERS

A widower is a man who has lost his wife by death and who has not remarried. A divorced man is not a widower. He is a divorcé. By dictionary definition, a "grass widower" is (1) a man who is divorced or separated from his wife, (2) a man whose wife is temporarily away from him. A widower continues to wear his wedding ring if he wishes, or may take it off after any period of formal mourning.

*See* separate listings, such as ENGAGEMENTS TO WED; MOURNING; WEDDING ANNOUNCEMENTS.

## WIDOWS

A divorcée is not correctly described as a "widow." A widow is a woman who has lost her husband by death and who has not remarried. "Grass widow" for "divorcée" is seldom heard today, possibly because the dictionary gives all the following meanings for that term: (1) a discarded mistress, (2) a woman who has had an illegitimate child, (3) a woman divorced or separated from her husband, (4) a woman whose husband is temporarily away from her.

A widow usually continues to wear her wedding ring. She continues to use her husband's full name after his death. Personal mail is addressed to her, and her social calling cards are engraved Mrs. Henry York Brown—never Mrs. Mary Greene Brown.

See NAMES, for certain exceptions now widely used by women in business, and other separate listings such as ENGAGEMENTS TO WED; MOURNING; WEDDINGS.

**WIFE.**  See HUSBAND AND WIFE.

**WINES**

> And Noah he often said to his wife
> When he sat down to dine,
> I don't care where the water goes if
> It doesn't get into the wine.
> —*G. K. Chesterton*

So-called "wines" are made from many substances—fruits, berries, blossoms (dandelion wine), rice (the famous saki of Japan), but, technically, "wine" means the alcoholic beverage produced from grapes by fermentation.

The family of wines is huge, and the differences among even the closely related ones are enormous. It takes years of enjoyable investigation to master the subject. But, happily, it takes no more than the firm grasp of a few basic facts to serve wines with confidence.

Wines fall into three main categories: the strong apéritifs that are served before a meal to whet the appetite; the markedly sweet wines that are correctly served only with or immediately after dessert; and the table wines that go best with main courses. Following are the major guidelines that experienced wine drinkers use in choosing and serving wines within each of these three main divisions:

**AGED WINES.** After crushed grapes have fermented in open vats, the juice is drawn off and aged in wooden casks for varying lengths of time before it is bottled and stored to age further. Wine is the only alcoholic beverage that continues to age in glass (unless aging has been stopped by pasteurization or the addition of a specific quantity of spirits before bottling). However, age alone does not mean a fine wine. Different wines reach their prime after different lengths of time, and deteriorate if kept longer. Some wines reach their prime point when quite young. Others reach their peak only after many years of aging. But a poor wine remains a poor wine no matter what the date on the label. It is usually far more rewarding to choose a relatively young wine of a fine year than an older wine of a poor year.

The term "vintage wine" does not necessarily mean that a wine is old. It means that a wine was made in a year that had exceptionally favorable weather for the production of superior wine grapes.

**APERITIF WINES.** Wines in this division have other uses, but most commonly serve the same purpose as cocktails. Apéritif wines are fortified (see below), and therefore keep well without refrigeration after being opened. Their alcoholic content is about 20 percent. Most of them are sharply flavored with herbs and other ingredients. Among the best known are Vermouth, Dubonnet, and Campari, though very dry sherry is also an apéritif.

The highly flavored apéritifs are usually served in an Old-Fashioned glass on the rocks or with a splash of soda added. They also are served as a long drink between meals, with much soda and ice. When such a wine is served straight, an ounce or so is poured into a sherry or small cocktail glass. Sherry and kindred apéritif wines are always served straight. If several wines are offered during a meal, a dry sherry sometimes accompanies the appetizer and soup courses, but sherry is not served thereafter during a meal.

**CHAMPAGNES.** Champagnes are in a class by themselves, since they can be served on any occasion. They are correctly served before and during an entire meal, and are considered the most festive of drinks that can be served at a reception—though it is true that many people prefer cocktails or highballs on such between-meals occasions. Champagnes usually are very pale gold, but sometimes are pink.

Dry champagne is served with the main courses, and the sweet champagnes go best with desserts. The choicest champagnes are the driest. The very driest is marked "natural"; the next, "brut"; then "sec"; and "demi-sec." If the label does not carry one of these words, the champagne is sweet. The process that gives champagne its effervescence is a long one, and so all champagnes are expensive. Champagne is served very well chilled, and is opened just before it is served. See "Opening" below for the special techniques required by this wine.

**DESSERT WINES.** Wines markedly sweet in taste are appropriately served at table only with or immediately following the dessert course. They are served before, rather than with, coffee, which is so strong in taste that liqueurs, rather than dessert wines, go best with or following it. Dessert wines are also served, on occasion, in the afternoon with cookies or cake. Many, though by no means all, dessert wines are fortified, and run to about 20 percent alcohol. Among the better-known dessert wines are port, the sweet sherries, Tokay, muscatel, sweet sauterne, sparkling Burgundy, and champagne. With the exception of sparkling Burgundy and champagne, dessert wines are generally served in a small wine or sherry glass, though a two-ounce liqueur glass is also correct and often used for very sweet wines like muscatel.

**DRY AND SWEET.** "Dry" is applied to a wine that has been fermented until all the sugar in the grape has been converted to alcohol. "Sweet" is used more loosely. If fermentation is stopped by any means before the sugar is turned into alcohol (even so small an amount that the inexperienced wine drinker cannot detect it), the wine is described in some such words as "on the sweet side."

There is, in contrast to the term "dry wine," no such term as "wet wine," though it would avoid a certain amount of confusion if we had it or some other term to apply to the "less than dry" table wines, and so could make a clearer distinction between them and the emphatically sweet-tasting dessert wines.

**FORTIFIED WINES.** Wines to which a small amount of a spirit (usually brandy) has been added are known as "fortified." Wines are fortified for several reasons: to stop fermentation before all the sugar in the grape has been turned into alcohol, to act as a preservative and prevent souring after a bottle is opened, and to add strength and flavor. All sherries are fortified, and it can be taken for granted that apéritifs and most of the exceedingly sweet-tasting dessert wines are also. The range of strength in fortified wines is wide. The alcoholic content of sherries, for example, varies from 15 to about 25 percent.

**PROOF.** "Proof" is a technical term commonly used to denote the alcohol content of a distilled spirit. A whiskey that is virtually 45 percent alcohol is labeled "90 proof." On the other hand, it is the custom to give the alcohol content of beers and wines in percentages. In order to compare the strength of a wine with that of a hard liquor, double the figure given on the label of the wine. For example, a sherry labeled "20 percent alcohol by volume" is half as strong as an 80-proof rum.

**STORAGE.** Wine kept for any length of time should be stored in a dark, cool place that is not subject to wide variations in temperature—55 degrees is considered ideal. Wine should not be allowed to chill below 40 degrees or be stored next to heating pipes or in any other very warm place.

A bottle with a cork stopper is stored on its side to keep the cork moist. Otherwise, in due course, the cork will dry, the seal will be broken, and the wine will spoil. Bottles with screw tops or plastic stoppers do not require this kind of storage.

**TABLE WINES.** Some people use "table wine" to mean an unpretentious wine for everyday meals, but technically "table wines" is used to distinguish all wines, of any quality, that can be served during the major part of a meal, from the apéritif and dessert wines that do not go well with main courses. Table wines are not so strong as those in the other two categories; they contain from 10 to 14 percent alcohol. At an elaborate dinner, several wines are usually offered, chosen to match the different courses. On everyday occasions, it is customary and correct to offer only one wine—a red or a white, whichever goes best with the main course.

The range of possible choices is all but endless. Many people today just do not bother with the traditional rules governing the choice between red and white wine with certain specific foods. They find a wine they like, and serve it with everything. As they become more familiar with wines, however, they are likely to please themselves (and their guests) more if they follow the long-established choices outlined briefly here:

**Red Wines.** Generally quite dry and heavier than many white wines, red wines are traditionally served with meat, especially red meats, game, the dark-meat fowl like duck and goose, spaghettis and other pastas, strong cheeses, and other heavy or strongly seasoned foods. Red wines usually are served at what is called room temperature—about 65 degrees.

**Rosé Wines.** These pink wines fall between the reds and the dry whites. They are a little too light to be perfect with beef and rather too heavy for sea-food, but many people enjoy them with white meats and poultry. They usually are served well cooled.

**Sparkling Wines.** The sparkling wines range from champagne (see above), which is highly effervescent, to those that are called "crackling" (in France, *pétillant*), which do not foam and bubble as champagne does. Sparkling wines may be red, white, or pink. They are the most versatile of wines and can be served at any time—with or without food, but always chilled.

**White Wines.** The so-called "white" wines range in color from pale gold through amber to pale green. They are, in general, more delicate in flavor than red wines, and are the classic choice with lighter foods. White wines are traditionally served with seafood and with white meats like veal, chicken, and turkey, as well as with egg dishes and other lightly seasoned entrees. (Certain white wines are so full-bodied that they are correctly served with red meats and game. Any good wine dealer can advise on this matter. White wines are served chilled.

**WINE SERVICE.** Following are the main rules observed in both the formal and informal service of wines.

**Cooling.** It is important to bring each wine to its proper temperature before serving it. No wine is served warm. "Room temperature," for example, does not mean the actual temperature of a comfortably warm dining room. It means 60 to 65 degrees. "Cool'" or "cellar temperature" means about 55 degrees. "Chilled" does not mean near freezing—it means about 45 degrees.

A good general rule is that still red wines are served at room temperature; rosés are served cool; white, as well as champagne and other sparkling wines (red or white), is served chilled.

If a red wine has been stored in a cool place, it is brought to its proper temperature by being allowed to stand for several hours in a warmer room. If its temperature needs to be reduced rapidly, it may be cooled briefly in a refrigerator. (*See* "Decanting," below, for the handling of sedimented wines.)

White wines, rosés, and sparkling wines are usually cooled or chilled by varying times in a refrigerator or, in an emergency, by a very brief time in a freezer, though they should never be allowed to freeze. Wines can also be brought to the right temperature fairly quickly in a wine cooler packed with ice. Salt added to the ice will speed the chilling, so will twirling the bottle to bring the wine in its center in contact with the cold sides of the bottle. Wine coolers are also useful for keeping prechilled bottles cold during a meal, though they are more often used in restaurants than at home. A cooler is generally placed on a stand rather than on the table. When taken from a cooler, a bottle is wrapped in a napkin before the glasses are filled from it. (*See* "Pouring," below.)

Delightful long drinks are made with wine, ice, soda, and sometimes other ingredients, and a mixture like the noted *sangría* of Spain is occasionally served with informal meals. By the rule, however, ice is not added to a glass of wine at the table, though there is no reason for someone who likes wine diluted not to please himself in this fashion.

**Decanting.** Any wine is correctly served from its original bottle. On the other hand, any but the sparkling wines may be decanted. Wines are decanted for two reasons: for appearance' sake, either because the wine was bought in bulk or because the house has beautiful wine decanters that are a pleasure to use; and to prevent traces of the sediment that forms in old red wines or bits of cork that may have crumbled into the bottle from escaping into the glasses when the wine is poured. (White wines do not produce a sediment.) It is not necessary to decant a heavily sedimented wine. If the bottle is handled very carefully, the sediment will remain undisturbed in the bottom few ounces, which, of course, are not served. And, indeed, many people prefer to see a fine old wine served in its original bottle.

Fortified wines like sherry can be left in stoppered decanters for quite a while without suffering, but unfortified wines are best decanted only two hours, at most, before they are to be served.

Wines that need to be served cool are usually brought to the table in their original bottles. If they are decanted, the decanter is also chilled. A decanter of wine is set on the table without its stopper.

The process of decanting, though it requires care, is not a difficult one. To decant a wine is, purely and simply, to pour the clear liquid from its bottle into another container, leaving behind any sediment accumulated in the bottom of the original bottle. Naturally, the pouring must be done slowly and gently, without shaking the bottle or tilting it back and forth and thereby stirring up the sediment. If the bottle is held against a light during the slow pouring, the sediment is easy to see. Sometimes a piece of fine cloth is employed as a filter to make doubly sure that cork and sediment do not pass into the decanter.

**Formal and Informal Service.** At both formal and informal meals, wine is not poured until the diners are seated and food is before them, and glasses are replenished before they are empty.

At *formal* meals, wine is always poured from the right of a diner, and the server never picks up the glass, nor does the diner, during this operation. The host is the first to be served, though only a token amount. A very small quantity is poured into his glass so that he can sample it (if he has not done so previously) and also so that he, instead of a guest, will get any small flake of cork that may be floating on the top of the bottle. (He removes any bits of cork with the tip of a spoon or knife and puts them on the edge of his plate, or the server may bring him a fresh glass.) The wine is then poured for the guests, beginning with the woman on the host's right. Next, the server walks around behind the host and fills the glass of the woman on the host's left, and thereafter proceeds clockwise around the table, serving each guest in turn. Last of all, the host's glass is filled to the proper level for all table wines—one-half to two-thirds full. If there are more than ten at the table, service usually starts simultaneously from both ends of the table. Wine bottles or decanters are not put on the table in formal service.

At a formal dinner, a different wine may be served with each course (sherry with the soup, dry white wine with the fish, red wine with the meat, and champagne with the dessert, for example. Or sherry may be served with the soup, and champagne with the remainder of the meal. Or champagne may be served throughout). Today, even at formal dinners, more than three table wines are seldom offered. If several wines are served, the most important convention to be observed is that a sweet wine never precedes a dry one, nor a heavy wine a light one.

In formal service, water as well as wine is served. The water glasses are filled after the diners are seated and before a wine is poured. The water glass is set above the tip of the knife. One or two wineglasses are set to the right of the water glass, with the one to be used first at the farthest right. In the unlikely event that more than two wineglasses are on the table, they are grouped in any attractive way. If the usual two or at most three wines are to be served, all the glasses are on the table at the beginning of the meal, though if this would crowd the table, the dessert wineglass may be brought in with the dessert. However, if champagne is to be served with dessert, the glass is in place from the beginning (as a hint that champagne is coming and that the diner had best go easy on the preceding wines).

If sherry or another apéritif wine is served with the first course, the glass is removed before the next wine is served. Otherwise, wineglasses are left in place —for example, if white wine is served with the fish, its glass is not removed with the fish course, but remains on the table even if red wine is to be served with the meat course.

At an *informal* meal, the opened wine bottle most often is set on the table at the host's place before the guests are seated, and it remains on the table during the meal. It is usually put in a shallow wine holder rather than directly on the unprotected table or its covering. In the rare cases where a wine bucket or cooler is used, it is set elsewhere than on the table, often on a stand close to the host.

Water may be served, but frequently it is not provided with wine in informal service; no more than two wines are served, and usually only one. The host (or hostess if she is entertaining alone) usually takes charge of serving the wine even if there is a maid to serve the rest of the meal.

The host pours a little of the wine into his own glass first, takes a sample sip if he has not tasted it previously, and then serves it in any of the following ways that he prefers: He may remain seated, fill the glass of the woman at his right, then of the woman at his left, and, after that, give her the bottle to be passed clockwise around the table. Each man in turn fills the glass of the woman on his left before filling his own. Or the host may fill the glasses of the two women next to him, and then ask the others at the table to pass their glasses to him to be filled (or refilled). Or the host may follow the standard procedure for formal service and walk around the table for the first serving, filling each person's glass from the right.

At a buffet meal that has a choice of heavy and light main dishes, it is customary to provide a choice of red or white wine. Filled wineglasses may be on the buffet table or an auxiliary table, for guests to pick up after they have helped themselves to food. Or filled glasses may be passed on a tray after the guests have found seats. Or, if guests are to find places at set tables after serving their own plates, wine may be poured from its bottle into the glasses at the table.

See MEALS AND THEIR SERVICE for other details.

**Glasses.** Traditionally, certain wines are served in glasses of special shape, but today most households get by comfortably and correctly with an all-purpose wineglass. This is a stemmed, straight-sided goblet with a total capacity of six or more ounces. It can be used for any table wine, white or red, still or sparkling.

See GLASSES for illustrations.

The rule, not very widely observed, is that a glass carrying chilled wine is picked up by the stem to protect the liquid from the heat of the hand. A glass of wine served at room temperature is picked up by the bowl.

**Opening.** Red wines are best opened about an hour before serving to give them a chance to "breathe." White wines are generally opened just before the guests are seated. Sparkling wines are not opened until just before they are served. If metal foil covers the cork, it is cut off neatly to give a smooth edge below the lip. The cork is wiped first; then the corkscrew is inserted very gently to avoid knocking crumbs of cork into the wine. The cork is eased out gently rather than jerked out with a pop that will disturb the wine to some extent. The top of the bottle is again wiped, to remove stray bits of cork.

The opening of champagne is a little more complicated. Since champagne builds up quite a bit of pressure in the bottle, the cork is secured in place by wire. It is not necessary to cut this wire. Find a little loop in it, pull this up, and the whole wire cage will come off. Grasp the neck of the bottle firmly in both hands, aiming it away from all nearby targets, and slowly ease the cork out with both thumbs. Many people think a loud pop is a festive sound and also a sign of good champagne, but experts try for a muffled pop rather than a loud report, since the explosive release of the cork too often causes the wine to spurt and foam over. It is a good idea to have an ice-cold teaspoon handy in case a bottle does boil over. Insert the spoon handle into the neck of the bottle for a moment, and the fountain will stop.

**Pouring.** Bottles taken from a wine cooler are wrapped in a napkin for pouring because they are dripping wet. Otherwise, a napkin is not usually put around a bottle. The bottle is grasped around its middle, the glass filled to its proper level, and then the bottle is given a slight twist as the neck is raised, to keep the final drop from falling onto the cloth. The proper level is no more than half to two-thirds full, to leave room for the bouquet to rise into the empty top part of the glass. However, sherry glasses, being V-shaped, may be filled closer to the brim, since they will not retain the bouquet anyway.

A wine is not poured at table until the guests are seated and the first course is in front of them (as mentioned above). After that, wine for the succeeding course is poured as soon as the course is served.

Sedimented wines are often allowed to settle on their sides in a serving basket, but this equipment is not generally used otherwise.

For other details of serving, see "Formal and Informal Service," above.

**REFUSING WINE.** A guest who does not care to be served wine does best to allow a little to be poured into his glass before indicating that he does not want any (or any more). Having some wine in each glass prevents the host or hostess from thinking that a guest's needs have been overlooked. A diner signals to the server that he does not want more wine by raising his right hand slightly. It is not correct to turn a glass upside down or cover it with the hand to indicate a refusal.

**WOMAN, Use of Word.**  *See* LADY AND WOMAN.

**WOMEN IN THE ARMED SERVICES.**  *See* FORMS OF ADDRESS (Armed Services).

**WORDS COMMONLY MISUSED.**  *See* Problem Words in the Index, and also CONVERSATION.

### WORDS WITH "ESS" ENDINGS

"Lioness," "waitress," and "giantess" are among the words that end in "ess" to denote gender, but there is a sizable list of words that should not be qualified, either because the form is out of style or because the addition of "ess" gives a word a special limited meaning.

*Ambassadress.* An ambassadress is the wife of an ambassador. "Ambassador" is the correct word for both women and men serving in that capacity.

*Authoress.* Women writers object to this label. Use "author" in the same way as "reporter" is used—for both sexes.

*Jewess.* This word is displeasing to members of the Jewish faith. "She is a Jew" and "She is Jewish" are correct.

*Mayoress.* A mayoress is the wife of a mayor, though the word is rarely used. "Mayor" is the correct title for either a man or a woman serving in that capacity.

*Negress.* This word is displeasing to members of the Negro race. Say "She is a Negro."

*Poetess.* Like "authoress," this word is considered belittling by women writers and should no more be used than "editoress," "reporteress," or writeress."

*Sculptress.* Women who practice the art of sculpture consider "sculptress" as absurd as "paintress" would be. Use "sculptor" for both sexes.

**WRITERS.**  *See* CELEBRITIES.

**WRITING PAPER.**  *See* CORRESPONDENCE.


# Y

**YACHTING.**  *See* BOATING; BOATS AND SHIPS.

### YAWNING

When George Washington was a boy, he compiled his own "Rules of Civility and Decent Behavior," which are given under CHILDREN AND MANNERS. He had this to say about yawning, a rule just as good today as when he wrote it in careful longhand in his copybook: "If you yawn, do it not loud but privately and speak not in your yawning but put your handkerchief or hand before your face and turn aside."

Yawns are as difficult to suppress as sneezes, so the way a yawn is dealt with is of double importance. A wide, frank, uncovered noisy yawn is, at best, childishly ill-mannered. At worst, it can be insulting. A conspicuous yawn during a speech or sermon, at the theater, or at any other performance is rude not only to the entertainers, but also to those in the audience who do not share the yawner's reaction. If helplessly overcomed by a yawn during a conversation, a brief apology is necessary, and some such explanation is "Not enough sleep last night" to let a companion know the yawn is not an indication of boredom.

**YOM KIPPUR.** *See* HOLIDAYS.

# Z

## ZIP CODE

A zip-code number is a standard part of any address, and should be used in all correspondence, from the most formal announcements to postcards.

*See* CORRESPONDENCE; INVITATIONS; VISITING CARDS for illustrations.

# A

A.S.P.C.A, 405
À la carte, 1
Abbots, 216
Abbreviations, 1
  in addresses, 142
  on business mail, 141-144
  on envelopes, 133, 142
  French, 1
  of titles, 196-255
Academic degrees, *see* Degrees
Accents, changing, 132
Acceptances, *see* Invitations, 344 ff.; *see also* specific events
Accessories, use of word, 2; *see also* Clothes, 107-112
Accidents, 2
  apologies and excuses, 9
  and borrowed objects, 47
  and damage, 155
  motor, 16
  in restaurants, 424
  at table, 451
Actors and actresses
  applause, 12
  backstage visits, 478
  charity performances, 80
  fan mail, 81
  fans' behavior, 81
  opening nights, 478
  payment of, 81
  *see also* Celebrities, 80; Entertainers, 184
Address, forms of, 196-254
Addresses
  announcing change of, 2, 3, 388
  on business mail, 141-144
  on Christmas cards, 98 ff.
  on invitations, 348, 349
  return, 145, 349
  on social letters, 133, 135
  on visiting cards, 505, 506
Addressing officials, etc., *see* Forms of address, 196-254
Admirals, 200, 206
Admittance cards, 3
  to a ball, 24
  to banquets, etc., 31
Adoptions, 3 ff.
  announcements of, 3
  gifts following, 4
Advertisements, 5;
  *see also* Announcements (press)
Advice, 5, 130
Affectations, in speech, 5, 132
Afternoon tea, 465
Age, as dangerous topic, 6, 130
Age of consent, 6
Agents, real estate, 417
Air Force (forms of address), 200-205
Airmen, 200, 204
Airplane travel, 494

Alcoholic drinks
  ale, 39
  beer, 39
  punch, 415
  whiskies and other spirits, 589-593
  wine, 594-599
Alcoholics, 336
Ale, 39
Alfresco, 6
Alibis, 10
Allegiance, Pledge of, 410
Allergies, 6
  to animals, 7, 405
  and diet restrictions, 167
Allowances, 7
Altar boys, *see* Wedding
Ambassadors, 230
  foreign, 232
  precedence, 512 ff.
  to United Nations, 252
American, use of word, 7, 230
American plan, 309
Anecdotes, 129 ff.
Animals, allergies to, 7
Anniversaries
  birthdays, 42
  special holidays, 303
  wedding, 518
Announcements
  of adoption, 3
  birth, 41
  change of name, 391
  of death, 261, 266
  of divorce, 168
  engagement, 176 ff.
  of funeral, 261, 266
  graduation, 288
  of legal separation, 168
  marriage annulment, 8
  wedding, 521-525
  wedding cancellation, 535
  wedding postponement, 569, 577
  *see also* specific events
Announcers (receiving line), 418
Announcing guests, 375
Announcing a meal, 369
Annulments, 8
Answer cards, 73
Answers
  to invitations, 344 ff.
  to questions, 131
  *see also* separate events
Antipasto, 8, 11
Antiperspirants, 404
Antiques, 8, 83
  and auctions, 15
Apartments, 8
  bachelors asking girls to, 22
  complaints of neighbors, 8
  elevators in, 9, 175
  entering and leaving, 9

**627**

Vests
men's clothes, 107-112
use of word, 112
Veterans Day, 304
Veterinarians, 504
Vicar Bishops, 218
Vice Presidents, 244
Vigils, 270
Visas for travel, 493
Viscountesses, 234, 235, 240
Viscounts, 234, 235, 240
Visiting cards, 504-511
addresses on, 505, 506
business, 505-506
children's, 507
divorcées, name used, 392
envelopes, use of, 507
formal calls and, 64
in official Washington, 512
illustrations of use, 505 ff.
informals (fold-over), 507
introductions on, 509
invitations on, 347, 509
joint-name cards, 509
mailing regulations, 507
names, 390 ff.
and titles, 506, 509
social, 506-511
telephone numbers on, 511
Visitors
calls
business, 52 ff.
social, 63 ff.
and children, 87 ff.
in hospitals, 308
in hotels, 313
Visitors' registers, 511
Visits, see Calls
Vital statistics columns, see Newspapers
Vocabulary (good and bad), 132
Vodka, 592
Volunteers (in hospitals), 307

**W**

W.C., 512
Wages (use of word), 432
Waistcoat
men's clothes, 107-112
use of word, 112
Waiters and waitresses
household employees, 321 ff.
for meals at home, 369 ff.
in restaurants, 424 ff.
tipping, 483, 484, 485, 486, 487
whistling to attract, 593
see also Parties
Walking sticks, 111
Walking on street, 448
Warrant officers
Army 200, 204
Navy 200, 208
Washington, George
and Purple Heart, 164
"Rules of Civility," 89-94

Washington protocol
basic rules, 512
calls, 512
forms of address for government officials,
242 ff.
names and titles, 515
official functions, basic rules for, 512
precedence, in receiving lines, 421
rules for, 513-515
seating guests at table, 513
see also White House
Washington's Birthday, 303
Washrooms, 36-37
houseguests and, 315, 318
nicknames for, 36, 37
on planes, 496
in restaurants, 426
in theaters, 479
Watches, see Clothes, 106-114
Water, 517
glasses, 283
see also Meals and their service
Watermelons, 258
Water-skiing, 517
Wedding, 519-589
admittance (church) cards, 548
advice about (special consultants), 549
age of consent, 521
age and marriage license, 575
altar boys, 521
announcements, see Wedding
announcements, below
assembling at the church, 535
"At home" cards, 525
attendants, 520, 521, 526; see also Best
man; etc.
awning, canvas, carpet, 550
bachelor dinner, 526-527
banns, 527
best man, 527
clothes, 527
duties, 527
expenses, 527
Bible, bride carrying, 528
birth certificates, 575
blood tests, 528, 575
bouquets, 553; see also Bride, bouquet in
receiving line, 580
breakfast, 528, 583
bridal dinner, 528
bridal party, 526
assembling at church, 535
bride, 529
bouquet, 553; see Bridegroom
catching, 582
expense of, 530
cake, 533
clothes, 529
dinner, 528
dress, 520, 529
duties, 529
expenses, 530, 531
family of
expenses, 531